The Writer's Eye

NWIC #5

The Writer's Eye
Composition in the Multimedia Age

William V. Costanzo

Westchester Community College
State University of New York

 Higher Education

Boston   Burr Ridge, IL   Dubuque, IA   Madison, WI   New York   San Francisco   St. Louis
Bangkok   Bogotá   Caracas   Kuala Lumpur   Lisbon   London   Madrid   Mexico City
Milan   Montreal   New Delhi   Santiago   Seoul   Singapore   Sydney   Taipei   Toronto

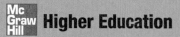

Higher Education

Published by McGraw-Hill, an imprint of The McGraw-Hill Companies, Inc., 1221 Avenue of the Americas, New York, NY 10020. Copyright © 2008. All rights reserved. No part of this publication may be reproduced or distributed in any form or by any means, or stored in a database or retrieval system, without the prior written consent of The McGraw-Hill Companies, Inc., including, but not limited to, in any network or other electronic storage or transmission, or broadcast for distance learning.

This book is printed on acid-free paper.

5 6 7 8 9 0 DOC/DOC 1 5 4 3 2

ISBN-13: 978-0-07-237260-1

MHID: 0-07-237260-5

Editor in Chief: Emily G. Barrosse
Publisher: Lisa Moore
Sponsoring Editor: Christopher Bennem
Marketing Manager: Tamara Wederbrand
Developmental Editor: Jesse Hassenger
Project Manager: Brett Coker
Manuscript Editor: Joan Pendleton
Art Director: Jeanne Schreiber
Interior and Cover Designers: Cassandra Chu and Amanda Kavanaugh
Art Editor: Robin Mouat
Photo Researcher: Nora Agbayani
Production Supervisor: Tandra Jorgensen
Composition: Electronic Publishing Services Inc., New York City
Printing: R. R. Donnelley & Sons
Credits: The credits section for this book begins on page C-1 and is considered an extension of the copyright page.

Library of Congress Cataloging-in-Publication Data
Costanzo, William V.
  The writer's eye: composition in the multimedia age / William V. Costanzo
    p. cm.
  Includes bibliographical references and index.
  ISBN: 978-0-07-237260-1
  MHID: 0-07-237260-5
    1. English language—Rhetoric. 2. Academic writing. 3. Popular culture—United States. I. Title
PE1408.C636 2006
808'. 042—dc22   2006048157

The Internet addresses listed in the text were accurate at the time of publication. The inclusion of a Web site does not indicate an endorsement by the author or McGraw-Hill, and McGraw-Hill does not guarantee the accuracy of the information presented at these sites.

www.mhhe.com

CONTENTS

Chapter 4   Close-Ups: Observing Our Environments   130

PREFACE FOR STUDENTS

You live in a world that's faster, closer, and in many ways more complex than it has ever been. Look in your backpack or take an inventory of your room, and you'll find many items not available to students just a generation ago. I-pods and cell phones, laptops and hand-held computers, cable television and the Internet, VCRs, CDs, DVDs and MP3s: your choices for entertainment, information, and communication grow greater every year. Not only does the world keep changing, but you are likely to contribute to those changes.

Where does writing fit into this expanding picture? How can a college course in composition prepare you for the kind of thinking and communicating you'll be doing in tomorrow's world? These are questions we'll be answering throughout this book while building bridges between the challenges of academic literacy and the ever-changing media environment.

The Writer's Eye takes a broad, inclusive view of composition. It begins with the idea that all forms of media—including movies, television, magazines, Web sites, and academic essays—are "composed." They are constructed by someone (or by several people) for an audience, usually with specific purposes in mind. They often have particular styles, follow recognizable formats, and organize their messages in familiar or unexpected patterns. We'll be referring to these compositions as texts, which may be articles or ads, talk shows or motion pictures. By comparing all kinds of texts, by learning how they are created and interpreted, or "read," you will learn how to use writing and reading as tools for realizing your goals.

This book takes your individuality and your cultural identity into account. It acknowledges who you are and builds on what you know. If you have special talents or interests in dancing or photography, for example, you'll have opportunities to relate these interests to what you read and write. If you've seen a lot of commercials (most Americans are exposed to more than a thousand ads a day) or have watched a lot of television, you'll be encouraged to apply your knowledge of those media to your academic work. In other words, you'll learn ways to connect your personal experiences, skills, and deep concerns—as well as those devices in your backpack—to what you'll be asked to do in all your college studies. And you'll learn to connect your college reading and writing to the challenges that face you beyond the campus as well.

The Writer's Eye is accompanied by a special Web site. Using the text and the Web site together will help you explore relationships among many kinds of visual and verbal texts. When you work with the Web site, you'll be screening documentaries and commercials, viewing magazine ads and Web pages, listening to radio shows, following Web links, and reading popular articles as well as college essays, poems, and stories. These visual and auditory texts will help to widen your definition of literacy and your command of broad literacy skills. As you begin thinking of these different texts as forms of composition, as you practice reading and viewing with a writer's eye, you will be writing more and more in sync with the expanding world of media.

At the same time, you'll be creating your own texts, including personal essays, reviews, research reports, persuasive papers, and possibly a video, Web site, or multimedia presentation. By comparing and contrasting different texts, you'll begin to see what they have in common and what is unique about each one. Through this kind of analysis, you'll come to understand the essential elements of all media. You'll learn to communicate effectively using any technique or technology, no matter what form it may take.

To be an effective writer and a proficient reader takes commitment. You will do your best work when something vital is at stake: a special interest, a deep concern, a pressing need. So choose projects based on your interest and experiences. Whether you're active in the community or dealing with personal issues or preparing for a career, there is a way to relate each chapter in the book to your ongoing concerns, so that your writing and reading move you forward toward your individual goals. At the same time, be open to new possibilities. The aim of good communication is not only to describe your world but also to extend it by including fresh ideas, information, and perspectives. My hope is that this book will help you make informed, effective contributions to your growth and the communities around you.

PREFACE FOR INSTRUCTORS

We live in a world permeated by visual and auditory media that not only compete with the written word but also continually influence the form it takes. In the twenty-first century, our students are bombarded by the messages of pop culture in the form of television, fast-paced movies, flashy magazines, carry-on music, and the ubiquitous Internet. The traditional school notebook has been replaced by a backpack full of electronic gadgets that call for new skills to operate. Many students prefer to do research by sitting at a computer, never opening a book. Some have learned to compose papers by cutting and pasting other people's texts together in a kind of postmodern pastiche. What's more, the boundaries between one medium and another keep getting blurred. Novels start to read like movies, movies look like video games or MTV, while television takes on features of talk radio and magazines. All this media convergence can be bewildering to faculty who are trying to teach sound principles of literacy. And it can be confusing for students who find themselves in an academic world that relies heavily on the critical thinking and reading skills of print-based culture.

This book offers new ways to bridge the gap between pop culture and academic writing. It acknowledges the new kinds of knowledge and competencies that today's media savvy students have acquired, and it builds on what they already know to make their transition to college easier. It shows them how the texts they are expected to read and write are in many ways like the media texts with which they are familiar. It gets them thinking about the audiences, purposes, and styles of Web sites and television shows. It shows how some documentaries are organized like research papers and how commercials use rhetorical strategies that may work in persuasive essays. It also leads students to examine the differences between academic texts and the media products turned out by the commercial world. The goal is to sharpen their understanding of how all texts are constructed so they can become more critical readers and more effective writers.

The Writer's Eye: Composition in the Multimedia Age is an outgrowth of more than thirty-five years of teaching, research, and publishing in the fields of English and media education. Much of the book's methodology is informed by recent developments in cognitive psychology, critical thinking, and cultural studies. Media literacy, a regular part of the curriculum in other countries for many years, has now taken firm roots in the United States. The importance of media literacy skills is now recognized by the NCTE, IRA, and a growing number of state standards.

Exploring the relationships between modern media and traditional literacies

What makes *The Writer's Eye* distinctive is the underlying principle that writing and reading, the traditional focus of first-year English courses, may be understood and practiced by students in the larger context of our media culture. By presenting the process of composition in contexts that are already familiar to students, this text validates students' accumulated knowledge, enlarges their resources for visual thinking, and applies their media literacy to the tasks of writing, reading, and reasoning in today's world.

Consider the conceptual similarities between writing and other media. Filmmakers, television producers, and Web designers, like writers, must make decisions about purpose, audience, content, format, arrangement, and style. They follow codes and conventions, observe time-honored rhetorical strategies, and create visual texts for many of the purposes that motivate writers: to recollect the past, describe the present, make proposals for the future, investigate issues, or take a stand.

The Writer's Eye approaches these ideas in a way that honors the principles of student-centered learning. In drawing on students' visual and auditory abilities as well as their facility with written language, this book enables them to draw from personal resources that are not always acknowledged in an English class. By reading and viewing texts in a variety of media, students learn that creative as well as critical thinking goes into composing and construing all kinds of texts.

Organization of *The Writer's Eye*

The Writer's Eye is arranged in two parts. Part One includes an introductory chapter, a section on Reading across the Media, and a section on Composing across the Media. Part Two includes seven chapters of Readings and Screenings arranged both rhetorically and thematically, each focusing on a particular kind of composing that is explored through written and visual texts.

The introduction, "Viewing with a Writer's Eye," presents some of the basic principles underlying the textbook and prepares students to make the kinds of connections between writing and visual media that they will be encountering in the course.

Chapter 1, "Reading across the Media," is about making sense of any text, printed or pictorial. It begins with a section on critical thinking, inviting students to explore the similarities and differences between verbal and visual languages. It demonstrates how what we get from the page or screen depends on personal experience, cultural expectations, familiarity with other texts, and our knowledge of dynamic sign systems. The chapter continues with sections on formal analysis and cultural perspectives before examining popular forms of parody. Students look closely at commercials, magazine ads, and selected passages of prose to sharpen their ability to understand and evaluate such documents. This section serves students as a foundation for the kinds of interpretation, response, and critical inquiry they will be doing in Part Two.

Chapter 2, "Composing across the Media," offers a closer look at the processes of composing as practiced by writers and producers of visual media. Using student and professional work as models, it shows how practitioners use the resources of written English or film language to clarify their impressions, how they arrive at a controlling theme, how they decide what to include, how they arrange and rearrange what they have into a meaningful sequence for a given audience. Students may return to this procedural information whenever they engage in the writing and media options of Part Two.

The composing chapter helps students tap the power of visual thinking. It shows them how to approach a new subject as a camera might, zooming in on a telling detail or shifting the angle to a new point of view. It suggests how students might organize thoughts and information in iconic patterns and visualize their compositions as storyboards, drawing on the familiar conventions of commercials, films, and television programs to help them begin, organize, and conclude their essays.

Part Two is divided into seven chapters, each focusing on an important rhetorical purpose: remembering, describing, explaining, reporting, evaluating, persuading, and predicting. This arrangement will be familiar to teachers who have organized their courses by traditional essay modes (like narration, description, and argument) or rhetorical patterns (definition, comparison and contrast, cause and effect), except that here the emphasis is on purpose and theme. The assignments, activities, and composing tips in each chapter are linked to a particular goal—such as evaluating a past experience, resolving a conflict, or predicting a future—and the readings and screenings center on a common theme—such as the environment, American cultures, or gender differences—so that students learn while engaging in specific projects of inquiry and communication linked to important issues. The intended outcome of each chapter is always a student composition of consequence, aligned with the writer's deepest interests and the world at large. Typically, the composition is an academic essay, but every chapter offers a media option as well, such as producing a video or creating a Web page. In this way, students are invited to engage in writing and composing in other media as forms of reflection and decision-making.

Although a writing course or a book is necessarily sequential, proceeding one unit and assignment at a time, Part Two assumes that competence in thinking and composing evolves more like a tree than like a chain of boxcars. That is, the many skills of writing develop simultaneously along many fronts, growing fuller and stronger through continual practice and mutual reinforcement. So while the rhetorical chapters in Part Two follow a recognizable trajectory, they may be assigned in any order.

Working with Part Two

Each chapter in Part Two guides students through a given writing project or media activity, taking care to place each project or activity in a larger context. While these seven chapters may be read in any combination, they offer various degrees of continuity. A student with a special interest in environmental issues, for example, might compose a video essay describing a local pond for Chapter 4, write an essay analyzing the threats to the pond's ecosystem for Chapter 5, and then produce a persuasive paper calling for decisive action for Chapter 8. Another student who writes about her teenage struggles with bulimia for Chapter 3 might pursue the topic further in an investigative report for Chapter 6. Or the same student might write a critique of modern fashion trends for Chapter 7, and create a Web site offering advice to teens and parents. In this way, *The Writer's Eye* encourages students to read and create purposeful compositions that are aligned with both their deepest individual concerns and the larger media environment in which they live.

Each chapter in Part Two offers the following features to help students understand a fundamental mode of composition and put it into effective practice.

- A brief introduction clarifies the rhetorical goals and thematic focus of each chapter. The theme is illustrated by a two-page photo montage.
- **Scenarios from Life** describe where the chapter's key purpose appears in school, at work, in personal life, and in the community.

- All chapters include a feature called **Why Write . . . ?** to provide further motivation and clarification. In Chapter 4, students learn about Sherlock Holmes' distinction between seeing and observing in "Why Write to Describe?"

- **Composing Options** describes the writing project and media assignment for the chapter.

- **Tips on Writing** offers guidelines for doing the project (from planning and collecting through drafting and revising) and for evaluating the final product.

- **Readings and Screenings** comprise the major part of each chapter in Part Two. Readings (essays and articles) and Screenings (commercials, documentaries, news programs, radio broadcasts, and Web sites) help to illustrate and model the kind of composing students are asked to do. Screenings are represented by video clips, storyboards, transcripts, and screen shots. As well, the texts are related by theme. For example, in Chapter 4, where the unifying theme is the environment, students can watch a video of Anna Quindlen on location at a New York City street fair, then read her description of the event in her weekly column. They can explore National Geographic's Web site on J. Michael Fay's Congo Trek and compare descriptions of his African journey in his journal, on the Web, and in the magazines. They can also read superb descriptive essays by a cross-section of writers like Annie Dillard, Diane Ackerman, Esmeralda Santiago, Linda Hogan, and Mark Twain. The preview section prepares students with background information on each author and gets them thinking about the topic. The follow-up questions guide them along four lines of inquiry: personal response, critical analysis, cultural perspectives, and ideas for their own writing.

- **Across the Media.** Each Readings and Screenings section is introduced by a brief list that shows the chapter's central purpose at work in popular culture.

- **A Student Writer in Action** provides student readers with a model essay by a college student like themselves. This section traces the student's composing process from start to finish with brainstorming ideas, draft materials, and comments on revision. It also includes follow-up questions to help students relate the model essay to their own work.

- An **Evaluation Checklist** is a convenient way for students to assess their own written work.

- **Weblinks** is a boxed feature that links students to reliable sources on the Internet where they can read more about the purpose of the chapter.

- **Taking Stock** is an opportunity for students to reflect on what they've learned from the chapter. At the end of Chapter 4, they briefly review how their descriptive skills have improved and where these skills will be useful in their lives.

Supplements

Online Learning Center: www.mhhe.com/costanzo
Integrated and cross-referenced in the book, the *Writer's Eye* Web site features the video and audio selections used in print form in the book, additional textbook material, related links, and downloads for both students and instructors.

The Writer's Eye Online Learning Center is also powered by Catalyst 2.0, McGraw-Hill's premier online tool for writing and research, featuring interactive writing tutors, as well as tutorials on visual rhetoric, avoiding plagiarism and evaluating sources, over 4,400 grammar exercises with personalized feedback, Bibliomaker software, and much more.

Teaching Composition Faculty Listserv: www.mhhe.com/tcomp

Offered by McGraw-Hill as a service to the composition teachers, this listserv brings together senior members of the college composition community with new members—junior faculty, adjuncts, and teaching assistants—in an online newsletter and accompanying discussion group that addresses issues of pedagogy in theory and in practice.

Acknowledgments

A textbook is not the work of a single person but a collaborative effort. My co-authors include colleagues, students, librarians, the staff at McGraw-Hill, and others who have each made valued contributions to *The Writer's Eye*.

For more than thirty-five years, Westchester Community College has been my academic home. I am grateful to Dr. Joseph N. Hankin, its dedicated president, for sustaining an environment that fosters excellence in teaching while supporting the efforts of faculty to grow through scholarship and publication. The library staff at WCC is first-rate, and I especially wish to thank Chris Kern, Alice DeWaters, Dorothy Freeman, Dale Leifeste, Sandy Schepis, and Una Shih for assisting me with my research. It has been my privilege to work alongside talented and trusted colleagues such as Michael Bobkoff, Greta Cohan, Frank Madden, Linda Sledge, and Maryanne Vent, who have generously shared their personal and professional lives with me these many years, as well as more recent members of my department, who continue to inspire with their commitment to good teaching: Richard Courage, Alan Devenish, Michael Downie, Elizabeth Gaffney, Rasma Koch, Mary Ellen LeClair, Craig Padawer, Richard Rodriguez, Mira Sakrajda, Patricia Sehulster, Christine Timm, James Werner, and Scott Zaluda.

The student essays that appear throughout the book were written by my first-year composition students at Westchester Community College: Melissa Ferreira, Stacey Whalen, Anna Tyutyunik, Nuala Lynch, Lisa Wess, Sylvia Pace, Mutsumi Oishi, James Gerace, Kathryn Diamond, and Monique Bonfiglio. Other student contributors include Holli Bundy, Shawnita Payne, and Dawn Turner, who graciously permitted me to interview them about their various media compositions.

A number of robust pioneers in the media literacy movement have influenced me directly and indirectly. I owe a deep debt of gratitude to Ralph Amelio, Neil Anderson, Frank Baker, David Bruce, Renée Cherow-O'Leary, Mary Christel, Barry Duncan, Ben Fuller, Steve Goodman, Renee Hobbs, Len Masterman, John Pungente, Marieli Rowe, Elizabeth Thoman, and Kathleen Tyner. To Jonathan Lovell, my cherished friend and fellow traveler, I am grateful for a lifetime of wise counsel and steadfast support.

I want to thank all the people at McGraw-Hill who helped to bring this book into being, coaxing it from a glimmer in this writer's eye into the light of day. I am especially grateful to Lisa Moore, who signed me on, to Tori Fullard, who started me off on the right track, to Laura Barthule and Alexis Walker, who guided me through much of the manuscript's progress with immeasurable patience and skill, and to Ben Morrison, who took up the reins with Tori for the final laps, managing a hundred hurdles with grace and ease. Brett Coker's many talents and tireless energy steered the book through the production process under the alert and practiced eyes of Christopher Bennem and his able assistant, Jesse Hassenger. Joshua Feldman and Alexander Rohrs lent their imagination and technical proficiency for the Web site. For assistance with clearing permissions, I am much obliged to Marty Granahan and Dorothy Wendel, as I am to Joan Pendleton for her judicious editing and to Nora Agbayani for her help with the photographs. I owe a special word of appreciation to Marlene Rubins, who contributed many of the photos and a great deal more.

Many colleagues across the country generously offered their expertise and feedback during the development of *The Writer's Eye*, and I acknowledge them most gratefully:

Maria Cahill, Abraham Baldwin Agricultural College
Terry Carter, Southern Polytechnic University
James Clark, UNC Greensboro
Jane Frick, Missouri Western State College
Lorie Goodman, Pepperdine University
Traci Kelly, University of Minnesota–Crookston
Karla Saari Kitalong, University of Central Florida
Argie Manolis, Arizona State University
Barry Mauer, University of Central Florida
Michael McDowell, Portland Community College
Michael Michau, Purdue University
Tamara Miles, State University of West Georgia
Megan O'Neill, Stetson University
Dana Perales, Mira Costa College
Stephanie Paterson, California State University–Stanislaus
Patricia Webb Peterson, Arizona State University
John Sapienza, City College of San Francisco
Nicholas Schevera, College of Lake County
Allison Smith, Louisiana Tech University
Janet Starner, East Stroudsburg University
John Tinker, Foothill College

Finally, I want to express my heartfelt appreciation to Diana for opening this writer's eye to alluring new prospects on the journey of life.

PART ONE

Foundations: Seeing, Reading, and Composing

Viewing with a Writer's Eye

Today's media environment throbs with a bewildering array of electronic messages. As technologies converge, words, images, and sounds combine to form new kinds of hybrid texts on countless screens. From the dazzling digital displays of Times Square to the wide-screen monitors that line the modern marketplace like wallpaper, visual and verbal languages interact, and animated characters talk with real actors. The traditional dividing lines between pictures and print, advertising and entertainment, fact and fiction grow dim and disappear. Meanwhile, more of us are using laptops, handheld computers, iPods, mobile phones, and other miniature marvels that mix and match the media even more.

How do these trends affect your daily life? What does it mean to be literate in a world where the screens that carry your visual and verbal texts continuously shrink, expand, cross-breed, and multiply? What skills and knowledge will you need in the years ahead? And what can you learn in a college composition class? This introductory chapter will help you to explore such questions, personally and in relationship to the world at large, laying the foundation for a lifelong course in reading and composing across the media.

We live in a world permeated by the media. The tunes and talk of radio wake us in the morning, escort us to work or school, and float us through the shopping mall. The pulsating images of television are pumped into our living rooms and bedrooms, our restaurants, barbershops, and fitness centers. In the doctor's office or the supermarket, racks of magazines divert us from the tedium of waiting. And the flickering computer screen is everywhere. Nearly all the spaces where we work and socialize and wait are filled with mediated messages.

Yet we are not all attuned to the same media. If you're like most students, you probably have spent more time watching television than reading books, more time communicating by cell phone than by writing letters. According to the National Association of Broadcasters, the time spent viewing television in the average U.S. home amounts to 7 hours and 40 minutes per day. Except for sleeping, that's more time than most Americans give to any other activity, including school. In contrast, the curriculum of higher education puts a heavy emphasis on print. In college, you're expected to critically analyze essays, articles, books, and other printed texts. This book is intended to prepare you for the writing, reading, speaking, and listening that you'll do in college and beyond by building connections between your viewing experience and your experience as a reader and a writer. It begins with the assumption that the task of producing an image, a film, or a television show is a lot like writing a story or an essay. The people who produce *20/20* or *The Evening News* must gather information, focus on a topic, select material, arrange what they've selected into a meaningful sequence, and present it in a style that will appeal to a particular audience, just as writers do when they compose an essay. In addition, the kind of mental work you do in order to make sense of what you watch on television—interpreting the images, anticipating what comes next, relating what you see to what you know about the world and about other television shows—is similar to what you do to make sense of a written text. This book makes explicit connections between the moving image and writing that will help you to explore and strengthen those connections: it will help you to apply what you already know about visual media to the task of becoming a better writer and reader.

An analogy may help to illustrate this point. Imagine that you're learning how to play tennis. You can usually return the ball when it is hit to your forehand side, but you have a lot of trouble with your backhand shot. The coach gives you precise instructions. She tells you where to look, how to tilt your racket, and when to plant your feet. But while you're busy looking, tilting, and planting, that ball keeps flying by you in a blur of yellow fuzz. The more you try to follow the instructions, the more frustrated you get. Then one day a friend stops by and notices your plight. Your friend offers a suggestion: the next time a ball comes to your backhand side, pretend you're throwing a Frisbee sidearm, something you can do well. So you try it. This time, your racket connects, driving the ball far into the opposing court.

The lesson in this story is not just about tennis. It's about learning. Generic instructions are made for everybody, but every individual is different. When you can make a personal connection between what you want to learn and what you already know, the task becomes easier. In the tennis analogy, all the physical and mental knowledge gained from years of playing Frisbee—the bent knees, the arm across the body, the follow-through—is applied instantly to the unfamiliar task of hitting a backhand shot. Furthermore, it is applied holistically instead of analytically. That is, the many movements and positions of a Frisbee throw are transferred to the backhand *as a whole*—in a fluid and unified action—instead of being analyzed as separate steps, one after the other, as they might be in an instruction book. The power of holistic learning is a feature of visual media, and it is one of the foundations of this book.

As you move through the following pages, you'll be encouraged to relate what you read and write to what you see. You'll have a chance to build on your knowledge of popular media by relating this knowledge of popular media to your general literacy. For example, it is likely that you already read the messages in commercials and interpret film techniques like close-ups, flashbacks, and fades. You make judgments about news broadcasters and talk show guests. You may know how to program a VCR or surf the Internet. In fact, you have already developed a certain degree of **media literacy,** the ability to access, understand, analyze, and evaluate messages in a variety of media. Although the chief aim of this book is to help you sharpen and strengthen your traditional literacy skills, it seeks to do so by widening the definition of literacy to include the whole spectrum of media by which human beings communicate with one another.

To understand literacy in this wider context, this book asks you to think of many things as **texts.** People usually speak of printed works as texts—essays, poems, books, and other documents that are composed entirely of written words. But movies, print advertisements, television programs, and commercials also can be considered texts. Film and television texts consist of images and sounds as well as words, but these images and sounds may be as carefully arranged, or composed, as the words on a page, and they may be interpreted, or read, with the same degree of skill. So in this text, you will be looking closely at both visual texts and written texts, at news programs, television shows, Web sites, radio documentaries, and advertisements as well as essays, in order to analyze how they work, how they differ, and how they are alike. You will discover more about the way these texts are put together, the way they use the codes and conventions of language to shape meaning, the strategies they adopt to inform, persuade, or entertain us, and why we respond to them the way we do. Meanwhile, you will learn how to create and shape your own texts, the kind that express your feelings, develop your thoughts, and communicate your messages with greater ease, power, and precision.

By becoming more aware of the skills you use when watching films, surfing the Web, and navigating other media texts, you will be better prepared to apply these skills to more academic texts. Like a Frisbee player on the tennis court, you'll see what can be transferred from the old, familiar sport to the new one—and you'll develop new strengths for the new game. When the Frisbee player and the tennis player begin to see themselves more broadly as athletes, they are ready to take on any game. That's what it means to read the media with a writer's eye. This book invites you to think of yourself as an active reader and composer of texts in many media. The next two chapters tell you how in more detail. The seven chapters in Part 2 offer guided practice reading and composing multimedia texts on a variety of captivating topics and in a range of useful forms. These are the kinds of texts that you will be encountering throughout your college career and the rest of your life.

WHY PAY CLOSE ATTENTION TO THE MEDIA?

In addition to helping you write, analyzing the media can reveal much about the inner workings of our culture. When we start to notice how media texts are put together, why they are constructed in certain ways, and who makes the decisions, we begin to understand the far-reaching influences that these decision makers have on our lives.

You might begin your own exploration by considering the choices that you make every day. What do you eat for breakfast? What clothes do you pick out to wear? Where do you get your daily news? Start with the items on your breakfast plate. Are your preferences for any products

First and nine.

Milk's number one in my playbook. It has the nine essential nutrients I need to go all the way. So ask somebody to pass the milk. It's your best call.

got milk?

PLAYERS INC

influenced by advertisements? Think beyond the cereal commercials and "Got Milk?" campaigns, which may or may not have introduced you to your favorite cereal or made you partial toward milk. Do you choose foods that are low in calories or high in protein? Are these choices connected to what you see reflected in the mirror or on the bathroom scale? In other words, are your eating habits linked to your body image, and if so, where does your assessment of this image come from? Chances are, the way you perceive yourself has a lot to do with the male and female bodies idealized in the movies, fashion magazines, and perfume ads. You might say that everyone wants to look thin or well toned, that this is healthy, but if you compare our best-paid models to those in other countries or even to those at other times in American history, you'll see that body images are shaped by culture. And our culture is largely shaped by the media.

What is true of foods and fashions is also true of news. Researchers speak of "news consumers" as if current events were some kind of product to be packaged and sold. They point out that most Americans get most of their news from television, although many also learn about world events from newspapers, the radio, and the Internet. Who decides which events make the front page or the evening news report? And how are such decisions made? Here again, the medium shapes the message. Television favors moving images, so dramatic, easy-to-get pictures are more likely to be broadcast than thoughtful commentaries on complex issues. A violent protest will usually preempt a peaceful demonstration. Or, as they say in the broadcast business, "If it bleeds, it leads." Radio is more partial to spoken language, so radio news programs feature lots of interviews and chatty editorials. Still, it's hard to follow intricate arguments while listening or to digest large quantities of data, which explains why radio tends to simplify the news. For more comprehensive coverage and multiple perspectives, we need newspapers, magazines, or some other printed form of media. We also need more time to select and read the details.

While the kind of news we get depends partly on the medium, it also depends on other factors that are often hard to discern. The daily news lineup is created by a team of editors, people who decide what we'll see on CNN or Fox 5, what we'll hear on CBS radio or NPR, or what we'll read in *Newsweek, USA Today,* or the *New York Times.* Their decisions may be guided by deeply held convictions, by their sense of what audiences want, and by policies set by people higher up. In this age of corporate mergers, more and more producers of the news are owned by giant conglomerates with interests that reach across the media spectrum. To take one example, businesses as varied as book publishing (Time Inc.; Warner Books; Little, Brown), cable television (HBO, CNN), online services (AOL Instant Messenger, MapQuest), film and television production (Warner Bros., Castle Rock, New Line Cinema, TBS Superstation, Turner Classic Movies), and magazines (*Time, Life, Fortune, People, Mad* magazine, and more than fifty other titles) all belonged to one vast parent company in 2005, Time Warner. In 1995, Disney bought Capital Cities/ABC, adding the huge music and television company to its six film production and distribution companies, two record companies, four theme parks, and more than a hundred magazines, as well as book publishers, cable networks, cruise line, and hockey team. Do these mergers affect what we see on the news? When Disney's *Good Will Hunting* came to movie screens, ABC's *World News Sunday* ran a feature on the Boston bar where it was filmed. When *Armageddon* was released, ABC did a science feature on asteroids, including clips from the Disney film. The opportunities for promoting products across the media are many.

This illustrates an important point about media authorship. When we ask who produces a particular movie, television show, or publication, the question is larger than asking who is the author of an essay or a book. By exploring the business interests that operate behind the scene, we may begin to understand that while television and magazines may bring us information and entertainment, they also bring us to the sponsors and advertisers who pay for the commercials and ads. The answer to the question "Who gains something from this text?" is often a business concern, and more broadly it is the commercial system itself. The answer to the question "Who pays?" may all too often be those of us who buy into the system. Such questions make us more aware. We begin to see how Barbie dolls, designer jeans, and action heroes shape our images of what it is to be attractive. We realize that the sources of our news about the world are themselves subject to internal and

Photographers—and protestors—know that news editors favor images of conflict and controversy. How does the medium shape the message?

external pressures, which explains why current events are represented differently by mainstream American television and newspapers than by the news media in other countries. In other words, reading the media with a critical eye gives us insight into ourselves as citizens, consumers, and social beings. The more we know about the choices others make to influence us, the more real choices *we* have. In today's society, where so much depends on those who mold the media, awareness of the media and how they work can free us to shape our own lives.

WHAT MEDIA CHOICES DO *YOU* MAKE?

The rest of this introduction will help you understand your daily choices in our media-driven world. You'll learn how to construct your personal media profile and compare it to others. You'll be invited to keep a media log and participate in a media fast. You'll have an opportunity to write a media memoir. These activities will prepare you for the kinds of critical thinking about media that you'll be practicing throughout this book.

Media Survey (Individual Project)

A good place to start is with a survey of your own experience with media. How much time do you spend watching television, going to the movies, listening to the radio, or reading books and magazines? Which radio and television programs do you like most? What kinds of books and movies do you prefer? How do you interact with the media in your life? Do you usually watch movies with friends or alone? Do you read with the radio on? When you write, do you seek a quiet place or do you prefer some background noise? Such questions will help you to prepare a personal media profile so you can see revealing patterns in your media experience and compare those patterns to the experience of others.

After surveying your present connections to the media, you'll be in a good position to write a media memoir that regards those connections from a historical perspective. You'll also be better situated to ask questions about what the media you consume say about you or others. This book gives you a map of the territory and a set of useful tools.

Personal Media Profile (Individual Project)

When you have completed the questionnaire, write a few paragraphs to summarize your general observations. Which media are most important in your life? What do you expect from these media? How do you go about getting what you want from them? What features of your favorite media do you appreciate most? Do you see any changes in your media habits over the last few years? What further changes would you like to make?

A few sample quotes will give you an idea of the range of observations other students make while exploring their responses to the questionnaire:

- "Radio is the most important medium in my life. I listen to music during my drive to school and when I clean house. It keeps life from being boring."
- "Growing up, I always thought television was my friend."
- "As a teenage girl in Jamaica in an all-girl school, you were popular if you were seen reading the latest *Sweet Dreams* or Danielle Steele romance. Now living in the United States, I consider television and radio the most important popular media in my life."
- "Television gives me quick updates on society."
- "Magazines keep me informed about the latest styles and fashions. Books, on the other hand, allow me to escape from my life and enter a fantasy land."
- "The written word is patient."
- "When you have read a novel that later is produced into a movie, it never is as good as the book."
- "I usually spend about 40 hours a week watching television. If I'm not watching TV, I listen to the radio. I do not spend any time at the movies because I don't have time."

Like some students, you may be surprised by your heavy use of electronic media. When you add up all the hours that you spend with radio, television, computers, videos, and elec-

Media Questionnaire

1. Time Spent with Media

Estimate the time you spend each week with these media:

  a. Movies (on video, DVD, TV, cable, the Internet, and at the theater)

  b. Television (other than movies)

  c. Radio (music, talk shows, news)

  d. Reading (newspapers, magazines, books, instructions)

  e. Writing (letters, e-mail, class assignments, journals, blogs, job reports, notes)

  f. Other (Identify any important media not listed above. Where do computers fit in? What about cell phones? iPods? Handhelds?)

2. Media Preferences

  a. People use media selectively (they pick out particular movies, watch only certain television shows, read books they've chosen for a special reason) or unselectively (they just "go to the movies," channel surf, read whatever comes along). Are you selective or unselective with each medium you use?

  b. Identify the kinds of choices that you make:

    Favorite movie genres (adventure, comedy, romance, horror)

    Television (news, game shows, talk shows, sitcoms, drama, soaps)

    Computers (Internet, games, e-mail, schoolwork)

    Reading (local newspaper, fashion magazines, mysteries)

    Writing (lists, reports, letters, e-mail, journal, lyrics, poetry)

3. Media Habits

  a. How do you usually watch TV? (alone, with family, while doing homework, munching on potato chips)

  b. When you see a movie, is it usually alone or with others? (with family, friends, a date)

  c. Where and when do you do most of your reading? (in a quiet section of the library, at night in bed before sleep, in the doctor's office, in the dorm)

  d. Under what conditions do you generally write? (in your bedroom with the radio on, at your home computer, on the dining room table, in your favorite park, at work)

tronic games, you may realize that much of your waking life has been lived in the presence of these media, and you may wonder what you have absorbed from them. Or, like other students, you may find that you no longer watch as much television or play as many video games as you once did. Changes in your lifestyle—including the new pressures of school, work, and community—may have led to changes in your media habits.

You may also notice that you rely on media for different needs. You might tune to particular programs or check familiar magazines for specific information—the weather, for example, or advice on personal relationships—while at other times you might just scan the channels for "the right mood." As one student put it, "If I'm feeling sad or lonely, I expect the radio to cheer me up. Sometimes the radio or TV will motivate me to do something—get me interested in reading more about a topic or in trying a new product." Another student wrote, "When there's nothing to do, I search for the remote."

Questions about genre can be revealing too. Do you watch a lot of soap operas, talk shows, comedy, or action movies? When you enter a bookstore or a library, which section do you head for? What kind of CDs do you own? Consider what your answers say about you as a person or about your purposes for using media. Since this book is organized according to different purposes for writing (to reconstruct memories, to explain things, to inform, to persuade, to solve problems, and so on), knowing what media you choose for different purposes will help you to make stronger connections to your writing.

The section on media habits may be the most revealing. One student noted that "The first thing I do when I get home is turn on the TV." She realized that television is a substitute for family, a way to feel connected to other human beings, and she began to see how television encourages this feeling with laugh tracks, folksy news teams, and group-oriented sitcoms. Another student observed, "I can't concentrate on homework without the radio or TV." He wondered why he needs background sounds and images while others require unanimated quiet for their work. Many students observe that they like to use the media interactively. They watch TV with the remote control at hand, call in to radio shows, program their stereos and VCRs, and enjoy controlling their computers with a joystick or keyboard. Such behavior suggests a trend away from the stereotype of passive viewing. You'll have a chance to explore this and other trends when you compare your Personal Media Profile to the profiles of others in the class. In this way, you can begin to create a profile of your personal learning styles.

Group Media Profile (Group Activity)

One way to see how your media habits compare to the experience of others is to share your personal observations with a small group of students. Use the following questions to pool your information and create a Group Media Profile. Look for areas of common agreement, but keep track of any split responses too. Whenever the group seems to divide into two or more subgroups, try to find reasons for these trends. Does the group profile surprise you in any way?

You may find it worthwhile to make a formal tabulation. To do this, record everyone's response to every question on a chart. First, you'll need to decide how to sort the answers. For example, take the first item in Part 1: time spent each week watching movies. Here, your group's

Group Media Profile Questions

1. **Time Spent**
   a. Rank the media in order of time spent with each.
   b. Is your group oriented more toward viewing, listening, or reading?

2. **Preferences**
   a. Is your group generally selective or unselective in its use of media?
   b. List the most popular genres for movies, television, radio, and reading material in your group. What kind of writing do you choose to do?

3. **Media Habits:** Describe any interesting patterns that you find in your group's media habits: why you use various media and how you interact with them.

Group Media Profile Display

You can create a table, graph, pie chart, or other visual display to clarify your group profile. Here are some examples, created with a computer.

GROUP PROFILE—TABLE

Time Spent with Media (estimated hours per week)

	Movies	Television	Radio	Reading	Writing
Danny	9	15	15	4	1
Clarissa	4	2	1	7	5
Jasmine	2	3	10	2	2
Brian	4	10	2.5	4	6
Tim	5	8	10	1	7
Total Time	24	38	38.5	18	21
Average Time	4.8	7.6	7.7	3.6	4.2

Group Genre Preferences

Movies	Action, Romance, Comedy
Television	Sports, Sitcoms, Drama (24, Lost)
Radio	Rock music, Talk shows
Reading	Textbooks, Romantic novels, Newspapers, Fashion magazines, Internet
Writing	Schoolwork, E-mail, Journal writing

Common Media Habits

- Our group watches more movies on video and DVD than in the theater. We can talk, eat, and socialize more comfortably this way.
- We like to have the radio or television on when we do schoolwork. It seems to help our concentration. Does that mean that we are multitasking learners?
- We watch movies and TV mostly for entertainment.
- We read mostly for information, sometimes for pleasure.
- We write partly for ourselves to help us record information and organize our thoughts (lists, journals, notes), partly for others (schoolwork, job reports, e-mail).

(continued)

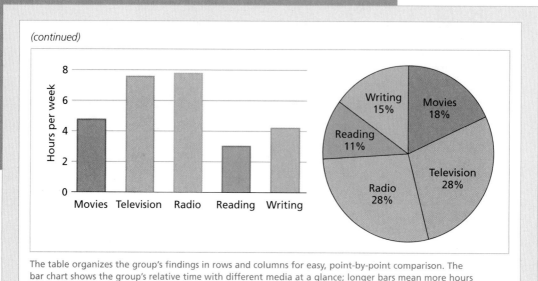

(continued)

The table organizes the group's findings in rows and columns for easy, point-by-point comparison. The bar chart shows the group's relative time with different media at a glance; longer bars mean more hours per week. The pie chart represents these hours as part of the group's total time with media, each slice showing the percentage of time spent with a given medium.

responses may fit into three categories: fewer than two hours, from two to six hours, more than six hours. These can be the headings for your tally. Or, as an alternative, you might add up all the hours and divide by the number of students to obtain an average for each item. For the questions in Part 2, you might count the number of selective and unselective users for each medium. Then you might list the most popular genres (romance or adventure novels, MTV, or talk shows) within each medium, using check marks to register each time someone prefers that genre. Part 3 doesn't lend itself to easy tabulation, but you can jot down any revealing trends. For example, do most students in your group prefer background sound or silence when they read or write? Do they turn on the radio or the TV as soon as they come home? Which media seem to be the focal points of social gatherings?

Discuss genres with your group and try to identify the larger purposes behind your preferences. If you prefer mostly comedies and action movies, are you choosing movies largely for entertainment and escape? If you like watching talk shows and sitcoms, does this mean that television fills a need for being in the company of other people? If you read only newspapers and how-to books, is reading more a source of information than of pleasure?

You may be surprised, even amused to learn how closely you're connected through the media. Our media constitute a common culture, a core of shared experience, so that we can talk about movie stars and sitcoms with distant strangers as if we're talking about close friends. How many times have you started a popular song or a commercial jingle and heard a dozen voices take up the tune? On the other hand, you may be surprised by the differences within your group. Someone may be an enthusiastic reader; someone else may watch thirty movies a

MEDIA USE BY CONSUMERS (HOURS PER PERSON PER YEAR)

	1990	1995	2000	2005
Broadcast TV	1120	1019	999	679
Cable TV	350	556	651	869
Radio	1135	1091	961	978
Recorded Music	235	289	357	179
Newspapers	175	165	107	183
Books	95	99	90	106
Magazines	90	84	71	124
Home Video	42	53	59	76
Movies in Theaters	12	12	12	12
Online/Internet	<1	7	124	183

Source: Veronis, Suhler, & Associates, Inc., *Communication Industry Forecast.*

month. Books or movie titles that are commonplace to one member of your group may sound like a foreign language to the other. Further probing may reveal different levels of trust in different media. Are the people in your group more likely to believe what they read or what they see on television? Does greater familiarity with a particular medium make them more or less critical of it?

Just as your individual choices change, national trends shift with the times. The polls show that Americans watch less broadcast television today than they did ten years ago. During the same period, they have come to spend more time with home video, cable television, and computers. Above is a national comparison of time spent with media since 1990.

Media Log (Individual Project)

How much time do you really spend with different media? One way to find out is to keep a media log. Select a time span (one week will give you a good sampling), and assign a page to each date. On each page, list every medium you use: writing, radio, television, computer, magazines, newspapers, books, movie theater, telephone, VCR, DVD, and so on. If you use the computer for different activities, you may want to divide that entry into parts, like computer games, word processing, and the Internet. At the end of each day, record the number of minutes you spent with each medium. Don't forget to include exposure to media in public places or time you listened to the radio while driving. Then add up your totals at the end of the week.

What did you discover? How close does the actual logged time come to your estimates in the Media Questionnaire? What portion of your waking time is spent with one or another form of media? Which media take up most of this time? Are you satisfied with this arrangement? Are there any decisions to make?

Media Fast (Individual Project)

One choice available to you is to pull the plug. Try this experiment for a day. Avoid exposure to any electronic medium for twenty-four hours. This means no television, no radio, no recorded music, nothing that connects you to the media culture with batteries or an electric cord. You may even want to avoid writing or reading as well. No pens or pencils. No newspapers or magazines.

After the fast, report on your experience. What was it like to be deprived of all those things you take for granted in your daily life? What did you miss the most? the least? What did you learn about the media? What did you learn about yourself? Are there any resolutions to be made?

Media Memoirs (Individual Project)

A media memoir tells the history of your relationship to the media. It is a way to reminisce about the role of various media in your life: the television programs you watched as a child, the video games you used to play, the books you used to read under the covers at night. You might begin by recalling your earliest memories of writing, or being read to, or of going to the movies with family or friends. What do you remember about those experiences? Were they chiefly positive or negative? Who else did they involve? What places do you associate with those memories? What changed as you got older? What influences contributed to the changes? Such questions can add a biographical dimension to your media profile. They can also help you to understand your personal development within the ongoing evolution of media culture.

Here is how the author of this book approached this task by writing an entry in his regular journal:

BILL COSTANZO'S JOURNAL ENTRY: WHY DO I LIKE TO READ?

What is my connection to reading? Where did that drive come from to read anything in sight when I was growing up: cereal boxes, Little Golden Books, comics, magazines—or that friendship with the printed word that kept me happily occupied for hours on the back porch in Brooklyn, typing stories on a black iron Remington about *Rip Reynolds, Space Cadet* or the endlessly amazing stories of the Costanzo family?

As far back as I can remember, I have always loved words, the magic of releasing sound and meaning from those cryptic symbols on the page, loved the rhythms and sonorities of language, even foreign languages, whose meanings eluded me but whose music could be played just by sounding out their melodies on the page, syllable by syllable. Somehow I knew that the meanings would come, in time, as they eventually did, from a persistence born of pleasure.

I sometimes think that pleasure has a personal beginning, rooted in moments of connection to important people in my life. I remember one moment when I was sick, tucked in bed with blankets to the chin, the sweet smell of a fever hovering above the scene, my mother sitting by the bedside reading from the story of "Uncle Wiggily and the Red Giant." I can't remember much about the story except that sweet smell and the comfort of the covers and the soothing voice, enveloping and warm, and a circle of soft lamplight dancing lightly round the two of us, like waves at the edges of our private world.

Funny how some pleasures stay with us long after the lamp has gone out, and we keep floating somehow on the current that connects us through the flow of words to people whom we love, connects us to people whom we've never had a chance to meet, to people long since gone and people yet to come, people linked together through the continuity of writing.

This journal entry gave me a chance to reflect on the source of pleasure that I take in reading. When I started writing it, I didn't know where it would lead. The image of my mother came to me while I was thinking back to books that I loved as a child. As that image grew brighter, as I began to capture it in words, to sharpen it, I realized how important that personal connection was for me. I realized how reading and writing were, and continue to be, bridges to other lives.

What follows was written by Melissa Ferreira, a college student. Melissa began by listing her early memories of video games and television shows in her journal, then developed these notes into a more reflective essay. Notice that Melissa chose to make general observations about her generation as well as describing her personal media habits. As you read, jot down any thoughts about your own history with media that come to mind.

STUDENT MEDIA MEMOIR BY MELISSA FERREIRA

We live in an ever-changing world where technology seems to be passing us by with every new day. It is sometimes hard to keep up with advances made in media. I can remember when *Donkey Kong* and *Frogger* were the most popular video games to play on my Atari game system. Now the graphics of some video games are so real that it's hard to tell the difference between fantasy and reality.

Years ago kids were told if they sit too close to the television they'll damage their eyes. They weren't discouraged from watching television; instead they watched as a family. Today kids are told they are watching too much television and that it will rot their brain. We no longer sit down as family units to do family activities. The computer has replaced television. Instead of watching television we're filling our heads with the high-powered Internet through our computers, cell phones, and Palm Pilots. The information superhighway is far and wide and taking advantage of it is easier than ever.

It is apparent to me that not only is changing technology upon us, but so is the task of keeping up with it. Being immersed in technology certainly does help; however, learning what to do with it is the real key. I believe that as we get older or "grow up," we begin to take media a bit more seriously. At least I did.

In elementary school I remember going to my grandmother's house after school and watching *Thunder Cats* and reruns of *Gilligan's Island*. In the evening my favorite shows to watch were *Three's Company* and *The Facts of Life*. It was the same routine every day. My mother would be cooking dinner while my sister and I watched television and did homework at the same time. After dinner we'd watch more TV as my mom would read yet another novel.

Sunday was cleaning day in my house. We'd listen to WNEW–FM, which used to be a classic rock station. My mom knew all the lyrics of artists like Stevie Nicks, Mick Jagger, and Bruce Springsteen. It's no surprise to me that these are some of my favorite artists today. It has become a ritual for me to listen to this type of music whenever I clean.

By the time I got to high school, the shows had changed, but the routine remained the same. My step-father and I enjoyed watching shows like *Married with Children* for its truly tasteless quality. When *90210* hit television, it made a big impact on every teenager in America. The evening soap opera brought us together with true-to-life scenarios and events to gossip over the next day at school. MTV was one of the most watched stations for teens to sit and stare at for hours on end. Comedy Central was also popular for airing reruns of *Saturday Night Live* and cult classics like *Pretty in Pink* and *The Breakfast Club*. Weeknights I would put myself to sleep by watching repeats of *Seinfeld* or *Cheers*. Of course we can't forget everyone's all-time favorite sitcom, *Friends*. After all, Chandler and Monica are some of the best friends I've ever had.

At some point I became addicted to the Discovery Channel and the Learning Channel. These channels provided me with information about things I would never really seek out to learn. They stimulated my mind and imagination with shows about forensic science and the Roswell incident. It was the reality that was appealing. I wasn't just sitting down in front of the television escaping life; I was immersing myself in the reality of the world.

As I grew older and went through new experiences and met new people, my tastes began to change. I had a friend named Jonathan who wanted to be a screenwriter. We would watch movies together and then discuss them. I found the conversation stimulating. I began to take film more seriously and appreciate what goes into the making of a good film. Movies tend to affect us powerfully by getting a point across in a way that nothing else can. Some films are so realistic that the emotions evoked are unspeakable. For example, *American History X* had some of the most powerful images I've ever seen captured on the big screen. To me that's what makes a good film. If I feel sick to my stomach or like I want to cry my eyes out afterwards, then the writer and director accomplished their goals.

In my mid-twenties I decided to further my education by going back to school. It was there that I met teachers who encouraged me to seek out more truths. I had never really been interested in watching the news or reading up on world events. Perhaps voting in my second presidential election changed my perspective. I started to become involved in what was really going on in the world around me and how it affects my life and my future. I began to pay attention to CNN and watched the nightly news regularly. I also began to read the science section of the *New York Times* in order to watch the development of the Human Genome Project. I realized that it never stops. The world continues to change and the only thing to do is pay attention.

Media are all around us. It is the individual's responsibility to decide what to do with them. We can take them at face value for entertainment purposes or we can use them to educate ourselves. With the ongoing development of media culture it seems we have no choice but to move forward. This reminds me of a line from what can be considered a classic film of my generation, *Ferris Bueller's Day Off*, when Ferris says, "Life moves quickly. If you don't stop to notice, you might miss it."

QUESTIONS TO CONSIDER

1. How much can you tell about Melissa's childhood from her media memoir? How do her media choices reflect her changing interests or those around her?

2. Compare Melissa Ferreira's memoir with your own memoir. Did you watch the same shows, listen to the same recording artists, or play similar video games? What major differences do you see in the shows you enjoyed while growing up and the way you watched them? How do you account for these differences?

3. What did Melissa learn about media as she got older? What conclusions does she come to about the role of technology in her life?

4. Melissa observes that changes in technology have accompanied changes in the family. To what extent do you agree with her? What patterns of change do you see today?

5. Reread Melissa's final statement about technology and individual responsibility. What options does she offer for confronting the media? What other options do you believe we have?

INVITATION TO WRITE

Write your own media memoir. Your writing may be as brief and casual as a journal entry or as long and formal as an academic essay, but let it be an exploration of your past experiences with the world of mediated messages. Here are some prompts to get you started:

1. What is your earliest memory of reading? Writing? Television? Movies? Computers?

2. Which forms of media (books, magazines, sitcoms, cartoons, video games) were most important to you growing up? What attracted you to those particular forms?

3. How did friends and family shape your early media experiences? Were there house rules about television or reading material? What tastes or habits did you pick up from others around you?

4. What recent changes do you notice in your use of media? What might account for the differences?

Now that you've read this introduction and completed some of the activities, you should have a clearer understanding of your place in our media environment. You should be more aware of the choices that you make each day involving various media and the reasons for your choices. We have begun to look at movies and television shows as texts, similar in some ways to printed texts but also different in significant ways. For example, visual texts are more holistic. The news reports on television favor instant, lively imagery rather than the detached, sequential thinking of newspaper reporting. More important, although visual texts seem closer to reality, they are constructed just as essays are. How they are constructed, by whom, and why are questions we'll be asking in the chapters ahead. As we explore such questions about visual and verbal texts, you'll be developing your ability to read critically and compose texts creatively in a variety of media. You'll be doing all these things from the perspective of a writer. In the process, you'll be making positive connections between popular media and academic literacy while reading and viewing with a writer's eye.

CHAPTER 1

Reading across the Media

How do we read moving images? This sequence of shots from Sergei Eisenstein's celebrated film *Battleship Potemkin* (1925) continues to stir the hearts and minds of movie audiences. As you interpret what you see, ask yourself how the director's cinematic choices—a screaming child, the rigid row of rifles, bodies falling across the horizontal lines of steps, a woman's shattered eyeglass lens, a woman carrying her dead son—contribute to your reading. Notice how you construct a story from these details.

Eisenstein set the scene in the Russian city of Odessa, the site of a massacre in 1905 when czarist troops fired on hundreds of civilians during a worker's revolt. He filmed this sequence on the city steps, although the actual event took place elsewhere, carefully composing and arranging each image for maximum effect. Notice how he alternates close-ups and long shots, high and low angles, groups and individuals, random figures and orderly lines. Eisenstein called this style of film editing a "montage of collision," stressing that new ideas arise from the conflict between frames. What ideas emerge as your mind connects the shots? Where else have you seen this kind of editing at work? Chapter 1 asks how you interpret images and read between the shots. It compares these acts of mind to the thinking you do when you read words in a book, browse through a magazine, or navigate a Web site. What you learn will help you to become a more critical, imaginative, proficient reader in any medium.

You already know that you're expected to do a lot of reading in college, for this and other courses. You may be wondering how you'll handle all those textbooks and supplementary readings on the syllabus. This chapter will help to lighten the load by showing you how to use your previous experience and your individual learning styles to read more efficiently.

First, we'll be taking a close look at the reading process, the steps you go through when you read and the steps that other readers take when they read. Successful readers use different strategies for different kinds of texts, so we'll look at how they read for information or pleasure, to understand complex ideas, or to argue with the author. You'll see that reading at its best is active, not a spectator sport. It's when you actively relate your reading to your liveliest interests that you're most likely to comprehend and remember what you read.

Since much of what we learn comes from movies, television, and the Internet as well as books, newspapers, and magazines, we'll look at reading across the media. That is, we'll see what is involved in understanding messages in any medium, whether they are delivered through drawings, motion pictures, speeches, Web sites, or print.

The learning curve you face is not as steep as you may think. It may comfort you to know that some researchers estimate the average high school student knows around 45,000 words, more than twice as many as used by Shakespeare in his writing. That doesn't mean that you know all the words in Shakespeare's works, of course, or how to use them, but it does suggest that you already have a broad working knowledge of the language: a good foundation on which to build the specialized vocabularies of the subjects you'll be studying. In addition to this verbal database, you also have an understanding of how certain texts work. You know how to use the layout of a magazine, a phone book, a novel, or a Web site, for example, to get what you want. You're familiar with the conventions of such texts—things like alphabetical listings, chapter headings, contents pages, and pull-down menus, which help you to find your way around. If you know a lot about a given subject, you also know it's easier to read within that field because the key names and ideas that keep coming up are already part of your mental storehouse. There's no need to make new room for them in memory.

Consider this: What makes unfamiliar kinds of reading seem difficult is only their unfamiliarity. If you're comfortable with one kind of reading material, you can develop confidence with other kinds. If you've learned how to read efficiently in one subject area, you can learn to read in other disciplines as well. The trick is to apply what you already know to what is new. It's a matter of building on the foundation of your previous experience.

CRITICAL THINKING: READING WHAT YOU SEE

Critical thinking is important for solving problems. Your abilities to frame a problem clearly, to delineate its parts, explain its causes, investigate its history, and appreciate its importance are all critical thinking skills. When you find, gather, and interpret information, separating facts from opinions, evaluating their merit and relevance to the task at hand, you are thinking critically. You think critically when you size up a problem in all its complexity, consider it from different viewpoints, weigh competing proposals, imagine their consequences, and come up with alternative solutions. Good readers use these instruments of thought whenever they encounter a challenging text. It's not just that they puzzle out the meaning of the text, as if it were a problem; they are always reading texts as possible solutions to the problems in their lives. Experienced readers know that any text—an article in *Popular Mechanics,* a short story before bedtime, a half hour of *Oprah* in the waiting room—may offer clues to their day-to-day dilemmas if they bring their critical facilities to the text.

Critical thinking can be visual or verbal. Some psychologists believe that visual information is stored and processed differently than verbal information. Visual memory works holistically. Our memories of faces, cars, and scenes are mental configurations of shapes, lines, and colors. These composite pictures are not static copies. They undergo transformations in the mind. We can imagine our best friend with a new hair color or a different nose. In our mind's eye, we can alter the shape of the family Ford or anticipate a change in weather. This is also true of verbal memory, which works sequentially. We remember written and spoken language as sequences of letters, words, and phrases; we process them internally as a series of mental objects, much like building blocks. This inner speech is flexible too. We have the capacity to transform language in our head, changing a word here and there, reorganizing sentences, or translating a phrase from English into Spanish or pig Latin. This ability to modify our mental models—whether visual or verbal—is a powerful tool for thinking and an important part of reading. It helps us to envisage new possibilities: to anticipate what might be coming next in life as well as in a text and to visualize alternatives to what is.

Try to solve these visual puzzles:

Puzzle 1 tests your ability to separate simple figures from a complex background. Did you find the mouse, rabbit, fish, and duck embedded in the tree? To do this, you may have mentally erased irrelevant twigs and leaves. This capacity to isolate relevant information is an important critical thinking skill.

Puzzle 1. Find the hidden animals. From William Costanzo, *Double Exposure*, pp. 128, 131, 132. Copyright © 1984 Boynton/Cook.

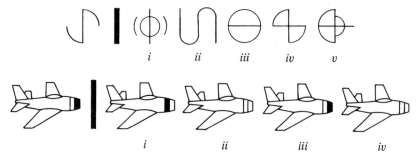

Puzzles 2 and 3. Find the left-hand figure in the designs pictured on the right. From William Costanzo, *Double Exposure*, pp. 128, 131, 132. Copyright © 1984 Boynton/Cook.

Puzzles 2 and 3 test your ability to match identical images. If you chose items iii and iv for Puzzle 2 and item iii for Puzzle 3, you have a good eye for detecting patterns, another critical thinking skill.

Puzzles 4 and 5 require you to visualize objects in three dimensions. Only ropes ii and iii can be pulled into knots; the others will come loose. When the box pattern is folded, it will look like box C; the other boxes do not have the right shape. These problems in spatial thinking ask you to imagine the consequences of certain actions, a critical ability for projecting the present into the future.

Notice that finding concealed figures, matching designs, and predicting knots and boxes are mental equivalents of physical operations. That is, you could have actually drawn, erased, or traced the figures with a pencil, or you could have used a real string or cut out paper boxes.

Don't worry if you found these puzzles hard to solve. You may have developed other visual skills or other learning styles. Maybe you're very good at word games, can assemble a flashlight in the dark, or can taste every ingredient in a French soufflé. The point is that critical thinking works through different senses and can be applied to different media. In this book, you'll be encouraged to think critically about food commercials, print ads, Web sites, film reviews, speeches, and songs as well as articles and academic essays. Think of these as flexible texts, compositions that were constructed one way for a particular purpose but that are capable of being analyzed, rotated, and reshaped by your active, critical imagination. And as you exercise

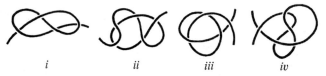

Puzzle 4. Which strings will form knots if pulled? From William Costanzo, *Double Exposure*, pp. 128, 131, 132. Copyright © 1984 Boynton/Cook.

Example X

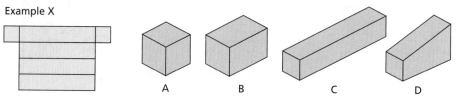

Puzzle 5. If the pattern on the left were folded to form a cube, what would it look like? *Differential Aptitude Tests, Form L.* Copyright © 1947, 1948, 1972 by Harcourt Assessment, Inc. Reproduced with permission. All rights reserved.

your critical abilities, you'll be enlarging your mental models, enabling you to handle texts and problems of greater complexity.

Thinking Critically about Visual Images

What we call seeing isn't automatic. It involves the mind as well as the eyes, a mind that has been trained to look for meaning. Consider this cartoon by Gary Larson before you read the caption:

What do you see in the cartoon? How do you make sense of it? At what point do you get the joke?

Most people see a couple of cats in a living room. One cat is reading a piece of paper. The other cat is looking out through a broken window. You might notice that the paper says "Arf arf arf . . . " and is composed of letters cut out of newspaper headlines, like those found in an anonymous threat or ransom note. You might also notice the bone on the floor among the shards of glass and conclude that the figure just beyond the window is a dog. Did you imagine this to be a case of kidnapping—or rather catnapping? Or did you think the message in the cat's paws represents a threat, something along the lines

THE FAR SIDE® BY GARY LARSON

Dog threat letters

of "We don't like cats in our neighborhood" or "Your kind aren't welcome here"—readings suggested by the caption. How much of the drawing were you able to understand without the words "Dog threat letters"?

Whether or not you find it funny, the cartoon depends largely on your visual literacy. Consider the kinds of knowledge that come into play. First, there is knowledge about **visual language,** the conventions of drawing that enable you to interpret slanted lines as window panes and triangles as bits of broken glass. Then there is **knowledge of the natural world,** like the fact that dogs like bones and cats have paws and pointed ears. Finally, there is **cultural knowledge,**

like the way kidnappers and hostile neighbors paste together ransom notes or hate mail to disguise their handwriting. People from a very different culture might see cats and a window, but they might imagine a different story. Of course, a certain amount of meaning depends on your individuality: your experience and imagination, for example, and whether you're in a mood for Gary Larson humor. But all this visual thinking takes place instantly, holistically. You're probably not even aware that you're thinking at all.

On page 25 is a *New Yorker* drawing by Saul Steinberg. Like all Steinberg *New Yorker* images, it never had a caption. Create your own caption and compare yours to those of others in your class. Did you "read" the image exactly as your classmates did? What assumptions about visual language, culture, and the natural world informed your reading? How else can you explain the caption you arrived at?

Thinking Critically about Moving Images

Movies add another dimension, the element of time. When motion pictures were invented, filmmakers created ways to tell stories in a sequence of moving images. They learned to use flashbacks to show the past, close-ups to represent a character's point of view, and reverse angle shots to dramatize an exchange between two speakers. Today, you probably don't think twice about such filmmaking techniques, but they often confused early film audiences. According to anecdotal accounts, when people in Iran were shown close-ups of mosquitoes for the first time, they thought they were watching giant insects on the screen. Some audiences in Africa were confused by panning shots; they wondered if the houses were moving. When a scene ended in a fade-out, they turned to see what was wrong with the projector. In other words, these beginning viewers did not understand the language of motion pictures. They might have been sophisticated readers of books, but their film literacy was largely undeveloped.

Chances are, if you've grown up in our multimedia culture, you take your film literacy for granted. So let's slow down the process of reading movies and analyze what you already know.

The storyboard on page 27 is for a Jell-O Pudding commercial featuring Bill Cosby. The storyboard breaks down the commercial into its individual shots, displaying the images and sounds in sequence for easy reading.

The storyboard contains some technical terms for familiar film conventions. A **low-angle shot** shows the subject from below. Typically, this makes the subject seem more impressive, maybe even menacing, as it does for Cosby's image in the first shot. The camera may **track** horizontally through space or **zoom** in and out in order to guide our attention, as it does when Cosby leans forward toward the desk and when the second boy opens the safe. Or the camera may **cut** to a new shot, reframing the subject in a **close-up** or a **medium shot,** as it does to focus on Cosby's shifting eyes or to reveal the heads of his young audience. Some techniques are sound-track conventions, like the **background music** or the **voice-over narrator** who speaks to us directly about the product but is never seen. Close-ups, zooms, and voice-overs belong to the vocabulary of film language, the system of visual and audible signs that make a movie meaningful.

But to understand the Jell-O commercial properly, we must do more than read the sequence of events. We must also read the **tone.** How serious is the story, and how do we know how to take it? One clue is the choice of language. If you've ever seen *The Godfather,* the 1972 gangster film (or its godchild, *The Sopranos,* on HBO), you know that to make "an offer that you can't refuse" is the crime boss's way of offering to kill you if you don't follow his advice. The formal decor and dress are also clues, reminding moviegoers of the scene in which Marlon Brando, as the Godfather, speaks to his devoted followers in his private office. Even the commercial's background music is reminiscent of the film. The language, set design, costumes,

1. Low-angle shot of Bill Cosby in formal attire. The camera tracks back as Cosby leans over the desk, revealing the backs of two boys. Music from *The Godfather*.

Cosby: *"Sonny, I want you to do me a favor. I want you to help your mother with the dishes."*

2. Cut to medium shot of three boys behind the desk, all dressed in black ties and white carnations. Two of them turn to face a third, who leans forward on the desk.

Boy: *"I can't do that Godfather."*

3. Cut to medium shot of Cosby bending toward the boy and sitting down.

Cosby: *"I want you to clean up your room."*

4. Cut to close-up of boy waving his hand.

Boy: *"Sorry Godfather."*

5. Cut to close-up of Cosby. His eyes shift left and right. Second boy crosses the screen from left to right.

Cosby: *"Okay, I'm going to make you an offer you can't refuse: smooth, creamy Jell-O pudding."*

6. Cut to second boy opening a safe. The camera zooms in as he reaches to retrieve a glass of chilled chocolate pudding.

7. Cut to medium shot of second boy placing pudding on the desk before the other two. He licks his fingers quickly and moves away.

8. Cut to close-up of a glass of Jell-O chocolate pudding, two packages, and a pitcher of milk. A lamp and plants are in the background just out of focus

Voice-Over: *"Jell-O Instant Pudding. Kids love it. And you make it up fresh in just five minutes."*

9. Cut to third boy reaching for pudding as Cosby pushes it toward him. Camera slowly pans left, revealing a subtle smile on Cosby's face as he looks into the camera and the first boy digs in.

Cosby: *"Godfather, you have my every loyalty."*

and music act as **allusions**—references beyond the text of the commercial to another text, the movie. Much of the commercial's humor depends on viewers making this connection. Yet even if you've never seen *The Godfather,* there are other hints that what you're watching is a parody, a spoof. A black-tie meeting about house chores? Pudding in a safe? Such contradictions are the stuff of **irony,** an opposition between what is expected and what shows up. In our culture, safes

are for valuables, not desserts. And of course, there is the playful way that Cosby acts the part: those shifty eyes and the mock-solemn voice. Even Cosby's reputation as a comedian and his popularity with children contribute to our reading, reminding us again how other texts—the other shows and ads in which Cosby appears—influence our reading of a given text.

To summarize, responding to a drawing or a filmed commercial is not as automatic as it seems. Seeing is an act of interpretation, a learned behavior. You couldn't understand a drawing or a movie if you hadn't learned the relevant languages—the systems of visible and audible signs with which artists and filmmakers communicate their messages. And you wouldn't get the joke in Larson's cartoon or in the Jell-O ad if you were unfamiliar with the world, the cultures, and the media texts to which they refer.

Reading and Evaluating Web Sites

Most books are checked carefully by editors before they're published. Television shows and movies are screened by many eyes before being released for public view. In contrast, nearly anyone can publish something on the Web without regard to accuracy. So the challenge of assessing information on the Web generally falls to you. Is the author knowledgeable and trustworthy? Is the information relevant and important to your research? Is the Web site reliable or a hoax? Such questions are essential for any serious reading on the Web. The sequence of a helicopter rescue and a leaping shark are circulated widely on the Internet as National Geographic's "Photo of the Year." It turned out to be a fake, a composite image spliced together from a U. S. Air Force photo taken near the Golden Gate Bridge and the photo of a great white shark from South Africa. It's easy to be misled by information on the Internet. In these days of computer-manipulated graphics, even photographs can lie.

Here are some hints to avoid being taken in:

- Look for the author or sponsor of the Web site in the header or footer. Is the author someone well known and respected in the field? Even if you're unfamiliar with the author's name, you can sometimes check that person's credentials or reputation on the Web. If the Web site was created by an organization, is the sponsor known as an authority on the topic? Is the sponsor likely to be biased on this topic? What does the sponsor have to gain by publishing this document on the Internet?

- Check the URL. The Internet address is often a clue to a Web site's real identity. Make sure that it matches the name on the home page. An Internet site like *whois.net* or *dnslookup.com* can help you find out who is behind the Web site you are evaluating.

- Pay attention to the way information is presented. Be wary of broad generalizations ("Most Americans . . ." "As everybody knows, . . . ") and biased language ("The foolhardy leadership of the Senate . . . "). Be skeptical of undocumented data and unsupported claims. A careful researcher will cite verifiable sources and acknowledge opposing points of view.

- How does the author refer to the literature of the field? People with a thorough understanding of a topic reveal that depth of knowledge by referring to other sources, citing current theories, and acknowledging the limits of their own knowledge. Their Web site may include their credentials, a professional biography, or an annotated bibliography.

- Is the information current? Check the header or footer to see when the Web site was published or last updated. This is especially important for some topics, like demographics and technology, where information changes rapidly.

Use one of the many services that screen Web sites for reliability, such as professional organizations or libraries that offer links to reputable sites. There are several good anti-hoax sites like Scambusters (http://www.scambusters.org/index.html) and Hoaxbusters (http://hoaxbusters.ciac.org/).

David Braun Stentor Danielson/National Geographic Image Collection. Used with permission. Shark photo used with permission by Underwater Video Services, Cape Town, South Africa.

ANALYZING TEXTS

Many of the things we've noticed about visual texts are also true of verbal texts. Let's start by looking at some sentences to understand how you make sense of them. We'll begin with a few riddles:

> Five men are trying to stand under an umbrella, but one doesn't fit. Yet he isn't getting wet. Why not?

> A doctor had a brother who went out West. But the man who went out West had no brother. How is this possible?

Both riddles depend on the mental pictures that you form. To solve them, your imagination must be flexible enough to see beyond the usual assumptions: that it's raining and the doctor is a man. Like the Larson cartoon, these jokes play on your real-world knowledge (about rain and umbrellas) and on cultural knowledge (about gender in the medical profession, particularly in the Old West). In fact, they trick you by challenging traditional expectations. Open umbrellas don't always mean it's raining, and doctors aren't always men.

The riddles also depend on your knowledge of the medium. While the cartoon relies on your familiarity with visual **conventions** (how artists draw windows and cats), the riddles require knowledge of verbal language, the codes and conventions by which things are represented in written speech. This verbal knowledge includes the ability to translate letters into words and words into meanings. The meanings may take the form of mental pictures ("five men," "an umbrella") or logical relationships ("but," "yet"), but they are always governed by **syntax,** the order of words.

Unlike drawings, which are generally interpreted holistically, verbal texts are analytic and sequential; they represent things, events, and ideas by breaking them into parts and stringing the parts into sentences. That's why a picture may be worth a thousand words. It's also why learning to read written texts takes so much effort. There are all those words to learn as well as the conventions for putting those words into a meaningful grammatical sequence.

Yet learning to read *well* is more than a matter of converting letters into words, more than assembling words into the logic of sentences. Words often have more than one meaning, and even identical sentences can mean different things if spoken by different people or on different occasions. So good readers learn to "read between the lines," guessing at the writer's tone, circumstances, and intentions. What would you guess from the following passage?

> Alas, poor Yorick! How surprised he would be to see how his counterpart of today is whisked off to a funeral parlor and is in short order sprayed, sliced, pierced, pickled, trussed, trimmed, creamed, waxed, painted, rouged, and neatly dressed—transformed from a common corpse into a Beautiful Memory Picture. This process is known in the trade as embalming and restorative art, and is so universally employed in the United States and Canada that the funeral director does it routinely, without consulting corpse or kin.

It probably didn't take you long to recognize the subject of this piece. In addition to the word "embalming," there are enough direct references to person ("funeral director"), place ("funeral parlor"), and thing ("common corpse") to help you get your bearings. But what is the writer's attitude toward the "restorative art" of embalming? How do you read the writer's tone? Much of the last sentence ("This process is known in the trade . . . ") might be spoken in a neutral, informative voice, but it would be hard to keep a straight face while pronouncing the final words ("without consulting corpse or kin"). Even earlier, you probably detected mockery or ridicule. That list of verbs in the second sentence, with terms borrowed from the workbench, the beauty parlor, and the kitchen, is too long and too specific to be entirely serious. You can almost *see* the irony, a pointed discrepancy between the image of a "Beautiful Memory Picture" and the image of a body being sliced, pierced, pickled, and rouged. There are other clues to the tone. The corpse is "whisked off" and handled "in short order." The opening reference to Yorick is an allusion to the graveyard scene in Shakespeare's *Hamlet,* when Hamlet lifts the battered skull of Yorick, the old court jester, from its untidy burial place. The allusion invites us to imagine the scene if Yorick had enjoyed the "benefits" of today's embalming and restorative art.

So what's the point of this grim humor? What's the larger meaning of the text? And for whom is it intended? What kind of reader would be likely to understand and appreciate the writer's purpose? You don't have to know that the writer is Jessica Mitford and that the passage comes from her book, *The American Way of Death,* which criticized the funeral business in 1963. Nor must you know that the book drew bitter attacks from mortuary professionals. But it helps to know something about Mitford's subject, to share her outrage and her sense of humor. It also helps to have the reading experience and skills that allow you to recognize literary allusions or hear a writer's tone.

READING IS A PROCESS

Whether we're reading visual or verbal texts, we're always engaged in a process of constructing meaning. The words, pictures, sound effects, and other signs are associated in the mind with preexisting mental categories and converted into thoughts. For example, a photo of the Yankee uniform might trigger an idea about the baseball team that we already have in our memory. The word *pitcher* might activate the idea of a baseball player or a water jug. Such photographs and words are meaningful to the extent that they can be correlated to established pathways in the brain. The interpretive acts that we call reading can be thought of as a conversion of information from a particular sign system to the language of thought.

But reading is more than just pouring information from a text into memory. Reading is a dynamic process. When we read a book or watch a television show, our brains are busy decoding what we see, assimilating new messages into the established structures of our brain and changing the old ideas to fit new information. We relate what we read to past experiences, comparing the new text to what we know of other texts, making interpretations, analyzing, predicting, and evaluating.

Think of reading as a kind of dialogue, a lively exchange between the reader and the text instead of as a one-way conversation. The text offers an idea and you respond. You might consider the idea, turning it over in your mind. You might accept or question what is said, maybe offering your own thoughts to confirm or challenge it. Perhaps you don't get the point right away. So you search your memory for help, try to reconstruct the idea in your own words or mental images, or ask for more information. At some point in the dialogue, you may lose track of the conversation. Something diverts your attention, and you drift on your own course for a while; then you tune in again, refocusing on the text.

Experienced readers learn to predict the flow of conversation. If you're familiar with a magazine or a film director or a television show, you already have some idea of how the dialogue will go. You may know what you want from the text, and you may anticipate much of what it has to offer. Since you've had many encounters of this kind, you have a storehouse of expectations to draw on. This can be a great help when you read. If you know the usual format for an article in *Rolling Stone* or an episode of *The Office,* you can get into the flow of it quickly and comfortably. But familiarity can also be a problem. Sometimes your expectations can prevent you from seeing what is really there. You already have an idea of what the text is likely to say, and the preconception blinds you to the text itself. This also happens in conversations with people we think we know well. We think we're listening to them when we're really hearing our own expectations.

Scientists who study the workings of the brain use the term **mental models** to explain this phenomenon. Our brains construct models of the world: mental replicas that correspond to our experience. We can think of these models as internalized copies of what we see, hear, taste, touch, and smell, molded in the flexible material of thought. We are continually shaping

these models to fit experience. For example, our idea of a ball may be shaped by our experiences with rubber balls, baseballs, billiard balls, and Ping-Pong balls. Our memories of how they look, feel in our fingers, and bounce against a wall form a mental picture that is associated in our mind with the word *ball*. The picture in our mind may be round until someone throws us a football. Then we must change our model to fit the new experience. This process of adjusting our thoughts in response to new information received through the senses is an important part of how we learn. Reading anything—an essay, documentary film, or *National Geographic* magazine—contributes to the process when we allow our preconceptions of the world to be expanded, reshaped, and refined.

Sometimes our experience is shaped by our internal models. An artist who has words for thirty different shades of the spectrum may experience colors differently than someone who only has only seven words. The artist may distinguish shades of crimson, scarlet, ruby, cherry, and burgundy where the other person sees only red. Both may see the same objects with equally good vision, but the artist's larger vocabulary results in a richer sensory experience. It's a matter of seeing what you're looking for.

What do you see in the picture to the left? Some people see an old woman, some see a young one, and some see only dark and light spots. Once someone has pointed out the two women, however, you can't avoid seeing them.

It's your mind that gives meaning to the spots, and the meaning that it gives depends on the expectations activated in your memory: the visual models of two women.

Here's another example, in words instead of pictures: Read the following sentence out loud.

> Go to the window and
> and see if anyone
> is looking back at you.

Now count the words in the sentence that you read and count the words on the page. Most people miss the extra *and* in line 2 because they expect a grammatically correct sentence. Their mental model of standard English imposes itself on what is actually written. This is one reason why it's hard to see our mistakes when proofreading what we write. We tend to read what's in our mind instead of what's really on the page.

You can probably come up with your own examples of visual and verbal miscues, reading mistakes you made because you imposed what you expected on the text. One student remembers saying "I pledge allegiance to the flag and the republic for Richard Stands" each school day morning because he heard his friend's name instead of the words "and which it stands" when he learned the Pledge of Allegiance. Another thought that the world's great journalists were awarded a "Pullet Surprise" instead of a Pulitzer Prize. Another thought the title of George Gershwin's "Rhapsody in Blue" was really "Rap City in Blue." You can imagine what the four-year-old pictured when told that his older brother grew another foot.

Such misunderstandings also happen on a larger scale. Psychologists use the term **schema** to describe the way we reconstruct events in the form of familiar stories. A schema is a kind of script, a set of expectations that we have in mind about the way a particular happening should go. Take the dating schema, for example. What do you expect to happen on a first date? Your schema might begin with a phone call to set the time and place. It might continue with a bouquet of flowers at the door, dinner at a romantic restaurant, an evening stroll along the river, and a good night kiss at the door. Your partner, however, may have another schema in mind. When your *schemata* (plural of schema) don't agree, you're likely to be surprised, disappointed, insulted, or angry.

We have schemata for family dinners, summer camp, frat parties, bank robberies, Westerns, horror films, and sitcoms. Whenever we attend a graduation, read about a basketball game, watch the evening news, or listen to Oprah, we anticipate a certain sequence of events to occur in a certain order. These schemata are important when we read. It's much easier to understand a new text once we know that it's written in the recognizable form of a recipe, an editorial, or a lab report. The schemata in our head provide familiar frameworks for understanding the new material. The same holds true for reading Web sites, listening to rap songs, or watching how-to shows on television. Your mind already knows so much about these formats that relatively little work is required to understand them compared to a completely unfamiliar format. This book emphasizes the format of different kinds of texts in order to make reading and writing easier for you. It seeks to build on the schemata already established in your mind so you can apply them to new tasks in any media.

READING STRATEGIES

These theories about sign systems, mental models, and schemata may seem a bit abstract, but they can be put to good practical use. When you really know how reading works, your reading can be more efficient and engaging. The following strategies will help you put into practice the concepts you've been learning about visual and verbal texts.

CLARIFY YOUR PURPOSE Before reading anything, consider why you're reading it. Are you looking to purchase a new computer? Are you writing a paper on global warming? Do you need evidence to win an argument? Use the text to solve a problem or support a project. Set specific reading goals.

TALK TO THE TEXT Keep up a running conversation as if the authors were in front of you. Pose questions and look for answers. Do you agree or disagree with what is being said? Are you skeptical of any data? Do you think there may be errors or misjudgments in the text? Take a stand at the beginning and notice how your position shifts or grows more solid as you read.

WRITE AN ACCOMPANIMENT Keep an ongoing record of your interaction within the text itself. Comment in the margins. Annotate new terms by checking their meanings and defining them on the page in your own words. Underline important passages. Highlight memorable or questionable statements in different colors.

KEEP A RESPONSE JOURNAL OR DOUBLE-ENTRY LOG Record your responses in a separate place. A journal keeps track of your thoughts, feelings, and associations while they're still fresh. It's a good way to talk to the text or to yourself in writing. A double-entry log allows for more reflection. Jot down your immediate responses on one side of the log. Come back later, and on the other side—opposite each original response—describe your thoughts after rereading the text, talking it over with others, or considering it more carefully.

PREVIEW THE TEXT Get the general layout before you plunge in. Skim over the details to see where it will take you. Use the headings and subheadings as clues. Check any photographs,

graphs, sidebars, and captions. The bird's-eye view that you form by skimming may make it easier to find your way through the text when you read it sentence by sentence.

CONNECT THE TEXT TO WHAT YOU KNOW Before reading, take stock of your previous knowledge of the topic. What have you heard, read, or seen about it in other media? What do you already know from personal experience? What's missing from your picture; what do you need to know?

SUMMARIZE, PARAPHRASE, REFRAME A good way to test your understanding is to put what you have learned into your own words. A concise summary will help to fix it in your memory, integrating the new information into your existing mental framework. For particularly technical or complicated passages, it is often useful to paraphrase, to rephrase the original sentence by sentence in ordinary language. If you decide to use your paraphrase later in a research essay, be sure to mark down the page numbers so you can cite the original passage properly. Reframing means seeing the text afresh, perhaps from a different point of view. When you read a corporate earnings report from the perspective of ecology, you might notice things that most investors miss. When you read the sports page as an anthropologist looking for cultural cues, you might find some odd social behaviors that sports fans take for granted.

NOTICE THE FORMAT How is the text organized? Can you recognize a familiar pattern or format? Does it belong to an established genre? It's easier to place yourself in a text when you have a mental map, or schema. Some texts have a linear arrangement (like fix-it manuals or training films): they tell a story, follow a process, explore causes and effects, or pose a problem followed by solutions. Some texts are hierarchical (like directories and genealogy charts), with levels of subheadings arranged under a main heading. Some texts are more cyclical (some game shows, for example), returning to the beginning, like a snake biting its own tail.

USE VISUAL ORGANIZERS Many texts use visual organizers like pie charts and graphs to present information clearly and concisely. You can create your own visual organizers as memory aids to reading. Make an outline or concept map of the main concepts and related material, like the one on *The Writer's Eye* Web site: www.mhhe.com/costanzo. Use a time line or flowchart to represent a linear process. Draw Venn diagrams for texts that compare and contrast, using overlapping circles to show how things are similar and different. See examples and definitions on *The Writer's Eye* Web site: www.mhhe.com/costanzo.

REDUCE YOUR MENTAL LOAD BY CHUNKING When you dial 911 or say SCUBA (Self Contained Underwater Breathing Apparatus), you're using chunking. Chunking compresses lots of information into a smaller space so you can store it more easily in memory. Since our short-term memory typically has room for only seven (give or take a few) items at a time, it helps to repack multiple items (like the digits of your area code) as a single item. Use this memory technique when you read. Sometimes you can reorganize key terms to form a familiar word or memorable name. For example, you might use the word HOMES to remember the Great Lakes (Huron, Ontario, Michigan, Erie, and Superior) or the name ROY G. BIV to recall the colors of the rainbow (Red Orange Yellow Green Blue Indigo Violet).

EVALUATE THE ARGUMENTS A rhetorical analysis examines persuasive techniques. How does the author set out to convince you of something? Can you find moments of emotional manipulation, misleading information, or faulty logic? How have the writers or filmmakers framed their subject, established their credibility, and justified their reasoning? Look beyond what is actually presented. What has been omitted? Are you convinced? What do you see as the logical consequences of the argument?

FORMAL ANALYSIS

A formal analysis examines the basic forms and features that are common to all texts, whether they are written essays, magazine ads, television commercials, Web sites, or documentaries. As you become more skillful in identifying the subject, audience, purpose, format, structure, style, and other elements of different texts, you will begin to see how messages are constructed in different media, often through a series of choices and decisions. By understanding the decisions behind what you watch and read, you will be able to construct your own messages more knowledgeably and deliberately in any medium.

1. **Subject**—what the text is about. All those references to corpses and the art of embalming tell us that Mitford's passage is about funerals. The Jell-O commercial seems to be about the appeal of chocolate pudding, judging from the shots of hungry kids, close-ups of the product, and words like "smooth" and "creamy."

2. **Audience**—who the text is intended for. Mitford is writing for a well-read audience, people who might know *Hamlet,* recognize words like "trussed" and "rouged," and appreciate grim irony. The Jell-O ad is intended for adults with kids (the voice-over speaks to these adults directly) and probably the kids themselves, who are likely to recognize Bill Cosby and identify with the children in the ad.

3. **Purpose**—why the text was produced. We conclude that Mitford wants to criticize the funeral industry, exposing its pretensions and exploitative practices. We assume that Jell-O wants to sell its product.

4. **Format**—the category or genre to which the text belongs. Mitford's book is an exposé; it exposes the dark side of a public institution. The Jell-O text is a commercial; it is also a parody.

5. **Structure**—how the text is organized. For a drawing or a full-page ad, this means the layout: the position of words and images on the page. For an essay or a book, it means the order in which ideas and information are presented. Mitford's book follows the step-by-step process of embalming, among other things. The Jell-O ad presents a miniature drama, starting with the conflict and ending with a resolution.

6. **Style**—the manner in which the text's message is conveyed. Mitford's style is literary, darkly ironic, and occasionally angry. The Jell-O ad might be described as cute and playful; it spoofs the tense dramatic style of modern gangster movies.

Simply describing these six elements is not the end, but the beginning of a good text analysis. What will make your observations worthwhile are the conclusions you arrive at by thinking carefully, critically, and creatively about what you observe. How do these and other elements work together to send messages? Are there deeper motives beneath the author's announced purpose? When you pay attention to the content of a text, you may notice that what a writer does *not* say about the subject may be as important as what that writer includes. Does the text promote a particular point of view? When you examine the structure of a documentary film, you may see that the angle from which each shot is filmed and the order in which the shots are arranged are deliberate decisions: someone's version of reality out of many possible versions. Often you'll want to know more about the person or persons who produced the text. If you're familiar with the author, what do you already know about the author's life, beliefs, or other works? If the text does not have a clearly identified author, the way a Web site or a television show might not, who is responsible for the decisions? Who is paying the costs and what motives might those people have? Even if a text seems neutral, it is never value-free. Attitudes and beliefs—about good and evil, about men and women, about young people and old, about money and power—are always stitched into the fabric of the text.

So analyzing texts can be an eye-opening activity. It can teach you a lot about both commonplace and unfamiliar texts: what they are, where they come from, how they work, and why. It can also teach you about yourself and others, since the way people read a text depends a lot on who they are. Additionally, you can examine texts from a cultural perspective, which will help you dig even deeper as you read.

Analyze a Magazine Ad (Individual Project)

Select an advertisement from a magazine, and examine it for the six elements described above: subject, audience, purpose, format, structure, and style. Write a paragraph or two about each element. Comment on the choices that were made in order to construct the text. Why do you think these particular images (faces, setting, colors, actions) and words (the words themselves, their shape and size, their density on the page) were selected and arranged in this particular way? Given the audience and purpose of the text, how well do the visual and verbal elements work together?

Here are some questions to guide your analysis.

1. **Subject. What does the ad seem to be about? What are its messages? Does it promote a particular attitude or lifestyle as well as a product? How do you know?**

2. **Audience. For whom is the message intended? To what age group, gender, ethnic group, or socioeconomic status might the ad appeal? Consider where the ad is found (what kind of magazine) as well as its subject and style.**

3. **Purpose. What effect does the ad seek to achieve on the readers? How are its messages likely to affect such readers or reflect their values?**

4. **Format. What other kinds of ads are similar to this one? What is typical of such ads?**

5. **Structure. How is the ad constructed? (Try turning the page upside down to get a fresh perspective on its layout.) Notice its visual elements (photography, drawings, and lettering; color, shape, and contrast) as well as the words. Why were these particular elements chosen? How are they arranged on the page? Why are they arranged this way?**

6. **Style. Describe the overall mood or feeling you get from the ad. Is it elegant, carefree, clownish, or seriously scientific? What contributes to this mood?**

7. **Evaluation. Finally, give your appraisal of the ad. How effectively does it achieve its purpose? What can you say about the format, structure, and style that make it particularly effective or ineffective? Did you find yourself resisting the ad's messages? If so, explain why you don't buy what the ad is offering.**

Here is how one student analyzed an ad for cigarettes.

STUDENT TEXT ANALYSIS OF CIGARETTE AD

by Stacey Whalen

Subject. This ad is about smoking and the end of the world. It presents a typical American couple and their dog at a time of irrevocable fate. They were enjoying a peaceful evening of barbecuing until the fireball of death and destruction entered the serene blue sky. At a time of intense and unexpected turmoil such as this, one only has enough time to grab the necessities of survival. In this case, the couple carries with them as many cartons of cigarettes as possible into the shelter where they may be for a long time. Even the dog grabs a box of lights.

Audience. The ad is directed at smokers. Because it appeared in *Glamour* magazine, it might be targeted at young women who care about their personal appearance, although this particular woman doesn't seem too glamorous. It probably appeals to people who are interested in the topic of the new millennium and the theories that come with it.

Purpose. The main purpose is to sell cigarettes. The creator of the ad wants to emphasize the value of cigarettes. When the planet is under attack, you only have time to take what is really important.

Format. The text is a magazine advertisement. Many cigarette ads are similar to this one. They all have smokers, the company logo, a close-up of the product, and the Surgeon General's warning. Camel ads tend to be offbeat and funny, appealing to younger smokers. This one also follows the format of a disaster movie. It tells an exciting story with lots of action.

Structure. The ad is organized like a movie or television show. You can imagine what they were doing before and what will happen after the clip they give you. It uses bright colors and dramatic angles to capture our attention and draw us in. The Camel logo is stamped in the upper left corner and some fine print appears

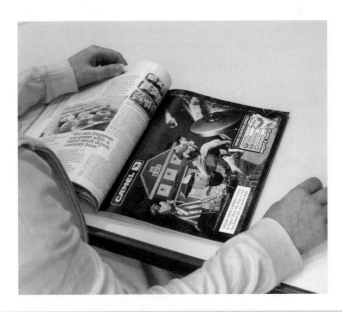

along the edges. Also included in the advertisement is a "viewer discretion advised" box evaluating its content, as many movies do, only with fake categories like FR (for Falling Rock), CH (for Cigarette Hoarding), and UM (for Undercooked Meat). This makes fun of people who stamp warnings on things, like the Surgeon General. The whole idea is to undermine the warning that cigarettes are dangerous.

Style. The Camel advertisement is comical. The picture takes a humorous approach to a serious situation. There is something ironic about this conservatively dressed couple in a suburban backyard running from a meteor. They seem like level-headed, down-to-earth people, yet the only thing they are taking into the shelter with them is an abundance of cigarettes.

In conclusion, I believe this advertisement is clever and manipulative. It takes a dangerous product like cigarettes and makes that product seem like a valuable item, necessary for survival. It uses bold colors and animated figures to capture the reader's attention. It uses the familiar format of an action movie to dramatize the story for a young audience. And it uses ironic humor to poke fun at a serious warning. The real irony is never stated. The cigarettes that this couple and their dog are taking to the shelter are a bigger hazard than the meteor.

CULTURAL ANALYSIS

A cultural analysis examines a text in terms of the culture that produced it. It looks beyond the individual authors and asks what larger forces are behind them. Who hired the team that created the Camel ad? What lifestyles, values, or perspectives do they represent? A cultural analysis also looks deeply into the nature of audience. It asks not only who is the intended audience, but who is excluded from the text as well. It questions whether readers, listeners, or viewers embrace the text's messages, reject them, or resist them. It regards every text as an interplay between authors and audiences, with both engaged in the enterprise of asserting power, deriving pleasure, and constructing meaning.

Here are some basic questions for a cultural analysis:

1. Who is the author or producer of the message?
2. What is the purpose of the message?
3. How might different people interpret the message?
4. What type of text is it? Does it belong to any genres?
5. How is it produced? What technologies and techniques are used in its production?
6. What beliefs, ideologies, or points of view are implied?
7. Who or what is left out?

As a reader and a viewer, you might begin by looking at your own interaction with the text. Are you a fan of such works or do you dislike them? How do you know what they mean? Do any personal characteristics come into play when you interpret the messages, perhaps some special knowledge, ability, or disability? When and where do you spend time with the text? How does the physical environment (your living room, the movie theater, a quiet corner of the library) influence your attitude? Are you influenced by your race, ethnicity, age, gender, family income, or membership in any special group?

When focused on the text itself, a cultural analysis assumes that media construct reality. It might look as if you're only seeing what is out there in front of the lens, but someone is always pointing the camera, framing the image, deciding what sounds you hear and what you don't. Media depend on identifiable techniques (camera angles, editing, and music in a film; layout, color, and lettering in one-page ads; irony, humor, and metaphors in writing) to convey their messages. Their messages are communicated through the codes and conventions of a sign system. And these messages often serve rhetorical purposes. Their aim is to persuade people to buy, to vote, to believe. They are never value-free.

Cultural analysts generally regard media producers as businesses with commercial interests. They look at the authors, agents, and industries behind each text, and they look behind these to the culture itself. From this perspective, the purpose of television is not to bring programs to the viewers but the other way around, to deliver consumers to the sponsors. And many films, while presenting themselves as simple entertainment, promote name-brand products and distinctive lifestyles. Who stands to gain from such promotions, and who loses in the process?

One value of cultural analysis is that we learn more about a culture through close readings of its texts. Another value is that awareness gives us choices. When we recognize the intentions behind a text, when we realize how it works, we have more ways to respond.

Let's apply some of the principles of cultural analysis to the Camel ad on page 37.

1. Who is the author or producer of the message?

The ad was paid for by the R.J. Reynolds Tobacco Company, the makers of Camel cigarettes since 1913. R.J. Reynolds is the nation's second largest manufacturer of cigarettes, producing one out of every four cigarettes in the United States, including Winston, Salem, and Doral. In an important sense, R.J. Reynolds authorized the Camel campaign by hiring an advertising agency, setting its agenda, and approving the ads created by the agency. From a cultural perspective, however, the originator of the message might be said to be much larger than a single company. Behind R.J. Reynolds is a multibillion-dollar tobacco industry with its enormous advertising budget, and beyond this a practice of smoking tobacco that is deeply rooted in our culture. Cigarettes have played many roles in American life, defining character in movies, mediating social intercourse, and serving as icons of sophistication, sex appeal, or rebellion at various times and places.

2. What is the purpose of the message?

A little research reveals an interesting history. In 1988, R.J. Reynolds launched one of its most successful ad campaigns, featuring Joe Camel. Joe Camel appeared on billboards and in magazines as a cool, sexy cartoon character. He sported sunglasses, rode a motorcycle, and knew how to handle his cue stick in the pool halls. Joe proved to be especially appealing to youngsters. In one study, more than 90 percent of six-year-olds were able to match his image with a picture of a cigarette, making him as well known as Mickey Mouse. Although the manufacturers denied that they were targeting children, during the first three years of the campaign Camel's share of the under-eighteen cigarette market jumped from 0.5 percent to 32.8 percent, representing a $470 million increase in annual sales. Antismoking critics began to protest, and the Federal Trade Commission threatened to take legal action. In 1997, under pressure from the FTC, R.J. Reynolds Tobacco Company announced the end of its twenty-three-year Joe Camel campaign.

The ad on page 37 is part of Camel's new campaign designed to replace Joe Camel with something more resistant to the critics. It uses humor as a weapon and defense. The mock warning, "Viewer Discretion Advised," is not only a sendup of movie ratings (FR for Falling Rock, CH for Cigarette Hoarding, UM for Undercooked Meat) but also pokes fun at the Surgeon General's warning that is required by law. The situation is so obviously absurd—a family with armloads of cigarettes running from a falling asteroid to the backyard shelter—that it might provoke a laugh. But who are we laughing at? And while we're laughing, do we become more receptive to the message of the ad?

3. How might different people interpret the message differently?

A cultural analysis might offer reasons why this ad would appeal to a young audience. Young people don't like to be told what to do. They enjoy making fun of authorities and their adult world. That's why parody is a popular art form among teenagers. Young viewers might also appreciate the comic references to disaster movies, which were particularly popular at the end of the millennium when this ad appeared. Not all readers would have the same reaction, though. A few might not understand the film allusions or get the joke. Nonsmokers and antitobacco activists would probably resist the implication that cigarettes are such a valuable commodity that even the family dog would want to save them from doom. They might point out that smoking in a fallout shelter is probably not the best way to insure survival. But since the ad doesn't take its own premise seriously, it is difficult to criticize on logical grounds.

4. What type of text is it? Does it belong to any genres?

We've seen that the ad is a kind of joke, a parody. It plays with familiar cultural objects (the grill, the fallout shelter, the game of croquet) and familiar stories (the family barbecue, doomsday). It belongs to an ad campaign that applies the same idea to different genres. In one ad, some women are bathing two men in a giant cast-iron pot. Two of the women are preparing vegetables; two are adding water to the pot in a seductive way. A Viewer Discretion box warns that the ad contains "HW (Hungry Women)," "HG (Hot Guys)," and "MS (Man Stew)." In another ad, a servant girl is about to flick cigarette ashes into a dish that she's preparing for her upper-class employers. The Camel symbol appears on her cap. The Viewer Discretion box warns that the ad contains "IR (Idle Rich)" and "PA (Premeditated Ashing)." These allusions to well-known movie scenes (the big-game hunters being cooked, the servant's revenge) are all about turning the tables, scenes that might appeal to those who want to blow smoke in the face of authority.

5. How is it produced? What technologies and techniques are used in its production?

Paying attention to the layout of the ad shows how carefully it was composed. The Camel logo appears in the upper left, where most readers look first. The man, woman, and dog are traveling from left to right (the way we read), drawing our eyes from the Surgeon General's warning to the fake Viewer Discretion advisory and the open pack of Camel cigarettes in the lower right. Although the scene is filled with details, bright colors (blue, yellow, red, and green) and a sense of motion (all three figures are leaping in mid-air) make the ad lively and dynamic.

6. What beliefs, ideologies, or points of view are implied?

There is no question what this couple believes in. They're clutching the Camel cartons for dear life. But while we are invited to smile at their excessive product loyalty, are we also laughing at the silly rules made for our "protection"? If we're going to be hit by a flaming meteor, who cares if we light up a few Camels?

7. Who or what is left out?

The point of this question is to notice who and what are not represented. The man and woman look like fairly young, white, middle-class suburbanites. Their home and clothing appear to be conventional. Is there a reason that other groups are not included in the picture? The ad appeared in *Glamour* magazine in March 1999. Is there a special connection between the readers of this magazine and the advertiser's choice of characters and setting? Finally, consider what could *not* be left out. The Surgeon General's warning is here because law requires it, but its serious message is diminished by a ludicrous comparison. The ad-makers have followed the law while flaunting it in a way that will appeal to their target audience.

READING PARODIES

The advertising agency that created the Camel ad campaign is not the first or last to use parody as a persuasive technique. A **parody** is a comic imitation. It imitates the form and style of another work for humorous effect. Parodies can be commercials, like the thirty-second spot for "Jooky Junk" that offers kids free gifts like chain saws, halibuts, and hernia belts in exchange for empty cans of Jooky soda. Knowledgeable viewers recognize this as a take-off on the Pepsi campaign that advertises "free stuff." The Jooky parody mimics the neon colors, rapid cuts, and trick editing used in the Pepsi campaign. It turns out that "Jooky Junk" is really a promotion for Sprite, which ends the spot with its main message: "Image is nothing. Taste is everything."

Parodies can also be movies, like *Scary Movie* (a parody of horror films) and *Not Another Teen Movie* (a parody of teen movies). There are parodies on television, like *Saturday Night Live* and *Mad TV.* In fact, the tradition of parody spans many media and many centuries, reaching back past eighteenth-century novels like *Tom Jones,* past medieval songs cycles, like the *Carmina Burana,* past classical drama, like the satyr plays that made fun of ancient Greek tragedies like *Oedipus Rex.* What all these parodies have in common is their delight in deflating other texts. By exaggerating the format and style of the texts they copy, they undercut the serious messages of those texts.

www.mhhe.com/costanzo

The Web site features examples of parody commercials, including Little Caesars Pizza's "Training Camp."

When you read a parody as it was intended to be read, there is pleasure in being in on the joke. Usually, the more you know about the target—the text being parodied—the more pleasure you derive from seeing the target take hits. You can also read parodies across the grain, with a critical eye. In this kind of reading, you're more focused on critical questions: what is being made fun of, who is behind the parody, what are the parodists' motives? Either way, reading parodies is different from simply reading for information.

Every year, aspiring writers enter literary parody competitions. There is an Imitation Hemingway Contest, a Faux Faulkner Contest, and even a Bulwer-Lytton Fiction Contest. The BLFC (as the latter competition is called) challenges contestants to compose the opening sentence to the worst possible novel. It is named after the unfortunate author who began his work with the immortal words, "It was a dark and stormy night. . . . "

Here is a recent Imitation Hemingway Contest winner by Kathryn Bold, a freelance writer from Coto de Caza, California. It parodies Ernest Hemingway's novella, *The Old Man and the Sea.*

The Old Man and the Flea by Kathryn Bold

He had been bad. He knew that. He had been bad and peed on her bed and in the end there was nothing anybody could do about it. She had yelled at him that time, screaming terrible things in that way women do when you have broken their trust and trampled on their hearts and urinated on their pillow. Bad dog, she'd said. He remembered it now. Bad dog. And he was a bad dog. A bad, old dog with a cranky disposition and a weak bladder.

It was at times like this that he feared life had no meaning. What was life anyway, but lying around on one's blankie, waiting for the next bowl of kibble. Life was nothing. Nada. Nada y nada y pues nada. Woof nada. Then she came along and gave him a treat and for a brief time life was good. Then he puked the treat on the rug and life was bad again.

At times he would strike out in frustration. How vividly he recalled the day he bit a man, drawing blood as he had so many times before. He had been sitting in Harry's Bar on a hot August afternoon when the strange man approached. "Go," said the man. "Go fetch." The man had tossed a tennis ball across the tile floor. It was an old tennis ball, and yellow, and he remembered liking the way the lights from the bar reflected off the ball's fuzzy skin. So he had chased the ball, and the ball offered no resistance as he put it in his mouth. Then the man wanted the ball back. So he had bit him. He had earned the ball. It belonged to him. He knew it and the people in the bar knew it and the ball knew it and now the man with the bloody hand knew it, too.

Yes, he was a bad dog but one could blame his poor health for his surly disposition. There was the ear trouble in August. She had taken him to the vet that time, just as she had on so many other occasions. She took him to the vet and the vet had performed surgery and he had spent the next couple weeks walking around with a cone on his head. It was a large white cone, and plastic, and when people saw him they laughed. They laughed at him and they laughed at the cone and there was nothing he could do about it. Life was bad.

Now it is Christmastime. He will try not to eat an ornament off the tree and land in the emergency room, as he had done with such reckless abandon the previous year. He will try, but the ornaments are very tasty, and time is very short. It is Christmastime, and he has already consumed half a red candlestick from the candelabra she had sitting by the fireplace. Life is good.

If you're familiar with the works of Ernest Hemingway, you'll appreciate Kathryn Bold's ability to capture the flavor of his prose while having fun with it. She mimics Hemingway's short, simple sentences—all nouns and verbs—to the point of absurdity. She imitates his use of repetition. She gently mocks his efforts to use sensory detail ("the way the lights from the bar reflected off the ball's fuzzy skin") and his tendency to join phrases with "and." Bold's parody also plays with themes and motifs familiar to most of Hemingway's readers, such as alcohol (Harry's Bar), the existential angst of nothingness (*nada y nada y pues nada*), and the author's questionable insights about women ("screaming terrible things in that way that women do when you have broken their trust and trampled on their hearts and urinated on their pillow"). Furthermore, by applying Hemingway's style to a subject as mundane as her dog, the parody has a deflating effect. The famous novelist's claims to literary greatness seem a little less grand.

"WASH YOUR BLUES AWAY," FROM *ADBUSTERS*

The parody ad to the left appeared in *Adbusters,* a not-for-profit, reader-supported magazine based in Vancouver, Canada.

Even if you don't recognize the product being spoofed and its bright, familiar package, you'll probably see the humor in trying to sell Prozac as if it were a soap detergent. Parody often works through incongruity: the absurdity of applying a familiar format to something unexpected, like the layout of a soap ad to an antidepressant or Hemingway's literary style to a dog with bladder problems. What really makes this spoof work is that such an absurdity is not far from the truth. We can almost imagine the makers of Prozac pitching their product as if it could brighten moods as easily as Tide brightens faded laundry. Notice how the *Adbusters* parody captures so many elements of real detergent ads: the colorful package dominating the layout, the catchy jingle (cleverly handwritten in blue ink), and the model dressed like a 1950s housewife. If you visit Adbusters' Web site, you'll see that the real subject is bigger than pharmaceuticals or soaps; it's nothing less than "the erosion of our physical and cultural environments by commercial forces."

Create a Parody (Group Project)

Besides being subversive, parodies can be entertaining and instructive. Creating a parody is a good way to test your understanding of how texts work. By parodying a car commercial or a Shakespearean play, you get to see how such commercials or plays are put together: what their language sounds like, how they're organized, how they appeal to a given audience. You get to play with the particular codes and conventions that these texts depend on to communicate their messages. So creating your own parody becomes a playful alternative to analyzing texts.

Consider two options for your parody: a magazine advertisement or a commercial. If your group chooses to design an ad, you might begin by brainstorming some key decisions. What kind of product will you sell? You might make up a new product with its own brand name. You might draw some prototypes to experiment with its shape, color, and other features. In what magazine will you place your ad? What kinds of people read that magazine? Why would they want to buy your product? How might you dramatize the features of your product that will most appeal to them? Whatever you decide, take your cues from advertisements that you know. That's the point of parody. What do such ads look like? How are they laid out on the page? What kind of printing, images, celebrities, or language do they generally use? What are their usual messages? There's no need to be painstakingly methodical here. Play with your ideas. Enjoy the freedom that you have to poke fun at something you know all too well.

If your group decides to create a parody commercial, you'll be making similar decisions. Instead of choosing a magazine, though, you'll want to specify your audience by thinking of a time slot, channel, and perhaps the television program where your commercial might be placed. Use a storyboard to plan the look of your commercial. (Refer back to page 27 for a sample storyboard.) This enables you to visualize the story shot by shot, adding dialogue, musical directions, or voice-over narration under each picture. Remember that each shot represents a new camera setup. If you're comfortable with technical terms like close-up and zoom, you might add camera directions as well. Your completed storyboard should be sufficient to give anyone a clear idea of what your parody would look like on TV. However, if you have the time and equipment to videotape your storyboard, try bringing it to life. (Chapter 3 and the *Writer's Eye* Web site, www.mhhe.com/costanzo, offer guidelines for composing with visual media.) Find a location for the shoot. Gather or build any props you'll need. Cast your actors in the leading roles and give them any costumes that they'll need. Then prepare the set, adjust the lighting, set up the camera, and get ready to roll.

CHAPTER 2

Composing across the Media

Writing, music, movies, dance, photography, and painting are all forms of composition. The building blocks of meaning—words, musical notes, images, or gestures—may differ, but there are important similarities in how these basic elements are selected, altered, and arranged. Writers often engage in research, brainstorming, or freewriting in the early stages of a manuscript, then shape their thoughts into a more coherent draft, revising and polishing it for final publication. Filmmakers do the scripting, scouting, casting and other preparatory work of preproduction before the actual shooting or the postproduction tasks of editing and sound mixing. Some choreographers work out the movements of a ballet mentally and on paper, then go back to the drawing board for changes once they see how things actually work out on the dance floor. Of course, the creative process may differ from individual to individual as it does from one art form to another. But it is worth looking closely at the correspondences as well as the differences.

Where in your life do you compose? Do you have a composing style? How can you apply what you already know to written composition? Chapter 2 will guide you through such questions while it helps you to compose more confidently and effectively in any medium.

A lot of people tell themselves they can't write because they think of writing as some kind of mysterious creative act. To them, writing is a gift, and they were absent on the day when this particular talent was distributed. While there's no denying that some writers, like William Shakespeare and Virginia Woolf, were extraordinarily talented with words, the truth is that most good writing is learned. As with any sport or art form, it takes some knowledge of the basics, good coaching, and lots of practice.

In basic terms, writing is a form of composing—a way to organize your thoughts and feelings through the medium of language so that others may be informed, inspired, and moved by your written words. This chapter is intended to help you understand the process of composing and how your mind engages in that process, whether you're producing an essay, a movie, a dance, or some other composition. It's based on the assumption, widely supported by research, that individuals learn best by relating new skills and information to what they already know. Therefore, you'll be encouraged to observe your mind in action, to take stock of the mental habits you've acquired, to notice the composing techniques you already use effectively in other areas of your life.

What makes a person effective in any area often is a sense of ownership. Taking active control makes you a driver rather than a passenger. This means getting familiar with the dashboard and taking hold of the wheel. "Composing across the Media" puts you in the writer's seat and offers you a close look at the choices available to you as a writer.

While there is a wealth of choices available, you won't employ every strategy in your composing process. Think of this chapter as a reference manual or a toolbox. It offers you much more than you'll need for any single composition. Read or skim through the entire chapter to get a sense of the whole process of composing. Notice which ideas and techniques appeal to you most, which best suit your own composing style. (To read more about learning styles, visit www.mhhe.com/costanzo.) Refer back to particular sections whenever you need help with those phases of your writing. You'll find tools to help you discover a topic and a point of view, plan the structure of your essay, develop a sound draft, write a good beginning or conclusion, strengthen paragraphs, support ideas, and revise for clarity, completeness, unity, continuity, organization, or style.

Near the end of this and other chapters, you'll find a sample student essay with accounts of how the writer proceeded step by step. These samples are intended to demonstrate the composing process in action. At the end of this chapter, you'll find screens from student examples of multimedia composition. On *The Writer's Eye* Web site, you'll also find full accounts of these media compositions, including a video documentary, a television production, and a Web site. These media projects are options that illustrate how much of the composing process applies to media other than writing. For guidelines to complete your own multimedia assignment, refer to the appendix, "Composing with a Camera." You don't need to undertake a media project in order to get the full value of this book. However, in addition to the regular writing assignments you'll be asked to do, Part 2 of this book offers media options for those who have the interest and the equipment to try composing in a different medium.

COMPOSING IS A PROCESS

Composing in any medium—whether it is writing, filmmaking, choreography, painting, dressmaking, or Web design—involves certain common steps or phases of development. This is because composing is a way of thinking, and the mind has a limited repertoire for examining events and reshaping them into meaningful arrangements. People follow similar patterns of thought whether they are behind a podium, a pen, a movie camera, or a computer keyboard.

For example, the process of writing, like the making of a documentary film, may be thought of as a succession of stages:

Discovering. Writers may make lists or do exploratory writing. Filmmakers explore with a camera.

Planning. Writers prepare an outline. Filmmakers plan a shooting script.

Developing. Writers draft paragraphs. Filmmakers shoot scenes.

Revising. Writers rework their draft. Filmmakers edit their footage.

Completing. Writers proofread their final draft. Filmmakers make a fine cut of the film.

Though these stages sometimes go by different names, you will find them in almost any creative activity. By drawing parallels between the way you work in a medium that you know well and the steps that writers follow, you'll be able to bring your general knowledge of the process of composing to the specific task of writing. You'll also be able to apply what you learn about writing in this book to other media that you'd like to work with.

DISCOVERING

The first stage of nearly any creative process is exploratory. Writers or filmmakers might not be familiar with their topic or might not have chosen one yet. At this stage, they may need to explore potential subjects or familiarize themselves with the subjects they have chosen. A group of filmmakers interested in music, for example, might decide to shoot a documentary about a rock concert. After considering which rock group most appeals to them or to their potential audience, they learn more about the group by listening to albums, reading magazines, and watching videos about the group. They may even do interviews. Equipped with their new knowledge, they arrive early at the concert hall, setting up their cameras to get footage of the empty stage, photographing fans as they arrive, and setting up their cameras to view the group from different distances and angles. Although they don't know precisely what will happen when the concert starts, they have been exploring their subject in depth. Writers prepare themselves in similar ways. They use language as their instrument of discovery. They might list phrases that describe their subject or jot down associated words and ideas (brainstorming), working from direct observation, memories, or research notes. If you have experience with filmmaking or some other medium of expression—say painting or cooking—think of how you usually begin exploring a new idea in that medium. There are probably useful parallels to writing.

Finding a Topic and a Point of View

Most college writing starts with an assignment. You're given a broad subject area to write about (violence and the media, the American family, women in sports) or a particular kind of writing to do (a memoir, a book review, a research paper). In the case of an assigned topic, your first task is to discover what you want to say about the topic. At this point, it's a matter of finding a particular perspective on that subject, what journalists call a *slant*. You may decide to look at contemporary American families from the perspective of colonial times, for example, or you may want to test your suspicion that modern media are isolating family members from each other. In the second case, when you're assigned a specific type of writing but no particular topic, your task is to find a suitable area of interest. What personal memories would be worth writing about? What book should you review? What hobbies or issues would you like to learn more about through careful research? In either case, the challenge is to make a promising connection between the assignment and your active interests. It's your distinctive point of view, your fresh slant, that will keep you vigorously focused on the task of writing, and it's what will make your writing most worth reading.

Here are some ideas for this discovery stage. Look for opportunities to cross from one medium to another medium as a way of tailoring your own composing process.

BRAINSTORMING Jot down quickly whatever comes to mind in the order that it comes to you. You might write single words or phrases or even sketch a rough drawing or two. Don't worry if your ideas seem silly or bizarre. Don't worry about spelling or grammar. The point of brainstorming is to turn off your internal censor and let your imagination flow. Later on, you can sift through the stream and pick out any unpolished gems.

FREEWRITING This is similar to brainstorming, except that you write in a continuous stream of sentences, oblivious to spelling or grammar. Write without interruption for about fifteen or twenty minutes. Later, go back and underline any sentences that might serve as seeds for an essay or another freewriting exercise.

LISTING This technique is a little more organized than brainstorming. Try listing your ideas in categories related to your topic. For example, if you're writing an essay on media and violence, you might begin by listing different media (video games, television, movies, music) and then list examples in each category that might be considered violent. If one or two items on a list seem promising, try some focused freewriting about each.

IMAGING Your visual imagination is a source of great creative power and control. Athletes sometimes prepare for a game by picturing themselves shooting hoops, one perfect shot after another. Look for opportunities to use your mind's eye at any stage of writing. When you're considering a topic, you might flip through an imaginary album of images associated with that topic. What pictures spring to mind when you think of the topic, and what do these pictures suggest for your writing?

VISUAL PROMPTS Let the visible world prime the pump of your imagination. If you're looking for ideas about a new topic, thumb through a magazine with that topic in mind. Or think about that topic while cruising through the mall or watching television. Sometimes, an accidental pairing between your topic and something you see will trigger a promising idea. For instance, does that Barbie doll you notice in the toy store (p. 49) have anything to do with the American family, women in sports, or your own past?

CAMERA STYLO In French, this term means "the camera as a pen." For some kinds of writing, you may want to approach your subject as if you had a camera in your hand. Like any writer, a filmmaker must frame what he is filming, choosing what to focus on and what to leave off screen. These camera techniques are good ways to guide your attention as you explore a topic or to guide your reader's attention later on when you develop your draft.

QUESTIONING Journalists are taught to answer five questions about their topic in any article they write: what, who, where, when, and why. This simple trick of the trade can help you plan your essays too. Say you're writing about the popularity of hip-hop music. What, exactly, is hip-hop? What makes it different from other kinds of music? Who likes it and who doesn't? Where is it performed? Where did it originate? When did it arrive on the scene? Why is it so popular? Some writers add an H, for How. How does hip-hop sound, or how did it develop?

DIALOGUING Talk with someone else about your topic. Team up with a partner and pose questions to each other. Or simply tell that person what your topic is, what you're planning to write, and where you're stuck. Just hearing your thoughts spoken aloud can often help to clarify your thinking and loosen those sticking points. Composing doesn't have to be a solitary activity. A good deal of writing is collaborative, especially in the early stages.

PERFORMANCE Another way to play out your ideas is to get other people to test them in performance. This works especially well for persuasive writing, where you must argue for or against a position. Stage a public debate, with each side defending its position. Then switch sides. This is a way to test the strength of your reasoning and evidence before committing them to paper.

READING Don't overlook reading as a form of exploration and a source of inspiration. Reading what others have written on your topic not only makes you better informed but also gives you a sense of how the topic has been treated. If you take notes, be careful to identify the source (author, publication, page) of any words or ideas that you jot down. This will help you avoid plagiarism as you begin to write.

JOURNALING Some writers keep a regular journal, a place where they record impressions of the day, responses to what they read, long-range plans, and brilliant middle-of-the-night ideas.

PLANNING

At some point in the exploratory stage, something may click. For example, the filmmaker may arrive at a distinctive vision of the subject: a unique point of view, a revealing angle, or a new way to represent what she sees. The sculptor suddenly may see a knot of wood as the eye of a whale struggling to emerge from the wood. The dancer, moving to a new piece of music, may be inspired to choreograph a new dance on flight. As for the writer, those notes or lists may suddenly suggest a pattern, something larger than the parts.

On the other hand, both filmmakers and writers might start with a more formal plan: a rough script or outline to be filled in and methodically developed. In this case, the filmmaker already has a sense of what footage is needed; the writer knows what material to look for. Now the task may be to film those shots that best tell the story or find good examples to support the thesis.

Seeing Patterns

Things become meaningful when we see them in relation to a pattern. The tiny dots that make up a photographic portrait acquire meaning only when we step back and recognize the pattern of a face. This ability to make connections, to find a unifying pattern in the tangle of events, allows us to make sense of an otherwise unruly world.

NOTATE YOUR LIST If you use listing in your discovery process, look for patterns in your list. Check the items that seem to go together, or rearrange them in new groups.

CONCEPT MAPS This technique, variously called clustering or idea trees, gives you a way to diagram your evolving thoughts in words and pictures on the page. Typically, a concept map has several key ideas, each forming the center of a cluster of related ideas and details. (See *The Writer's Eye* Web site at www.mhhe.com/costanzo.)

OUTLINING Experienced writers often use a **working outline** to help visualize the structure of an essay. By listing the main ideas in order, they see more clearly how their essay is shaping up. At this stage, any outline should be flexible. Once you have outlined the main elements, you can decide how to present them to the reader, perhaps in a different order. More **formal outlines,** with numbered sections and subsections, usually come later in the writing process. These can be especially helpful after completing a first draft to clarify the structure of what you've already written. Some writers even use **sentence outlines,** in which each section is a statement rather than a heading. Reading such an outline sentence by sentence lets you follow the whole story, the evolving thesis, or the argument without reading the entire draft. (For examples of some types of outlines, visit *The Writer's Eye* Web site at www.mhhe.com/costanzo.)

VISUAL ORGANIZERS Use visual aids like graphs, charts, maps, and sketches to help organize your thinking. Computer software now makes these tools particularly easy to use. If you're working with a lot of data, try using pie charts or bar graphs, like those that represent the media survey results in the Introduction.

FLOWCHARTS Computer programmers learn to use flowcharts to represent the flow of information in a program. They use lines, arrows, and other graphic symbols to trace the program's pathways, showing how each part of the process fits into the whole. If you're familiar with this method of notation, try using it to plan the flow of logic in an essay.

STORYBOARDING Do you remember the storyboard for the Jell-O commercial in Chapter 1? This is another way to do your planning, one favored by filmmakers and other visual artists. Start with a sequence of boxes large enough to draw in. Each box depicts a moment in your story or a stage in your report. You can add a few words at the bottom of each box, but sometimes it's your drawing that will capture the concept best. What's more, you'll be able to see the whole structure of your composition at a glance.

THESIS STATEMENTS Once you've grasped the special focus or key concept of your essay, it often helps to put this concept in a nutshell. This concise statement—what you'll be demonstrating or developing more completely in your essay—serves to guide your planning, drafting, and revising. It can also clarify your purpose to your readers if you include it in an introductory paragraph.

DEVELOPING / DRAFTING

The next broad stage is developing. Each medium has its methods for realizing the main idea in concrete terms, usually in rough form, before adding the final touches. This stage involves some shaping. Painters might sketch broad shapes on the canvas in charcoal before applying paint. Filmmakers prepare a rough cut of the film, writers a rough draft. Gradually, through a time-honored process of editing, the filmmakers arrange each day's yield of film (known as "dailies" or "rushes") into a sequence, as the rough cut takes on a recognizable shape. Similarly, writers work the fragments of their composition into a unified whole, guided by the thesis as well as growing sense of purpose, audience, and the subject itself.

Although filmmakers and writers work with different instruments, they often follow comparable strategies for organizing their material. They might use the principle of narration to tell a story (the rock group's rise to stardom, for example) or to chronicle an event (publicity, setting up the concert, ticket lines, arrival of the stars). They might group their shots or notes into categories (regular fans, curious onlookers, fanatics, bouncers). They might develop an analogy, comparing and contrasting their subject with something similar (moving back and forth between the views of the performers and circus animals). We'll be looking more closely at these strategies for development later in this chapter.

Paragraphing

Paragraphs are the basic building blocks of written composition, similar to scenes in a movie or stanzas in music. Writers regularly use **topic sentences** to clarify the focus of a paragraph. A topic sentence identifies the paragraph's main idea so that readers get the point quickly. It usually comes first, announcing the issue or subject matter that will be developed further in the paragraph with more detailed reasoning, description, examples, comparisons, or facts.

Topic sentence (italicized) in a student paragraph:

> *I am a Jamaican, not a movie stereotype.* I am not loud and brawling. I do not smoke weed. I am not a Rastafarian. I do not live by the beach or own a machete. I do not say "Mon" at the end of every sentence. So why are we Jamaicans portrayed that way in the movies? Why does the Jamaican in a film have to be a drug dealer who is in a gang and practices voodoo? Why do we quibble with the cruel, biased comments from people on the street when we should be complaining to the people who produce such films?
>
> "Route 40," by Nicholas Duncan, student

Transitions

Effective writers also learn to use **transitions** to help readers follow the flow of thought. Transitions link the parts of a paragraph together and one paragraph to another. Like good bridges, they offer smooth passage across the breaks and divisions of a composition. Filmmakers use transitions too. One scene might dissolve into another, indicating the passage of time. Or the camera might shift scenes with a swish pan, transporting us from one location to a new part of town in blur of rapid motion.

Over time, writers have developed a stock of standard transitions to do this work. They use words and phrases like the following to signal shifts in time, space, or logic.

Transitions of Time:

- Items in a series: First, second, third / for one thing, for another thing / next, then, finally
- Duration of time: during / for a long time / hour by hour / instantly
- Pointing to specific times: once / at that moment / two weeks ago
- Beginnings: at first /in the beginning / at the start / even before
- Middles: meanwhile / in the meantime / at that moment / at the same time
- Endings: finally / at last / eventually / in the end / afterwards

Spatial Transitions:

- Direction: to the left / on the right / behind / above / below / inside / across
- Distance: beyond / far below / in the distance / there / away
- Closeness: near / next to / alongside / adjacent to / here / close to

Logical Transitions:

- To illustrate: for example / for instance
- To conclude: finally / all in all / to sum up / in conclusion / of course / clearly
- To identify a cause: because / since
- To indicate an effect: consequently / as a result / accordingly / therefore / hence / so
- To offer a qualification: it is true / of course / naturally / to be sure / granted
- To name an alternative: but / however / yet / nevertheless / on the contrary / on the other hand / to put it another way / in contrast / still
- To return to the original idea: still / nonetheless / yet / all the same / nevertheless

Conventional transitions, if chosen carefully, can strengthen the coherence of your composition. They're quick, recognizable cues to guide the reader. Too many, though, can make your writing sound artificial and automatic. It's often better to create your own linking phrase or bridge sentence, one that fits the particular passages you want to connect.

Beginnings, Middles, Ends

Almost any composition has a beginning, middle, and end. As you move into the drafting stage of writing, you'll be writing paragraphs that introduce, develop, and conclude the main body of your essay.

Some writers compose their beginning paragraph last, reasoning that they have a better idea of what to introduce after they've written the body. Others don't feel ready to write the body until they've finished their first paragraph, which acts as a kind of launching pad. Beginnings should grab the reader, middles should support your thesis, and endings should clinch the essay.

START WITH AN INVITING OPENING A good beginning paragraph orients your readers. It may establish the topic, declare your purpose, set an appropriate style, forecast what will come, or explain how the essay is organized. This is the place to clarify your thesis, either by announcing it directly in an opening thesis statement or leading up to it at the end of your first paragraph.

- Direct thesis statement: "Paganism is one of the most misunderstood religions of the modern world." ("What Is Paganism" by Robert Robertson, student)
- Gradual buildup to thesis statement: "To law abiding citizens, they are a necessary evil. To activists, they are symbols of repressive authority. To criminals, they are objects of fear and hatred. From their first day of training, police officers become unwitting targets of public antipathy. . . . The increasing pressure from politicians and the media only adds bricks of secrecy to the ever growing Blue Wall of Silence. ("The Blue Wall of Silence" by Jane Wilson, student essay on code of secrecy used by police officers to protect themselves)

BUILD THE MIDDLE: STRATEGIES FOR SUPPORTING AN IDEA Over the years, people have fashioned familiar strategies for developing their ideas, making them clearer, stronger, more convincing. Writers use these methods to nurture the seed of a topic into one or more paragraphs. Filmmakers and advertisers use them, too. Here is a short inventory of strategies and examples gathered from television commercials and professional writers. Use this section as a reference for your writing. When you're faced with the task of supporting an idea, one or more of these strategies may work for your topic.

Example / Demonstration One of the great strengths of visual media lies in their power to illustrate abstract ideas with concrete instances: the particular images and sounds that memorably demonstrate what otherwise might be vague or difficult to grasp. A recent Super Bowl commercial (2002) plays with this technique—and mocks the typical vacation ad—in a series of illustrative vignettes:

Woman #1: "I want to feel the wind in my hair." (She is blown off her feet by a wind machine.)

Man #1: "I want to taste something exotic." (A bucket of green liquid pours down into his face.)

Man #2: "I want to take part in a native ritual." (He's hand-wrestling with Popeye.)

Woman #2 on ride: "I want to get closer to my children." (As a dinosaur rises from a lake, she screams and she presses her two kids to her ample bosom.)

Clincher: Universal Orlando Resorts: "A vacation from the ordinary"

You can bring some of this concreteness to your writing with examples taken from your personal experience, the media, or even your imagination.

Comparison / Contrast Advertisers are always comparing their products to the competition, often side by side. Two shirts with identical stains are treated with different detergents and run through the washer. In seconds we watch how Brand A removes the stubborn stain while Brand B leaves the shirt spotted. The contrast in product effectiveness is easy to see.

Another familiar marketing strategy is the before and after ad. A heavy woman loses thirty pounds; a balding man restores his head of hair. The contrasting pictures tell the story in an

instant. The California Department of Health Services used this strategy effectively when it wanted to dramatize the risks of smoking. Each excuse for not quitting smoking is echoed by a living cancer victim:

> Man on street: "I can't go more than a few hours without a cigarette."
>
> Man in hospital: "I can't go more than a few feet without the oxygen tank."
>
> First young woman: "I tried to stop, and I put on five pounds."
>
> Second young woman: "I've lost 25 pounds."
>
> Man in kitchen: "I have trouble getting out of bed without a smoke, man."
>
> Man in sick bed: "I have trouble getting out of bed."
>
> Driver: "No, I don't think I can quit."
>
> Surgeon: "I don't think I can operate."
>
> Clincher (titles on screen): Quitting is hard. Not quitting is harder.
>
> "Echo" / Ground Zero, Los Angeles

Classification / Division An automobile, a basketball team, or the World Wide Web can be explained by analyzing its parts. This need not be a lifeless lesson in anatomy. Sony Pictures used such a technique to advertise its film, *Not Another Teen Movie.* Spoofing the typical teenage movie, the ad divided the film's cast into all-too-familiar roles: Popular Jock; Pretty Ugly Girl; Cocky Blond Guy; Desperate Virgins; Obsessed Best Friend; Token Black Guy. Sony's publicity Web site features a mock yearbook with quotes from each character. Pretty Ugly Girl: "I read Sylvia Plath. I listen to Bikini Kill, and I eat tofu. I'm a unique rebel." Nasty Cheerleader: "Let's get one thing straight—this is not a cheerocrasy."

Such analysis is sometimes called **classification** because it classifies, or sorts, a seemingly unorganized array of items into systematic groupings. Much of the fun and insight comes from classifying vaguely familiar patterns into sharp, new categories, giving catchy names to each category.

Division is a variation of classification. In division, something is divided into its component parts. That's what Taco Bell did to advertise its new food product for the Super Bowl in 2002. The commercial begins with dramatic music, dynamic close-ups, and an enthusiastic voice announcing a "revolutionary S-class steak." It goes on to divide the product into three parts: "The new 2002 *quesadilla* has unmatched flavor dispersion thanks to marinated carne-Asada steak . . . three melted cheeses to rev up your taste buds . . . and a toasty grilled tortilla." Each ingredient is shown in separate close-ups before the whole *quesadilla* is put back together again, "a tasty triumph of culinary engineering." The clincher accompanies the Taco Bell logo: "Bite into the new steak quesadilla today and see how it feels to think outside the bun."

Process Analysis A breakdown of an activity into its component steps is called process analysis. The "Training Camp" commercial for Little Caesars Pizza (in Chapter 5) uses this technique in an entertaining way by slicing up the process of delivering pizzas into steps like Exiting the Car, Running from the Dog, Knocking on the Door, and Pronouncing the Product.

Definition A **formal definition** consists of the term to be defined, a category to which the term belongs, and defining features that distinguish the term from others in the same category. For example, Webster defines *anaconda* as "a very long, heavy, South American snake." The term is *anaconda,* the category is snake, and the defining features are "very long, heavy, South American."

An **extended definition** is more informative. It can include examples, etymologies (the origins of words), history, and other background information, as does this definition of *weasel words* from William Lutz's book on deceptive language:

> Advertisers use weasel words to appear to be making a claim for a product when in fact they are making no claim at all. Weasel words get their name from the way weasels eat the eggs they find in the nests of other animals. A weasel will make a small hole in the egg, suck out the insides, then place the egg back in the nest. Only when the egg is examined closely is it found to be hollow. That's the way it is with weasel words in advertising. Examine weasel words closely and you'll find that they're as hollow as any egg sucked by a weasel. Weasel words appear to say one thing when in fact they say the opposite, or nothing at all.
>
> William Lutz, *Doublespeak,* 1990

Cause and Effect Is the oil industry ruining our environment? Does television violence promote crime? Can a butterfly in Singapore cause a tornado in Kansas? Such questions require a careful look at the connections between events to see if one thing really leads to another. If it can be shown that A is the reason for B, then A is the cause and B is the effect. The logic of cause and effect explains why something happens and what the result is.

When Continental Insurance wanted to remind people that unexpected accidents may be expensive, it borrowed a story about cause and effect from an old nursery rhyme, "The House That Jack Built." The children's rhyme builds Jack's house by adding one item at a time, stanza after stanza, in a chain of causes and consequences. Continental's commercial does the opposite:

> "This is the foot that hit the plant that swung the door that hit the vase that hit the plant that pushed the light that struck the picture that toppled the table that knocked the radio that scared the dog that bumped the chair that shoved the piano that collapsed the wall that belonged to the lucky guy who was insured by Continental Insurance. Continental doesn't just insure the things that can happen. We can insure the things that just can't happen. But they do."

The commercial shows us close-ups of one thing leading to another, frame by frame, until the piano crashes through the outside wall—a dramatic visual clincher to the thesis that unforeseen mishaps can be costly.

Problem Solving A common strategy for developing a topic is to pose a problem and offer a solution. Many advertisements work this way, like the medicine ads offering relief from physical distress. According to these commercials, heartburn or colds are the problem; Tums or Nyquil are the solutions.

Chronology Sometimes it makes sense to arrange events in the order they occurred, chronologically. When Pepsi wanted to advertise the enduring popularity of its soft drink at the Super Bowl in 2002, it staged a retrospective of old Pepsi commercials, using the popularity of Britney Spears to express a lively message. The ad begins with Spears imitating Marilyn Monroe in a simulated black and white commercial, singing the 1955 jingle, "For those who think young." Then she's the star of a Miss Hit TV show from 1963, inviting us to "come alive" with Pepsi. Next she's at a beach party where "Pepsi pours it on." In a neat visual transition, Britney is thrown up in the air from a beach blanket. She rises in a bikini (1966) and comes down in hippie clothes (1970), singing "You've got a lot to live and Pepsi's got a lot to give." The commercial concludes with a montage of shots from earlier years as the lyrics spell out the ad's underlying theme: "Come feel the joy all around. Each generation has found. They've got their—own sound." The whole composition is nailed down with a familiar clincher: "The joy of Pepsi."

Testimonial When Apple Computers wanted to attract PC users to its expanding line of computers, the company launched its award-winning "Apple Switchers" ad campaign, featuring personal testimonies by real people. Each commercial features a different kind of person sharing his or her reasons for switching to an Apple.

Ellen (student) explains how a PC devoured her paper, and she had to write it again, but it wasn't as good.

Jamie (the girl who saved Christmas) tells how her Powerbook automatically transferred family photos from her camera while her dad spent the holiday downloading a Windows driver on his PC.

Liza (DJ) complains that her parents made her buy a PC, which was so unwieldy that she got rid of it and bought her own iMac. "It never crashed or nothing. It was great."

Kelly (surfer) shows a surfing video he made on his Apple computer in an hour, with sound and titles included. "It's so simple to use."

Yo Yo Ma (cellist): "I like to get in . . . and noodle with things. My G4 allows that to happen. It's beautiful."

"Apple Switchers" / TBWA\Chiat\Day, Los Angeles

Analogy It is often easier to understand something new by placing it alongside something familiar that is similar. Stephen King, the master of horror fiction, uses several analogies to help describe the psychological function of his favorite film genre. By comparing horror films to dirty jokes, he implies that they tempt our darker, secret impulses, as if these impulses were primitive creatures lurking in our unconscious minds—a horrid image even for Stephen King:

The mythic horror movie, like the sick joke, has a dirty job to do. It deliberately appeals to all that is worst in us. It is morbidity unchained, our most base instincts

let free, our nastiest fantasies realized . . . , and it all happens, fittingly enough, in the dark. For those reasons, good liberals often shy away from horror films. For myself, I like to see the most aggressive of them—*Dawn of the Dead,* for instance—as lifting a trap door in the civilized forebrain and throwing a basket of raw meat to the hungry alligators swimming around in that subterranean river beneath.

Stephen King, "Why We Crave Horror Movies" Playboy, 1982

Examples, comparison/contrast, classification/division, process analysis, definition, cause and effect, problem solving, testimonial, and analogy are among the most widely used techniques for building the body of an essay. Learn to use them to your advantage. But beware of mistaking formula for form. Formulaic writing, the kind in which a writer mindlessly fits words into a standard mold, can stunt your new perceptions and exploratory thoughts before they have a chance to grow into their natural shapes. Experienced writers usually find forms to fit their meanings rather than the other way around.

END WITH A CLINCHER The conclusion is one of the hardest parts of an essay to write. The concept of a clincher can help. In carpentry, a clincher is a tool used for fastening something together by means of a nail or bolt. Clinching nails are specially made to hold firm, sealing the whole project together. In filmmaking and writing, a clincher is a strong, decisive ending, the final stroke that wraps up the movie, ties the essay together, and drives the main point home. Most of the commercials described above end with clinchers:

Taco Bell: "Think outside the bun."

Continental Insurance: "Continental doesn't just insure the things that can happen. We can insure the things that just can't happen. But they do."

The next time you watch a film, read an article, or listen to a radio feature, notice how they're clinched. How well do the final words or images bring things to a close and leave a memorable impression on the audience? Here are some ideas for clinching your own work.

- **Summarize.** "Indeed, conservationists will tell you this remote atoll's real treasure wasn't buried by pirates 200 years ago. It's open and apparent for all to see—Palmyra holds the seeds of paradise." (Concludes an article on "The Treasured Islands of Palmyra" in *National Geographic,* March 2001.)

- **Return to the beginning.** "In short, these companies rose to the occasion. And that, too, is what being one of the 100 Best is all about." (Concludes an article on "The 100 Best Companies to Work For" in *Fortune,* February 4, 2002. The article begins: "It's not easy being good these days, at least if you're an employer.")
- **Call for action.** "Maybe we should find it, before it finds us." (From "All Fall Down," an article on the Black Plague in *New Scientist,* November 24, 2001. The article begins: "The disease that spread like wildfire throughout Europe between 1347 and 1351 is still the most violent epidemic in recorded history.")
- **Tie the topic to a familiar title or phrase.** "We'll miss you, George. Eight days in a week." (From "All Things Must Pass," a memorial article on Beatles guitarist George Harrison in *Guitarist,* January 2002.)
- **Leave your audience with a striking image.** "Being in Flagstaff was like being in a planetarium, but as the cold night air crept under my jacket, I was aware of an acute difference. The Flagstaff sky was real, and it went on forever." (Concludes "Dark Skies," Radio feature about reducing light pollution in Flagstaff, Arizona. *Morning Edition,* NPR, March 25, 2002.)

What type of ending is best for you? Let your final purpose be your guide. If you're developing a case in an editorial or persuasive essay, you'll probably want to conclude with a decisive argument or an inspiring call to action. If you're reporting information in a research paper or investigative report, it might make sense to summarize your most important findings. Thinking from your reader's point of view is the key. In an essay, unlike many conversations, you always get to have the last word, but it's the reader who decides what happens next. If you want your words to make a lasting difference, choose an ending that contributes to your reader's goals as well as yours.

REVISING

With almost any composition, a time comes when the interest shifts from discovery, planning, and development to communication. Here the underlying question is not "What is there to learn about my subject?" but "How well is it coming across to others?" This is the revision stage, a chance to test whether your intentions are likely to be realized. That's why there are dress rehearsals, preview screenings, and preliminary drafts. By watching how an audience responds to the composition at this stage, the creators get a better sense of what is clear and what still needs to be done. Here are six ways to help you see your work from a fresh perspective.

READ ALOUD Sometimes just reading your work aloud enables you to notice things you didn't see when you wrote silently. You might hear a choppy sentence more easily this way or become aware of a certain stiffness in your tone. If you're stumbling over your own words at some point, imagine what your readers might be hearing.

USE PEER REVIEWS Often the best person to check out your draft is another writer: a student who is working on a similar assignment. Throughout Part 2 of this book, in the Tips for Writers section of each chapter, you'll find a checklist of peer response questions tailored to the specific assignment in that chapter. Use this checklist as a guide to revision.

CHANGE THE LOOK After many readings, any work may start to appear unalterable. A simple computer trick will remind you that your words are not written in stone. Try changing the appearance of your document by setting new margins, selecting a new font, or experimenting with the layout. You might see opportunities for change that were invisible before.

LET IT SIMMER Since a watched pot never boils, it's wise to put your draft on the back burner when nothing's cooking. Take a walk or see a movie. The mind has a way of working on a project just below the threshold of awareness. When you get back to it, you may find that your writing has taken on a new flavor.

Revision often means returning to an earlier stage of the composing process. A filmmaker might have to reshoot a scene that was too dark or out of focus. A writer might want to adjust a misleading introduction, find a more powerful example, or reorganize the essay to accommodate the reader's expectations. Be willing to take a few steps back so you can move forward toward a stronger final product.

PROOFREADING

The final phase of a composition varies from medium to medium. A painter might add shadows and highlights before covering the canvas with a clear glaze. A filmmaker typically adds transitions and blends the soundtracks before making the final release print. A writer might proofread the revised version to produce a final draft free from errors. The important point here is that the overall composition is essentially complete—developed, organized, revised—before adding the finishing touches. Proofreading is a matter of correcting errors in spelling, grammar, punctuation, and mechanics.

SPELLING Some people seem to have a knack for spelling, but most of us have to check the dictionary for unfamiliar words. The spell-check function on most word processors will catch many of your typos and spelling errors automatically, but not all. Be alert to homonyms, words that sound alike but are spelled differently, such as *it's* and *its* or *there, they're,* and *their.* Watch out for words that are commonly confused because they sound similar, like *affect* and *effect* or *accept* and *except.* If you're not certain, this is a good time to consult a handbook or dictionary.

GRAMMAR In order to avoid making the same errors in verb tenses, pronoun agreement, sentence fragments, and the like, it's a good idea to learn the specific errors that you make repeatedly and look for them when you proofread. Computers are becoming better at finding grammatical errors, but they are not yet foolproof. They still miss many mistakes, and they often mark perfectly good sentences as wrong.

PUNCTUATION Punctuation was invented to clarify the meaning of your words without your voice. Check your sentences for misplaced or missing commas. Avoid fragments, run-on sentences, and comma splices errors. Be sure that you use colons and semicolons properly. See that apostrophes and quotation marks are correctly placed. These and other points of usage are clarified in later chapters when they are likely to come up in your writing.

MECHANICS The layout of your writing is important too. Check your margins and spacing. Be sure that all paragraphs are indented half an inch. If you use a heading or a title, follow the format prescribed by your instructor.

PRINCIPLES OF EFFECTIVE COMPOSITION

Good compositions are clear, unified, coherent, and well organized, with a suitable, consistent style. These qualities are relative, however, depending on the writer's **topic, audience,** and **purpose.** Take the topic of sports mascots. You might be writing a humorous account of your personal experiences as the high school's team mascot (a memoir). You might be exploring the history of mascot names (a research paper), arguing that some team names are hurtful to Native Americans (a persuasive essay) or dissecting the reasons for mascots in sports (an analysis). For each of these different purposes, you would probably organize your essay differently and write in a different style. The memoir might be chronological and lighthearted. The persuasive essay might build a serious case, using testimonials and examples to compare the pros and cons. In each case, the gauge will be your audience. You'll want to adapt your language, structure, and tone to your final readers. As you revise, keep asking this question: "Given my topic, how well will I achieve my purpose with this audience?"

Let the following six principles guide your revision work.

Clarity in Composition

In the visual arts, clarity refers to the distinctness of an image, how easily it can be made out. A drawing or a photograph is clear if it shows us plainly and sharply what the artist saw. Clarity in writing generally means precision. A sentence or a word is clear if it gives the reader a precise idea of what the writer had in mind. Or, to look at it another way, clear writing accurately represents the writer's view.

SAY IT ANOTHER WAY Sometimes, all it takes is a simple variation. Keep rephrasing the fuzzy phrase until your listening partner gets it. Then write down the last thing you said. Chances are it will be clearer to your readers.

ACTIVATE ALL YOUR SENSES If your subject is something tangible—an object, person, or place—try cycling through the full range of your senses. What are the colors, shapes, and sizes? What are the sounds, smells, textures, and tastes?

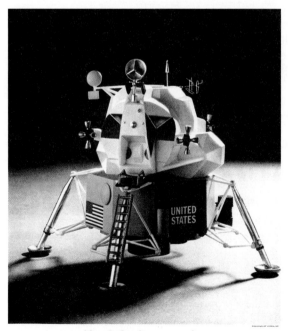

It's ugly, but it gets you there.

EXPERIMENT WITH SYNONYMS Slim, slender, lean, lanky, and skeletal are synonyms for thin. Each variation has a different shade of meaning, or **connotation,** which can put your subject in a very different light. Words with different connotations may share the same **denotation,** their dictionary definition. For example, the words *cop, flatfoot, fuzz,* and *officer of the law* all refer to members of the police force (their denotation) but reflect varying attitudes (their connotations) toward police.

USE ANALOGIES Is your reader having trouble understanding a new concept or unfamiliar object? Try comparing it to something already familiar. The old ads for the Volkswagen Beetle (left) introduced its odd shape to skeptical consumers with humorous comparisons.

AVOID CLICHÉS A **cliché** is like a rubber stamp that is used so often it no longer leaves a sharp impression. In fact, it was originally a printing term for a stereotype plate. We've all seen film clichés that have lost their freshness, like the shot of two lovers running in slow motion through a field of flowers. Steer clear of such tired expressions.

Completeness in Composition

How do you decide when to stop writing? Do you count pages or words? Do you run out of steam? Some assignments carry length requirements, like a ten-page research paper for biology or a thousand-word column for a magazine. Usually, though, a composition generates its own measures of completeness. It's a matter of recognizing when you have achieved your purpose.

One way of looking at a composition is to think of it as a kind of map or course of action. The filmmaker or writer wants to get the audience from point A to point B. Point A may be the beginning of a process, as when someone writes instructions for cooking an omelet or repairing a bicycle. Research papers and persuasive essays can be regarded in this manner if you think of writing as a way of moving readers from one level of understanding to another or from attitude A to attitude B.

Of course, this oversimplifies the process of composing. Movies and essays are usually richer, more complex than maps. But the analogy serves to clarify the nature of that three-way traffic that links writers to their subject, audience, and purpose. If your purpose is to get your readers from Brooklyn to the Bronx, you need to know how much they already understand about your subject. Are they familiar with the streets or subway lines? Are they good at following place names, or are they more successful when they count the number of blocks or train stops? For some readers you may need to add extra steps. For others, you can safely leave out information you assume they know. Completeness, then, is a relative term. It depends on what your readers need to know to get from here to there.

PREPARE THE GROUND Any composition builds on a foundation of knowledge. Storytellers often start by setting the scene, introducing characters, and clarifying other details that readers need to know in order to follow the story. This background information is called **exposition.** Whatever kind of writing you do, you'll need to decide how much to tell your readers. Can they understand your research paper on cloning without a basic grasp of genetics? Can they appreciate your case against smoking without the vital statistics on lung cancer? Can they follow your film review without knowing the director's early work? If not, you'll need to supply what's missing from their mental maps.

CLEAR THE DECK At the same time, you don't want to litter your writing with unnecessary information or needless repetition. Why bore readers with what they already know? Why say something in twenty words when you can say it in five? Blaise Pascal, the French essayist, once apologized for a very long letter, explaining that he didn't have the time to make it shorter. Brevity takes work. You can make this work worthwhile by practicing a few revising tricks.

PRUNE YOUR COMPOSITION SENTENCE BY SENTENCE Cut out the deadwood, those unnecessary words and phases that clutter your writing and sap its energy.

Cluttered: "In the story 'Mothers' that I have read by Anna Quindlen it deals with a young lady who lost her mother when she died young and she wants to know how things would have been between her and her mother so she imagines how they would have interacted if the mother was alive."

Revised: "Anna Quindlen's 'Mother' is about a child's struggle to cope with her mother's early death through her active imagination."

Trim overgrown phrases:

"at this point in time" use *now*

"along the lines of" use *like*

"are of the opinion that" use *believe*

"due to the fact that" use *because*

"in spite of the fact that" use *although*

"in the final analysis" use *finally*

Avoid unnecessary repetition:

Our house is a beautiful ~~house~~.

We learned to cooperate ~~together~~.

Another interesting fact about Sophocles's ~~life that I found quite interesting~~ was that ~~it was believed that~~ he was thought to be gay.

FILL IN THE PICTURE Early filmmakers learned that they could leave out parts of a story without losing the audience. They could cut from a shot of Papa leaving home to a shot of his arrival at the office without showing all the steps between. This is quite different from storytelling in a three-act play, which typically has only two cuts. Modern film audiences have become quite resourceful about filling in the missing moments, though directors keep testing their ability with movies like *Memento* and *Mulholland Drive*. Writers, too, must decide how much detail to include or how much logical guidance to give.

Consider the following three sentences:

Sabrina and Charlie walked into a restaurant.

They ordered Peking duck.

They paid the check and left.

These statements tell a story longer than the sentences themselves. Most of us would assume that something happened "between the lines." The words don't state that Sabrina and Charlie ate a meal. Nor do they tell us, directly, how much either ate or what kind of restaurant they entered. We fill in the information automatically. We assume, from past experience, that people go to restaurants to eat, that they eat what they order, and that they pay after they've eaten. If we recognize that Peking duck is a Chinese specialty, we may also assume that the incident did not take place in Beefsteak Charlie's or Pizza Hut. What other assumptions did you make?

Notice what happens if we change the final sentence:

Charlie paid the check, and they left.

or:

Sabrina paid the check and left.

or:

Sabrina left, and Charlie paid the check.

In each case, the story changes. A reader might assume that something interesting occurred between the lines: a dispute, an agreement, a sudden call on the cell phone. Leaving out this information may create interest, but it can also cause confusion. As a writer, you should consider the assumptions that your readers are likely to make. If you have a good reason to keep them guessing, fine. But if you fear they'll lose your line of thought, you may need to connect the dots for them.

Unity in Composition

Since your draft may have evolved gradually, it probably reflects the shifts in your thinking over time. It's only when you arrive at the end that you get a sense of the whole. This is the time to revise it as a unified composition.

CHECK EACH PARAGRAPH AGAINST YOUR MAIN IDEA Use your thesis statement as a point of reference. A peer review can help you spot where you go off on tangents or introduce irrelevant details. Delete those passages, or save them for another composition.

CHECK EACH PARAGRAPH FOR INTERNAL CONSISTENCY Check that each sentence relates to the paragraph's main point. Each should describe, develop, or qualify the point you're making in that paragraph. Remove unrelated passages, or move them to another paragraph where they belong. Or you might revise the topic sentence itself to match what the paragraph actually says.

CHECK THE COMPOSITION FOR ACCIDENTAL SHIFTS IN TENSE AND POINT OF VIEW Have you ever watched a movie that keeps alternating between past and present actions, like *Memento,* or that swings unexpectedly into the future, like *Pulp Fiction* or *Run Lola Run?* If so, you know how dislocating such shifts in tense can be. To avoid confusion, filmmakers sometimes use black and white photography or still images to signal the changes. Writers give similar attention to verb tense and point of view. Verb tenses clarify the time of actions: the past (*he went*), the present (*he goes*), the future (*he will go*), and other variations. Point of view is expressed grammatically in the first person (*I* or *we*), second person (*you*), or third person (*he/she/it/one* or *they*). The aim here is consistency. Avoid distracting jumps from one tense or person to another. Unless you have good reason to shift your reader to a different time frame or perspective, choose a suitable tense and point of view, and stay with them.

Continuity in Composition

In filmmaking, unintentional disruptions in continuity are called **jump cuts.** Jump cuts interrupt a movie's flow, its continuity. Something similar occurs in writing when the mind works faster than the pen. The stream of words, like the film inside a camera, starts and stops while the writer's thoughts race on ahead. The results, at least in a first draft, are likely to seem jumpy. Readers are left wondering what they missed.

USE TRANSITIONS Transitions can help to restore integrity and continuity to your original ideas. Review the transitions described earlier in the section on paragraphing. Use them to bridge the jump cuts in your writing.

TEST YOUR LOGIC Logic is the glue that holds an argument together. When you revise, pay close attention to the steps in your reasoning process. A reader should be able to follow your train of thought from start to finish. A quick way to check this is with a **topic sentence test.** Highlight the topic sentence of each paragraph. If a paragraph has no explicit topic sentence, create one. By reading through the marked sentences, you should be able to trace the logic of your whole composition.

Structure in Composition

Reading your draft with a fresh eye sometimes exposes problems with structure. Even though the draft may seem complete, unified, and cohesive, it may not be organized as well as it could be. The discussion of paragraphing earlier in this chapter offered ideas for organizing your composition (see the sections titled "Beginnings, Middles, Ends" and "Strategies for Supporting an Idea").

Style in Composition

When people say "I like your style," they may be referring to the way you dress, sing a song, or throw a ball. Most likely, what they have in mind is a combination of ingredients: those distinctive traits that give a personal touch to everything you do. It's what makes one person bounce and another person shuffle to the same dance tune.

It's also true that individuals vary their style of dancing when the music changes. Frequently, matters of style depend on the occasion. We dress one way for a formal evening, another for the beach. We speak to an employer differently than we speak to an old friend. In this sense of the word, style is more a reflection of our purpose and audience than an expression of our personality.

In writing, style involves many elements, such as the selection of words, the rhythm of sentences, or the choice of imagery, which may set a formal, comic, or ironic tone. These are all choices. The process is not as simple as choosing a tuxedo or a pair of jeans, but in some ways it is like learning to dress for the occasion. If you're like most people, you learned to anticipate how people would respond to what you chose to wear, and you worked out a middle course between external factors and inner needs. Something similar happens with composing. When you're first taught to write an academic essay, a research report, or a music review, you conform to expectations and follow a given format. Eventually, you learn to add your own spin.

When you revise for style, ask yourself these questions. First, is the style appropriate for your topic, purpose, and audience? Second, does the writing voice reflect your personal style, the way you want to sound? Third, is the voice consistent throughout? If not, do you have good reason to change the style at any point?

STUDENT ESSAY: "MY HISTORY LESSON"

Anna Tyutyunik wrote this essay as a first-year student at Westchester Community College in Valhalla, New York. Born in Kiev, Ukraine, Anna had moved to the United States when she was six years old. The move was difficult, she says, because of the language barrier and culture shock. It was also hard to leave behind close family members and friends. Despite these challenges, Anna adjusted quickly to her new lifestyle and made new friends.

"My History Lesson" was Anna's response after reading "'Indians': Textualism, Morality, and the Problem of History" by Jane Tompkins. No special guidelines were given for this assignment, only the simple prompt: "Write about your history lesson." Here is how Anna describes the process of writing her essay.

DISCOVERING

Q: How did you arrive at the idea for your essay?

A: It took me a long time to come up with the idea for this essay. I asked myself, was there something I was taught as a child that I later learned wasn't quite true? In thinking about this, I found that my Russian heritage was an interesting topic to explore. So many things that children were taught to believe in the former Soviet Union were incredibly biased and not fully true. This idea was the basic catalyst for my essay. I jotted down notes about the many misconceptions that I was taught, even at the young age of six. My next problem was figuring out how this idea of mine was going to become an essay. I thought about the former Soviet Union, about communism, and then thoughts of my communist grandfather came to mind. When I get this many ideas in my head, my best bet is simply to start writing and see where it takes me. I began with a sort of flashback to one day I remember spending with my grandfather. After writing about this event, I figured that I should give the reader a little bit of my own history. The part about my paternal grandfather (the one who died in one of Stalin's labor camps) was simply something that came up in my mind all of a sudden and I decided to weave it into the essay. This essay came about as the result of a focused freewriting exercise. I started with an idea and just wrote and let it flow.

PLANNING

Q: Say a little about how you prepare yourself to write and how you organize your thoughts.

A: I usually have to be in the mood to write. I'm not the kind of person who can take out a pen and write on command. For me, preparing to write usually requires reading. It has always been easier for me to write responses to things I've read than to simply write for a random prompt. Before I write, I need to sit down quietly and organize thoughts and ideas in my head. Sometimes I write these thoughts down as quick notes, and other times I just formulate a plan in my head. I like to do my writing in a quiet, comfortable environment with no clocks. Once I sit down to write something, I always write the first draft in one sitting. I do this because I feel that my style and my tone changes slightly every time I sit down to write. So, to keep whatever I'm writing flowing, I need to get it done in one sitting. I also rarely write by hand. Instead, I usually settle into bed or onto a comfortable couch and type everything on my laptop. This comes from a need to be neat and organized—I hate eraser marks and cross-outs on my paper. With a computer, I can just go back and delete something or add something in without a problem.

DEVELOPING

Q: How did you develop your first draft? Do you have any methods for building paragraphs? How did you arrive at your beginning and ending?

A: My first draft was something of a focused freewriting exercise. I didn't worry much about transitions or a smooth flow. As far as paragraphing is concerned, I stick to the rule that if you change topics or ideas, you automatically start a new paragraph. My beginning was the result of exactly what I was picturing in my mind when thinking about what to write. I had been thinking about that day with my grandfather, and I thought it would be interesting to try to put the memories in my mind on paper. When that was done, the rest just flowed.

I admit that I got stuck on the ending for a little while. I wasn't sure where to end or what to end with because I had too many thoughts running through my mind. What finally helped me write the ending was returning to the assignment itself. The original prompt (*write about your history lesson*) reminded me that there was a lesson to be derived from my story. I wanted to leave the reader with that lesson. So, instead of just ending with my personal experience, I decided to put things in a broader perspective. I shifted from "I" to "we" in my conclusion to bring my message closer to the reader. By including my readers in the essay, I hope to make them realize that the lesson I learned applies to them as well. Maybe they, like me, will reconsider the world around them and figure things out for themselves. This new conclusion really tied the whole essay together, clarifying and summarizing my point very directly.

REVISING

Q: Tell me about your process of revising. What did you delete, add, move around, or otherwise change? And what were you thinking when you made the changes?

A: I did more revising on this piece than I usually do with my writing. My usual approach is to simply write the essay and put it aside for several days. By putting it aside, I allow myself time to clear confusing thoughts out of my head. When I pick up the essay again, it seems like something new to me. I try to look at my writing from the reader's perspective, always keeping my audience in mind. I begin by simply reading the essay, without making any corrections. Reading the whole thing gives me a complete sense of what I'm trying to say and where I'm trying to go with it. This way, if there is some kind of confusion in the way my thoughts are written, I can catch it right away. The first thing I do when I edit is smooth out the flow of my writing and make sure the ideas are clear.

There were several places in the essay where I really struggled when editing:

- "She has to keep reminding herself to listen as they head toward the market, his steady voice a *contradiction* to her constant stumbling and tripping."

   The word "contradiction" may seem like an odd choice. I wanted to show contrast between the old man and the little girl, but the word "contrast" just didn't sound strong enough in my mind. There is more at play here than just his stability pitted against her lack of stability. There is also an underlying idea of power, which the old man represents; he is powerful, and she is not. In hindsight, I think that the reason I used "contradiction" in my first draft was because this essay is, in a sense, about the contradictions and juxtapositions of thoughts, actions, and ideology. After changing the word several times, I decided to stick with the original wording of the sentence because I felt that there was a reason behind it.

- I often struggle with comma usage in the form of comma splices. I think this stems from my need to get thoughts down on paper very quickly when I write my first draft. When in doubt, I try to separate the sentence in question into two separate sentences. If this works, I usually make the change. I also keep a style and mechanics reference guide around when I edit.

- As I mentioned before, perfecting the ending of this essay was a huge struggle for me. I rewrote the conclusion at least five times before I settled on a compromise between my own personal experience and sending my message out to the reader. I find that often I have to reread my essays several times before I can come up with a great ending. Rereading the essay really helps me absorb what I'm trying to say, which makes it easier to draw conclusions and sum up the piece.

PROOFREADING

Q: Do you give any special attention to completeness, unity, structure, continuity, or style? How do proofread your work for errors?

A: My main focus in editing is on unity and continuity, as well as clarity. I think that these are the key elements in a well-written piece. I read a lot, so I have developed a keen sense when it comes to the flow of a piece of writing. I can almost always tell if I am missing a transition. My feeling is that all the different thoughts and ideas that go into an essay should be interlaced so tightly that it becomes difficult for the reader to focus on one without needing to include the others. I think that style is also very important in writing.

I proofread my work for errors by reading slowly and out loud. Often, when reading silently, I miss simple errors because my mind's eye automatically corrects them. Reading out loud forces me to pronounce everything that's written on the paper, making it much easier to find mistakes. Another helpful tool for me is the spellchecker on my computer, but I have learned countless times that I still need to check my writing for spelling mistakes after it has gone through the spellchecker.

Q: Looking back, what would you say was your most important goal in writing the essay? What were your biggest obstacles, and how did you tackle them? How do you feel now about the results?

A: At first, my goal was simply to complete the assignment I was given. But this particular essay soon became more personal than that. In this case I felt a strong connection to the assignment and my ideas for answering the prompt were very dear to me. I think that by the time I actually began writing, my goal was to tell my story so well that it would force the readers to think about the misconceptions in their own lives. My greatest obstacle when it comes to writing is to simply let my ideas flow without constantly trying to perfect them as I write. In the past I often tried too hard to make things perfect the first time around and eventually found that this hindered the flow of my ideas. I realize that there is room for editing and revising later on. Although this has been a struggle for me, I find that by not editing as I write I get better results in the end.

Q: Finally, did you learn anything about yourself while writing "My History Lesson"? What advice would you give to other student writers?

A: The most important lesson I learned from writing "My History Lesson" was that sometimes a vague idea can really blossom into something wonderful. I also learned that as a writer I have to trust my instincts. For the most part, if whatever I'm writing feels right, it probably is.

My advice to other student writers is to simply write. Many people don't write because they are afraid that they aren't good enough, but they need to realize that something is always better than nothing when it comes to writing. The more people write, the better they get at it. Also, when writing, don't be too hard on yourself. Just do your best and remember that there is always time and room for improvement later.

Anna's First Draft (with instructor's comments)

MY HISTORY LESSON[1]

by Anna Tyutyunik

[First Draft]

Four years old. Sun-kissed blonde hair, a pouty mouth, and porcelain white skin. Large gray eyes—too serious.[2] She almost has to run to keep up with him, carrying her plump little ball of a body on short, stubby legs. Concentrating hard, she never lets go of his

1. I like the way your title sums up the main idea of your essay.

2. Your first two lines contain three fragments. Try writing complete sentences to create a smoother flow. Sometimes fragments can be effective, though, if used deliberately for a good reason.

3. Comma splice
error. Use a
semicolon or a
linking word to
join these sen-
tences. Or make
them two sepa-
rate sentences.

4. Your use of
the present
tense here gives
the scene a qual-
ity of immediacy,
but watch your
tense forms care-
fully. Here you
have slipped into
the past tense.

5. Watch your
verb tenses in this
section. If you are
telling this as if it
happened today,
use the present
tense until you
begin to talk
about a previous
action, as you do
in the sentence
that begins, "She
had told herself
that morning."

6. This forecast-
ing of events
makes me want
to read more.

7. Is this the
word you want?

8. Do you want
to take such a
long while to get
to your point?
Consider con-
densing this part
of the story. You
can still make the
point about a
stagnant econo-
my to prepare us
for your grand-
father's Stalinist
nostalgia, but
maybe with
fewer words.

hand. It's an old wrinkled hand, but strong and dominant: a hand of power. Today is special, every moment is like magic.[3] On any other day she's[4] be at school right now, but not today. No, today he took[5] the day off work. Not only did he take the day off, but he decided to spend it with her. She had told herself that morning that not a moment of the day should be forgotten. Even at her age, she already knew that the only thing that brings results and possible success in life is knowledge. He was the wisest man she had ever met. Today, there would be a lot to learn.[6]

She has to keep reminding herself to listen as they head toward the market, his deep steady voice a contradiction[7] to her constant stumbling and tripping. When they get to the market, the little girl knows just by quickly looking around that it is going to be a long while[8] before they head home again—the place is packed. It's a cold, bitter, winter day in Kiev. Hopefully her thick worn stocking and small fox fur coat will keep her from freezing. Slowly, the man starts filling a satchel with various produce. She watches him and listens carefully, wondering when she too will be as wise as him. Finally, all they need is milk and butter. They had already stood in lines for sausage, eggs, and bread, but the dairy line was always the longest with no guarantee that you would get what you needed when your turn came. The man takes her little hand and they get in line to wait. Fifteen minutes, twenty . . . tick-tock, tick-tock . . . forty-five minutes go by. It seems like they're going to be there for days. The man turns to the little girl and says, "If Stalin were alive, we wouldn't be waiting." Her large solemn gray eyes register every word that comes out of his mouth as absolute truth. If Josef Stalin were still alive, we wouldn't work so hard just to try to make ends meet.

The man with the strong wrinkled hand was my grandfather, and I am the little blonde with gray eyes. My grandfather was a communist. For as long as I can remember, my grandfather could find no fault with communism. He only found fault in every leader of the Soviet Union since Stalin. So, from a very young age I learned to believe that when Stalin was alive and in power, there was no better place in the world than Communist Russia.

Shortly after I turned six, my family moved to the United States, and I was faced with a rude awakening. America was nothing like my grandfather has described. It seemed to me to be a land of plenty populated by nice, intelligent people. My family lived in a neat condo in suburban Cheshire, Connecticut and I went to a public school. Every Sunday I would sit down and write my grandfather a detailed letter. I would tell him all about my life and, most importantly, my education. In my letters I always tried hard to show him that I had everything I could possibly need and that life here wasn't so bad after all. But, when his replies came I was always heartbroken. He always found a way to tell me that I was simply young and naïve, that I didn't understand what was going on around me, and that by mov- ing our family to the US from Kiev, my parents were basically condemning us to death.

I was eight years old when I first studied the Holocaust in school. When I found out about Hitler and his concentration camps, I cried for almost a week straight. Soon thereafter I heard, in passing, some mention of my other grandfather being held in a concentration camp for six years of his life. Automatically I assumed that he had been one of Hitler's many victims (since he was Jewish, it made sense to me).[9] But, I decided to investigate the matter no further since I knew that talking about my grandfather was an incredibly sensitive subject for my father.

Later that year I went back to Kiev for the first time since I had left in 1991. During the two weeks that I was there my grandfather and I spent a lot of time together. Every single day he had something different and interesting for us to do. We frequented many museums and visited every historical site in Kiev. My grandfather told me all about Russia's history, especially the period when Josef Stalin was in power. He told me that Stalin had picked up a country that was in shambles, pieced it together, and put it back on its feet. That Stalin had successfully gotten the U. S. S. R. through WWII and then dragged it out of starvation and poverty.[10] He told me about all the great and wonderful things Stalin had accomplished and my entire return trip was spent pondering the matter. I later often wondered why it was that the things I learned in school were always such a contradiction to what the wisest man in the world had once told me. Three years ago,[11] my grandfather passed away. His death was a very painful time for me because we had left off on terrible terms. We had long stopped writing to each other and every conversation we had would ultimately turn into a full-blown political argument. But, it wasn't until recently that I decided to set the record straight for myself, and in honor of his memory.

Last summer I ended up with more free time on my hands than I knew what to do with. In July, a few days after my birthday, we celebrated what would have been my grandfather's ninetieth birthday.[12] With his memory and our arguments weighing heavily on my mind I decided to do some reading about my mother country and my culture. I read numerous books and soon got bored. Then, in August I went to Cape Cod and ended up with no reading material. I asked my brother if he had anything good to read and he told me that I would probably find something lying around in his car. So I went in search of what was to become one of the missing pieces to my puzzle. Inside the car, all I found was an old tattered copy of Aleksander Solzhenitsyn's "One Day in the Life of Ivan Denisovich."[13] My interest in the book grew after I read the back cover. I had known for several years at this point that Hitler wasn't the only one who had set up concentration camps. Stalin too had forced labor camps set up all over the taiga in Siberia. Reading Ivan Denisovich's story, the horror of Stalin's labor camps settled into my bones. I was shocked and appalled; how could my grandfather have praised this demon of a man? How could the wisest man in the world have called this murderer the savior of our country? I was a complete emotional wreck.

9. Consider making this a separate sentence instead of a parenthetical afterthought.

10. This is a fragment.
11. This marks such a big break in the story that I wonder why you didn't start a new paragraph or provide a transition between your grandfather's "wisdom" and his death.

12. There may be more opportunities to trim your sentences here. What is most important for the reader to know?

13. Underline or italicize the titles of books.

My father saw what I was reading and asked me how I liked it. I told him about the dilemma I was faced with and we ended up having a long discussion. This is when I learned that my other grandfather hadn't been in one of Hitler's concentration camps, but actually had served out his term in one of Stalin's labor camps. He had been sentenced to ten years simply because he had been sitting in a bar with two friends and one of them had told a political joke. My grandfather had only listened to the joke, but someone told a government official about the incident and all three were called in for questioning. The man who had told the joke didn't admit to it, but he gave the names of my grandfather and the other man as the two people listening. When my grandfather was questioned, he refused to give out the names of his two friends and to betray them. Thus, the other two betrayed him and he was the only one given a sentence. Here was my family torn before my eyes: one of my grandfathers had died at the hands of the man who my other grandfather worshipped.[14] How could this be?

It was only after the long discussion with my father that I realized that my grandfather,[15] the wisest man in the world, actually didn't know everything there was to know. There is no doubt in my mind that he was incredibly intelligent, well educated, and well read, but his views were biased and clouded by years of conditioning and brainwashing. I don't blame him any longer for being the way he was; he was only trying to teach me what he thought was the truth and was best for me. All his life he was taught that communism was wonderful and that Stalin had saved our country. I now have no contradicting views on the situation. I know what really happened with Josef Stalin and I know what kind of man he was. There are definite facts that support my view. But, I have also learned how things work in life. Oftentimes, the things we take to be true are not quite so; they are simply a biased or opinionated version of the truth. Is it so wrong to say that Stalin did good things? No. He did some great things for the Soviet Union, but that statement simply contains an omission.[16] It is the truth, but not the whole truth. And so, we go through life every day trying to find little pieces of the truth about different things. Maybe one day as a society we will be able to piece together those little sections of the puzzle and create a real history of the world.[17]

Anna's Revision

MY HISTORY LESSON

by Anna Tyutyunik

[Revised]

She's four years old[18] with sun-kissed blonde hair, a pouty mouth, and porcelain white skin. Her large gray eyes are too serious. She almost has to run to keep up with him, carrying her plump little ball of a body on short, stubby legs. Concentrating hard, she never

14. You do a fine job of summing up the central idea of this essay in a single sentence.

15. Since you have two grandfathers, it might be less confusing if you identified him here in some distinctive way.

16. Since this is a rather large omission, it might help readers unfamiliar with Soviet history to explain the enormity of his crimes.

17. I wonder if you can link this ending more directly to your personal experience. In what way would your history lesson be useful to the world?

18. Fragments changed to complete sentences

lets go of his hand. It's an old wrinkled hand, but strong and dominant: a hand of power. Today is special;[19] every moment is like magic. On any other day she'd be at school right now, but not today. No, today he's decided to take[20] the day off from work. Not only did he take the day off, but he's also decided to spend it with her. She had told herself that morning that not a moment of the day should be forgotten. Even at her age, she already knew that the only thing that brings results and possible success in life is knowledge. He was the wisest man she had ever met. Today, there would be a lot to learn.

She has to keep reminding herself to listen as they head toward the market, his deep steady voice a contradiction[21] to her constant stumbling and tripping. When they get to the market, the little girl knows just by quickly looking around that it is going to be a long while[22] before they head home again—the place is packed. It's a cold, bitter, winter day in Kiev. Hopefully her thick, worn stockings and small fox fur coat will keep her from freezing. Slowly, the man starts filling a satchel with various produce. She watches him and listens carefully, wondering when she too will be as wise as he is. Finally, all they need is milk and butter. The man takes her little hand and they get in line to wait. Fifteen minutes, twenty . . . tick-tock, tick-tock . . . forty-five minutes go by. It seems like they're going to be there for days. The man turns to the little girl and says, "If Stalin were alive, we wouldn't be waiting." Her large solemn gray eyes register every word that comes out of his mouth as absolute truth. In her little mind she can almost hear his unspoken words as well—if Josef Stalin were still alive, we wouldn't work so hard just to try to make ends meet.[23]

The man with the strong, wrinkled hand was my maternal grandfather, and I am the little blonde with gray eyes. My grandfather was a communist. For as long as I can remember, my grandfather could find no fault with communism. He found fault only with the leaders—with every leader of the Soviet Union since Stalin. So, from a very young age I learned to believe that when Stalin was alive and in power, there was no better place in the world than Communist Russia.

Shortly after I turned six, my family moved to the United States, and I was faced with a rude awakening. America was nothing like my grandfather had described. It seemed to me to be a land of plenty populated by nice, intelligent people. My family lived in a neat condo in suburban Cheshire, Connecticut, and I went to a public school. Every Sunday I would sit down and write my grandfather a detailed letter. I would tell him all about my life and, most importantly, my education. In my letters I always tried hard to show him that I had everything I could possibly need and that life here wasn't so bad after all. But when his replies came, I was always heartbroken. He always found a way to tell me that I was simply young and naïve, that I didn't understand what was going on around me, and that by moving our family to the United States from Kiev, my parents were basically condemning us to death.

19. Comma replaced by semicolon

20. Verb tenses corrected for consistency

21. Anna decides to keep this word, as she explains in her description of her revision process.

22. This section is tightened by the removal of several unnecessary lines.

23. Anna revises the first part of the sentence to make it clear that this part represents her grandfather's thoughts.

I was eight years old when I first studied the Holocaust in school. When I found out about Hitler and his concentration camps, I cried for almost a week straight. Soon thereafter I heard, in passing, some mention of my other grandfather being held in a concentration camp for six years of his life. Automatically I assumed that he had been one of Hitler's many victims. Since he was Jewish, this made sense to me.[24] But, I decided to investigate the matter no further since I knew that talking about my grandfather was an incredibly sensitive subject for my father.

Later that year I went back to Kiev for the first time since I had left in 1991. During the two weeks that I was there, my grandfather and I spent a lot of time together. Every single day he had something different and interesting for us to do. We frequented many museums and visited every historical site in Kiev. My grandfather told me all about Russia's history, especially the period when Josef Stalin was in power. He told me that Stalin had picked up a country that was in shambles, pieced it together, and put it back on its feet and that he had successfully gotten the U.S.S.R. through WWII and then dragged it out of starvation and poverty.[25] He told me about all the great and wonderful things Stalin had accomplished, and my entire return trip was spent pondering the matter. I later often wondered why it was that the things I learned in school were always such a contradiction to what the wisest man in the world had once told me.

Three years ago,[26] my grandfather passed away. His death was a very painful time for me because we had left off on terrible terms. We had long stopped writing to each other, and every conversation we had would ultimately turn into a full-blown political argument. But it wasn't until recently that I decided to set the record straight for myself, and in honor of his memory.

Last summer, we celebrated what would have been my grandfather's ninetieth birthday. With his memory and our arguments weighing heavily on my mind I decided to do some reading about my mother country and my culture. Inside the family car, I found an old tattered copy of Aleksander Solzhenitsyn's One Day in the Life of Ivan Denisovich.[27] My interest in the book grew after I read the back cover. I had known for several years at this point that Hitler wasn't the only one who had set up concentration camps. Stalin too had set up forced labor camps all over the taiga in Siberia. Reading Ivan Denisovich's story, the horror of Stalin's labor camps settled into my bones. I was shocked and appalled; how could my grandfather have praised this demon of a man? How could the wisest man in the world have called this murderer the savior of our country? I was a complete emotional wreck.

My father saw what I was reading and asked me how I liked it. I told him about the dilemma I was faced with, and we ended up having a long discussion. This is when I learned that my other grandfather hadn't been in one of Hitler's concentration camps, but actually had served out his term in one of Stalin's labor camps. He had been sentenced to

24. By making this a separate sentence, Anna gives the idea more importance. It is no longer a parenthetical afterthought.

25. The fragment is repaired by the addition of "and" to connect it to previous sentence.

26. Anna starts a new paragraph here.

27. Book title underlined

ten years simply because he had been sitting in a bar with two friends and one of them had told a political joke. My grandfather had only listened to the joke, but someone told a government official about the incident and all three were called in for questioning. The man who had told the joke didn't admit to it, but he gave the names of my grandfather and the other man as the two people listening. When my grandfather was questioned, he refused to name his two friends. Thus, the other two betrayed him, and he was the only one given a sentence. Here was my family torn before my eyes: one of my grandfathers had died at the hands of the man whom my other grandfather worshipped. How could this be?

It was only after the long discussion with my father that I realized that my maternal grandfather,[28] the wisest man in the world, actually didn't know everything there was to know. There is no doubt in my mind that he was incredibly intelligent, well educated, and well read, but his views were biased and clouded by years of conditioning and brainwashing. I don't blame him any longer for being the way he was—he was only trying to teach me what he thought was the truth and what was best for me. All his life he was taught that communism was wonderful and that Stalin had saved our country. I now have no conflicting views on the situation. I know what really happened with Josef Stalin, and I know what kind of man he was. There are concrete facts that support my view. But I have also learned how things work in life. Oftentimes, the things we take to be true are not quite so; they are simply a biased version of the truth. Is it so wrong to say that Stalin did good things? No. He did some great things for the Soviet Union, but that statement contains an important omission.[29] It is the truth, but not the whole truth. Stalin may have done great things for the U.S.S.R., but he also murdered around 20 million of his own people while he was in power. And so we go through life every day trying to find little pieces of the truth about different things. We are usually only taught or shown one side of the story, and we must make it our duty to search for the other sides. Maybe one day as a society we will be able to piece together those little sections of the puzzle and reveal a true history of the world.

28. Anna solves the problem (how to distinguish between her two grandfathers) by referring to her mother's father as her maternal grandfather.

29. Anna underscores the magnitude of her grandfather's "omission" by adding the word "important."

30. Anna's new ending broadens the original perspective to include the reader in her history lesson. See her commentary on revision.

STUDENT MULTIMEDIA PROJECTS

The principles of effective communication can be applied to documentary films, commercials, song lyrics, Web site content, and other forms of media. Throughout the chapters that follow, you will be invited to compose in various media, including film. For guidelines to composing in film, see the Web site appendix to this book, "Composing with a Camera." To see examples of how other students have applied these principles to their multimedia projects, visit www.mhhe.com/costanzo.

Holli Bundy created her first Web site while enrolled in a course on hypertext at Illinois State University. Her online portfolio, "The Holli Bundy Story," is available on *The Writer's Eye* Web site together with Holli's description of nonlinear composing.

Dawn Turner learned how to shoot and edit movies as a student at Westchester Community College in New York. When her mother began showing symptoms of a little-known environmental illness, Dawn took her digital camera to the medical community and produced a documentary film, *What Is MCS?* She tells about her composing process in an interview on *The Writer's Eye* Web site.

A student from Bermuda, Shawnita Payne joined a college video club that produces biweekly cable television shows. When sexual harassment became a major campus issue, she cowrote the script, edited, and hosted a special program on the topic. Read an interview with Shawnita on *The Writer's Eye* Web site.

PART TWO

Connections: Readings, Screenings, and Invitations to Compose

CHAPTER 3

Flashbacks: Longing and Belonging

Human beings are social creatures. We long to belong. Much of our lives is spent trying to fit in—to groups at the playground, cliques at school, special organizations, our family, the workplace, a community where we can feel at home. Many of the world's best stories are based on memories about making or breaking a crucial human bond. For the storyteller, each narrative becomes a kind of expedition through the past. Scientists tell us that our past experiences are stored as neural pathways in the brain. Sometimes we get caught in these pathways unaware. By exploring memories deliberately and reconstructing them as stories, we have more choice over the paths we take.

The essays, videos, and Web sites in this chapter were composed by people seeking to retrieve the past. Some embarked on literal journeys to the place where they grew up. Others made the voyage in mind only, revisiting moments from childhood through the power of imagination. For all of them, the past unveils a lesson about longing and belonging, some connection desired, found, forgotten, or lost. As you read, you'll be invited to join the club by contributing your own story. What are your most vivid memories? What was it like to be you as a child? When did you want, discover, or lose something so important that it shaped the person you are today? This chapter will help you bring that moment back to life for yourself and others to appreciate.

Why are our libraries populated with so many histories and memoirs? Why does television carry so many documentaries about people from the past? Why do we enjoy hearing and telling anecdotes about the good old days—or harder times? The fact that our media are full of memories reflects the high value that we place on the act of remembering in everyday life.

SCENARIOS FROM LIFE

At school, in the community, in personal relationships, and at work, people reconstruct memories for a variety of reasons. Consider the times in your own life when you are asked to recount previous experiences in writing or through some other medium. The following scenarios—all true—illustrate some of the day-to-day events that call for a focused use of memory.

1. A student of psychology is asked write a paper that describes key incidents from each stage of her life: infancy (0–2), the toddler years (2–4), childhood (5–10), puberty (11–13), and so on. In her paper, she must distinguish between what she was told about these moments by others and what she herself remembers. These memories will serve as the personal foundation for a course in mental health.

2. A witness to a crime is asked by different people to recall a significant event. A detective questions the witness for a police report. A legal attorney prepares a written deposition based on the witness's testimony under oath to be used when the case comes to court. At the trial, an attorney examines the witness with pointed questions of fact, character, and motive. Family and friends also want to know what happened. Each version of the story differs, depending on the audience, the witness's expectations, and what the witness remembers at the time.

3. After the death of a young woman, her friends plan a special funeral. They invite each guest to bring an object that represents the deceased. At the funeral, the chairs are arranged in a circle around a Navajo rug that she cherished when she was alive. As the guests place their chosen objects on the rug, they each tell a story that connects the object to the woman's memory. A softball glove, a knitted shawl, a clay pot, a sheet of music—each object generates a story that helps to reconstruct the unique character of her life. At the end of the ceremony, the objects are wrapped in the rug and buried with the casket. But those shared stories keep her memory alive.

4. A self-employed accountant wants to boost his business at the end of the year. Much of his success comes from the personal attention that he gives to clients, getting to know their habits, likes, dislikes, and needs. Yet many of his best clients have been out of touch for years. So he decides to contact them one by one. First, he writes a profile of every individual, recalling hobbies, family names, and anecdotes. Then he writes a letter to these former clients, inviting them back and drawing on his profiles to make each invitation personal.

WHY WRITE TO REMEMBER?

In this chapter, you'll be practicing the twin activities of **remembering** and **reconstructing.** Memory keeps our past alive. Sometimes memories sustain us through tough times. Sometimes they haunt us, preventing us from seeing new possibilities. Awareness is one way to take hold of our past, so that we—and not our history—may guide our future.

Distance can lend perspective necessary to the past. A memory may never be quite as intense, as vivid, as the original experience, but through memory we may see the experience more distinctly, in a clearer light. So remembering can be a path to self-discovery, a way to find out who we are by revisiting where we've been. Memories are not always true to the original, however. Even when we try to be as accurate as possible, we may recall events differently than others involved remember them; we may even remember the same events differently at different times, depending on our state of mind.

This kind of writing can reach beyond the boundaries of a private diary, enabling you to share part of yourself with an audience. How many times have you joined a group of people telling stories when your own story becomes a ticket of admission, establishing a bond? You offer something of yourself, and you receive the validation of response. You might get appreciation, moral support, perhaps sympathy or admiration, perhaps fresh insights. You get to test your self-discoveries in the mirror of an audience.

WRITING OPTION: WRITING TO REMEMBER

The writing option in this chapter is about memory. It is a chance to recapture something significant from your past, to explore its importance, and to reconstruct it in writing for others to appreciate.

Your topic should be something *consequential* that happened to you: perhaps an incident during which you felt threatened, a personal triumph, a lesson that you learned, or a turning point in your life. Try telling the story to a friend before you begin writing. Your friend's response and questions may help you shape the story for others to read. You might also try to list important moments and details as a way to see what should be included in your story. The Tips on Writing from Memory that follow will help to guide you through this process.

When you write your first draft, give attention to organization: the way you build your story. Decide what the reader needs to know in the beginning. Think about the order in which things happened and how much to tell the reader at each point. Pay attention also to the pictures you create. Try to reconstruct key moments by showing what happened rather than merely telling that it happened. Dialogue and scene descriptions often help to make important moments come alive. Finally, give careful thought to the story's theme or controlling idea. It should be more than a chronology of incidents. It should add up to something meaningful. By the time your readers reach the end, they should understand why the event was so important to you.

MEDIA OPTION: VIDEO JOURNAL

Is there a special place from the past that you haven't seen in a long time? Maybe it's the neighborhood you used to live in, your grandmother's house in the country, the old school, or a vacation spot from childhood. The media assignment is a chance to return to the scene with a video camera and record what you see, think, and feel. It's a good idea to take someone with you, someone who can ask you questions and film your reactions, as Bill Moyers does for the writer Maya Angelou when she returns to the town of Stamps where she grew up (see "Maya Angelou's Journey Home" on page 87).

Your final video will be a document about the place you visit and its significance for you. It may include your immediate responses, recorded on the spot by the camera and the microphone. It may involve interviews with people you meet there, perhaps a former teacher or old friend who remembers you from earlier times. It may use voice-over narration to accompany the images: memories that you recall while the camera is running or words that you write down later and add to the final soundtrack. Like any well-made composition, your video should have a beginning, middle, and end. After watching it, your audience should come away with a strong impression of this place from your past and its special meaning in your life.

TIPS ON WRITING FROM MEMORY

As you saw in Chapter Two, "Composing across the Media," experienced writers rarely follow a rigid, step-by-step procedure to produce an essay. Yet it often helps to think of your progress in stages—discovering, planning, drafting, revising, and proofreading—bearing in mind that the boundaries between stages are always flexible and recursive. This section offers strategies for reconstructing your memory in essay form and refers to the readings and screenings that you will encounter later in this chapter. Refer back to Chapter Two for more detailed guidelines.

DISCOVERING

Sometimes you can look for memories by calling on an old friend or by revisiting a place from the past, like your childhood neighborhood. Sometimes memories will find you, if you let yourself be open to discovery. The idea for Marcel Proust's *In Search of Time Past,* probably the longest memoir ever written, came to him unexpectedly when he dipped a madeleine biscuit into a cup of tea. The scent from the tea-soaked biscuit revived strong memories of childhood that had been lost for years. Once stirred by these recollections, Proust was ready to follow the scent.

Try one or two of these discovery techniques to start your journey back in time.

1. VISUAL PROMPTS. Old photos, family videos, or other visual prompts can often prime your memory. Check the walls and shelves for mementos of your past. Or flip through a magazine. Sometimes a random photograph will activate a long-forgotten story. If no visual prompts are at hand, create one. Walk through your old neighborhood in your imagination, make a map, draw a house you once lived in or a favorite toy.

2. READING. Some writers get ideas by reading or viewing texts about other people's memories, like the documentaries, essays, and Web sites discussed in this chapter. Does Langston Hughes's description of his childhood church or Esmeralda Santiago's story about ironing with her mother trigger special memories for you? What personal images come to mind while you watch Maya Angelou return to her childhood home in Arkansas?

Visual Prompt

3. LISTING. Try listing your ideas in categories. For example, list all the "first times" (rites of passage) you can think of: your first job, first date, first car, and so on. Other lists might include turning points, big surprises, funny stories, and tough decisions.

4. CONNECTING WITH OTHER WRITERS. A good way to explore topics for your writing is with a partner or a group of other writers. You might begin by talking about familiar "rites of passage," those predictable events that mark a person's progress from one stage of life to another. What can you recall about your high school prom or your driver's license test? What initiation rituals did you face before being accepted into a club, congregation, or some other group? Do you share any life-altering experiences, like a serious illness, the loss of someone close, or a divorce? Consider how each person in your group responded to these moments. How were your personal experiences alike or different? How did your families and cultures shape or interpret these landmark events? Ultimately, what did the experience mean for you? How did it affect your life?

5. FOCUSED FREEWRITING. Deep down, locked in the chambers of your memory, there is a lot of energy waiting to be released. Sometimes you don't know what's there until you explore it with a steady flow of words. Begin writing freely on two or three items from your list of possible topics. Once you tap into the right reservoir, you may feel a surge of power in your writing, a signal that you've struck something vigorous and meaningful to you.

PLANNING

1. QUESTIONING. Test your topic with questions. Is the topic really important to you? Will it be interesting to others? How comfortable will you feel writing on this topic for an audience? Do you have enough to say, enough details to make the story come alive? What should be included? How should it be organized? Does the story fit into a larger picture? How does it relate to the history, music, personalities, or media events of the time? If you have trouble questioning yourself, try teaming up with someone else and pose questions to each other.

2. CONRASTING THEN AND NOW. To help you establish a point of view and clarify the story's meaning for you, compare your past and current perspectives. What did it look like to you then? What does it look like now? Do you still feel the same way? Would you handle things differently today? What has changed? What do the changes tell you about yourself? In "Two Views of the River" (page 151), Mark Twain's description of the Mississippi becomes a reflection on certain changes in his life. Similarly, a significant object, place, or incident from your past can serve as a yardstick for measuring how far you've come.

3. OUTLINING. Some writers use a working outline to help them visualize the structure of an essay. By listing the main ideas in order, they see more clearly how their essay is shaping up. At this stage, any outline should be flexible. You might begin by identifying the incidents of your story in the order that they happened. You might consider where the incidents took place and who was involved. Once you have outlined the main elements, you can decide how to present them to the reader.

DRAFTING

1. CREATE A SCRIPT. Bring out the drama in your story by including elements that you'd expect to find in a play. Where is the story set? Who are the leading actors? Are there any

important props? Most plots lead to a climactic action, building tension and suspense along the way. They usually begin with a conflict that disrupts the status quo and show how people respond to the conflict, one action leading to another, until the problem is resolved. At the drama's end, life returns to normal, but with a difference. The progression of events has caused a change—in knowledge, in perception, in relationships, in fact. Don't worry about the formal requirements for writing scripts. The point here is to see your story in dramatic terms.

2. BUILD KEY SCENES. Try to bring your memory to life so that readers will feel what the experience was like for you. Show them the important moments as if you had a camera. You control their focus of attention by framing every scene. Give them close-ups of significant details but also pull back for a long shot of the scene when you want to put those details in perspective. Use dialogue to let the people in your story speak in their own language. Try to capture their gestures and intonation with a few descriptive terms, as Hughes does when he describes the preacher's "wonderful rhythmical sermon, all moans and shouts and lonely cries and dire pictures of hell" or his friend Wesley "sitting proudly on the platform, swinging his knickerbockered legs and grinning down at me." In other words, use your visual and auditory imagination to *show* what happened.

3. FIND YOUR VOICE. In addition to showing past events, your essay should *tell* readers about their significance to you. Think of yourself as a voice-over narrator, introducing the story, commenting on the action, clarifying its implications, filling in the background information necessary to understand the story's deeper meanings. Your writing voice will set the tone for the entire essay, creating a relationship between you and your readers. Like your speaking voice, your writing voice is partly a matter of personal style, partly of the mood you're in, partly of the situation. Whether your writing is formal or informal, angry or humorous, confessional or ironic, it should fit your subject, audience, and purpose.

4. USE TRANSITIONS. Transitions move you from one section of a text to the next. Visual transitions can signal relationships between segments of a film, like the fades from and to black in Deann Borshay Liem's documentary or her use of different filters to distinguish her three identities in the introductory sequence. Writers tie their paragraphs together with verbal transitions. Maya Angelou uses this sentence to link a paragraph about food to one about the holidays: "Although the syrupy golden rings sat in their exotic cans on our shelves year round, we only tasted them during Christmas." Nuala Lynch shifts the focus from her inner thoughts to her physical surroundings this way: "While all these thoughts were racing through my head, there was a lot of noise above me." Such links help to clarify the logical connections in an essay, giving the reader a smooth path from beginning to end.

5. MAKE UP A WORKING TITLE. The essay's title is the first thing your readers come to. Some titles are flatly descriptive ("Ironing"), some thematic ("Salvation"), some evocative ("A Night of Terror"). Creating a fitting title can be an opportunity to test the broad meaning of your essay. While considering titles, ask yourself the following questions: What does it all add up to? What dominant impression do you want it to make on your audience?

REVISING

Remember that revising your essay means seeing it again, usually from a certain distance. You can distance yourself by putting the draft aside for a while, letting it simmer on the back burner while your attention is focused elsewhere, then returning to it with a fresh eye, rewriting, trimming, and polishing the text into a final draft. Or you can try a more direct approach.

1. READ ALOUD. When you read your draft aloud to someone else, you often hear what should be changed. Sometimes your listener's responses are clues to what is coming through, what is unclear, or what is missing. Sometimes just hearing the words in your own voice tells you where those words are most and least connected to the underlying thoughts and feelings.

2. PLAY WITH THE TEXT. If you write with a computer, try changing the appearance of your text. Experiment with different margins, line spacings, or fonts. If you've been looking at your words on the screen, print out a copy to see how they would look on paper. Simply altering the visual layout can often help you see misspellings, repetitious phrasing, faulty logic, and other rough spots that you didn't notice before. This also helps you see what you actually wrote, not what you intended to write but didn't.

3. LOOK FOR STRUCTURE. One way to see the structure of your essay is to make a skeletal outline. List the main ideas in the order they occur. When you visualize the bare bones of your story in this way, you may discover that you left something out or that you'd like to rearrange events, maybe starting with a flashback. As an alternative to outlining, try reading only the first sentence of each paragraph. This gets you to notice whether you're using "lead sentences," sentences that lead the reader into the main topic of a paragraph. It also draws attention to transitions, phrases that link the sections of your essay into a smoothly flowing narrative.

4. USE PEER PREVIEWS. Film producers like to test early versions of a new film with preview screenings. Sometimes actors, directors, and other moviemakers sit in with the audience to gauge its various reactions. Sometimes questions are distributed to pinpoint specific features of the film. It's a good idea to find a preview audience for your first draft. Other students are a natural audience because they know the assignment and can tell you what came through in your writing. Ask them about those passages that concern you most. Or use the Peer Preview Checklist to help you measure their response.

After you use preview audiences a few times, you may find that their responses continue to influence your writing long afterward. Their faces and voices stay with you, guiding your decisions and shaping what you write.

Peer Preview Checklist

Give this checklist to a "committed reader," someone interested in helping you shape your rough draft into a final essay.

1. **Where were you most or least engaged? What helped you to experience the writer's memory as if you were there?**

2. **Did anything seem to be missing? What would make the essay more complete?**

3. **What came across as the essay's main idea, its central focus? Where is the memory's significance most clearly presented?**

4. **List any problems you had following the text from start to finish.**

5. **What do you remember most after reading it?**

Reconstructing Memories across the Media

Readings and Screenings: Longing and Belonging

A box of treasured objects sets the nostalgic mood for *To Kill a Mockingbird,* adapted for the movie screen by Horton Foote from Harper Lee's fictionalized autobiography. A young aspiring filmmaker, Stephen Frankfurt, composed these shots on his kitchen table from details of the story—and his own memories of childhood—for the movie's famous title sequence. Consider this evocative movie moment and other media that reflect on the past. What other examples can you add to the list?

In this section, you'll be examining texts in a variety of media—essays, Web sites, poetry, documentary videos—that reconstruct memories for particular reasons. Some, like the selections about Maya Angelou and Deann Borshay Liem, revisit places from the past in order to clarify the present. Angelou writes about her hometown in Arkansas and returns to it in a video interview with Bill Moyers. Borshay Liem's search for her Korean roots is explored in her documentary video and its companion Web site. Other texts, like Robert Hayden's poem about his father, Esmeralda Santiago's piece about ironing with her mother, and Nicholas Gage's essay about his high school teacher, help us to appreciate the role of important people in the authors' lives—and in our own. Many of the readings in this chapter are connected by the theme of longing and belonging. They recall key moments when the author learned something about belonging to—or being excluded from—a group. Langston Hughes, Dick Gregory, and Sandra Cisneros recall childhood incidents when they were separated from others by the sting of shame. The need to belong led Hughes to claim that he saw Jesus, and it set Borshay Liem on a journey to Korea.

As you view and read these texts, notice how each one uses the resources of its medium to narrate events purposefully.

- How does each text distinguish between past and present?
- How does each text organize key incidents and create a mood?
- Are there general guidelines for telling a successful story, whether it's told on television or in writing?
- What makes a story interesting and significant?
- What makes the story worth remembering?

When poet-writer Maya Angelou returned to her hometown of Stamps, Arkansas, after a thirty-year absence, Bill Moyers accompanied her with a video team. "I feared the ghosts I was about to bestir," Angelou said. "I was terribly hurt in this town . . . and vastly loved." The resulting hour-long documentary was originally broadcast on PBS as part of the television series, *Creativity with Bill Moyers*. "Maya Angelou's Journey Home" is an excerpt from that documentary. As Moyers reminds us, every journey home is also a journey inward.

Maya Angelou became a national celebrity when she read her poem, "On the Pulse of Morning," at President Clinton's 1993 inauguration. Well before then, however, many readers appreciated her inspiring poetry and autobiographical works, which include *I Know Why the Caged Bird Sings* and *The Heart of a Woman*. Others knew her as an international journalist, a screenwriter, a dancer, a composer of music (recorded by B. B. King), and an actor (she played Kunta Kinte's grandmother in *Roots*) as well as a poet. In her rich and varied life, she spent five years in Africa, worked with Dr. Martin Luther King, Jr., and was appointed to national commissions by Presidents Ford and Carter. Yet, as we learn from Angelou's story, such an extraordinary career might not have been predictable from her early years. Born black in the segregated South, raped at eight, and pregnant at sixteen, Marguerite Johnson (her given name) somehow found strength and inspiration in the very town that injured and constrained her.

Angelou is accompanied on her journey by Bill Moyers. As a broadcast journalist for more than twenty-five years, Moyers has earned wide-ranging respect and recognition for his honest, intelligent reporting on subjects ranging from history and politics to mythology and medicine. Born in Oklahoma and raised in Texas, Moyers began reporting for a local paper at the age of sixteen. After college, he served in the White House under two administrations, as deputy director of the Peace Corps for President Kennedy and as special assistant to President Johnson, before becoming publisher of *Newsday* and working for CBS and public television. He has won more than 120 awards for broadcast journalism, including thirty Emmys.

www.mhhe.com/costanzo

To view the video excerpt, visit this book's Web site.

PARTIAL TRANSCRIPT OF DOCUMENTARY, "MAYA ANGELOU'S JOURNEY HOME"

Maya Angelou: In my memory, Stamps is a place of light, shadow, sounds, and entrancing odors. The earth's smell was pungent, spiced with the odor of cattle manure, the yellowish acid on the ponds and rivers, the deep pots of greens and beans cooking for hours with smoked or cured pork. Flowers added their heavy aroma. And above all, the atmosphere was pressed down with the smell of old fears and hates and guilt.

I am a writer, and Stamps must remain for me in that nebulous, unreal reality, because I'm a poet and I have to draw from these shadows, these densities, these phantasmagories for my poetry. I don't want it to become a place on the map, because the truth is you never can leave home. You take it with you everywhere you go. It's under your skin, it moves the tongue, or slows it, colors the thinking, impedes upon the logic. So as the time came for me to actually come to Stamps, I started to dread it, I started to really fear the ghosts who I was about to bestir.

Is that all the size of the bridge? Miss Lizzy used to live there, Willie Williams' store was there. My lord, I used to come to fish on the pond there, and people were also baptized right there.

5 I was terribly hurt in this town and vastly loved.

[She reads:] We lived with our grandmother and uncle in the rear of the store. Until I was 13 and left Arkansas for good, the store was my favorite place to be. Alone and empty in the mornings, it looked like an unopened present from a stranger. Opening the front doors was pulling the ribbon off an unexpected gift.

Bill Moyers: If anyone has never been to an old country store, you just can't imagine what it did to the imagination. I can remember right now the feel of the seed bags in Hillary's Grocery and the smell of old T. J. Taylor's potato bags. It just made you feel so good to go into there. It was a wonderful world for a child, black or white.

Maya Angelou: Well, you can imagine it now, but it used to be filled with shelves, which had all sorts of exciting, exotic things, like sardines from Portugal—Port-u-gual. That's the way we pronounced it. We pronounced it as carefully as we pronounced the game we played, which was Mono-poly.

Bill Moyers: Mono-poly?

Maya Angelou: Well, we found out when we got to California that it was really Monopoly.

10 Bill Moyers: What else did you see here? What else was on the shelf? It was kind of like an enchanted land.

Maya Angelou: It was an enchanted land. There were things from Kansas that had, you know, were canned in Kansas and Louisiana, and even things from New York City. And we had matches from Ohio. So there, I mean—

Bill Moyers: That was living.

Maya Angelou: That was big time.

All the whites who picked up cotton pickers would pick them up at the front of our store. And about dawn the wagons would come rolling in. We'd open the store early so they could buy peanut patties, cans of sardines, hunks of cheese, and take them out to the cotton fields. And then they would bring them back at dusk, just about dark. We would fold out these wagons dead tired, beat. But on Saturday, big day Saturday at the store, then the people would talk and they would be so sassy. And then if a white person would come, they'd become meek and "sho, yessir, thas righ'." And you would see this thing that happened, this mask, or these masks. And Paul Lawrence Dunbar helped me to understand that with the poem:

> We wear the mask that grins and lies,
> It shades our cheeks and hides our eyes.
> This debt we pay to human guile;
> With torn and bleeding hearts we smile,
> And mouth myriad subtleties.
> Why should the world be overwise,
> In counting all our tears and sighs?
> Nay, let them only see us, while
> We wear the mask.

* * *

15 Bill Moyers: So many people here who touched you.

Maya Angelou: Yes, there was one woman in particular. There was one woman, Mrs. Flowers. Mrs. Flowers was the lady of well-to-do Stamps. She was very, very black and very, very beautiful. I thought she was—she was pretty. Now that was a pretty woman. And she seemed to me always to wear voile, which is an old cloth, old material. It's like a cotton chiffon which sways. And she'd wear talcum powder, and there'd always be a little of the talcum on this pretty black skin. And she spoke as softly as my grandmother. She'd walk up the road and pass going to her house; she had a summer house here. One day she stopped and she talked a few minutes with my grandmother. My grandmother would come off the porch. Now, that was a big step for my grandmother, but Momma used to stand on the porch to talk to people. But when Mrs. Flowers came, Momma would come out the door and step down and they would stand together and talk. So this day Mrs. Flowers said she wanted to invite me to her home. It was during the time when I couldn't talk and wouldn't talk.

Bill Moyers: How old were you?

Maya Angelou: I guess I was about eight. And Momma said, "Sister, Mrs. Flowers is inviting you to her home." Well, the beauty of the town, the most wonderful person in town to invite me? I couldn't believe it. It was just—it was as if someone said here's a million dollars, do anything you want with it. I followed her to her house, and all the shades were drawn. It was very cool in there, just like her, dark and cool. She raised the shades. And she had already made these big tea cookies that we make in the South, anyway in Arkansas, huge flat things, and they smell of vanilla. And the house smelled of vanilla. And she served me, which was very unusual because children usually served the older. And she served me—I couldn't speak all the way up to her house, which must be a half mile—and gave me iced lemonade. And then she sat down and she said, "Now. Margaret, I'm going read a book to you. It's called *A Tale of Two Cities*." This is the very way she talked. *[Slow and deliberate]* "It was the best of times. It was the worst of times." I thought—I had already seen that in my house, I had that book. But I didn't know it sounded like that. So she read to me. And then she told me that poetry was music written for the human voice. She told me that fifty times. Then she said, "Now, what I want you to do is, I want you to try by yourself to say a poem." So I'd get under my grand-mother's bed—she has a high bed, you know, the mattresses are high up—and I would get under the bed and try saying some of the poems out loud. I could hear them in my head, but to say them out loud. And finally it was through her and poetry that I began to talk.

Bill Moyers: You said you would not talk.

Maya Angelou: No.

Bill Moyers: Why, what was it?

Maya Angelou: Well, I had had a difficulty in St. Louis when I was seven and a half, and I had been—I had been raped. And the person who had raped me was killed. I said—I called his name and he was killed. And I thought at the time that it was my voice that caused the man to be dead, and so I just refused to put my voice out and put anybody else in danger.

Bill Moyers: And Mrs. Flowers—

Maya Angelou: Mrs. Flowers gave me back my voice.

RESPONSE QUESTIONS

1. What moments in the video made the strongest impression? How do you explain their effect on you?

2. Does Stamps remind you of your own hometown? What particular locations or people in the town bring your childhood to mind?

3. Do you agree with Angelou that "you can never leave home"? What do you think she means by saying "I don't want it [Stamps] to become a place on the map"?

4. After recalling Saturdays at her grandmother's store, Angelou recites a poem by Lawrence Dunbar about masks. What connection do you see between the poem and life at the store? Describe your response to Angelou's reading of the poem.

GUIDELINES FOR ANALYSIS

1. Compare "Journey Home" to Angelou's written account of her childhood in *I Know Why the Caged Bird Sings* (excerpted on pages 93–94). What does the video version add? What does it leave out?

2. During certain segments of the video, we hear Angelou's voice while the camera shows us scenes of the town. Find these voice-over segments and notice what images accompany her words. (In two of these segments, the words are taken from her book.) Why do you think these particular images were chosen? How effective is this combination of images and spoken language?

3. Sometimes, while Maya Angelou is talking about people and places from her past, the camera focuses on her face instead of showing us old photographs or mementos. Where does this happen? Should the film editors have inserted other images at these points? Why or why not?

4. At one point, Angelou says, "So as the time came for me to actually come to Stamps, I started to dread it, really fear the ghosts who I was about to bestir." Why did she dread returning home? What ghosts might she be referring to?

5. Angelou also says that she was "vastly loved." Where do you find evidence of that love in her reminiscence?

6. There is a moment when Angelou and Moyers reminisce together about the sights and smells of the old country store, "an enchanted land" for children. Where else does Moyers's presence make a difference? What role, or roles, does he play in reviving Angelou's memories?

QUESTIONS OF CULTURE

1. Moyers remembers the country store as "a wonderful world for a child, white or black." To what extent can his memories and Angelou's be shared across racial boundaries? Where else in the video does Moyers's presence raise issues about race?

2. When Angelou lived in Stamps, the town was divided by the railroad tracks into two separate districts, one for whites and one for blacks. From what you see and hear, how has this situation changed?

3. In order to understand Maya Angelou's experiences, how important is it to have lived in a small Southern town? to have lived during segregation? to be a woman? to be African American?

IDEAS FOR YOUR JOURNAL

www.mhhe.com/costanzo

For a link to online memory maps, visit this book's Web site.

1. Make a list of places you have not visited in a long time. Pick one and write about it in your journal. What do you remember most about it? Do you associate any special smells, sounds, or tactile sensations with this place? Imagine what it might be like to return there now.

2. Is there a Momma or a Mrs. Flowers in your past? Did anyone make such a difference in your life as those two individuals did for Maya Angelou? Describe those people in your journal. What did they look like? What mannerism will you never forget? What words do you still carry in your head? What moment had the most dramatic impact on your life?

Visual Prompt

My childhood, seen by Google Maps

Tri-City Park, a city park I was lucky enough to live near. I would ride my bike around it and run around it while on the cross country team. I used to feed the ducks old bread when my grandparents would visit.

Used with permission from Matthew Haughey and Flickr.com.

3. Are there any ghosts in your old neighborhood? Begin writing a ghost story, an imaginative journey home where someone or something that you feared as a child takes on an imaginary form. Be inventive. Be playful. Now that you are older, you may find yourself to be a good match for the ghost.

4. Go to Google Maps or another online service that provides satellite photos, and look at a satellite photo of your old neighborhood. Make a memory map by taking a virtual walk around your neighborhood. What locations, pathways, buildings, and other locations have vivid memories for you?

In the video excerpt, "Maya Angelou's Journey Home" (transcript on page 87, video online at www.mhhe.com/costanzo), Bill Moyers followed the writer back to Stamps, Arkansas. Returning after thirty years to the town where she grew up, she reminisced about the sights and smells of her grandmother's country store as they had appeared to her childhood imagination. Although her memories were full of wonder and delight, they were laced with the anger and resentment expressed in Lawrence Dunbar's poem, "We Wear the Mask."

Here, in an excerpt from her 1969 autobiography, *I Know Why the Caged Bird Sings*, Angelou describes those early years in Momma's store in more detail. Notice how she re-creates the events entirely through written language. Notice too how she mixes the pleasure and pain of coming of age in the segregated South. If you have already seen the video, be prepared to talk about the differences between the experience of viewing—listening to her voice, watching her move among the people and locations of Stamps—and the experience of reading her words on the page.

Momma's Store
by Maya Angelou

Weighing the half-pounds of flour, excluding the scoop, and depositing them dust-free into the thin paper sacks held a simple kind of adventure for me. I developed an eye for measuring how full a silver-looking ladle of flour, mash, meal, sugar or corn had to be to push the scale indicator over to eight ounces or one pound. When I was absolutely accurate our appreciative customers used to admire: "Sister Henderson sure got some smart grandchildrens." If I was off in the Store's favor, the eagle-eyed women would say, "Put some more in that sack, child. Don't you try to make your profit offa me."

Then I would quietly but persistently punish myself. For every bad judgment, the fine was no silver-wrapped Kisses, the sweet chocolate drops that I loved more than anything in the world, except Bailey. And maybe canned pineapples. My obsession with pineapples nearly drove me mad. I dreamt of the days when I would be grown and able to buy a whole carton for myself alone.

Although the syrupy golden rings sat in their exotic cans on our shelves year round, we only tasted them during Christmas. Momma used the juice to make almost-black fruitcakes. Then she lined heavy soot-encrusted iron skillets with the pineapple rings for rich upside-down cakes. Bailey and I received one slice each, and I carried mine around for hours, shredding off the fruit until nothing was left except the perfume on my fingers. I'd like to think that my desire for pineapples was so sacred that I wouldn't allow myself to steal a can (which was possible) and eat it alone out in the garden, but I'm certain that I must have weighed the possibility of the scent exposing me and didn't have the nerve to attempt it.

Until I was thirteen and left Arkansas for good, the Store was my favorite place to be. Alone and empty in the mornings, it looked like an unopened present from a stranger. Opening the front doors was pulling the ribbon off the unexpected gift. The light would come in softly (we faced north), easing itself over the shelves of mackerel, salmon, tobacco, thread. It fell flat on the big vat of lard and by noontime during the summer the grease had softened to a thick soup. Whenever I walked into the Store in the afternoon, I sensed that it was tired. I alone could hear the slow pulse of its job half done. But just before bedtime, after numerous people had walked in and out, had argued over their bills, or joked about their neighbors, or just dropped in "to give Sister Henderson a 'Hi y'all,'" the promise of magic mornings returned to the Store and spread itself over the family in washed life waves.

5   Momma opened boxes of crispy crackers and we sat around the meat block at the rear of the Store. I sliced onions, and Bailey opened two or even three cans of sardines and allowed their juice of oil and fishing boats to ooze down and around the sides. That was supper. In the evening, when we were alone like that, Uncle Willie didn't stutter or shake or give any indication that he had an "affliction." It seemed that the peace of a day's ending was an assurance that the covenant God made with children, Negroes and the crippled was still in effect.

Throwing scoops of corn to the chickens and mixing sour dry mash with leftover food and oily dish water for the hogs were among our evening chores. Bailey and I sloshed down twilight trails to the pig pens, and standing on the first fence rungs we poured down the unappealing concoctions to our grateful hogs. They mashed their tender pink snouts down into the slop, and rooted and grunted their satisfaction. We always grunted a reply only half in jest. We were also grateful that we had concluded the dirtiest of chores and had only gotten the evil-smelling swill on our shoes, stockings, feet and hands. Late one day, as we were attending to the pigs, I heard a horse in the front yard (it really should have been called a driveway, except that there was nothing to drive into it), and ran to find out who had come riding up on a Thursday evening when even Mr. Steward, the quiet, bitter man who owned a riding horse, would be resting by his warm fire until the morning called him out to turn over his field.

The used-to-be sheriff sat rakishly astraddle his horse. His nonchalance was meant to convey his authority and power over even dumb animals. How much more capable he would be with Negroes. It went without saying.

His twang jogged in the brittle air. From the side of the Store, Bailey and I heard him say to Momma, "Annie, tell Willie he better lay low tonight. A crazy nigger messed with a white lady today. Some of the boys'll be coming over here later." Even after the slow drag of years, I remember the sense of fear which filled my mouth with hot, dry air, and made my body light.

The "boys"? Those cement faces and eyes of hate that burned the clothes off you if they happened to see you lounging on the main street downtown on Saturday. Boys? It seemed that youth had never happened to them. Boys? No, rather men who were covered with graves' dust and age without beauty or learning. The ugliness and rottenness of old abominations.

10   If on Judgment Day I were summoned by St. Peter to give testimony to the used-to-be sheriff's act of kindness, I would be unable to say anything in his behalf. His confidence that my uncle and every other Black man who heard of the Klan's coming ride would scurry under their houses to hide in chicken droppings was too humiliating to hear. Without waiting for Momma's thanks, he rode out of the yard, sure that things were as they should be and that he was a gentle squire, saving those deserving serfs from the laws of the land, which he condoned.

Immediately, while his horse's hoofs were still loudly thudding the ground, Momma blew out the coal-oil lamps. She had a quiet, hard talk with Uncle Willie and called Bailey and me into the Store.

We were told to take the potatoes and onions out of their bins and knock out the dividing walls that kept them apart. Then with a tedious and fearful slowness Uncle Willie gave me his rubber-tipped cane and bent down to get into the now-enlarged empty bin. It took forever before he lay down flat, and then we covered him with potatoes and onions, layer upon layer, like a casserole. Grandmother knelt praying in the darkened Store. It was fortunate that the "boys" didn't ride into our yard that evening and insist that Momma open the Store. They would have surely found Uncle Willie and just as surely lynched him. He moaned the whole night through as if he had, in fact, been guilty of some heinous crime. The heavy sounds pushed their way up out of the blanket of vegetables and I pictured his mouth pulling down on the right side and his saliva flowing into the eyes of new potatoes and waiting there like dew drops for the warmth of morning.

RESPONSE QUESTIONS

1. Maya Angelou gives close attention to the pleasures of choc-olate Kisses, canned pineapples, and other foods. Where do her descriptions best convey the look, taste, smell, or feel of those edible obsessions? Were you reminded of anything you especially enjoyed eating as a child? What do you remember most about your favorite childhood food?

2. Angelou's writing is populated with individuals as well as inanimate things. Which people stand out most clearly? What makes them seem memorable to you?

3. In your reading, where did you feel most connected to Angelou's experience? What were your thoughts and feelings at the time? Were you left with any questions or unsettled feelings?

GUIDELINES FOR ANALYSIS

1. If you have seen the Bill Moyers documentary of Maya Angelou, you may recognize the description of Momma's store in paragraph 4, which was used as voice-over narration in the video. Compare the experience of hearing it read aloud and reading it yourself in the original context. What is the effect of comparing the front doors to "the ribbons of an unexpected gift"? Where else does Angelou use comparisons to create particular visual and emotional effects?

2. Angelou refers to her grandmother as Momma and Sister Henderson. What attitudes or points of view are implied by these names? How is her grandmother's character represented in the essay? What view of Momma are you left with?

3. What do you imagine to be Uncle Willy's "affliction"? Does this make any difference in the way he is treated by the "used-to-be-sheriff"? How do you relate this to Angelou's assurance, in paragraph 5, about "the covenant God made with children, Negroes and the crippled"?

4. Although this is an excerpt, a chapter taken from a book, it has a certain self-contained organization. How would you describe its structure? Notice the roles that food plays in this arrangement. How do the descriptions of food differ at the beginning and the end?

QUESTIONS OF CULTURE

1. When do you think the events described here took place? What clues can you find to locate it in history? Could such things happen today? What would be different now? What hasn't changed?

2. Angelou uses dialogue and local terms to re-create the special character of Stamps. Did you find any of this language amusing, confusing, or troubling? Explain.

IDEAS FOR YOUR JOURNAL

1. Make a list of foods that you loved when you were younger but that seem to have disap-peared or to be unavailable in other parts of the country. Choose one and describe it to someone who has never seen or heard of it before.

2. Who were your heroes growing up? Describe one individual you looked up to as a role model and explain what you admired. Now that you are older, do you recognize any of those qualities in yourself?

3. Remember a time when you felt powerless. What were the circumstances? What were your feelings? What did you do or fail to do? What was the result?

PREVIEW

When Deann Borshay Liem began having recurring dreams about Korea, she wondered whether they were really memories of childhood. Adopted by an American family, she had been told she was an orphan, that both of her Korean parents had died when she was very young, but the official record didn't match her memories. Borshay Liem's determined search for the truth about her birth led her on a journey to her homeland, where she sought to reconcile her conflicting identities by uniting her biological and adoptive families. Her extraordinary journey is documented in a video, titled "First Person Plural," which was broadcast on PBS's award-winning program, *P.O.V.* A partial transcript of the video is reproduced below. Excerpts from the video itself are included on this book's Web site.

www.mhhe.com/costanzo

To view the video excerpts, visit this book's Web site.

If you read the transcript before viewing the video, jot down some notes to record your thoughts, feelings, and questions along the way. Why does Borshay Liem seem so driven to reconstruct her past? What would you ask or say if you could speak to her? What do you expect the video will show that is missing from the transcript? You may find answers to such questions in the program's Web site, part of which appears later in this chapter.

PARTIAL TRANSCRIPT OF DOCUMENTARY, "FIRST PERSON PLURAL"

Deann: My name is Kang Ok Jin. I was born on June 14, 1957. I feel like I've been several different people in one life.

My name is Cha Jung Hee. I was born on November 5, 1956. I've had three names, three different sets of histories.

My name is Deann Borshay, I was born on March 3, 1966, the moment I stepped off the airplane in San Francisco.

I've spoken different languages and have had different families.

5   Deann: When I was 8 years old, I was adopted by Arnold and Alveen Borshay, who lived in Fremont, California.

* * *

Alveen (Mother): Daddy had gone into real estate and was doing really well. And we'd bought a new house and we were unhappy with the church, the way they treated the minister. And they came to get more money. We said, "No." So then I felt bad. I said, "But we should do something for somebody because life's been really good for us." And I watched the TV and Gary Moore came on.

Gary Moore (voice-over from old television show): Winter is the natural enemy of the thousands of needy children in Europe and Asia.

Alveen: And he was talking about the Foster Parents Plan. And he said for fifteen dollars a month you can help some child. I said to Daddy, I said "Let's do that." Then we got a letter saying that they had a little girl in Korea, in a Sun Duck orphanage. We wrote for two and a half years, I think. You know, we just became attached to you through the mail and I found myself saying, every time we did something, I wonder what Cha Jung Hee would think about this, I wish Cha Jung Hee was here. It finally got to be an obsession with me. And I said to Daddy, I said, "You know, I'd like to adopt her." And this way you were going to have a family was all we thought about.

Deann: Right before I got on the plane in South Korea, the director of the orphanage told me, "Don't tell your new parents who you really are, until you're old enough to take care of yourself." The next thing I knew, he nudged me toward the plane and walked away.

* * *

10 Alveen: Well, when you arrived, little stoic face and bundled up in all those clothes, and we couldn't talk to you, you couldn't talk to us, and I realize now that you were terrified, but because we were so happy, you know, we just didn't think about that.

Denise (Sister): From the moment you came here, you were my sister and we were your family and that was it. And even though maybe we looked different and different nationality or whatever, we were your family.

Arnold (Father): I remember very clearly your first meal. Mother prepared something that was very nice, and we were sitting at the table, and you just kind of dropped your head and the tears started to come down. No words were spoken. Mother could see what was happening. And she simply took you away from the table, and you were excused, and from then on it was perfect.

Alveen: You didn't sleep very well at night in the beginning. And you knew all the nursery rhymes that we know, but you would say them in Korean. I used to stay awake and listen to you. Some people would ask, and others would kind of look, you know, and you knew they were wondering but we didn't care.

Arnold: You were so determined to learn, I guess to please us, whatever, I'm not sure. You actually made yourself ill, and you became jaundiced, you'd gotten kind of yellow looking. And only thing we could think of was that you tried too hard, and were trying too hard.

15 Deann: I think at some point as a child I made a decision that I would never forget Korea. Every now and then, I would stop whatever I was doing, close my eyes, and picture the road from the orphanage to the house.

Denise: I remember the day that she took you to school and you freaked out like I guess you'd been left behind, or left in an orphanage. And I remember the principal coming to get me out of class. And I went to your class, and you were so upset you didn't even know who I was. And it took a while, and then I remember I carried you kinda like a little monkey, your little arms and legs were just kinda wrapped around me and we just started walking home.

Alveen: We were together a lot, and you went from being stoic to smiling and you just blossomed like a flower. You know, every day you did something else. And so we were regaling Duncan and Denise with it, you know. So Duncan finally used to come home and say, "Well, what did Miss Wonderful do today?" "Well, she did this." Denise was the baby. Then you came along and you were the baby. Denise was very quiet, you know. She never said, never said a word.

Deann: You feel like I'm your sister? Do you ever question that I'm your sister?

Duncan (Brother): As much as Denise is. You didn't come from my mommy's womb, but I don't care. You don't have the family eyes, but I don't care. You've got the family smile. Color and look doesn't make any difference. It's who you are. You're my sister.

20 Alveen: We just had some great times on vacations. You were always willing to go with us where Duncan and Denise, really, they were looking for another

girl or another boy to spend their time with, but you, you were always happy to go sightseeing with us.

Deann: When I had learned enough English to talk to my parents, I decided that I should tell them who I really was. I remember going up to my mother and telling her, "I'm not who you think I am. I'm not Cha Jung Hee. And I think I have a mother and brothers and sisters in Korea still." And she turned to me and said, "Oh honey, you've just been dreaming. You don't have a mother. And you never had brothers and sisters. Look at these adoption documents. It says that you're Cha Jung Hee and that your mother died giving birth to you." And she said, "You know what? This is just a natural part of you getting used to living in another country. Don't worry about it. They're just bad dreams. They're going to go away soon."

Deann: It was getting more and more difficult to remember how to get home. I remember closing my eyes and saying, "Okay, don't forget." But the last memory of Korea was starting to fade.

* * *

Deann: My life could have probably continued on the track that I had been in Fremont, and you know, I would have married somebody in Fremont, I would have lived a few blocks from my parents and stayed near them and, you know, it would have been an okay life.

Deann: I think what was significant for me was I moved away from my American family and started living by myself. And dreams started coming to me. These images kept coming at me at different times of the day. Sometimes they were at night, I would just wake up, and there would be something. Sometimes I would be walking down the streets of Berkeley, and I would just, then something would just come into my head. And over the course of a year or so, I started realizing that these must be, these must be memories coming back from Korea, that they weren't just dreams, that there had to be something about them that were real.

25 Deann: One time I was driving home and all of a sudden my father jumped into my seat, the ghost of my Korean father, I mean I was going a hundred miles an hour, drove into the driveway of my house, and ran out of the car, ran up the steps and shut the door. And then all of a sudden he was in the house, and he was flying around, and I thought at that moment that it was the moment where I would have probably have gone to the other side.

Deann: My parents have no idea actually this whole period where I was, I would say, depressed.

I started searching through my adoption papers. Everything said I was Cha Jung Hee, and that I was an orphan—no parents, no family. But then I found this picture. On the back it said Cha Jung Hee. And then I found a second picture, and on the back it also said Cha Jung Hee. The problem was, only one of them looked like me, but we were both being passed off as Cha Jung Hee.

In May 1981, I decided to write to the Sun Duck orphanage. Six weeks later, I received a letter from Korea: "My dear Sister Ok Jin, You don't know how happy I am to be writing a letter to you now. I'm your second brother and my name is Ho Jin. Your mother, who used to think of you days and night, is so happy to read the letter you wrote. Your family name is Kang and your name is Ok Jin. There are five brothers and sisters in our family. You are the fourth. I'm certain you are Kang Ok Jin, not Cha Jung Hee.

I was beginning to unravel the mysteries of my past. The Korean War ended in 1953, leaving the country devastated. A huge international relief effort began, aimed at helping thousands of destitute families and orphans. In 1955, Harry Holt began a small rescue operation of children orphaned by the war. Tens of thousands of orphans were subsequently sent overseas for adoption by American and European families. As the years [passed], the South Korean government began rebuilding the country, but there was no plan to deal with widespread poverty, orphans, or families in need. Even though the war was long over, the number of orphans in orphanages continued to multiply. The more children orphanages had, the more money they received from abroad. By the 1960s when I was adopted, the government was expediting overseas adoptions at an unprecedented rate. What Harry Holt began as a humanitarian gesture right after the war became big business in the decades that followed. South Korea became the largest supplier of children to developed countries in the world, causing some to argue that the country's economic miracle was due in part to the export of its most precious natural resource, its children.

30   In 1965, the adoption procedure for Cha Jung Hee was completed. My parents signed the papers and sent money to the adoption agency in Korea. One month before Cha Jung Hee was scheduled to go to the U.S., her father found her at the Sun Duck orphanage and took her home. Cha Jung Hee was no longer available for adoption. Assuming nobody would notice, the adoption agency falsified her paperwork and I was sent in her place. I had been given a history and an identity that didn't belong to me.

RESPONSE QUESTIONS

1. Borshay Liem begins her video by giving three different names and birth dates. How do you explain her "three sets of histories"? Have you ever felt that you have more than one identity? If so, how would you represent these various identities in a video?

2. To what extent does Borshay Liem seem driven by a need to belong? Compare her narrative to the other stories about belonging in this chapter or to other stories you have read or seen. What advice would you give to each narrator as a child and as an adult?

3. Which of Borshay Liem's American family members seems best able to understand her point of view? Please explain. How sensitive is she to the needs and feelings of her family?

4. Borshay Liem's personal investigation takes her to Korea, where she meets her biological parents and unites them with her adoptive parents. View the complete version of her documentary, if you can, or read about it on the Web site. What journeys—to actual places or in your mind—have you undertaken in search of your identity?

GUIDELINES FOR ANALYSIS

1. As Borshay Liem's account unfolds, the film keeps shifting back and forth in time. Do you find these shifts helpful or confusing? What visual records does Borshay Liem use to represent the past? What does each one contribute to her story?

2. Do you think this is the kind of narrative that makes a single point or develops one central theme? If so, what would it be? If not, what different ideas does the narrative explore?

3. The film's title is "First Person Plural." Why do you think Borshay Liem used this name?

QUESTIONS OF CULTURE

1. Nearly all young people must find an identity distinct from their parents. How much of Borshay Liem's struggle for identity is typical of adolescence? How much of her struggle do you attribute to her Korean background, her adoption, her personality, or the lies about her birth?

2. Borshay Liem's personal story intersects with history at the point when she introduces newsreel footage of the Korean War. What do you learn about this historical period from

the video? What is she implying when she says, "the country's economic miracle was due in part to the export of its most precious resource, its children"?

IDEAS FOR YOUR JOURNAL

1. If you were going to videotape the story of your own search for identity, whom would you interview? Where would you get photographs, old movies, letters, and other documents to represent the past? Start sorting through these mementos and jot down your thoughts about them. Why is each important in your story? How might you arrange them in the video?

2. The orphanage's lies about Borshay Liem's identity had major consequences for her life. Have deceptions in your own past affected you in lasting ways? Explore their impact on you in your journal.

3. Has your own life ever been connected with historical events as Borshay Liem's was with the Korean War? If so, when? What were the connections? Looking back now, what did you learn about the power—or powerlessness—of individuals to influence the course of history?

PREVIEW

Like many online resources that support television shows, the Web site for "First Person Plural" offers a vast and varied wealth of information beyond the one-hour program. Among other things, it includes a summary of the program, background about Borshay Liem, and the making of her video, filmed interviews, several bulletin boards for viewer responses, historical facts, and links to other sites. Although the Web site presents a complex network of multimedia documents, it can be read and analyzed like any other text. First, though, you must be able to find your way around.

The parent Web site, at www.pbs.org, is the Internet branch of Public Broadcasting Service, a private, nonprofit media enterprise owned and operated by the nation's 347 public television stations. Its mission is to bring quality programs and educational services to the public through a variety of media, including the World Wide Web and noncommercial television programs like *P.O.V.* Although *P.O.V.* is known chiefly as a television showcase for independent nonfiction films, it encourages active audience involvement through *P.O.V. Interactive,* an initiative that uses the Web and other new media tools to continue the thoughtful exchange of information and ideas well after a show is broadcast.

www.mhhe.com/costanzo

To view the complete Web site, visit this book's Web site.

Working the Web: "First Person Plural"

1. Begin at the home page for "First Person Plural" created by *P.O.V. Interactive* (http://www.pbs.org/pov/pov2000/firstpersonplural/index.html) to see a capsule summary of the program, photographs, and various links.
2. Go to the site map (bottom of the screen) to see how its Web site is organized. This is often the quickest way to get a bird's eye view of most Web sites and decide where you want to go. Typically, you'll find a

site map link at the top or bottom of a Web site's home page. Judging from this site map, where are you likely to find a summary of the program? Where might you find more information about Deann Borshay Liem? Where would you look for different perspectives on adoption? What sorts of information would you expect from the Resources link? Explore some of these links.

3. At the bottom of the home page there are links to Web sites for the organizations that helped present "First Person Plural." Visit ITVS, NAATA, and POV to find out more about what they do.

4. Back on the "First Person Plural" Web site, you can select Filmmaker, then click on Filmmaker Interview to watch film clips of Borshay Liem speaking about her project. These interviews were filmed exclusively for the Web site in answer to specific questions about her experience. (Note that RealPlayer or Quicktime software must be installed on your computer to run the clips.) You can also view selections from Borshay Liem's scrapbook to see how she gathered photographs, documents, and journal notes in preparation for the final film.

5. Another option is the Voices of Adoption, which includes more memories by other Korean Americans. These stories, poems, and videos were submitted to the Web site in a nationwide call for different points of view on the topic.

6. Check out the Resources page and follow any links to related sites on the Web that interest you.

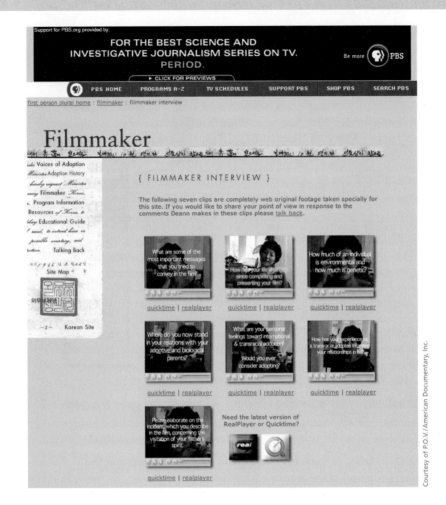

Courtesy of P.O.V./American Documentary, Inc.

7. Find the detailed description, or synopsis, of the one-hour program "First Person Plural." When was the program first aired? How can you learn when the program will be rebroadcast in your area or how to order a copy on videocassette? Where would you find a complete list of programs produced by *P.O.V.*?

RESPONSE QUESTIONS

1. Describe your first impressions of the "First Person Plural" Web site. What features grabbed your immediate attention? Why do you think you focused on those features first?

2. In one of the Filmmaker Interview clips on NAATA's Web site (http://www.pbs.org/pov/pov2000/firstpersonplural/filmmaker/filminterview.html), Borshay Liem answers the question, "What are some of the most important messages that you tried to convey in the film?" Among other things, she says the film is "about reconciling loss and coming to terms with

our parents." What loss is she referring to? What other themes or messages do you find in the film clips and on the Web site as a whole?

3. In another clip, when asked to elaborate on the incident, Borshay Liem talks about a visit from her Korean father's ghost. She describes the ghost as "swooping down," "a very definable energy in the seat next to me," and speculates that it might have been "a manifestation of my psychological state," "a kind of hallucination" or a form of "Shaman ritual" but still "a very real, very live experience." What other explanations can you offer? To what extent can such visitations be considered forms of memory?

4. Compare Borshay Liem's return to her homeland and Maya Angelou's "Journey Home." What fears and expectations do they have about revisiting the past? How do their visits to Korea and Arkansas help to revive old memories? What would they have missed if they had not made the visits?

5. Like many of the readings in this chapter, "First Person Plural" is about a break in belonging. When does this break occur in Borshay Liem's story? Why is it so important for her to connect her two families? Compare her narrative to other stories in this chapter that deal with a sudden separation from family, friends, or group identity.

GUIDELINES FOR ANALYSIS

1. In the Filmmaker Interview section of the NAATA Web site (http://www.pbs.org/pov/pov2000/firstpersonplural/filmmaker/filminterview.html), Borshay Liem talks about the unexpectedly strong reception to her video. What began as a small personal project intended for her two mothers developed into a one-hour film shown at festivals and on television, where it continues to provoke "intense conversations" about identity, assimilation, immigration, and adoption for a broad audience. What groups of people do you think this Web site most appeals to? What particular features of the Web site's content, arrangement, and style do you think appeal to them?

2. Behind the Lens (accessible through *POV*'s home page menu (http://www.pbs.org/pov/behindlens_director.php?page=6) offers an interview with Borshay Liem in printed, audio, and video forms. Focus on each one separately. Try viewing the video with no sound so you can keep your attention on the visuals. Describe the differences between reading the transcript, listening to her voice, and watching her speak. What do you get from each medium? What do you find yourself focusing on? What do you remember most from each one?

3. Talking Back (http://www.pbs.org/pov/talkingback.html) gave viewers a chance to interact with *P.O.V.* programs and one another. What other parts of the Web site would you consider interactive? How well do these features support the goal of *P.O.V.* to promote "the thoughtful exchange of information and ideas"?

4. Click on Site Credits for a list of the team members who created the Web site. How many individuals were involved, and what did they contribute? Given the Web site's purpose, subject, and audience, how would you rate it for overall organization, content, and style?

CONNECTING TO CULTURE

1. Go to the Voices of Adoption page (http://www.pbs.org/pov/pov2000/firstpersonplural/voices.html) for more accounts by Korean Americans. Do you notice any patterns in their

stories? What obstacles faced them growing up in this country? How did they deal with these obstacles? Compare their efforts to balance conflicting cultures to those of other immigrants, like Nicholas Gage and Esmeralda Santiago. How much of these stories is unique to Koreans, to immigrants, to adopted children? How much is universal?

2. Go to the Adoption History page and click on Overview of International Adoption (http://www.pbs.org/pov/pov2000/firstpersonplural/historical/transracial.html). Here you'll find a broader picture of the 16,000 children adopted from fifty different countries in just one year. How have conflicts like the wars in Korea and Vietnam affected adoption patterns over the years? What disruptive events elsewhere in the world have changed the picture of adoption in more recent times?

IDEAS FOR YOUR JOURNAL

1. Review the photos, journal entries, and documents of Borshay Liem's scrapbook in the Web site's Filmmaker Photo Album section (http://www.pbs.org/pov/pov2000/firstpersonplural/filmmaker/album.html). Do you have any similar mementos that might help to tell a story about your past? List them and describe what each one says about you at that time.

2. Watch or read the Filmmaker Interviews with your own past in mind. Notice the driving force behind Borshay Liem's project, what personal talents she brought to it, how she proceeded, and what the payoff was for her and her unanticipated audience. Sketch out a plan for turning your own memory into an essay, a video, a Web site, or some other form to share it with others.

PREVIEW

Langston Hughes (1902–1967), poet, playwright, and fiction writer, was a major figure of the Harlem Renaissance. His ear for dialect and his simple, direct manner helped to bring the lifestyles and concerns of African Americans into the mainstream of world literature. In this excerpt, "Salvation," taken from his autobiography, *The Big Sea,* Hughes recalls an incident that shook his childhood faith.

As you read the essay, you may be reminded of your own beliefs and the early experiences that shaped them. What expectations did you have about religion at the age of twelve? What expectations did your family and peers have about your part in the community of believers? How did these expectations affect your faith?

The word *salvation* has both religious and non–religious meanings. What does it mean to you? What do you expect from an essay with this title?

Salvation
by Langston Hughes

I was saved from sin when I was going on thirteen. But not really saved. It happened like this. There was a big revival at my Auntie Reed's church. Every night for weeks there had been much preaching, singing, praying, and shouting, and some very hardened sinners had been brought to Christ, and the membership of the church had grown by leaps and bounds. Then just before the revival ended, they held a special meeting for children, "to bring the young lambs to the fold." My aunt spoke of it for days ahead. That night I was escorted to the front row and placed on the mourners' bench with all the other young sinners, who had not yet been brought to Jesus.

My aunt told me that when you were saved you saw a light, and something happened to you inside! And Jesus came into your life! And God was with you from then on! She said you could see and hear and feel Jesus in your soul. I believed her. I have heard a great many old people say the same thing and it seemed to me they ought to know. So I sat there calmly in the hot, crowded church, waiting for Jesus to come to me.

The preacher preached a wonderful rhythmical sermon, all moans and shouts and lonely cries and dire pictures of hell, and then he sang a song about the ninety and nine safe in the fold, but one little lamb was left out in the cold. Then he said: "Won't you come? Won't you come to Jesus? Young lambs, won't you come?" And he held out his arms to all us young sinners there on the mourners' bench. And the little girls cried. And some of them jumped up and went to Jesus right away. But most of us just sat there.

A great many old people came and knelt around us and prayed, old women with jet-black faces and braided hair, old men with work-gnarled hands. And the church sang a song about the lower lights are burning, some poor sinners to be saved. And the whole building rocked with prayer and song.

5   Still I kept waiting to *see* Jesus.

Finally all the young people had gone to the altar and were saved, but one boy and me. He was a rounder's son named Westley. Westley and I were surrounded by sisters and deacons praying. It was very hot in the church, and getting late now. Finally Westley said to me in a whisper: "God damn! I'm tired o' sitting here. Let's get up and be saved." So he got up and was saved.

Then I was left alone on the mourners' bench. My aunt came and knelt at my knees and cried, while prayers and songs swirled all around me in the little church. The whole congregation prayed for me alone, in a mighty wail of moans and voices. And I kept waiting serenely for Jesus, waiting, waiting—but he didn't come. I wanted to see him, but nothing happened to me. Nothing! I wanted something to happen to me, but nothing happened.

I heard the songs and the minister saying: "Why don't you come? My dear child, why don't you come to Jesus! Jesus is waiting for you. He wants you. Why don't you come? Sister Reed, what is this child's name?"

"Langston," my aunt sobbed.

10   "Langston, why don't you come? Why don't you come and be saved? Oh, Lamb of God! Why don't you come?"

Now it was really getting late. I began to be ashamed of myself, holding everything up so long. I began to wonder what God thought about Westley, who certainly hadn't seen Jesus either, but who was now sitting proudly on the platform, swinging his knickerbockered legs and grinning down at me, surrounded by deacons and old women on their knees praying. God had not struck Westley dead for taking his name in vain or for lying in the temple. So I decided that maybe to save further trouble, I'd better lie, too, and say that Jesus had come, and get up and be saved.

So I got up.

Suddenly the whole room broke into a sea of shouting, as they saw me rise. Waves of rejoicing swept the place. Women leaped in the air, My aunt threw her arms around me. The minister took me by the hand and led me to the platform.

When things quieted down, in a hushed silence, punctuated by a few ecstatic "Amens," all the new young lambs were blessed in the name of God. Then joyous singing filled the room.

15   That night, for the last time in my life but one—for I was a big boy twelve years old—I cried. I cried, in bed alone, and couldn't stop. I buried my head under the quilts, but my aunt heard me. She woke up and told my uncle I was crying because the Holy Ghost had come into my life, and because I had seen Jesus. But I was really crying because I couldn't bear to tell her that I had lied, that I had deceived everybody in the church, that I hadn't seen Jesus, and that now I didn't believe there was a Jesus any more, since he didn't come to help me.

RESPONSE QUESTIONS

1. What motivates young Langston Hughes to get up to be saved at the end of the essay? What does he mean when he says, in the second sentence, "But not really saved"?

2. What else could Hughes have done instead of pretending to be saved? What might be the consequences if he chose another alternative?

3. Compare Hughes to the others in the church: his aunt, the preacher, Westley, and the congregation. Do you find yourself judging them? If so, what judgments do you make?

4. Hughes admits to lying. Is he basically an honest person despite this? How do you judge him?

5. How does your own experience with religion influence your reading? Compare your childhood pressures and beliefs with those of Hughes and your classmates.

GUIDELINES FOR ANALYSIS

1. Is the incident told chiefly from the perspective of a child or an adult? How does Hughes shape this point of view? How does it affect your reading?

2. Do you ever feel that you are there with the author in the church? What helps to create this feeling of a lived experience?

3. What kinds of information does Hughes choose to tell us? What does he leave out? Why do you think he begins and ends the essay where he does?

4. Hughes uses short sentences, simple language, and repetition to tell the story. What else do you notice about his language?

5. Does Hughes explain why this experience was so important for him? Where does its significance come through with the greatest force and clarity?

QUESTIONS OF CULTURE

1. List the references to church and religion in the text. Can you tell what kind of church service Hughes is attending? Does this setting limit your connection to his story? How universal is his experience?

2. Hughes does not explain the language and rituals around him; he simply describes what he hears and sees. Which words or events are unfamiliar to you? Find out what these words refer to, and explain what they tell you about the culture in which Langston Hughes grew up.

IDEAS FOR YOUR JOURNAL

1. What kinds of expectations did your family or community have for you? Did you feel these expectations as pressure or encouragement? How did you respond to them?

2. Recall your early encounters with religion. What did you believe at the time? Have your beliefs changed much since then? If so, what accounts for the change? What different religious groups and customs have you experienced in your life?

PREVIEW

Dick Gregory, the celebrated comedian, civil rights activist, and outspoken proponent of health care, was born to a poor African American family in St. Louis, Missouri, in 1932. An outstanding athlete in school, he won an athletic scholarship to Southern Illinois University but left to join the army in 1953. He put on comedy shows for military personnel, then went on to perform in nightclubs and on television, gradually gaining a national reputation for his biting wit. In the early 1970s, his attention turned to politics. He became an active voice against racism, world hunger, capital punishment, and drug abuse. He also launched several initiatives in the health food business, seeking to change the unhealthy diets of Americans.

In this selection from his autobiography, Gregory recalls a schoolroom incident when he learned about shame. As you read, notice how he reconstructs the factual and emotional details so that we experience them through his eyes.

Shame
by Dick Gregory

I never learned hate at home, or shame. I had to go to school for that. I was about seven years old when I got my first big lesson. I was in love with a little girl named Helene Tucker, a light-complexioned little girl with pigtails and nice manners. She was always clean and she was smart in school. I think I went to school then mostly to look at her. I brushed my hair and even got me a little old handkerchief. It was a lady's handkerchief, but I didn't want Helene to see me wipe my nose on my hand. The pipes were frozen again, there was no water in the house, but I washed my socks and shirt every night. I'd get a pot, and go over to Mister Ben's grocery store, and stick my pot down into his soda machine. Scoop out some chopped ice. By evening the ice melted to water for washing. I got sick a lot that winter because the fire would go out at night before the clothes were dry. In the morning I'd put them on, wet or dry, because they were the only clothes I had.

Everybody's got a Helene Tucker, a symbol of everything you want. I loved her for her goodness, her cleanness, her popularity. She'd walk down my street and my brothers and sisters would yell, "Here comes Helene," and I'd rub my tennis sneakers on the back of my pants and wish my hair wasn't so nappy and the white folks' shirt fit me better. I'd run out on the street. If I knew my place and didn't come too close, she'd wink at me and say hello. That was a good feeling. Sometimes I'd follow her all the way home, and shovel the snow off her walk and try to make friends with her Momma and her aunts. I'd drop money on her stoop late at night on my way back from shining shoes in the taverns. And she had a Daddy, and he had a good job. He was a paper hanger.

I guess I would have gotten over Helene by summertime, but something happened in that classroom that made her face hang in front of me for the next twenty-two years. When I played the drums in high school it was for Helene and when I broke track records in college it was for Helene and when I started standing behind microphones and heard applause I wished Helene could hear it, too. It wasn't until I was twenty-nine years old and married and making money that I finally got her out of my system. Helene was sitting in that classroom when I learned to be ashamed of myself.

It was on a Thursday. I was sitting in the back of the room, in a seat with a chalk circle drawn around it. The idiot's seat, the troublemaker's seat.

The teacher thought I was stupid. Couldn't spell, couldn't read, couldn't do arithmetic. Just stupid. Teachers were never interested in finding out that you couldn't concentrate because you were so hungry, because you hadn't had any breakfast. All you could think about was noontime, would it ever come? Maybe you could sneak into the cloakroom and steal a bite of some kid's lunch out of a coat pocket. A bite of something. Paste. You can't really make a meal of paste, or put it on bread for a sandwich, but sometimes I'd scoop a few spoonfuls out of the paste jar in the back of the room. Pregnant people get strange tastes. I was pregnant with poverty. Pregnant with dirt and pregnant with smells that made people turn away, pregnant with cold and pregnant with shoes that were never bought for me, pregnant with five other people in my bed and no Daddy in the next room, and pregnant with hunger. Paste doesn't taste too bad when you're hungry.

The teacher thought I was a troublemaker. All she saw from the front of the room was a little black boy who squirmed in his idiot's seat and made noises and poked the kids around him. I guess she couldn't see a kid who made noises because he wanted someone to know he was there.

It was on a Thursday, the day before the Negro payday. The eagle always flew on Friday. The teacher was asking each student how much his father would give to the Community Chest. On Friday night, each kid would get the money from his father, and on Monday he would bring it to the school. I decided I was going to buy me a Daddy right then. I had money in my pocket from shining shoes and selling papers, and whatever Helene Tucker pledged for her Daddy I was going to top it. And I'd hand the money right in. I wasn't going to wait until Monday to buy me a Daddy.

I was shaking, scared to death. The teacher opened her book and started calling out names alphabetically. "Helene Tucker?"

10 "My daddy said he'd give two dollars and fifty cents."

"That's very nice, Helene. Very, very nice indeed."

That made me feel pretty good. It wouldn't take too much to top that. I had almost three dollars in dimes and quarters in my pocket. I stuck my hand in my pocket and held onto the money, waiting for her to call my name. But the teacher closed her book after she called everybody else in the class.

I stood up and raised my hand.

"What is it now?"

15 "You forgot me."

She turned toward the blackboard. "I don't have time to be playing with you, Richard."

"My Daddy said he'd . . ."

"Sit down, Richard, you're disturbing the class."

"My Daddy said he'd give . . . fifteen dollars."

20 She turned around and looked mad. "We are collecting this money for you and your kind, Richard Gregory. If your Daddy can give fifteen dollars you have no business being on relief."

"I got it right now, I got it right now, my Daddy gave it to me to turn in today, my Daddy said . . ."

"And furthermore," she said, looking right at me, her nostrils getting big and her lips getting thin and her eyes opening wide, "we know you don't have a Daddy."

Helene Tucker turned around, her eyes full of tears. She felt sorry for me. Then I couldn't see her too well because I was crying, too.

"Sit down, Richard."

25 And I always thought the teacher kind of liked me. She always picked me to wash the blackboard on Friday, after school. That was a big thrill, it made me feel important. If I didn't wash it, come Monday the school might not function right.

"Where are you going, Richard?"

I walked out of school that day, and for a long time I didn't go back very often. There was shame there.

Now there was shame everywhere. It seemed like the whole world had been inside that classroom, everyone had heard what the teacher had said, everyone had turned around and felt sorry for me. There was shame in going to the Worthy Boys Annual Christmas Dinner for you and your kind, because everybody knew what a worthy boy was. Why couldn't they just call it the Boys Annual Dinner; why'd they have to give it a name? There was shame in wearing the brown and orange and white plaid mackinaw the welfare gave to three thousand boys. Why'd it have to be the same for everybody so when you walked down the street the people could see you were on relief? It was a nice warm mackinaw and it had a hood, and my Momma beat me and called me a little rat when she found out I stuffed it in the bottom of a pail full of garbage way over on Cottage Street. There was shame in running over to Mister Ben's at the end of the day and asking for his rotten peaches, there was shame in asking Mrs. Simmons for a spoonful of sugar, there was shame in running out to meet the relief truck. I hated that truck, full of food for you and your kind. I ran into the house and hid when it came. And then I started to sneak through alleys, to take the long way home so the people going into White's Eat Shop wouldn't see me. Yeah, the whole world heard the teacher that day, we all know you don't have a Daddy.

RESPONSE QUESTIONS

1. Dick Gregory's memory focuses on a single incident at school. What, exactly, was he ashamed of? What does he say he learned from it? Do you think there are other lessons to be learned from the experience?

2. Gregory describes himself as "a kid who made noises because he wanted someone to know he was there." How does he describe his teacher and her perception of him? Considering Dick Gregory's career, how would you say he finally channeled his need for attention?

3. In paragraph 7, Gregory says, "I decided I was going to buy me a Daddy right then." What intention do you see behind this decision? Considering his teacher's response, how did this intention contribute to his shame?

GUIDELINES FOR ANALYSIS

1. Unlike some writers, Gregory is very explicit about the theme of his story. He names it in his title, introduces it in his first sentence, and elaborates on it in the final paragraph. Do you think this explicitness adds or detracts from the story's overall effect? Compare Gregory's approach to Langston Hughes's narration in "Salvation."

2. Gregory does not use dialogue until more than halfway through the story. Reread the exchange of words between him and his teacher. How does the shift from narration to dialogue affect your involvement as a reader? What do you imagine young Gregory thinks and feels at that moment, even if he doesn't say so?

3. Gregory refers to Helene Tucker as a symbol. What does she represent? Would you know this if the author didn't tell you?

QUESTIONS OF CULTURE

1. What does Gregory mean when he says, "I was pregnant with poverty"? What specific facts describe just how poor he was? What connections do you see between poverty and shame?

2. Gregory begins with the statement, "I never learned hate at home, or shame. I had to go to school for that." How much can you tell about Gregory's family from the story? What is there about his school environment that makes him feel like an outsider?

IDEAS FOR YOUR JOURNAL

1. How do you define shame? How does it differ from guilt? Can you recall an incident in your own life when you were made to feel shame? Describe the circumstances and the outcome. How long did the feeling last?

2. Gregory claims, "Everybody's got a Helene Tucker, a symbol of everything you want." Who was your Helene Tucker? What made her or him so important to you at the time? Gregory went out of his way to impress Helene. How did you behave in the presence of your Helene Tucker? Do you have any regrets?

Robert Hayden (1913–80) grew up in a Detroit ghetto, where he was raised by foster parents in a perpetually troubled household. Nearsighted and physically slight, he found refuge and release in the reading and writing of poetry. In the 1930s, he became interested in black history and folk culture, which he researched for the Federal Writers' Project. His research fueled much of his best writing in years to come. Inspired by authors like Langston Hughes and Countee Cullen, Hayden shaped his writing voice into a clear, precise, and powerful instrument for self-expression and political change.

"Those Winter Sundays," published in 1966, reminds us that poetry can be an especially intense and intimate medium for reconstructing memories. In a few words, a poem can evoke resonant feelings and leave indelible impressions on the mind.

Those Winter Sundays
by Robert Hayden

Sundays too my father got up early
and put his clothes on in the blueblack cold,
then with cracked hands that ached
from labor in the weekday weather made
5   banked fires blaze. No one ever thanked him.
I'd wake up and hear the cold splintering, breaking.
When the rooms were warm, he'd call,
and slowly I would rise and dress,
fearing the chronic angers of that house.
10   Speaking indifferently to him,
who had driven out the cold
and polished my good shoes as well.
What did I know, what did I know
of love's austere and lonely offices?

RESPONSE QUESTIONS

1. Describe the speaker in this poem. Which details give you the sharpest picture of the situation?

2. Although Hayden doesn't tell us how he feels, we can guess at his emotions from certain passages. What do you imagine he is thinking and feeling?

3. Does the poet's father remind you of anyone? How does your memory affect your response to the poem?

GUIDELINES FOR ANALYSIS

1. Unlike the essays in this chapter, "Those Winter Sundays" describes only one recurring moment in the writer's life. What makes this moment so memorable? What does it remind Hayden of now that he is older?

2. What might "the chronic angers of that house" refer to? What is meant by "love's austere and lonely office"?

3. Like most poems, this one has a visible shape. What difference would it make if the sentences were written out in paragraph form? What is gained by arranging them into three stanzas and these fourteen lines?

QUESTIONS OF CULTURE

1. Hayden's father has "cracked hands that ached from labor in the weekday weather." What kind of work might his father do? To what extent does this limit the poem's messages to a particular social or economic class?

2. If you did not know that the poet was African American, would you be able to guess from details in the poem? Compare these details to the ethnic references in the writing by Maya Angelou, Langston Hughes, Sandra Cisneros, Esmeralda Santiago, and Nicholas Gage. Check out Hayden's other works to see how his cultural awareness comes through elsewhere.

IDEAS FOR YOUR JOURNAL

1. Now that you're older, do you have a different understanding of the household rituals you experienced as a child? Write about one of these recurring moments as you saw it then and as you see it now.

2. Select one memory from your journal and write a poem about it. Give special attention to your choice of words and phrasing. Concentrate on re-creating the experience rather than telling about it.

PREVIEW

At the age of thirteen, Esmeralda Santiago left her native Puerto Rico and arrived in New York with her single mother and eleven younger siblings. Despite the pressures of her family's poverty, she stayed in school, attending Manhattan Community College and eventually graduating from Harvard with high honors. Esmeralda's struggles and successes have inspired readers around the world. In addition to a novel, *America's Dream* (1997), she has written three memoirs: *When I Was Puerto Rican* (1993), *Almost a Woman* (1998), and *The Turkish Lover* (2004). Her family life, work ethic, and creative process are revealed in the PBS documentary *Esmeralda Santiago: Writing a Life* (2006), an intimate portrait of the writer and a demonstration of the power of words to transform lives (available from http://www.esmeraldasantiago.com).

In *When I Was Puerto Rican,* Esmeralda remembers her childhood struggles with her mother, a strict disciplinarian, realizing only later that the rules she had resisted were for her own protection. In the following excerpt, Santiago recalls an incident that brought her closer to her mother. Before reading "Ironing," reflect back on your childhood and those routine household chores that had to be done in your household. Was any job particularly distasteful or attractive to you? Can you tell why?

Ironing

by Esmeralda Santiago

Because of all the running around she had to do with Raymond, Mami couldn't work a steady job anymore. Still, his medications and doctor visits meant we needed money, so Mami talked our landlord into paying her for cooking a daily *caldero* of rice and beans and a stack of fried chicken pieces or pork chops, which he then sold at the bar. Sometimes she left the house, not in her work clothes but dressed a little better than what she wore around the house. She didn't tell us where she was going on those days, and it was years before I learned that she went to clean other people's houses. One day I came back from school to find a rope stretched across the front room and men's white shirts, lean and crisp, hanging in a row.

"Don't touch them. They're not ours."

"Whose are they?"

"They belong to the laundry down the street."

5   She spritzed some water from a bottle onto the cuff of a shirt and pressed the iron against it, making the steam rise up to her face.

"How come you're doing their ironing?"

"They were very nice and let me bring the work home instead of do it there." She finished the shirt and put it on a wire hanger alongside the others.

Of all the things in the world Mami had to do, this was her least favorite. She liked cooking, sewing, mopping, even dusting. But she always complained about how much she hated ironing.

"Can I try?"

10   "Her eyebrows formed a question mark over her round eyes. Her mouth toyed with a smile. This was probably the first time I'd ever volunteered to learn anything useful.

She turned off the iron and looked for one of Papi's old shirts in her clean laundry hamper. "We wouldn't want you burning a customer's shirt," she chuckled. She stretched it on the board.

Quietly she showed me how to set the temperature for linen or cotton, how to wet my finger on my tongue and listen for the sizzle when I touched the flat bottom of the iron, and how to keep the electric cord from touching the hot metal, which could cause a fire. She turned over the bottle of cold water and sprinkled the inside of my wrist.

"This is how little moisture you need to get the steam to rise." She curved my fingers around the handle, pressing the iron against the fabric while with the other hand she pulled the cloth taut.

"Always iron the inside button and hole plackets first, then the inside and outside collar, then the cuffs." We danced around the ironing board, with Mami guiding my hand, pressing down on the iron, and standing away for a minute to see me do as she'd taught. The steam rose from the shirt and filled my head with the clean fresh scent of sun-dried cotton, and bubbles of perspiration flushed along my hair line and dripped down my neck. But I pressed on, absorbed by the tiny squares in the weave, the straight, even stitches that held the seams in place, the way the armhole curved into the shoulder.

15   "You're doing a good job," Mami murmured, a puzzled expression on her face.

"This is fun," I said, meaning it.

"Fun!" she laughed. "Then from now on you do all the ironing around the house." She said it with a smile, which meant she was teasing. And she never asked me to do it. But after that, whenever I wanted to feel close to Mami, I stacked wrinkled clothes into a basket, and, one by one, ironed them straight, savoring the afternoon when she taught me to do the one thing she most hated.

RESPONSE QUESTIONS

1. How would you describe the author's relationship with her mother? What clues to that relationship do you find in the essay? Do you think their rapport changes as a result of the ironing incident?

2. Santiago writes, "Of all the things in the world Mami had to do, this was her least favorite." How does Mami's attitude toward ironing affect the outcome of the story?

3. Compare Santiago's portrait of her mother to Hayden's portrait of his father. What do the two writers appreciate most in their parents? How does each arrive at this appreciation?

4. Were you reminded of events in your own life while reading this selection? If so, identify the passages that triggered your memory. If not, try to explain why.

GUIDELINES FOR ANALYSIS

1. Although this selection is taken from a chapter in Santiago's book, it can stand alone as a separate essay. What gives it that stand-alone quality? Would any changes make it even more coherent and complete?

2. Much of the essay is in the form of dialogue. What does this contribute to your reading? How can you tell who is speaking and in what tone of voice?

3. Santiago gives close attention to the process of ironing. Where does she show how it is done? Where does she describe the way it feels? Mark any passages you find particularly descriptive and precise.

QUESTIONS OF CULTURE

1. How much of the author's Puerto Rican roots are visible in her story? Notice how Santiago includes references to clothing, food, and language.

2. What attitudes about "women's work" do you find in the essay? How does ironing fit in with these attitudes? From what you see of Mami's life, how much of her role as a woman is shaped by her being Puerto Rican, a single parent, an immigrant, or poor?

IDEAS FOR YOUR JOURNAL

1. Make a list of common household chores. Are deep-seated feelings attached to any of these chores for you? Begin writing about one that evokes strong feelings. Where do you think those feelings originate?

2. Recall a task that you learned about from someone important in your life. What were you taught? What did you learn? How did the experience affect your relationship?

Sandra Cisneros was born in Chicago in 1954 to a large family of Mexican descent. As the only girl among six brothers, unsettled by frequent moves between Mexico and the United States, she retreated into her imagination and became an alert observer of life. She discovered writ-

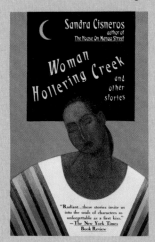

ing as a form of self-expression, a way to weave imagination, observation, and memory into stories people wanted to read. But first she had to find her own distinctive writing voice. By her own account, this happened when a writing assignment about a house left her feeling different from the other students. She realized that their proud homes were different from the shabby bungalow where she grew up. "That's when I decided I would write about something my classmates couldn't write about." The result was her first novel, *The House on Mango Street,* which was hailed for its originality and is widely read for its insights into childhood.

Cisneros, who has been a teacher as well as a writer, has become a strong voice for Latino and Latina literature. While much of her work explores the uniqueness of Mexican culture and her estrangement from the American mainstream, her stories speak to everyone who has ever felt like an outsider. "Eleven" is taken from her collection of short stories, *Woman Hollering Creek,* published in 1991. In it, a schoolgirl named Rachel is made to feel ashamed of a sweater that does not belong to her.

Eleven
by Sandra Cisneros

What they don't understand about birthdays and what they never tell you is that when you're eleven, you're also ten, and nine, and eight, and seven, and six, and five, and four, and three, and two, and one. And when you wake up on your eleventh birthday you expect to feel eleven, but you don't. You open your eyes and everything's just like yesterday, only it's today. And you don't feel eleven at all. You feel like you're still ten. And you are—underneath the year that makes you eleven.

Like some days you might say something stupid, and that's the part of you that's still ten. Or maybe some days you might need to sit on your mama's lap because you're scared, and that's the part of you that's five. And maybe one day when you're all grown up maybe you will need to cry like if you're three, and that's okay. That's what I tell Mama when she's sad and needs to cry. Maybe she's feeling three.

Because the way you grow old is kind of like an onion or like the rings inside a tree trunk or like my little wooden dolls that fit one inside the other, each year inside the next one. That's how being eleven years old is.

You don't feel eleven. Not right away. It takes a few days, weeks even, sometimes even months before you say Eleven when they ask you. And you don't feel smart eleven, not until you're almost twelve. That's the way it is.

5   Only today I wish I didn't have only eleven years rattling inside me like pennies in a tin Band-Aid box. Today I wish I was one hundred and two instead of eleven because if I was one hundred and two

I'd have known what to say when Mrs. Price put the red sweater on my desk. I would've known how to tell her it wasn't mine instead of just sitting there with that look on my face and nothing coming out of my mouth.

"Whose is this?" Mrs. Price says, and she holds the red sweater up in the air for all the class to see. "Whose? It's been sitting in the coatroom for a month."

"Not mine," says everybody. "Not me."

"It has to belong to somebody," Mrs. Price keeps saying, but nobody can remember. It's an ugly sweater with red plastic buttons and a collar and sleeves all stretched out like you could use it for a jump rope. It's maybe a thousand years old and even if it belonged to me I wouldn't say so.

Maybe because I'm skinny, maybe because she doesn't like me, that stupid Sylvia Saldivar says, "I think it belongs to Rachel." An ugly sweater like that, all raggedy and old, but Mrs. Price believes her. Mrs. Price takes the sweater and puts it right on my desk, but when I open my mouth nothing comes out.

10 "That's not, I don't, you're not . . . Not mine," I finally say in a little voice that was maybe me when I was four.

"Of course it's yours," Mrs. Price says. "I remember you wearing it once." Because she's older and the teacher, she's right and I'm not.

Not mine, not mine, not mine, but Mrs. Price is already turning to page thirty-two, and math problem number four. I don't know why but all of a sudden I'm feeling sick inside, like the part of me that's three wants to come out of my eyes, only I squeeze them shut tight and bite down on my teeth real hard and try to remember today I am eleven, eleven. Mama is making a cake for me for tonight, and when Papa comes home everybody will sing Happy birthday, happy birthday to you.

But when the sick feeling goes away and I open my eyes, the red sweater's still sitting there like a big red mountain. I move the red sweater to the corner of my desk with my ruler. I move my pencil and books and eraser as far from it as possible. I even move my chair a little to the right, Not mine, not mine, not mine.

In my head I'm thinking how long till lunchtime, how long till I can take the red sweater and throw it over the schoolyard fence, or leave it hanging on a parking meter, or bunch it up into a little ball and toss it in the alley. Except when math period ends Mrs. Price says loud and in front of everybody, "Now, Rachel, that's enough," because she sees I've shoved the red sweater to the tippytip corner of my desk and it's hanging all over the edge like a waterfall, but I don't care.

15 "Rachel," Mrs. Price says. She says it like she's getting mad.

"You put that sweater on right now and no more nonsense."

"But it's not—"

"Now!" Mrs. Price says.

This is when I wish I wasn't eleven, because all the years inside of me—ten, nine, eight, seven, six, five, four, three, two, and one—are pushing at the back of my eyes when I put one arm through one sleeve of the sweater that smells like cottage cheese, and then the other arm through the other and stand there with my arms apart like if the sweater hurts me and it does, all itchy and full of germs that aren't even mine.

20 That's when everything I've been holding in since this morning, since when Mrs. Price put the sweater on my desk, finally lets go, and all of a sudden I'm crying in front of everybody. I wish I was invisible but I'm not. I'm eleven and it's my birthday today and I'm crying like I'm three in front of everybody. I put my head down on the desk and bury my face in my stupid clown-sweater arms. My face all hot and spit coming out of my mouth because I can't stop the little animal noises from coming out of me, until there aren't any more

tears left in my eyes, and it's just my body shaking like when you have the hiccups, and my whole head hurts like when you drink milk too fast.

But the worst part is right before the bell rings for lunch. That stupid Phyllis Lopez, who is even dumber than Sylvia Saldivar, says she remembers the red sweater is hers! I take it off right away and give it to her, only Mrs. Price pretends like everything's okay.

Today I'm eleven. There's a cake Mama's making for tonight, and when Papa comes home from work we'll eat it. There'll be candles and presents and everybody will sing Happy birthday, happy birthday to you, Rachel, only it's too late.

I'm eleven today. I'm eleven, ten, nine, eight, seven, six, five, four, three, two, and one, but I wish I was one hundred and two. I wish I was anything but eleven, because I want today to be far away already, far away like a runaway balloon, like a tiny *o* in the sky, so tiny-tiny you have to close your eyes to see it.

RESPONSE QUESTIONS

1. Why is the red sweater so important to Rachel? What does it represent for her? Can you think of any articles of clothing or some other material possession that had strong symbolic meanings for you in the past? Do they still bear any special power for you today?

2. Cisneros likens aging to the rings inside a tree trunk and to little wooden dolls that fit one inside the other. When in your life have you felt more like one of the inner rings or smaller dolls? What incident triggered this feeling of being a younger version of yourself? Do you agree with the author that it's okay for an adult to cry like a three-year-old?

3. What do you think Rachel feels in the last paragraph when she wishes she were "far away like a runaway balloon"? What in the story might account for her feelings?

4. Unlike other selections in this chapter, "Eleven" is a work of fiction. Would it have made a different impact on you if it were true? Explain why or why not. Generally speaking, do you prefer reading fiction or nonfiction?

QUESTIONS FOR ANALYSIS

1. Cisneros speaks through the voice of an eleven-year-old. How does her vocabulary, sentence structure, and comparisons reflect this age? Do any passages seem inconsistent with a young person's use of language or frame of mind?

2. Find two or three moments in the story that seem particularly vivid to you. How does the author's use of dialogue or description make them come alive for you?

QUESTIONS OF CULTURE

1. Rachel says of Mrs. Price, "because she's older and the teacher, she's right and I'm not." Should one always yield to an older person or someone in authority? What were you taught about asserting yourself with elders or authority figures? Compare what you were taught in your English class to the teachings of other cultures represented in the class.

2. Cisneros is the child of a Mexican father and a Mexican American mother. Does her Chicana background appear anywhere in the story?

1. At several points in the story, Rachel can't bring herself to speak up and yet has a running conversation in her mind of what she'd like to say. When has this happened to you? Tell the story. What were you thinking at the time, and what did you actually do or say? What might have happened if you had spoken your mind?

2. Imagine Rachel's story if she had spoken her true thoughts. How might Mrs. Price have responded? What would the other girls have done? How would Rachel's birthday have turned out? Rewrite "Eleven" with a new twist.

PREVIEW

Nicholas Gage was born in 1939, in a Greek village far from electricity and automobiles. His father was then an immigrant working in Massachusetts to send money home to his family. First

World War II and then the occupation of his village by Communist guerrillas kept his father away from the family for Gage's entire childhood, until his mother was finally able to plan an escape. Nicholas and his four sisters managed to evade their captors and cross the minefields to safety, but his mother was imprisoned, tortured, and executed by the guerillas. Finally united with his father in the United States, Nicholas struggled to learn a new language in a new land until an English teacher recognized his talents and encouraged him to write. He became an award-winning journalist, publishing several books on organized crime, and landed a post in Athens, where he sought to realize his lifelong dream of investigating the circumstances of his mother's death. His investigation led to his award-winning book, *Eleni,* published in 1983 and made into a film two years later with John Malkovich and Kate Nelligan. President Reagan cited the book as an inspiration for foreign policy under his administration. Gage still lives in Massachusetts, where he continues to write and work on film projects. Buried near his home are his father and his mother, who were united only after death.

The following selection is taken from Gage's book about his father, *A Place for Us,* which recounts the struggle to adjust to his new home in the United States. In it, he recalls his mother's sacrifice and pays tribute to the teacher who helped transform his difficulties with English into a celebrated career in writing.

The Teacher Who Changed My Life
by Nicholas Gage

The person who set the course of my life in the new land I entered as a young war refugee—who, in fact, nearly dragged me onto the path that would bring all the blessings I've received in America—was a salty-tongued, no-nonsense schoolteacher named Marjorie Hurd. When I entered her classroom in 1953, I had been to six schools in five years, starting in the Greek village where I was born in 1939.

When I stepped off a ship in New York Harbor on a gray March day in 1949, I was an undersized 9-year-old in short pants who had lost his mother and was coming to live with the father he didn't know. My mother, Eleni Gatzoyiannis, had been imprisoned, tortured and shot by Communist guerrillas for sending me and three of my four sisters to freedom. She died so that her children could go to their father in the United States.

The portly, bald, well-dressed man who met me and my sisters seemed a foreign, authoritarian figure. I secretly resented him for not getting the whole family out of Greece early enough to save my mother. Ultimately, I would grow to love him and appreciate how he dealt with becoming a single parent at the age of 56, but at first our relationship was prickly, full of hostility.

As Father drove us to our new home—a tenement in Worcester, Mass.—and pointed out the huge brick building that would be our first school in America, I clutched my Greek notebooks from the refugee camp, hoping that my few years of schooling would impress my teachers in this cold, crowded country. They didn't. When my father led me and my 11-year-old sister to Greendale Elementary School, the grim-faced Yankee principal put the two of us in a class for the mentally retarded. There was no facility in those days for non-English-speaking children.

5   By the time I met Marjorie Hurd four years later, I had learned English, been placed in a normal, graded class and had even been chosen for the college preparatory track in the Worcester public school system. I was 13 years old when our father moved us yet again, and I entered Chandler Junior High shortly after the beginning of seventh grade. I found myself surrounded by richer, smarter and better-dressed classmates who looked askance at my strange clothes and heavy accent. Shortly after I arrived, we were told to select a hobby to pursue during "club hour" on Fridays. The idea of hobbies and clubs made no sense to my immigrant ears, but I decided to follow the prettiest girl in my class—the blue-eyed daughter of the local Lutheran minister. She led me through the door marked "Newspaper Club" and into the presence of Miss Hurd, the newspaper adviser and English teacher who would become my mentor and my muse.

A formidable, solidly built woman with salt-and-pepper hair, a steely eye and a flat Boston accent, Miss Hurd had no patience with layabouts. "What are all you goof-offs doing here?" she bellowed at the would-be journalists. "This is the Newspaper Club! We're going to put out a *newspaper*. So if there's anybody in this room who doesn't like work, I suggest you go across to the Glee Club now, because you're going to work your tails off here!"

I was soon under Miss Hurd's spell. She did indeed teach us to put out a newspaper, skills I honed during my next 25 years as a journalist. Soon I asked the principal to transfer me to her English class as well. There, she drilled us on grammar until I finally began to understand the logic and structure of the English language. She assigned stories for us to read and discuss; not tales of heroes, like the Greek myths I knew, but stories of underdogs—poor people, even immigrants, who seemed ordinary until a crisis drove them to do something extraordinary. She also introduced us to the literary wealth of Greece—giving me a new perspective on my war-ravaged, impoverished homeland. I began to be proud of my origins.

One day, after discussing how writers should write about what they know, she assigned us to compose an essay from our own experience. Fixing me with a stern look, she added, "Nick, I want you to write about what happened to your family in Greece." I had been trying to put those painful memories behind me and left the assignment until the last moment. Then, on a warm spring afternoon, I sat in my room with a yellow pad and pencil and stared out the window at the buds on the trees. I wrote that the coming of spring always reminded me of the last time I said goodbye to my mother on a green and gold day in 1948.

I kept writing, one line after another, telling how the Communist guerrillas occupied our village, took our home and food, how my mother started planning our escape when she learned that the children were to be sent to reeducation camps behind the Iron Curtain and how, at the last moment, she couldn't escape with us because the guerrillas sent her with a group of women to thresh wheat in a distant village. She promised she would try to get away on her own, she told me to be brave and hung a silver cross around my neck, and then she kissed me. I watched the line of women being led down into the ravine and up the other side, until they disappeared around the bend—my mother a tiny brown figure at the end who stopped for an instant to raise her hand in one last farewell.

10   I wrote about our nighttime escape down the mountain, across the minefields and into the lines of the Nationalist soldiers, who sent us to a refugee camp. It was there that we learned of our mother's execution. I felt very lucky to have come to America, I concluded, but every year, the coming of spring made me feel sad because it reminded me of the last time I saw my mother.

I handed in the essay, hoping never to see it again, but Miss Hurd had it published in the school paper. This mortified me at first, until I saw that my classmates reacted with sympathy and tact to my family's story. Without telling me, Miss Hurd also submitted the essay to a contest sponsored by the Freedoms Foundation at Valley Forge, Pa., and it won a medal. The Worcester paper wrote about the award and quoted my essay at length. My father, by then a "five-and-dime-store chef," as the paper described him, was ecstatic with pride, and the Worcester Greek community celebrated the honor to one of its own.

For the first time I began to understand the power of the written word. A secret ambition took root in me. One day, I vowed, I would go back to Greece, find out the details of my mother's death and write about her life, so her grandchildren would know of her courage. Perhaps I would even track down the men who killed her and write of their crimes. Fulfilling that ambition would take me 30 years.

Meanwhile, I followed the literary path that Miss Hurd had so forcefully set me on. After junior high, I became the editor of my school paper at Classical High School and got a part-time job at the Worcester *Telegram and Gazette*. Although my father could only give me $50 and encouragement toward a college education, I managed to finance four years at Boston University with scholarships and part-time jobs in journalism. During my last year of college, an article I wrote about a friend who had died in the Philippines—the first person to lose his life working for the Peace Corps—led to my winning the Hearst Award for College Journalism. And the plaque was given to me in the White House by President John F. Kennedy.

For a refugee who had never seen a motorized vehicle or indoor plumbing until he was 9, this was an unimaginable honor. When the Worcester paper ran a picture of me standing next to President Kennedy, my father rushed out to buy a new suit in order to be properly dressed to receive the congratulations of the Worcester Greeks. He clipped out the photograph, had it laminated in plastic and carried it in his breast pocket for the rest of his life to show everyone he met. I found the much-worn photo in his pocket on the day he died 20 years later.

15   In our isolated Greek village, my mother had bribed a cousin to teach her to read, for girls were not supposed to attend school beyond a certain age. She had always dreamed of her children receiving an education. She couldn't be there when I graduated from Boston University, but the person who came with my father and shared our joy was my former teacher, Marjorie Hurd. We celebrated not only my bachelor's degree but also the scholarships that paid my way to Columbia's Graduate School of Journalism. There, I met the woman who would eventually become my wife. At our wedding and at the baptisms of our three children, Marjorie Hurd was always there, dancing alongside the Greeks.

By then, she was Mrs. Rabidou, for she had married a widower when she was in her early 40s. That didn't distract her from her vocation of introducing young minds to English literature, however. She taught for a total of 41 years and continually would make a "project" of some balky student in whom she spied a spark of potential. Often these were students from the most troubled homes, yet she would alternately bully and charm each one with her own special brand of tough love until the spark caught fire. She retired in 1981 at the age of 62 but still avidly follows the lives and careers of former students while overseeing her adult stepchildren and driving her husband on camping trips to New Hampshire.

Miss Hurd was one of the first to call me on Dec. 10, 1987, when President Reagan, in his television address after the summit meeting with Gorbachev, told the nation that Eleni Gatzoyiannis' dying cry, "My children!" had helped inspire him to seek an arms agreement "for all the children of the world."

"I can't imagine a better monument for your mother," Miss Hurd said with an uncharacteristic catch in her voice.

Although a bad hip makes it impossible for her to join in the Greek dancing, Marjorie Hurd Rabidou is still an honored and enthusiastic guest at all family celebrations, including my 50th birthday picnic last summer, where the shish kebab was cooked on spits, clarinets and *bouzoukis* wailed, and costumed dancers led the guests in a serpentine line around our Colonial farmhouse, only 20 minutes from my first home in Worcester.

20   My sisters and I felt an aching void because my father was not there to lead the line, balancing a glass of wine on his head while he danced, the way he did at every celebration during his 92 years. But Miss Hurd was there, surveying the scene with quiet satisfaction. Although my parents are gone, her presence was a consolation, because I owe her so much.

This is truly the land of opportunity, and I would have enjoyed its bounty even if I hadn't walked into Miss Hurd's classroom in 1953. But she was the one who directed my grief and pain into writing, and if it weren't for her I wouldn't have become an investigative reporter and foreign correspondent, recorded the story of my mother's life and death in *Eleni* and now my father's story in *A Place for Us,* which is also a testament to the country that took us in. She was the catalyst that sent me into journalism and indirectly caused all the good things that came after. But Miss Hurd would probably deny this emphatically.

A few years ago, I answered the telephone and heard my former teacher's voice telling me, in that won't-take-no-for-an–answer tone of hers, that she had decided I was to write and deliver the eulogy at her funeral. I agreed (she didn't leave me any choice), but that's one assignment I never want to do. I hope, Miss Hurd, that you'll accept this remembrance instead.

RESPONSE QUESTIONS

1. What qualities does Gage admire in his English teacher, Marjorie Hurd? Did you ever have a teacher who influenced you the way she influenced him? If so, tell what made that teacher so important in your life.

2. Compare Gage's school experience to Dick Gregory's in "Shame." What do you think each writer wanted most as a young student? How did their teachers respond to these needs? What were the results?

3. Gage says of the United States, "This is truly the land of opportunity." What evidence does he give to support this statement? Based on your own experience and your observations of others, would you agree?

4. Gage learns the power of language with the help of Miss Hurd. Where in the essay is this lesson most strikingly reinforced? Describe a moment in your own life when you learned that writing can have a strong impact on others.

5. Miss Hurd submitted Gage's personal essay to the school paper and a national contest without telling him. Do you think she should have done this? What issues of privacy and student rights are raised by her action?

GUIDELINES FOR ANALYSIS

1. Gage's essay is a story within a story. One story is about his escape from Greece and focuses on his mother. The other story is about becoming a writer and focuses on Marjorie Hurd. How does he link these two stories? What common threads or themes can you find in them?

2. Reread the description of Miss Hurd and her manner of speaking in paragraph 6. What would your impression of her be from this paragraph alone? How does Gage's introduction help to shape your impression and explain her role in his life?

QUESTIONS OF CULTURE

1. In the 1950s, Gage and his sisters were placed in a class for mentally retarded students. How would non-English-speaking children be taught in your elementary school today? How have attitudes toward immigrants changed in this country since Gage was a student? How have they stayed the same?

2. The land that Gage's family came from contrasts sharply with his home in the United States. Describe some of the differences in education, politics, and daily life. If you have time, read *Eleni* or watch the movie to find out more about Greece after World War II and the death of Eleni Gatzoyiannis.

IDEAS FOR YOUR JOURNAL

1. Do you have a special talent or interest like writing, music, or athletics? How did you become aware of it? What (or who) helped you discover or develop this talent or interest in yourself? How might you pursue it further?

2. Miss Hurd advises her students to write about what they know, and she tells Gage specifically to write about a painful personal moment. Based on your own experience of writing about painful moments, what do you think of her advice?

3. Gage was placed with mentally retarded students because he did not speak English well. Were you ever misplaced or misunderstood in school because of a problem in communication? What was the problem?

4. Gage's mother gave her life for her children's freedom. Can you remember a time when someone sacrificed herself or himself in some way for your benefit? Describe that moment. Did the sacrifice make a difference in your life? How did you feel toward that person at the time? How do you feel toward that person now?

A STUDENT WRITER IN ACTION

Preview

Nuala Lynch, a student enrolled in a first-year composition class, chose to reconstruct a memory that had been troubling her for years. Born and raised in Northern Ireland, she knew what it was like to live with violence all around her, but it was not until she moved to New York that she experienced terror face to face. Writing her essay became an opportunity to reexamine a key incident in her life and to understand its lessons about fear and survival.

Nuala's essay is followed by a description of her writing process. As you trace her steps of planning, drafting, and revising the essay, notice how she moves from uncertainty about the subject to a more focused sense of purpose and audience. Watch how she makes decisions about where to begin, what to include, and how to organize her story.

Later chapters will feature other student essays along with early drafts and the students' own commentaries. These glimpses into the writing practices of others can give you useful ideas for your own writing. They also can be comforting reminders that effective essays are not necessarily produced in one sitting.

"A NIGHT OF TERROR"

by Nuala Lynch

I spent the first twenty-two years of my life in Northern Ireland, a country justifiably known as one of the most heavily militarized in Europe.

As a citizen of that country, I am perceived to have lived every day with the constant threat of violence or even death. This is an understandable perception due to the fact that on a daily basis the sight of bombed-out buildings and armed men walking around was as common a sight as a pretzel stand on a New York City street corner. On the contrary, though, New Yorkers don't feel fear when they hear about a murder in New Jersey. Neither did I. Death was in my country—not on my street or in my home. That's the difference between perception and reality.

Despite growing up surrounded by these images I don't ever recall having been afraid for my life. Terror is not a word that springs to mind when recalling my childhood. Perverse as it may seem to many, the sight of guns was an accepted part of the society in which I lived. Only when these images were personalized did I experience terror.

One balmy May evening in 1993, while working as a bartender in the Bronx, I was robbed at gunpoint by three men. Never before or since have I felt such terror. I truly believed for the first time in my life that I was about to die.

5   I was alone in the bar at the time. The door was hooked open as the air conditioner was broken and it was quite humid. At approximately 10:30 p.m. two well-dressed men entered the bar. I noticed a third man on the doorstep attempting to unhook the door. I asked him to leave it open and explained why. One of the men inside the bar nodded to the third man, as if indicating to him that he should do as I asked. He remained on the doorstep. I remember he looked left and right down the street. In hindsight, this action should have triggered alarm bells for me, but it didn't. The two men inside the bar refused my offer of a drink. They asked me if I had a telephone. I directed them to the phone and continued to wash glasses.

Then, out of the corner of my eye I noticed one of the men looking into the adjoining poolroom, which I knew to be empty. Suddenly, the proverbial penny dropped and I realized what was about to happen. The actions of the three men, while taken individually, did not alarm me; combined, they immediately posed a threat. Without speaking another word, I dropped the glasses I was holding and ran for the door in an attempt to escape.

About three feet from the door I came face to face with the barrel of a gun. I froze, stared at the gun, and immediately my body started to involuntarily tremble and perspire. Although used to the sight of guns all my life, this time the barrel was pointing directly at my head. While guns had always been a part of my childhood, in an indirect way, they were now an extremely unpleasant part of my life, in a very direct way. My mouth felt like someone had laid carpet in it. I could feel tears running down my cheeks but can't recall hearing myself cry. My chest felt like it was in some sort of vise-grip. I was struggling to breathe. I was completely and utterly overcome with terror. Everything around me was blurred. I remember a distant voice shouting, "Get back! Get back!" This strange voice was mingled with my own, alternately pleading for mercy and calling for my mother.

Looking back, obviously my pleas for mercy were directed at my assailants. On the other hand my calls for my mother, who had always protected me, were, I believe, some sort of verbalized wish that she would sweep into the room like a Rambo figure and save her baby when she needed her most.

The next thing I remember was standing behind the bar being ordered to open the register. I don't recall walking from the door to the register but I doubt my assailants carried me.

After opening the register I was ordered onto the floor. I knelt down amid the broken glass. When my ordeal was over I had a nasty cut on my hand but I don't remember feeling any pain. While on the floor I pressed my palms and knees into the floorboards in an effort to control my trembling. I assume this was when I sustained my cut.

It was in this position that I felt most vulnerable and totally helpless. My mind was racing with ideas. "Jesus they'll kill me if they don't get enough money! Protect your head! There's more money hidden in the bar! Take my handbag! Take my tips! If you let me up, I can get you more money?" I must have been simultaneously thinking out loud, because next I heard a voice, telling me not to be stupid and to keep my head down. I realized that they did not wish to be identified, always willing to oblige I tried to stick my head under the sink as far as I could. I couldn't identify anyone from under there. More importantly the sink offered protection for my head. I figured I might survive a bullet to the body but not one to the head.

While all these thoughts were racing through my head, there was a lot of noise above me: the rattle of money, the clanging of bottles then suddenly a voice saying, "Don't move for five minutes!" Next there was silence except for the sound of my heart thumping.

I don't know how long I lay on the floor, nor do I recall getting up, locking the door, or calling the police. But somehow logic went hand in hand with fear, because I performed all these necessary motions. The police arrived to find me sitting on a barstool, still trembling.

I now know what it's like to experience pure terror. My assailants made sure of that with the business end of a gun; nonetheless, I returned to work the following night as normal.

Today I can recall the specifics of the incident only when I force myself to. Some might see that as denial. I consider it a sign of survival, a determination to go on as I had before. To survive something—not forget it—still means you have to erase some memory, if not all of it. Denial is keeping it locked inside, even from yourself. Survival is when the story means more to others than to you. Long after the incident, I was able to look back on this episode and realize that it was never about me. A certain amount of self-flattery comes with being a victim; thankfully, victim is not a role I play well. It was always about the bar. Only when I was able to look at the big picture, did I see the whole story. While it was an experience that taught me a lot about my own strengths and weaknesses, it is one that I would never care to relive.

A Writer's Progress

Nuala began by listing and evaluating several possible topics from her past.

> getting my green card—too trivial
>
> mother's funeral—too personal
>
> winning the cross country race—too far back to remember?
>
> the holdup—too painful?

After eliminating the first two topics, which she considered too inconsequential or private for a college essay, Nuala weighed the remaining two options. She had won a cross-country race in Ireland when she was twelve years old, a long time ago, so the experience might be hard to reconstruct. Besides, she reasoned, that story would be only a chronology of events. It lacked a message and was not likely to move most readers. So she chose to write about the time that she was robbed at gunpoint while working in a Bronx bar. This event was more recent, and although it was still painfully vivid, she decided that the impact on her was significant enough to face the discomfort of reliving it.

Once she had chosen her topic, Nuala took stock of what she had to say about it by recalling what had happened moment by moment. She had told the story several times: to the police, to the owner of the bar, to friends, and to several customers. She realized that each retelling changed with her audience. The police wanted facts, her friends were eager for the emotional details, and the owner was interested in the damage to his bar. Sifting through these different versions, she began picking out particulars she might include for a general audience:

> gun pointing at my face
>
> broken glass pressing into my skin
>
> forced to lie on the floor
>
> man's voice, calm, ordering my head down
>
> voices in my head calling my mother

From these fragments of memory, chosen from her oral versions of the story, she began composing her first draft. The facts were relatively easy. What was most difficult to write about was her fear. She knew she was no hero—she was terrified—and she was hesitant to recall in writing the terror that she had tried to avoid thinking about for six years. Yet, when it came to writing a conclusion, to summarizing the meaning of the whole experience, this fear is precisely what she focused on. She realized that her fear was the emotional center of the essay and that she learned to manage it when she decided not to take the holdup personally. She was not the target; she was just a means to an end, a conduit to cash for some people looking for fast money. If there was a lesson to be learned, it was how to depersonalize the terror in order to move on with her life.

Nuala wrote the body of her essay first, because it was factual and familiar, the easiest to write. Then she drafted a conclusion, asking the question, "Where am I now?" This is where she had to stand back from the events and evaluate their significance to her. What did they add up to? How did they contribute to the trajectory of her life? Finally, she wrote the introduction, asking, "Where was I before?" Her opening paragraphs offer background information, the violence in Northern Ireland where she grew up, which contrasts with the violence that occurred in the Bronx.

While writing and revising her draft, Nuala also had to decide what to leave out. In her words, "I write on a need-to-know basis." She decided that some details were unnecessary, like the name of the bar, the outcome of a dart contest that had taken place before the theft, and the police photos that she was later asked to identify. These details did not contribute directly to the ongoing story. She also chose to leave out certain emotional details. As she explained, "It's still my personal experience, and I want to keep some files private."

While composing her essay, Nuala made selective use of this chapter. For example, she drew on certain ideas from the "Tips on Writing" section. The writing voice she found is formal and objective, a fitting style for an essay about depersonalizing fear (see "Find Your Voice," page 84). Yet she used descriptive close-ups and some dialogue to create a sense of drama (see "Build Key Scenes," page 84). When she wrote about victims, denial, and survival, she recalled Maya Angelou's struggle with the childhood memory of rape. The break-in by three armed men had felt like a deeply personal violation to her, but eventually she came to the conclusion that "it was never about me."

Considerations for Your Own Writing

While Nuala listed only four topics before selecting one, it often helps to list as many as you can. Try the brainstorming technique described in Chapter 2 (page 48). Let the ideas pour out without stopping the flow. Then examine your list and check the likely prospects. Notice what helps you decide. What are your criteria for eliminating topics? Will your topic appeal to your audience? Do you have enough to say about it? Are you likely to be overwhelmed by unsorted feelings? Can this process be therapeutic for you?

Your topic need not be as dramatic as a holdup. It's not what you write about that counts so much as how you write about it. Seemingly ordinary events, such as stoking the furnace (remember Robert Hayden's poem) or a child's day in church (remember Langston Hughes's "Salvation"), or ironing, can become significant when they are reconstructed in the light of a new understanding.

The Web of Memory

The Internet offers a worldwide web of writers—beginners and professionals—who share their memories through diaries, journals, memoirs, scrapbooks, and other forms. Their Web sites feature advice, discussion groups, bibliographies, and large databases of resources. Most are linked to other Web sites. So get online and follow the web.

Here are a few Web sites to get you started.

The Diary Registry
http://diarist.net/registry/
Calling itself "The Definitive Directory of Online Journals and Diaries," this site indexes (at last count) over 4,000 online journals and diaries arranged by title, name, location, sex and age, and birthdays.

The Center for Autobiographic Studies (CAS)
http://storyhelp.com/
CAS identifies itself as "a not-for-profit educational organization dedicated to promoting the knowledge, appreciation, creation and preservation of contemporary autobiographic works." The site posts events and offers a menu of resources that includes writing exercises, tips on forming writing groups, and help with choosing the right form of autobiographical writing.

Conversations Within
http://www.journal-writing.com/
This popular "on-line workshop on journal writing" offers a step-by-step program for creating your journal as "an inner dialog."

Association of Personal Historians
http://www.personalhistorians.org/index.html
Here is a Web site for professionals. It has membership fees but also offers useful links and hints for anyone interested in writing memoirs.

Taking Stock

Before closing the book on your completed composition, take a moment to consider where it has led you as a writer.

1. What did you learn from this assignment?
2. What composing problems did you solve? What problems remain?
3. What would you do differently the next time?
4. Review your own composing process at this stage. What seems to work best for you? Do you have a particular approach or style? Remember that certain methods may work better for certain kinds of composing. Be prepared to experiment and try new strategies with each assignment.

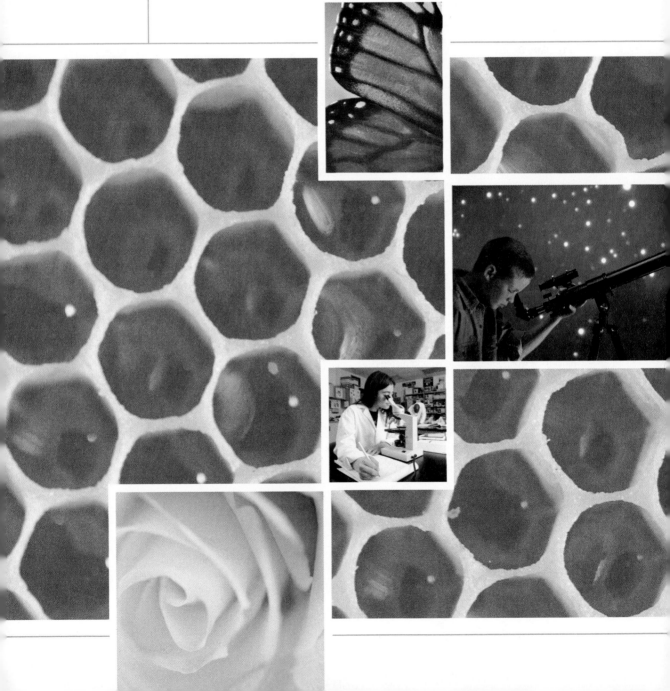

CHAPTER 4

Close-ups—
Observing Our
Environments

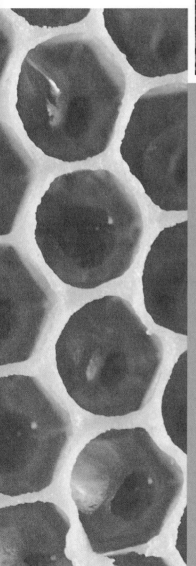

Technology sharpens and expands the reach of human vision. With modern telescopes and microscopes, we can explore the shapes of distant galaxies or peer into the mysteries of a water droplet. Technology also gives us tools for re-envisioning our world. A simple camera with a zoom lens enables us to frame familiar things as close-ups and wide-angle shots, making ordinary things seem extraordinary, sometimes even unrecognizable. Words are tools as well. With focused practice, we can learn to use the technology of language to observe and describe our surroundings with greater precision and imagination.

How would you describe what you see on this page? One approach is to give each photograph a name. Another is to clarify your impressions in terms of colors, shapes, patterns, or metaphors: what these images look like rather than what they might be called. How else might you respond? Notice the difference between naming and describing, between precise language and fuzzy words. What are the benefits and disadvantages of these approaches? Chapter 4 is about observing and describing your environments. You'll be exploring the people and places around you with one of the most powerful instruments available, the writer's eye.

This chapter will help to sharpen your observation skills and your powers of description. It will help you write with an educated eye. We'll begin by looking at the need for careful observation and description in your life. We'll continue with a set of exercises that explore the relationships between images and words. Then we'll look closely at a variety of descriptive texts: a video about Manhattan's Sullivan Street, a National Geographic Webcast on the Congo, and selections by observant writers on the topic of the environment. Meanwhile, you'll be applying what you learn about observation and description by focusing on a particular person, place, or object. This might be a colorful person in your neighborhood, an interesting member of your family, an environment that fascinates you, or a prized possession. You might use a camera or a sketchpad to help you focus on your subject, but the final description will take one of two forms. If you choose the media option, you will be composing a collage: a display of drawings, photographs, or other images that show your subject in a fresh, new way. If you choose the writing option, you'll be composing a descriptive essay, one that will make your readers hear, feel, and above all see that subject as distinctly, as completely, and as revealingly as you do.

SCENARIOS FROM LIFE

Here are some instances that call for purposeful descriptive writing in school, in the community, at work, and in personal relationships.

1. You've just learned that merchants in your town want to build a new shopping mall on undeveloped property. The land—a plot of stately fir trees and majestic oaks—is one of the last unspoiled retreats for you and others who appreciate the sanctity of nature. You decide to write in protest to your local newspaper. To build your case, you want to describe your sanctuary in such a way that readers will see the beauty, hear the gentle sounds, and feel the peaceful rhythms that would be destroyed by the construction of a mall.

2. Chatting with the new teller at your bank job, you decide that he would be a great match for your best friend. So you begin describing your friend's appearance, personality, and interests in order to set up a blind date. You want to be as honest and persuasive as possible because you feel that they'd be perfect for each other. Meanwhile, you're pumping the teller for personal information so you can e-mail a complete description to your friend.

3. Standing at the corner waiting for the light to change, you're startled by the squeal of rubber followed by a thud. You turn your head just in time to see a red convertible speeding away from the scene. A child lies on the street, dazed and injured but alive: a hit-and-run. Your first instinct is to help the child. However, you also know that you're a witness to a crime. Will you be able to describe the car and its driver clearly and completely enough to help the police find the hit-and-run driver?

4. In biology class, you've been studying human anatomy, learning how to distinguish different forms of tissue by the sizes, shapes, and structures of their cells. As a lab exercise, your instructor gives you a set of "mystery slides." Your task is to describe the cells on these slides so that another student can tell what part of the body they are from. You need to write down what you see accurately and precisely—as if your lab report were crucial in a medical emergency.

WHY WRITE TO DESCRIBE?

In one of Arthur Conan Doyle's murder mysteries, detective Sherlock Holmes turns to his assistant, Dr. Watson, who has been surveying the scene of the crime with discouraging results. For all his poking and prying, Watson has failed to find a single clue. Holmes tells him, "You see, but you do not observe." What Watson lacks is Holmes's educated eye: the imagination that enables the sleuth to behold ordinary objects from unusual angles, the skill of focusing attention on significant details, the vision to rearrange those details into a revealing picture of events.

Joseph Conrad, the novelist, put it another way. After twenty years at sea and sailing many times around the world, Conrad chose to write about his experiences in English, his third language. "My task," he declared, "is by the power of the written word, to make you hear, to make you feel—it is, before all, to make you see." Conrad's statement broadens the field of observation to include sound, touch, and emotions, suggesting that the sense of sight is our most important way to understand the world. Conrad also reminds us that one of the writer's central activities is describing: the task of putting observations into words. Of course, you observe things and describe them every day. When your doctor asks you how you feel, when your friends want to know about the new guy on the block, or when your science teacher asks you to report the results of an experiment, they are calling on your powers of observation and description. In this chapter, you'll be strengthening those powers. In contrast to remembering and reconstructing, the emphasis here is on a subject outside yourself: not an inward-looking memory but an object, person, place, or event that exists out there in the world to be explored, carefully examined, and portrayed in written language.

This may involve a combination of detective work and celebration. The verb *observe* implies a close adherence, like the times when you observe a holiday. When you truly observe something, you get to look at it more closely and more steadily than usual. Even the most familiar objects and events begin to radiate new meanings when observed in a fresh light. And since it's nearly impossible to describe anything without revealing something of yourself, the act of describing is as interesting for what it reveals about the writer as for what it says about the subject.

While this may seem like a great challenge, think of the experience that you already bring to it. If you draw or paint or use a camera, you have already developed useful visual skills. If you have an ear for music or a special sensitivity to touch, you can apply those skills as well. Even if you don't think of yourself as particularly skillful or creative, consider what you've learned by living in our modern media environment. Movies model eye and body movements, demonstrating how to shift our gaze by panning the horizon or tilting up from foot to face, how to concentrate attention through a close-up, how to alternate between two points of view by reversing camera angles. Computer simulations show us how to move through imaginary spaces, mentally rotating objects, shifting our perspective from ground level to an aerial view, or experimenting with a spectrum of colors and shadings. Research has shown that we learn from these mediated experiences. *What* we see on the screen, again and again, influences *how* we see the world and how we transform its images in the mind.

Good descriptive writing usually serves a purpose beyond description for its own sake. A journalist may describe an execution in grim detail in order to make a case against capital punishment. A biologist may describe a new moth so that other scientists will understand its place within the insect world. Advertisers want to sell the products they describe. You'll notice that the texts included in this chapter do more than simply describe their subject. They may set it in a wider framework, provide background information, or use it to advance an argument. So don't feel that you must limit your descriptive essay to the way your subject looks or sounds. Few people like to read long catalogs of sensory detail. Instead, be clear about your larger purpose—whether to characterize the quality of life in your neighborhood or to show how you misjudged your ninth-grade teacher—and describe what is most likely to achieve that purpose.

COMPOSING OPTIONS

Writing Option: Writing to Describe

This assignment is an opportunity to practice writing in sync with all your senses. You will be describing something—a special object, person, location, or event—so that readers can imagine your subject just as you observed it, including any odors, sounds, tastes, or tactile sensations that were part of the experience. However, your writing should do more than simply catalogue your sense impressions. It should *characterize* your chosen subject, giving your readers enough distinctive details to form a picture of the whole, leaving them with a strong, dominant impression of its character.

Your essay will be most worth reading if you care about your subject. So choose something, someone, or some place that is important to you. It may be related to the writing option in Chapter 3, "Writing to Remember," but avoid a subject that is only a distant memory. For this option, you should have direct access to your subject so you can observe it closely and describe precisely what you see.

Media Option: Collage

A collage is an assembly of odds and ends—such as photographs, magazine clippings, pressed flowers, or bits of cloth—mounted on a flat surface like wood or poster board. Although the pieces come from different sources, their placement together can create new meanings and make strong statements. A collage about your campus, for example, or about love or human rights can describe these subjects with power and precision. It can be an effective way to compose thoughts and feelings on a topic that are hard to put into words.

For this option, focus on an object, person, place, or concept as your subject. Start gathering visual materials that illustrate or characterize this subject for you. Be creative. Follow your imagination. A snapshot, a headline, or a leaf that seems unrelated to your subject may turn out to say something important about it when placed in your collage. When you assemble the fragments, consider how their relationship to one another affects the overall message. How deliberately do you want to spell out those relationships? How much will you leave to the viewers? Notice the tone of your composition: whether it's funny, angry, preachy, or carefree. Before deciding that your collage is complete, you may want to ask a few people what it means to them. Do their responses surprise you? Are you moved to add, delete, or rearrange anything—to reenvision or revise your collage?

The media option can be an assignment by itself, or it can lead to a written essay on the same topic. Sometimes the process of collecting and arranging physical objects for a collage helps to channel your thoughts into words. Even if you don't write a formal essay, it's worth considering how the act of making a collage is like the process of composing an essay. What steps did you take? What were you thinking when you took these steps? Do the principles of good writing—unity, clarity, organization, continuity, and completeness—apply to visual composition as well?

TIPS ON DESCRIPTIVE WRITING

DISCOVERING

1. Try brainstorming alone or in a group. Jot down possible subjects in any order they occur to you.

   Why I Could Live in My Car

   My Sister the Sorceress

   The Church on Times Square

2. List ideas by category. Think of the interesting people you know: an intriguing personality in your family, someone with an unusual problem, a community activist who makes a difference. Think of places that might be worth a closer look, or think of upcoming events that you may be attending soon. List some of the different points of view from which your subject might be seen. What would it look like to a child, a lawyer, an insect, or a twenty-foot giant?

3. Select one or two of these subjects and try freewriting about them. Ask exploratory questions: What do you already know about the subject? What do you expect to discover?

PLANNING

1. When you have chosen a promising subject, make arrangements to observe it firsthand. Your observations may require several visits and interviews. Try to avoid premature judgments at this stage. Keep an open mind, all your senses alert.

2. A double-entry log will help you separate direct observation (what you see, smell, hear, touch, and taste) from general impressions (what the observations cause you to think, feel, and remember). The log can tell you when you have a strong overall impression and enough distinctive details to support it.

DEVELOPING

You can learn a lot about developing your draft by observing other writers. Watch how Arthur Conan Doyle, William Faulkner, and N. Scott Momaday compose descriptive paragraphs for different purposes.

The Discerning Eye: Selecting the Revealing Details

In Arthur Conan Doyle's mystery, "The Red-Headed League," Dr. Watson finds Sherlock Holmes speaking with a visitor who claims to have witnessed a crime. Watson sizes up the guest this way:

> Our visitor bore every mark of being an average commonplace British tradesman, obese, pompous, and slow. He wore rather baggy gray shepherd's check trousers, a not over-clean black frock-coat, unbuttoned in the front, and a drab waistcoat with a heavy brassy Albert chain, and a square pierced bit of metal dangling down as an ornament. A frayed top-hat and a faded brown overcoat with a wrinkled velvet collar lay upon a chair beside him. Altogether, look as I would, there was nothing remarkable about the man save his blazing red head, and the expression of extreme chagrin and discontent upon his features.

Watson's description is extensive and specific. He notices lots of details about the stranger's clothes and a few physical traits. His dominant impression is of an unremarkable person, a common British tradesman. Holmes comes to different conclusions. Says Holmes, "Beyond the obvious facts that he has at some time done manual labor, that he takes snuff, that he is a Freemason, that he has been in China, and that he has done a considerable amount of writing lately, I can deduce nothing else." He's teasing Watson about the "nothing else," but all of his conclusions are based on observation. He has noticed that the man's right hand is larger than his left, a sign of manual labor. He's also noticed that the man's right cuff and left elbow are shiny, indicating that he writes with his right hand while resting on his left elbow. He sees that what is hanging from the watch-chain is a Chinese coin found only in China. And so on. This is what makes Sherlock Holmes such a good detective and Dr. Watson a good foil. Watson sees, but Holmes observes.

Good descriptive writing also works this way. The point is not to give an exhaustive list of details but to zero in with a discerning eye on the most telling features of a subject, what is most distinctive, most revealing, most pertinent to the purpose at hand. This is much like sketching. You draw just enough particulars to convey what's special about the subject and allow the reader to fill in the rest.

The Subjective Lens

Watch how William Faulkner describes the heroine of "A Rose For Emily," his short story about a Southern woman whose pride, isolation, and obsession with the past have consumed her life:

> They rose when she entered—a small, fat woman in black, with a thin gold chain descending to her waist and vanishing into her belt, leaning on an ebony cane with a tarnished gold head. Her skeleton was small and spare; perhaps that was why what would have been merely plumpness in another was obesity in her. She looked bloated, like a body long submerged in motionless water, and of that pallid hue. Her eyes, lost in the fatty ridges of her face, looked like two small pieces of coal pressed into a lump of dough as they moved from one face to another while the visitors stated their errand.

Much of the description in this passage is **subjective.** It comes from a personal perspective, reflecting the feelings and imagination of the narrator. Faulkner uses metaphors that emphasize Emily's lifelessness and detachment from the world: the image of a body steeped in stagnant water, the comparison of her eyes to bits of coal in lumpy dough. Holmes is more **objective.** He remains unbiased and emotionally detached, describing what a camera might observe in terms that anyone might use. Objectivity is a feature of police reports, technical writing, and scientific studies. You wouldn't expect a police officer to compare a victim's eyes to chunks of coal. But if you're writing fiction or a personal essay, you may want to describe your subject subjectively in order to accentuate your individual perspective. In fact, it is this subjectivity that gives you authority as a writer. Nobody else can describe what you've observed from your particular point of view.

Notice how objective and subjective description work together in the following passage by N. Scott Momaday. Momaday, a member of the Kiowa tribe from Oklahoma, describes the place where he grew up. His description opens *The Way to Rainy Mountain,* a book that traces the migration of his tribe and his return to the land of his roots.

> A single knoll rises out of the plain in Oklahoma, north and west of the Wichita Range. For my people, the Kiowas, it is an old landmark, and they gave it the name Rainy Mountain. The hardest weather in the world is there. Winter brings blizzards,

hot nomadic winds arise in the spring, and in summer the prairie is an anvil's edge. The grass turns brittle and brown, and it cracks beneath your feet. There are green belts along the rivers and creeks, linear groves of hickory and pecan, willow and witch hazel. At a distance in July or August the steaming foliage seems almost to writhe in fire. Great green-and-yellow grasshoppers are everywhere in the tall grass, popping up like corn to sting the flesh, and tortoises crawl about on the red earth, going nowhere in the plenty of time. Loneliness is an aspect of the land. All things in the plain are isolate; there is no confusion of objects in the eye, but *one* hill or *one* tree or *one* man. To look upon that landscape in the early morning, with the sun at your back, is to lose the sense of proportion. Your imagination comes to life, and this, you think, is where Creation was begun.

As you can see, sometimes Momaday's words are more objective, as when he names the types of trees along the rivers or identifies the colors of the grass, the grasshoppers, and the earth. While most of his description is visual, he also appeals to the ear and sense of touch, directly addressing you, the reader, in order to draw you into the setting. The brittle grass "cracks beneath your feet" and grasshoppers pop up "like corn to sting the flesh." By the time you've come to the conclusion of this paragraph, if Momaday's words have done their job, you are ready to agree with his *subjective* phrases: your imagination *has* come to life, and this place "is where Creation was begun."

REVISING

Revising your writing starts with seeing it afresh from the audience's point of view. Put yourself in the position of your readers, who are coming to your essay for the first time with their particular knowledge, backgrounds, and interests. Will they be able to understand your language and really see, hear, or feel what you want them to see, hear, or feel? Where would it help to add more distinctive details or to sharpen them? Do the descriptive details serve a larger purpose? Have you characterized your subject as a whole instead of merely offering lots of close-ups? Will readers easily follow the flow of your essay? Is it organized in some consistent way, perhaps chronologically, spatially, as a running comparison? Have you guided your reader's discerning eye, making clear connections along the way?

Peer Preview Checklist

Give this checklist to a "committed reader," someone interested in helping you shape your rough draft into a final essay.

1. **Where did the subject come into sharpest focus for you? What helped you to see, hear, smell, taste, or feel things as if you were there?**

2. **Did anything seem to be missing? What would make the description more complete?**

3. **What came across as the essay's main idea, its central focus? Where is the subject characterized most clearly?**

4. **List any problems you had following the essay from start to finish.**

5. **What do you picture after reading it? What are you likely to remember most?**

PRINT

Poets, novelists, and journalists vividly and evocatively describe.

Magazines like *National Geographic, Nature, Travel.*

Personal ads

TELEVISION

Detective shows: *Mystery!*

Nature programs: *Animal Planet, National Geographic Channel, Blue Planet*

Travel: *Globe Trekker*

MOVIES

Microcosmos

Winged Migration

RADIO

Nature Watch

Radio Expeditions

Traveler's Journal

INTERNET

Ecotourism
http://www.ecotourism.org/

Envirolink
http://www.envirolink.org/

naturalist.com
http://www.naturalist.com/

Readings and Screenings: Observing the Environment

The French filmmaking team Claude Nuridsany and Marie Perennou made cinematic history by taking their camera where no man has gone before, not into outer space but on our own planet. In *Microcosmos* (1996) they used a high-powered lens to bring the tiny, fascinating world of insects to the big screen. In *Winged Migration* (2001), they followed the astonishing journey of migratory birds in flight from continent to continent. The extreme close-ups and extraordinary wide-angle shots of these two largely wordless films demonstrate the descriptive power of visual technology when guided by a discerning eye and respect for the environment. Where else do masters of the media observe and describe?

Our thematic focus in this section is on the environment. We'll be following an ecologist's trek across Africa (as recounted on the Internet), three reporters on assignment in Manhattan (captured on video), and essays that span a wide range of different settings, from an Indian reservation in the American Southwest to the woodlands of the Northeast. Each of these texts relies on careful observation and description to make a strong statement about the environment.

Visual Prompt

PREVIEW

Born in Pittsburgh, Pennsylvania, in 1945, Annie Dillard attended Hollins College in Virginia before becoming a celebrated writer on the beauty and mystery of nature. She has described herself as "a wanderer with a penchant for quirky facts," but she endows those facts with a lyrical grace and spiritual significance. Her poems and essays continue to inspire readers with a deep appreciation of the natural environment. The following excerpt is taken from her book, *Pilgrim at Tinker Creek,* which was awarded the Pulitzer Prize in 1974.

Seeing

by Annie Dillard

When I was six or seven years old, growing up in Pittsburgh, I used to take a precious penny of my own and hide it for someone else to find. It was a curious compulsion; sadly, I've never been seized by it since. For some reason I always "hid" the penny along the same stretch of sidewalk up the street. I would cradle it at the roots of a sycamore, say, or in a hole left by a chipped-off piece of sidewalk. Then I would take a piece of chalk, and, starting at either end of the block, draw huge arrows leading up to the penny from both directions. After I learned to write I labeled the arrows: SURPRISE AHEAD or MONEY THIS WAY. I was greatly excited, during all this arrow drawing, at the thought of the first lucky passer-by who would receive in this way, regardless of merit, a free gift from the universe. But I never lurked about. I would go straight home and not give the matter another thought, until, some months later, I would be gripped again by the impulse to hide another penny.

It is still the first week in January, and I've got great plans. I've been thinking about seeing. There are lots of things to see, unwrapped gifts and free surprises. The world is fairly studded and strewn with pennies cast broadside from a generous hand. But—and this is the point—who gets excited by a mere penny? If you follow one arrow, if you crouch motionless on a bank to watch a tremulous ripple thrill on the water and are rewarded by the sight of a muskrat kit paddling from its den, will you count that sight a chip of copper only, and go your rueful way? It is dire poverty indeed when a man is so malnourished and fatigued that he won't stoop to pick up a penny. But if you cultivate a healthy poverty and simplicity, so that finding a penny will literally make your day, then, since the world is in fact planted in pennies, you have with your poverty bought a lifetime of days. It is that simple. What you see is what you get.

I used to be able to see flying insects in the air. I'd look ahead and see, not the row of hemlocks across the road, but the air in front of it. My eyes would focus along that column of air, picking out flying insects. But I lost interest, I guess, for I dropped the habit. Now I can see birds. Probably some people can look at the grass at their feet and discover all the crawling creatures. I would like to know grasses and sedges—and care. Then my least journey into the world would be a field trip, a series of happy recognitions. Thoreau, in an expansive mood, exulted, "What a rich book might be made about buds, including, perhaps, sprouts!" It would be nice to think so. I cherish mental images I have of three perfectly happy people. One collects stones. Another—an Englishman, say—watches clouds. The third lives on a coast and collects drops of sea-water which he examines microscopically and mounts. But I don't see what the specialist sees, and so I cut myself off, not only from the total picture, but from the various forms of happiness.

Unfortunately, nature is very much a now-you-see-it, now-you-don't affair. A fish flashes, then dissolves in the water before my eyes like so much salt. Deer apparently ascend bodily into heaven; the brightest oriole fades into leaves. These disappearances stun me into stillness and concentration; they say of nature that it conceals with a grand nonchalance, and they say of vision that it is a deliberate gift, the revelation of a dancer who for my eyes only flings away her seven veils. For nature does reveal as well as conceal: now-you-don't-see-it, now-you-do. For a week last September migrating red-winged blackbirds were feeding heavily down by the creek at the back of the house. One day I went out to investigate the racket; I walked up to a tree, an Osage orange, and a hundred birds flew away. They simply materialized out of the tree. I saw a tree, then a whisk of color, then a tree again. I walked closer and another hundred blackbirds took flight. Not a branch, not a twig budged: The birds were apparently weightless as well as invisible. Or, it was as if the leaves of the Osage orange had been freed from a spell in the form of red-winged blackbirds; they flew from the tree, caught my eye in the sky, and vanished. When I looked again at the tree the leaves had reassembled as if nothing had happened. Finally I walked directly to the trunk of the tree and a final hundred, the real diehards, appeared, spread, and vanished. How could so many hide in the tree without my seeing them? The Osage orange, unruffled, looked just as it had looked from the house, when three hundred red-winged blackbirds cried from its crown. I looked downstream where they flew, and they were gone. Searching, I couldn't spot one. I wandered downstream to force them to play their hand, but they'd crossed the creek and scattered. One show to a customer. These appearances catch at my throat; they are the free gifts, the bright coppers at the roots of trees.

5   It's all a matter of keeping my eyes open. Nature is like one of those line drawings of a tree that are puzzles for children: Can you find hidden in the leaves a duck, a house, a boy, a bucket, a zebra, and a boot? Specialists can find the most incredibly well-hidden things. A book I read when I was young recommended an easy way to find caterpillars to rear: You simply find some fresh caterpillar droppings, look up, and there's your caterpillar. More recently an author advised me to set my mind at ease about those piles of cut stems on the ground in grassy fields. Field mice make them; they cut the grass down by degrees to reach the seeds at the head. It seems that when the grass is tightly packed, as in a field of ripe grain, the blade won't topple at a single cut through the stem; instead, the cut stem simply drops vertically, held in the crush of grain. The mouse severs the bottom again and again, the stem keeps dropping an inch at a time, and finally the head is low enough for the mouse to reach the seeds. Meanwhile, the mouse is positively littering the field with its little piles of cut stems into which, presumably, the author of the book is constantly stumbling.

If I can't see these minutiae, I still try to keep my eyes open. I'm always on the lookout for ant-lion traps in sandy soil, monarch pupae near milkweed, skipper larvae in locust leaves. These things are utterly common, and I've not seen one. I bang on hollow trees near water, but so far no flying squirrels have appeared. In flat country I watch every sunset in hopes of seeing the green ray. The green ray is a seldom-seen streak of light that rises from the sun like a spurting fountain at the moment of sunset; it throbs into the sky for two seconds and disappears. One more reason to keep my eyes open. A photography professor at the University of Florida just happened to see a bird die in midflight; it jerked, died, dropped, and smashed on the ground. I squint at the wind because I read Stewart Edward White: "I have always maintained that if you looked closely enough you could see the wind—the dim, hardly-made-out, fine debris fleeing high in the air." White was an excellent observer, and devoted an entire chapter of *The Mountains* to the subject of seeing deer: "As soon as you can forget the naturally obvious and construct an artificial obvious, then you too will see deer."

But the artificial obvious is hard to see. My eyes account for less than one percent of the weight of my head; I'm bony and dense; I see what I expect. I once spent a full three minutes looking at a bullfrog that was so unexpectedly large I couldn't see it even though a dozen enthusiastic campers were shouting directions.

Finally, I asked, "What color am I looking for?" and a fellow said, "Green." When at last I picked out the frog, I saw what painters are up against: The thing wasn't green at all, but the color of wet hickory bark.

The lover can see, and the knowledgeable. I visited an aunt and uncle at a quarter-horse ranch in Cody, Wyoming. I couldn't do much of anything useful, but I could, I thought, draw. So, as we all sat around the kitchen table after supper, I produced a sheet of paper and drew a horse. "That's one lame horse," my aunt volunteered. The rest of the family joined in: "Only place to saddle that one is his neck"; "Looks like we better shoot the poor thing, on account of those terrible growths." Meekly, I slid the pen and paper down the table. Everyone in that family, including my three young cousins, could draw a horse. Beautifully. When the paper came back it looked as though five shining, real quarter horses had been corralled by mistake with a papier-mâché moose; the real horses seemed to gaze at the monster with a steady, puzzled air. I stay away from horses now, but I can do a creditable goldfish. The point is that I just don't know what the lover knows; I just can't see the artificial obvious that those in the know construct. The herpetologist asks the native, "Are there snakes in that ravine?" "Nosir." And the herpetologist comes home with, yessir, three bags full. Are there butterflies on that mountain? Are the bluets in bloom, are there arrowheads here, or fossil shells in the shale?

Peeping through my keyhole I see within the range of only about thirty percent of the light that comes from the sun; the rest is infrared and some little ultraviolet, perfectly apparent to many animals, but invisible to me. A nightmare network of ganglia, charged and firing without my knowledge, cuts and splices what I do see, editing it for my brain. Donald E. Carr points out that the sense impressions of one-celled animals are not edited for the brain: "This is philosophically interesting in a rather mournful way, since it means that only the simplest animals perceive the universe as it is."

10   A fog that won't burn away drifts and flows across my field of vision. When you see fog move against a backdrop of deep pines, you don't see the fog itself, but streaks of clearness floating across the air in dark shreds. So I see only tatters of clearness through a pervading obscurity. I can't distinguish the fog from the overcast sky; I can't be sure if the light is direct or reflected. Everywhere darkness and the presence of the sunset appalls. We estimate now that only one atom dances alone in every cubic meter of intergalactic space. I blink and squint. What planet or power yanks Halley's Comet out of orbit? We haven't seen that force yet; it's a question of distance, density, and the pallor of reflected light. We rock, cradled in the swaddling band of darkness. Even the simple darkness of night whispers suggestions to the mind. Last summer, in August, I stayed at the creek too late.

RESPONSE QUESTIONS

1. How would you describe Annie Dillard's view of nature? Which of her experiences best supports this view? Compare her experiences with your own.

2. Where in the essay do you see Dillard's natural surroundings most vividly? How does Dillard's use of language help you to see this moment as she did?

3. What does Dillard mean in the last paragraph by "the artificial obvious"? Give an example from her essay or your own life.

GUIDELINES FOR ANALYSIS

1. Why do you think Dillard begins her essay with the story about pennies? How is this connected to her statement in paragraph 2: "What you see is what you get?"

Visual Prompt

2. Identify any unfamiliar words or phrases that you would like to understand more clearly. Look them up or bring them in for class discussion. What does knowledge of their meaning add to your reading of the essay?

3. Dillard's writing style is neither scientific nor didactic; she doesn't analyze or preach. How would you describe her style? Where in the essay are you most aware of her distinctive voice?

QUESTIONS OF CULTURE

1. When you see a penny on the ground, do you stop to pick it up? What about the people you know? What does this say about our values in today's world?

2. Monarch pupae, muskrat kits, and Osage trees are not common sights in the urban and suburban landscapes of America. They are not even part of our general vocabulary. What, essentially, has been lost, according to Annie Dillard? Can you make a case that contemporary American culture, with its modern conveniences and technological advances, is worth the loss?

IDEAS FOR YOUR JOURNAL

1. Try to recall your earliest memories of nature. Where were you? Who were you with? What do you remember seeing, hearing, smelling, tasting, touching? What made the most lasting impression on you?

2. Do you have a favorite place to wander, away from the stress and commotion of everyday life? Describe the place and its appeal to you.

3. Take your journal on a hike. Sit down somewhere quiet and wait. Watch. Listen. Take a deep breath. Describe what you find hidden in the puzzle.

4. In *The Writing Life* (1989), Dillard cautions writers against the impulse to hold on to impressions and ideas, advising them to "spend it all, shoot it, play it, lose it, all, right away, every time." "Anything you do not give freely and abundantly," she says, "becomes lost to you." Use your journal to give away something you have been holding on to.

In "Before the First Word," three writers walk through Manhattan's Sullivan Street with pen and pad in hand. Anna Quindlen is covering the annual street festival of St. Anthony for her weekly column in the *New York Times*. The other writers, both students, have been assigned to "write about the street." The video follows their progress through the early stages of composing as they piece together tentative assumptions, observations, interviews, and speculations into working drafts. It's a rare opportunity to watch a professional writer at work and listen to her thoughts as she composes. At the same time, it's a chance to see how different writers interpret and represent the same events in different ways. Quindlen's finished essay appears on page 148.

www.mhhe.com/costanzo

To view the video excerpt, visit www.mhhe.com/costanzo.

PARTIAL TRANSCRIPT OF DOCUMENTARY, "BEFORE THE FIRST WORD"

ANNA QUINDLEN (at computer): It's the hardest thing in the world I think to look at a blank sheet of paper, but it's one of the most satisfying things when you're finished with the paper and there's something on it. So when you're sitting there with the blank sheet just think of what's going to come later. Don't think of how empty it is right now.

(Shots of Quindlen on the street with notepad, interviewing residents, with people passing by)

QUINDLEN: My name's Anna Quindlen and I do a column for *The New York Times*. Right now I'm doing a story about the Feast of St. Anthony, which takes place every year on Sullivan Street. These two New York City high school students, Wilmer Ortiz and Maria Hampton, are on assignment too. They've been asked to observe as much as they can about this street, Sullivan Street, so they can write about it.

(Shots of Ortiz and Hampton walking, talking)

QUINDLEN: Even though they're doing it in school and about the street and my piece is for the newspaper and it's about the feast, the process they go through in observing a neighborhood is a lot like the one I use to write my column.

(Students with notepads. Shots of the street)

HAMPTON: Actually, I mostly wondered what the neighborhood would look like. I expected it to be a little larger, maybe a few houses with grass and small streets and tall buildings, and everything's connected. I hadn't expected that.

WILMER ORTIZ: I thought this would be a very diverse neighborhood.

QUINDLEN: When you have to write about anything, particularly if it's something you're not too familiar with, you have to start by doing a lot of looking and a lot of listening and questioning. You might be confused by what you find out at first, but that's okay. Eventually some patterns will start to appear.

(Shots of Ortiz and Hampton discussing where to look)

When I'm getting ready to write I look for details. I talk to people and I try not to make up my mind about what it all means.

(Ortiz and Hampton exchange observations about the neighborhood)

HAMPTON (to residents in window): My name's Marie Hampton and I've been assigned a writing project about Sullivan Street, and I thought that perhaps through the course of the day you notice a lot of different things that happened on Sullivan Street and could you tell me a few of the things that happened or that are exciting.

WOMAN IN WINDOW: Sure, what would you like to know?

HAMPTON: You know, what type of people come here, and why do they come? Is it because of the shops?

WOMAN: Yes, since we have Soho in the neighborhood, we get a different clientele of people than we had many years ago. We have a lot of boutiques and a lot of galleries, and they come and go, in groups, all week long.

(Cut to Ortiz waiting to speak to balloon vendor)

WOMAN (to Hampton): We originally were all Italians. We have a lot of Portuguese people . . . mostly Portuguese. It seems that they've taken over now, the Portuguese people.

HAMPTON: Is that a threat to you in any way?

WOMAN: Oh no, they're beautiful people.

HAMPTON: Do you have any living in your building now?

MAN: Oh yes, the building is loaded with them.

WOMAN: We were thirty-five Italian families. We're about eight, ten Italian families left. The rest are all Portuguese.

(Ortiz is still following the balloon man)

HAMPTON: If you could at any point, would you leave Sullivan Street?

WOMAN: No way.

MAN: No.

HAMPTON: Why?

WOMAN: I was born up the next block. I won't move from Sullivan Street.

HAMPTON: You've stayed here the whole time, the entire time? Did you at any point move away?

WOMAN: No, no. All in the neighborhood. Always in the neighborhood.

HAMPTON: You also?

MAN: I was born on West Broadway.

WOMAN: And we're here. We're always here.

MAN: Seventy-two years.

HAMPTON: The same place.

MAN: Same neighborhood. And I wouldn't change it.

(The balloon man finally finishes loading the balloons and turns to Ortiz.)

MAN WITH BALLOONS: We wanted to send balloons as a present to somebody, and we shopped around. We didn't like anything we could have bought so we made them ourselves, and we found how much fun it was.

WOMAN: People liked receiving them.

MAN: They loved it. So we decided it was a good outlet for a company to get involved with. So we opened up "Balloons."

ORTIZ: Do you live in the neighborhood?

35 WOMAN: No.

MAN: Neither of us do, no. I think being in one neighborhood, working and playing and living and cooking and sleeping is a little rough. I wouldn't like that. I like the fact that I go home to a different place.

ORTIZ: Were the people supportive of this business when you first came here?

WOMAN: Yeah, they liked seeing a different kind of concept for the neighborhood. I think they did.

ORTIZ: How about the other shop owners? How did they feel about this?

40 WOMAN: Everybody on the block gets along terrific. We have no problems with any of our neighbors.

MAN: Everybody's very nice on the block. There's no problems on this block at all, ever.

ANNA QUINDLEN: When you're on a street like Sullivan Street, is someone who's lived there forty years talking to you about the street now or the street the way it used to be? You have to ask the kinds of questions that elicit those answers. Who are the powerful people on the street? Who are the people who exercise some influence? You have to weigh their answers to questions about the street versus the answers of people who have just gotten there.

RESPONSE QUESTIONS

1. Come up with a working definition of a neighborhood. Describe some neighborhoods you know, and compare them to Sullivan Street. What makes these neighborhoods distinctive?

2. Anna Quindlen begins with the problem of the blank page and suggests how to move past it. What other advice does she offer about writing? Which of her suggestions seem most helpful to you?

3. Watch the video clip again, paying close attention to the interviews. Which questioning techniques work best? What could be improved? If you were on the scene, what questions would you ask, and how would you present them?

GUIDELINES FOR ANALYSIS

1. Compare the three writers in the video: Anna Quindlen, Wilmer Ortiz, and Maria Hampton. How does each individual approach the assignment of writing about Sullivan Street? What expectations do they begin with? What leads do they follow? What helps them establish a point of view on the topic? Speculate where you think their inquiries will lead, and watch the entire video, if you can, to see how your speculations turn out.

2. The video itself is a form of composition. It took three months to edit, with a 36:1 ratio of original footage to finished film. Notice which scenes were selected and how they are arranged. How are the three storylines (the three writers) integrated? How is sound (dialogue, background noises, voice-over narration) used? How would you rate the video in the categories of clarity, unity, organization, continuity, and style?

QUESTIONS OF CULTURE

1. Do you see any signs of prejudice among the residents of Sullivan Street? For example, how accepting of the Portuguese are the Italians being interviewed? How do they feel about other ethnic groups?

2. The balloon vendors say that the established residents welcome newcomers like themselves. How well is this claim validated by their body language and in the rest of the video? What attitudes do these two groups seem to share or not share?

3. Watch the rest of the video with an eye on potential conflicts. What evidence of disagreement or tension do you see? In your view, are there any serious threats to the values of the old neighborhood? Where would you look for these conflicts if you were writing a column titled "Sullivan Street Revisited: There Goes the Neighborhood"?

IDEAS FOR YOUR JOURNAL

1. If you live within traveling distance of Manhattan, visit Sullivan Street for yourself. Does it look to you today as it did to Anna Quindlen in 1982? If you were to update her essay or the video, what changes would you describe?

2. Take a notepad into a neighborhood near you and record your observations. Use a double-entry format, jotting down your specific observations in one column and your general ideas in the other. Before you begin, anticipate what you expect to find. Later, you can compare these expectations to the actual facts. As you walk around the neighborhood, don't leap to generalities too quickly. Practice using your "discerning eye" to capture precisely what you see, smell, hear, and feel. See if you can find a special "slant," a perspective on the topic that is uniquely your own.

3. Instead of a notebook, work with a scrapbook. Collect things from the neighborhood that represent its distinctive character: flyers, ticket stubs, leaves and flowers, newspaper clippings and photographs. Use what you have found to create a collage (page 134).

PREVIEW

This essay first appeared in Anna Quindlen's column in the *New York Times,* "About New York," in 1982. Her assignment was to write about the Feast of St. Anthony, a celebration that takes place every June on Sullivan Street in Manhattan's "Little Italy." Quindlen describes the early stages of her writing process in "Before the First Word" (see page 143).

Anna Quindlen continues to expand her writing repertoire. Her column was awarded a Pulitzer Prize in the 1990s, but she chose to leave the *Times* in order to concentrate on fiction. Her best-selling novels now include *Object Lessons* (1991), *One True Thing* (1994, made into a movie with Meryl Streep in 1998), *Black and Blue* (1998), and *Blessings* (2002). Quindlen recounts her lifelong dance with books in a book-length essay, *How Reading Changed My Life* (1998). She is also a columnist for *Newsweek.*

On a SoHo Street, a Feast for Body and Soul
by Anna Quindlen

As sure as the sun will come up in the morning and the three-card monte men will play on Broadway in the afternoon, so there will be crowds on Sullivan Street this week. That is because the Feast of St. Anthony of Padua has begun, and even if it rains—God forbid, as they say on the street—there will be sausage, and zeppole, and ragtag games of chance with stuffed-animal prizes that look something like dogs, something like cats, something like nothing at all.

Feasts and festivals and fairs have become a torturous tradition in this city, blocking intersections and bringing indigestion and skewered meat to what sometimes seems like every sociable block and every proud parish in New York.

But St. Anthony's is an old and respected feast, and it is just exactly the sort of thing that people expect from New Yorkers: booths in red and green, tinsel minarets strung across the street, crabs and lobsters slapped on outdoor counters with their sidekick lemon, sausage and peppers spitting on shiny grills, a Ferris wheel so close to tenement windows that a woman hanging wash could hitch a ride, peaches in wine, cherries in brandy, bilingual repartee, bands, back-slapping, dancing in the street. The feast combines many ingredients for which the city is justly known: commerce, food, noise, crowds and conflict. And so it is a New York City tradition.

While many of the newer street festivals are strictly secular, this feast remains devoted to St. Anthony himself, wearing the traditional tonsure and carved in stone above the doorway of the Roman Catholic church that bears his name at Sullivan and Houston Streets. The Rev. Paul Rotondi, the pastor, does not want anyone to forget the saint in temporal transports over the sausage. There are novenas and masses all day on June 13, which is the final day of the feast; there are votive lights and visits to be made. "It's a nice combination of the spiritual, the religious and the human," said Father Rontandi, who oversees the first two.

5   Ralph Tardi takes care of the last, although he, too, is ever mindful of St. Anthony, for whom he toils without pay. The 13th-century monk is the feast's patron saint, but Mr. Tardi has been, since its beginnings 31 years ago, its patron human being, and "Where's Ralph?" is the feast motto.

Mr. Tardi, who is a bank guard most of the time, begins in January, doling out sites for stands, careful not to put pasta next to pasta, candy with candy. In June he becomes driven, pacing the street with a cigar stub and a nervous stomach. Mr. Tardi, who hates crowds and goes home for dinner, loses from five to six pounds every June.

He works in the shadow of San Gennaro, the monster Mulberry Street feast held in September, which many at St. Anthony's insist is too crowded and draws tourists. Nevertheless, Mr. Tardi is a satisfied man, as he walks between stands and free calzone is pressed upon him. "After so many years you get like a figure of the feast," said Mr. Tardi, meaning no disrespect to St. Anthony.

And there are other feast figures, too. There is Bea Cannetti, who sits at the window of her ground-floor apartment feast or famine. She has lived on Sullivan Street for decades and keeps her oven hot for days as she and her daughter churn out baked ziti and eggplant Parmesan for the stand manned by her son. There are Marion Talamini, Mamie Caviglia, Teresa Croce, Margaret Basso and Jenny Liccione, all in a row, at a long table by the church, selling chances on a car like they have done at the feast for almost 30 years. They have never won a thing. There is John Romano of Johnny's Bar-B-Q stand—not to be confused with Vincent's Bar-B-Q, farther up the block, which is not to be confused with Vincent's clam bar next to it. Mr. Romano's father was one of the first vendors at the feast. "It's one of the best little feasts in New York," said Mr. Romano.

Of course, the feast would not be a true New York event if it did not have controversy. Sullivan Street is just on the edges of SoHo, and it has become fashionable in recent years, gaining boutiques and young single people. Some of those people—as well as cabdrivers, who complain of the traffic—do not like the feast.

10 There are complaints that the food is unhealthy, the crowded conditions unsafe, the buying and selling benefiting only the concessionaires, the normally quiet street turned into a sideshow. There are complaints that the odor of frying sausage gets into the silks and suedes in the shops. Mary Arnold, who runs a wholesale clothing business on Sullivan Street, says she hates the feast. "I ignore it," she said. "I pretend it's not there."

But, judging by the crowds, more people like the feast than do not, and Mr. Tardi says the others will just have to be tolerant for 11 days each year. Fashionable neighborhoods come and go, but Mr. Tardi believes the feast is immutable.

It is also lucrative, but no one at the feast wants to be too specific about money. Mr. Tardi says the stall proprietors pay $620 rent and $70 to the city for cleanup, but he says he has no idea of their profits.

John Romano says it depends on the weather, and Bea Cannetti says it depends on the crowds. Father Rotondi says the church receives enough in contributions to keep its elementary school open, but says he isn't sure just how much that it is from year to year.

All that can be said for certain is that a sausage sandwich costs $2, all the beer is advertised as ice cold, and, for the next eight days, as sure as the sun goes down at night and hot dog stands have umbrellas, Sullivan Street will be filled with food, and noise, and money, and complaints and prayers to St. Anthony.

RESPONSE QUESTIONS

1. When asked about her methods as a writer, Anna Quindlen explained, "My problem is to pick and choose the telling details that will make [my reader] feel he's on the street with me." Select passages from the essay where you felt that you were with her on the street. What makes those descriptive passages successful?

2. Quindlen recognizes that descriptive details by themselves are meaningless. "Show them a whole bunch of little points," she advises, "so they'll see a whole picture." What does the "big picture" add up to in this essay? Does Quindlen ever sum up her overall view of the feast in a single statement? Imagine another title that might reflect her main idea.

3. What were you thinking, seeing, and feeling as you read the essay? Use a double-entry reading log to separate your responses from the words and phrases that triggered those responses: direct quotes from the reading on the left side, your responses on the right. Did any particular segments trigger an unusual response? Where in the essay were you most engaged?

4. Did the essay remind you of people, places, or events in your own life? Imagine how you might begin if you were on assignment to describe them for a newspaper or a writing class.

GUIDELINES FOR ANALYSIS

1. This essay was written for the *New York Times* in 1982. What do you suppose Quindlen's readers were like? How are the interests and expectations of such an audience reflected in her writing style?

2. Quindlen wrote the essay as a columnist rather than as a news reporter. How does a regular column differ from a news report? Consider what Quindlen chooses to include and leave out. What do her choices tell you about her conception of a column called "About New York"?

3. Notice how the essay is organized. How does Quindlen arrange her information and ideas? Notice, for example, how the first and final paragraphs relate to one another. Notice, too, how she moves between details and generalities or from objects and activities to people and community.

QUESTIONS OF CULTURE

1. Quindlen speaks of the Feast of St. Anthony as "a New York City tradition," and her references to place names, local personalities, and the Statue of Liberty support that view. What other details give this story a distinctly New York flavor?

Visual Prompt

2. Sullivan Street is in a section of Manhattan known as Little Italy. How do you know that this "Feast for Body and Soul" is Italian? What might be different if the subject were a festival in Chinatown, Harlem, El Barrio, or another ethnic neighborhood? How universal is Quindlen's main message?

IDEAS FOR YOUR JOURNAL

1. Is a festival or local event taking place in your area? Make a visit and report on what you see. In addition to describing the sights, sounds, and smells that you encounter, interview some of the people and include them in your report just as Quindlen does.

2. In the video, Quindlen says that becoming a writer depends more on confidence in your personality than in your skills, a recognition that you can write a story differently than anybody else. List the things that make you different from the people you know. Start with your family. How are you distinct from your siblings, your parents, cousins, aunts, or uncles? What makes you stand out from your friends, classmates, or the people in your neighborhood? These special experiences and traits make you one of a kind. They are why nobody else in the world can write from your unique perspective.

PREVIEW

In his youthful years, Mark Twain served as a cub pilot on a Mississippi River steamboat. While his exploits were fictionalized in novels like *The Adventures of Tom Sawyer* and *The Adventures of Huckleberry Finn,* he remembered them more factually in his 1883 memoir, *Life on the Mississippi.* The following excerpt describes how the river changed as he grew older.

Two Views of the River
by Mark Twain

Now when I had mastered the language of this water, and had come to know every trifling feature that bordered the great river as familiarly as I knew the letters of the alphabet, I had made a valuable acquisition. But I had lost something, too. I had lost something which could never be restored to me while I lived.

All the grace, the beauty, the poetry, had gone out of the majestic river! I still keep in mind a certain wonderful sunset which I witnessed when steamboating was new to me. A broad expanse of the river was turned to blood; in the middle distance the red hue brightened into gold, through which a solitary log came floating black and conspicuous; in one place a long, slanting mark lay sparkling upon the water; in another the surface was broken by boiling, tumbling rings, that were as many-tinted as an opal; where the ruddy flush was faintest, was a smooth spot that was covered with graceful circles and radiating lines, ever so delicately traced; the shore on our left was densely wooded, and the somber shadow that fell from this forest was broken in one place by a long, ruffled trail that shone like silver; and high above the forest wall a clean-stemmed dead tree waved a single leafy bough that glowed like a flame in the unobstructed splendor that was flowing from the sun. There were graceful curves, reflected images, woody heights, soft distances; and over the whole scene, far and near, the dissolving lights drifted steadily, enriching it every passing moment with new marvels of coloring.

I stood like one bewitched. I drank it in, in a speechless rapture. The world was new to me, and I had never seen anything like this at home. But as I have said, a day came when I began to cease from noting the glories and the charms which the moon and the sun and the twilight wrought upon the river's face; another day came when I ceased altogether to note them. Then, if that sunset scene had been repeated, I should have looked upon it without rapture, and should have commented upon it, inwardly, after this fashion: "This sun means that we are going to have wind to-morrow; that floating log means that the river is rising, small thanks to it; that slanting mark on the water refers to a bluff reef which is going to kill somebody's steamboat one of these nights, if it keeps on stretching out like that; those tumbling 'boils' show a dissolving bar and a changing channel there; the lines and circles in the slick water over yonder arc a warning that that troublesome place is shoaling up dangerously; that silver streak in the shadow of the forest is the 'break' from a new snag, and he has located himself in the very best place he could have found to fish for steamboats; that tall dead tree, with a single living branch, is not going to last long, and then how is a body ever going to get through this blind place at night without the friendly old landmark?"

No, the romance and beauty were all gone from the river. All the value any feature of it had for me now was the amount of usefulness it could furnish toward compassing the safe piloting of a steamboat. Since those days, I have pitied doctors from my heart. What does the lovely flush in a beauty's cheek mean to a doctor but a "break" that ripples above some deadly disease? Are not all her visible charms sown thick with what are to him the signs and symbols of hidden decay? Does he ever see her beauty at all, or doesn't he simply view her professionally, and comment upon her unwholesome condition all to himself? And doesn't he sometimes wonder whether he has gained most or lost most by learning his trade?

RESPONSE QUESTIONS

1. Describe what you already know about Mark Twain (Samuel Clemens) and his works. How does this previous knowledge help you understand this selection from his autobiography?

2. What "valuable acquisition" does Twain refer to in the opening sentence? What did he gain and lose by mastering the river? Compare Twain's observation about nature to Dillard's insights in "Seeing."

GUIDELINES FOR ANALYSIS

1. Select two passages that you find particularly descriptive. What makes them so effective?

2. This excerpt can be read as an essay. How is it organized? What is the main idea? What does each paragraph contribute to this idea?

3. From the opening metaphor of "the language of the river" to the comparison of a river's ripple to a beauty's cheek in the last paragraph, Twain uses analogies to help us see familiar things in new ways. What points does he make with this poetic language? Would more analytic language be more effective here?

QUESTION OF CULTURE

Writing in the nineteenth century, Twain uses a style that is rare today. Why do you think he writes such long, complex sentences? How does he use punctuation to control the rhythm and meanings of his words? Does this style of writing help or interfere with his purpose? Explain.

IDEAS FOR YOUR JOURNAL

1. If you were to film Twain's essay, what would you show? Identify the close-ups, long shots, pans, and zooms.

2. Can you think of any place in your life that you see differently now than you once did? If so, describe it and explain what has changed.

For more than a year, ecologist J. Michael Fay journeyed through central Africa in search of environmental information and adventure. Armed with cameras and a pen, Fay and his team hiked some 1,200 miles through dense forests that had been untouched by humans for hundreds of years. They surveyed the wildlife and the terrain from coast to coast, recording their observations in journals, photographs, and videos.

www.mhhe.com/costanzo

To view the Web site, visit this book's Web site.

You can follow Fay's journey on the National Geographic Society's Web site. Congo Trek features a 360-degree virtual image of the Congo Basin, maps, and dispatches from Africa in Fay's own voice as well as links to related sites. For guidelines about navigating the Internet and understanding information on the Web, see Reading Web sites on www.mhhe.com/costanzo.

Congo Trek:
National Geographic Web Site

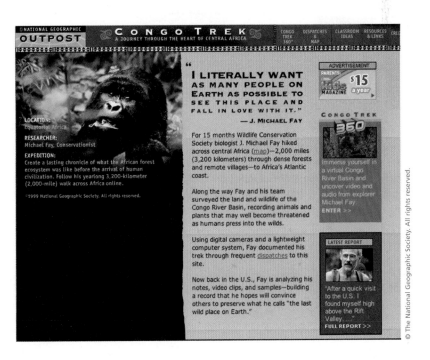

Also on the Web site is The Green Abyss, which gives excerpts of an article about Fay's "Megasect" (his term for crossing the large midsection of Africa) published by journalist David Quammen in *National Geographic* magazine.

Another way to learn about Michael Fay's activities is by listening to the radio. National Public Radio has been following his work for years, updating his progress with regular broadcasts. Check out NPR's Web site at http://www.npr.org to hear stories about Fay's role in helping the government of Gabon to create a new national park (September 4, 2002) or Fay's narrow escape from death in an elephant attack (December 8, 2003). Transcripts of the broadcasts are also available from NPR.

RESPONSE QUESTIONS

1. Visit Congo Trek and explore what it has to offer. Describe your first impression of the Web site. Does your impression change as you spend more time with the site?

2. What feeling does the Web site give you for the Congo Basin? How does this view compare with what you already knew about jungle environments?

GUIDELINES FOR ANALYSIS

1. Where do you find Michael Fay's writing most descriptive? Select a particularly powerful passage from his report and explain what makes it so vivid for you. Which words capture your attention? How does Fay make his experience come alive in your imagination?

2. Visit The Green Abyss and read Quammen's version of events. How successful is he in capturing the flavor of Fay's experience? Here is Quammen's description of Fay himself:

Fay is a compact 43-year-old American with a sharp chin and a lean, wobbly nose. Behind his wire-rimmed glasses, with their round, smoky lenses, he bears a disquieting resemblance to the young Roman Polanski. Say something that's dolt-ish or disagreeable, and he'll gaze at you silently the way a heron, hungry or not, gazes at a fish. But on the trail he's good company, a man of humor and generous intellect. He sets a punishing pace, starting at daylight, never stopping for lunch or rest, but when there are field data to record in his yellow notebook, fortunately, he pauses often.

Quote another passage in Quammen's writing that you find particularly descriptive, and explain why you chose it.

3. Consider the use of text, graphics, sound, video, and virtual images in this Web site. Tell what makes these features effective or ineffective.

4. Notice how the Web site is organized. In what ways is it similar to a collage? How easy is it to find your way around the site? What helps you to navigate? What would make navigation easier?

5. Compare the experience of reading this Web site to other kinds of reading. What would you gain—or lose—if you read about Fay's journey in a magazine or watched a documentary film?

QUESTIONS OF CULTURE

1. "It's pretty easy for us . . . in a developed country to think . . . they shouldn't cut down trees and kill all these poor animals, but then when you get over there . . . where there are no hospitals and no schools and a lack of food, it's not so cut and dry." These are the words of Robin Freeman, who produced *Africa Extreme,* a documentary film about Fay's journey, for Explorer TV. Do you agree with Freeman? Is it fair for a developed country like the United States to impose its ecological values on a poor country like Gabon?

2. National Geographic's online Forum posts positive and negative comments by the public about the trans-African expedition. Some see Fay as a heroic figure, out to rescue an endangered environment from destruction. Others see him as an ambitious egotist, exploiting native labor and intruding on the rights of poor Africans to use their natural resources. Read some of these views online. What is your own opinion of Fay and his project?

IDEAS FOR YOUR JOURNAL

1. Select a photograph or video from the Web site to write about. Observe closely (some pho-tos let you zoom in or pan around in a full circle) and describe what you see so that readers will be able to picture precisely what you do.

2. Describe a journey you have taken. Use your memory as well as any photographs, tape recordings, videos, maps, and other memorabilia to help you reconstruct the experience for others.

PREVIEW

Born on a Kiowa reservation in Oklahoma in 1934, N. Scott Momaday came of age in an environment rich in the stories and heritage of his Native American culture. At the age of two, he moved from the Oklahoma home of his grandparents to Arizona, where he lived with his parents among the Navajo, Apache, and Pueblo Indian cultures of the Southwest. A close observer of his surroundings with a keen ear for language, Momaday became a painter, printmaker, novelist, poet, and scholar dedicated to exploring humanity's place in the natural world. He studied at the University of New Mexico and earned a doctorate in English from Stanford University in 1963. His books of folk tales, essays, memoirs, and speeches are steeped in both Native American and Anglo-American traditions. Momaday's work gained international attention when he received the Pulitzer Prize for Fiction for his first novel, *House Made at Dawn*, in 1969. In the following excerpt from *The Way to Rainy Mountain*, also published in 1969, he embarks on a journey to rediscover the land and people of his childhood, inviting us to look and listen as the landscape reveals its secrets.

The Way to Rainy Mountain
by N. Scott Momaday

A single knoll rises out of the plain in Oklahoma, north and west of the Wichita Range. For my people, the Kiowas, it is an old landmark, and they gave it the name Rainy Mountain. The hardest winter in the world is there. Winter brings blizzards, hot tornadic winds arise in the spring, and in summer the prairie is an anvil's edge. The grass turns brittle and brown, and it cracks beneath your feet. There are green belts along the rivers and creeks, linear groves of hickory and pecan, willow and witch hazel. At a distance in July or August, the steaming foliage seems almost to writhe in fire. Great green and yellow grasshoppers are everywhere in the tall grass, popping up like corn to sting the flesh, and tortoises crawl about on the red earth, going nowhere in the plenty of time. Loneliness is an aspect of the land. All things in the plain are isolate; there is no confusion of objects in the eye, but *one* hill or *one* tree or *one* man. To look upon that landscape in the early morning, with the sun at your back, is to lose the sense of proportion. Your imagination comes to life, and this, you think, is where Creation was begun.

I returned to Rainy Mountain in July. My grandmother had died in the spring, and I wanted to be at her grave. She had lived to be very old and at last infirm. Her only living daughter was with her when she died, and I was told that in death her face was that of a child.

I like to think of her as a child. When she was born, the Kiowas were living the last great moment of their history. For more than a hundred years they had controlled the open range from the Smoky Hill River to the Red, from the headwaters of the Canadian to the fork of the Arkansas and Cimarron. In alliance with the Comanches, they had ruled the whole of the southern Plains. War was their sacred business, and they were among the finest horsemen the world has ever known. But warfare for the Kiowas was pre-eminently a matter of disposition rather than of survival, and they never understood the grim, unrelenting advance of the U.S. Cavalry. When at last, divided and ill-provisioned, they were driven onto the Staked Plains in the cold rains of autumn, they fell into panic. In Palo Duro Canyon they abandoned their crucial stores to pillage and had nothing then but their lives. In order to save themselves, they surrendered to the soldiers of Fort Sill and were imprisoned in the old stone corral that now stands as a military museum. My grandmother was spared the humiliation of those high gray walls by eight or ten years, but she must have known from birth the affliction of defeat, the dark brooding of old warriors.

Her name was Aho, and she belonged to the last culture to evolve in North America. Her forebears came down from the high country in western Montana nearly three centuries ago. They were a mountain people, a mysterious tribe of hunters whose language has never been positively classified in any major group. In the late seventeenth century they began a long migration to the south and east. It was a journey toward the dawn, and it led to a golden age. Along the way the Kiowas were befriended by the Crows, who gave them the culture and religion of the Plains. They acquired horses, and their ancient nomadic spirit was suddenly free of the ground. They acquired Tai-me, the sacred Sun Dance doll, from that moment the object and symbol of their worship, and so shared in the divinity of the sun. Not least, they acquired the sense of destiny, therefore courage and pride. When they entered upon the southern Plains they had been transformed. No longer were they slaves to the simple necessity of survival; they were a lordly and dangerous society of fighters and thieves, hunters and priests of the sun. According to their origin myth, they entered the world through a hollow log. From one point of view, their migration was the fruit of an old prophecy, for indeed they emerged from a sunless world.

5   Although my grandmother lived out her long life in the shadow of Rainy Mountain, the immense landscape of the continental interior lay like memory in her blood. She could tell of the Crows, whom she had never seen, and of the Black Hills, where she had never been. I wanted to see in reality what she had seen more perfectly in the mind's eye, and traveled fifteen hundred miles to begin my pilgrimage.

Yellowstone, it seemed to me, was the top of the world, a region of deep lakes and dark timber, canyons and waterfalls. But, beautiful as it is, one might have the sense of confinement there. The skyline in all directions is close at hand, the high wall of the woods and deep cleavages of shade. There is a perfect freedom in the mountains, but it belongs to the eagle and the elk, the badger and the bear. The Kiowas reckoned their stature by the distance they could see, and they were bent and blind in the wilderness.

Descending eastward, the highland meadows are a stairway to the plain. In July the inland slope of the Rockies is luxuriant with flax and buckwheat, stonecrop and larkspur. The earth unfolds and the limit of the land recedes. Clusters of trees, and animals grazing far in the distance, cause the vision to reach away and wonder to build upon the mind. The sun follows a longer course in the day, and the sky is immense beyond all comparison. The great billowing clouds that sail upon it are shadows that move upon the grain like water, dividing light. Farther down, in the land of the Crows and Blackfeet, the plain is yellow. Sweet clover takes hold of the hills and bends upon itself to cover and seal the soil. There the Kiowas paused on their way; they had come to the place where they must change their lives. The sun is at home on the plains. Precisely there does it have the certain character of a god. When the Kiowas came to the land of the Crows, they could see the dark lees of the hills at dawn across the Bighorn River, the profusion of light on the grain shelves, the oldest deity ranging after the solstices. Not yet would they veer southward to the caldron of the land that lay below; they must wean their blood from the northern winter and hold the mountains a while longer in their view. They bore Tai-me in procession to the east.

A dark mist lay over the Black Hills, and the land was like iron. At the top of the ridge I caught sight of Devil's Tower upthrust against the gray sky as if in the birth of time the core of the earth had broken through its crust and the motion of the world was begun. There are things in nature that engender an awful quiet in the heart of man; Devil's Tower is one of them. Two centuries ago, because they could not do otherwise, the Kiowas made a legend at the base of the rock. My grandmother said:

Eight children were there at play, seven sisters and their brother. Suddenly the boy was struck dumb; he trembled and began to run upon his hands and feet. His fingers became claws, and his body was covered with fur. Directly there was a bear where the boy had been. The sisters were terrified; they ran, and the bear ran after them. They came to the stump of a great tree, and the tree spoke to them. It bade them climb upon it, and as they did so it began to rise into the air. The bear came to kill them, but they were just beyond its reach. It reared against the tree and scored the bark all around its claws. The seven sisters were borne into the sky, and they became the stars of the Big Dipper. From that moment, and so long as the legend lives, the Kiowas have kinsmen in the night sky. Whatever they were in the mountains, they could be no more. However tenuous their well-being, however much they suffered and would suffer again, they had found a way out of the wilderness.

My grandmother had a reverence for the sun, a holy regard that is all but gone out of mankind. There was a wariness in her, and an ancient awe. She was a Christian in her later years, but she had come a long way about, and she never forgot her

birthright. As a child she had been to the Sun Dances; she had taken part in those annual rites, and by them she had learned the restoration of her people in the presence of Tai-me. She was about seven when the last Kiowa Sun Dance was held in 1887 Washita River above Rainy Mountain Creek. The buffalo were gone. In order to consummate the ancient sacrifice—to impale the head of a buffalo bull upon the medicine tree—a delegation of old men journeyed into Texas, there to beg and barter for an animal from the Goodnight herd. She was ten when the Kiowas came together for the last time as a living Sun Dance culture. They could find no buffalo; they had to hang an old hide from the sacred tree. Before the dance could begin, a company of soldiers rode out from Fort Sill under orders to disperse the tribe. Forbidden without cause the essential act of their faith, having seen the herds slaughtered and left to rot upon the ground, the Kiowas backed away forever from the medicine tree. That was July 20, 1890, at the bend of the Washita. My grandmother was there. Without bitterness for as long as she lived, she bore a vision of deicide.

10   Now that I can have her only in memory, I see my grandmother in the several postures that were peculiar to her: standing at the wood stove on a winter morning and turning meat in a great iron skillet; sitting at the south window, bent above her beadwork, and afterwards, when her vision failed, looking down for a long time into the fold of her hands out upon a cane, very slowly as she did when the weight of ages came upon her; praying. I remember her most often at prayer. She made long, rambling prayers out of suffering and hope, having seen many things. I was never sure that I had the right to hear, so exclusive were they of mere custom and company. The last time I saw her she prayed standing by the side of her bed at night, naked to the waist, the light of a kerosene lamp moving upon her dark skin. Her long, black hair, always drawn and braided in the day, lay upon her shoulders and against her breast shawl. I do not speak Kiowa, and I never

understood her prayers, but there was something inherently sad in the sound, some merest hesitation upon the syllables of sorrow. She began in a high and descending pitch, exhausting her breath to silence; then again and again—and always the same intensity of effort, of something that is, and is not, like urgency in the human voice. Transported so in the dancing light among the shadows of her room, she seemed beyond the reach of time. But that was illusion; I think I knew then that I should not see her again.

Houses are like sentinels in the plain, old keepers of the weather watch. There, in a very little while, wood takes on the appearance of great age. All colors wear soon away in the wind and rain, and then the wood is burned gray and the grain appears and the nails turn red with rust. The windowpanes are black and opaque; you imagine there is nothing within, and indeed there are many ghosts, bones given up to the land. They stand here and there against the sky, and you approach them for a longer time than you expect. They belong in the distance; it is their domain.

Once there was a lot of sound in my grandmother's house, a lot of coming and going, feasting and talk. The summers there were full of excitement and reunion. The Kiowas are a summer people; they abide the cold and keep to themselves, but when the season turns and the land becomes warm and vital they cannot hold still; an old love of going returns upon them. The aged visitors who came to my grandmother's house when I was a child were made of lean and leather, and they bore themselves upright. They wore great black hats and bright ample shirts that shook in the wind. They rubbed fat upon their hair and wound their braids with strips of colored cloth. Some of them painted their faces and carried the scars of old and cherished enmities. They were an old council of warlords, come to remind and be reminded of who they were. Their wives and daughters served them well. The women might indulge themselves; gossip was at once the mark and compensation of their servitude. They made loud and elaborate talk among themselves, full of jest and gesture, fright and false alarm. They went abroad in fringed and flowered shawls, bright beadwork and German silver. They were at home in the kitchen, and they prepared meals that were banquets.

There were frequent prayer meetings, and great nocturnal feasts. When I was a child I played with my cousins outside, where the lamplight fell upon the ground and the singing of the old people rose up around us and carried away into the darkness. There were a lot of good things to eat, a lot of laughter and surprise. And afterwards, when the quiet returned, I lay down with my grandmother and could hear the frogs away by the river and feel the motion of the air.

Now there is a funeral silence in the rooms, the endless wake of some final word. The walls have closed in upon my grandmother's house. When I returned to it in mourning, I saw for the first time in my life how small it was. It was late at night, and there was a white moon, nearly full. I sat for a long time on the stone steps by the kitchen door. From there I could see out across the land; I could see the long row of trees by the creek, the low light upon the rolling plains, and the stars of the Big Dipper. Once I looked at the moon and caught sight of a strange thing. A cricket had perched upon the handrail, only a few inches away from me. My line of vision was such that the creature filled the moon like a fossil. It had gone there, I thought, to live and die, for there, of all places, was its small definition made whole and eternal. A warm wind rose purled like the longing within me.

15   The next morning I awoke at dawn and went out on the dirt road to Rainy Mountain. It was already hot, and the grasshoppers began to fill the air. Still, it was early in the morning, and the birds sang out of the shadows. The long yellow grass on the mountain shone in the light, and a scissortail hied above the land. There, where it ought to be, at the end of a long and legendary way, was my grandmother's grave. Here and there on the dark stones were ancestral names. Looking back once, I saw the mountain and came away.

1. In one of his poems, N. Scott Momaday writes, "Once in his life a man ought to concentrate his mind upon the remembered earth." Where in this excerpt does he focus your attention on the land? In what sense is it a "remembered earth"? Whose memory is being revived?

2. Compare the landscape of Rainy Mountain to the place where you grew up. What are the chief landmarks and characteristics of the Oklahoma plain? What colors, creatures, vegetation, and surface features predominate?

3. In paragraph 8, Momaday quotes the Kiowa legend of Devil's Tower told by his grandmother. Does this seem like an appropriate story for children? What does Momaday believe this legend meant for the Kiowa people?

4. How does Momaday describe his grandmother? What is her special relationship to Rainy Mountain? What does she represent for Momaday? Does she remind you of anyone in your own life?

GUIDELINES FOR ANALYSIS

1. Momaday has said that he pays close attention to tone. "I think that the voice of my writing is very much like the voice of my speaking. And I think in both cases it's distinctive." How would you describe this voice? What makes it distinctive? What kind of person do you imagine when you read his words?

2. How is this selection organized? Does it have a clear beginning, middle, and end? Is there a traditional thesis statement? Why do you think Momaday arranges his writing in this way?

3. Momaday likes to give the names of specific locations, animals, trees, and plants. Is this a good technique for describing his surroundings? Where are these names particularly effective or ineffective?

4. Momaday uses a great many comparisons in his description. The summer prairie is "an anvil's edge." The foliage seems to "writhe in fire." Find other examples of metaphors and analogies in the selection. What is the effect of comparing one thing to another in each case?

5. Nearly every paragraph in this excerpt begins and ends deliberately. Notice how much care the writer gives to introducing and clinching the topic of each paragraph. How much of the excerpt would you be able to understand just by reading these opening and closing sentences? What would you miss?

QUESTIONS OF CULTURE

1. What do you learn about the history of the Kiowas from Momaday's essay? Where did they come from, and why did they leave to come to Rainy Mountain? How is this history reflected in their myths, legends, and Momaday's images of his grandmother?

2. How does Momaday characterize the Kiowa people? How does his depiction compare to your own idea of Native Americans? Momaday was educated in prestigious universities and does not speak the Kiowa language. Do these facts make his portrayal less reliable?

1. Do all families have their Rainy Mountain? Identify a place that has special meaning for your family. What landmarks, place names, plants, animals, and sounds do you associate with this site? Try to include the distinctive voices, songs, stories, and dialects in your journal.

2. Visit a historical site, a place that bears the imprint of the past. Get in touch with the place and its memories. Explore it from different angles. Take stock of its colors, shapes, and shades. Close your eyes and take in all the sounds. Use your hands. Taste the air. And write what you find.

3. Did you grow up with stories like the legend of Devil's Tower? Try to remember one, and retell it in words that come as close as possible to the original storyteller's voice.

PREVIEW

Linda Hogan's Native American lineage (her father was a member of the Chickasaw nation) is embedded in her writing. She takes a holistic view of the environment, based on the belief that all life—human, plant, and animal—is interconnected. Through observation, meditation, and a return to the tribal wisdom of her ancestors, she has fashioned a strong and resonant voice for healing the earth.

Born in 1947 in Colorado, Hogan moved with her family many times. While working with children in her twenties, she discovered the expressive power of writing and reading during lunch breaks. Her discovery led to college, teaching, and a prolific writing career. She has published novels, plays, essays, and many volumes of award-winning poetry. The following essay is taken from *Dwellings: A Spiritual History of the Living World,* published in 1995.

Dwellings
by Linda Hogan

Not far from where I live is a hill that was cut into by the moving water of a creek. Eroded this way, all that's left of it is a broken wall of earth that contains old roots and pebbles woven together and exposed. Seen from a distance, it is only a rise of raw earth. But up close it is something wonderful, a small cliff dwelling that looks almost as intricate and well made as those the Anasazi left behind when they vanished mysteriously centuries ago. This hill is a place that could be the starry skies at night turned inward into the thousand round holes where solitary bees have lived and died. It is a hill of tunneling rooms. At the mouths of some of the excavations, half-circles of clay beetle out like awnings shading a doorway. It is earth that was turned to clay in the mouths of the bees and spit out as they mined deeper into their dwelling places.

This place is where the bees reside at an angle safe from rain. It faces the southern sun. It is a warm and intelligent architecture of memory, learned by whatever memory lives in the blood. Many of the holes still contain gold husks of dead bees, their faces dry and gone, their flat eyes gazing out from death's land toward the other uninhabited half of the hill that is across the creek from the catacombs.

The first time I found the residence of the bees, it was dusty summer. The sun was hot, and land was the dry color of rust. Now and then a car rumbled along; the dirt road and dust rose up behind it before settling back down on older dust. In the silence, the bees made a soft droning hum. They were alive then, and working the hill, going out and returning with pollen, in and out through the holes, back and forth between daylight and the cooler, darker regions of the inner earth. They were flying an invisible map through air, a map charted by landmarks, the slant of light, and a circling story they told one another about the direction of food held inside the center of yellow flowers.

Sitting in the hot sun, watching the small bees fly in and out around the hill, hearing the summer birds, the light breeze, I felt right in the world. I belonged there. I thought of my own dwelling places, those real and those imagined. Once I lived in a town called Manitou, which means "Great Spirit," and where hot mineral springwater gurgled beneath the streets and rose into open wells. I felt safe there. With the underground movement of water and heat a constant reminder of other life, of what lives beneath us, it seemed to be the center of the world.

5 A few years after that, I wanted silence. My daydreams were full of places I longed to be, shelters and solitudes. I wanted a room apart from others, a hidden cabin to rest in. I wanted to be in a redwood forest with trees so tall the owls called out in the daytime. I daydreamed of living in a vapor cave a few hours away from here. Underground, warm, and moist, I thought it would be the perfect world for staying out of cold winter, for escaping the noise of living.

And how often I've wanted to escape to a wilderness where a human hand has not been in everything. But those were only dreams of peace, of comfort, of a nest inside stone or woods, a sanctuary where a dream or life wouldn't be invaded.

Years ago, in the next canyon west of here, there was a man who followed one of those dreams and moved into a cave that could only be reached by climbing down a rope. For years he lived there in comfort, like a troglodite. The inner weather was stable, never too hot, too cold, too wet, or too dry. But then he felt lonely. His utopia needed a woman. He went to town until he found a wife. For a while after the marriage, his wife climbed down the rope along with him, but before long she didn't want the mice scurrying about in the cave, or the untidy bats that wanted to hang from the stones of the ceiling. So they built a door. Because of the closed entryway, the temperature changed. They had to put in heat. Then the inner moisture of earth warped the door, so they had to have air conditioning, and after that the earth wanted to go about life in its own way and it didn't give in to the people.

In other days and places, people paid more attention to the strong-headed will of earth. Once homes were built of wood that had been felled from a single region in a forest. That way, it was thought, the house would hold together more harmoniously, and the family of walls would not fall or lend themselves to the unhappiness or arguments of the inhabitants.

An Italian immigrant to Chicago, Aldo Piacenzi, built birdhouses that were dwellings of harmony and peace. They were the incredible spired shapes of cathedrals in Italy. They housed not only the birds, but also his memories, his own past. He painted them the watery blue of his Mediterranean, the wild rose of flowers in a summer field. Inside them was straw and the droppings of lives that layed eggs, fledglings who grew there. What places to inhabit, the bright and sunny birdhouses in dreary alleyways of the city.

10　　One beautiful afternoon, cool and moist, with the kind of yellow light that falls on earth in these arid regions, I waited for barn swallows to return from their daily work of food gathering. Inside the tunnel where they live, hundreds of swallows had mixed their saliva with mud and clay, much like the solitary bees, and formed nests that were perfect as a potter's bowl. At five in the evening, they returned all at once, a dark, flying shadow. Despite their enormous numbers and the crowding together of nests, they didn't pause for even a moment before entering the nests, nor did they crowd one another. Instantly they vanished into the nests. The tunnel went silent. It held no outward signs of life.

But I knew they were there, filled with the fire of living. And what a marriage of elements was in those nests. Not only mud's earth and water, the fire of sun and dry air, but even the elements contained one another. The bodies of prophets and crazy men were broken down in that soil.

I've noticed often how when a house is abandoned, it begins to sag. Without a tenant, it has no need to go on. If it were a person, we'd say it is depressed or lonely. The roof settles in, the paint cracks, the walls and floorboards warp and slope downward in their own natural ways, telling us that life must stay in everything as the world whirls and tilts and moves through boundless space.

One summer day, cleaning up after long-eared owls where I work at a rehabilitation facility for birds of prey, I was raking the gravel floor of a flight cage. Down on the ground, something looked like it was moving. I bent over to look into the pile of bones and pellets I'd just raked together. There, close to the ground, were two fetal mice. They were new to the planet, pink and hairless. They were so tenderly young. Their faces had swollen blue-veined eyes. They were nestled in a mound of feathers, soft as velvet, each one curled up smaller than an infant's ear, listening to the first sounds of earth. But the ants were biting them. They turned in agony, unable to pull away, not yet having the arms or legs to move, but feeling, twisting away from, the pain of the bites. I was horrified to see them bitten out of life that way. I dipped them in water, as if to take away the sting, and let the ants fall in the bucket. Then I held the tiny mice in the palm of my hand. Some of the ants were drowning in the water. I was trading one life for another, exchanging the lives of the ants for those of mice, but I hated their suffering, and hated even more that they had not yet grown to a life, and already they inhabited the miserable world of pain. Death and life feed each other. I know that.

Inside these rooms where birds are healed, there are other lives besides those of mice. There are fine gray globes the wasps have woven together, the white cocoons of spiders in a corner, the downward tunneling anthills. All these dwellings are inside one small walled space, but I think most about the mice. Sometimes the downy nests fall out of the walls where their mothers have placed them out of the way of their enemies. When one of the nests falls, they are so well made and soft, woven mostly from the chest feathers of birds. Sometimes the leg of a small quail holds the nest together like a slender cornerstone with dry, bent claws. The mice have adapted to life in the presence of their enemies, adapted to living in the thin wall between beak and beak, claw and claw. They move their nests often, as if a new rafter or wall will protect them from the inevitable fate of all our returns home to the deeper, wider nests of earth that houses us all.

15   One August at Zia Pueblo during the corn dance I noticed tourists picking up shards of all the old pottery that had been made and broken there. The residents of Zia know not to take the bowls and pots left behind by the older ones. They know that the fragments of those earlier lives need to be smoothed back to earth, but younger nations, travelers from continents across the world who have come to inhabit this land, have little of their own to grow on. The pieces of earth that were formed into bowls, even on their way home to dust, provide the new people a lifeline to an unknown land, help them remember that they live in the old nest of earth.

It was in early February, during the mating season of the great horned owl. It was dusk, and I hiked up the back of a mountain to where I'd heard the owls a year before. I wanted to hear them again, the voices so tender, so deep, like a memory of comfort. I was halfway up the trail when I found a soft, round nest. It had fallen from one of the bare-branched trees. It was a delicate nest, woven together of feathers, sage, and strands of wild grass. Holding it in my hand in the rosy twilight, I noticed that a blue thread was entwined with the other gatherings there. I pulled at the thread a little, and then I recognized it. It was a thread from one of my skirts. It was blue cotton. It was the unmistakable color and shape of a pattern I knew. I liked it, that a thread of my life was in an abandoned nest, one that had held eggs and new life. I took the nest home. At home, I held it to the light and looked more closely. There, to my surprise, nestled

into the gray-green sage, was a gnarl of black hair. It was also unmistakable. It was my daughter's hair, cleaned from a brush and picked up out in the sun beneath the maple tree, or the pit cherry where the birds eat from the overladen, fertile branches until only the seeds remain on the trees.

I didn't know what kind of nest it was, or who had lived there. It didn't matter. I thought of the remnants of our lives carried up the hill that way and turned into shelter. That night, resting inside the walls of our home, the world outside weighed so heavily against the thin wood of the house. The sloped roof was the only thing between us and the universe. Everything outside of our wooden boundaries seemed so large. Filled with the night's citizens, it all came alive. The world opened in the thickets of the dark. The wild grapes would soon ripen on the vines. The burrowing ones were emerging. Horned owls sat in treetops. Mice scurried here and there. Skunks, fox, the slow and holy porcupine, all were passing by this way. The young of the solitary bees were feeding on the pollen in the dark. The whole world was a nest on its humble tilt, in the maze of the universe, holding us.

RESPONSE QUESTIONS

1. Hogan (whose name in Navajo refers to a house made of earth and timber) uses the word "dwelling" many times. How is a dwelling different from a house, residence, abode, or habitat? What does her choice of terms imply about her subject; what are its connotations?

2. In her first paragraph, Hogan describes something that looks unremarkable from a distance, but "up close it is something wonderful." What makes this thing so special? Where else does she give us close-ups of the environment?

3. The author compares the dwelling place of bees to the cliff dwellings of the Anasazi people and her former home in Manitou. Elsewhere, she compares a barn swallow's nest to a potter's bowl and the mud-and-saliva constructions of the bees. What other things does she compare? What do such comparisons suggest to you?

4. At the end of paragraph 11, Hogan writes, "The bodies of prophets and crazy men were broken down in that soil." Does she mean this literally or figuratively? What do the bodies of men have to do with the mud in a bird's nest? What "marriage of elements" is she referring to? Relate this idea to the paragraph in which she describes her daughter's hair in an abandoned nest.

5. Hogan shares her dreams and her past as well as her direct observations. How well do you come to know her after reading the essay? What can you say about her view of dwellings, of human beings and the environment, of life and death? What seem to be the guiding principles of her beliefs?

GUIDELINES FOR ANALYSIS

1. The essay is not a straightforward narrative. It weaves back and forth in time, zooms in for close-ups and out again for long views of the universe. What other essays are you reminded of? How does this form of composition affect your reading? Why do you think Hogan writes this way?

2. Look closely at the paragraph in which the author describes an abandoned house (paragraph 12). Notice the way she develops the analogy to a human being. What fresh insights does the analogy give you about houses and people?

3. Select a descriptive passage from the essay and imagine how a scientist might describe the same scene. How is Hogan's use of language different from a scientist's description?

4. Does it surprise you to know that Linda Hogan has written several books of poetry? In what ways does her writing here reflect the style and sensibility of a poet?

QUESTIONS OF CULTURE

1. Reread the story of the cave man and the woman (paragraph 7). Does the story have a moral? What does it say about the needs of men and women and the needs of the earth? What other stories do you know that either confirm or contradict this view of male and female attitudes?

2. How does Hogan characterize the tourists who visit the Zia Pueblo for the corn dance? What do the residents of Zia know that the visitors do not? What judgments, if any, do you find behind this anecdote?

3. Compare "Dwellings" to "The Way to Rainy Mountain." Linda Hogan and N. Scott Momaday are both descendants of Native Americans. How is this fact reflected in their writing?

IDEAS FOR YOUR JOURNAL

1. Give some thought to the idea of dwellings. What kinds of dwellings have you lived in? Have any of them reminded you of an animal's habitat? If so, what points of resemblance do you see?

2. Linda Hogan's descriptions of the environment are also meditations on the place of human beings in the natural world. Use a double-entry format in your journal to capture these two kinds of writing. Use one side for your close-up descriptions of what you see, smell, hear, touch, and taste. Use the other side for reflections: step back from the sensory details and consider what they mean to you.

PREVIEW

Sometimes a single object can represent a whole environment. In the prologue to her 1993 memoir, *When I Was Puerto Rican,* Esmeralda Santiago writes about guavas. She has picked one while shopping in a supermarket in the United States. As she holds it to her nose, she is reminded of the guavas of her childhood in Puerto Rico. Her description of the fruit in her hand and the guavas she remembers helps to define two important times and places in her life.

Esmeralda Santiago left Puerto Rico at the age of thirteen and arrived in New York with her single mother and eleven younger siblings. Despite the pressures of her family's poverty, she stayed in school, attending Manhattan Community College and eventually earning degrees from Harvard and Sarah Lawrence. Santiago is also the author of a novel, *America's Dream* (1997), and two other memoirs, *Almost a Woman* (1998) and *The Turkish Lover* (2004). An award-winning film adaptation of *Almost a Woman* was produced for PBS's *Masterpiece Theatre* in 2002.

How to Eat a Guava
by Esmeralda Santiago

Barco que no anda, no llega a puerto.

***

A ship that doesn't sail, never reaches port.

There are guavas at the Shop & Save. I pick one the size of a tennis ball and finger the prickly stem end. It feels familiarly bumpy and firm. The guava is not quite ripe; the skin is still a dark green. I smell it and imagine a pale pink center, the seeds tightly embedded in the flesh.

A ripe guava is yellow, although some varieties have a pink tinge. The skin is thick, firm, and sweet. Its heart is bright pink and almost solid with seeds. The most delicious part of the guava surrounds the tiny seeds. If you don't know how to eat a guava, the seeds end up in the crevices between your teeth.

When you bite into a ripe guava, your teeth must grip the bumpy surface and sink into the thick edible skin without hitting the center. It takes experience to do this, as it's quite tricky to determine how far beyond the skin the seeds begin.

Some years, when the rains have been plentiful and the nights cool, you can bite into a guava and not find many seeds. The guava bushes grow close to the ground, their branches laden with green then yellow fruit that seem to ripen overnight. These guavas are large and juicy, almost seedless, their round-ness enticing you to have one more, just one more, because next year the rains may not come.

5   As children, we didn't always wait for the fruit to ripen. We raided the bushes as soon as the guavas were large enough to bend the branch.

A green guava is sour and hard. You bite into it at its widest point, because it's easier to grasp with your teeth. You hear the skin, meat, and seeds crunching inside your head, while the inside of your mouth explodes in little spurts of sour.

You grimace, your eyes water, and your cheeks disappear as your lips purse into a tight O. But you have another and then another, enjoying the crunchy sounds, the acid taste, the gritty texture of the unripe center. At night, your mother makes you drink castor oil, which she says tastes better than a green guava. That's when you know for sure that you're a child and she has stopped being one.

I had my last guava the day we left Puerto Rico. It was large and juicy, almost red in the center, and so fragrant that I didn't want to eat it because I would lose the smell. All the way to the airport I scratched at it with my teeth, making little dents in the skin, chewing small pieces with my front teeth, so that I could feel the texture against my tongue, the tiny pink pellets of sweet.

Today, I stand before a stack of dark green guavas, each perfectly round and hard, each $1.59. The one in my hand is tempting. It smells faintly of late summer afternoons and hopscotch under the mango tree. But this is autumn in New York, and I'm no longer a child.

10   The guava joins its sisters under the harsh fluorescent lights of the exotic fruit display. I push my cart away, toward apples and pears of my adulthood, their nearly seedless ripeness predictable and bit-tersweet.

RESPONSE QUESTIONS

1. Which parts of Santiago's description give you the strongest sense of what guavas are like? If you are familiar with guavas, what would you add to make her description more complete?

2. Why do you think the author chooses guavas to begin her memoir? What contrasts is she making between Puerto Rico and New York?

3. Paragraph 7 ends with an observation about Santiago's mother: "That's when you know for sure that you're a child and she has stopped being one." What do you think she means by this?

4. At the end of the essay, Santiago pushes her cart away from the exotic fruit display and steers toward the apples and pears. What do you make of this gesture?

GUIDELINES FOR ANALYSIS

1. Make a list of the five senses and jot down descriptions from the essay that appeal to each. Which senses seem to be most active in Santiago's impressions of the guava?

2. Santiago describes a process as well as an object. What suggestions does she give for eating a guava? What does she say should be avoided?

3. What is the effect of shifting from first person ("I") to second person ("you") and back again? Is it a good idea to change the reader's point of view like this?

4. Santiago uses short paragraphs and simple words. How would you describe the tone set by her language? What purpose might be served by this tone?

QUESTIONS OF CULTURE

1. The guava might be called a cultural icon because it embodies so much of the people and traditions of Puerto Rico. What does it seem to represent about Santiago's homeland? What cultural icons can you think of that might stand for your cultural heritage?

2. Compare "How to Eat a Guava" to Mark Twain's "Two Views of the Mississippi" (page 151). How does each writer use description to evoke a place, a culture, and a remembered past?

IDEAS FOR YOUR JOURNAL

1. For Santiago, the scent of guavas stirs up memories of "later summer afternoons and hopscotch under the mango tree." Describe a fruit, candy, or other food that holds special memories for you of another time and place.

2. Santiago begins her description of the guava with a quotation in Spanish, translated into English. Why do you think she has chosen this passage? Use your journal to collect quotations that say something important about you.

PREVIEW

Diane Ackerman uses writing to "return to the textures of life." For her, language is not just a tool for describing sense experience but also a way to experience the natural world with heightened sensitivity. Readers of her book *A Natural History of the Senses* often say that the world seems a more vibrant place after spending time with her chapters on smell, touch, taste, hearing, vision, and synesthesia. Ackerman's deep interests in both nature and human nature lead her to explore her subjects from artistic and scientific points of view, refining her appreciation through close personal encounters and deepening her knowledge through meticulous research. As a result, her essays are difficult to classify, an original fusion of journalism, science, poetry, history, mythology, and environmental awareness.

Diane Ackerman was born in 1948 in Waukegan, Illinois. Even as a child, she liked to write, starting a spy novel at the age of twelve, then switching to a story about a girl and a horse she loved. She kept journals and wrote poems. After graduating from Pennsylvania State University, she earned degrees from Cornell University, settling in Ithaca, New York with her husband, Paul West, a fiction writer. Her doctoral committee at Cornell included a poet and a scientist, the renowned astronomer Carl Sagan, reflecting the unusual cross-disciplinary breadth of her work. Ackerman has written more than twenty books of essays, poems, and memoirs, including *Deep Play, A Slender Thread, The Rarest of the Rare, A Natural History of Love, The Moon by Whale Light,* and *On Extended Wings.* The following excerpt is from *A Natural History of the Senses,* published in 1990.

How to Watch the Sky
by Diane Ackerman

I am sitting at the edge of the continent, at Point Reyes National Seashore, the peninsula north of San Francisco, where the land gives way to the thrall of the Pacific and the arching blue conundrum of the sky. When cricket-whine, loud as a buzz saw, abruptly quits, only bird calls map the quiet codes of daylight. A hawk leans into nothingness, peeling a layer of flight from thin air. At first it flaps hard to gain a little altitude, then finds a warm updraft and cups the air with its wings, spiraling up in tight circles as it eyes the ground below for rodents or rabbits. Banking a little wider, it turns slowly, a twirling parasol. The hawk knows instinctively that it will not fall. The sky is the one visual constant in all our lives, a complex backdrop to our every venture, thought, and emotion. Yet we tend to think of it as invisible—an absence, not a substance. Though we move the air's glassy fathoms; we rarely picture it as the thick heavy arena it is. We rarely wonder about the blue phantasm we call the sky: "*Skeu,*" I say out loud, the word that our ancient ancestors used; I try to utter it as they might have, with fear and wonder: "*Skeu.*" Actually, it was their word for a covering of any sort. To them, the sky was a roof of changing colors. Small wonder they billeted their gods there, like so many quarrelsome neighbors who, in fits of temper, hurled lightning bolts instead of crockery.

Look at your feet. You are standing in the sky. When we think of the sky, we tend to look up, but the sky actually begins at the earth. We walk through it, yell into it, rake leaves, wash the dog, and drive cars in it. We breathe it deep within us. With every breath, we inhale millions of molecules of sky, heat them briefly, and then exhale them back into the world. At this moment, you are breathing some of the same molecules once breathed by Leonardo da Vinci, William Shakespeare, Anne Bradstreet, or Colette. Inhale deeply. Think of *The Tempest.* Air works the bellows of our lungs, and it powers our cells. We say "light as air," but there is nothing lightweight about our atmosphere, which weighs 5,000 trillion tons. Only a clench as stubborn as gravity's could hold it to the earth; otherwise it would simply float away and seep into the cornerless expanse of space.

Without thinking, we often speak of "an empty sky." But the sky is never empty. In a mere ounce of air, there are 1,000 billion trillion gyrating atoms made up of oxygen, nitrogen, and hydrogen, each a menagerie of electrons, quarks, and ghostly neutrinos. Sometimes we marvel at how "calm" the day is, or how "still" the night. Yet there is no stillness in the sky, or anywhere else where life and matter meet. The air is always vibrant and aglow, full of volatile gases, staggering spores, dust, viruses, fungi, and animals, all stirred by a skirling and relentless wind. There are active flyers like butterflies, birds, bats, and insects, who ply the air roads; and there are passive flyers like autumn leaves, pollen, or milkweed pods, which just float. Beginning at the earth and stretching up in all directions, the sky is the thick, twitching realm in which we jive. When we say that our distant ancestors crawled out onto the land, we forget to add that they really moved from one ocean to another, from the upper fathoms of water to the deepest fathoms of air.

The prevailing winds here are from the west, as I can see from the weird and wonderful shapes of the vegetation along the beach. A light steady breeze blowing off the Pacific has swept back the wild grasses into a sort of pompadour. A little farther back, in a more protected glade, I find a small clump of them, around which a circle runs in the dirt. It looks as if someone pressed a cookie cutter down in the ground, but the wind alone has done it, blowing the grass around and turning it into a natural protractor. We think of the wind as a destructive force—a sudden funnel that pops a roof off a schoolhouse in Oklahoma—but the wind is also a gradual and powerful mason that carves cliffs, erodes hillsides, re-creates beaches, moves trees and rocks down mountains or across rivers. Wind creates waves, as in the sensuously rippling dunes of Death Valley or along the changing shorelines. The wind hauls away the topsoil as if it were nothing more than a dingy tablecloth on the checkerboard fields of the Midwest, creating a "dust bowl." It can power generators, gliders, windmills, kites, sailboats. It sows seeds and pollen. It sculpts the landscape. Along rugged coasts, one often sees trees dramatically carved by the relentless wind.

5   The north wind is shown on ancient maps as a plump-cheeked man with tousled hair and a strained expression, blowing as hard as he can. According to Homer, the god Aeolus lived in a palatial cave, where he kept the winds tied up in a leather bag. He gave the bag to Odysseus to power his ship, but when Odysseus's comrades opened the bag the winds raced free throughout the world, squabbling and whirling and generally wreaking havoc. "The children of morning," Hesiod called the Greek winds. To the ancient Chinese, *fung* meant both wind and breath, and there were many words for the wind's temperaments. *Tiu* meant "to move with the wind like a tree." *Yao* was the word for when something floated on the breeze like down. The names of winds are magical, and tell a lot about the many moods the sky can take. There's Portugal's hillside *vento coado;* Japan's demonic *tsumuji,* or soft pine-grove-loving *matsukaze;* Australia's balmy *brickfielder* (which first described dust storms blowing off brickyards near Sydney); America's moist warm *chinook* drifting in from the sea, and named after the language of Indians who settled Oregon; or snow-clotted *blizzard* or fierce *Santa Ana,* or Hawaii's humid *waimea;* North Africa's hot, sand-laden desert *simoom* (from the Aramaic word *samma,* "poison"); Argentina's baking, depleting *zonda,* which pours down

from the Andes to sweep the pampas; the Nile's dark, gloomy *haboob;* Russia's gale-force *buran,* bringing a storm in the summer or a blizzard in the winter; Greece's refreshing summer *etesian;* Switzerland's warm, gusty *foehn* blowing off the leeward slopes of a mountain; France's dry cold *mistral* ("master wind") squalling through the Rhone Valley and down to the Mediterranean coast; India's notorious *monsoon,* whose very name means a whole season of monsoons; the Cape of Good Hope's *bull's-eye squall;* Alaska's petulent *williwaw;* Gibraltar's easterly-blowing *datoo;* Spain's mellifluous *solano;* the Caribbean's *hurricane* (derived from the Taino word *huracan,* which means "evil spirit"); Sweden's gale-level *frisk vind;* China's whispering *I tien tien fung,* or first autumn breeze, the *sz.*

Storms have been fretting the coast here for days, and now thick gray clouds stagger across this sky. I watch mashed-potato heaps of cumulus (a word that means "pile") and broad bands of stratus (which means "stretched out"). As author James Trefil once observed, a cloud is a sort of floating lake. When rising warm air collides with descending cold air, the water falls, as it does now. I take shelter on a porch, while a real toad-strangler starts, a full-blooded, hell-for-leather thunderstorm, during which the sky crackles and throbs. Lightning appears to plunge out of it, a pitchfork stabbing into the ground. In fact, it sends down a short electrical scout first, and the earth replies by arcing a long bolt up toward the sky, heating the air so fast that it explodes into a shock wave, or *thunder*, as we call it. Counting the seconds between a lightning flash and the thunder, I then divide by five, and get a rough idea of how far away it is—seven miles. In one second, sound travels 1,100 feet. If the lightning flash and the thunder arrive at the same time, one doesn't have much of a chance to count. In a little while the storm quiets, as the thunder bumpers roll farther up the coast. But some clouds still stalk the sky. A cloud rhinoceros metamorphoses into a profile of Eleanor Roosevelt; then a bowl of pumpkins; then a tongue-wagging dragon. Parading hugely across the sky, clouds like these have squatted above people of all times and countries. How many vacant afternoons people have passed watching the clouds drift by. The ancient Chinese amused themselves by finding shapes in the clouds just as Inuits, Bantus, and Pittsburghers do now. Sailors, generals, farmers, ranchers, and others have always consulted the crystal ball of the sky to foretell the weather (lens-shaped clouds—severe winds aloft; dappled or "mackerel" sky—rain is near; low, thick, dark, blanketlike clouds—a stormy cold front may be coming), devising jingles, maxims, and elaborate cloud charts and atlases, graphics as beautiful as they are useful. On a train through Siberia, Laurens van der Post looked out the window at the huge expanse of flat country and endless sky. "I thought I had never been to any place with so much sky and space around it," he writes in *Journey into Russia,* and was especially startled by "the immense thunder clouds moving out of the dark towards the sleeping city resembling, in the spasmodic lightning, fabulous swans beating towards us on hissing wings of fire." As van der Post watched the lightning from the train, the Russian friend accompanying him explained that they had a special word in his language for just that scene: *Zarnitsa.*

Throughout time and place, people have been obsessed with the many moods of the sky. Not just because their crops and journeys depended on the weather, but because the sky is such a powerful symbol. The sky that gods inhabit, the sky whose permanence we depend on and take for granted, as if it really were a solid, vaulted ceiling on which stars were painted, as our ancestors thought. The sky that can fall in nursery rhymes. In the nuclear disarmament marches of the sixties, some people wore signs that read: CHICKEN LITTLE WAS RIGHT. We picture the sky as the final resting place of those we love, as if their souls were perfumed aerosol. We bury them among pine needles and worms, but in our imaginations we give them a lighter-than-air journey into some recess of the sky from which they will watch over us. "High" is where lofty sentiments dwell, where the "high and mighty" live, where choirs of angels sing. I don't know why the sky symbolizes our finest ideals and motives, unless, lacking in self-confidence, we think our acts of mercy, generosity, and heroism are not intrinsic qualities, not characteristics human beings alone can muster, but temporary gifts from some otherworldly power situated in the sky. Stymied by events, or appalled by human nature, we sometimes roll our eyes upward, to where we believe our fate is dished out in the mansions of the stars.

RESPONSE QUESTIONS

1. Ackerman points out that we generally think of the sky as "an absence, not a substance." What does she mean by this? What evidence does she offer to disprove the notion of an empty sky? How convincing do you find her argument?

2. Throughout her writing, Ackerman uses unusual words or familiar words in unusual ways. In her first two sentences, she speaks of "the *thrall* of the Pacific," "the arching blue *conundrum* of the sky," and "the quiet *codes* of daylight." What other examples can you find? How do you respond to such language? Are you confused or curious? Are you moved to look up new words or skip over them? Compare your classmates' responses to your own.

3. Ackerman likes thought-provoking statements. "Look at your feet. You are standing in the sky" (paragraph 2). "But the sky is never empty" (paragraph 3). "A cloud is a sort of floating lake" (paragraph 6). Find a statement that you like, and explain what it means to you. Ackerman is often quoted in books and on the Internet. Make a list of sentences you might include on a Web site of provocative quotes.

4. "How to Watch the Sky" draws material from a variety of sources, including science, literature, mythology, etymology (the origins of words), geography, and personal observation. Which kinds of information interest you most? What are the most valuable insights or information that you get from the essay?

GUIDELINES FOR ANALYSIS

1. Ackerman says, "There is no way in which to understand the world without first detecting it through the radar-net of our senses." Where in the essay are her sense impressions of the sky described most clearly? What does she add to these impressions to make them fit together, to give us more than an array of random blips on a radar screen?

2. Paragraph 1 offers a motion picture of a hawk in flight. How does Ackerman convey the sensations of movement with her words? Compare this passage with other extended descriptions, like the thunderstorm in paragraph 6.

3. At the beginning of the essay, the author situates herself in a particular time and place. Where is she? Where does she go from here? What are the advantages of shifting her location in this way? What are the possible risks of this composing strategy?

QUESTIONS OF CULTURE

1. The fifth paragraph is a catalog of names for winds in different countries. How many of these winds do you know from personal experience? What do the names suggest about each culture's view of the sky?

2. Where else in the essay do you find cultural beliefs expressed through language, myth, or religion? How do you explain the differences and similarities?

3. How does your own location—city or countryside, mountain or desert, Northwest or Southeast—influence your attitudes and those around you about the sky?

IDEAS FOR YOUR JOURNAL

1. Does some aspect of nature interest you the way the sky interests Diane Ackerman? What do you know or want to know about ponds, salt marshes, the prairie, bamboo forests, or the ocean? Create a catalog of your current knowledge, drawing from as many different areas as

possible: memories, history, environmental science, mythology, literature, geography, and so on. Make a list of areas for possible research.

2. Get a copy of Ackerman's book, *A Natural History of the Senses*, and skim through it. Use your journal to jot down memorable quotes or ideas for your own personal history of the senses.

A STUDENT WRITER IN ACTION

Preview

Lisa Wess describes herself as "an aspiring poet, writer, and teacher with an intense love for all languages." After living for six years in Canberra, Australia, she recently moved back to the United States, which she says will always be her home. When not traveling, camping, or attending college classes, she works diligently on her Web site, where she showcases her writing and photography. When she graduates, Lisa hopes to make her career in a field where she can effect positive change while helping other people. One of her favorite sayings is ". . . in the distant, early morning all things are possible."

What follows is an account of Lisa's writing process followed by her first and final draft. Notice how much she added to her earliest version to make the descriptive passages more purposeful.

DISCOVERING

Q: How did you arrive at the idea for your essay?

A: I like to write poetry, so when a descriptive essay was assigned, it was a natural step for me. Two weeks before this essay was due I spent a weekend in Harrison, Vancouver, B.C., and this description is of a place where I actually spent many hours. Turning it into a description and making it "real" to the reader was a bit more difficult than enjoying the scenery, but it was rewarding and due to my experience with poetry turned out to be not so difficult.

PLANNING

Q: Say a little about how you prepare yourself to write and how you organize your thoughts.

A: The planning process for this type of writing is different than for a research essay, at least for me. I write often and I often have creative spurts. To add to that I have a stash of one-liners and paragraphs, as well as half-written poems and stories that I never finished or was too tired or busy when the idea came up. I keep those around and read those or build on them when I need to. But for this particular essay the trip to Canada was fresh in mind, as was the beauty of the area, and so inspiration was not a problem. The moment I read the assignment I knew what I was to write about.

I then spent several days formulating the descriptions. During classes, or wandering around, I would sometimes come up with what I thought, at least, was a good line. I would write that down or dictate it into my digital recorder for later use. I've long made a habit of carrying around a recorder because my creativity crops up at the worst, most inconvenient times.

When it finally came time to actually write the essay, it was rather a necessity of putting together bits and pieces into a comprehensible, flowing essay. That was not very difficult since it was mostly written.

DEVELOPING

Q: How did you develop your first draft? Do you have any methods for building paragraphs? How did you arrive at your beginning and ending?

A: This is a harder question for me to answer. When I write my poetry, it is rather random, and my poetry is very free-form although I've been told that it does have rhythm. Because the essay was of a descriptive nature, I simply applied my poetry skills to that. For the first draft I paid absolutely no attention to what I was writing, I simply wrote. Then I left that and went back to it two days later. The bits and pieces I'd collected and finally put together in the first draft were surprising to me, as while I had written it, because I had written it randomly, I was not fully aware of what I had written.

That made revision a bit easier, since I could immediately see the incongruities. But the essay also flowed well and I did not reorganize it much after the first draft. For the most part it was the technical aspects of writing that needed revision, not the content. Reading it out loud helped to get rid of my overuse of sentence fragments, which are a layover from writing free-form poetry. That was the largest problem with the first draft.

As to arriving at the beginning and ending, this wasn't really a matter of thought. I simply started from when I sat down on that rock until shortly before I returned to the cabin. The beginning and ending came from real experience, so it was easy to place them into the context of an essay.

REVISING

Q: Tell me about your process of revising. What did you add or change, and what were you thinking when you made the changes?

A: This essay was a strange one. I wrote the first, basic descriptive essay for class and only later was the plot added to it, to make it a full-fledged story.

Since the feedback on the original essay was very positive, I elected not to revise that at all. When I first wrote that essay it went through many revisions mostly in the way I worded sentences. For me, the most important aspect of a piece of writing is for it to flow. That is, it is important to me that the essay be readable in a very natural manner. I hate it when I have to read, then go back to a prior paragraph to understand a later one. I avoid this in my writing and since I had written in a "stream of consciousness" style, I had a lot of reworking to do.

I didn't really rearrange the paragraphs much. Since I had ordered them chronologically and it was nonfiction, they already followed properly. I pulled out a thesaurus and made the rhythm and scansion of the paragraphs flow more naturally and used more descriptive words that held more emphasis. I attempted to avoid too many words that a basic reader would have to look up, however. That would destroy the reading for many people.

It was more difficult to re-create the context for the piece—to tell what led up to my description of the glacial park and what it meant for me. When I went back and added the plot, it was a challenge. I find it much harder to incorporate a new storyline into an existing piece than to write "from scratch." Because I had written some nonfiction, I felt that I wanted to capture the reality of the situation. It is hard to reflect back and truly capture the emotions of the moment, but I did my best to integrate the narrative and personal details into the essay and to continue its original flow.

PROOFREADING AND ADVICE

Q: How do you proofread your work for errors?

A: I don't proofread. The problem that I have with that is that my eyes skip the writing, because my mind knows what I've written. To get around this, I "proof-speak." That is, I read the paper out loud, sometimes to an audience and sometimes not. When I do this, because I am following the punctuation as I read, it is a lot easier to catch errors, especially sentence fragments.

Q: Looking back, what would you say was your most important goal in writing the essay? What were your biggest obstacles, and how did you tackle them? How do you feel now about the results?

A: The most important goal for me in writing this essay was easily to capture and portray the gravity and importance of a very short span of time. The essay itself only covers approximately five to ten minutes. Yet, those few minutes had a profound impact on me. It was most important to make sure that the reader understood, and hopefully felt, that impact.

Because I had no restriction on adjectives and description (since it was a descriptive essay) I simply took my time. I drew out the descriptions of little things that would often not be noticed. I spent paragraphs relating the most minor of details. But that was a potential obstacle. I did not wish the essay to bore anyone to tears, and so I couldn't spend too long worshipping a single rock. I had to rely on strong words and use them appropriately and in a well-placed manner to convey the imagery appropriately.

Q: Finally, did you learn anything about yourself while writing "In the Distant, Early Morning"? What advice would you give to other student writers?

A: I learned that I could write poetry in the form of an essay or short story rather than in the fragmented fashion that I normally follow. I also learned that by drawing on my own experience, and placing myself back into the context of the writing, I could make it clearer to the audience. This helped me in later classes for stories and essays, to draw the essay into a whole package. I found that by looking holistically at a paper, rather than at the minute details, the paper itself metamorphosed into a whole piece.

To other students I would say "Don't stress the small things." When you're writing an essay, get the whole idea; then write it. Ignore technicalities and flow, just get the paper out there in some sort of draft form. Look at it holistically. If you run a magnifier over every word during the first stages, you will stagnate and lose track of the purpose of the essay. If you at least get the main point written out, the technicalities can be fixed up any time.

In short, listen to yourself and trust yourself and your essay will naturally flow from you and become a work to be proud of.

1. This is good descriptive writing, attentive and evocative. You really help us to see the details of this place through your eyes and feel its impact on you. However, your description might be much more powerful if it served a clearer purpose. Consider giving us more background about this environment, what it means to you, and why it is worth observing so carefully.

2. This is a fragment.

3. This is a good verb to use here.

4. Why do you shift to the past tense here?

5. Apostrophe needed

IN THE DISTANT, EARLY MORNING

By Lisa Wess

First Draft (with Instructor's Comments)

I sit upon a smooth, curved rock.[1] The rock is large and flat, curved and smoothed at its edges, anchored firmly within the ground. Other rocks surround me, spread around. A veritable mountain of rock, corners rounded smoothly like marble.[2] They do not chafe[3] when sat upon, as a normal rock would.

There are millions of small crevices, softened by time, depressions in the rock where once water collected. Look in that depression and see the growth of moss. It exists in hues of deep green and brown, a soft fur covering along the shadowed portions of the rock. The moss is slippery and slick in patches of fuzz strewn randomly. No shadows now, however! Look up and see the soft clouds spread sporadically across the sky. Next to the hot, orange sun a wild hare sits; long legs, ears perked watching the world below it.

In front of me upon the rock an arm of the sun reaches out to me. The arm is hot and translucent, too bright to have color. Within its translucence, suspended, are millions of motes of dust. They dance, ensconced within the warmth of the sun's ray. A slight breeze lifts my hair. My hair surrounds my face as if it were threads spread over my nose, across my eyes, a strand of hair in my mouth. I brush the hair away; the motes of dust in front of me dance wildly, embraced within the arms of the sun.

Listen to the wind, the soft breeze causes the leaves to rustle softly; a sound akin to silk on silk. The water runs past, moving swiftly through the rocks below me. As the water hits a rocky edge it jumps gracefully, dancing in the air. The water turns into droplets twirling before my eyes in a private ballet.

I watch the water run below, caressing the rocks softly. It whispers secrets as it passes. The water hugs the rock, molding it, softening the corners, smoothing out its rough edges.

Within the rocks below the water is a small bowl, collecting water, cradling it within the rock. Within this pool smaller pebbles glistened[4] promising beauty. Broken pieces of quartz reflect the suns[5] hues, glittering through the waves of the cascading water.

I scoot carefully down the smooth, wizened edges of the rock. I reach into the pool, gasp and pull away. The water ignores the suns warmth, the suns attempts to heat the world. The stream runs from the mountains above, its source a glacier. Glacier and sun are in constant competition. There is no winner here; the water runs quickly and smoothly, no longer ice. Only barely, however, is it not ice; the water so cold it stings, biting sharply any flesh it contacts.

I steel myself, my breath held, and reach again into the shallows of the pool. My hand grasps a rock;[6] its edges not yet fully softened by time. This rock has been opened, the inside a glitter of sharp quartz, beautifully reflecting the sun back out into the world.

It seems to be, as I sit upon the rock that the entire world flows ceaselessly from this stream. There is endless variation in how the water crashes over the rocks, and yet the variations repeat, same as yet different. It strikes me as the world at large, endless variation yet similar and recognizable.

A water beetle swims, weaving its way through the melted glacier. It swims strongly with an unknown goal. Yet as he swims he is pushed by the water in an endless battle against the nature of the beast which encompasses him.

The wind picks up, the small of the distant forest engulfing the surroundings. My skin tingles; my heart pulses; my eyes seek out new experiences.[7] But I am not just my eyes, and even as I close my eyes, I still see.

IN THE DISTANT, EARLY MORNING
by Lisa Wess

Final Draft

It is a late, June afternoon. The last few weeks have been incredibly hectic and I feel a pressing need to get away from everything. I need time. I need time to be alone and to consider the events of the past few months. I need space and silence, the entwining embrace of nature and the lack of rush that surrounds everyday life. With this in mind, I pack my bags, gather up a nice spread of food for the weekend, and hop into the car.

As I drive up the highway, the music is pressing in around me. The windows are shut against the unnaturally cool wind outside. The speedometer is telling me that the car is running at seventy miles per hour. There is no one in the car but myself; I am cocooned, ensconced by the safety of the metal cage that embraces me. The trees to the side of the road whip by, an almost hypnotic dance of time going full throttle.

I come to the gravel road, an hour and a half away from where I left. I slow the car down so that I can control it. I am nearly there, to that place of ultimate safety and comfort; to be alone with myself.

As I drive I remember, vaguely, a story that I read in elementary school. I do not clearly remember the details and yet the fabric of the story, the threads are still winding

6. Why do you use a semicolon here when you are not joining two independent clauses?

7. This is lovely, but what do these sensations mean to you?

their way through my head. It was a beautiful, fantastic, impossible story that went something like this:

A man is visiting a strange town. In that town no one ever speaks, and if anyone makes any noise he or she is rapidly hushed. Finally one of the inhabitants of that strange town speaks to him and says that if he would just be silent for a few days, he too would understand.

So, the man—rather annoyed at this obstruction, but needing the village inhabitants' help, undertakes this silence. A few days later he is walking in the town when he suddenly hears in his head a beautiful, lilting music. It is nothing like that he had ever heard before, in all his life, and finally, he understands.

I laugh to myself, amazed at the impossibility of the dream; a common thread, constant communication in the throngs of silent reverie. How utterly absurd!

I arrive at the cabin and unpack the car. I light the propane tank and turn on the old refrigerator. The humming soothes me and relaxes me, but it soon quiets down into an unnoticeable background purr.

Finally, the dreary work of unpacking is done, and I can relax, and allow the comfort of the mountains to embrace me. However, it is still early afternoon, and after months in classrooms, cubicles, and rooms I no longer wish to be trapped inside. Only a few feet from the cabin is a beautiful river, fed by the glaciers up from the cabin. I find the trail, it having hidden itself from humans in the hopes of staying pure, and I follow it to the lake.

I thread my way through the moss-covered rocks. I look and see the smoothness of the rocks, the green fuzz like a beard covering the lower edges. The time-worn wrinkles tell tales as filled with meaning as the greatest of poetry. At long last, I see the spot where I may finally find peace.

Looking around, I find my place and sit upon a smooth, curved rock. The rock is large and flat, curved and smoothed at its edges, anchored firmly within the ground. Other rocks surround me, spread around in a veritable mountain of rock, corners rounded smoothly like marble. They do not chafe when sat upon, as a normal rock would.

My mind wanders again to the trifles of the few past weeks. I consider the stresses and unending hassles. I contemplate the constant ringing of the telephone, almost as though it were a music that one could not live without: the drone of people discussing this and that, the squeals as the discussions escalated from boring banter to frenzied fighting.

No longer do I need to hear that constant droning. Instead now I hear the beautiful tinkle of the river as it winds its merry way through the rocks, on a goal that may never end. The water knows it is the journey that counts. I wish that I could be so easily convinced.

Although the rock that I am perched upon is smooth, there are millions of small crevices, softened by time, depressions in the rock where once water collected. Look in that depression and see the growth of moss. It exists in hues of deep green and brown, a soft fur covering along the shadowed portions of the rock. The moss is slippery and slick in patches of fuzz strewn randomly. There are no shadows now, however! I look up and see the soft clouds spread sporadically across the sky. Next to the hot orange sun a wild hare sits; long legs, ears perked watching the world below it.

In front of me upon the rock an arm of the sun reaches out to me. The arm is hot and translucent, too bright to have color. Within its translucence, suspended, are millions of motes of dust. They dance within the warmth of the sun's ray. A slight breeze lifts my hair. My hair surrounds my face like threads spread over my nose, across my eyes, a strand of hair in my mouth. I brush the hair away; the motes of dust in front of me dance wildly as they are embraced within the arms of the sun.

The sun, too, seems to have no boundaries. It is not rushed by the desires of people. It shines when and where it will, oblivious to comfort or discomfort. It has only one care in the world, and that is to be that beautiful, shining star that we all look up to. Even without trying, it succeeds.

I listen to the wind. The soft breeze causes the leaves to rustle softly, a sound akin to silk on silk. The water runs past, moving swiftly through the rocks below me. As the water hits a rocky edge it jumps gracefully, dancing in the air. The water turns into droplets twirling before my eyes in a private ballet.

As I listen to the sibilating hisses and hums of the wind as it whips the leaves in the adjacent trees, my mind wanders back to the story. I close my eyes, but can still see those motes of dust twirling to their private ballet, illuminated by the rays of the sun. My brow furrows with concentration and I take a deep breath and make a conscious effort to just let go. There is no danger here; I am being held by the sun. The wind whispers to me and the lake creates a moat, embracing my shelter.

Then I hear it. It is not some fanciful music out of a Disney fairy tale, but it is the music that nature sings to us. It persists in the rush of the lake as it caresses the rocks. It reverberates with the wind pushing the leaves out of its way, making the branches swing and sway. Nature's music resounds with the twinkling of splashes of water as they hit the rock-pools. It explodes with frenzy as the motes of dust twirl madly in the sun's rays. Yet it is silent. The music is as silent as a person contemplating life. Its profoundness moves me and I open my eyes again.

I watch the water run below, caressing the rocks softly. It whispers secrets as it passes. The water hugs the rock, molding it, softening the corners, smoothing out its rough edges.

Within the rocks below the water is a small bowl, collecting water, cradling it within the rock. Within this pool smaller pebbles glisten, promising beauty. Broken pieces of quartz reflect the sun's hues, glittering through the waves of the cascading water.

I scoot carefully down the smooth, wizened edges of the rock. I reach into the pool, gasp, and pull away. The water ignores the sun's warmth, the sun's attempts to heat the world. The stream runs from the mountains above, its source a glacier. Glacier and sun are in constant competition. There is no winner here; the water runs quickly and smoothly, no longer ice. Only barely, however, is it not ice, the water so cold it stings, biting sharply into any flesh it contacts.

I steel myself, my breath held, and reach again into the shallows of the pool. My hand grasps a rock whose edges are not yet fully softened by time. This rock has been opened, the inside is a glitter of sharp quartz, beautifully reflecting the sun back out into the world.

It is not only the music, but the feel of the world that embraces, comforts, and calms me. I touch the rock and rejoice in its contrariness, the feeling of rough, jagged edges of quartz contrasting sharply with the smoothened rock, and even more sharply with the fluid grace of the racing river.

It seems to me, as I sit upon the rock, that the entire world flows ceaselessly from this stream. There is endless variation in how the water crashes over the rocks, and yet the variations repeat, identical yet different. It strikes me as the world at large, endless variation yet related and recognizable in each of its intertwining parts.

Not even a day into my trip I feel relaxed, refreshed, and revived. I have two more days here, and I will relish them. But with that comes the sure knowledge that when I return, I can relish the race of humanity. I will finally be able to revel in the constant buzz, the constant joy, and even the constant hassle that makes it all worthwhile. Finally I realize that in the distant, early morning every aspect of life is beautiful if I can take but a moment to inhale a deep breath, relax, and absorb it. I finally understand that the music of life, in nature or in the hustle and bustle of the city, is what fulfills, entertains, enriches, and extends me. It is not the silence that the man in the story had sought, but it is a recognition of the beauty of that which is the human experience and which, once embraced, becomes that blissful, beautiful, lilting tune.

Considerations for Your Own Writing

1. Lisa's first draft was highly descriptive, but the purpose served by her description was not immediately clear. When pressed for more information about the moment she described, Lisa recalled the circumstances that led up to her experience in Vancouver. She explained the reasons for her trip to Canada, remembered the story she had read in high school about a traveler to a silent village, and got in touch with the deeper insights about nature and

humanity inspired by the natural beauty of a glacial park. What does she add to her final version that was missing in her first draft? What can you add to your draft that would make it more meaningful and complete?

2. Descriptive writing often runs a risk of being too detailed, repetitious, or extravagant. Does Lisa's writing seem overdone at any point? If so, what changes would you suggest? Where in your own writing might your description be improved by careful pruning?

Evaluation Checklist

Use the following checklist to evaluate your descriptive essay. The categories used here are from the text analysis assignment in Chapter 1 (page 35), but they can apply to any form of composition.

Purpose. How clear is the purpose of your composition? Good descriptive writing always serves some larger intention. Does your essay add up to something more than a gathering of details? Does it truly characterize your subject? What is the big picture?

Topic and content. Have you focused on your topic without going off track? Is your description complete enough to give your readers a full picture for your purposes?

Audience. Who are your intended readers? Why would they find your essay interesting? What are you offering to make them read on? Have you explained any terms that they might find unfamiliar or confusing? Have you taken into account what they already know?

Format. There may be no set format for description as there are for other kinds of writing. Description is not so much a genre in itself (like memoirs, research papers, or advice columns) as it is a set of tools for other purposes. Have you used tools such as sense impressions, metaphors, and perspective to good advantage?

Structure. The essays in this chapter follow a wide range of organizing patterns. Quindlen returns to the beginning of her essay after exploring the history, people, sights, and sounds of St. Anthony's feast. Momaday and Ackerman alternate between close-ups and long shots, moving back and forth among personal observation, history, and legend. Santiago and Twain compare their subjects (guavas and the Mississippi River) as they seemed in childhood and in adulthood. Have you used any of these strategies in your writing? What guides the arrangement of material in your essay?

Style. Does your essay have a distinctive style or tone? If so, how would you describe it? Does your style shift throughout the essay? If so, are there good reasons for the shifts?

Description on the Web

The Internet is full of helpful Web sites on descriptive writing. Teachers, consultants, and professional writers offer the benefit of their experience free of charge. Here are a few links to get you started.

Things to Consider as You Write Your Descriptive Essay
http://leo.stcloudstate.edu/acadwrite/descriptive.html
St. Cloud State University's LEO (Literacy Education Online) offers these guidelines and sample paragraphs.

Descriptive Writing Techniques
http://www.montanalife.com/writing/descriptive_writing_techniques.html
A business consultant suggests tips for using memory, sketching, listing, and data charts to help with descriptive writing.

Photographic Prompts
http://www.kodak.com/global/en/consumer/education/lessonPlans/lessonPlan040.shtml
Kodak's educational Web site shows how to incorporate photography into descriptive writing projects.

Writing to Describe—Examples
http://www.englishbiz.co.uk/extras/describeexample1.htm
A writing teacher shows what to look for in excerpts from *Hard Times,* "Shooting an Elephant," and *Out of Africa.*

Descriptive Writing
http://teacher.scholastic.com/writewit/diary/index.htm
A writer's journey to South Africa prompted her to use description in her travel diary. In this Web site, hosted by Scholastic, Inc., she offers ideas for student journals.

Taking Stock

Take a moment to review what you have learned about observing and describing from this chapter.

1. Where in your future work, personal life, and community activities will you likely need to use descriptive writing?

2. In what ways do you now feel better equipped for these needs? How have you sharpened your powers of observation and descriptive skills?

3. Based on the feedback from your instructor, classmates, and "committed reader," what methods and techniques seem to work best for you?

4. What did you learn about descriptive writing from the readings? Consider the way these readings are organized, characterize their subject, focus on particular details, and use devices like comparison, alliteration, and place names.

5. What did you learn about the person, place, or thing that you wrote about or described in your collage? What would you still like to learn about this topic?

6. Think about the various environments described in the readings and screenings. What did you learn about the Congo, the Mississippi River, Sullivan Street, the woods, or the sky?

7. Consider the process you went through during the composition assignment. What steps will you probably take again in future writing? What will you do differently?

American culture is a patchwork quilt composed of various materials and stitched together from a variety of traditions and subcultures. Our national identity—who we are as a people—is reflected in our skylines and our hemlines, the foods and music we enjoy together, our common pastimes and holidays, the television shows and movies that permeate our daily conversation. Some traditions seem to be uniquely American; some were imported and assimilated into American rituals and icons. Others remain separate and distinct, reflecting the diversity of our original roots.

How much of the American quilt is truly native, unique to the land between the Atlantic and Pacific oceans? Is it accurate to speak of the United States as a single nation, one people, one culture? Do we really share a common heritage? Scan the radio at a given moment or flip through the channels on your television set, and notice how many sounds and images you can recognize in an instant. From the brash voice of Beyoncé to Jon Stewart's sacrastic wit, from the roar of NASCAR to the celebrated Apple logo, these mediated icons describe a vast cultural spectrum. What connects the pieces to each other, and how do we come to learn about them?

One of the best ways to learn something well is to explain it to someone else. We've all had the experience of improving a familiar skill by teaching it to people who lack our experience and competence. Yet communicating even well-known information can be tricky. If you have ever tried to give directions to a stranger or to explain your family's rituals to a new friend, you probably know how challenging such tasks can be. Part of the challenge is making your knowledge explicit, getting it out in the open for others to see. That's when you often notice which pieces are most important, which are missing, and which are unnecessary. That's when you recognize the strengths and limits of your knowledge.

Another challenge is telling just how much your audience needs to know. Would you give the same directions to someone from another state as you would to someone from the other side of town? Some years back, a researcher at Harvard University tried an experiment. One day, he appeared at Harvard Square dressed in cowboy boots and a Texan hat. When he asked for directions, people gave the most detailed responses. In slow, deliberate English, they would explain how to find the nearest entrance to the subway, called the T, how to put a token in the turnstile, and where to board the T for Central Square. On another day, the researcher dressed in local clothes. This time, the directions were casual and clipped: "Take the T one stop east to Central Square."

In this chapter, we'll be examining different ways that people pass along their knowledge: how they give instructions, offer advice, clarify ideas, and explain relationships. We'll be looking at different strategies for analyzing and explaining as they are practiced in a variety of media. If you pay attention to your media environment, you'll see that the art of explaining can take many forms, from advice columns in magazines and how-to shows on television to instruction manuals and chapters in textbooks. Meanwhile, you will be preparing an essay of your own in which you analyze something you know well and explain it to someone unfamiliar with your topic. As you notice the strategies used by other writers and producers, as you discuss their works with classmates, you will be discovering—maybe rediscovering—methods to try out in your essay. The goal is to give you access to options that you can put to good use in your academic writing and in your daily life whenever you are called upon to communicate what you know or think you know.

SCENARIOS FROM LIFE

Here are some everyday moments that call for analysis and explanation. Ask yourself when you might need to analyze something and explain it to others—at work, at school, in your community, or in your personal life. Keep these scenarios in mind when you select a topic for the composing option in this chapter.

- Your boss hires two new workers. Since you know the job well, you are asked to explain things to the new employees. Not only are you expected to show them how the job is done, but the two employees also want a scorecard of the personnel: who has the power, who has seniority, and whom they can turn to for help.

- A visitor from out of town is spending a few days with a religious friend who attends church every Sunday. The host realizes that her familiar rituals and beliefs will be unfamiliar to her visitor. She needs to analyze and explain the service—what people do in her church and why they do it—in order to prepare her guest.

- After several years of dating, a young couple is ready for marriage. Their relationship is so special that they want to pledge themselves to one another for life. The young man wonders, however, whether his relationships with old friends will change after the wedding. He finds himself thinking a lot about the meaning of friendship, loyalty, love, and commitment. To help clarify these thoughts for himself and for the others in his life, he tries to define these complex terms in his diary.

■ A class in environmental studies has just taken field trips to a local wetland and a forest. The students have carefully recorded what they saw, including the terrain, common plants, and animals. Their next task is to compare the different forms of life they found in each setting and to think of reasons for these differences. They need to explain how a particular environment favors particular species.

WHY WRITE TO ANALYZE?

To **analyze** something is to loosen it up, to break it down into its parts in order to discover more about its nature. By separating a thing into its components, by looking closely at the parts and their relationship to one another, we sometimes see more clearly what it is and how it works. That's what happens, for example, when we break down a word into its components. Our word *analysis* comes from two Greek terms, *ana* (meaning "up") and *lysis* (meaning "loosening"). Our word **explain** comes from two Latin terms, *ex* (meaning "out") and *planere* (meaning "to make level"). The idea is that a thing is easier to understand when it is spread out flat in front of us, plain for all to see. That's why biology texts explain the three-dimensional complexities of the pulmonary system with a two-dimensional map of the heart, arteries, and veins. A good explanation is a simple way of representing something messy; it depicts the main arteries, veins, and heart of the matter without all the obscuring blood and guts.

Analyzing and explaining typically go hand in hand. In order to explain the game of soccer, for example, you might first have to analyze for yourself the kinds of players, strategies, and rules that make up the sport. Then you might explain these components to your audience by likening them to features of a game that the audience is likely to know already. An explanation of prejudice might begin with your analysis of different forms of prejudice or the factors you believe contribute to prejudiced behavior, offering examples to which your audience can readily relate. In each case, a complex process or concept is broken down (analyzed) into its component parts in order to simplify and clarify (explain) what it is and how it works.

Words themselves are analytic tools. Language separates experience into bits: into nouns, verbs, and adjectives that isolate the actor from the action, the person from the personal qualities. When I say "My sister washed her dirty dog," I am picking out certain elements—sister, dog, the act of washing, dirt, and much more—that are not so distinct from one another in the flow of real events. A picture or a film might give us a messier image of Lassie's bath. Yet photographers and filmmakers also use analytic tools. They adjust the camera's frame to isolate an image from the larger scene and refocus the lens to sharpen significant details against the background. They select particular photographs or takes, arranging them to highlight particular relationships. Such strategies help to center and guide our attention. They fix a subject on the page or screen, giving us time and space to absorb it, study it, understand it better, before the pause control kicks in, returning it, and us, to the undifferentiated mainstream.

Here is a list of analytic tools that we'll be highlighting in this chapter. You have probably used most of them at one time or another. This chapter is an opportunity to watch closely how other composers, skilled in the crafts of writing or filmmaking, use such tools to produce explanatory texts. As you put them into practice in your essay and elsewhere, you should find yourself adding new resources to your toolbox and sharpening those you already have.

Definition: a statement of what something is; the power of a lens to show an object in clear, sharp outline

Example: something selected to show the nature or character of the rest; a pattern or model for others to imitate

Comparison and Contrast: pointing out similarities and differences

Cause and Effect: chain of actions and reactions; how one thing leads to another

Division and Classification: separation into parts and systematic groupings

For more description and examples of these analytic tools, see "Build the Middle: Strategies for Supporting an Idea" in Chapter 2.

Of course, tools are useless by themselves. Their value lies in the use to which they are put. What will make your essay most worth writing—and reading—is your special slant on the topic that you choose. This is the unique perspective or theme that you want to communicate. It guides the way you analyze the topic and shapes the way you represent it to your readers for your own particular purpose.

COMPOSING OPTIONS

Writing Option: Analyze a Cultural Concept, Icon, or Ritual

Your goal in this assignment is to explain something that you already know to someone unfamiliar with your subject. What you write about should be something interesting and fairly intricate that you have come to know well over time. Your topic might be a group that you belong to, a sport or hobby you enjoy, the organization of your workplace, or a complex idea, like love or friendship. First, you'll need to analyze the topic for yourself. That may mean dividing it into its parts, looking closely at the parts, and seeing how those parts relate to each other. Then you'll explain what you have come to understand in a formal essay so that readers can begin to share your knowledge. This is where definitions, examples, and comparisons may help.

The essay may take the form of advice ("How to Win a Family Argument"), an extended definition ("What Does Success Mean?"), an informative account ("How Does a Rock Group Rock?"), or a combination of essay forms. Whatever its format, your final draft should maintain a clear, engaging focus. It should be sensibly organized, with a distinct beginning, middle, and end. It should lead your readers to an informed understanding of your topic: what it is, what it is not, how it operates, and why this information is worth knowing.

This assignment does not require extensive outside research. It does require that you observe closely and think carefully about something in your life to which you may not normally pay much attention. Choose a topic that you really want to analyze so you can understand it better. Consider how much you already know about it. What are its component parts? What are the features of each part? How do the parts fit together? Consider, too, what your readers need to know. How do outsiders see it? What do they already know or believe about your topic? What key terms or concepts need explaining? How can you get them to see your topic as you see it? Be sure to give attention to your writing style. If you're too technical or too confrontational, you may lose some readers. Think of yourself as a knowledgeable guide who wants your followers to appreciate and understand something that you genuinely care about. Finally, be clear about your unique perspective on the topic, your theme. Have you found an unusual way to get a job? Do you have strong feelings about friendship based on personal experience? Let your distinctive viewpoint guide the essay. Remember that you are the expert here. Nobody else can write from your point of view. It is the source of your power as a writer, and it is your chief contribution to your reader.

Media Option: Illustrated Speech

An illustrated speech is a good means for analyzing and explaining something. Since the talk is accompanied by visual aids—charts, drawings, photographs, or even props—the speaker can show as well as tell about the topic. An illustrated speech about hockey might include face masks and a hockey stick as well as pictures of a team in action and drawings to show defensive strategies. A speaker on scuba diving might talk about her diving techniques, illustrating them with underwater photos and demonstrating certain movements with real scuba gear. The visual and verbal components of the illustrated speech work hand in hand to analyze the activity and explain how it works.

As with the writing option, choose a topic with which you are familiar. Select an artifact or an activity that you knew very well, an article or practice of American culture that lends itself to a classroom demonstration. It is a good idea to pick a topic unfamiliar to your class, since this will challenge your communication skills. The goal is not only to describe your topic, but also to break it down so that your audience understands its nature—what it is, how it functions, and why it works the way it does. Although you'll be mostly talking and pointing, you can use the same analytic tools that writers use, including definitions, examples, comparison and contrast, cause and effect, division and classification.

A good speech follows many of the same principles of good writing. It should be interesting, unified, organized, continuous, and complete. Plan out the subtopics that you want to cover, and decide what is important to say about each one. Start with an engaging introduction that sets the tone and lets your listeners know what you'll be covering. Stay focused on your topic without straying to irrelevant side issues. Move smoothly from one part of the speech to the next. Wrap it up when you have covered the main points, perhaps with a summary or a memorable punch line.

Since a speech is given before a live audience, you won't be able to revise it like an essay. You will, however, be able to rehearse. Step through the whole presentation before a mirror or a practice audience. Record your performance with a microphone or camcorder, and play it back to hear and see what might be improved. Be sure that your charts or other visual aids are clear and large enough to be seen by everyone. Use them only if they contribute to your topic. If your speech includes special gear, check to see that everything is working and complete. If you'll be giving a demonstration, run through the demo several times until you're fully comfortable. Once you've given a successful speech, consider putting it into essay form. Since you've already worked out much of the language, organization, and key ideas, it should be easier to write.

TIPS ON WRITING AN ANALYSIS

DISCOVERING

1. **CHOOSE A TOPIC.** Consider where in your schoolwork, job, or daily life you find yourself explaining things to people.

2. **THINK LIKE AN ANTHROPOLOGIST.** Cultural anthropologists study the social customs and practices of different cultural groups. What *subcultures* or special groups do you belong to? Can you explain the way this group is organized and how it functions to a stranger? Besides a group, you might analyze a *cultural site,* like a beauty salon, pool hall, or shopping mall. Or you might analyze a *cultural artifact,* like baseball caps, skateboards, Phat fashions, or jeans. What might someone make of this site or artifact if it were discovered in the distant future?

3. **GATHER YOUR THOUGHTS.** What do you already know about your chosen topic? Sift through your memory to gather your knowledge and analyze it methodically. If your topic is a process, what steps are involved? If it is a complex object or group, what are its component parts? If it is a concept, what other concepts contribute to its meaning?

PLANNING

1. DRAW ON YOUR VISUAL IMAGINATION. Your topic may lend itself to visual exploration. You might sketch an object from different angles. You might picture a process as if it were being filmed, using an imaginary camera to focus, frame, and track the topic as it moves along. You might illustrate a concept with mental snapshots, each snapshot representing an example that helps to clarify the main idea.

2. CLARIFY YOUR FOCUS. As you collect and organize more details, your topic may seem too broad, too narrow, or too fuzzy. Ask yourself what you really want to write about. What is your particular interest in explaining the topic? What special experience and point of view do you bring to it that will make your essay unique? That will be the theme or focused purpose that shapes whatever you write about.

3. THINK ABOUT STRUCTURE. Find examples of explanatory texts in various media, such as radio, television, magazines, and the Internet. Check TV guides, radio schedules, tables of contents, and other listings. Make a list of formats that regularly use some form of advice, such as advice columns, self-help books, how-to shows, and science programs. Do any of these formats give you ideas about organizing an essay or an illustrated lecture?

DRAFTING

1. DEVELOP YOUR ANALYSIS. At this point, you may already be drafting paragraphs, or you may still be listing, clustering, and outlining your thoughts. In either case, keep in mind the analytic tools of definition; example; comparison and contrast; cause and effect; and division and classification described above in "Why Write to Analyze?"

2. USE TRANSITIONS. Writers of explanatory essays draw on a repertoire of standard transitions to track a process (*first, second, before, then, next, finally*), to compare and contrast (*in the same way, similarly, likewise; yet, however, by contrast, on the other hand*), to illustrate (*for example, for instance*), to define (*technically, more precisely*) and to relate cause and effect (*because, consequently, as a result, in order to*).

3. INTRODUCE YOUR ESSAY. A good introduction arouses interest, establishes a mood, and leads us to the body of the essay. It may frame the topic, establish its importance, give background for what follows, or start with an incident that the text will expand and explain. Some writers like to write their introduction last, after they have a complete picture of what they are introducing. Others prefer to write the opening paragraph first because it opens a door and liberates a flow of words.

4. DRAW IT ALL TOGETHER. When the flow ends, your readers should experience a satisfying sense of closure. Your explanatory essay, like good instructions or a successful tour, should leave the readers with a clearer understanding of your topic.

REVISING

A good visual aid to revising is your ability to picture a real audience. Imagine your readers as you go through your first draft aloud or to yourself. What do their imagined faces and voices tell you? If you know these readers well enough to anticipate responses, you will know which sections to revise. What do they already know about the topic? Are you explaining too little or too much? Do any terms or concepts need elaboration? Given their backgrounds and temperaments, are your readers likely to be interested, amused, or surprised in the way you hope? Read or show your draft to your peers and get their feedback.

Readings and Screenings: American Cultures

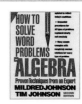

In his acclaimed documentary film, *An Inconvenient Truth,* director Davis Guggenheim focuses his camera on Al Gore and a large computer screen. Gore, who introduces himself by saying, "I used to be the next president of the United States," goes on to deliver some disturbing news about global warming. In an impassioned multimedia presentation, he unravels the complexities of climate change, using graphs, maps, video clips, and interviews to show how the planet is heading toward an ecological disaster. His anatomy of environmental trends shows an inquiring mind at work: probing, comparing, defining, and dissecting in order to reveal truths that he believes are too critical to be ignored. *How to Solve Word Problems in Algebra,* one of the many self-help books to be found on bookstore shelves these days, is not as earthshaking in its implications, but it too shows how to break down challenging problems into manageable parts. Gore may well have consulted similar books in his formative education to prepare him for the challenges ahead. Documentary films and self-help books are among the most common tools we have to analyze and explain the world around us. Radio shows like *Car Talk* and TV shows like *Nova* or *Dr. Phil* perform similar services in the areas of automotive technology, science, and psychology. What they have in common is the principle of analysis, the rhetorical focus of Chapter 5.

Our thematic focus in this chapter is on American culture, which spans a broad spectrum of practices and products. The cultural landscape of the United States is so wide and varied that it might be more accurate to speak of American cultures, acknowledging the plurality of multicultural experiences, highbrow art and popular entertainment, time-honored traditions and the countercultures that make this country such a fascinating mosaic to analyze and explain.

In the following readings and screenings, you'll have opportunities to analyze a variety of cultural icons and traditions from quite different points of view. You'll listen to a radio broadcast about hip-hop music and watch a commercial for a new pizza delivery service. You'll read an essay on horror films by a master of the genre, and you'll find a study of weddings by a family therapist. Among other things, you'll get a traveler's perception of conversational styles, a journalist's perspective on sport utility vehicles, and an adult woman's inquiry into the world of a ten-year-old boy. What makes each topic interesting is the spectacle of an inquiring mind at work: probing, comparing, defining, and dissecting in order to reveal new things about our cultural environment. Keep your own mind open and alert for something you might like to analyze.

Analyzing and Explaining across the Media

PRINT
Psychology Today
The Economist
College textbooks

TELEVISION
Nova
The Dog Whisperer
Dr. Phil
Emeril Live
This Old House

MOVIES
Instructional videos and DVDs
An Inconvenient Truth

RADIO
Car Talk
Healthy Talk Radio
Heart Talk Live
A Chef's Table

INTERNET
How Stuff Works
www.howstuffworks.com
Advice for Undergraduates
Applying to Graduate School
http://polaris.gseis.ucal.edu/
pagre/grad-school.html

From its local roots in the African American and Latino ghettos of New York City, hip-hop music has risen to become a strong current in the American mainstream. Todd Boyd believes that hip-hop culture defines a generation much as rock or jazz once did. According to Boyd, hip-hop performers like Def Jam and DMX are also potent political forces, replacing Martin Luther King's civil rights agenda of the 1960s with vigorously modern messages about poverty, suffering, and power in our own times.

Dr. Boyd is a professor of critical studies at the University of Southern California School of Cinema and Television. In his book, *The New H.N.I.C.: The Death of Civil Rights and the Reign of Hip Hop*, Boyd writes, "Hip hop has now revolutionized the times precisely because it is music from the margins that has grown up to consume the mainstream. As Jay-Z says, '[W]e brought the suburbs to the hood.'" The following transcript is taken from a radio interview of Dr. Boyd by National Public Radio's Scott Simon. The interview was originally aired on *Weekend Edition Saturday* on March 1, 2003.

www.mhhe.com/costanzo

Visit the Web site to listen to the radio interview.

TRANSCRIPT OF RADIO INTERVIEW—
HIP HOP: TODAY'S CIVIL RIGHTS MOVEMENT?

(Soundbite of music)

SCOTT SIMON, host: This is "Ruff Ryders Anthem" from DMX's 1998 release, "It's Dark and Hell is Hot." In his latest book, Todd Boyd writes, "I would suggest that you might get a better read of what's going on in the world of black people today by listening to DMX on 'It's Dark and Hell is Hot' than by listening to repeated broadcasts of Martin Luther King speeches."

(Soundbite of "Ruff Ryders Anthem")

DMX: (Singing) Niggers want to try, niggers want to lie, then niggers wonder why niggers want to die. All I know is pain, all I feel is vain, how can I maintain with that (censored) on my brain. I resort to violence, my nigger's moving silent. Like you don't know when I'm silent. New York think it's the wildest, . . . (unintelligible) is with it. You want it? Come and get it. Took it, then we split it. (Censored) right, we did it.

SIMON: Dr. Boyd says that hip-hop has become a new kind of mass movement. Todd Boyd teaches at the University of Southern California's School of Cinema and Television. He just published a new book, "The New H.N.I.C.: The Death of Civil Rights and the Reign of Hip Hop." He joins us from the studios of NPR West in Los Angeles.

Professor Boyd, thanks so much for being with us.

5   Dr. TODD BOYD (Author, "The New H.N.I.C.: The Death of Civil Rights and the Reign of Hip Hop"): Thank you for having me.

SIMON: And I've got to ask you to explain the "H.N.I.C.," for people for whom it's not immediately apparent.

Dr. BOYD: OK. It actually refers to originally a phrase in the 1970s, "head nigger in charge." N-I-G-G-E-R, for so long, was considered a derogatory word. Of course, it's rooted in slavery and racism and some very odious things. But what hip-hop has done is come along and changed the meaning of that word. N-I-G-G-A, Tupac said, stands for "never ignorant, getting goals accomplished." So the word, I think, now for many people is a word of affirmation.

SIMON: And to be sure, you're not saying that there's no inspiration or instruction to be found in Martin Luther King, just that times have changed and there's instruction and inspiration in hip-hop now.

Dr. BOYD: Certainly. I think that, you know, Martin Luther King is a historical figure. We celebrate his birthday as a holiday, so I would suggest that Martin Luther King and his politics are very specific to a certain time and it's important for us to learn from that. But if we want to talk about the present and the future, hip-hop is much more immediate and much more relevant. We're in a moment when we can't simply look at things from that 1960s perspective and expect for it to hold up in the present day.

10 SIMON: Let me ask you about, I guess, what you've called perhaps the most important song in the history of hip-hop, and that's "The Message" by Grandmaster Flash & The Furious Five.

Dr. BOYD: An incredible song.

(Soundbite of "The Message")

GRANDMASTER FLASH & THE FURIOUS FIVE: (Singing) Broken glass everywhere, people pissin' on the stairs, you know, they just don't care. I can't take the smell, I can't take the noise, got no money to move out; I guess I got no choice. Rats in the front room, roaches in the back, junkie's in the alley with a baseball bat. I tried to get away, but I couldn't get far 'cause the man with the tow-truck repossessed my car. Don't push me 'cause I'm close to the edge. I'm trying not to lose my head.

SIMON: That's a very powerful song.

Dr. BOYD: Amazingly powerful. It's as powerful now as it was when it came out in the summer of 1982.

15   SIMON: And looking back on it, did "The Message," in a sense, kind of pick up from Dr. King's rhetoric when it was stilled in 1968?

Dr. BOYD: You know, I think that where "The Message" picks up is maybe on Malcolm X. So when I hear "The Message," what I hear is an evolution of the Black Power Movement, in which by the early '80s, the sort of dawn of the Reagan era, you had individuals—in this case in New York City, but it could be applicable throughout the country in urban areas—who saw the plight of poor working-class black people who had been displaced by America's move from an industrial economy to a service economy and then to a sort of technologically computer-based economy. And in this displacement, when Grandmaster Flash & The Furious Five and Melle Mel looked around, what they saw was very much like a jungle; and in a jungle, you have predator and you have prey. So when they say "broken glass everywhere, people pissin' on the stairs," you know, "they just don't care. Got no money to move out. I guess I got no choice" . . .

(Soundbite of "The Message")

GRANDMASTER FLASH & THE FURIOUS FIVE: (Singing) It's like a jungle some-times. It makes me wonder how I keep from going under. It's like a jungle sometimes. It makes me wonder how I keep from going under.

Dr. BOYD: I mean, it really captures a life from that perspective at that time, I think, in a most compelling fashion.

SIMON: And it is different from—I remember the phrase from Dr. King to the effect that "We will wear you down by our capacity to suffer," famous speech he gave.

20 Dr. BOYD: Certainly. And I think what black power did, what hip-hop would pick up on later, was move away from, you know, that sort of passive sense of suffering, "We shall overcome." Hip-hop is political in a different way. You know, when I look at the Fortune 40, Richest Under 40, you have figures like Master P, Sean "P. Diddy" Combs. And to me, you know, if we're going to be honest about it, in America it's about capitalism. It's like, you know, Barzini says in "The Godfather," "After all, we're not Communists." And all the obstacles placed in front of young black men for them to overcome these obstacles and become wealthy and powerful and influential, to me, that's very political, and political maybe in a different sense than a march, you know, or a sit-in or a protest would be.

SIMON: Let me ask you about the song "One Mic."

(Soundbite of "One Mic")

Unidentified Singer: (Singing) All I need is one mike, yeah. All I need is one blunt, one page, of one pen, one prayer—tell God forgive me for one sin, matter of fact, maybe more than one. Look back at all the hatred against me (censored). Jesus died at age 33, there's 33 shots from twin Glocks. There's 16 apiece; that's 32, which means one of my guns was holding 17. Twenty-seven hit your crew, six went into you. Everybody got to die sometime. Hope your funeral . . .

Dr. BOYD: I love this idea of oneness, if you will, the connection between the artist and the art form: "All I need is one mike." You know, the mike allows you to express yourself, and that's what hip-hop is about; it's about expression. It's about, you know, self-representation, self-determination, even. And, yes, you could say it's like a gun. A gun is power in a very direct sense. The microphone is power in a different sense, but ultimately it can be equally as devastating and have as much impact as a gun if used properly.

SIMON: There are some people who will never listen to hip-hop except to get upset about it. I don't think the words are used casually. I think, in fact, they're there to lift people out of their seats.

25 Dr. BOYD: Yes. Yes. I wonder if those people who wouldn't listen to hip-hop because it uses certain language [watch] "The Sopranos." I wonder if they, you know, go to see movies that have profanity and if they have a problem with that. The point is hip-hop is inherently political. The language is

political. It uses language, you know, like we were talking about with Nas; it's using language as a weapon, but not a weapon to violate or not a weapon to offend, but a weapon that pushes the envelope, that provokes people, makes people think.

SIMON: In fact, you cite a Shakespeare verse towards the end of your book that you think discloses something about the inspiration of hip-hop.

Dr. BOYD: Yeah, I mean, you know, very much like Shakespeare said, "The sweetness of adversity, ugly and venomous like the toad, yet wears a precious jewel in its crown"—you know, to me, that's very much what hip-hop is about. It's about coming up. It's about overcoming obstacles. It's about, you know, transforming a bad situation into a good situation. So the sweetness of adversity, to me, is very relevant in the world of hip-hop. And I would suggest that if Shakespeare were alive today, he'd be a hip-hop artist, he'd be an emcee—you know, emcee Shakespeare on the mike, doing his thing. You know, I would say that Shakespeare is very relevant, and that sweetness of adversity is something I carry with me everywhere I go.

SIMON: Professor Boyd, thank you very much.

Dr. BOYD: Thank you.

30 SIMON: Todd Boyd, who's a professor of critical studies at the University of Southern California School of Cinema and Television. His latest book is "The New H.N.I.C.: The Death of Civil Rights and the Reign of Hip Hop." You can find more on our Web site at npr.org.

This is WEEKEND EDITION from NPR News. I'm Scott Simon.

RESPONSE QUESTIONS

1. How would you describe hip-hop to somebody who has never been exposed to it? What words best express its sounds, attitudes, and messages? To what degree is hip-hop a form of music or a larger cultural phenomenon?

2. Boyd says that DMX gives a "better read" of the world of black people than do Martin Luther King's speeches. What does he mean by this comparison? Explain why you agree or disagree. Dr. King's famous "I Have a Dream" speech is reprinted in Chapter 9.

3. If hip-hop has become "a new kind of mass movement," as Boyd believes, what might explain its general popularity? What reasons does Boyd offer for the movement's early origins and current commercial success?

4. Read the passage where Boyd explains the meaning of *H.N.I.C.* Why do you think he uses this term in the title of his book?

5. Parts of the broadcast and the transcript are censored. What case can you make for or against censorship of this kind? Given what Dr. Boyd says about *The Sopranos* and the political nature of language, what would be his views on censorship?

GUIDELINES FOR ANALYSIS

1. Does the interview contain anything resembling a thesis statement? Find a sentence in the transcript that comes closest to stating Boyd's main thesis or idea.

2. What role should an interviewer play in a radio show? How well does Scott Simon perform his role in this broadcast?

3. Boyd makes a number of provocative comments about Martin Luther King, Malcolm X, and William Shakespeare. At one point, Dr. Boyd says, "If Shakespeare were alive today, he'd be a hip-hop artist." What point is he making here? Do you agree with this assertion about the English Renaissance playwright?

4. Compare the radio broadcast and the transcript. What is the effect on you of listening as opposed to reading? What is added by the music and the spoken word? What do you gain by reading (and rereading) the words on the page? What would you expect to get from reading Todd Boyd's book?

QUESTIONS OF CULTURE

1. While speaking about American capitalism, Todd Boyd refers to Francis Ford Coppola's film, *The Godfather,* in which Italian immigrants seek power, wealth, and influence outside a system that excludes them from the usual channels for pursuing the American dream. What parallels can you draw between the aspirations of hip-hop artists and those of recent immigrant groups?

2. Hip-hop came from the margins of society but is now part of the American mainstream. How did this transformation come about? What changes in the music were involved in the transition? Do you see the shift from an isolated subculture to a mass market as a positive or negative development?

IDEAS FOR YOUR JOURNAL

1. Write out the words to a hip-hop song like "The Message" or "One Mic." Then analyze it as a musician, a literary critic, a sociologist, a concerned parent, or a political activist. What messages would you find in the lyrics from this particular point of view?

2. If you were a hip-hop performer, what aspects of your life or the world around you would you include in your performances? Try writing your own lyrics.

As the creative director of a new advertising agency, you are competing with other agencies for a lucrative account with a national pizza company that seeks to advertise its new pizza delivery service. Before creating a commercial, what kinds of decisions do you need to make about purpose, audience, content, format, organization, and style? If your class splits into rival agencies, you may experience some of the challenge and variety that come from real-world competition.

For your commercial, you decide to dramatize the process of delivering pizza. What do you know or imagine about this process? What steps in the process might you include? What features of the delivery process might you want to emphasize?

Once you have settled on a concept, decide what you would need to film the commercial. Consider things like casting, location, props, music, dialogue, and sound effects. Make a list of your options and decisions.

Now screen "Training Camp," the commercial made for Little Caesars Pizza in 1995. How does it compare to the pizza ad you just designed?

www.mhhe.com/costanzo

Visit the Web site to view the video of this sketched storyboard.

ORIGINAL STORYBOARD FOR "TRAINING CAMP"

Title: *Training Camp* Date: 1995

Production Company: Propaganda Films

Agency: Cliff Freeman & Partners, NY

Client: Little Caesars Pizza

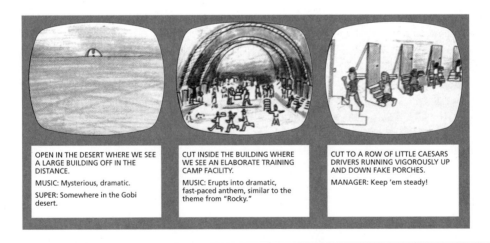

OPEN IN THE DESERT WHERE WE SEE A LARGE BUILDING OFF IN THE DISTANCE.

MUSIC: Mysterious, dramatic.

SUPER: Somewhere in the Gobi desert.

CUT INSIDE THE BUILDING WHERE WE SEE AN ELABORATE TRAINING CAMP FACILITY.

MUSIC: Erupts into dramatic, fast-paced anthem, similar to the theme from "Rocky."

CUT TO A ROW OF LITTLE CAESARS DRIVERS RUNNING VIGOROUSLY UP AND DOWN FAKE PORCHES.

MANAGER: Keep 'em steady!

CUT TO THE "CHANGE-MAKING STATION" WHERE WE SEE A SERIES OF FAKE HANDS.

SPEAKER: I get change?

THE DRIVERS ARE FRANTICALLY MAKING CHANGE, THEN HITTING THE RED BUZZER TO STOP THE CLOCK.

SPEAKER #2: Change?
SPEAKER #3: Change?
SPEAKER #4, etc.: Change?

CUT TO DRIVERS AT FAKE DOORS, PRACTICING THEIR KNOCKING TECHNIQUES.

MANAGER: Bell, knocker, hand! Bell, knocker, hand!

VO: It's been a long time coming, but we needed time to prepare.

CUT TO A DRIVER SAYING "Pizza! Pizza!"

MANAGER: No, no, no!

HE PUSHES THE BOY'S CHEEKS IN.

MANAGER: Pi-zza! Pi-zza!

CUT TO A DRIVER HOLDING A PIZZA BOX IN THE AIR. HE RAISES THE BOX ABOVE HIS HEAD MOMENTS BEFORE A STREAM OF WATER HITS HIM IN THE FACE.

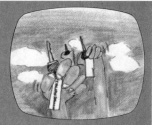

PULL BACK TO REVEAL DRIVER AT THE "SPRINKLER STATION."

VO: Little Caesars intrduces. . .

CUT TO A DRIVER RUNNING FROM A MECHANICAL DOG.

CUT TO THE BLUE SKY WHERE WE SEE DRIVERS' HANDS VICTORIOUSLY WAVING CAR KEYS IN THE AIR.

MUSIC BUILDS TO A TRIUMPHANT FINALE.

VO: . . . delivery!

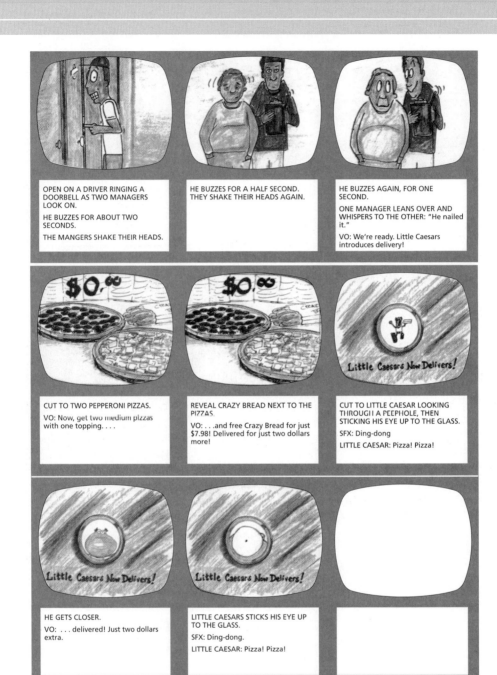

OPEN ON A DRIVER RINGING A
DOORBELL AS TWO MANAGERS
LOOK ON.

HE BUZZES FOR ABOUT TWO
SECONDS.

THE MANGERS SHAKE THEIR HEADS.

HE BUZZES FOR A HALF SECOND.
THEY SHAKE THEIR HEADS AGAIN.

HE BUZZES AGAIN, FOR ONE
SECOND.

ONE MANAGER LEANS OVER AND
WHISPERS TO THE OTHER: "He nailed
it."

VO: We're ready. Little Caesars
introduces delivery!

CUT TO TWO PEPPERONI PIZZAS.

VO: Now, get two medium pizzas
with one topping. . . .

REVEAL CRAZY BREAD NEXT TO THE
PIZZAS.

VO: . . .and free Crazy Bread for just
$7.98! Delivered for just two dollars
more!

CUT TO LITTLE CAESAR LOOKING
THROUGH A PEEPHOLE, THEN
STICKING HIS EYE UP TO THE GLASS.

SFX: Ding-dong

LITTLE CAESAR: Pizza! Pizza!

HE GETS CLOSER.

VO: . . . delivered! Just two dollars
extra.

LITTLE CAESARS STICKS HIS EYE UP
TO THE GLASS.

SFX: Ding-dong.

LITTLE CAESAR: Pizza! Pizza!

RESPONSE QUESTIONS

1. What is your general impression of this commercial? Did you find it funny, clever, silly? Try to capture the overall feeling or idea in a few words.

2. Locate specific moments that contributed to your impression. What were the funniest, cleverest, or silliest moments in the commercial?

3. Does "Training Camp" remind you of other commercials or movies you have seen? What are the points of similarity? How are they different?

4. Did anything about the commercial confuse you? Did you get the point at the beginning, or did it become clear later in the sequence?

GUIDELINES FOR ANALYSIS

1. If you did the preview activities in this section, compare "Training Camp" to your original ideas. What choices about setting, casting, camera placement, acting, and organization were made for this commercial? How well do these choices contribute to the goal of advertising Caesars Pizza's delivery service?

2. Much of the filmed commercial's appeal comes from its implied comparisons. What familiar activities does it remind you of? What is the effect of comparing pizza delivery to these activities?

3. Consider how the film divides the delivery process into steps. How many steps can you remember? Why do you think these particular steps were chosen?

4. How does the film begin and end? How does the beginning set the mood? What statement about Caesars Pizza does the ending make?

5. The film is composed of more than two dozen different shots. Notice how it alternates among close-ups, medium shots, long shots, and different angles. What does the camera placement emphasize? How do the editing and sound track create a sense of continuity from one shot to the next?

6. Compare the original storyboard (page 198) to the actual commercial on this book's Web site (www.mhhe.com/costanzo). What changes were made in the final cut? Why do you think the editor made these revisions?

CONNECTING TO CULTURE

1. The employees in this commercial are wearing uniforms. In what other jobs are uniforms worn regularly? Why? What cultural beliefs might explain our culture's preference for uniforms?

2. What attitudes do Americans have about the rigorous kind of training illustrated in this commercial? Consider how such discipline is represented in military films, sports magazines, and other popular media. How does "Training Camp" fit into these traditions?

3. Pizza delivery is part of our fast-food culture. Do you think it is a healthy trend? What accounts for the popularity of fast-food service in our country? What are the benefits and risks?

1. Keep a record of the commercials you see. Classify them by consumer categories. How many advertise fast foods, fast cars, quick solutions to health problems, and so on? Besides the products themselves, what values or beliefs are these ads promoting?

2. Classify the kinds of uniforms you see in a single day. Are more uniforms worn by men or women? Are more uniforms worn by professional people, business employees, or blue-collar workers? Are the wearers older or younger? Based on your observations, what can you say about gender, age, and social class with respect to uniforms?

PREVIEW

Nancy Masterson Sakamoto's name reflects the two cultures she knows best. An American born in 1931, she married a Japanese man and moved with him to Osaka, Japan. While living there, she was both fascinated and bewildered by the differences between Japanese and American ways of doing things as simple as having a conversation. Her efforts to explain these cultural distinctions led to a textbook on conversational English, *Polite Fictions: Why Japanese and Americans Seem Rude to Each Other* (by Nancy Sakamoto and Reiko Naotsuka; Kinseido, Tokyo, 1982). The following essay is taken from her book.

Conversational Ballgames
By Nancy Masterson Sakamoto

After I was married and had lived in Japan for a while, my Japanese gradually improved to the point where I could take part in simple conversations with my husband and his friends and family. And I began to notice that often, when I joined in, the others would look startled, and the conversational topic would come to a halt. After this happened several times, it became clear to me that I was doing something wrong. But for a long time, I didn't know what it was.

Finally, after listening carefully to many Japanese conversations, I discovered what my problem was. Even though I was speaking Japanese, I was handling the conversation in a western way.

Japanese-style conversations develop quite differently from western-style conversations. And the difference isn't only in the languages. I realized that just as I kept trying to hold western-style conversations even when I was speaking Japanese, so my English students kept trying to hold Japanese-style conversations even when they were speaking English. We were unconsciously playing entirely different conversational ballgames.

A western-style conversation between two people is like a game of tennis. If I introduce a topic, a conversational ball, I expect you to hit it back. If you agree with me, I don't expect you simply to agree and do nothing more. I expect you to add something—a reason for agreeing, another example, or an elaboration to carry the idea further. But I don't expect you always to agree. I am just as happy if you question me, or challenge me, or completely disagree with me. Whether you agree or disagree, your response will return the ball to me.

5   And then it is my turn again. I don't serve a new ball from my original starting line. I hit your ball back again from where it has bounced. I carry your idea further, or answer your questions or objections, or chal-

lenge or question you. And so the ball goes back and forth, with each of us doing our best to give it a new twist, an original spin, or a powerful smash.

And the more vigorous the action, the more interesting and exciting the game. Of course, if one of us gets angry, it spoils the conversation, just as it spoils a tennis game. But getting excited is not at all the same as getting angry. After all, we are not trying to hit each other. We are trying to hit the ball. So if we attack only each other's opinions, and do not attack each other personally, we don't expect anyone to get hurt. *A* conversation is supposed to be interesting and exciting.

If there are more than two people in the conversation, it is like doubles in tennis, or like volleyball. There's no wait line. Whoever is nearest and quickest hits the ball, and if you step back, someone else will hit it. No one stops the game to give you a turn. You're responsible for taking your own turn.

But whether it's two players or a group, everyone does his best to keep the ball going, and no one person has the ball for very long.

A Japanese-style conversation, however, is not at all like tennis or volleyball. It's like bowling. You wait for your turn. And you always know your place in line. It depends on such things as whether you are older or younger, a close friend or a relative stranger to the previous speaker, in a senior or junior position, and so on.

When your turn comes, you step up to the starting line with your bowling ball, and carefully bowl it. Everyone else stands back and watches politely, murmuring encouragement. Everyone waits until the ball has reached the end of the alley, and watches to see if it knocks down all the pins, or only some of them, or none of them. There is a pause, while everyone registers your score.

Then, after everyone is sure that you have completely finished your turn, the next person in line steps up to the same starting line, with a different ball. He doesn't return your ball, and he does not begin from where your ball stopped. There is no back and forth at all. All the balls run parallel. And there is always a suitable pause between turns. There is no rush, no excitement, no scramble for the ball.

No wonder everyone looked startled when I took part in Japanese conversations. I paid no attention to whose turn it was, and kept snatching the ball halfway down the alley and throwing it back at the bowler. Of course the conversation died. I was playing the wrong game.

This explains why it is almost impossible to get a western-style conversation or discussion going with English students in Japan. I used to think that the problem was their lack of English language ability. But I finally came to realize that the biggest problem is that they, too, are playing the wrong game.

10

Whenever I serve a volleyball, everyone just stands back and watches it fall, with occasional murmurs of encouragement. No one hits it back. Everyone waits until I call on someone to take a turn. And when that person speaks, he doesn't hit my ball back. He serves a new ball. Again, everyone just watches it fall.

15 So I call on someone else. This person does not refer to what the previous speaker has said. He also serves a new ball. Nobody seems to have paid any attention to what anyone else has said. Everyone begins again from the same starting line, and all the balls run parallel. There is never any back and forth. Everyone is trying to bowl with a volleyball.

And if I try a simpler conversation, with only two of us, then the other person tries to bowl with my tennis ball. No wonder foreign English teachers in Japan get discouraged.

Now that you know about the difference in the conversational ballgames, you may think that all your troubles are over. But if you have been trained all your life to play one game, it is no simple matter to switch to another, even if you know the rules. Knowing the rules is not at all the same thing as playing the game.

Even now, during a conversation in Japanese I will notice a startled reaction, and belatedly realize that once again I have rudely interrupted by instinctively trying to hit back the person's bowling ball. It is no easier for me to "just listen" during a conversation, than it is for my Japanese students to "relax" when speaking with foreigners. Now I can truly sympathize with how hard they must find it to try to carry on western-style conversation.

If I have not yet learned to do conversational bowling in Japanese, at least I have figured out one thing that puzzled me for a long time. After his first trip to America, my husband complained that Americans asked him so many questions and made him talk so much at the dinner table that he never had a chance to eat. When I asked him why he couldn't talk and eat at the same time, he said that Japanese do not customarily think that dinner, especially on fairly formal occasions, is a suitable time for extended conversation.

20 Since westerners think that conversation is an indispensable part of dining, and indeed would consider it impolite not to converse with one's dinner partner, I found this Japanese custom rather strange. Still, I could accept it as a cultural difference even though I didn't really understand it. But when my husband added, in explanation, that Japanese consider it extremely rude to talk with one's mouth full, I got confused. Talking with one's mouth full is certainly not an American custom. We think it very rude, too. Yet we still manage to talk a lot and eat at the same time. How do we do it?

For a long time, I couldn't explain it, and it bothered me, until after I discovered the conversational ballgames, I finally found the answer. Of course! In a western-style conversation, you hit the ball, and while someone else is hitting it back, you take a bite, chew, and swallow. Then you hit the ball again, and then eat some more. The more people there are in the conversation the more chances you have to eat. But even with only two of you talking, you still have plenty of chances to eat.

Maybe that's why polite conversation at the dinner table has never been a traditional part of Japanese etiquette. Your turn to talk would last so long without interruption that you'd never get a chance to eat.

RESPONSE QUESTIONS

1. Midway through her essay, Sakamoto comes to the realization that she was "playing the wrong game." Explain what she means. Does she offer any solutions to the problem? Why or why not?

2. Sakamoto originally wrote this essay for Japanese students. What difference does it make when you read it from their point of view?

3. Did Sakamoto's essay remind you of any personal experiences with speakers of another language? Describe what happened. What expectations about communication did you or

the other speakers bring to the experience? What problems did you encounter? What was the outcome?

GUIDELINES FOR ANALYSIS

1. What exactly is Sakamoto analyzing in this essay? What is her primary purpose in doing this analysis?
2. The author uses several analogies to make her case. What is she comparing? Trace the main points of her comparisons. How does she use these analogies to organize her essay?

QUESTIONS OF CULTURE

1. Compare two groups that you know well in terms of the games they play, literal or figurative. What are the rules of the game? What are the goals? How do the players respond to winning or losing?
2. In *Polite Fictions,* Sakamoto gives an example of cultural misunderstanding related to the media. One day, her husband ruined the suspense in a popular television drama by telling her that one of its main characters was going to die. He had read about it in the newspaper. At first she was astonished that the Japanese press would reveal such a big part of the plot. Then she realized that Japanese audiences were less concerned about what would happen to the character than they were in how the other characters would behave at his death. They were more interested in form than in content. Judging from your own knowledge of the popular media here and abroad, what can you infer about the differences between American culture and other cultures?
3. What broad generalizations about Japanese and American culture are implied in Sakamoto's discussion of conversational styles? Has she given you enough information to convince you of the differences she finds? Does she resort to stereotypes? Explain. What are the risks of trying to generalize about such a large population of individuals?

IDEAS FOR YOUR JOURNAL

1. Compare the conversational styles of two different groups: men and women, teens and middle-aged adults, artists and techies, or the people on this side of town and the people on that side. Think of how they address each other, the words they use for everyday experience, their use of jargon, and the kinds of sentences that pass for acceptable speech. Consider any body language and rituals that characterize their speech. Based on your analysis of speech patterns, what conclusions can you come to about the underlying values of these groups?
2. Can you think of any customs in your family or neighborhood that differ from those of other families or neighborhoods? How would you explain these customs to a stranger using analogies?

PREVIEW

Born in Saint Paul, Minnesota, in 1912, Horace Miner became interested in anthropology while studying in Paris, Munich, and Kentucky. After serving as a museum curator, he moved to Canada to study a modern French-speaking community, the subject of his first book. Much of his life was divided between fieldwork and teaching at various academic institutions. He died in 1993 in Ann Arbor, Michigan.

Webster's New World Dictionary defines anthropology as "the study of man, especially of the variety, physical and cultural characteristics, distributions, customs, social relationships, etc. of mankind." What do you expect from an essay titled "Body Ritual among the Nacirema" and written by an anthropologist? Before reading Miner's essay, consider how the human body is regarded throughout the world. What do you already know about various customs of dress, health, art, and daily life that define the body in different cultures?

Body Ritual among the Nacirema
By Horace Miner

The anthropologist has become so familiar with the diversity of ways in which different people behave in similar situations that he is not apt to be surprised by even the most exotic customs. In fact, if all of the logically possible combinations of behavior have not been found somewhere in the world, he is apt to suspect that they must be present in some yet undescribed tribe. The point has, in fact, been expressed with respect to clan organization by Murdock.[1] In this light, the magical beliefs and practices of the Nacirema present such unusual aspects that it seems desirable to describe them as an example of the extremes to which human behavior can go.

Professor Linton[2] first brought the ritual of the Nacirema to the attention of anthropologists twenty years ago, but the culture of this people is still very poorly understood. They are a North American group living in the territory between the Canadian Cree, the Yaqui and Tarahumare of Mexico, and the Carib and Arawak of the Antilles. Little is known of their origin, although tradition states that they came from the east. . . .

Nacirema culture is characterized by a highly developed market economy which has evolved in a rich natural habitat. While much of the people's time is devoted to economic pursuits, a large part of the fruits of these labors and a considerable portion of the day are spent in ritual activity. The focus of this activity is the human body, the appearance and health of which loom as a dominant concern in the ethos of the people. While such a concern is certainly not unusual, its ceremonial aspects and associated philosophy are unique.

The fundamental belief underlying the whole system appears to be that the human body is ugly and that its natural tendency is to debility and disease. Incarcerated in such a body, man's only hope is to avert these characteristics through the use of ritual and ceremony. Every household has one or more shrines devoted to this purpose. The more powerful individuals in the society have several shrines in their houses and, in fact, the opulence of a house is often referred to in terms of the number of such ritual centers it possesses. Most houses are of wattle and daub construction, but the shrine rooms of the more wealthy are walled with stone. Poorer families imitate the rich by applying pottery plaques to their shrine walls.

5   While each family has at least one such shrine, the rituals associated with it are not family ceremonies but are private and secret. The rites are normally only discussed with children, and then only during the period when they are being initiated into these mysteries. I was able, however, to establish sufficient rapport with the natives to examine these shrines and to have the rituals described to me.

The focal point of the shrine is a box or chest which is built into the wall. In this chest are kept the many charms and magical potions without which no native believes he could live. These preparations are secured from a variety of specialized practitioners. The most powerful of these are the medicine men, whose assistance must be rewarded with substantial gifts. However, the medicine men do not provide the curative potions for their clients, but decide what the ingredients should be and then write them down in an ancient and secret language. This writing is understood only by the medicine men and by the herbalists who, for another gift, provide the required charm.

The charm is not disposed of after it has served its purpose, but is placed in the charm-box of the household shrine. As these magical materials are specific for certain ills, and the real or imagined maladies of the people are many, the charm-box is usually full to overflowing. The magical packets are so numerous that people forget what their purposes were and fear to use them again. While the natives are very vague on this point, we can only assume that the idea in retaining all the old magical materials is that their presence in the charm-box, before which the body rituals are conducted, will in some way protect the worshiper.

Beneath the charm-box is a small font. Each day every member of the family, in succession, enters the shrine room, bows his head before the charm-box, mingles different sorts of holy water in the font, and proceeds with a brief rite of ablution.[3] The holy waters are secured from the Water Temple of the community, where the priests conduct elaborate ceremonies to make the liquid ritually pure.

In the hierarchy of magical practitioners, and below the medicine men in prestige, are specialists whose designation is best translated as "holy-mouth-men." The Nacirema have an almost pathological horror of and fascination with the mouth, the condition of which is believed to have a supernatural influence on all social relationships. Were it not for the rituals of the mouth, they believe that their teeth would fall out, their gums bleed, their jaws shrink, their friends desert them, and their lovers reject them. They also believe that a strong relationship exists between oral and moral characteristics. For example, there is a ritual ablution of the mouth for children which is supposed to improve their moral fiber.

10   The daily body ritual performed by everyone includes a mouth-rite. Despite the fact that these people are so punctilious[4] about care of the mouth, this rite involves a practice which strikes the uninitiated stranger as revolting. It was reported to me that the ritual consists of inserting a small bundle of hog hairs into the mouth, along with certain magical powders, and then moving the bundle in a highly formalized series of gestures.[5]

In addition to the private mouth-rite, the people seek out a holy-mouth-man once or twice a year. These practitioners have an impressive set of paraphernalia, consisting of a variety of augers, awls, probes, and prods. The use of these items in the exorcism of the evils of the mouth involves almost unbelievable ritual torture of the client. The holy-mouth-man opens the client's mouth and, using the above mentioned tools, enlarges any holes which decay may have created in the teeth. Magical materials are put into these holes. If there are no naturally occurring holes in the teeth, large sections of one or more teeth are gouged out so that the supernatural substance can be applied. In the client's view, the purpose of these ministrations[6] is to arrest decay and to draw friends. The extremely sacred and traditional character of the rite is evident in the fact that the natives return to the holy-mouth-men year after year, despite the fact that their teeth continue to decay.

It is to be hoped that, when a thorough study of the Nacirema is made, there will be careful inquiry into the personality structure of these people. One has but to watch the gleam in the eye of a holy-mouth-man, as he jabs an awl into an exposed nerve, to suspect that a certain amount of sadism is involved. If this can be established, a very interesting pattern emerges, for most of the population shows definite masochistic tendencies. It was to these that Professor Linton referred in discussing a distinctive part of the daily body ritual which is performed only by men. This part of the rite includes scraping and lacerating the surface of the face with a sharp instrument. Special women's rites are performed only four times during each lunar month, but what they lack in frequency is made up in barbarity. As part of this ceremony, women bake their heads in small ovens for about an hour. The theoretically interesting point is that what seems to be a preponderantly masochistic people have developed sadistic specialists.

The medicine men have an imposing temple, or *latipso,* in every community of any size. The more elaborate ceremonies required to treat very sick patients can only be performed at this temple. These ceremonies involve not only the thaumaturge [7] but a permanent group of vestal maidens who move sedately about the temple chambers in distinctive costume and headdress.

The *latipso* ceremonies are so harsh that it is phenomenal that a fair proportion of the really sick natives who enter the temple ever recover. Small children whose indoctrination is still incomplete have been known to resist attempts to take them to the temple because "that is where you go to die." Despite this fact, sick adults are not only willing but eager to undergo the protracted ritual purification, if they can afford to do so. No matter how ill the supplicant or how grave the emergency, the guardians of many temples will not admit a client if he cannot give a rich gift to the custodian. Even after one has gained and survived the ceremonies, the guardians will not permit the neophyte to leave until he makes still another gift.

15   The supplicant entering the temple is first stripped of all his or her clothes. In everyday life the Nacirema avoids exposure of his body and its natural functions. Bathing and excretory acts are performed only in the secrecy of the household shrine, where they are ritualized as part of the body-rites. Psychological shock results from the fact that body secrecy is suddenly lost upon entry into the latipso. A man, whose own wife has never seen him in an excretory act, suddenly finds himself naked and assisted by a vestal maiden while he performs his natural functions into a sacred vessel. This sort of ceremonial treatment is necessitated by the fact that the excreta are used by a diviner to ascertain the course and nature of the client's sickness. Female clients, on the other hand, find their naked bodies are subjected to the scrutiny, manipulation and prodding of the medicine men.

Few supplicants in the temple are well enough to do anything but lie on their hard beds. The daily ceremonies, like the rites of the holy-mouth-men, involve discomfort and torture. With ritual precision, the vestals awaken their miserable charges each dawn and roll them about on their beds of pain while performing ablutions, in the formal movements of which the maidens are highly trained. At other times they insert magic wands in the supplicant's mouth or force him to eat substances which are supposed to be healing. From time to time the medicine men come to their clients and jab magically treated needles into their flesh. The fact that these temple ceremonies may not cure, and may even kill the neophyte, in no way decreases the people's faith in the medicine men.

There remains one other kind of practitioner, known as a "listener." This witchdoctor has the power to exorcise the devils that lodge in the heads of people who have been bewitched. The Nacirema believe that parents bewitch their own children. Mothers are particularly suspected of putting a curse on children while teaching them the secret body rituals. The counter-magic of the witchdoctor is unusual in its lack of ritual. The patient simply tells the "listener" all his troubles and fears, beginning with the earliest difficulties he can remember. The memory displayed by the Nacirema in these exorcism sessions is truly remarkable. It is not uncommon for the patient to bemoan the rejection he felt upon being weaned as a babe, and a few individuals even see their troubles going back to the traumatic effects of their own birth.

In conclusion, mention must be made of certain practices which have their base in native esthetics but which depend upon the pervasive aversion to the natural body and its functions. There are ritual fasts to make fat people thin and ceremonial feasts to make thin people fat. Still other rites are used to make women's breasts larger if they are small, and smaller if they are large. General dissatisfaction with breast shape is symbolized in the fact that the ideal form is virtually outside the range of human variation. A few women afflicted with almost inhuman hyper-mammary development are so idolized that they make a handsome living by simply going from village to village and permitting the natives to stare at them for a fee.

Reference has already been made to the fact that excretory functions are ritualized, routinized, and relegated to secrecy. Natural reproductive functions are similarly distorted. Intercourse is taboo as a topic and scheduled as an act. Efforts are made to avoid pregnancy by the use of magical materials or by limiting intercourse to certain phases of the moon. Conception is actually very infrequent. When pregnant, women dress so as to hide their condition. Parturition takes place in secret, without friends or relatives to assist, and the majority of women do not nurse their infants.

20   Our review of the ritual life of the Nacirema has certainly shown them to be a magic-ridden people. It is hard to understand how they have managed to exist so long under the burdens which they have imposed upon themselves. But even such exotic customs as these take on real meaning when they are viewed with the insight provided by Malinowski [8] when he wrote:

> Looking from far and above, from our high places of safety in the developed civilization, it is easy to see all the crudity and irrelevance of magic. But without its power and guidance early man could not have mastered his practical difficulties as he has done, nor could man have advanced to the higher stages of civilization.

---

1. George Peter Murdock (1897–1985), famous ethnographer.

2. Ralph Linton (1893–1953), best known for studies of enculturation (maintaining that all culture is learned rather than inherited; the process by which a society's culture is transmitted from one generation to the next), claiming culture is humanity's "social heredity."

3. A washing or cleansing of the body or a part of the body. From the Latin *abluere,* to wash away.

4. Marked by precise observance of the finer points of etiquette and formal conduct.

5. It is worthy of note that since Prof. Miner's original research was conducted, the Nacirema have almost universally abandoned the natural bristles of their private mouth-rite in favor of oil-based polymerized synthetics. Additionally, the powders associated with this ritual have generally been semi-liquefied. Other updates to the Nacirema culture shall be eschewed in this document for the sake of parsimony.

6. Tending to religious or other important functions.

7. A miracle-worker.

8. Bronislaw Malinowski (1884–1942), famous cultural anthropologist best known for his argument that people everywhere share common biological and psychological needs and that the function of all cultural institutions is to fulfill such needs; the nature of the institution is determined by its function.

RESPONSE QUESTIONS

1. Miner offers the Nacirema as "an example of the extremes to which human behavior can go." Which of their practices and institutions seem most extreme to you?

2. What fundamental belief about the human body does Miner say explains the bizarre rituals of Nacirema culture?

3. Where in the essay was your interest highest? Where was it lowest? Why? For what kind of reader is Miner writing? How can you tell? Did you feel included in his audience?

4. At what point in the essay did you begin to understand the author's real subject? What clues help to identify the Nacirema? Where is Miner's purpose most clearly expressed? Ultimately, what theme or underlying messages come through?

GUIDELINES FOR ANALYSIS

1. What particular aspects of Nacirema culture seem to interest the author? To which of these does he pay most attention?

2. "Body Ritual among the Nacirema" was written in a particular style and format. How would you describe them? How did these conventions affect your reading of the essay?

3. How has Miner organized his analysis? What are his subdivisions of Nacirema culture and how are they arranged in the essay?

CONNECTING TO CULTURE

1. Go back and select specific terms that Miner uses to identify the significant features of Nacirema life, such as "curative potions," "charm-box," and "mouth-rite." What does each term reveal about the Nacirema people?

Visual Prompt

2. If you have been in another country or a different part of the United States, compare the attitudes of people in that region toward the human body to your own view. How are these attitudes expressed in clothing, hairstyles, and ideal body types? How are they reflected in the foods, health care, and medical institutions of the region?

IDEAS FOR YOUR JOURNAL

1. Identify one ritual of American culture that we take for granted (birthday parties, Super Bowl Sunday, the workout room) and write about it from the point of view of a cultural anthropologist. Without being judgmental, describe the practices you observe and speculate on the underlying beliefs that might explain them.

2. Try pitching a common artifact of American culture (a video game, a backpack, Barbie dolls) to several distinctly different readers in terms they would appreciate and understand. For example, how would you sell it to a child, a businessman, an actor, a politician, or a forest ranger?

PREVIEW

Few popular writers have been as successful or well known as Stephen King. Nearly all his books have been best sellers, and many have been turned into movies, from *Carrie* and *The Shining* to *The Dead Zone* and *The Green Mile*. Born in 1947, King grew up with his mother and brother in Portland, Maine, after his father left one night and never returned. He began writing stories at an early age, developing a special flair for horror and science fiction. After graduating from the University of Maine with a major in English, he started sending his manuscripts out to publishers while working at odd jobs. *Carrie* was bought by Doubleday and released in 1974 to great acclaim, launching a career that now includes more than thirty novels, five story collections, nine screenplays, and nonfiction.

Stephen King's success attests to the widespread appeal of horror as a genre. Stories of the supernatural have captivated audiences for centuries, and horror films have found a distinctive if unsettling niche in our culture. In the following essay, King analyzes the underlying reasons for our fascination with the macabre. The essay originally appeared in *Playboy* magazine.

Why We Crave Horror Movies

By Stephen King

I think that we're all mentally ill; those of us outside the asylums only hide it a little better—and maybe not all that much better, after all. We've all known people who talk to themselves, people who sometimes squinch their faces into horrible grimaces when they believe no one is watching, people who have some hysterical fear—of snakes, the dark, the tight place, the long drop . . . and, of course, those final worms and grubs that are waiting so patiently underground.

When we pay our four or five bucks and seat ourselves at tenth-row center in a theater showing a horror movie, we are daring the nightmare.

Why? Some of the reasons are simple and obvious. To show that we can, that we are not afraid, that we can ride this roller coaster. Which is not to say that a really good horror movie may not surprise a scream out of us at some point, the way we may scream when the roller coaster twists through a complete 360 or plows through a lake at the bottom of the drop. And horror movies, like roller coasters, have always been the special province of the young; by the time one turns 40 or 50, one's appetite for double twists or 360-degree loops may be considerably depleted.

We also go to re-establish our feelings of essential normality; the horror movie is innately conservative, even reactionary. Freda Jackson as the horrible melting woman in *Die, Monster, Die!* confirms for us that no matter how far we may be removed from the beauty of a Robert Redford or a Diana Ross, we are still light-years from true ugliness.

And we go to have fun.

Ah, but this is where the ground starts to slope away, isn't it? Because this is a very peculiar sort of fun indeed. The fun comes from seeing others menaced—sometimes killed. One critic has suggested that if pro football has become the voyeur's version of combat, then the horror film has become the modern version of the public lynching.

It is true that the mythic, "fairytale" horror film intends to take away the shades of gray. . . . It urges us to put away our more civilized and adult penchant for analysis and to become children again, seeing things in pure blacks and whites. It may be that horror movies provide psychic relief on this level because this invitation to lapse into simplicity, irrationality and even outright madness is extended so rarely. We are told we may allow our emotions a free rein . . . or no rein at all.

If we are all insane, then sanity becomes a matter of degree. If your insanity leads you to carve up women like Jack the Ripper or the Cleveland Torso Murderer, we clap you away in the funny farm (but neither of those two amateur-night surgeons was ever caught, heh-heh-heh); if, on the other hand your insanity leads you only to talk to yourself when you're under stress or to pick your nose on your morning bus, then you are left alone to go about your business . . . though it is doubtful that you will ever be invited to the best parties.

The potential lyncher is in almost all of us (excluding saints, past and present; but then, most saints have been crazy in their own ways), and every now and then, he had to be let loose to scream and roll around in the grass. Our emotions and our fears form their own body, and we recognize that it demands its own exercise to maintain proper muscle tone. Certain of these emotional muscles are accepted—even exalted—in civilized society; they are, of course, the emotions that tend to maintain the status quo of civilization itself. Love, friendship, loyalty, kindness—these are all the emotions that we applaud, emotions that have been immortalized in the couplets of Hallmark cards and in the verses (I don't care call it poetry) of Leonard Nimoy.

When we exhibit these emotions, society showers us with positive reinforcement; we learn this even before we get out of diapers. When, as children, we hug our rotten little puke of a sister and give her a kiss, all the aunts and uncles smile and twit and cry, "Isn't he the sweetest little thing?" Such coveted treats as chocolate-covered graham crackers often follow. But if we deliberately slam the rotten little puke of a sister's fingers in the door, sanctions follow—angry remonstrance from parents, aunts and uncles; instead of a chocolate-covered graham cracker, a spanking.

But anticivilization emotions don't go away, and they demand periodic exercise. We have such "sick" jokes as, "What's the difference between a truckload of bowling balls and a truckload of dead babies? (You can't unload a truckload of bowling balls with

a pitchfork . . . a joke, by the way, that I heard originally from a ten-year-old.) Such a joke may surprise a laugh or a grin out of us even as we recoil, a possibility that confirms the thesis: If we share a brotherhood of man, then we also share an insanity of man. None of which is intended as a defense of either the sick joke or insanity but merely as an explanation of why the best horror films, like the best fairy tales, manage to be reactionary, anarchistic, and revolutionary all at the same time.

The mythic horror movie, like the sick joke, has a dirty job to do. It deliberately appeals to all that is worst in us. It is morbidity unchained, our most base instincts let free, our nastiest fantasies realized . . . and it all happens, fittingly enough, in the dark. For those reasons, good liberals often shy away from horror films. For myself, I like to see the most aggressive of them—DAWN OF THE DEAD, for instance—as lifting a trap door in the civilized forebrain and throwing a basket of raw meat to the hungry alligators swimming around in that subterranean river beneath.

Why bother? Because it keeps them from getting out, man. It keeps them down there and me up here. It was Lennon and McCartney who said that all you need is love, and I would agree with that.

As long as you keep the gators fed.

RESPONSE QUESTIONS

1. What is your experience with horror movies? Do you enjoy them or avoid them? Give examples of horror films that made the biggest impression on you one way or the other, and describe your reaction to them.

2. King begins by saying, "we're all mentally ill." Later he adds, "sanity becomes a matter of degree." What do you think he means by this? How seriously is he proposing that everyone is mad?

3. What reasons does the essay offer for our preoccupation with horror? With which of these explanations, if any, do you agree? What other reasons can you give?

GUIDELINES FOR ANALYSIS

1. Where does King come closest to expressing his main idea in a thesis statement?

2. In paragraph 11, King asserts, "the best horror films, like the best fairy tales, manage to be reactionary, anarchistic, and revolutionary all at the same time." Explain what he means. What evidence does he offer to support his claim?

3. The essay is filled with analogies like the comparison between horror movies and roller coasters or sick jokes. Find one such analogy and follow its implications. What does the analogy contribute to the analysis of horror films?

4. King is a master of beginnings and endings. What does he achieve with the opening and closing lines of the essay? Which paragraphs end with a good "clincher"—a final sentence that affirms the main idea and drives it home?

5. At times, King seems to be having fun while he writes. He tells a few jokes, refers to "our rotten little puke of a sister," and at one point inserts a "heh-heh-heh" into his narrative. How does humor function in the essay? Does King use this playful tone in any other works you may have read? What connections can you make between humor and horror?

QUESTIONS OF CULTURE

1. King's essay does not seem to ask whether horror movies appeal more to men or women, to Americans or non-Americans, or to some ethnic groups more than others. Are these important questions to ask? What might such questions lead to?

2. Movies like *The Rocky Picture Horror Show* (1975) and *Night of the Living Dead* (1968) have large cult followings. Visit some of the Web sites dedicated to them or conduct interviews with fans as if you were a researcher studying a foreign culture. What conclusions can you draw from your study?

IDEAS FOR YOUR JOURNAL

1. Think of horror films that you have seen. Can you apply Stephen King's ideas to any of them? Try to analyze one or two films as if you were the author. What does this analysis explain about the films or your response to them?

2. Explore another popular genre, such as gangster films, animal house comedies, true romance novels, or reality television. Consider the same kinds of questions that King asks about horror films, but give your own answers. What are the characteristics of the genre you have chosen? What reasons can you find for its popularity? What does the genre reveal about American culture?

PREVIEW

It is nearly impossible to drive these days without seeing an SUV. Whether you own a sport utility vehicle, would like to, or would never buy one in your life, you probably have opinions about this new phenomenon of the American road. In the following essay, a journalist brings humor and insight to this ubiquitous icon of American culture.

Jack Hitt, born in 1957, is a contributing writer for *GQ, Harper's, Lingua Franca,* and National Public Radio. He also writes for the *New York Times Magazine.* An award-winning journalist with wide interests and a sharp wit, Hitt is a keen observer of cultural barometers. *Off the Road: A Modern Walk down the Pilgrim's Route into Spain* (Simon & Schuster, 2005) is an irreverent pilgrimage through Iberian history. "The Hidden Life of SUVs" originally appeared in the July/August 1999 issue of *Mother Jones* magazine.

The Hidden Life of SUVs

By Jack Hitt

What's in a name? What do you make of a passenger vehicle called a Bronco?

Or one dubbed a Cherokee? How about a Wrangler? Are they just chrome-plated expressions of sublimated testosterone flooding the highways? Check out the herd that grazes the average car lot these days: Blazer, Tracker, Yukon, Navigator, Tahoe, Range Rover, Explorer, Mountaineer, Denali, Expedition, Discovery, Bravada. Besides signaling that we're not Civic or Gallant, they indicate there's something else going on here.

These are, of course, all names of sport utility vehicles, the miracle that has resurrected Motown. Think back to the dark days of the previous decade when the Japanese auto industry had nearly buried Detroit. In 1981, only a relative handful of four-wheel-drives traveled the road, and the phrase "sport utility vehicle" hadn't entered the language. Today, they number more than 14 million, and that figure is growing fast. If you include pickups and vans, then quasi trucks now constitute about half of all the vehicles sold in America. Half. They're rapidly displacing cars on the highways of our new unbraking economy.

Go to any car lot and jawbone with a salesman, and you'll find that big is once again better. Any savvy dealer (clutching his copy of Zig Ziglar's *Ziglar on Selling*) will try to talk you up to one of the latest behemoths, which have bloated to such Brobdingnagian dimensions as to have entered the realm of the absurd.

Ford, in fact, has unveiled a new monster, the Excursion, due to hit the showrooms before the millennium. With a corporate straight face, its literature touts as selling points that the Excursion is "less than 7 feet tall . . . and less than 20 feet long" and is "more fuel efficient . . . than two average full-size sedans."

These Big Berthas have even spawned new vocabulary words. The biggest of the big, for instance, can no longer fit comfortably in a standard-size garage or the average parking space. So salesmen will often sell you on one of the "smaller" SUVs by praising its "garageability."

What, then, explains the inexorable advance of these giant SUVs into our lives? Why do we want cars that are, in fact, high-clearance trucks with four-wheel drive, an optional winch, and what amounts to a cowcatcher?

The answer, in part, lies in the vehicles themselves. Cars are not fickle fashions. They are the most expensive and visible purchases in an economy drenched in matters of status and tricked out with hidden meanings.

Some people will tell you that the shift from car to truck can be explained simply: We Americans are getting, um, bigger in the beam. We aren't comfortable in those Camrys, so we trade up to a vehicle we can sit in without feeling scrunched. Here's a new buzzword for Ziglar disciples: fatassability.

But I think the key is found not so much in their size or expense (although both keep ballooning) but in those ersatz Western names. The other day, I saw an acquaintance of mine in a boxy steed called a Durango. Say it out loud for me: "Durango." Can you get the syllables off your tongue without irony? In the post-"Seinfeld" era, can anyone say Durango without giving it an Elaine Benes enunciation at every syllable? Doo-RANG-Go.

The true irony comes from the fact that this thoroughly market-researched word no longer has any core meaning. No one comprehends its denotation (Colorado town) but only its vague connotations (rugged individualism, mastery over the wilderness, cowboy endurance). The word does not pin down meaning so much as conjure up images.

These names are only the end product of the intense buyer-profiling that the car companies and the marketing firms continuously carry out. By the time they make it to the lot, these cars are streamlined Frankensteinian concoctions of our private anxieties and desires. We consumers don't so much shop for one of these SUVs as they shop for us.

A typical focus-group study might be one like the "cluster analysis" conducted by college students for Washington, D.C.-area car dealers in 1994 and reported in *Marketing Tools.* The analysts coordinated numerous databases, mail surveys, and census information to profile the typical "Bill and Barb Blazers," whose consumer apprehensions can shift from block to block, but can be pinpointed down to the four-digit appendix on the old zip code.

Each Bill and Barb then got tagged as "Young Suburbia" or "Blue-Collar Nursery" or "Urban Gentry." Translation, respectively: "college-educated, upwardly mobile white" or "middle-class, small-town" or "educated black" people. The students next identified what images spoke to the underlying appeal of an SUV for each group (prestige, child space, weekend leisure). Then they developed targeted ads to run in the media most favored by each group: the *Wall Street Journal, National Geographic,* Black Entertainment Television.

Many of the ads they developed were directed at women. For example, the one meant for upscale homeowners depicted a "woman architect standing next to her four-door [Blazer] at a Washington-area construction site" and "conveyed her professional leadership in a city with one of the highest rates of labor force participation for women."

Sport utility vehicles are quickly becoming women's cars. In fact, current statistics show that 40 percent of all SUV sales are to women, and the proportion is growing. (More men, on the other hand, are buying bigger, tougher pickup trucks.) But one wonders what's going on in the mind of that female architect or that soccer mom, high above the world in her soundproof, tinted-glass SUV, chatting on her cellular phone as she steers her mobile fortress down the street.

When GMC decided to launch the Denali (an SUV named for the Alaskan mountain), the auto-trade papers discussed the subtleties of that outdoorsy name: Even though most buyers "will never venture into territory any less trampled than the local country club parking lot," wrote *Ward's Auto World,* "the important goal of the Denali marketing hype is to plant the image in customers' minds that they can conquer rugged terrain. The metaphor of Alaska is particularly apt because SUVs, especially the larger of the species, depend on the myth that we have new frontiers yet to pave. Perhaps we're trying to tame a different kind of wilderness. Indeed, in an age of gated communities the SUV is the perfect transportation shelter to protect us from fears both real and imagined."

In one focus group, female drivers confessed they hesitated even to exit the interstate "because they are afraid of what they are going to find on some surface streets."

G. Clotaire Rapaille, a French medical anthropologist and student of the consumer mind, practices a more advanced marketing technique called "archetype research." In one session he has consumers lie on the floor and lulls them into a relaxed alpha state with soothing music. Then he asks them to free-associate from images of different vehicle designs and write stories about what they hoped the design would become. Overwhelmingly,

Rapaille told the *Wall Street Journal,* his participants had the same reaction: "It's a jungle out there. It's Mad Max. People want to kill me, rape me. Give me a big thing like a tank."

More and more, SUVs give us that tanklike security, and part of the feeling derives from their literal altitude. Down there is the old working class, the new peasants who haven't figured out how to snatch a six-figure income out of our roaring economy—the little people who don't own a single Fidelity fund. There's a brutal Darwinian selection at work: They huddle down in their wretched Escorts and their Metros—not merely because they are poor but because they deserve to be.

These are the new savages: people who drive cars. They scrape and fetch about in their tiny compacts, scuttling along on surface streets. But above it all, in their gleaming, skyscraping vehicles, is the new high society—the ambitious, the exurban pioneers, the downtown frontiersmen.

It's been said that the most distinctive feature of the American character is that we continually define ourselves as pilgrims facing a new frontier. In their darkest hearts, the members of the new-money bourgeoisie have convinced themselves that we live in an unforgiving wilderness of marauders and brutes. The hidden meaning of our new conveyances can be found right on the surface. Once upon a time, Trailblazers, Explorers, and Trackers tamed the Wild West. Now, through the sorcery of focus groups, the bull-market gentry have brought the Pathfinders and Mountaineers back into their lives in the belief that they need to conquer the savage land one more time.

RESPONSE QUESTIONS

1. What were your views on SUVs before reading Jack Hitt's essay? What were they based on? Did any of your views change as a result of what you read?

2. What do you think Hitt means at the end of paragraph 12 when he says, "We consumers don't so much shop for one of these SUVs as they shop for us"? How does he support this claim? Which of his arguments or facts do you find most convincing?

3. Near the end of the essay, the author relates the SUV to American myths about frontiers and the wilderness. What leads him to these conclusions?

4. Hitt wrote this essay in 1999 at the end of a period of economic prosperity. How many of his observations still hold true today?

GUIDELINES FOR ANALYSIS

1. The author begins with a series of questions. How does he answer them? Where else in his writing does he use questions to focus his thoughts or organize the essay?

2. Notice how Hitt uses the tools of analysis. Where does he define his subject? Where does he use history or statistics to explain what caused the popularity of SUVs? Where does he give examples to illustrate his points?

3. Paragraphs 13 and 14 describe a cluster analysis of "Bill and Barb Blazers" by college students. See if you can explain what the students did. What did they expect to gain by breaking down SUV consumers into component groups? What does Hitt think of this kind of marketing research?

4. Jack Hitt writes in a lively style. He uses short, peppy sentences; plays with brand names ("we're not Civic or Gallant"); makes exaggerated use of alliteration ("the latest behemoths, which have bloated to such Brobdingnagian dimensions"); and finds a dozen comic ways to say "too big." What do you think he gains by writing this way? What would he have accomplished (or lost) by writing in a more serious style?

QUESTIONS OF CULTURE

1. At the end of paragraph 17, Hitt writes, "Indeed, in an age of gated communities the SUV is the perfect transportation shelter to protect us from fears both real and imagined." What fears is he referring to? In your opinion, do such fears justify big vehicles that look like tanks?

2. According to Hitt's research, 40 percent of all SUV sales are to women. How does he explain this statistic? What reasons can you give to explain the fact that "sport utility vehicles are quickly becoming women's cars"?

3. Take another look at Hitt's references to social class (paragraphs 20 and 21). What distinction does he make between "the new high society" and "the new peasants"? Where else do you find evidence of this distinction besides the open road?

IDEAS FOR YOUR JOURNAL

1. List the people you know who drive SUVs. What reasons can you give for their choice of a sport utility vehicle? Do the same for sports cars, convertibles, and other models. To what degree do you think an automobile reflects the owner's personality, gender, social status, or ambitions? You might try to test your theory by speculating about the vehicles owned by your classmates and professors. Then find out how close you came.

2. Make up some names for an imaginary vehicle. Consider the denotation and connotations of these names (as Hitt does with the "Durango."). If you were a marketing specialist, what names would you select for the "Young Suburbia," "Blue Collar Nursery," or the "Urban Gentry" groups described in paragraph 14?

3. Have you ever thought of a new product that might sell? Plan a focus-group study to pilot-test your idea. Who are your potential consumers? What questions would you ask them?

PREVIEW

Rituals say a lot about a culture. This is particularly true of American wedding ceremonies, which have followed predictable patterns for generations. In the following essay, a family therapist examines these patterns and finds some curious contradictions. He explains how the familiar rituals of weddings came about and why they cause such family stress.

William J. Doherty directs the Marriage and Family Programs at the University of Minnesota, where he is a professor. His many publications cover a range of topics, from responsible fatherhood to community-parenting partnerships. "Rituals of Passage: Weddings" is excerpted from his book, *The Intentional Family,* published in 1997 by Addison-Wesley.

Rituals of Passage: Weddings
By William J. Doherty

Most family rituals occur at home, away from the gaze and judgment of the community. No one is around to evaluate the quality of your family dinner or bedtime rituals. But weddings and funerals are planned by the family to share with their community, which is why they are so packed with meaning and stress.

Weddings and funerals have always been public events because they are too important to be left to individuals. We all have a stake in the start of a new family and in the death of a member of the community. But being intentional about these two central family rituals, in the face of community, traditions and pressures, is a major challenge for families.

Weddings

Wedding rituals occur in every human society because marriage in its various forms has enormous social significance. In the Western world, the weddings of royalty and the upper class were always highly ritualized because of their political importance. By the eighteenth century, families of the middle class were also celebrating weddings in a big way. But it wasn't until the nineteenth century in Europe and America that almost all families, rich and poor, began putting substantial time and resources into weddings. It was during this period that what we think of as the "traditional wedding" came into being.

The traditional wedding is American society's classic example of a rite of passage. Anthropologists studying premodern cultures realized that rituals served as transitions from one state of being to another, for example, from childhood to adolescence. (Confirmations and bar mitzvahs serve the same purpose today for Christians and Jews, respectively.) Traditional rites of passage involved a separation from the community, a transitional event, and then reemergence with a new social identity. In other words, you go away, you are transformed, and you return with a new role in the community.[1] Traditional wedding ceremonies involved all three stages.

5   Although there are regional, ethnic, and religious variations, the general outline of a traditional American wedding ceremony is as follows: At the outset, the groom stands at the front of the church with his best man, awaiting his bride. Before that, he has been mingling about, whereas the bride is in seclusion getting prepared. Immediate family members are escorted to their assigned places on either side of the aisle. There is a pause. The rite of transition begins in earnest when the music shifts and the bride's party starts walking down the aisle. The first high point of the ritual occurs when the bride appears, resplendent in a white gown, accompanied by her father or other significant man. The couple are reunited at the front when the parents hand her over to her groom. The rite of transition culminates with the couple's exchange of vows in solemn

tones in front of a member of the clergy. Sometimes at the end of the service, particularly if the woman has taken the man's family name, the clergyperson introduces the couple to the congregation as Mr. and Mrs. They are now legally and religiously married, with all the accompanying rights and responsibilities, before God and the state. The transformation of identity now complete, the couple walk back down the aisle in more informal fashion to joyous music. The receiving line then initiates the postceremony rituals of congratulations and celebration.

However, this traditional wedding ritual is packed with a number of fascinating contradictions:[2]

- *Traditional weddings are public ceremonies that are nevertheless organized by individual families.* Virtually every other public ceremony in our society is organized by clergy, officials, or other professionals. No wonder families feel so much pressure, and why they rely on wedding guides and other "expert" opinions.

- *Weddings follow strict guidelines of propriety, with a personal touch.* Dear Abby and Ann Landers have made a living responding to irate family members and guests who all have complaints about violations of wedding protocol, everything from the invitations to what the bride wore and the lack of thank-you notes. Although there are clear rights and wrongs in traditional weddings, the couple is also expected to put its own stamp on the ritual in details such as the invitations, flowers, cake, music, wedding attire, vows, and order of service. These personal choices must also be "correct," that is, not out of line with community expectations. The double-bind is thus manifest: To be unoriginal is to not measure up, but to be too original is to invite social disapproval.

- *Even couples with little religious affiliation often want religious weddings.* Couples who do not make time for the "sacred" in their daily lives nevertheless frequently want this religious aspect to their weddings. In American society, only religious surroundings make possible the traditional wedding pomp and circumstance of the majestic bridal procession up a long aisle, high-vaulted ceilings, the engulfing organ music, and the sense that something profound and holy is occurring. An office wedding by a justice of the peace carries far less ritual power. The traditional wedding ritual is even more potent if held at the place of one's baptism, bar mitzvah or bat mitzvah, and the weddings and funerals of loved ones. The walls reverberate with family memories.

10
- *Traditional religious weddings combine the sense of the sacred and the sexual, elements that are rarely connected in society.* In all cultures and all religions, the sexual bond is what makes marriage unique. Sexual themes, therefore, pervade the wedding ritual, from the presumed virginity of the bride in her white gown and the readings from the erotic Song of Songs in the Bible to the expectation that the bride and groom will exchange a lover's kiss. The couple is expected to consummate their union on the wedding night. Traditional religious rituals also refer to the outcome of their sexual activity—children, the continuity of the family, and the community. Failure to consummate the marriage is in fact grounds for annulment in most religions. This combination of the sacred and the sexual gives weddings special power in our consciousness.

- *The couple are elevated and celebrated by the community, but also teased and embarrassed.* After honoring the bride and groom with gifts and special attention, guests at the traditional wedding reception expect the couple to submit to embarrassing, silly rituals such as feeding each other cake, dancing on command, having people pay to dance with them, removing and tossing a garter belt, having to kiss whenever the guests tinkle their glasses, and enduring practical jokes as they prepare to leave for their honeymoon. The same kinds of rituals occur in many other cultures; in Hindu weddings, for example, the couple is required to play various games for the benefit of the guests. It is as if the community wants to remind the couple not to feel above those who know and love them the best.

- *Weddings in contemporary society are expected to bring a man and woman together as equal partners in marriage, but the traditional ceremony suggests an imbalance.* The bride's white dress is the key symbol. The white color symbolizes youth and virginity, two elements not regarded as important for the groom. She purchases her dress, often at considerable expense, and is expected to keep it. The groom generally rents his tuxedo unless he happens to own one. The bride is the object of much more attention than the groom before, during, and after the ceremony. In the traditional ceremony, she is given away by her family; no one gives him away. In the past, she received a ring; he did not. In many cases, she still changes her family name to his. All of these elements make it clear that the change in identity is more significant for the woman than for the man, implying that her status in the world will be dependent on his. Although most contemporary couples aspire to equality in marriage, they enthusiastically go through a ritual that emphasizes the woman's inequality.[3]

- *Traditionally only first marriages are allowed the full ritual.* Actually, the key is the bride's prior marriages, not the groom's. A woman supposedly only has the right to wear white once. After that, she is expected to be more discreet about what she wears—she is clearly no longer a virgin—and what she expects in the way of attention and gifts. If the man has been married three times before but the woman has never been married, they are still eligible to have a traditional wedding—another clear illustration of how a wedding is thought to change a woman's identity more than a man's. But Intentional Couples today sometimes ignore these strictures for second marriages and have all the bells and whistles at their wedding. I know one woman who had eloped for her first wedding and decided to make the second one a grand production. It was her groom's first marriage and he was all for it.

Notes

1. Arnold van Gennep was the anthropologist who pioneered the study of rites of passage. See *The Rites of Passage* (Chicago: University of Chicago Press), 1960, originally published in 1900.
2. See Diana Leonard Barker, "A Proper Wedding," in Marie Corbin (ed.), *The Couple* (New York: Penguin Books), 1978, pp. 56–77; and Diana Leonard Barker, *Sex and Generation: A Study of Courtship and Wedding* (New York: Tavistock Publications), 1980.
3. Ibid., p. 71.

RESPONSE QUESTIONS

1. William Doherty outlines a traditional American wedding in paragraph 5. How much of his description sounds familiar to you? How does your own experience of weddings differ from this outline? Explain the differences, if any.
2. Doherty finds several "fascinating contradictions" in American wedding rituals. Which of these contradictions seem most interesting to you? Tell what makes them so remarkable.
3. If you are married or plan to be, have you felt any of the stress about your wedding that Doherty believes is felt by American families? What accounts for such stress?

GUIDELINES FOR ANALYSIS

1. Doherty begins with a general statement and narrows his focus. Where does he make the clearest statement of the essay's thesis or main idea?
2. The author defines terms, gives a little history, outlines the basic stages of a wedding, and contrasts the contradictory elements of wedding rituals. How well does he use these tools

of analysis? What does each tool contribute to our understanding of weddings as rituals of passage?

3. On the whole, do you consider the author of this essay to be neutral or judgmental? Where do you find evidence of his neutrality or judgment? Do you think his stance is appropriate for an essay of this kind?

QUESTIONS OF CULTURE

1. At one point, Doherty mentions the "embarrassing, silly rituals" of American weddings that contrast with the solemnity of the occasion, adding that similar contradictions occur in other cultures. How many of these contradictory practices occur in other cultures that you know?

2. The author has a lot to say about the way wedding rituals treat men and women differently. What examples does he offer? What conclusions does he come to about traditional attitudes toward gender? Explain why you agree or disagree.

IDEAS FOR YOUR JOURNAL

1. Apply Doherty's analysis to a wedding you have recently attended. Compare your outline of the ceremony to his. What do you see differently now that you have read the essay?

2. The opening two paragraphs suggest that Doherty will talk about funerals as well as weddings. If you were to complete his project, what rituals of passage would you write about concerning traditional American funerals?

PREVIEW

What does American culture look like to a ten-year-old boy from Glen Ridge, New Jersey? Writer Susan Orlean decided to find out by following Colin Duffy day by day. She sat through his first fifth-grade class, tagged along while he played with his pals, and listened while he talked about his dreams and fears. Her humorous essay offers serious insights into one child's world and the kind of adult he—and others like him—may become.

Born in Cleveland, Ohio, in 1955, Susan Orlean attended the University of Michigan in Ann Arbor, where she studied literature and history while dreaming of becoming a writer. She found a job writing features and music reviews for a magazine in Portland, Oregon, then began writing for the *Village Voice* and *Rolling Stone*. In 1982, she moved east to Boston and New York, eventually becoming a staff writer for the *New Yorker*. Meanwhile, she worked on her first book, *Saturday Night* (1991), a lively account of how people all across America spend the sixth night of the week. Her book about an eccentric plant dealer in Florida, *The Orchid Thief* (1999), became a national best seller and was adapted into the Oscar-winning movie *Adaptation* in 2003. "The American Man at Age Ten" originally appeared in *Esquire* in 1992.

The American Man at Age Ten

By Susan Orlean

If Colin Duffy and I were to get married, we would have matching superhero notebooks. We would wear shorts, big sneakers, and long, baggy T-shirts depicting famous athletes every single day, even in the winter. We would sleep in our clothes. We would both be good at Nintendo Street Fighter II, but Colin would be better than me. We would have some homework, but it would not be too hard and we would always have just finished it. We would eat pizza and candy for all of our meals. We wouldn't have sex, but we would have crushes on each other and, magically, babies would appear in our home. We would win the lottery and then buy land in Wyoming, where we would have one of every kind of cute animal. All the while, Colin would be working in law enforcement—probably the FBI. Our favorite movie star, Morgan Freeman, would visit us occasionally. We would listen to the same Eurythmics song ("Here Comes the Rain Again") over and over again and watch two hours of television every Friday night. We would both be good at football, have best friends, and know how to drive; we would cure AIDS and the garbage problem and everything that hurts animals. We would hang out a lot with Colin's dad. For fun, we would load a slingshot with dog food and shoot it at my butt. We would have a very good life.

Here are the particulars about Colin Duffy: He is ten years old, on the nose. He is four feet eight inches high, weighs seventy-five pounds, and appears to be mostly leg and shoulder blade. He is a handsome kid. He has a broad forehead, dark eyes with dense lashes, and a sharp, dimply smile. I have rarely seen him without a baseball cap. He owns several, but favors a University of Michigan Wolverines model, on account of its pleasing colors. The hat styles his hair into wild disarray. If you ever managed to get the hat off his head, you would see a boy with a nimbus of golden-brown hair, dented in the back, where the hat hits him.

Colin lives with his mother, Elaine; his father, Jim; his older sister, Megan; and his little brother, Chris, in a pretty pale-blue Victorian house on a bosky street in Glen Ridge, New Jersey. Glen Ridge is a serene and civilized old town twenty miles west of New York City. It does not have much of a commercial district, but it is a town of amazing lawns. Most of the houses were built around the turn of the century and are set back a gracious, green distance from the street. The rest of the town seems to consist of parks and playing fields and sidewalks and backyards—in other words, it is a far cry from South-Central Los Angeles and from Bedford-Stuyvesant and other, grimmer parts of the country where a very different ten-year-old American man is growing up today.

There is a fine school system in Glen Ridge, but Elaine and Jim, who are both schoolteachers, choose to send their children to a parents' cooperative elementary school in Montclair, a neighboring suburb. Currently, Colin is in fifth grade. He is a good student. He plans to go to college, to a place he says is called Oklahoma City State College University. OCSCU satisfies his desire to live out west, to attend a small college, and to study law enforcement, which OCSCU apparently offers as a major. After four years at Oklahoma City State College University, he plans to work for the FBI. He says that getting to be a police officer involves tons of hard work, but working for the FBI will be a cinch, because all you have to do is fill out one form, which he has already gotten from the head FBI office. Colin is quiet in class but loud on the playground. He has a great throwing arm, significant foot speed, and a lot of physical confidence. He is also brave. Huge wild cats with rabies and gross stuff dripping from their teeth, which he says run rampant throughout his neighborhood, do not scare him. Otherwise, he is slightly bashful. This combination of athletic grace and valor and personal reserve accounts for considerable popularity. He has a fluid relationship to many social groups, including the superbright nerds, the ultrajocks, the flashy kids who will someday become extremely popular and socially successful juvenile delinquents, and the kids who will be elected president of the student body. In his opinion, the most popular boy in his class is Christian, who happens to be black, and Colin's favorite television character is Steve Urkel on *Family Matters,* who is black, too, but otherwise he seems uninterested in or oblivious to race. Until this year, he was a Boy Scout. Now he is planning to begin karate lessons. His favorite schoolyard game is football, followed closely by prison dodge ball, blob tag, and bombardo. He's crazy about athletes, although sometimes it isn't clear if he is absolutely sure of the difference between human athletes and Marvel Comics action figures. His current athletic hero is Dave Meggett. His current best friend is named Japeth. He used to have another best friend named Ozzie. According to Colin, Ozzie was found on a doorstep, then changed his name to Michael and moved to Massachusetts, and then Colin never saw him or heard from him again.

He has had other losses in his life. He is old enough to know people who have died and to know things about the world that are worrisome. When he dreams, he dreams about moving to Wyoming, which he has visited with his family. His plan is to buy land there and have some sort of ranch that would definitely include horses. Sometimes when he talks about this, it sounds as ordinary and hard-boiled as a real estate appraisal; other times it can sound fantastical and wifty and achingly naive, informed by the last inklings of childhood—the musings of a balmy real estate appraiser assaying a wonderful and magical landscape that erodes from memory a little bit every day. The collision in his mind of what he understands, what he hears, what he figures out, what popular culture pours into him, what he knows, what he pretends to know, and what he imagines, makes an interesting mess. The mess often has the form of what he will probably think like when he is a grown man, but the content of what he is like as a little boy.

He is old enough to begin imagining that he will someday get married, but at ten he is still convinced that the best thing about being married will be that he will be allowed to sleep in his clothes. His father once observed that living with Colin was like living with a Martian who had done some reading on American culture. As it happens, Colin is not especially sad or worried about the prospect of growing up, although he sometimes frets over whether he should be called a kid or a grown-up; he has settled on the word *kid-up.* Once I asked him what the biggest advantage to adulthood will be, and he said, "The best thing is that grown-ups can go wherever they want." I asked him what he meant, exactly, and he said, "Well, if you're grown-up, you'd have a car, and whenever you felt like it, you could get into your car and drive somewhere and get candy."

Colin loves recycling. He loves it even more than, say, playing with little birds. That ten-year-olds feel the weight of the world and consider it their mission to shoulder it came as a surprise to me. I had gone with Colin one Monday to his classroom at Montclair Cooperative School. The Coop is in a steep, old, sharp-angled brick building that had served for many years as a public school until a group of parents in the area took it over and made it into a private, progressive elementary school. The fifth-grade classroom is on the top floor, under the dormers, which gives the room the eccentric shape and closeness of an attic. It is a rather informal environment. There are computers lined up in an adjoining room and instructions spelled out on the chalkboard— BRING IN: (1) A CUBBY WITH YOUR NAME ON IT, (2) A TRAPPER WITH A 5-POCKET ENVELOPE LABELED SCIENCE, SOCIAL STUDIES, READING/LANGUAGE ARTS, MATH, MATH LAB/COMPUTER; WHITE LINED PAPER; A PLASTIC PENCIL BAG; A SMALL HOMEWORK PAD, (3) LARGE BROWN GROCERY BAGS—but there is also a couch in the center of the classroom, which the kids take turns occupying, a rocking chair, and three canaries in cages near the door.

It happened to be Colin's first day in fifth grade. Before class began, there was a lot of horsing around, but there were also a lot of conversations about whether Magic Johnson had AIDS or just HIV and whether someone falling in a pool of blood from a cut of his would get the disease. These jolts of sobriety in the midst of rank goofiness are a ten-year-old's specialty. Each one comes as a fresh, hard surprise, like finding a razor blade in a candy apple. One day, Colin and I had been discussing horses or dogs or something, and out of the blue he said, "What do you think is bet-ter, to dump garbage in the ocean, to dump it on land, or to burn it?" Another time, he asked me if I planned to have children. I had just spent an evening with him and his friend Japeth, during which they put every small, movable object in the house into Japeth's slingshot and fired it at me, so I told him I wanted children but that I hoped they would all be girls, and he said, "Will you have an abortion if you find out you have a boy?"

At school, after discussing summer vacation, the kids began choosing the jobs they would do to help out around the classroom. Most of the jobs are humdrum—putting the chairs up on the tables, washing the chalkboard, turning the computers off or on. Five of the most humdrum tasks are recycling chores—for example, taking bottles or stacks of paper down to the basement, where they would be sorted and prepared for pickup. Two children would be assigned to feed the birds and cover their cages at the end of the day.

I expected the bird jobs to be the first to go. Everyone loved the birds; they'd spent an hour that morning voting on names for them (Tweetie, Montgomery, and Rose narrowly beating out Axl Rose, Bugs, Ol' Yeller, Fido, Slim, Lucy, and Chirpie). Instead, they all wanted to recycle. The recycling jobs were claimed by the first five kids called by Suzanne Nakamura, the fifth-grade teacher; each kid called after that responded by groaning, "Suzanne, aren't there any more recycling jobs?" Colin ended up with the job of taking down the chairs each morning. He accepted the task with a sort of resignation—this was just going to be a job rather than a mission.

On the way home that day, I was quizzing Colin about his world views.

"Who's the coolest person in the world?"

"Morgan Freeman."

"What's the best sport?"

"Football."

"Who's the coolest woman?"

"None. I don't know."

"What's the most important thing in the world?"

"Game Boy." Pause. "No, the world. The world is the most important thing in the world."

Danny's Pizzeria is a dark little shop next door to the Montclair Cooperative School. It is not much to look at. Outside, the brick facing is painted muddy brown. Inside, there are some saggy counters, a splintered bench, and enough room for either six teenagers or about a dozen ten-year-olds who happen to be getting along well. The light is low. The air is oily. At Danny's, you will find pizza, candy, Nintendo, and very few girls. To a ten-year-old boy, it is the most beautiful place in the world.

One afternoon, after class was dismissed, we went to Danny's with Colin's friend Japeth to play Nintendo. Danny's has only one game, Street Fighter II Champion Edition. Some teenage boys from a nearby middle school had gotten there first and were standing in a tall, impenetrable thicket around the machine.

"Next game," Colin said. The teenagers ignored him.

"Hey, we get next game," Japeth said. He is smaller than Colin, scrappy, and, as he explained to me once, famous for wearing his hat backward all the time and having a huge wristwatch and a huge bedroom. He stamped his foot and announced again, "Hey, we get next game."

One of the teenagers turned around and said, "Fuck you, *next game,*" and then turned back to the machine.

"Whoa," Japeth said.

He and Colin went outside, where they felt bigger.

"Which street fighter are you going to be?" Colin asked Japeth.

"Blanka," Japeth said. "I know how to do his head-butt."

"I hate that! I hate the head-butt," Colin said. He dropped his voice a little and growled, "I'm going to be Ken, and I will kill you with my dragon punch."

"Yeah, right, and monkeys will fly out of my butt," Japeth said.

Street Fighter II is a video game in which two characters have an explosive brawl in a scenic international setting. It is currently the most popular video-arcade game in America. This is not an insignificant amount of popularity. Most arcade versions of video games, which end up in pizza parlors, malls, and arcades, sell about two thousand units. So far, some fifty thousand Street Fighter II and Street Fighter II Championship Edition arcade games have been sold. Not since Pac-Man, which was released the year before Colin was born, has there been a video game as popular as Street Fighter. The home version of Street Fighter is the most popular home video game in the country, and that, too, is not an insignificant thing. Thirty-two million Nintendo home systems have been sold since 1986, when it was introduced in this country. There is a Nintendo system in seven of every ten homes in America in which a child between the ages of eight and twelve resides. By the time a boy in America turns ten, he will almost certainly have been exposed to

Nintendo home games, Nintendo arcade games, and Game Boy, the hand-held version. He will probably own a system and dozens of games. By ten, according to Nintendo studies, teachers, and psychologists, game prowess becomes a fundamental, essential male social marker and a schoolyard boast.

The Street Fighter characters are Dhalsim, Ken, Guile, Blanka, E. Honda, Ryu, Zangief, and Chun Li. Each represents a different country, and they each have their own special weapon. Chun Li, for instance, is from China and possesses a devastating whirlwind kick that is triggered if you push the control pad down for two seconds and then up for two seconds, and then you hit the kick button. Chun Li's kick is money in the bank, because most of the other fighters do not have a good defense against it. By the way, Chun Li happens to be a girl—the only female Street Fighter character.

I asked Colin if he was interested in being Chun Li. There was a long pause. "I'd rather be Ken," he said.

The girls in Colin's class at school are named Cortnerd, Terror, Spacey, Lizard, Maggot, and Diarrhea. "They do have other names, but that's what we call them," Colin told me. "The girls aren't very popular."

"They are about as popular as a piece of dirt," Japeth said. "Or, you know that couch in the classroom? That couch is more popular than any girl. A thousand times more." They talked for a minute about one of the girls in their class, a tall blonde with cheerleader genetic material, who they allowed was not quite as gross as some of the other girls. Japeth said that a chubby, awkward boy in their class was boasting that this girl liked him.

"No way," Colin said. "She would never like him. I mean, not that he's so . . . I don't know. I don't hate him because he's fat, anyway. I hate him because he's nasty."

"Well, she doesn't like him," Japeth said. "She's been really mean to me lately, so I'm pretty sure she likes me."

"Girls are different," Colin said. He hopped up and down on the balls of his feet, wrinkling his nose. "Girls are stupid and weird."

"I have a lot of girlfriends, about six or so," Japeth said, turning contemplative. "I don't exactly remember their names, though."

The teenagers came crashing out of Danny's and jostled past us, so we went inside. The man who runs Danny's, whose name is Tom, was leaning across the counter on his elbows, looking exhausted. Two little boys, holding Slush Puppies, shuffled toward the Nintendo, but Colin and Japeth elbowed them aside and slammed their quarters down on the machine. The little boys shuffled back toward the counter and stood gawking at them, sucking on their drinks.

"You want to know how to tell if a girl likes you?" Japeth said. "She'll act really mean to you. That's a sure sign. I don't know why they do it, but it's always a sure sign. It gets your attention. You know how I show a girl I like her? I steal something from her and then run away. I do it to get their attention, and it works."

They played four quarters' worth of games. During the last one, a teenager with a quilted leather jacket and a fade haircut came in, pushed his arm between them, and put a quarter down on the deck of the machine.

Japeth said, "Hey, what's that?"

The teenager said, "I get next game. I've marked it now. Everyone knows this secret sign for next game. It's a universal thing."

"So now we know," Japeth said. "Colin, let's get out of here and go bother Maggie. I mean Maggot. Okay?" They picked up their backpacks and headed out the door.

Psychologists identify ten as roughly the age at which many boys experience the gender-linked normative developmental trauma that leaves them, as adult men, at risk for specific psychological sequelae often manifest as deficits in the arenas of intimacy, empathy, and struggles with commitment in relationships. In other words, this is around the age when guys get screwed up about girls. Elaine and Jim Duffy, and probably most of the parents who send their kids to Montclair Cooperative School, have done a lot of stuff to try to avoid this. They gave Colin dolls as well as guns. (He preferred guns.) Japeth's father has three motorcycles and two dirt bikes but does most of the cooking and cleaning in their home. Suzanne, Colin's teacher, is careful to avoid sexist references in her presentations. After school, the yard at Montclair Cooperative is filled with as many fathers as mothers—fathers who hug their kids when they come prancing out of the building and are dismayed when their sons clamor for Supersoaker water guns and war toys or take pleasure in beating up girls.

In a study of adolescents conducted by the Gesell Institute of Human Development, nearly half the ten-year-old boys questioned said they thought they had inadequate information about sex. Nevertheless, most ten-year-old boys across the country are subjected to a few months of sex education in school. Colin and his class will get their dose next spring. It is yet another installment in a plan to make them into new, improved men with reconstructed notions of sex and male-female relationships. One afternoon I asked Philip, a schoolmate of Colin's, whether he was looking forward to sex education, and he said, "No, because I think it'll probably make me really, really hyper. I have a feeling it's going to be just like what it was like when some television reporters came to school last year and filmed us in class and I got really hyper. They stood around with all these cameras and asked us questions. I think that's what sex education is probably like."

At a class meeting earlier in the day:

Suzanne: "Today was our first swimming class, and I have one observation to make. The girls went to their locker room, got dressed without a lot of fuss, and came into the pool area. The boys, on the other hand, the *boys* had some sort of problem doing that rather simple task.

Can someone tell me exactly what went on in the locker room?"

Keith: "There was a lot of shouting."

Suzanne: "Okay, I hear you saying that people were being noisy and shouting. Anything else?"

Christian: "Some people were screaming so much that my ears were killing me. It gave me, like, a huge headache. Also, some of the boys were taking their towels, I mean, after they had taken their clothes off, they had their towels around their waists and then they would drop them really fast and then pull them back up, really fast."

Suzanne: "Okay, you're saying some people were being silly about their bodies."

Christian: "Well, yeah, but it was more like they were being silly about their pants."

Colin's bedroom is decorated simply. He has a cage with his pet parakeet, Dude, on his dresser, a lot of recently worn clothing piled haphazardly on the floor, and a husky brown teddy bear sitting upright in a chair near the foot of his bed. The walls are mostly bare, except for a Spiderman poster and a few ads torn out of magazines he has thumbtacked up. One of the ads is for a cologne, illustrated with several small photographs of cowboy hats; another, a feverish portrait of a woman on a horse, is an ad for blue jeans. These inspire him sometimes when he lies in bed and makes plans for the move to Wyoming. Also, he happens to like ads. He also likes television commercials. Generally speaking, he likes consumer products and popular culture. He partakes avidly but not indiscriminately. In fact, during the time we spent together, he provided a running commentary on merchandise, media, and entertainment:

"The only shoes anyone will wear are Reebok Pumps. Big T-shirts are cool, not the kind that are sticky and close to you, but big and baggy and long, not the kind that stop at your stomach."

"The best food is Chicken McNuggets and Life cereal and Frosted Flakes. "

"Don't go to Blimpie's. They have the worst service."

"I'm not into Teenage Mutant Ninja Turtles anymore. I grew out of that. I like Donatello, but I'm not a fan. I don't buy the figures anymore."

"The best television shows are on Friday night on ABC. It's called TGIF, and it's *Family Matters, Step by Step, Dinosaurs,* and *Perfect Strangers,* where the guy has a funny accent."

"The best candy is Skittles and Symphony bars and Crybabies and Warheads. Crybabies are great because if you eat a lot of them at once you feel so sour."

"Hyundais are Korean cars. It's the only Korean car. They're not that good because Koreans don't have a lot of experience building cars."

"The best movie is *City Slickers,* and the best part was when he saved his little cow in the river."

"The Giants really need to get rid of Ray Handley. They have to get somebody who has real coaching experience. He's just no good."

"My dog, Sally, costs seventy-two dollars. That sounds like a lot of money but it's a really good price because you get a flea bath with your dog.

"The best magazines are *Nintendo Power,* because they tell you how to do the secret moves in the video games, and also *Mad* magazine and *Money Guide*—I really like that one."

"The best artist in the world is Jim Davis."

"The most beautiful woman in the world is not Madonna! Only Wayne and Garth think that! She looks like maybe a . . . a . . . slut or something. Cindy Crawford looks like she would look good, but if you see her on an awards program on TV she doesn't look that good. I think the most beautiful woman in the world probably is my mom."

Colin thinks a lot about money. This started when he was about nine and a half, which is when a lot of other things started—a new way of walking that has a little macho hitch and swagger, a decision about the Teenage Mutant Ninja Turtles (con) and Eurhythmics (pro), and

a persistent curiosity about a certain girl whose name he will not reveal. He knows the price of everything he encounters. He knows how much college costs and what someone might earn performing different jobs. Once, he asked me what my husband did; when I answered that he was a lawyer, he snapped, "You must be a rich family. Lawyers make $400,000 a year." His preoccupation with money baffles his family. They are not struggling, so this is not the anxiety of deprivation; they are not rich, so, he is not responding to an elegant, advantaged world. His allowance is five dollars a week. It seems sufficient for his needs, which consist chiefly of quarters for Nintendo and candy money. The remainder is put into his Wyoming fund. His fascination is not just specific to needing money or having plans for money: It is as if money itself, and the way it makes the world work, and the realization that almost everything in the world can be assigned a price, has possessed him. "I just pay attention to things like that," Colin says. "It's really very interesting."

He is looking for a windfall. He tells me his mother has been notified that she is in the fourth and final round of the Publisher's Clearinghouse Sweepstakes. This is not an ironic observation. He plays the New Jersey lottery every Thursday night. He knows the weekly jackpot; he knows the number to call to find out if he has won. I do not think this presages a future for Colin as a high-stakes gambler; I think it says more about the powerful grasp that money has on imagination and what a large percentage of a ten-year-old's mind is made up of imaginings. One Friday, we were at school together, and one of his friends was asking him about the lottery, and he said, "This week it was $4 million. That would be I forget how much every year for the rest of your life. It's a lot, I think. You should play. All it takes is a dollar and a dream."

Until the lottery comes through and he starts putting together the Wyoming land deal, Colin can be found most of the time in the backyard.

Often, he will have friends come over. Regularly, children from the neighborhood will gravitate to the backyard, too. As a technical matter of real-property law, title to the house and yard belongs to Jim and Elaine Duffy, but Colin adversely possesses the backyard, at least from 4:00 each afternoon until it gets dark. As yet, the fixtures of teenage life—malls, video arcades, friends' basements, automobiles—either hold little interest for him or are not his to have.

He is, at the moment, very content with his backyard. For most intents and purposes, it is as big as Wyoming. One day, certainly, he will grow and it will shrink, and it will become simply a suburban backyard and it won't be big enough for him anymore. This will happen so fast that one night he will be in the backyard, believing it a perfect place, and by the next night he will have changed and the yard as he imagined it will be gone, and this era of his life will be behind him forever.

Most days, he spends hours in the backyard building an Evil Spider-Web Trap. This entails running a spool of Jim's fishing line from every surface in the yard until it forms a huge web. Once a garbage man picking up the Duffys' trash got caught in the trap. Otherwise, the Evil Spider-Web Trap mostly has a deterrent effect, because the kids in the neighborhood who might roam over know that Colin builds it back there. "I do it all the time," he says. "First I plan who I'd like to catch in it, and then we get started. Trespassers have to beware."

One afternoon when I came over for a few rounds of Street Fighter at Danny's, Colin started building a trap. He selected a victim for inspiration—a boy in his class who had been pestering him—and began wrapping. He was entirely absorbed. He moved from tree to tree, wrapping; he laced fishing line through the railing of the deck and then back to the shed; he circled an old jungle gym, something he'd outgrown and abandoned a few years ago, and then crossed over to a bush at the back of the yard. Briefly, he contemplated making his dog, Sally, part of the web. Dusk fell. He kept wrapping, paying out fishing line an inch at a time. We could hear mothers up and down the block hooting for their kids; two tiny children from next door stood transfixed at the edge of the yard, uncertain whether they would end up inside or outside the web. After a while, the spool spun around in Colin's hands one more time and then stopped; he was out of line.

It was almost too dark to see much of anything, although now and again the light from the deck would glance off a length of line, and it would glint and sparkle. "That's the point," he said. "You could do it with thread, but the fishing line is invisible. Now I have this perfect thing and the only one who knows about it is me." With that, he dropped the spool, skipped up the stairs of the deck, threw open the screen door, and then bounded into the house, leaving me and Sally the dog trapped in his web.

RESPONSE QUESTIONS

1. Did any passages surprise you? Given what you already know about ten-year-old boys, which of Colin's actions, statements, or beliefs seemed unexpected?

2. Some readers laugh out loud when they read this essay. What parts did you find funny? Why? Did any passages seem genuinely serious, even troubling to you?

3. What do Colin and his friends think about girls? How and when do you predict these attitudes will change?

4. Reread Orlean's descriptions of Danny's Pizzeria, Colin's bedroom, and his yard. What do they reveal about Colin's personality and values? What judgments did you find yourself making about him as you read?

5. Occasional references are made to the adults in Colin's world. What kind of teacher is Suzanne? How would you describe his parents? What do you think of the way they are raising him?

GUIDELINES FOR ANALYSIS

1. The essay begins with an imaginary depiction of married life. In whose mind would this be "a very good life"? How does the opening paragraph set the tone and point of view for what follows?

2. Compared to the other essays in this chapter, how analytic is Orlean's writing? How much of her essay is given to assessment, interpretation, description, prediction, or some other mode of writing? Where does she make judgments and where does she simply report what she observes? Do you feel at any point that she should have taken on another role?

3. How well does Susan Orlean capture the spirit and imagination of a ten-year-old boy? Point to specific words, sentences, and topics that might have come from Colin himself. Where does she step back into the mind of an adult?

QUESTIONS OF CULTURE

1. Look closely at the passages that describe Colin's preoccupation with money, consumer goods, and video games. What critique of American culture can you see in these passages?

2. How typical does Colin seem to you? To what degree is he the product of his family, his age, his social class, American culture, or his unique individuality?

IDEAS FOR YOUR JOURNAL

1. Susan Orlean chose to write about a young boy. How different would her essay have been if she had followed a ten-year-old girl? Write your own version of "The American Woman at Age Ten."

2. Part of the appeal of Orlean's writing lies in her ability to project herself into Colin's mind, to see the world through his eyes. Try to imagine a typical day in the life of someone very different from you: a police officer, a professor, a blind man, or perhaps an eighty-year-old Native American woman. What would contemporary pop culture look like to such a person?

A STUDENT WRITER IN ACTION

Preview

Sylvia Pace was born and raised in Brooklyn, New York, and lives in Westchester County, north of New York City. As the child of Puerto Ricans, she spent three years in the homeland of her parents, from the age of six to nine. In her first-year composition course at Westchester

Community College, Sylvia was assigned to write an essay about customs. "I have always wanted to share my childhood experiences from Puerto Rico," she writes. "This essay was an opportunity to analyze one of those experiences, my grandmother's funeral, and explain it to others." Sylvia is currently pursuing a liberal arts degree with the goal of becoming an elementary school teacher.

What follows is a brief account of Sylvia Pace's writing process together with her first and final draft. Her first draft includes the instructor's comments so you can trace the changes that she made.

DISCOVERING

Q: How did you come up with the idea for your essay?

A: It didn't take me long to find the topic. My grandmother's funeral left a big impression on me. I thought it might be interesting to describe the customs that are traditional in Puerto Rico but seem strange to us in the United States.

PLANNING

Q: Say a little about how you prepare yourself to write and how you organize your thoughts.

A: I meditate on experiences I've had and try to visualize them. I enjoy writing either early in the morning or late in the evening, when it's quiet. Once I have the subject, I write down all my thoughts and as many details as I can. Then I proceed to put the essay together like a puzzle.

DEVELOPING

Q: How did you develop your first draft?

A: I develop the first draft by trying to convey all my thoughts about the specific subject. In the first paragraph of the essay, I introduce the topic. My goal for the ending is to sum up the main idea in order to help readers remember what the essay was about.

REVISING

Q: Tell us about your process of revising.

A; To be honest, I find it difficult to critique my own writing, even though I read it over four or five times. So I asked others to look over my draft of the essay. My friends asked questions that helped me see what was missing. My instructor gave me advice about organization, grammar, and punctuation.

Q: What did you learn about yourself while writing this essay? What advice would you give to other student writers?

A: I never thought that I could write an essay that others would find interesting. My advice would be, "If you enjoy writing, do not give it up." Writing is a tool that can be used to express our deepest fears and greatest victories.

FUNERAL CUSTOMS IN GUAYAMA

By Sylvia Pace

Sylvia's First Draft (with Instructor's Comments)

I was a kid[1] living in a little town called Guayama in Puerto Rico. My family and I resided there for about a year. The houses were made of cinder blocks, cement, and tin roofs. The homes had outhouses and shower stalls outside in their back yards. That town was referred to as the village of the witches. The nickname was quite suitable for most of the local folks practiced witchcraft.

My parents decided[2] to move to Puerto Rico to live near my father's mother. She was ill with diabetes. A few months when[3] by and she became terminally ill and died due to complications from the disease. My father and his brothers took care of all the funeral arrangements. They had to be very careful as to what arrangements they made. The Hispanic customs for burials vary. They had to do their utmost to respect my grandmother's wishes and her religious beliefs.

The day of the wake was quite eerie. Being just a kid and having to contend with the fact that it was my first funeral, I can recollect quite a bit of what took place. Unlike the American custom of viewing the deceased in a funeral home, my grandmother's viewing took place at her house. The reason why some viewed the deceased at their home was due to monetary reasons or[4] they felt that they should be home as long as possible with their deceased loved one. The viewing took place for two to three days around the clock. The casket was velvet and light blue. My grandmother was encased in glass. This was done to prevent any contamination from the deceased. I think it was air tight shut[5] as well. After all, she was laid out for half a week.[6] Being in a tropical island where the temperature is in the 90's most of the time was a bit disconcerting to me. How long can they[7] linger on with the viewing and keep it safe environmentally?

The people have[8] arrived and the show must begin. They were women, professional mourners as I called them. They sat by the casket crying and praying. There were candles that were lit.[9] They were not your ordinary Yankee Candles. These candles were in a tall clear glass. Different colors had different meanings to them. They were mostly white candles. The significance of the white candle was for her soul to go to heaven (though I am almost positive that there were a few ladies that lit a black candle at home). So these ladies cried and carried on for hours chanting aloud the "Hail Mary prayer".[10] They would then say her name in ululation. These women were also spirit mediums, so in their religious rituals they had the power to do this task.

Sitting by me were other individuals and family members sobbing quietly. Some held their rosary beads while praying for grandma's new heavenly life (they hoped). I

---

1. Your opening paragraph does a good job of describing the conditions of your childhood. (Who would have pictured this small town after seeing you now?) However, it gives us no idea about the topic of your essay. It might help if you linked this image of Guyama (or the idea of witchcraft) to the subject of funeral customs.

2. Consider changing the verb tense to show more clearly that this decision was made before the other events took place.

3. Spelling

4. Do you need to repeat the word "reasons" in this sentence?

5. Is this word necessary?

6. I see why you were concerned about contamination.

7. Will it be clear who "they" refers to?

8. Keep to the past tense.

9. Can you say this more directly?

10. Place all periods and commas inside quotation marks.

must take this moment to share a bit of our inside family secret. Grandma was quite contentious and used to getting her way. She owned the only grocery store in the area and this gave her a warped sense of superiority. Needless to say, she did not have too many friends.[11] Grandma lived in Guayama all her life and so the neighbors all had to pay their respect.

It is[12] now the last day of her viewing. It was so sad to see my uncles in despair. My father did not shed a tear. He just held it all in. The photographer came and took the pictures. This was another custom. We had to memorialize this occasion and what better way than with pictures.[13] A bit shocking or morbid perhaps for a family to get a photographer for a funeral, but this is how it was done. The casket was now carried out and put in the back of a pick up. We drove to Ponce, Puerto Rico. The casket was exposed to the elements and everyone could see it while we drove over two hours into Ponce. Upon our arrival to Ponce she was taken to the church for a quick Mass[14] and eulogy. The professional mourner's job was over. Now it was time for the family to show their grief. We drove her to the cemetery. It was a hot sunny day as I watched my favorite grandmother's casket lowered into the ground. While that was taking place we all had to throw a flower in and say a prayer. The significance of the flower and prayer was to hopefully stop her spirit from haunting us. Pretty frightening for a kid to hear such a thing.[15]

Having to say goodbye was very difficult. Now that I think about it all, I am glad I was exposed to my Latin heritage and customs. I feel it gives me a sense of completeness as a Hispanic person. I do not follow these customs today due to having different religious belief's,[16] but that time it was important to follow the traditional funeral customs. It brought the family closer together, at least for that week. We moved back to New York shortly after that and I never saw my uncles or relatives again. I am impressed with how I can remember that week so distinctly. I was eight years old at the time. I guess it is a gift;[17] a gift that I will always cherish (in a way).[18]

Sylvia's Final Draft

Years ago I lived in a little town called Guayama in Puerto Rico. My family and I resided there for about a year. The houses were made of cinder blocks, cement, and tin roofs. The homes had outhouses and shower stalls outside in their back yards. That town was referred to as the village of the witches. The nickname was quite suitable, for most of the local folks practiced witchcraft. In fact, many of their customs still seem strange to me.

My parents had decided to move to Puerto Rico to live near my father's mother. She was ill with diabetes. A few months went by, and she became terminally ill and died due

---

11. Does this account for the "professionals"?

12. Use the past tense throughout.

13. Remember to use a question mark for this question.

14. No capital letter is needed unless this is a proper noun.

15. This is a good clincher, although it is a fragment.

16. Apostrophe error

17. Use a semicolon only to join independent clauses (full sentences).

18. This sounds like an afterthought. Can you think of a stronger ending, one that sums up the main concept of the entire essay and leaves us with something to remember?

to complications from the disease. My father and his brothers took care of all the funeral arrangements. They had to be very careful as to what arrangements they made. The Hispanic customs for burials are very particular. They had to do their utmost to respect my grandmother's wishes and her religious beliefs.

The day of the wake was quite eerie. Being just a kid and having to contend with the fact that it was my first funeral, I can recollect quite a bit of what took place. Unlike the American custom of viewing the deceased in a funeral home, my grandmother's viewing took place at her house. The folks in that town viewed the deceased at their homes due to monetary reasons. They felt that their dead loved one should be home as long as possible before saying goodbye to them. The viewing took place for two to three days around the clock. The casket was velvet and light blue. My grandmother was encased in glass. This was done to prevent any contamination from the deceased. I think it was airtight as well. After all, she was laid out for half a week. Being in a tropical island where the temperature is in the 90s most of the time was a bit disconcerting to me. How long can people linger on with the viewing and keep it safe environmentally?

The people had arrived, and the show was about to begin. They were women, professional mourners as I called them. They sat by the casket crying and praying. Candles were lit. They were not your ordinary Yankee Candles. These candles were in a tall, clear glass. Different colors had different meanings to them. They were mostly white candles. The white candle meant that her soul would go to heaven (though I am almost positive that a few ladies lit a black candle at home). So these ladies cried and carried on for hours, chanting aloud the "Hail Mary" prayer. They would then say her name in ululations, a wave of mournful cries. These women were also spirit mediums, so in their religious rituals they had the power to do this task.

Sitting by me were other individuals and family members sobbing quietly. Some held their rosary beads while praying for grandma's new heavenly life (they hoped). I must take this moment to share a bit of our inside family secret. Grandma had been quite contentious and used to getting her way. She had owned the only grocery store in the area, and this gave her a warped sense of superiority. Needless to say, she did not have too many friends. But since Grandma had lived in Guayama all her life, the neighbors all had to pay their respect.

It was now the last day of her viewing. It was so sad to see my uncles in despair. My father did not shed a tear. He just held it all in. The photographer came and took the pictures. This was another custom. We had to memorialize this occasion, and what better way than with pictures? It may seem a bit shocking or morbid, perhaps, for a family to get a photographer for a funeral, but this is how it was done. The casket was now carried out and put in the back of a pickup. We drove to Ponce, Puerto Rico. The casket was exposed to the elements and everyone could see it while we drove over two hours into Ponce. Upon our arrival at Ponce she was taken to the church for a quick mass and eulogy. The professional mourners' job was over. Now it was time for the family to show their grief.

We drove her to the cemetery. It was a hot sunny day as I watched my favorite grandmother's casket lowered into the ground. While that was taking place we all had to throw a flower in the grave and say a prayer. The significance of the flower and prayer was to hopefully stop her spirit from haunting us. It can be very scary for a kid to hear that a dead person's spirit can haunt people. I wanted to throw in a whole bouquet.

Having to say goodbye was very difficult. Now that I think about it all, I am glad I was exposed to my Latino heritage and customs. I feel it gives me a sense of completeness as a Hispanic person. I do not follow these customs today due to having different religious beliefs, but at that time it was important to follow the traditional funeral customs. It brought the family closer together, at least for that week. We moved back to New York shortly after that and I never saw my uncles or relatives again. I am impressed with how I can remember that week so distinctly. I was just eight years old. I was a little girl being exposed to new customs and the facts of life and death. It was an experience that I will never forget.

CONSIDERATIONS FOR YOUR OWN WRITING

1. Compare your own experiences with funerals to Sylvia's account of Puerto Rican customs. Which practices seem strange to you? What helped you most to visualize these practices and understand their significance? What additional information might help you as a reader?

2. Although the writer was only eight years old during the funeral, she is looking back on the event now as an adult. Where in the essay were you most aware of this difference in perspective?

3. Sylvia describes her grandmother's life as well as her death. What kind of person does she seem to have been? How much can you tell about Sylvia's attitude toward her grandmother and the others in her family?

4. Compare the first and final drafts of Sylvia's essay. What changes has she made to her opening and closing paragraphs? How has she modified her use of verb tenses and punctuation? How effective are these changes? What other changes would you suggest?

5. Think of cultural traditions that you know well but that may be unfamiliar to other students. How might you explain them to your classmates?

Analyze This on the Web

The Internet is a vast resource of explanations and advice, both sound and suspicious. For clear explanations, models of analysis, or simply to find out how things work, try these popular Web sites:

How Stuff Works
http://www.howstuffworks.com/
This popular Web site features explanations on a wide range of topics, from lock picking and wine making to auto transmissions and nuclear bombs.

Free Legal Advice
http://freeadvice.com/
Looking for explanations of the law? This site, founded by attorneys, uses a Q & A format to clarify matters of litigation, accidents, real estate, intellectual property, and other legal issues.

How to Analyze an Advertisement
http://www.medialit.org/reading_room/article227.html
The Center for Media Literacy offers tips for finding hidden messages in ads and other forms of media analysis.

Advice Guide
http://www.adviceguide.org.uk/
This British Web site offers citizens advice about money, family, human rights, and daily life.

Composition Patterns
http://grammar.ccc.commnet.edu/grammar/composition/organization.htm
Capitol Community College in Hartford, Connecticut, hosts this online guide to organizing strategies, using such common patterns as definition, examples, comparison and contrast, cause and effect, and division and classification.

Evaluation Checklist

Use this checklist to help you—or another student—evaluate your explanatory essay.

Purpose. Your primary purpose should be to explain something familiar by analyzing it part by part. Have you done this while giving your particular view or slant on the topic?

Content. The essay should include enough details to explain the nature of your topic and how its parts relate to one another. Consider whether examples, definitions, comparisons, causal relationships, or more subdivisions would help to accomplish this.

Audience. Given your readers' previous knowledge, have you explained too much or too little? Have you missed an opportunity to explain your topic in terms they are familiar with? What terms still need to be defined for them?

Format. Does the essay use a traditional format, like the step-by-step chronology of a how-to essay or the logical structure of a formal definition? Will readers be able to recognize and follow the format?

Structure. Does the first paragraph set the tone and lead into the topic? Is the body of the essay organized in a way that reflects your analysis? Do transitions help to link parts of the essay? Does the conclusion clinch the main idea?

Style. How would you describe the essay's tone? Is the writing voice engaging? Is it appropriate to your topic and point of view?

Taking Stock

Take a moment to review what you have learned about analyzing and explaining from this chapter.

1. Where in your future work, personal life, and community activities will you need to analyze something and explain it to someone else?

2. How has this chapter helped to prepare you for these needs? How have you sharpened your powers of analysis? What new tools have you acquired?

3. Based on the feedback from your instructor, classmates, and peer reader, what methods and techniques seem to work best for you?

4. What did you learn about analytic writing from the readings? Consider the way these readings present their subject, focus on particular perspectives, arrange material, and use strategies like definition, examples, classification and division, comparison and contrast, or cause and effect. What methods appealed most to your writer's eye?

5. What did you learn about the topic that you wrote about or described in your illustrated speech? What would you still like to learn about this trend in American culture?

6. Think about the various topics presented in the readings and screenings. What did you learn about conversational styles, facial expressions, horror films, ten-year-olds, the food we eat, and the habits of the Nacirema?

7. Consider the process you went through during the composing assignment. What steps will you probably take again in future writing? What will you do differently?

CHAPTER 6

Documented Investigations: The Changing Family

The six groupings pictured here depict families from different eras in our nation's history. Can you guess which periods they represent? Clearly the image of the American family—whether real or ideal—has gone through many changes within the past one hundred years. You might begin by asking what these pictures show. First, what values does each photo seem to affirm? What beliefs about family relationships and the role of family in people's lives do you see reflected in the photos? Notice how these family members are dressed, arranged, and photographed. Second, how typical do you think these families are? Does anyone or anything appear to be missing from the pictures? Third, describe any trends you observe. Where do you think the family might be heading?

Notice how you arrived at your conclusions. They might be educated guesses based on personal experience. They might be carefully composed theories, deduced through principles of logic and analysis. They might be mere hunches or wild stabs in the dark. Whether theories or hunches, one way to test your ideas is to do some research. That means moving beyond the photographs themselves to learn what experts say about the family. It might mean investigating historical documents, conducting interviews, maybe finding other family photographs from the same periods. Research is one of the best ways to test, confirm, qualify, revise, and deepen what you think you know.

Writing that is based on research—variously called research papers, documented essays, or investigative reports—is a central part of most college composition courses. But it is not just academic. A facility to search purposefully for information, gather it around a central focus, arrange it in an organized sequence, and present it clearly to others involves life skills that are indispensable in the modern world. In this chapter, we'll be focusing on family issues. By investigating books, articles, and television programs that document recent changes in family structure, we'll see how the tools of modern research help to illuminate an important area of American life.

SCENARIOS FROM LIFE

Here are some moments that call for investigative research and reporting in school, in the community, at work, and in personal relationships:

- During a trip to Ellis Island, you learn that millions of immigrants arrived here by boat between 1892 and 1924. You wonder if your great-great-grandparents were among them. A quick search of the Ellis Island Web site turns up passenger lists, photos of ships, and other fascinating records of your ancestors. You decide to combine this material with genealogical information in a multimedia presentation. It will make a great gift for your family on a CD.

- In a changing job market, it is difficult to know what kind of career to pursue. You have a good idea of your aptitudes and interests, but what positions are really suitable for you, and which of these positions are likely to be open when you're ready? To find out, you set up visits to several work sites. You arrange to interview employers and employees. And you begin some broader research in the library.

- A research assignment in your history class happens to coincide with a campus screening of *Glory*, the 1989 film about an all-black regiment that fought in the American Civil War. It might be interesting to write your paper on the topic of African Americans in the armed forces. How much of the movie is based on fact? When were fighting units fully integrated? What is the status of African Americans—men and women—in the service today?

- One day, your younger sister comes home from school in tears. Kids on the school bus have been harassing her and her friends. As she talks to you, you realize that this experience may be the sign of a bigger problem. Children don't feel safe in her school. You decide to investigate. You interview school officials, conduct a survey of the children in her grade, and read about other school systems. Within a few weeks, you have gathered enough information to write an article for the local newspaper.

WHY WRITE TO INVESTIGATE?

An investigation is a systematic search. The Latin word *investigare* originally meant to follow tracks, like a hunter in pursuit of prey. When you investigate a topic, you pose questions that focus your interest in the topic. You follow various lines of inquiry hoping that they'll lead you to some illuminating answers. If you've done your hunting well, you can bring back what you find in the form of a report. The final draft of your report may take the form of Option 1 (the I-Search Paper) or Option 2 (the academic research paper).

Whatever it is called and whatever final form it takes, an essay that involves research can be the most time-consuming and anxiety-provoking assignment in any course. But consider this: you already know a lot about investigating and reporting. Take a moment to acknowledge your readiness for the challenge of the hunt.

First, you do research all the time. Whenever you look for the best buys or seek more information about your favorite hobby, you practice strategies and skills that can be useful in a research paper. You talk to people, read manuals and magazines, and jot down important information. Your talk may not take the form of an interview and your jottings may not seem very systematic, but you can build methodically on their foundation.

Second, the earlier assignments in this book have prepared you for research in several ways. If you know how to reconstruct a memory, describe your observations, or analyze something, you have important research tools at your disposal. When I began reading Daniel Goleman's best seller, *Emotional Intelligence,* I noticed that he uses all these tools to report on his research. His book begins with the memory of a Manhattan bus driver whose contagious good nature transformed an irritable pack of New Yorkers into a busload of smiles. Later he describes a shy preschooler with extraordinary social skills and analyzes the steps of an "emotional hijacking" to explain how emotions and reason can compete or cooperate for control of human behavior. In other words, he investigates the nature of emotional intelligence through memory, direct observation, and analysis as well as through interviews and documented readings. A section from Goleman's book is reprinted in this chapter as "The Family Crucible."

A third way that you are primed for the assignment lies in your accumulated experience with printed and electronic texts. Many best sellers, articles, and television programs report on research. If you're familiar with programs like *Nightline, Dateline,* or *60 Minutes,* for example, you already know about the role of anchors in broadcast news. You know that they announce the evening's topic, tie together bits of information contributed by experts and reporters in the field, and wrap up the show with some tentative conclusions. What you may not have considered is that the anchor's role on television is much like your role in a research report. You may not be the leading expert on your topic, but you're the one who introduces it and leads the audience through a lineup of selected information, clarifying, explaining, comparing, and qualifying as you go along. Once you begin to make analogies like this, you will be able to apply your reading and viewing experience more directly to your writing. The *Dateline* report and essays in this chapter will help you to look at such texts with the eye of an investigative writer.

Finally, there is your own natural curiosity, the driving force of all research. The students whom I interviewed while preparing this chapter told me that they are most motivated by a genuine connection to their topic. The teachers all agreed. We do our best when something of value is at stake. So choose a topic that really interests you. What are the burning questions in your life? What do you want to know at this moment? What do you need to know? While your final report will be written for other eyes, remember that your own eyes are the real center of your investigation. Nobody expects your paper to be the final word on your topic. Nobody expects it to be comprehensive or exhaustive. In fact, what will make it valuable to others is the way you frame and limit your search. Your particular slant on the topic, what you find most engaging, is your chief contribution to your readers.

As you follow your own investigative path, you may find it helpful to check in with fellow travelers from time to time. Many students tell me that they benefit from working with a partner or in groups. Some pair up with an investigative partner who is exploring the same topic, though from a different point of view. Others form a support group of students who have different topics but share similar concerns about sources, notes, and documentation. Some students submit their work in stages to their instructor, getting useful feedback about narrowing their topic, choosing sources, forming interview questions, designing surveys, and so on. In my own work, I have formed a habit of taking colleagues out to lunch. This gives me a chance to test my half-baked ideas with someone who shares my appetite for the topic but has different tastes. By the time we get to dessert, my dining partner's responses have helped me to revise the recipe for my research. I also regularly submit successive drafts to my editor, who sends back comments and suggestions. Often, these responses open possibilities that I would otherwise have missed. Ultimately, though, I know that I bear the ownership and responsibility for what I write. The last word is always mine.

Several of the teachers whom I interviewed told me that their most successful students learn to read books, magazines, and other printed works actively. That is, they learn to "talk to the text" as if talking to a live person. Active readers routinely question and challenge the authority of secondary sources, holding the writer's reasoning and reported facts up to critical judgment and the authority of other source materials. This kind of reading is easiest when the topic is something you truly care about, when you can see how your own life "intersects with the text."

I don't know at what point in my career I learned to question the authority of sources. I do know that when I read or watch a film, part of me is usually engaged in an ongoing dialogue with the author or the filmmakers. I ask the kinds of questions I might ask if the author were in front of me. "How do you know you're right about X? What about Y and Z? What you say here conflicts with my experience or what I just read in another source. What you say there fascinates me. I'd like to know more. This is the clearest statement of that point that I've ever come across. Let me write it down." Perhaps you do this already. Perhaps you're used to questioning some kinds of sources but not others. You critique your friends or you talk back to your television set. I'd like to encourage you to form the habit of challenging all kinds of texts. Students who select Option 1 for their assignment find that the format promotes this habit. As they describe their encounters with various sources, one by one, they learn about the nature of authority. The investigative "I" helps them to see that they have choices. Even if you select Option 2, you still decide which sources are most reliable, which facts most credible, which ideas most sensible. And as you acquire a greater understanding of your topic and more experience as an investigator, you develop a certain confidence in your own authority. Instead of being a passive recipient of other people's knowledge, you gain active membership in the communities that share and create knowledge.

www.mhhe.com/costanzo

Visit the Web site for more information on research and working with sources.

More guidelines for your research and writing are offered in this chapter in the section on Tips on Writing from Research and on the Web site that accompanies this book.

WRITING OPTIONS: WRITING TO INVESTIGATE

Option 1: The I-Search Paper (Investigative Story)

When you present your report in the form of an investigative story, the tone is relatively informal. Since it is essentially the story of *your* investigation, you regularly use the first-person pronoun "I" to trace your progress, as I have done in the previous section of this chapter. This approach has been called the I-Search Paper by Ken Macrorie, a gifted teacher with a knack for folksy eloquence. In contrast to the traditional research paper, the I-Search Paper is personal and chronological; it includes the researcher's "I" as the principal investigator of an ongoing quest. "The I-Search comes out of a student's life and answers a need in it," Macrorie wrote. "Textbooks imply that reference works are tools for dull people. Yet true investigators are excited, sustained in their work not by instructions but by curiosity."

Typically, the story's basic organization is sequential because you describe your discoveries in the order they occurred. You might begin by telling how you became interested in the topic, illustrating it with a personal incident or an example that you read about. You might explain what you already knew about the topic when the incident occurred and list the unanswered questions that it raised for you. Then you might describe the steps you took to answer them. These might include primary sources, like a survey or interviews, and secondary sources, like books and movies. Each source that you consulted will be documented; that is, you will let your readers know certain details that will help them locate or evaluate your source. What these details are and how they are presented will depend on the specific guidelines that you follow. The MLA documentation guidelines, widely used in college English departments, can be found online or in libraries or bookstores.

Option 2: The Academic Research Paper

A traditional academic research paper presents your findings in a more objective manner. Instead of narrating your investigation in the first person as if telling a story, you are more likely to organize the essay by subtopics. For example, if your topic is children of gay couples, you might write one section on the growing number of families with gay parents, another on their legal status, a third on the ethical debates, a fourth on the social consequences, and so on. To help focus your research, it is often wise to pose your topic as a research question. For example, if you're writing a paper on divorce, you might start with the question "Why do parents of girls divorce more often than parents of boys?" Then you might divide your investigation, and your essay, into smaller questions that help to answer the main question. What do statistics show? Do fathers and mothers show favoritism toward children of the same sex? Do race, ethnicity, and education play a role? What are the effects on individual families and the national economy? Subquestions like these will occur to you as you begin to organize your thoughts, and more will arise as you continue your research.

Like other expository essays, an academic research paper may describe, analyze, and evaluate your topic, but it also documents your sources of information. Be sure to follow the prescribed guidelines for citing sources in your essay and for listing them at the end.

MEDIA OPTION: MULTIMEDIA PRESENTATION

Modern technology now enables us to do research and report our findings using a variety of media. With computer software like Microsoft *PowerPoint,* one of the most popular multimedia programs, we can compose a presentation using words, graphics, sounds, animation, and video. If we want to report on interfaith marriages, for example, such software allows us to include pictures of the couples, statistical animations, sound recordings of family members, and video clips of religious events.

The media option for this chapter requires that you have a working knowledge of a multimedia program such as *PowerPoint.* As with the writing option, you'll be combining primary and secondary research to investigate your chosen topic and present what you have learned to an audience. The difference is that a multimedia presentation lets you incorporate material beyond the words on a page. This means you can scan in documents and graphics, capture photos from the Internet, or transfer video and sound to a CD if you have the right equipment. Keep track of all your sources, though. You'll need to document them in your final presentation.

Your report will probably be organized as a series of slides, so you'll need to arrange things in a sequence. Consider whether to start with an overview or a captivating detail. What is the best way to introduce the questions you'll be answering? Should you present them question by question, answering each one in turn as you might in a conventional research essay? Or should you trace your investigation chronologically,

www.mhhe.com/costanzo

For a tutorial on using *PowerPoint,* visit the book Web site.

in the manner of an I-Search essay or an "In Search Of" television show? Either way, you'll be making similar decisions to those for written compositions. And your purpose will be the same: to inform your audience with carefully selected facts and ideas about your topic.

TIPS ON WRITING FROM RESEARCH

Since research reports generally involve more steps than other forms of writing, the "Tips on Writing" in this chapter are more substantial than they are in other chapters. Yet in most other ways, the basic stages are already familiar to you. You make plans by selecting a topic, focus on a particular aspect of that topic, and gather information about it. You draft an essay that reports your findings in an organized way, following an appropriate format for integrating and documenting your sources. You revise the essay in response to other readings and your own developing understanding of the topic. And you proofread the final draft, paying particular attention to the way you handle quotations and references to sources.

DISCOVERING

1. USE A TIMETABLE. Planning backward from the final deadline, decide what tasks should be completed by certain dates in order to complete the project on time. This helps keep you on schedule and avoids the last-minute panic brought on by procrastination.

2. FIND A TOPIC. Investigate a topic that truly interests you. It may be a topic that you explored in an earlier assignment as a memory, an observation, or the subject of an analysis. One student who analyzed his college fraternity for Chapter 5 went on to investigate the culture of American fraternities. A different student, who reconstructed some painful childhood memories for Chapter 3, pursued her interest by researching the consequences of child abuse. Another fruitful source for topics is your recent reading, viewing, or listening experience. What kinds of books or magazines do you spend time with? What kinds of radio or television shows do you enjoy?

PLANNING

1. BRING YOUR TOPIC INTO FOCUS. Chances are that the topic you've chosen is broad enough to write a book about it. Eventually, you'll need to limit your investigation to a particular part or aspect of the topic. Focused freewriting, the five W's, and considering the scope of your topic can help you locate the nerve center of your interest.

2. FOCUSED FREEWRITING. Write on your general topic, recalling personal experiences, describing those you've heard about, and analyzing different aspects of the topic until you discover what you are most curious about.

3. FIVE W's (Who, what, when, where, why). Do you want to know more about the *what* of your topic? (What exactly is bulimia? What constitutes violent crimes? What are fraternities like across America?) Do you want to know more about *who?* (Who suffers from bulimia? Who commits or is victimized by violent crimes? Who joins frat houses?) Are you more interested in *why?* (Why do people become bulimic, get involved in violent crime, or join fraternities?)

4. DETERMINING THE SCOPE OF YOUR PAPER. The scope of your final paper will depend on external constraints as well as your inner motivation. Consider how much time you have, the essay's length, and other guidelines provided by your instructor. If you know that you must include five outside sources, a topic like your local firehouse might be too narrow. If you can or must include a personal interview, you may want to limit the focus to take advantage of local sources.

RESEARCH

1. GATHER RELEVANT MATERIAL There are many ways to take stock of your knowledge. Some people write informally. Some people make inventory lists. What facts do you know about the topic? What assumptions and opinions do you bring to it? Who are the people you can

contact? What are the special journals, magazines, pamphlets, or authoritative books related to your topic? Where can you go for more information? You may be surprised by how much you already know, even if that knowledge consists mostly of sources who know more than you do.

2. **CREATE A PRELIMINARY PLAN.** Draw up a plan to organize your search. This may include some general reading to acquaint you with the topic. Every field has its special terms, its defining questions, its history and big names. A few articles or an encyclopedia entry can give you a working knowledge of the field that will serve you well during interviews and more specialized readings. Your plan may also include the names of agencies or individuals for potential interviews, sites to visit, libraries, and Web sites.

3. **WORK WITH PRIMARY SOURCES. Primary sources** are people, places, and artifacts from which you get information firsthand. Since these are original sources of information, in contrast to the secondhand accounts you derive from secondary sources like books and documentaries, working with primary sources can be especially lively and creative. You might visit a site, conduct interviews and surveys, or browse original documents to further your research.

4. **WORK WITH SECONDARY SOURCES. Secondary sources** consist of books, documents, or Web sites on your topic that have already been published. You'll usually find such sources in a library or online. Keep a working bibliography to document these sources so you won't have to scurry around for that information at deadline time. For more information on citing sources, visit www.mhhe.com/costanzo.

DRAFTING

1. **INTRODUCTIONS.** Some writers compose their introductions last, after drafting the main body of their essay. For these writers, it is easier to orient the reader once the writers know the terrain themselves. Others prefer to start their draft at the beginning because the introduction gives impetus and direction to their writing. For them, finding the opening words is like discovering the key to the right door.

2. **ORGANIZATION AND DEVELOPMENT.** Research essays offer this challenge: how to winnow down mounds of information into a focused report. If you are writing an I-Search investigative story (Option 1), you will be retracing your investigation step by step. The main ordering principle will be chronological, starting with how you became interested in the topic and moving through your stages of inquiry. An investigative report (Option 2) offers more organizing options. You have already seen how a topic question can be broken down into subquestions. By answering these subquestions one by one, you can arrive at a larger answer to your central inquiry. The standard journalistic what-who-where-when-why questions can be helpful here, but every topic question can be analyzed differently.

3. **CONCLUSIONS.** The conclusion of your essay should create a sense of closure. Don't just trail off. Assure the reader that you have arrived at your destination, or at least a recognizable rest spot.

REVISING

Much of the revising for an investigative story or report is like revising other kinds of essays. You reread your drafts with a fresh eye, or through the lens of someone else's reading, to check for clarity, completeness, unity, continuity, organization, and correctness. But since a research paper includes references to outside sources, you also need to **document** those sources so that readers will be able to tell exactly where you found your information. The standard methods for documenting have been compiled by the Modern Language Association (MLA); however, some disciplines and organization follow their own formats. Check with your instructor for the preferred format in your course.

PRINT
Newspapers
Research essays
Business reports
Scientific American
Newsweek
Time

TELEVISION
60 Minutes
Geraldo at Large
Frontline

MOVIES
Control Room
The Fog of War
Who Killed the Electric Car?

RADIO
All Things Considered
Morning Edition
No Place to Hide

INTERNET
The Smoking Gun
http://www.thesmokinggun.com
Investigative Reporters and
Editors
http://www.reporter.org/

Readings and Screenings: The Changing Family

Some investigative reporters are household names. They do the detective work behind current events, searching through the dark corners of the world, uncovering its secrets, and bringing the news to light each day on television, on the radio, in print, and on the Internet. Other investigators are less well known, although their research is also indispensable. We depend on their investigative and reporting skills to bring us what we need to know about health, business, education, sports, and every other topic of importance in our lives. In the following pages, we'll be learning what leading researchers have discovered about one of the most fundamental components of American life, the family.

For most of human history, and throughout the world, the family has been the basic training ground for life. Our first lessons in language, thinking, and behavior begin here. Many of our most fundamental beliefs and much of our personality can be traced to these early years. What happens, then, when the basic structures of the family begin to change? How will such changes affect society and the individuals that we become? Such questions have generated much speculation and investigation. Psychologists, sociologists, anthropologists, news reporters, and others have used the instruments of their disciplines to take the pulse of the American family and make various pronouncements about its health.

You'll find the fruits of their research in the following readings and screenings. Historian Frank Sulloway's studies of evolution and revolution support the claim that personality is shaped by our rank in the family. A *Dateline* televised report features an interview with Sulloway and investigates the influence of birth order on our daily lives. Psychologist Daniel Goleman explores the impact of parenting on emotional intelligence. Several writers use research to fuel the ongoing debate about family values. Shere Hite offers a theory about new family forms based on thousands of interviews. Barbara Dafoe Whitehead, drawing on statistics and the evidence of popular culture, argues that disruptions in the modern family are undermining the well-being of our children. Stephanie Coontz questions the literature on divorce, asserting that the research can be misleading. Many of these issues are woven into the fabric of "Everyday Use," Alice Walker's short story about a single mother who must decide which of her daughters will get a treasured family heirloom.

For more than ten years, NBC's *Dateline* has been reporting on a wide range of interesting topics using the popular format of a weekly television magazine. This format combines background information, interviews, on-location shooting, and the presence of a commentator to anchor a story. In many ways a *Dateline* program resembles an investigative essay. Like the writer of an essay, the anchorperson introduces the topic and ties together material from various sources, including primary sources (on-site visits, interviews, surveys) and secondary sources (articles, books, Web sites). In "Out of Order," Maria Shriver examines the research on birth order. As she discovers, "a child's eventual place in the world has a lot to do with their place in the family."

Maria Shriver was born in Chicago in 1955. A member of the prominent Kennedy family (she is the former president's niece), she entered journalism after graduating from Georgetown University and worked as a reporter for CBS and NBC. She married Arnold Schwarzenegger in 1986 and supported his successful race for governor of California in 2003. Maria Shriver has written a self-help book, *Ten Things I Wish I'd Known before I Went into the Real World* (2000), and a children's book about disabilities, *What's Wrong with Timmy?* (2001).

www.mhhe.com/costanzo
Visit the Web site to see the video.

Before watching the video, ask some of your classmates to tell you their birth order. Are you surprised by what they say? What preconceptions do you and others have about birth order and personality? Do the family rankings in your class confirm these preconceptions? Make a list of well-known historical and contemporary figures, and try to guess their birth order based on what you know about them. If you wanted to test your hunches about these people and about birth order in general, how would you go about doing so?

TRANSCRIPT FOR "OUT OF ORDER"

SHOW: Dateline

DATE: April 14, 1996

OUT OF ORDER

Announcer: From our studios in Los Angeles, here again is Maria Shriver.

MARIA SHRIVER: If you're like most parents, you work hard every day to help your kids grow up to be successful adults. But there is something else that plays a vital role in whether your child turns out to be the class leader or the class clown, a factor you may not even be aware of. There is new research showing that a child's eventual place in the world has a lot to do with their place in the family.

(Voiceover) Winston Churchill, a born leader and a firstborn. Martin Luther King, a peacemaker, a middle child. And Jay Leno, the class cut-up. Yep, the youngest child. None of this is surprising to social historian Dr. Frank Sulloway.

(File footage of Winston Churchill speaking; Martin Luther King accepting Nobel Peace Prize; Jay Leno on "Tonight Show")

Dr. FRANK SULLOWAY: The pervasive tendency is for youngest siblings to be radical, rebellious. And that's been true for the last 500 years.

5 SHRIVER: (Voiceover) Dr. Sulloway knows this after having spent 25 years searching for common links among thousands of radical thinkers. His research, soon to be published in the book "Born to Rebel" found birth order to be the key. "That," he says, "helps explain why innovators like Darwin and Copernicus, last-born both, were such independent thinkers."

(Dr. Sulloway typing on computer; computer screen; research papers)

Dr. KENNETH HARDY: (Voiceover) The position you're born in shapes your personality and shapes your behavior and shapes your relationships with other people.

(Children playing in room; man taking notes as children play)

SHRIVER: (Voiceover) Dr. Kenneth Hardy is director of Syracuse University's Department of Child and Family Studies.

Dr. HARDY: It informs professions, jobs we choose. I think it impacts who we select as marital partners, people we date. I think it's pervasive.

SHRIVER: I've talked to some people about this story, and they said "Oh, it's pop psychology."

10 Dr. HARDY: I've heard it before. I hear it all the time, people likening it to, "Oh you may as well read a horoscope." You know, I think that there's some caution that has to be exercised. I don't think that birth order explains every possible dimension of one's personality or one's behavior, but I don't think it can be ignored.

SHRIVER: (Voiceover) To see what role birth order plays in forming personality, we spent several months following 12-year-old Carrie, 10-year-old Katie, and nine-year-old Jessie Gaetano. The three sisters have three distinct personalities, personalities that psychologists say are typical of their birth order.

(Carrie, Katie, and Jessie playing)

Dr. HARDY: The first is very competitive, controlling, very—very conscious of rules and doing things the right way.

SHRIVER: (Voiceover) It's Carrie, the oldest, who makes sure her sisters follow the rules.

(Gaetano sisters playing together)

Dr. HARDY: Middles tend to be the forgotten children. They go through life sort of struggling with these sort of questions about, "Where is my place? What is my place?," and their behavior tends to suggest that.

15   SHRIVER: And it's Katie, the middle child, who sits with her back to her sisters, playing alone.

(Katie)

Dr. HARDY: (Voiceover) And then the youngest are very playful, very free spirited, usually great entertainers.

(Jessie playing with friends)

SHRIVER: (Voiceover) Not surprisingly, Jessie prefers playing with friends, while Katie likes to make things by herself. And it's Carrie who's a leader at the youth group at her church.

(Gaetano sisters)

Miss CARRIE GAETANO: (Working with youth group) What is the da—dinner theater?

SHRIVER: (Voiceover) They were also true to their birth order roles when they went pumpkin picking. Firstborn Carrie and middle-born Katie found pumpkins right away . . .

(Gaetano sisters in pumpkin patch)

20   Miss JESSIE GAETANO: (In pumpkin patch) What about this one?

SHRIVER: (Voiceover) . . . while Jessie kept looking and looking and looking.

(Gaetano sisters in pumpkin patch)

Dr. HARDY: Those behaviors are—are so typical of each of their respective birth orders. We expect the firstborn to kind of hone in and make a decision very—very quickly, very decisively, and for the youngest to be more free-spirited and to be more exploratory.

SHRIVER: (Voiceover) And a trip to the toy store found Katie acting very much the middle . . .

(Katie in toy store)

Ms. DEBBIE GAETANO: (To Katie) Why aren't you picking out dominoes? Isn't that what you wanted for Christmas?

25   SHRIVER: (Voiceover) . . . not wanting to voice much of an opinion . . .

(Gaetano sisters in toy store)

Miss J. GAETANO: (In toy store) Look at that dog. Oh, come here!

SHRIVER: (Voiceover) . . . while Jessie acted like a typical last-born.

(Gaetano sisters and mother in toy store)

Miss J. GAETANO: (In store) Mommy, how come she gets to sit here and I didn't get to look at my car that . . .

Ms. GAETANO: (In toy store) Jessie, we've looked at every Harley-Davidson in the store.

30 Dr. HARDY: Jessie screamed what is the—many youngest children's national anthem, "That's not fair. Why is she getting more attention than I'm getting?" And that's pretty typical for the youngest to respond that way.

SHRIVER: (Voiceover) Chuck and Debbie Gaetano are the girls' parents.

(Chuck and Debbie)

Ms. GAETANO: The rules that we have and the way that we act towards each other and towards the children, I think we were the same with the three of them. I don't see how it could be so different.

SHRIVER: Chuck and Debbie said to me, "I don't understand how we could have three such different kids. We're exactly the same, we treat them exactly the same, we didn't change the rules, and we've got three different kids."

Dr. HARDY: Each of those three children were born into different families, so that when they had the first child, and I typically think of these first babies as experimental babies, you know.

35 (Voiceover) They're the ones whose parents are so incredibly anxious about doing everything the right way, and then—so you have the second child that's born into a family where there's already an older sibling.

(Carrie Gaetano looking at babies in hospital beds; Katie and Carrie in grocery store)

Dr. HARDY: That, by any stretch of imagination, psychologically, emotionally, experientially, is a different family for that second-born.

(Voiceover) And then you have Jessie, of course, who's born into a family where she has two older siblings. Not only that, she has parents who now have experienced raising two children, so they're not quite the same parents.

(Gaetano sister)

SHRIVER: (Voiceover) This different introduction to the family can be seen in each of the girls' baby albums. Firstborn Carrie's is completely filled.

(Gaetano family looking at baby albums)

Ms. GAETANO: (Looking at album) These are all the things that she did first, the date that she did them.

40   SHRIVER: (Voiceover) Katie's album is somewhat smaller.

(Katie)

Ms. GAETANO: (Holding baby hat) We have a hat for Katie, look.

SHRIVER: (Voiceover) And then by the time Jessie came along . . .

(Jessie)

Ms. GAETANO: (Flipping through album) We don't have your first picture. We really don't have a lot, do we?

Miss J. GAETANO: No.

45   SHRIVER: Of course, not all families come in threes or stay frozen in time. A new baby can come along and all of a sudden a youngest child becomes a middle child, or a little girl can be born into a family of all boys. These changes do affect family dynamics, but there are certain traits that you can count on.

(Voiceover) Dr. Hardy has seen these traits in his lab at Syracuse University where he observes interactions of children through a one-way mirror. He showed DATELINE one such experiment. The children here are brothers and sisters from several families. They've been asked to draw a picture and make a collage, and who is it that takes charge? This boy, a firstborn.

(Hardy observing children in observation lab; boy)

Unidentified Boy #1: Can I show you my pictures?

SHRIVER: (Voiceover) Here he's showing not only his picture . . .

(Boy #1 holding picture)

Boy #1: This is Barry the banana.

50   SHRIVER: (Voiceover) . . . but also those of his brothers. And off to the side, it's a middle child working quietly. And the last-borns, they're playful and they seek attention.

(Children playing)

HUEY: Guys, I need the scissors and I order you to give them to me now.

SHRIVER: (Voiceover) Sometimes to the extreme.

(Huey taking scissors from other boy)

Boy #1: Hey, give me those!

SHRIVER: (Voiceover) Watch here, as Huey, in the green, the youngest of three brothers in the room, dissolves into tears.

(Huey crying)

55 ARNOLD: Come on, Huey.

HUEY: I keep asking people to give me the scissors. And finally, when I get the scissors, I cut something out, all you say is, "No, it doesn't fit."

SHRIVER: (Voiceover) And it's a firstborn who takes control.

Boy #1: Arnold—Arnold, you're wrong. Now where is it?

Dr. HARDY: After this was over, one of our colleagues interviewing the children asked, you know, each of them what was their favorite part of the process. And when she asked Huey, he said, with a big, bright, wonderful smile on his face, "Oh when I was crying, that was the best part for me." And I'm sure it was in part the best part for him because, you know, it was very effective in getting him lots of attention.

60 SHRIVER: He said that?

Dr. HARDY: He—he—those were his words, verbatim, "Oh, the part when I was crying."

SHRIVER: (Voiceover) If that's the way birth order is displayed in children, what happens when we become adults? We decided to try an experiment we thought seemed impossible. Could Dr. Hardy meet a group of DATELINE producers for the first time, and by observing them for just a few minutes determine their place in their family pecking order? The group was asked to decide where to give 1 million in aid.

(Huey crying; Dr. Hardy sitting at table with group of DATELINE producers)

DIANE: I guess we have to identify what we look at as the problems.

Unidentified Man #1: Drug abuse.

65 STEVE: Drugs.

MARTI: Homelessness.

MIAH: Yeah, homelessness.

BRUCE: Violence.

DIANE: Should we pick one area or should we divide it?

70 BRUCE: Well, I think we have to pick one topic and then decide . . .

SHRIVER: (Voiceover) Dr. Hardy watched the interaction.

(Hardy and producers)

STEVE: This money is clean money, by the way. We don't have to worry about where it came from?

MIAH: What is it within these programs that it would be useful?

SHRIVER: (Voiceover) After 10 minutes, Dr. Hardy's time was up.

(Hardy and producers)

75 BRUCE: How'd we do, Doctor?

SHRIVER: Hey, did you figure this whole situation out now? What is she?

Dr. HARDY: Well, actually, let me start with me because this group was a difficult one.

(Speaking to Steve) Well, I actually thought you—that you're a youngest.

STEVE: That's pretty amazing. Yeah, by quite a bit.

80 Dr. HARDY: Are you?

STEVE: Mm-hmm.

Dr. HARDY: (Speaking to Steve) I really—throughout this process, even before we started, really appreciated your great sense of humor. My thought was that Diane was a firstborn.

DIANE: Yep.

Dr. HARDY: I'm a firstborn myself, so there was some very recognizable, familiar . . .

85 SHRIVER: Which were?

Dr. HARDY: You know, from the very beginning, she was the only person who took down notes, who—who . . .

SHRIVER: (Voiceover) In the end, Dr. Hardy guessed four out of five correctly.

He missed on Marti, who was unusually quiet that day, but did pick out Bruce as an oldest . . .

(Producers)

Dr. HARDY: (Speaking to Bruce) I saw a lot of firstborn traits in you.

90 SHRIVER: (Voiceover) . . . and Miah as a middle-born.

(Miah)

Dr. HARDY: (Speaking to Miah) I was reading your confronting, sort of challenging questions as, "Hey, notice me. I'm a part of this process too. I'm over here. Hey, don't forget about me over here."

SHRIVER: How right did you think he was about all of you?

STEVE: Right on the money for me.

SHRIVER: Right on the money for you.

STEVE: Absolutely, right on the money.

SHRIVER: (Voiceover) And, says Dr. Hardy, it's helpful to recognize that some of our behavior is influenced by our birth order.

(Hardy and producers)

Dr. HARDY: See, I'm hoping that having some increased awareness of birth order would enlighten an individual, because firstborns are—are—are packaged as being authoritative and controlling. Doesn't mean that a firstborn shouldn't challenge that part of their personality, particularly if they find it's not especially helpful or useful.

SHRIVER: (Voiceover) And it's especially important for parents to pay attention to birth order.

(Gaetano family in grocery store)

SHRIVER: Is there anything that Carrie, Jessie, and Katie's mom and dad can do to make these kids aware of their birth order, to perhaps help them so that they don't, perhaps fit into this specific mold that might be preordaineded for them?

Dr. HARDY: I think continue to have expectations of each of their children that pushes them beyond their birth order.

(Voiceover) So there's no reason why Jessie can't take charge, or take control somewhat simply because she's the youngest.

(Jessie and Debbie)

Dr. HARDY: One clip where I actually saw the mother actively trying to engage Katie in an interaction. . . .

Ms. GAETANO: (Speaking to Katie in grocery store) OK, do you like what you picked out?

Miss KATIE GAETANO: Yeah.

Dr. HARDY: (Voiceover) It's helpful for parents to do that, to have expectations of the children that challenge their birth order stereotypes.

(Gaetano family in grocery store)

Ms. GAETANO: If you would have told me that I was going to have three girls, I would have said, "Oh, they'll be like little triplets, and I'll dress them all the same."

(Voiceover) It's as far from that as—as can be possible.

> (Katie, Carrie, and Jessie playing with dog)
>
> SHRIVER: And where do only children fit in the birth order puzzle? Dr. Hardy says they tend to share many of the same traits as firstborn. They like to be in the spotlight and they tend to mimic adult behavior.

RESPONSE QUESTIONS

1. Rate your interest in this video from 1 (lowest) to 10 (highest). How does your rating compare to the response of others in the class? How do you explain any patterns of response? Did you find your own birth order making a difference in how you watched the video?

2. What moments in the video stand out as particularly memorable? What makes them stand out?

3. What did you learn about birth order from watching this video? What surprised you or made you want to learn more? Where would you go to find the kind of information in which you are most interested?

4. Have you read or seen other reports on this subject? If so, compare them with *Dateline's* coverage. How would you decide on their relative reliability?

5. What other programs are you familiar with that resemble *Dateline?* What do they have in common? Why do you think they are organized this way? What purposes do they serve in your life? Who else benefits from them?

GUIDELINES FOR ANALYSIS

1. Maria Shriver is not an expert on the topic of birth order. How is her authority established? What is her role in this report? How well does she perform that role?

2. Like other television programs that use a magazine format, *Dateline* reports typically have two openers. One opener is part of the pre-taped video "package," which often includes a visual introduction to the topic, like the file footage of Winston Churchill, Martin Luther King, and Jay Leno. The other is a live introduction by the program's anchor, addressed to the viewer and introducing the package. What does Shriver's introduction contribute to our understanding of the topic? What does the taped introduction contribute?

3. Make a rough outline to see the major segments of the video. What does each segment add to your understanding of birth order? What kinds of sources support each segment? Which of these sources do you find most helpful, engaging, and trustworthy?

4. Refer to the transcript to find the boundaries of these segments. How does Shriver link one segment to another? How does she conclude the report? Does her wrap-up leave you with a satisfying sense of closure?

5. Describe the target audience for this program. How well does the program's style fit its audience? What particular decisions do you think were made with this audience in mind?

6. Compare the video and the transcript. What do you get from each version that seems lost or missing in the other? In general, what are the differences between reading and viewing investigative reports?

QUESTIONS OF CULTURE

1. Describe the Gaetano family and its environment. In addition to the influence of birth order, what other factors (social class, ethnic background, location) might account for the way the three girls behave?

2. Compare the children in the observation lab and the producers at NBC. How is Dr. Hardy able to apply what he has learned about children at play to adults in a work environment?

3. How well do you think the generalities about birth order made in this report can be applied to Chinese families, Muslim families, or families in other cultures? Where would you look for answers to this question if you were doing your own investigative report?

IDEAS FOR YOUR JOURNAL

1. Make a chart of your family, and arrange the people in it according to their birth order. How much of the *Dateline* report can you apply to your family? What does the research on birth order fail to explain?

2. Go someplace where you can observe children at play. Write down what you notice about their interaction, trying to guess which children are the oldest, middle, or youngest in their family.

PREVIEW

Frank Sulloway spent more than twenty-five years preparing for his book, *Born to Rebel: Birth Order, Family Dynamics, and Creative Lives.* He retraced Darwin's historical voyage on the *Beagle,* and he researched the history of 121 different revolutions—political, scientific, social, and religious—to test his idea that revolutions begin within families as a consequence of birth order. A former MacArthur Fellow with a Ph.D. from Harvard in the history of science, Sulloway gained national prominence for his meticulous work and striking ideas. In addition to his interview by *NBC Dateline,* he has appeared on *Nightline,* the *Today Show,* the *Charlie Rose Show,* and the Discovery Channel.

The following excerpt from Sulloway's book is an opportunity to watch an experienced researcher in action. Sulloway goes beyond the casual interest of a magazine article to meet the rigorous demands of academic research. His purpose is not simply to report on his topic to a general audience but also to develop and support a **hypothesis,** that is, a tentative theory to explain certain observed facts. As he says at one point, his hypothesis is formulated in answer to a question about sibling rivalry: "In competing for parental investment, what strategies are children most likely to employ, given differences in their birth order?" To answer this topic question, Sulloway investigates relevant research in several fields. He examines studies of animal behavior, human personality, and Darwinian evolution looking for clues, gathering theories, statistics, and examples that might help to answer his key questions. Once he forms a working hypothesis, he builds a case to support it, systematically arranging what he has learned from his research to explain, develop, and test his claims. In this respect, he is writing to persuade as well as to inform.

The following selection is also an opportunity to compare two kinds of media: scholarly writing and television reporting. As you read, notice the differences in format, content, and presentation style between Sulloway's essay and Maria Shriver's *Dateline* report on birth order.

Birth Order and Personality
By Frank Sulloway

Psychologists have been studying birth order for more than a century and have documented many intriguing results. Firstborns are reported to be more responsible and achievement oriented than laterborns, who are in turn reported to be more socially successful than their older siblings.[1] Although numerous explanations have been offered to account for these findings, no theory has commanded general acceptance. Alfred Adler, an early follower of Freud's who broke away in 1911 to found his own school of "individual psychology," had a strong interest in birth order.[2] The firstborn child, Adler argued, is "dethroned" by the birth of the next siblings.[3] Firstborns who manage to overcome this trauma try to emulate parents. In their role as surrogate parents, firstborns may overemphasize the importance of law and order and become "power-hungry conservatives."[4] As Adler reasoned, "Sometimes a child who has lost his power, the small kingdom he ruled, understands better than others the importance of power and authority."[5] If firstborns are unable to regain parental favor, Adler claimed, they sometimes rebel.

A secondborn himself, Adler considered individuals from this birth rank to be more cooperative than firstborns. Secondborns try harder than their older siblings, he maintained, because they are always playing catch-up. The secondborn "behaves as if he were in a race, is under full steam all the time, and trains continually to surpass his older brother and conquer him."[6] As a result, secondborns are "rarely able to endure the strict leadership of others."[7]

Youngest children are not subject to dethronement and are said to become lazy and spoiled. "A spoiled child can never be independent," Adler insisted.[8] Those lastborns who feel particularly overshadowed by their older siblings may experience a sense of inferiority. When lastborns do decide to compete with other siblings, Adler argued, they are often successful later in life.

Adler's hypotheses can accommodate themselves to almost any psychological outcome. Adlerian firstborns can be conservative or rebellious. Adlerian laterborns can be competitive or lazy. To be useful, these hypotheses need to be stated in ways that are refutable. Psychoanalytic approaches to human behavior have largely foundered on their propensity to forgo hypothesis testing.[9] Systematic studies, not clinical anecdotes, are required to validate such claims.[10] Anecdotal evidence plays a different role in science. For example, it helps to generate hypotheses and can illustrate tendencies that have already been validated through statistical testing.

Darwinian Guidance
Evolutionary Conflicts

5 Evolutionary theory offers a compelling answer to the question of why birth order should affect personality. Evolution is governed by a small number of biological conflicts. Organisms are in continual conflict with their environments, including predators and pathogens. This insight led Charles Darwin to his celebrated theory of natural selection. In the relentless struggle for existence, even minor individual differences can alter the balance between survival and death. Individuals who possess advantageous traits have a greater chance of passing them on to their progeny. Over time, natural selection adapts species to the dangers that lurk within their environments.

Darwin recognized a second principle, sexual selection, as a powerful mechanism of evolutionary change. In the *Origin of Species* (1859) and especially in the *Descent of Man* (1871), he used this principle to explain secondary sexual characteristics. The peacock has evolved his beautiful tail in response to competition for mates. Although peacocks suffer greater predation owing to this cumbersome objet d'art, the discerning preferences of peahens have overridden the pressures of natural selection. Structures such as the peacock's tail, which detract from classical Darwinian "fitness," demonstrate that natural and sexual selection are independent processes.

It took more than a century for biologists to go beyond Darwin's two fundamental insights. In recent years, biologists have begun to rethink the subject of evolution from the point of view of the gene. In 1963 William Hamilton, a graduate student, proposed a resolution to a problem that had stymied the greatest minds in biology since Darwin.[11] Because natural selection acts only for the good of the individual, the outcome is inherently selfish. Why, then, do organisms sometimes cooperate? Hamilton's solution to this problem was the theory of "kin selection." Copies of an altruist's genes are typically present in close kin. Because kin benefit from altruistic acts, genes coding for these behaviors will tend to spread within the population, despite occasional costs to the altruist.

This line of reasoning led Hamilton to the notion of "inclusive fitness." This measure of fitness is calculated as an individual's own reproductive success, together with his contribution to the reproductive success of relatives, discounted according to their coefficient of relatedness.[12] Based on the logic of inclusive fitness, J. B. S. Haldane once quipped that he would lay down his life for more than two brothers, four half-brothers, or eight cousins—a formula that closely approximates the genetic costs of sacrificing oneself for close kin.[13]

Hamilton's solution to this problem has been called "the most important advance in evolutionary theory since Charles Darwin and Gregor Mendel."[14] Curiously, Hamilton's ideas were not immediately appreciated, and they were judged insufficient for a doctoral degree at the University of London.[15] His theory of kin selection has inspired a staggering amount of empirical research, which has confirmed and extended his central idea. Foremost among the extensions of Hamilton's principle are those explaining conflicts over parental investment.

10   Based on a cost-benefit approach to kin selection, Robert Trivers developed the principle of "parent-offspring conflict."[16] In most organisms that reproduce sexually, parents and offspring share only one-half their genes. As a consequence, parents will sometimes disagree with offspring about the optimum level of investment. One prominent manifestation of these disagreements is conflict over weaning. At the time of weaning, the offspring wants to continue being fed. The parents' genetic interests are usually better served by having, and nurturing, other offspring. In many species, weaning conflicts involve considerable physical violence as parents inflict prohibitive costs on offspring who resist this process.[17] When these costs become high enough, the offspring finally agrees with the parent.

Implicit in the theory of parent-offspring conflict is another basic evolutionary principle. Because siblings share, on average, only one-half their genes, altruism among siblings—while considerable—has its limits. Siblings will tend to disagree about the allocation of shared resources. Whereas parents will normally encourage equal sharing among their offspring, offspring will generally prefer to acquire more of any scarce resource than they give to a sibling. As a rule, an offspring's idea of "fairness" is to give a sibling only one-third of any shared item, not half. This allocation follows from the fact that offspring are twice as related to themselves as they are to their siblings.[18]

The notion of "sibling conflict" is generally subsumed under the principle of parent-offspring conflict. Although these two principles are biologically inseparable, treating them as a single process obscures an important point: Parent-offspring conflict is driven by conflict between siblings. If parents could have only one offspring, their genetic interests would coincide with their offspring's and there would be no parent-offspring conflict in the Darwinian sense of the term. It is not necessary for an individual to have a sibling in order to experience sibling conflict. As disputes over weaning demonstrate, future siblings represent a powerful source of conflict over parental investment.[19] When resisting the weaning process, only children are engaged in sibling competition. . . .

Adaptive Strategies for Siblings

In all societies, parents make discriminations about the potential of their children and invest in them accordingly. When confronted by parental discrimination, siblings respond in strategic ways. One well-established finding about siblings is how exquisitely sensitive they are to any favoritism by parents.[46] Siblings can spend hours debating who got the better gift. No evolutionary psychologist should be surprised by such behavior. Sibling rivalry is Darwinian common sense. To keep parents on their toes, siblings even compete when parents have no intention of treating them differently. The *anticipatory* nature of sibling rivalry betrays its evolutionary roots.

In their efforts to maximize parental investment, siblings avail themselves of certain basic strategies. First, offspring can try to promote parental favor directly—for instance, by helping and obeying parents. Offspring can also attempt to dominate their rivals, reducing their demands for parental investment. Finally, offspring who find that they are being dominated can adopt various countermeasures, including appeasement, rebellion, or a combination of both tactics. Depending on age and physical size, some of these strategies are more effective than others. Here is where birth order comes in.[47]

Birth Order and the "Big Five" Personality Dimensions

To determine whether birth order is a proximate cause of sibling differences, it is useful to consider a general taxonomy for personality traits. Most personality traits can be grouped under five global "dimensions." These five dimensions emerge consistently in personality tests administered in different countries and languages around the world.[48] Called the "Big Five," these dimensions encompass (1) Extraversion, (2) Agreeableness, (3) Conscientiousness, (4) Neuroticism, and (5) Openness to Experience.[49]

Using the Big Five as my guide, I offer here a psychodynamic account of birth-order differences. Although more research is needed to validate some of these hypotheses, they are reasonably consistent with the evidence. My hypotheses take the form of answers to a question: In competing for parental investment, what strategies are children most likely to employ, given differences in their birth orders? Although my hypotheses are informed by a Darwinian perspective, they must stand or fall on their own empirical merits.

1. *Extraversion.* As a dimension of personality, extraversion involves at least six facets, which can be grouped under the dual headings of temperamental and interpersonal traits. The three temperamental facets of extraversion include activity level, excitement-seeking, and positive emotions such as self-confidence. Shyness is closely associated with these temperamental features of extraversion. The three interpersonal attributes of extraversion are warmth, friendliness, and gregariousness—all aspects of sociability.[50] The birth-order prediction that one might make for temperamental features of extraversion is not the same prediction that one might make for the interpersonal features.

   I first address the issue of birth order and temperament. Throughout most of childhood, firstborns enjoy the advantages of being bigger, stronger, and smarter than their younger siblings. The possession of these attributes makes it natural for firstborns to feel more self-assured than laterborns. Firstborns are also likely to try to minimize the costs of having siblings by dominating them. Firstborns should therefore score higher than laterborns on those behaviors that tend toward "assertiveness" and "dominance." With some qualifications to be discussed later in this chapter, the existing research supports these expectations. For example, firstborns are reported to be more self-confident than laterborns, and they are overrepresented among political leaders, including American presidents and British prime ministers.[51]

When extraversion is measured as sociability, an attribute that is associated with lower social status, laterborns ought to score higher than firstborns. For this reason, one cannot make a global prediction about birth order and extraversion, although one can make predictions with regard to some of this dimension's six facets.

2. *Agreeableness /Antagonism.* Again based on physical superiority, firstborns ought to be more antagonistic than laterborns, and firstborns are rated higher, by themselves and their siblings, in the physical uses of power. Among laterborns, lesser physical size suggests strategies that minimize physical confrontations. Prudent laterborn strategies include acquiescing to firstborn demands, cooperating, pleading and whining, and appealing to parents for protection. These "low-power" strategies are well documented in studies of laterborn behavior.[53] Relative to firstborns, laterborns are also reported to be more altruistic, empathetic, and peer-oriented.[54]

3. *Conscientiousness.* Given their special place within the family constellation, firstborns should be more amenable than laterborns to their parents' wishes, values, and standards. One effective way for firstborns to retain parental favor is by assisting with child-rearing tasks and by trying to be the "responsible" child of the family. As a consequence, firstborns should score higher than laterborns on Conscientiousness. The tendency for firstborns to excel in school and in other forms of intellectual achievement is consistent with their strong motivation to satisfy parental expectations.[55] Studies have repeatedly found that firstborns are "more strongly identified with parents and readier to accept their authority."[56]

4. *Neuroticism.* My psychodynamic hypotheses for Neuroticism are more restricted than for other Big Five dimensions. The reason is that Neuroticism (or Emotional Instability) does not apply across the board. Firstborns are not likely to be more "nervous" or "neurotic" than laterborns.[57] Still, Neuroticism is closely tied to jealousy, a trait that is instrumental to the preservation of valued resources.[58] From a Darwinian point of view, siblings are a threat to survival. One of the most common causes of childhood mortality is malnourishment, which tends to increase with sibship size. Negative emotions, including jealousy, are natural responses to this threat.

Firstborns have more reason than laterborns to be jealous of their siblings. Every firstborn begins life with 100 percent of parental investment. For laterborns, who share parental investment from the beginning, the reduction in parental care owing to a new sibling is never suffered to the same degree. Parents try to discourage jealousy, and firstborns may often suppress this trait. Still, when parents are not watching, a firstborn's display of jealous rage can be an effective means of intimidating younger siblings.

The literature on birth order is consistent with these expectations. For example, firstborns are described as being more anxious about their status.[59] They are also more emotionally intense than laterborns and slower to recover from upsets.[60] Among males, firstborns are more likely than laterborns to exhibit anger and vengefulness.[61] The Bible tells the same story. It was Cain, not his younger brother Abel, whose jealousy precipitated the first biblical murder.

5. *Openness to Experience.* Laterborns should score higher than firstborns on Openness to Experience, a dimension that is associated with being unconventional, adventurous, and rebellious. This prediction stems from the lesser identification that laterborns have with parents, as well as their history of domination by older siblings. As family "underdogs," laterborns should empathize with other downtrodden

individuals and generally support egalitarian social change. Effecting social change usually requires taking risks, so we would expect laterborns to be more adventurous than firstborns.[62]

The literature on birth order accords closely with these expectations. Laterborns are more inclined than firstborns to question authority and to resist pressure to conform to a consensus. Firstborns, in contrast, tend to endorse conventional morality. Studies also reveal that laterborns are more risk oriented than firstborns. For instance, laterborns are more likely to engage in dangerous physical activities, such as contact sports.[63]

Although the literature on birth order is generally consistent with these five trends, this body of research has not compelled widespread agreement. Indeed, accomplished psychologists have vigorously contested the existence of any general trends. The reasons for their objections need to be considered.

Testing Birth-Order Claims

It has been more than two decades since Carmi Schooler published his damning review of the birth-order literature under the title "Birth Order Effects: Not Here, Not Now!"[64] Since then several other reputable scholars have reached the same conclusion: birth-order effects are a mirage. In a noteworthy 1983 book, Cecile Ernst and Jules Angst reviewed more than a thousand publications on the subject. Most birth-order effects, they concluded, are artifacts of poor research design.[65]

According to Ernst and Angst, birth-order researchers have consistently failed to control for important background factors, such as social class and family size. On average, lower-class families are larger than upper-class families, creating spurious cross-correlations with birth order. Ernst and Angst have summed up their assessment of the literature with the blunt conclusion: *"Birth order influences on personality and IQ have been widely overrated."*[66] Other careful scholars, working with independent data, have agreed. Birth order, assert Dunn and Plomin, "plays only a bit-part in the drama of sibling differences."[67] . . .

Conclusions

Helen Koch's pioneering study compellingly demonstrates that birth order shapes personality. Just as important, her findings indicate that gender and other systematic sibling differences are vital to the story of human development. This story involves numerous interaction effects—a phenomenon that underscores the "emergent" nature of personality. Besides gender, the most common sources of interaction effects are age gaps between siblings and the sex of siblings. In subsequent chapters I shall expand on this list, which, properly constituted, encompasses a wide variety of influences that define a child's family niche.

Like the alpha males of primate societies, firstborns covet status and power. They specialize in strategies designed to subordinate rivals. The Big Five dimensions of personality provide us with a convenient means of summarizing these strategies. Firstborns tend to be *dominant, aggressive, ambitious, jealous,* and *conservative.* At these five levels of behavior, the influence of birth order is consistent and unmistakable.

Like low-status primates, laterborns are at a disadvantage in direct confrontations with older siblings. Although laterborns often manifest a decided inclination to rebel, they also work hard to improve their lot through good-natured sociability and cooperation. Dominance and cooperation are timeworn strategies, created and perpetuated by different forms of Darwinian selection.[94] Success can be achieved by either route.

In the drama of sibling competition, birth order and gender appear to be the two most important players in the choice of sibling strategies. There is evolutionary aptness to this conclusion. As ancestral siblings tailored their competitive strategies to the cognitive and physical dictates of age, they increasingly conducted the business of sibling rivalry like a game of chess, coordinating tactics in age- and gender-sensitive ways.

Today's offspring continue to play out this evolutionary drama. All over the world, offspring strive to maximize parental investment, adapting their strategies to their own particular family niche. Ultimately, sibling rivalry is about surviving childhood. Even after this Darwinian hurdle has been cleared, siblings continue to compete over the right to reproduce. In attempting to achieve these two fundamental Darwinian goals, siblings become astute strategists. The end result is called personality.

Notes

1. See, for example, Steelman and Powell 1985.

2. Adler 1927, 1928, 1956:376–83; see also Ernst and Angst 1983:85–87. Freud and other early psychoanalysts mostly ignored the subject of birth order. Freud himself (1916–17:334) made only one brief reference to the topic.

3. Adler 1956:377.

4. Adler 1956:379; Ernst and Angst 1983:85.

5. Adler 1956:378–79.

6. Adler 1956:379.

7. Adler 1956:380.

8. Adler 1956:381.

9. On the numerous shortcomings of psychoanalytic theory, see Grünbaum 1984, 1993; Eysenck 1985; Crews 1986, 1995; Sulloway 1979b, 1991a. Psychoanalytic hypotheses cannot be tested in the clinical setting because therapist and patient are both contaminated by psychoanalytic expectations (Grünbaum 1984). It is worth noting that Adlerians, through their *Journal of Individual Psychology,* have done considerably more than Freudians to promote hypothesis testing, a method that they have sometimes brought to bear in birth-order research (Miley 1969; Vockell, Felker, and Miley 1973).

10. Adler's hypotheses have been expanded upon and refined by other psychologists. For a summary of other such extensions, see Sutton-Smith and Rosenberg 1970:4–10; Ernst and Angst 1983:86–87. One intriguing psychoanalytic account employs birth order to explain various historical tendencies, such as being holistic or atomistic, romantic or realistic, connected or disconnected, and so forth (Harris 1964). Although Harris's claims are largely impressionistic and based on small samples, many of his hypotheses are consistent with the general thrust of the empirical literature.

11. Hamilton 1963, 1964a,b.

12. Dawkins (1982:185–86), whose definition of inclusive fitness I have paraphrased, explains why this notion is properly defined in terms of an individual's *effects* on the reproductive success of relatives, rather than as an absolute property of the individual. Were inclusive fitness an absolute property, individual organisms would possess inclusive fitness even though deceased or not yet born.

13. For the Haldane anecdote, see Richards 1987:541. Writing in the 1950s, Haldane failed to grasp the full implications of this idea, so the honor for the insight fell to Hamilton a decade later. Building on Hamilton's ideas about inclusive fitness, Edward O. Wilson (1975) proposed the broad outlines of an evolutionary theory of social behavior under the term "sociobiology." During the two decades since Wilson's treatment of this subject, it has become a burgeoning research domain. Owing to the heated controversies that greeted Wilson's 1975 book, many researchers have abandoned Wilson's "sociobiology" label for other designations. Today's sociobiologists call themselves behavioral biologists, Darwinian anthropologists, and evolutionary psychologists. This tactic has tended to diminish intellectual credit where credit is due. The term "evolutionary psychology" is appropriate for use by psychologists, but the approach remains a subfield of the broader project that Wilson originally sketched under the term "sociobiology." Although he did not use the term, Darwin was a sociobiologist, which is why all sociobiologists are Darwinians. For additional publications on sociobiology, see Wilson 1978; Alexander 1979; Symons 1979; Trivers 1985; Buss 1994; Ridley 1994; Wright 1994. For a thoughtful critique of sociobiology, see Kitcher 1985.

14. Trivers 1985:47.

15. Trivers 1985:47.

16. Trivers 1974. The notion of parent-offspring conflict, like that of sibling conflict, is implicit in Hamilton's ideas about kin selection, and these two conflicts were fully appreciated by Hamilton himself (1964a,b). By using a cost-benefit approach to individual development (and to the parent-offspring relationship), Trivers extended these two principles in new and important ways.

17. Trivers 1985:145–55.

18. Genetic considerations also predict that siblings will share scarce resources whenever the benefits of doing so are more than twice the costs (Trivers 1985:148).

19. Based on Darwinian theory, identical twins ought to be angelic altruists, free of sibling rivalry. Twinning is too rare a phenomenon in our own species for behaviors to have evolved for such a special case (Alexander 1979:157; Daly and Wilson 1988a:11). Unlimited altruism prevails in many asexual organisms because siblings are usually twins (Wilson 1975). Some species of aphids give birth to two different forms of offspring, which are in fact twins. One form, a soldier caste, remains in the first larval stage and defends the lives of the second form. The second form, which is adapted to feeding on plant sap, grows to adulthood and reproduces. Soldier aphids are altruists because their siblings reproduce on their behalf (Trivers 1985:42).

A remarkable tendency toward cooperation has evolved among the social insects—ants, bees, and wasps. As William Hamilton grasped in 1963, the social insects owe their altruistic propensities to an unusual genetic arrangement called haplodiploidy (Hamilton 1964a,b; Wilson 1971). Females have two sets of chromosomes, whereas males, who develop from an unfertilized egg, have only one set of chromosomes derived from their mother. On average, sisters share ¾ of their genes, but they are related to their brothers by only ¼. As a result, social insects have evolved female-based societies in which sisters perform most of the work. In some species, sisters actively limit the queen's production of male offspring (Trivers 1985:178, 279–80). After all, who needs brothers who mostly loaf around and who are genetically like nephews.

47. I have discussed this topic elsewhere (Sulloway 1995).

48. McCrae and Costa 1987, 1990; see also Goldberg 1981, 1982; Digman 1990; John 1990.

49. The Big Five personality dimensions represent a folk taxonomy and need to be employed judiciously (Kagan 1994:42–46). Buss (1991) argues that these five dimensions have been shaped by evolutionary considerations to provide, in shorthand form, maximally useful information about people. This same logic applies to Osgood, Suci, and Tannenbaum's (1957) semantic differential (good–bad, strong–weak, and active–passive). These three dimensions, which overlap with the Big Five personality dimensions, convey a maximum of information about friend or foe with a minimum of mental activity. Among lower animals, protective mimicry makes frequent use of these three dimensions of biological "judgment." See also D. S. Wilson 1996.

50. See, for example, Koch 1956e:408; Brim 1958; Sutton-Smith and Rosenberg 1970:114–16; Ernst and Angst 1983:148.

51. Forbes 1971; Stewart 1977, 1992.

52. Sutton-Smith and Rosenberg 1970:59.

53. Sutton-Smith and Rosenberg 1970:39–68. Similar strategies by status are observed in primate dominance hierarchies (de Waal 1989).

54. Sutton-Smith and Rosenberg 1970:118–19; see also Batson 1991 on birth order and altruism. Especially in ancestral times, it would often have been in the interests of younger siblings to cooperate with older siblings, since older siblings were more likely to survive and reproduce. With high levels of childhood mortality in previous centuries, many younger siblings' genes were propagated only via older siblings. Among some species of birds, younger siblings help to raise the offspring of older siblings (Trivers 1985:184–85; Emlen, Wrege, and Demong 1995).

55. See Altus 1966, Belmont and Marolla 1973, and Zajonc 1976. Properly interpreted, birth-order differences in achievement reflect Conscientiousness rather than Openness on the Big Five personality dimensions. IQ is not a personality dimension and represents a sixth factor (McCrae 1994).

56. The quotation is noteworthy because it comes from Ernst and Angst (1983: 240), who are critical of most other claims about birth order. See also MacArthur 1956; Altus 1963; Palmer 1966; Harris and Howard 1968; Price 1969; Sutton-Smith and Rosenberg 1970:113–14; MacDonald 1969a,b, 1971a,b; Singer 1971; Smith 1971; Kagan 1971:148; 1977; Baskett 1984.

57. Ernst and Angst 1983:159. Firstborns may be more anxious about status than laterborns, but they are also more self-confident (Koch 1955a). These behavioral differences are strongly dependent on context.

58. Adjective pairs that define Neuroticism include "not envious–envious," "even-tempered–temperamental," and "unemotional–emotional" (McCrae and Costa 1987:85). On the psychological functions of jealousy, see DeKay and Buss 1992:187–88.

59. Koch 1955a:36.

60. Koch 1955a:24; 1956e:397–98, 406.

61. See, for example, Koch 1955a:26, 28, 36; Koch 1956a:17; Koch 1956e:407.

62. Relevant to my claim about laterborns being "champions of the underdog" is a curious finding in behavioral genetics (Eaves, Eysenck, and Martin 1989:323). In a 60-item questionnaire involving social attitudes, in which many items exhibit moderate heritability, the following item had almost no heritability: "The so-called underdog deserves little sympathy or help from other people." Most differences in answers to this item are attributable to the nonshared environment (and hence to sibling differences). Although the issue has not been investigated in behavioral genetic research, it is not hard to predict the direction of any birth-order difference.

63. On birth order and conformity, see Bragg and Allen 1970; Sampson and Hancock 1967; Sutton-Smith and Rosenberg 1970:83–84, 140–42. For birth order and conventional morality, see MacDonald 1969b; Sutton-Smith and Rosenberg 1970:110; Ernst and Angst 1983:124–26. On birth order and dangerous activities, see Sutton-Smith and Rosenberg 1970:82; Nisbett 1968.

64. Schooler 1972.

65. Researchers owe a considerable intellectual debt to Ernst and Angst (1983) for their systematic analysis of the birth-order literature. Their book convinced me of the need for controlling my own historical samples for important background factors such as social class and sibship size. For other useful reviews of the birth-order literature, see Miley 1969; Vockell, Felker, and Miley 1973; Schubert, Wagner, and Schubert 1976; Schubert, Wagner, and Schubert 1984.

66. Ernst and Angst 1983:242 (their emphasis).

67. Dunn and Plomin 1990:85. Similar critical conclusions about birth-order research have been reached by Scarr and Grajek 1982; Plomin and Daniels 1987; Blake 1989a,b; Somit, Arwine, and Peterson 1996.

94. On dominance versus cooperation in primate groups, see de Waal 1982 and Trivers 1985:363, 381.

RESPONSE QUESTIONS

1. Consider your rank in the birth order of your family. Are you a firstborn child, a middle child, the youngest, or a singleton (only child)? How has this position affected your life? How might your life have been different if your rank had been different?

2. Review Sulloway's summary of the "Big Five" dimensions of personality, and rate your own personality in each category. How closely do your personal traits correspond to Sulloway's predictions about birth order?

3. In some ways, Sulloway's writing is more challenging than most of the other readings in this book. What makes it so challenging? Compare his essay to the *Dateline* video on birth order. How do you account for the differences in format, structure, and style?

GUIDELINES FOR ANALYSIS

1. In the first paragraph, Sulloway distinguishes between the reported facts about birth order and the theories offered to explain the facts. What does he think of Alfred Adler's theories? Why does Sulloway introduce Adler's hypotheses before offering his own?

2. Sulloway uses a combination of direct quotation, paraphrase, and summary to describe Adler's ideas. What are the advantages of using each of these techniques? Notice the way he uses tag lines ("Adler argued," "as Adler reasoned," "Adler insisted") in his writing. What functions do these tag lines serve?

3. In paragraph 4, Sulloway stresses the importance of "hypothesis testing." What kinds of testing does he mean? How well does he apply these tests on his own hypotheses about birth order?

4. Review Sulloway's discussion of Darwinian evolution. According to Sulloway, what are the key principles of evolutionary theory, and how are they relevant to birth order? Why does he believe that "Sibling rivalry is Darwinian common sense"?

5. One test of a hypothesis is its ability to explain observed facts. What explanations does Sulloway offer for sibling rivalry? What fields of study does he draw on to support his claims? By the time he reaches the conclusion of his essay, how convincingly has he refuted those who believe that "birth-order effects are a mirage"?

QUESTIONS OF CULTURE

1. Is there an ideal American family? How many children are considered ideal? Is gender a factor? How well does Sulloway's essay help to explain why Americans would want a particular family size and male-female ratio at this time in our history?

2. At one point, Sulloway speaks of a "culture-sensitive theory of inheritance practices." What examples does he give to show that the value placed on siblings (firstborn, laterborn, sons, daughters) may vary with social class, historical period, or ethnicity? What examples can you offer from your personal experience or reading?

3. Give a cultural critique of Sulloway's hypothesis. How well does he account for cultural differences in his effort to provide general theory of birth order?

4. As a result of China's one-child policy, a high percentage of the young people in China are "singletons." According to Sulloway's findings, what kinds of social and psychological problems are these children likely to encounter as they grow up? Will China become a nation of "little emperors," as some people predict?

IDEAS FOR YOUR JOURNAL

1. Draw up a list of people in your family and apply the "Big Five" personality dimensions to their behavior. How do you explain their individual traits?

2. How has this essay influenced your view on parenting? What does it explain about your own upbringing? How has it affected your thoughts about raising a family?

PREVIEW

When Daniel Goleman's book *Emotional Intelligence* appeared in 1995, it challenged the widespread notion that success in life depends largely on I.Q. Goleman's research persuaded him that emotional factors such as empathy, self-awareness, and self-discipline can be more important than a person's fixed Intelligence Quotient. Furthermore, he argued, these emotional skills can be learned.

A nationally acclaimed psychologist, Goleman studied at Amherst College and Harvard University. For many years, he reported on the brain and behavioral sciences for the *New York Times*. Goleman's writings, which include *The Art of Meditation* (1996) and *Working with Emotional Intelligence* (2000), continue to expand our definition of intelligence, and they offer practical guidelines for anyone raising a family. The following selection is taken from *Emotional Intelligence*.

The Family Crucible
By Daniel Goleman

It's a low-key family tragedy. Carl and Ann are showing their daughter Leslie, just five, how to play a brand-new video game. But as Leslie starts to play, her parents' overly eager attempts to "help" her just seem to get in the way. Contradictory orders fly in every direction.

"To the right, to the right—stop. Stop. Stop!" Ann, the mother, urges, her voice growing more intent and anxious as Leslie, sucking on her lip and staring wide-eyed at the video screen, struggles to follow these directives.

"See, you're not lined up . . . put it to the left! To the left!" Carl, the girl's father, brusquely orders.

Meanwhile Ann, her eyes rolling upward in frustration, yells over his advice. "Stop! Stop!"

Leslie, unable to please either her father or her mother, contorts her jaw in tension and blinks as her eyes fill with tears.

Her parents start bickering, ignoring Leslie's tears. "She's not moving the stick *that* much!" Ann tells Carl, exasperated.

As the tears start rolling down Leslie's cheeks, neither parent makes any move that indicates they notice or care. As Leslie raises her hand to wipe her eyes, her father snaps, "Okay, put your hand back on the stick . . . you wanna get ready to shoot. Okay, put it over!" And her mother barks, "Okay. move it just a teeny bit!"

But by now Leslie is sobbing softly, alone with her anguish.

At such moments children learn deep lessons. For Leslie one conclusion from this painful exchange might well be that neither her parents, nor anyone else, for that matter, cares about her feelings.[1] When similar moments are repeated countless times over the course of childhood they impart some of the most fundamental emotional messages of a lifetime—lessons that can determine a life course. Family life is our first school for emotional learning; in this intimate cauldron we learn how to feel about ourselves and how others will react to our feelings; how to think about these feelings and what choices we have in reacting: how to read and express hopes and fears. This emotional schooling operates not just through the things that parents say and do directly to children, but also in the models they offer for handling their own feelings and those that pass between husband and wife. Some parents are gifted emotional teachers, others atrocious.

10   There are hundreds of studies showing that how parents treat their children—whether with harsh discipline or empathic understanding, with indifference or warmth, or so on—has deep and lasting consequences for the child's emotional life. Only recently, though, has there been hard data showing that having emotionally intelligent parents is itself of enormous benefit to a child. The ways a couple handles the feelings between them—in addition to their direct dealings with a child—impart powerful lessons to their children, who are astute learners, attuned to the subtlest emotional exchanges in the family. When research teams led by Carole Hooven and John Gottman at the University of Washington did a microanalysis of interactions in couples on how the partners handled their children, they found that those couples who were more emotionally competent in the marriage were also the most effective in helping their children with their emotional ups and downs.[2]

The families were first seen when one of their children was just five years old, and again when the child had reached nine. In addition to observing the parents talk with each other, the research team also watched families (including Leslie's) as the father or mother tried to show their young child how to operate a new video game—a seemingly innocuous interaction, but quite telling about the emotional currents that run between parent and child.

Some mothers and fathers were like Ann and Carl: overbearing, losing patience with their child's ineptness, raising their voices in disgust or exasperation, some even putting their child down as "stupid"—in short, falling prey to the same tendencies toward contempt and disgust that eat away at a marriage. Others, however, were patient with their child's errors, helping the child figure the game out in his or her own way rather than imposing the parents' will. The video game session was a surprisingly powerful barometer of the parents' emotional style.

The three most common emotionally inept parenting styles proved to be:

- *Ignoring feelings altogether.* Such parents treat a child's emotional upset as trivial or a bother, something they should wait to blow over. They fail to use emotional moments as a chance to get closer to the child or to help the child learn lessons in emotional competence.

- *Being too laissez-faire.* These parents notice how a child feels, but hold that however a child handles the emotional storm is fine—even, say, hitting. Like those who ignore a child's feelings, these parents rarely step in to try to show their child an alternative emotional response. They try to soothe all upsets, and will, for instance, use bargaining and bribes to get their child to stop being sad or angry.

- *Being contemptuous, showing no respect for how the child feels.* Such parents are typically disapproving, harsh in both their criticisms and their punishments. They might, for instance, forbid any display of the child's anger at all, and become punitive at the least sign of irritability. These are the parents who angrily yell at a child who is trying to tell his side of the story. "Don't you talk back to me!"

Finally, there are parents who seize the opportunity of a child's upset to act as what amounts to an emotional coach or mentor. They take their child's feelings seriously enough to try to understand exactly what is upsetting them ("Are you angry because Tommy hurt your feelings?") and to help the child find positive ways to soothe their feelings ("Instead of hitting him, why don't you find a toy to play with on your own until you feel like playing with him again?").

15   In order for parents to be effective coaches in this way, they must have a fairly good grasp of the rudiments of emotional intelligence themselves. One of the basic emotional lessons for a child, for example, is how to distinguish among feelings; a father who is too tuned out of, say, his own sadness cannot help his son understand the difference between grieving over a loss, feeling sad in a sad movie, and the sadness that

arises when something sad happens to someone the child cares about. Beyond this distinction, there are more sophisticated insights, such as that anger is so often prompted by first feeling hurt.

As children grow the specific emotional lessons they are ready for—and in need of—shift. The lessons in empathy begin in infancy, with parents who attune to their baby's feelings. Though some emotional skills are honed with friends through the years, emotionally adept parents can do much to help their children with each of the basics of emotional intelligence: learning how to recognize, manage, and harness their feelings; empathizing; and handling the feelings that arise in their relationships.

The impact on children of such parenting is extraordinarily sweeping.[3] The University of Washington team found that when parents are emotionally adept, compared to those who handle feelings poorly, their children—understandably—get along better with, show more affection toward, and have less tension around their parents. But beyond that, these children also are better at handling their own emotions, are more effective at soothing themselves when upset, and get upset less often. The children are also more relaxed biologically, with lower levels of stress hormones and other physiological indicators of emotional arousal (a pattern that, if sustained through life, might well augur better physical health). Other advantages are social: these children are more popular with and are better liked by their peers, and are seen by their teachers as more socially skilled. Their parents and teachers alike rate these children as having fewer behavioral problems such as rudeness or aggressiveness. Finally, the benefits are cognitive; these children can pay attention better, and so are more effective learners. Holding IQ constant, the five-year-olds whose parents were good coaches had higher achievement scores in math and reading when they reached third grade (a powerful argument for teaching emotional skills to help prepare children for learning as well as life). Thus the payoff for children whose parents are emotionally adept is a surprising—almost astounding—range of advantages across, and beyond, the spectrum of emotional intelligence.

Heart Start

The impact of parenting on emotional competence starts in the cradle. Dr. T. Berry Brazelton, the eminent Harvard pediatrician, has a simple diagnostic test of a baby's basic outlook toward life. He offers two blocks to an eight-month-old, and then shows the baby how he wants her to put the two blocks together. A baby who is hopeful about life, who has confidence in her own abilities, says Brazelton,

> will pick up one block, mouth it, rub it in her hair, drop it over the side of the table, watching to see whether you will retrieve it for her. When you do, she finally completes the requested task—place the two blocks together. Then she looks up at you with a bright-eyed look of expectancy that says, "Tell me how great I am!"[4]

Babies like these have gotten a goodly dose of approval and encouragement from the adults in their lives; they expect to succeed in life's little challenges. By contrast, babies who come from homes too bleak, chaotic, or neglectful go about the same small task in a way that signals they already expect to fail. It is not that these babies fail to bring the blocks together: they understand the instruction and have the coordination to comply. But even when they do, reports Brazelton, their demeanor is "hangdog," a look that says, "I'm no good. See, I've failed." Such children are likely to go through life with a defeatist outlook, expecting no encouragement or interest from teachers, finding school joyless, perhaps eventually dropping out.

The difference between the two outlooks—children who are confident and optimistic versus those who expect to fail—starts to take shape in the first few years of life. Parents, says Brazelton, "need to understand

20

how their actions can help generate the confidence, the curiosity, the pleasure in learning and the understanding of limits" that help children succeed in life. His advice is informed by a growing body of evidence showing that success in school depends to a surprising extent on emotional characteristics formed in the years before a child enters school. [According to a landmark study of delayed gratification,] the ability of four-year-olds to control the impulse to grab for a marshmallow predicted a 210-point advantage in their SAT scores fourteen years later.

The first opportunity for shaping the ingredients of emotional intelligence is in the earliest years, though these capacities continue to form throughout the school years. The emotional abilities children acquire in later life build on those of the earliest years. And these abilities are the essential foundation for all learning. A report from the National Center for Clinical Infant Programs makes the point that school success is not predicted by a child's fund of facts or a precocious ability to read so much as by emotional and social measures: being self-assured and interested; knowing what kind of behavior is expected and how to rein in the impulse to misbehave; being able to wait, to follow directions, and to turn to teachers for help; and expressing needs while getting along with other children.[5]

Almost all students who do poorly in school, says the report, lack one or more of these elements of emotional intelligence (regardless of whether they also have cognitive difficulties such as learning disabilities). The magnitude of the problem is not minor; in some states close to one in five children have to repeat first grade, and then as the years go on fall further behind their peers, becoming increasingly discouraged, resentful, and disruptive.

A child's readiness for school depends on the most basic of all knowledge, *how* to learn. The report lists the seven key ingredients of this crucial capacity—all related to emotional intelligence.[6]

1. *Confidence.* A sense of control and mastery of one's body, behavior, and world; the child's sense that he is more likely than not to succeed at what he undertakes, and that adults will be helpful.
2. *Curiosity.* The sense that finding out about things is positive and leads to pleasure.
3. *Intentionality.* The wish and capacity to have an impact, and to act upon that with persistence. This is related to a sense of competence, of being effective.
4. *Self-control.* The ability to modulate and control one's own actions in age-appropriate ways; a sense of inner control.
5. *Relatedness.* The ability to engage with others based on the sense of being understood by and understanding others.
6. *Capacity to communicate.* The wish and ability to verbally exchange ideas, feelings, and concepts with others. This is related to a sense of trust in others and of pleasure in engaging with others, including adults.
7. *Cooperativeness.* The ability to balance one's own needs with those of others in group activity.

Whether or not a child arrives at school on the first day of kindergarten with these capabilities depends greatly on how much her parents—and preschool teachers—have given her the kind of care that amounts to a "Heart Start," the emotional equivalent of the Head Start programs.

Getting the Emotional Basics

25 Say a two-month-old baby wakes up at 3 A.M. and starts crying. Her mother comes in and, for the next half hour, the baby contentedly nurses in her mother's arms while her mother gazes at her affectionately, telling her that she's happy to see her, even in the middle of the night. The baby, content in her mother's love, drifts back to sleep.

Now say another two-month-old baby, who also awoke crying in the wee hours, is met instead by a mother who is tense and irritable, having fallen asleep just an hour before after a fight with her husband. The baby starts to tense up the moment his mother abruptly picks him up, telling him, "Just be quiet—I can't stand one more thing! Come on, let's get it over with." As the baby nurses his mother stares stonily ahead, not looking at him, reviewing her fight with his father, getting more agitated herself as she mulls it over. The baby, sensing her tension, squirms, stiffens, and stops nursing. "That's all you want?" his mother says. "Then don't eat." With the same abruptness she puts him back in his crib and stalks out, letting him cry until he falls back to sleep, exhausted.

The two scenarios are presented by the report from the National Center for Clinical Infant Programs as examples of the kinds of interaction that, if repeated over and over, instill very different feelings in a toddler about himself and his closest relationships.[7] The first baby is learning that people can be trusted to notice her needs and counted on to help, and that she can be effective in getting help; the second is finding that no one really cares, that people can't be counted on, and that his efforts to get solace will meet with failure. Of course, most babies get at least a taste of both kinds of interaction. But to the degree that one or the other is typical of how parents treat a child over the years, basic emotional lessons will be imparted about how secure a child is in the world, how *effective* he feels, and how dependable others are. Erik Erikson put it in terms of whether a child comes to feel a "basic trust" or a basic mistrust.

Such emotional learning begins in life's earliest moments, and continues throughout childhood. All the small exchanges between parent and child have an emotional subtext, and in the repetition of these messages over the years children form the core of their emotional outlook and capabilities. A little girl who finds a puzzle frustrating and asks her busy mother to help gets one message if the reply is the mother's clear pleasure at the request, and quite another if it's a curt "Don't bother me—I've got important work to do." When such encounters become typical of child and parent, they mold the child's emotional expectations about relationships, outlooks that will flavor her functioning in all realms of life, for better or worse.

The risks are greatest for those children whose parents are grossly inept—immature, abusing drugs, depressed or chronically angry, or simply aimless and living chaotic lives. Such parents are far less likely to give adequate care, let alone attune to their toddler's emotional needs. Simple neglect, studies find, can he more damaging than outright abuse.[8] A survey of maltreated children found the neglected youngsters doing the worst of all: they were the most anxious, inattentive, and apathetic, alternately aggressive and withdrawn. The rate for having to repeat first grade among them was 65 percent.

30

The first three or four years of life are a period when the toddler's brain grows to about two thirds its full size, and evolves in complexity at a greater rate than it ever will again. During this period key kinds of learning take place more readily than later in life—emotional learning foremost among them. During this time severe stress can impair the brain's learning centers (and so be damaging to the intellect). Though as we shall see, this can be remedied to some extent by experiences later in life, the impact of this early learning is profound. As one report sums up the key emotional lesson of life's first four years, the lasting consequences are great:

> A child who cannot focus his attention, who is suspicious rather than trusting, sad or angry rather than optimistic, destructive rather than respectful and one who is overcome with anxiety, preoccupied with frightening fantasy and feels generally unhappy about himself—such a child has little opportunity at all, let alone equal opportunity, to claim the possibilities of the world as his own.[9]

Notes

1. Leslie and the video game: Beverly Wilson and John Gottman, "Marital Conflict and Parenting: The Role of Negativity in Families," in M. H. Bornstein, ed., *Handbook of Parenting*, vol. 4 (Hillsdale, NJ: Lawrence Erlbaum, 1994).

2. The research on emotions in the family was an extension of John Gottman's marital studies reviewed in Chapter 9. See Carole Hooven, Lynn Katz, and John Gottman, "The Family as a Meta-emotion Culture," *Cognition and Emotion* (Spring 1994).

3. The benefits for children of having emotionally adept parents: Hooven, Katz, and Gottman, "The Family as a Meta-emotion Culture."

4. Optimistic infants: T. Berry Brazelton, in the preface to *Heart Start: The Emotional Foundations of School Readiness* (Arlington, VA: National Center for Clinical Infant Programs, 1992).

5. Emotional predictors of school success: *Heart Start.*

6. Elements of school readiness: *Heart Start,* p. 7.

7. Infants and mothers: *Heart Start,* p. 9.

8. Damage from neglect: M. Erickson et al., "The Relationship Between Quality of Attachment and Behavior Problems in Preschool in a High-Risk Sample," in I. Betherton and E. Waters, eds., *Monographs of the Society of Research in Child Development* 50, series no. 209.

9. Lasting lessons of first four years: *Heart Start,* p. 13.

RESPONSE QUESTIONS

1. According to Goleman, "Family life is our first school for emotional learning." Describe the kind of emotional schooling you got at home. What lessons did you learn about feelings and relationships from what your parents said and did?

2. Although Goleman does not directly define emotional intelligence in this selection, he gives many examples. What characteristics of emotionally intelligent parents can you list after reading Goleman's essay?

3. Based on your own experience, what distinguishes good and bad parenting? Compare your distinctions to Goleman's summary of "the three most inept parenting styles."

GUIDELINES FOR ANALYSIS

1. The selection starts with a description of Leslie learning a new video game with her parents. What is Goleman's purpose in beginning this way? This example of "a low-key family tragedy" is taken from a book about parenting and marital conflict (see note 1). Where else does Goleman cite an example of observed family life? Where would other examples be appropriate?

2. Goleman cites a surprising report on school success made by the National Center for Clinical Infant Programs. How are the reported seven key ingredients of learning readiness related to emotional intelligence? Why does Goleman call this a "Heart Start" program?

3. Why does Goleman believe that parenting can influence a child's biological, social, and cognitive development as well as the child's emotional makeup? How can basic lessons about feelings have such sweeping consequences "across, and beyond, the spectrum of emotional intelligence?"

4. To what kinds of outside sources does Goleman refer? Which of these sources seem most reliable to you? What makes them reliable?

QUESTIONS OF CULTURE

1. Can you tell whether Goleman's research is limited to a particular socioeconomic group, or does it apply to families of all backgrounds?

2. What beliefs do you have about parenting and culture? Where did these beliefs come from? Do different cultural groups favor different parenting styles? To what extent does Goleman address such differences?

IDEAS FOR YOUR JOURNAL

1. What emotional ingredients were blended in the crucible of your own family? What insights about your emotional home schooling did you get from reading Goleman's research?

2. If you were to list three or four key principles to guide your behavior as a parent, what would they be? What sources of information might be helpful in supporting these principles or in expanding them?

PREVIEW

Research on the family is rarely neutral, although some researchers are more outspoken than others about their agenda. For some thirty years, Shere Hite has spoken and written widely about families and other topics from a distinctly feminist perspective. Her famous nationwide studies, known as "The Hite Reports," have published pioneering research on female sexuality (1976), male sexuality (1981), and the family (1994). She has also written *Women as Revolutionary Agents of Change* (1996), *Sex and Business* (2000), and *The Hite Report: A National Study of Female Sexuality* (2003).

Hite's study of 30,000 American families reveals new patterns of diversity that she argues may be healthier than traditional family forms. The following selection is from *The Hite Report on the Family: Growing Up under Patriarchy* (New York: Grove/Atlantic, 1994).

New Family Forms Are Emerging
By Shere Hite

Love and anger, love and obedience, love and power, love and hate. These are all present in family relationships. It's easy to say that they are inevitable, that stresses and strains are unavoidable, given "human nature." To some extent this is true, but these stresses and strains are exaggerated by a tense and difficult family system that is imposed upon our emotions and our lives, structuring them to fit its own specified goals.

Is the family as we have known it for so long the only way to create safe, loving, and caring environments for people? The best way? To understand the family in Western tradition, we must remember that much of what we see, say, and think about it is based on the archetypal family that is so pervasive in our society—Jesus, Mary, and Joseph. There is no daughter icon. This is the "holy family" model that we are expected, in one way or another, to live up to. But is this model really the right one for people who believe in equality and justice? Does it teach a good understanding of love and the way to make relationships work when we become adults?

One constantly hears that the family is in trouble, that it doesn't work anymore, that we must find ways to help it. If the family doesn't work, maybe there is something wrong with its structure. People must have reasons for fleeing the nuclear family: human rights abuses and the battering of women are well documented in many governments' statistics.

The "Democratized" Family

The family is changing because only in recent decades has the process of democratization, which began in Western political life more than two centuries ago, reached private life. Although John Stuart Mill wrote in favor of women's rights in the egalitarian democratic theory he helped develop, the family and women's role in the world were left out of most discussions of democracy, left in the "sacred" religious domain. Women and non-property owners, as well as "minorities," did not have the vote when democracy first began. Men made a fatal mistake. The democracy they thought they could make work in the public sphere would not really work without democracy in private life.

5   Some people, of course, are alarmed by changes in the family. Reactionary fundamentalist groups have gone on the offensive to try to stop this process. Yet most people are happier with their personal lives today than people were 50 years ago. Women especially have more choices and freedom than they did in the past. There is a positive new diversity springing up in families and relationships today in Western society. This pluralism should be valued and encouraged: far from signaling a breakdown of society, it is a sign of a new, more open and tolerant society springing up, a new world being born out of the clutter of the old.

Diverse Families Offer Healthy Possibilities

Democracy could work even better if we changed the aggressive personality that is being created by the patriarchal family system. Children brought up with choice about whether to accept their parents' power are more likely to be confident about believing in themselves and their own ideas, less docile or habituated to bending to power. Such a population would create and participate in public debate very differently. And there are many more advances we are on the threshold of achieving: naming and eliminating emotional violence, redefining love and friendship, progressing in the areas of children's rights and in men's questioning of their own lives.

My work salutes the gentler and more diverse families that seem to be arising. They are part of a system that does not keep its members in terror: fathers in terror lest they not be "manly" and able to support it all; mothers in terror lest they be beaten in their own bedrooms and ridiculed by their children; children in terror of being forced to do things against their will and having absolutely no recourse, no door open to them for exit.

A New Theory of the Family

What I am offering is a new interpretation of relationships between parents and children, a new theory of the family. My interpretation of the data from my questionnaires [given to more than 3,000 people primarily from Western nations] takes into account not only the individual's unique experiences, as is done in psychology, but also the cultural backdrop—the canvas of social "approval" or "disapproval" against which children's lives are lived. This interdisciplinary theory also takes into account the historical ideology of the family; those who took part in my research are living in a world where perception of "family" is filtered through the Christian model of the "holy family" with its reproductive icons of Jesus, Mary, and Joseph. But no matter how beautiful it appears (especially in its promise of "true love"), this family model is an essentially repressive one, teaching authoritarian psychological patterns, meekness in women, and a belief in the unchanging rightness of male power. In this hierarchical family, love and power are inextricably linked, a pattern that has damaging effects not only on all family members but on the politics of the wider society. How can there be successful democracy in public life if there is an authoritarian model in private life?

So used have we become to these symbols that we continue to believe—no matter what statistics we see in the newspapers about divorce, violence in the home, mental breakdown—that the icons and the system they represent are right, fair, and just. We assume without thinking that this model is the only "natural" form of family, and that if there are problems it must be the individual who is at fault, not the institution.

10   We need a new interpretation of what is going on. We may be at one of the most important turning points of the Western world, the creation of a new social base that will engender an advanced and improved democratic political structure.

The Patriarchal Family

Creating new, more democratic families means taking a clear and rational look at our institutions. We tend to forget that the family was created in its current form in early patriarchy for political, not religious, reasons. The new political order had to solve a specific problem: How could lineage or inheritance flow through men (and not women as it had previously) if men do not bear children?

The modern patriarchal family was created so that each man would "own" a woman who would reproduce for him. He then had to control the sexuality of "his" woman, for how else could he be sure that "his" child was really his? Restrictions were placed on women's lives and bodies by men; women's imprisonment in marriage was made a virtue, for example, through the later archetype of the self-sacrificing Mary, who was happy to be of service, never standing up for herself or her own rights. Mary, it is important to note, is a later version of a much earlier Creation Mother goddess. In her earlier form, she had many more aspects, more like the Indian goddess Kali than the "mother" whom the Christian patriarchal system devised.

Fortunately, the family is a human institution: humans made it and humans can change it. My research indicates that the extreme aggression we see in society is not a characteristic of biological "human nature" (as Freud concluded), nor a result of hormones. "Human nature" is a psychological structure that is carefully implanted in our minds—for life—as we learn the love and power equations of the family. Power and love are combined in the family structure: in order to receive love, most children have to humiliate themselves, over and over again, before power.

In our society, parents have the complete legal, economic, and social "right" to control children's lives. Parents' exclusive power over children creates obedience. Children are likely to take on authoritarian emotional, psychological, and sexual patterns, and to see power as one of the central categories of existence.

The Need for Family Love

15 Love is at the heart—so to speak—of our belief in the importance of the family. The desire for love is what keeps us returning to the icons. Even when they don't seem to work in our lives, we try and try again. We are told that we will never find love if we don't participate in the family. We hear repeatedly that the only place we will ever be able to get security, true acceptance, and understanding is in the family; that we should distrust other forms of family; that we are only "half a family" or a "pretend family" if we create any other human group; that without being a member of the family we will be forever "left out," lonely, or useless. No one would want to deny the importance of love, or of lasting relationships with other people. But the violent, distorted definitions of love created by the patriarchal family make it difficult for love to last, and to be as profound as it could be.

How confusing it is for children, the idea of being loved! They are so often told by their parents, "Of course we love you, why do you even ask?" It is easy for children to believe that the emotion they feel when faced with a powerful person is "love"—or that the inscrutable ways of a person who is sometimes caring and friendly, and other times punitive and angry, are loving. The problem then is that, since the parents are still the providers and "trainers" of the children, legally and economically the "owners" of the children, they exercise incredible power over the children—the very power of survival itself.

Children must feel gratitude, and so, in their minds, this gratitude is mixed with love. How much of the love they feel is really supplication before the power of the parents? How will they define love later in life? Won't they be highly confused by passion (either emotional or physical) and what it means, unable to connect it with other feelings of liking and concern? Of course, long-term caring for others is something positive that can also be learned in families, but it can be learned in other kinds of families, not just the nuclear model. . . .

Single-Parent Families

There are very few carefully controlled studies of the effects of single-parent families on children. Today, much popular journalism assumes that the two-parent family is better for children. My data show that there are beneficial effects for the majority of children living in single-parent families. It is more positive for children not to grow up in an atmosphere poisoned by gender inequality.

Do girls who grow up with "only" their mother have a better relationship with her? According to my study, 49 percent of such girls felt that it was a positive experience; 20 percent did not like it; and the rest had mixed feelings. Mothers in one-parent families are more likely to feel freer to confide in daughters because no "disloyalty to the spouse" is implied. Daughters in such families are less likely to see the mother as a "wimp"—she is an independent person.

20 Boys who grow up with "only" their mother experience less pressure to demonstrate contempt for things "feminine" and for nonaggressive parts of themselves. In *The Hite Report on Men and Male Sexuality,* I was surprised to find that boys who grow up with their mother alone were much more likely to have good relationships with women in their adult lives: 80 percent of men from such families had formed strong, lasting ties with women (in marriage or long-term relationships), as opposed to only 40 percent from two-parent families. This does not mean that the two-parent family cannot be reformed so that it provides a peaceful environment for children—indeed this is part of the ongoing revolution in the family in which so many people today are engaged.

Single-parent families are mostly headed by mothers, yet there is an increasing number of single-father families. Many single fathers don't take much part in child care but instead hire female nannies or ask their mothers, sisters, or girlfriends to take care of the children. Men could change the style of families by taking more part domestically, and by opening up emotionally and having closer contact with children. My research highlights men's traumatizing and enforced split from women at puberty. Healing this is the single most important thing we as a society could do to bridge the distance men feel from "family."

A Positive Pluralism

If you listen to people talk about their families, it becomes clear that we must give up on the outdated notion that the only acceptable families are nuclear families. We should not see the new society that has evolved over the last 40 years as a disaster simply because it is not like the past.

The new diversity of families is part of a positive pluralism, part of a fundamental transition in the organization of society that calls for open-minded brainstorming by all of us: What do we believe "love" and "family" are? Can we accept that the many people fleeing the nuclear family are doing so for valid reasons? If reproduction is no longer the urgent priority that it was when societies were smaller, before industrialization took hold, then the revolt against the family is not surprising. Perhaps it was even historically inevitable. It is not that people don't want to build loving, family-style relationships, it is that they do not want to be forced to build them within one rigid, hierarchical, heterosexist, reproductive framework. Diversity in family forms can bring joy and enrichment to a society: new kinds of families can be the basis for a renaissance of spiritual dignity and creativity in political as well as personal life.

Continuing this process of bringing private life into an ethical and egalitarian frame of reference will give us the energy and moral will to maintain democracy in the larger political sphere. We can create a society with a new spirit and will—but politics will have to be transformed. We can use the interactive frame of reference most often found today in friendships between women. Diversity in families can form the basic infrastructure for a new and advanced type of political democracy to be created, imagined, developed—a system that suits the massive societies that communications technology today has made into one "global village."

Promoting Justice

25 One cannot exaggerate the importance of the current debate: there has been fascism in societies before; it could certainly emerge again, alongside fascism in the family. If we believe in the democratic, humanist ideals of the last 200 years, we have the right, almost the duty, to make our family system a more just one; to follow our democratic ideals and make a new, more inclusive network of private life that will reflect not a preordained patriarchal structure, but our belief in justice and equality for all—women, men, and children. Let's continue the transformation, believe in ourselves, and go forward with love instead of fear. In our private lives and in our public world, let's hail the future and make history.

RESPONSE QUESTIONS

1. Paragraph 2 starts with a question: "Is the family as we have known it for so long the only way to create safe, loving, and caring environments for people?" How would you have answered this question before reading Hite's selection? To what extent does the reading affect your answer?

2. What is Hite's main purpose in this selection? To what extent is she seeking to inform, persuade, or otherwise influence her readers? Where is her agenda most apparent?

3. What connections does Hite make between democracy and patriarchy, between public politics and private family life? Is her analysis of power and love relationships between children and parents an accurate reflection of your family or families you know well?

1. In her opening paragraph, Hite makes a key statement about stress and families. How might this statement be formulated into a hypothesis, or theory, about family systems? Notice how she organizes her essay into subsections dealing with democracy, family theory, patriarchy, love, single-parent families, and pluralism. What does each subsection contribute to her hypothesis?

2. Hite begins this selection with a reference to "human nature." Where does she define this term? Do you agree with her definition?

3. Compare Hite's use of research to the other readings in this chapter. Is she more or less objective in reporting it? How neutral is her use of language? How many of her claims are backed by factual evidence? In your view, does Hite's investigative style and format strengthen or weaken her report?

QUESTIONS OF CULTURE

1. Hite refers to Jesus, Mary, and Joseph as "the archetypal family." What does she mean by this term? According to this "holy family" standard, what kinds of families are left out?

2. Most of Hite's research is based on families from Western nations. Which of her findings do you think might apply to non-Western cultures? On what basis do you think so?

3. In paragraph 4, Hite recalls a time when "Men made a fatal mistake." To what mistake is she referring? How do women figure in this interpretation of history?

IDEAS FOR YOUR JOURNAL

1. Hite refers to issues of love, anger, obedience, power, and repression throughout her essay. To what extent do you think these are inevitable features of human nature or the result of family relationships? Based on your personal experience and the observation of others, what dynamics of family structure influence a child's conception of love?

2. If you wanted to support or refute Hite's theory of the family, what primary and secondary sources would you consult?

PREVIEW

Writing in *The Atlantic Monthly* in 1993, Barbara Dafoe Whitehead stirred up a national controversy with her landmark essay on family values. Entitled "Dan Quayle Was Right," the essay defended the position taken by Vice President Quayle against a television series in which the unmarried heroine, Murphy Brown, chose to become a mother. Whitehead argued that the trend toward single parenthood was threatening the fabric of the family. A graduate of the University of Wisconsin with a Ph.D. in American social history from the University of Chicago, Whitehead became a leader of the family values movement, appearing on public television and writing for a wide variety of publications. Her books include *The Divorce Culture: Rethinking Our Commitments to Marriage and Family* (Vintage, 1998) and *Why There Are No Good Men Left: The Romantic Plight of the New Single Woman* (2002). The following selection is excerpted from "Dan Quayle Was Right."

From Death to Divorce

By Barbara Dafoe Whitehead

Across time and across cultures, family disruption has been regarded as an event that threatens a child's well-being and even survival. This view is rooted in a fundamental biological fact: unlike the young of almost any other species, the human child is born in an abjectly helpless and immature state. Years of nurture and protection are needed before the child can achieve physical independence. Similarly, it takes years of interaction with at least one but ideally two or more adults for a child to develop into a socially competent adult. Children raised in virtual isolation from human beings, though physically intact, display few recognizably human behaviors. The social arrangement that has proved most successful in ensuring the physical survival and promoting the social development of the child is the family unit of the biological mother and father. Consequently, any event that permanently denies a child the presence and protection of a parent jeopardizes the life of the child.

The classic form of family disruption is the death of a parent. Throughout history this has been one of the risks of childhood. Mothers frequently died in childbirth, and it was not unusual for both parents to die before the child was grown. As recently as the early decades of this century children commonly suffered the death of at least one parent. Almost a quarter of the children born in this country in 1900 lost one parent by the time they were fifteen years old. Many of these children lived with their widowed parent, often in a household with other close relatives. Others grew up in orphanages and foster homes.

The meaning of parental death, as it has been transmitted over time and faithfully recorded in world literature and lore, is unambiguous and essentially unchanging. It is universally regarded as an untimely and tragic event. Death permanently severs the parent-child bond, disrupting forever one of the child's earliest and deepest human attachments. It also deprives a child of the presence and protection of an adult who has a biological stake in, as well as an emotional commitment to, the child's survival and well-being. In short, the death of a parent is the most extreme and severe loss a child can suffer.

Because a child is so vulnerable in a parent's absence, there has been a common cultural response to the death of a parent: an outpouring of support from family, friends, and strangers alike. The surviving parent and child are united in their grief as well as their loss. Relatives and friends share in the loss and provide valuable emotional and financial assistance to the bereaved family. Other members of the community show sympathy for the child, and public assistance is available for those who need it. This cultural understanding of parental death has formed the basis for a tradition of public support to widows and their children. Indeed, as recently as the beginning of this century widows were the only mothers eligible for pensions in many states, and today widows with children receive more-generous welfare benefits from Survivors Insurance than do other single mothers with children who depend on Aid to Families with Dependent Children.

It has taken thousands upon thousands of years to reduce the threat of parental death. Not until the middle of the twentieth century did parental death cease to be a commonplace event for children in the United States. By then advances in medicine had dramatically reduced mortality rates for men and women.

At the same time, other forms of family disruption—separation, divorce, out-of-wedlock birth—were held in check by powerful religious, social, and legal sanctions. Divorce was widely regarded both as a deviant behavior, especially threatening to mothers and children, and as a personal lapse: "Divorce is the public acknowledgment of failure," a 1940s sociology textbook noted. Out-of-wedlock birth was stigmatized, and stigmatization is a powerful means of regulating behavior, as any smoker or overeater will testify. Sanctions against nonmarital childbirth discouraged behavior that hurt children and exacted compensatory behavior that helped them. Shotgun marriages and adoption, two common responses to nonmarital birth, carried a strong message about the risks of premarital sex and created an intact family for the child.

Consequently, children did not have to worry much about losing a parent through divorce or never having had one because of nonmarital birth. After a surge in divorces following the Second World War, the rate leveled off. Only 11 percent of children born in the 1950s would by the time they turned eighteen see their parents separate or divorce. Out-of-wedlock childbirth barely figured as a cause of family disruption. In the 1950s and early 1960s, five percent of the nation's births were out of wedlock. Blacks were more likely than whites to bear children outside marriage, but the majority of black children born in the twenty years after the Second World War were born to married couples. The rate of family disruption reached a historic low point during those years.

A new standard of family security and stability was established in postwar America. For the first time in history the vast majority of the nation's children could expect to live with married biological parents throughout childhood. Children might still suffer other forms of adversity—poverty, racial discrimination, lack of educational opportunity—but only a few would be deprived of the nurture and protection of a mother and a father. No longer did children have to be haunted by the classic fears vividly dramatized in folklore and fable—that their parents would die, that they would have to live with a stepparent and stepsiblings, or that they would be abandoned. These were the years when the nation confidently boarded up orphanages and closed foundling hospitals, certain that such institutions would never again be needed. In movie theaters across the country parents and children could watch the drama of parental separation and death in the great Disney classics, secure in the knowledge that such nightmare visions as the death of Bambi's mother and the wrenching separation of Dumbo from his mother were only make believe.

In the 1960s the rate of family disruption suddenly began to rise. After inching up over the course of a century, the divorce rate soared. Throughout the 1950s and early 1960s the divorce rate held steady at fewer than ten divorces a year per 1,000 married couples. Then, beginning in about 1965, the rate increased sharply, peaking at twenty-three divorces per 1,000 marriages by 1979. (In 1974 divorce passed death as the leading cause of family breakup.) The rate has leveled off at about twenty-one divorces per 1,000 marriages—the figure for 1991. The out-of-wedlock birth rate also jumped. It went from five percent in 1960 to 27 percent in 1990. In 1990 close to 57 percent of births among black mothers were nonmarital, and about 17 percent among white mothers. Altogether, about one out of every four women who had a child in 1990 was not married. With rates of divorce and nonmarital birth so high, family disruption is at its peak. Never before have so many children experienced family breakup caused by events other than death. Each year a million children go through divorce or separation and almost as many more are born out of wedlock.

Half of all marriages now end in divorce. Following divorce, many people enter new relationships. Some begin living together. Nearly half of all cohabiting couples have children in the household. Fifteen percent have new children together. Many cohabiting couples eventually get married. However, both cohabiting and remarried couples are more likely to break up than couples in first marriages. Even social scientists find it hard to keep pace with the complexity and velocity of such patterns. In the revised edition (1992) of his book *Marriage, Divorce, Remarriage,* the sociologist Andrew Cherlin ruefully comments: "If there were a truth-in-labeling law for books, the title of this edition should be something long and unwieldy like Cohabitation, Marriage, Divorce, More Cohabitation, and Probably Remarriage."

Under such conditions growing up can be a turbulent experience. In many single-parent families children must come to terms with the parent's love life and romantic partners. Some children live with cohabiting couples, either their own unmarried parents or a biological parent and a live-in partner. Some children born to cohabiting parents see their parents break up. Others see their parents marry, but 56 percent of them (as compared with 31 percent of the children born to married parents) later see their parents' marriages fall apart. All told, about three quarters of children born to cohabiting couples will live in a single-parent home at least briefly. One of every four children growing up in the 1990s will eventually enter a stepfamily. According to one survey, nearly half of all children in stepparent families will see their parents divorce again by the time they reach their late teens. Since 80 percent of divorced fathers remarry, things get even more complicated when the romantic or marital history of the noncustodial parent, usually the father, is taken into account. Consequently, as it affects a significant number of children, family disruption is best understood not as a single event but as a string of disruptive events: separation, divorce, life in a single-parent family, life with a parent and live-in lover, the remarriage of one or both parents, life in one stepparent family combined with visits to another stepparent family; the breakup of one or both stepparent families. And so on. This is one reason why public schools have a hard time knowing whom to call in an emergency.

Given its dramatic impact on children's lives, one might reasonably expect that this historic level of family disruption would be viewed with alarm, even regarded as a national crisis. Yet this has not been the case. In recent years some people have argued that these trends pose a serious threat to children and to the nation as a whole, but they are dismissed as declinists, pessimists, or nostalgists, unwilling or unable to accept the new facts of life. The dominant view is that the changes in family structure are, on balance, positive.

A Shift in the Social Metric

There are several reasons why this is so, but the fundamental reason is that at some point in the 1970s Americans changed their minds about the meaning of these disruptive behaviors. What had once been regarded as hostile to children's best interests was now considered essential to adults' happiness. In the 1950s most Americans believed that parents should stay in an unhappy marriage for the sake of the children. The assumption was that a divorce would damage the children, and the prospect of such damage gave divorce its meaning. By the mid-1970s a majority of Americans rejected that view. Popular advice literature reflected the shift. A book on divorce published in the mid-1940s tersely asserted: "Children are entitled to the affection and association of two parents, not one." Thirty years later another popular divorce book proclaimed just the opposite: "A two-parent home is not the only emotional structure within which a child can be happy and healthy. . . . The parents who take care of themselves will be best able to take care of their children." At about the same time, the long-standing taboo against out-of-wedlock childbirth also collapsed. By the mid-1970s three fourths of Americans said that it was not morally wrong for a woman to have a child outside marriage.

Once the social metric shifts from child well-being to adult well-being, it is hard to see divorce and nonmarital birth in anything but a positive light. However distressing and difficult they may be, both of these behaviors can hold out the promise of greater adult choice, freedom, and happiness. For unhappy spouses, divorce offers a way to escape a troubled or even abusive relationship and make a fresh start. For single parents, remarriage is a second try at marital happiness as well as a chance for relief from the stress, loneliness, and economic hardship of raising a child alone. For some unmarried women, nonmarital birth is a way to beat the biological clock, avoid marrying the wrong man, and experience the pleasures of motherhood. Moreover, divorce and out-of-wedlock birth involve a measure of agency and choice; they are man- and woman-made events. To be sure, not everyone exercises choice in divorce or nonmarital birth. Men leave wives for younger women, teenage girls get pregnant accidentally—yet even these unhappy events reflect the expansion of the boundaries of freedom and choice.

This cultural shift helps explain what otherwise would be inexplicable: the failure to see the rise in family disruption as a severe and troubling national problem. It explains why there is virtually no widespread public sentiment for restigmatizing either of these classically disruptive behaviors and no sense—no public consensus—that they can or should be avoided in the future. On the contrary, the prevailing opinion is that we should accept the changes in family structure as inevitable and devise new forms of public and private support for single-parent families.

The View from Hollywood

With its affirmation of the liberating effects of divorce and nonmarital childbirth, this opinion is a fixture of American popular culture today. Madison Avenue and Hollywood did not invent these behaviors, as their highly paid publicists are quick to point out, but they have played an influential role in defending and even celebrating divorce and unwed motherhood. More precisely, they have taken the raw material of demography and fashioned it into a powerful fantasy of individual renewal and rebirth. Consider, for example, the teaser for *People* magazine's cover story on Joan Lunden's divorce: "After the painful end of her 13-year marriage, the Good Morning America cohost is discovering a new life as a single mother—and as her own woman." *People* does not dwell on the anguish Lunden and her children might have experienced over the breakup of their family, or the difficulties of single motherhood, even for celebrity mothers. Instead, it celebrates Joan Lunden's steps toward independence and a better life. *People,* characteristically, focuses on her shopping: in the first weeks after her breakup Lunden leased "a brand-new six bedroom, 8,000 square foot" house and then went to Bloomingdale's, where she scooped up sheets, pillows, a toaster, dishes, seven televisions, and roomfuls of fun furniture that was "totally unlike the serious traditional pieces she was giving up."

This is not just the view taken in supermarket magazines. Even the conservative bastion of the greeting-card industry, Hallmark, offers a line of cards commemorating divorce as liberation. "Think of your former marriage as a record album," says one Contemporary card. "It was full of music—both happy and sad. But what's important now is . . . YOU! the recently released HOT, NEW, SINGLE! You're going to be at the TOP OF THE CHARTS!" Another card reads: "Getting divorced can be very healthy! Watch how it improves your circulation! Best of luck! . . . " Hallmark's hip Shoebox Greetings division depicts two female praying mantises. Mantis One: "It's tough being a single parent." Mantis Two: "Yeah . . . Maybe we shouldn't have eaten our husbands."

Divorce is a tired convention in Hollywood, but unwed parenthood is very much in fashion:

in the past year or so babies were born to Warren Beatty and Annette Bening, Jack Nicholson and Rebecca Broussard, and Eddie Murphy and Nicole Mitchell. *Vanity Fair* celebrated Jack Nicholson's fatherhood with a cover story (April, 1992) called "Happy Jack." What made Jack happy, it turned out, was no-fault fatherhood. He and Broussard, the twenty-nine-year-old mother of his children, lived in separate houses. Nicholson said, "It's an unusual arrangement, but the last twenty-five years or so have shown me that I'm not good at cohabitation. . . . I see Rebecca as much as any other person who is cohabiting. And she prefers it. I think most people would in a more honest and truthful world." As for more-permanent commitments, the man who is not good at cohabitation said: "I don't discuss marriage much with Rebecca. Those discussions are the very thing I'm trying to avoid. I'm after this immediate real thing. That's all I believe in." (Perhaps Nicholson should have had the discussion. Not long after the story appeared, Broussard broke off the relationship.)

As this story shows, unwed parenthood is thought of not only as a way to find happiness but also as a way to exhibit such virtues as honesty and courage. A similar argument was offered in defense of Murphy Brown's unwed motherhood. Many of Murphy's fans were quick to point out that Murphy suffered over her decision to bear a child out of wedlock. Faced with an accidental pregnancy and a faithless lover, she agonized over her plight and, after much mental anguish, bravely decided to go ahead. In short, having a baby without a husband represented a higher level of maternal devotion and sacrifice than having a baby with a husband. Murphy was not just exercising her rights as a woman; she was exhibiting true moral heroism.

On the night Murphy Brown became an unwed mother, 34 million Americans tuned in, and CBS posted a 35 percent share of the audience. The show did not stir significant protest at the grass roots and lost none of its advertisers. The actress Candice Bergen subsequently appeared on the cover of nearly every women's and news magazine in the country and received an honorary degree at the University of Pennsylvania as well as an Emmy award. The show's creator, Diane English, popped up in Hanes stocking ads. Judged by conventional measures of approval, Murphy Brown's motherhood was a hit at the box office.

Increasingly, the media depicts the married two-parent family as a source of pathology. According to a spate of celebrity memoirs and interviews, the married parent family harbors terrible secrets of abuse, violence, and incest. A bumper sticker I saw in Amherst, Massachusetts, read unspoken traditional Family Values: Abuse, Alcoholism, Incest. The pop therapist John Bradshaw explains away this generation's problems with the dictum that 96 percent of families are dysfunctional, made that way by the addicted society we live in. David Lynch creates a new aesthetic of creepiness by juxtaposing scenes of traditional family life with images of seduction and perversion. A Boston-area museum puts on an exhibit called "Goodbye to Apple Pie," featuring several artists' visions of child abuse, including one mixed-media piece with knives poking through a little girl's skirt. The piece is titled Father Knows Best.

No one would claim that two-parent families are free from conflict, violence, or abuse. However, the attempt to discredit the two-parent family can be understood as part of what Daniel Patrick Moynihan has described as a larger effort to accommodate higher levels of social deviance. "The amount of deviant behavior in American society has increased beyond the levels the community can 'afford to recognize,'" Moynihan argues. One response has been to normalize what was once considered deviant behavior, such as out-of-wedlock birth. An accompanying response has been to detect deviance in what once stood

as a social norm, such as the married-couple family. Together these responses reduce the acknowledged levels of deviance by eroding earlier distinctions between the normal and the deviant.

Several recent studies describe family life in its postwar heyday as the seedbed of alcoholism and abuse. According to Stephanie Coontz, the author of the book *The Way We Never Were: American Families and the Nostalgia Trap,* family life for married mothers in the 1950s consisted of "booze, bowling, bridge, and boredom." Coontz writes: "Few would have guessed that radiant Marilyn Van Derbur, crowned Miss America in 1958, had been sexually violated by her wealthy, respectable father from the time she was five until she was eighteen, when she moved away to college." Even the budget-stretching casserole comes under attack as a sign of culinary dysfunction. According to one food writer, this homely staple of postwar family life brings back images of "the good mother of the 50's . . . locked in Ozzie and Harriet land, unable to move past the canvas of a Corning Ware dish, the palette of a can of Campbell's soup, the mushy dominion of which she was queen."

Nevertheless, the popular portrait of family life does not simply reflect the views of a cultural elite, as some have argued. There is strong support at the grass roots for much of this view of family change. Survey after survey shows that Americans are less inclined than they were a generation ago to value sexual fidelity, lifelong marriage, and parenthood as worthwhile personal goals. Motherhood no longer defines adult wom-

anhood, as everyone knows; equally important is the fact that fatherhood has declined as a norm for men. In 1976 less than half as many fathers as in 1957 said that providing for children was a life goal. The proportion of working men who found marriage and children burdensome and restrictive more than doubled in the same period. Fewer than half of all adult Americans today regard the idea of sacrifice for others as a positive moral virtue.

Dinosaurs Divorce

It is true that many adults benefit from divorce or remarriage. According to one study, nearly 80 percent of divorced women and 50 percent of divorced men say they are better off out of the marriage. Half of divorced adults in the same study report greater happiness. A competent self-help book called *Divorce and New Beginnings* notes the advantages of single parenthood: single parents can "develop their own interests, fulfill their own needs, choose their own friends and engage in social activities of their choice. Money, even if limited, can be spent as they see fit." Apparently, some women appreciate the opportunity to have children out of wedlock. "The real world, however, does not

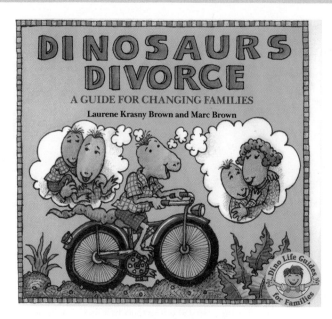

always allow women who are dedicated to their careers to devote the time and energy it takes to find—or be found by—the perfect husband and father wanna-be," one woman said in a letter to *The Washington Post*. A mother and chiropractor from Avon, Connecticut, explained her unwed maternity to an interviewer this way: "It is selfish, but this was something I needed to do for me."

There is very little in contemporary popular culture to contradict this optimistic view. But in a few small places another perspective may be found. Several racks down from its divorce cards, Hallmark offers a line of cards for children—To Kids With Love. These cards come six to a pack. Each card in the pack has a slightly different message. According to the package, the "thinking of you" messages will let a special kid "know how much you care." Though Hallmark doesn't quite say so, it's clear these cards are aimed at divorced parents. "I'm sorry I'm not always there when you need me but I hope you know I'm always just a phone call away." Another card reads: "Even though your dad and I don't live together any-

more, I know he's still a very special part of your life. And as much as I miss you when you're not with me, I'm still happy that you two can spend time together."

Hallmark's messages are grounded in a substantial body of well-funded market research. Therefore it is worth reflecting on the divergence in sentiment between the divorce cards for adults and the divorce cards for kids. For grown-ups, divorce heralds new beginnings (A HOT NEW SINGLE). For children, divorce brings separation and loss ("I'm sorry I'm not always there when you need me").

An even more telling glimpse into the meaning of family disruption can be found in the growing children's literature on family dissolution. Take, for example, the popular children's book *Dinosaurs Divorce: A Guide for Changing Families* (1986), by Laurene Krasny Brown and Marc Brown. This is a picture book, written for very young children. The book begins with a short glossary of "divorce words" and encourages children to "see if you can find them" in the story. The words include "family counselor," "separation agreement," "alimony," and "child custody." The book is illustrated with cartoonish drawings of green dinosaur parents who fight, drink too much, and break up. One panel shows the father dinosaur, suitcase in hand, getting into a yellow car.

The dinosaur children are offered simple, straightforward advice on what to do about the divorce. On custody decisions: "When parents can't agree, lawyers and judges decide. Try to be honest if they ask you questions; it will help them make better decisions." On selling the house: "If you move, you may have to say good-bye to friends and familiar places. But soon your new home will feel like the place you really belong." On the economic impact of divorce: "Living with one parent almost always means there will be less money. Be prepared to give up some things." On holidays: "Divorce may mean twice as much celebrating at holiday times, but you may feel pulled apart." On parents' new lovers: "You may sometimes feel jealous and want your parent to yourself. Be polite to your parents' new friends, even if you don't like them at first." On parents' remarriage: "Not everyone loves his or her stepparents, but showing them respect is important."

These cards and books point to an uncomfortable and generally unacknowledged fact: what contributes to a parent's happiness may detract from a child's happiness. All too often the adult quest for freedom, independence, and choice in family relationships conflicts with a child's developmental needs for stability, constancy, harmony, and permanence in family life. In short, family disruption creates a deep division between parents' interests and the interests of children.

One of the worst consequences of these divided interests is a withdrawal of parental investment in children's well-being. As the Stanford economist Victor Fuchs has pointed out, the main source of social investment in children is private. The investment comes from the children's parents. But parents in disrupted families have less time, attention, and money to devote to their children. The single most important source of disinvestment has been the widespread withdrawal of financial support and involvement by fathers. Maternal investment, too, has declined, as women try to raise families on their own and work outside the home. Moreover, both mothers and fathers commonly respond to family breakup by investing more heavily in themselves and in their own personal and romantic lives.

Sometimes the tables are completely turned. Children are called upon to invest in the emotional well-being of their parents. Indeed, this seems to be the larger message of many of the children's books on divorce and remarriage. *Dinosaurs Divorce* asks children to be sympathetic, understanding, respectful, and polite to confused, unhappy parents. The sacrifice comes from the children: "Be prepared to give up some things." In the world of divorcing dinosaurs, the children rather than the grown-ups are the exemplars of patience, restraint, and good sense.

RESPONSE QUESTIONS

1. As you were reading "From Death to Divorce," did you find yourself agreeing or arguing with the author? Explain.

2. How would you characterize the author's attitude toward recent changes in the American family?

3. Children who came of age during the 1960s, when family disruption was at its peak, are sometimes called "the me generation." How does this label relate to Whitehead's observation about the shifting social metric from child well-being to adult well-being?

4. Compare "From Death to Divorce" to the selections by Stephanie Coontz and Shere Hite in this chapter. Which selection seems best researched? Which seems most convincing? Explain your choices.

5. In paragraph 12, Whitehead says, "The dominant view is that the changes in family disruption are, on balance, positive." How accurate do you believe her statement is today?

GUIDELINES FOR ANALYSIS

1. Follow the development of Whitehead's essay. Why does she begin by focusing on death? What other forms of family disruption does she go on to discuss? How does she link these

forms to research data and trends in popular culture? What is the effect of ending with a reference to *Dinosaurs Divorce?*

2. In her opening paragraph, Whitehead states that the family unit based on both biological parents has been the most successful social structure for ensuring the welfare of the child. Does this assertion need to be supported by research, even though her essay first appeared in a popular magazine? Where else does she make unsupported claims—and with what degree of effectiveness?

4. Notice the way Whitehead constructs her paragraphs. Where does she use topic sentences most effectively? Where does she use transitional sentences to link sections of her essay? Where does she draw together the strands of an idea with a clinching statement?

5. Terms like "cohabiting couples," "unwed motherhood," and "divergent behavior" might be considered *loaded words,* words that carry deliberately negative connotations. Find other possible examples of loaded words. How might these ideas be expressed in more positive terms?

6. Whitehead quotes Stephanie Coontz in paragraph 23. Read Coontz's essay (page 287) to determine how fairly Whitehead represents her point of view.

QUESTIONS OF CULTURE

1. Whitehead sees a shift in attitude toward family disruptions from the 1950s to the 1970s. What reasons does she give to explain this "cultural shift"? Which of these reasons do you find most and least convincing? Why?

2. Throughout the essay, Whitehead refers to mass media like magazines, television, movies, children's literature, Hallmark cards, and even bumper stickers. What are these sources intended to document? Find other examples from popular culture that either confirm or contradict the author's main point.

3. Whitehead rarely mentions social class, race, or ethnicity when discussing family patterns. To what extent do you consider such factors important to an understanding of the issues raised in "From Family to Divorce"?

IDEAS FOR YOUR JOURNAL

1. Make a list of current films and television shows that center on family relationships. How many of these depictions represent the two-parent family in a favorable light? How are other family structures represented?

2. Design a survey to test Whitehead's assertions among people in your area. What questions would you ask to find out whether children of "disrupted families" do as well or believe they are as well off as children of two-parent families? To whom would you give your questionnaire?

3. Write an essay on family well-being and responsibility. Where do you put the blame or credit for the shifting family forms described by Whitehead?

PREVIEW

Stephanie Coontz is nationally known for her studies of the family. The author of several best-selling books and a frequent contributor to major magazines and newspapers, she appears regularly on television and has testified about her research before Congress. Coontz has taught in Japan and Hawaii and is currently a member of the faculty at the Evergreen State College in Olympia, Washington. Her books include *The Way We Really Are: Coming to Terms with America's Changing Families* (1997), *The Social Origins of Private Life: A History of American Families, 1600–1900* (1990), *The Way We Never Were: American Families and the Nostalgia Trap* (2000), and *Marriage, A History: From Obedience to Intimacy, or How Love Conquered Marriage* (2005). The following selection is from Chapter 5 of *The Way We Really Are*.

Putting Divorce in Perspective
By Stephanie Coontz

We have already accepted the fact that aging Americans are increasingly unlikely to live out their lives in "traditional" nuclear families, where they can be supported and cared for entirely by a spouse or a child. We can no longer assume that a high enough proportion of kids grow up with both biological parents that society can continue to ignore the "exceptions" that were there all along. Nor can our school schedules, work policies, and even emotional expectations of family life continue to presume that every household has a husband to earn the income and a wife to take care of family needs.

The social and personal readjustments required by these changes can seem awfully daunting. Here's what a spokesman for the Institute for American Values told me during a tape-recorded debate over whether it was possible to revive male breadwinning and restore permanent marriage to its former monopoly over personal life: "The strongest point in your argument is that the toothpaste is out of the tube. There's no longer the subordinate status of women to the extent there was in earlier eras—there is simply too much freedom and money sloshing around. We may be heading into what some sociologists call a 'postmarriage society,' where women will raise the children and men will not be there in any stable, institutional way. If so, we'd better build more prisons, even faster than we're building 'em now."[1]

I don't think the consequences of facing reality are quite so bleak. As my grandmother used to say, sometimes problems are opportunities in work clothes. Changes in gender roles, for example, may be hard to adjust to, yet they hold out the possibility of constructing far more honest and satisfying relationships between men and women, parents and children, than in the past. But this doesn't mean that every change is for the better, or that we don't pay a price for some of the new freedoms that have opened up. Divorce is a case in point. While divorce has rescued some adults and children from destructive marriages, it has thrown others into economic and psychological turmoil.

For the family values crusaders, this is where the discussion of how to help families begins and ends. "Let's face it," one "new consensus" proponent told me privately, "the interests of adults and children are often different, and there are too many options today for parents to pursue personal fulfillment at the expense of their children's needs. Sure there are other issues. But unless we keep the heat on about the dangers of divorce, parents will be tempted to put their own selfish concerns above the needs of their children." Fighting the "divorce culture" has to be the top priority, he argued, because "it's the one thing we can affect" by making parents realize what disastrous consequences divorce has for the future of their kids.

5   I have met only a tiny handful of divorced parents who didn't worry long and hard about the effects of divorce on their children (almost a third of divorced women, for example, attempted a reconciliation between the time of initial separation and the final divorce, according to data from 1987–1988).[2] And while it's true that a few pop psychologists have made irresponsible claims that divorce is just a "growth experience," I don't

believe we are really a culture that "celebrates" divorce, even if well-meaning people sometimes issue overly rosy reassurances to those who have undergone this trauma.

But for the record, let me be clear. Ending a marriage is an agonizing process that can seriously wound everyone involved, especially the children. Divorce can interfere with effective parenting and deprive children of parental resources. Remarriage solves some of the economic problems associated with divorce but introduces a new set of tensions that sometimes, at least temporarily, make things even more difficult.

Surely, however, it's permissible to put the risks in perspective without being accused of glorifying single parenthood or attempting, in Barbara Dafoe Whitehead's words, "to discredit the two-parent family." And the truth is that there has been a lot of irresponsible doom-saying about "disrupted" families. In a widely distributed article in the *Atlantic Monthly,* for example, Whitehead spends eight pages explaining why kids from divorced families face almost insurmountable deficits. Then, when she's convinced the average single mom to run out immediately to find a father for her child, she lowers the boom: Children in stepfamilies turn out even worse.[3]

While it is true that children in divorced and remarried families are more likely to drop out of school, exhibit emotional distress, get in trouble with the law, and abuse drugs or alcohol than children who grow up with both biological parents, most kids, from *every* kind of family, avoid these perils. And to understand what the increased risk entails for individual families, we need to be clear about what sociologists mean when they talk about such children having more behavior problems or lower academic achievement. What they really mean to say is *not* that children in divorced families have more problems but that more children of divorced parents have problems.

It's an important distinction, especially if you are a divorced or divorcing parent. It doesn't mean that all kids from divorced families will have more problems. There will be outstanding kids and kids with severe problems in both groups, but there will be a slightly higher proportion of kids from never-disrupted families in the outstanding group and a slightly lower proportion of them in the group with severe problems.

10   As family researcher Paul Amato notes, in measures of both achievement and adjustment, "a large proportion of children in the divorced group score *higher* than the average score of children in the nondivorced group. Similarly, a large proportion of children in the nondivorced group score *lower* than the average score of children in the divorced group." Comparing the average outcomes of children in various types of families obscures the fact that there is "more variability in the adjustment of children in divorced and remarried families than in nondivorced families." So knowing there are more divorced kids who do poorly is not really helpful. The question is how many more children from divorced and never-married parents are doing poorly, and what accounts for this, since some divorced children do exceptionally well and most are within normal range.[4]

Researchers who use clinical samples, drawn from people already in therapy because their problems are severe enough that they have sought outside help, tend to come up with the highest estimates of how many children are damaged by divorce. In 1989, for example, Judith Wallerstein published a long-term study of middle-class children from divorced families, arguing that almost half experienced long-term pain, worry, and insecurity that adversely affected their love and work relationships. Her work was the basis for Whitehead's claim in the *Atlantic Monthly* that "the evidence is in: Dan Quayle was right." But this supposedly definitive study, based on a self-selected sample of only sixty couples, did not compare the children of divorced couples with those of nondivorced ones to determine whether some of their problems might have stemmed from other factors, such as work pressures, general social insecurities, or community fragmentation. Moreover, the sample was drawn from families already experiencing difficulty and referred to the clinic for therapy. Only a third of the families were judged to be functioning adequately prior to the divorce.[5]

Research based on more representative samples yields much lower estimates of the risks. Paul Amato and Bruce Keith recently reviewed nearly every single quantitative study that has been done on divorce. Although they found clear associations with lower levels of child well-being, these were, on average, "not large." And the more carefully controlled the studies were, the smaller were the differences reported. The "large majority" of children of divorce, wrote eleven family researchers in response to Whitehead's misuse of their data, do not experience severe or long-term problems: *Most* do not drop out of school, get arrested, abuse drugs, or suffer long-term emotional distress. "Examining a nationally representative sample of children and adolescents living in four diverse family structures," write researchers Alan Acock and David Demo, "we find few statistically significant differences across family types on measures of socioemotional adjustment and well-being."[6]

Sara McLanahan, often cited by family values crusaders for her research on the risks of divorce, points out that divorce does not account for the majority of such social problems as high school dropout rates and unwed teen motherhood. "Outlawing divorce would raise the national high school graduation rate from about 86 percent to 88 percent. . . . It would reduce the risk of a premarital birth among young black women from about 45 percent to 39 percent."[7]

To be sure I'm not minimizing the risks, let's take a comparatively high estimate of divorce-related problems, based on the research of Mavis Hetherington, one of the most respected authorities in the field. She argues that "20 to 25 percent of kids from divorced families have behavior problems—about twice as many as the 10 percent from nondivorced families. You can say, 'Wow, that's terrible,'" she remarks, "but it means that 75 to 80 percent of kids from divorced families *aren't* having problems, that the vast majority are doing perfectly well."[8]

15   The fact that twice as many children of divorce have problems as children in continuously married families should certainly be of concern to parents. But it's important to remember that the doubling of risk is not evenly distributed among all families who divorce. Some of the families who contribute to these averages have had several divorces and remarriages. A study of boys who had been involved in divorce and remarriage found that those who had experienced many transitions, such as two or more divorces and remarriages, "showed the poorest adjustment." But even here the causal relationship involved more than divorce alone. It was "antisocial mothers" who were most likely *both* to experience many marital transitions and to engage in unskilled parenting practices that in turn placed their sons at risk for maladjustment.[9]

Many of the problems seen in children of divorced parents are caused not by divorce alone but by other frequently coexisting yet analytically separate factors such as poverty, financial loss, school relocation, or a prior history of severe marital conflict. When Rand Institute researchers investigated the relation between children's test scores and residence in a female-headed family, for example, the gross scores they obtained showed a significant deficit, but the disadvantage of children in mother-headed families was reduced to "essentially zero" when they controlled for other factors. "Apparently," they concluded, "a lot of the gross difference is . . . due to income, low maternal education, and other factors that frequently characterize single-parent families, rather than family structure itself."[10]

Income differences account for almost 50 percent of the disadvantage faced by children in single-parent homes. The tendency of less-educated women to have higher rates of divorce and unwed motherhood also skews the statistics. In fact, a mother's educational background has more impact on her child's welfare than her marital status. Other research suggests that the amount of television kids watch affects aggressive behavior whether or not their parents are divorced; one survey found that eating meals together was associated with a bigger advantage in school performance than was having two parents.[11]

Researchers who managed to disentangle the effects of divorce itself from the effects of a change in residence found that relocation and loss of peer support were more likely to interfere with school completion than parental separation. McLanahan's research with Gary Sandefur suggests that up to 40 percent of the increased risk of dropping out of school for children in single-parent families is attributable to moving after the divorce. A 1996 study found that the impact of family structure on schooling is "reduced substantially" when the number of school changes is controlled.[12]

Obviously, divorce often triggers financial loss, withdrawal of parental attention, and change of residence or schools. In this sense it is fair to say that divorce causes many childhood problems by creating these other conditions. But it makes more sense to adopt policies to minimize income loss or school and residence changes than to prohibit divorce across the board, for there are no hard and fast links between family structure, parental behaviors, and children's outcomes. One pair of leading researchers in the field conclude that there is "no clear, consistent, or convincing evidence that alterations in family structure per se are detrimental to children's development."[13]

20 The worst problems for children stem from parental conflict, before, during, and after divorce—or *within* marriage. In fact, children in "intact" families that are marked by high levels of conflict tend to do worse than children in divorced and never-married families. Two researchers who compared family types and child outcomes over a period of five years found that children who remained in highly conflicted marriages had more severe behavior problems than children in any other kind of family. They "were more depressed, impulsive, and hyperactive" than children from either low-conflict marriages or divorced families.[14]

In the first two years after a divorce, says Hetherington, children of divorce "look worse off than kids from intact families, even bad intact families." But after two or three years, "the kids who lived in one-parent households, with a competent mother, were doing better—with half as many behavioral problems—than the kids in the conflict-ridden homes."[15]

Furthermore, the problems found in children of divorced parents were often there months, or even years, prior to the parental separation. Eight to twelve years before a family breakup, researchers have found, parents who would eventually divorce were already reporting significantly more problems with their children than parents who ended up staying together. This finding suggests that "the association between divorce and poor parent-child relationships may be spurious; the low quality of the parents' marriage may be a cause of both." Alternatively, severely troubled children may help to precipitate a divorce, further distorting the averages.[16]

Some behaviors that make kids look worse off in the first few years after divorce may actually be the first steps toward recovery from damaging family patterns. For example, psychologist Richard Weissbourd cites the case of Ann, a 10-year-old girl who had become the family caretaker to cope with her father's alcoholism and her mother's long work hours. This role gave her many satisfactions and a strong sense of importance within the family, but it cut her off from friends and schoolmates. After the divorce, Ann's mother recovered from her own stress, spent more time at home, and resumed her parental role. Ann resented her "demotion" in the family and began to throw temper tantrums that landed her in a therapist's office. Yet her turmoil, far from being evidence of the destructive effects of divorce, was probably a necessary stage in the move to healthier relations with both parents and peers.[17]

One long-term study found that divorce produced extremes of *either* negative or positive behavior in children. At one end of the spectrum were children who were aggressive and insecure. These children were likely to have been exposed to a disengaged or inconsistently harsh parenting style. A significant number of these children were boys who had been temperamentally difficult early in life and whose behavior problems were made worse by family conflict or divorce.

At the other extreme were caring, competent children who were exceptionally popular, self-confident, well behaved, and academically adept. These children had the most stable peer friendships and solid relations with adults. And a high proportion—more than half—of the girls in this group came from divorced, female-headed families. Their mothers were typically warm, but not always available, and most of these girls had had to assume some caretaking responsibility for siblings, grandparents, or even their mothers at a young age. "Experiences in a one-parent, mother-headed family seemed to have a positive effect for these girls."[18]

As Mavis Hetherington sums up the research, most family members go through a period of difficulty after a divorce but recover within two to three years. Some exhibit immediate and long-term problems, while others adapt well in the early stages but have problems that emerge later. "Finally, a substantial minority of adults and children . . . emerge as psychologically enhanced and exceptionally competent and fulfilled individuals."[19] It should be reassuring for divorced parents to realize that such enhancement is possible, and that we also know a lot about how to avoid the worst outcomes for children.

Notes

1. David Blankenhorn, "Can We Talk? The Marriage Strategy," *Mirabella,* March 1995, p. 91.

2. Howard Wineberg and James McCarthy, "Separation and Reconciliation in American Marriages," *Journal of Divorce and Remarriage* 20 (1993).

3. Barbara Dafoe Whitehead, "Dan Quayle Was Right," *Atlantic Monthly,* April 1993, p. 55.

4. Paul R. Amato, "Life-Span Adjustment of Children to Their Parents' Divorce," *The Future of Children* 4, no. 1 (Spring 1994), p. 147; E. Mavis Hetherington, "An Overview of the Virginia Longitudinal Study of Divorce and Remarriage with a Focus on Early Adolescence," *Journal of Family Psychology* 7, no.1 (June 1, 1993), p. 53.

5. Judith Wallerstein and Sandra Blakeless, *Second Chances: Men, Women and Children a Decade After Divorce* (New York: Ticknor & Fields, 1989); Frank Furstenberg, Jr., and Andrew Cherlin, *Divided Families: What Happens to Children When Parents Part* (Cambridge, Mass.: Harvard University Press, 1991), p. 68; Andrew Cherlin and Frank Furstenberg, "Divorce Doesn't Always Hurt the Kids," *Washington Post,* March 19, 1989 (emphasis added). Wallerstein and Kelly suggested that there was a "sleeper effect" for young women, where problems caused by divorce were not evident until years later. But a ten-year Australian study found "no convincing evidence" for such an effect. Rosemary Dunlop and Ailsa Burns, "The Sleeper Effect—Myth or Reality?" *Journal of Marriage and the Family* 58 (May 1995), p. 375. It is possible that the young women who reported such effects to Wallerstein were engaging in an after-the-fact attempt to explain why they were having troubles.

6. Paul Amato, "Children's Adjustment to Divorce," *Journal of Marriage and the Family* 55 (1993); Paul Amato and Bruce Keith, "Parental Divorce and the Well-Being of Children: A Meta-Analysis," *Psychological Bulletin* 110 (1991); Arlene Skolnick and Stacey Rosencrantz, "The New Crusade for the Old Family," *American Prospect,* Summer 1994, p. 62; Rex Forehand, Bryan Neighbors, Danielle Devine, and Lisa Armistead, "Interparental Conflict and Parental Divorce: The Individual, Relative, and Interactive Effects on Adolescents Across Four Years," *Family Relations* 43 (1994), p. 387; Bonnie Thornton Dill, Maxine Baca Zinn, and Sandra Patton, "Feminism, Race, and the Politics of Family Values," *Report from the Institute for Philosophy and Public Policy* 13 (1993), p.17; Alan C. Acock and David H. Demo, *Family Diversity and Well-Being* (Thousand Oaks, Calif: Sage, 1994), p. 213; P. Lindsay Chase-Lansdale, Andrew Cherlin, and Kathleen Kiernan, "The Long-Term Effects of Parental Divorce on the Mental Health of Young Adults: A Developmental Perspective," *Child Development* 66 (1995).

7. Sara S. McLanahan, "The Two Faces of Divorce: Women's and Children's Interests," *Macro-Micro Linkages in Sociology* (Newbury Park, Calif: Sage, 1991), p. 202. She notes that these "estimates assume that all of the negative impact of family disruption is due to the disruption itself as opposed to preexisting characteristics of the parents."

8. Kathryn Robinson, "The Divorce Debate: Which Side Are You On?" *Family Therapy Networker* (May/June 1994), p. 20.

9. D. M. Capaldi and G. R. Patterson, "Relation of Parental Transitions to Boys' Adjustment Problems: I. A Linear Hypothesis. II. Mothers at Risk for Transitions and Unskilled Parenting," *Developmental Psychology* 27, no. 3 (1991), p. 489; William S. Aquilino, "The Life Course of Children Born to Unmarried Mothers: Childhood Living Arrangements and Young Adult Outcomes," *Journal of Marriage and the Family* 58 (May 1996), p. 306.

10. David Grissmer, Sheila Nataraj Kirby, Mark Berends, and Stephanie Williamson, *Student Achievement and the Changing American Family* (Santa Monica, Calif: Rand Institute on Education and Training, 1994), p. 66; Doris R. Entwisle and Karl L. Alexander, "A Parent's Economic Shadow: Family Structure Versus Family Resources as Influences on Early School Achievement," *Journal of Marriage and the Family* 57 (May 1995), p. 399.

11. Sara McLanahan and Gary Sandefur, *Growing Up with a Single Parent: What Hurts, What Helps?* (Cambridge, Mass.: Harvard University Press, 1995), pp. 2–3; Elizabeth Kolbert, "Television Gets a Closer Look as a Factor in Real Violence," *New York Times,* December 14, 1994; Rachel Wildavsky, "What's Behind Success in School?" *Reader's Digest,* October 1994, p. 52.

12. Sameera Teja and Arnold L. Stolberg, "Peer Support, Divorce, and Children's Adjustment," *Journal of Divorce and Remarriage* 20, no. 3/4 (1993); Robert Haveman, Barbara Wolfe, and James Spaulding, "The Relation of Educational Attainment to Childhood Events and Circumstances, *Institute for Research on Poverty Discussion Paper No.* 908-9o, Madison, Wisconsin, 1990, p. 28; David Demo and Alan Acock, "The Impact of Divorce on Children," in Alan Booth, ed., *Contemporary Families: Looking Forward, Looking Back* (Minneapolis: National Council on Family Relations, 1991), p. 185; Maxine Baca Zinn and Stanley D. Eitzen, *Diversity in American Families* (New York: Harper and Row, 1987), p. 317; "Frequent Moving Harmful, Study Says," *Olympian,* July 24, 1996, p. A3; Jay Teachman, Kathleen Paasch, and Karen Carver, "Social Capital and Dropping Out of School Early," *Journal of Marriage and the Family* 58 (1996), p. 782.

13. Adele Eskeles Gottfried and Allen W. Gottfried, eds., *Redefining Families: Implications for Children's Development* (New York: Plenum,1994), p. 224.

14. Furstenberg and Cherlin, *Divided Families,* p. 70; Amato and Keith, "Parental Divorce and the Well-Being of Children," p. 40; Andrew Cherlin, "Longitudinal Studies of Effects of Divorce on Children in Great Britain and the United States," *Science,* June 7, 1991, pp. 1386–1389; Joan Kelly, "Longer-Term Adjustment in Children of Divorce," *Journal of Family Psychology* 2 (1988); Larry Lettich, "When Baby Makes Three," *Family Therapy Networker* (January/February 1993), p. 66; Forehand et al., "Interparental Conflict and Parental Divorce," p. 387; Eileen S. Nelson, "The Relationship Between Familial Conflict and the Identity of Young Adults," *Journal of Divorce and Remarriage* 20, no. 3/4 (1993), p. 204.

15. Hetherington quoted in Robinson, "The Divorce Debate," pp. 27–28.

16. Furstenberg and Cherlin, *Divided Families,* p. 64; Paul R. Amato and Alan Booth, "A Prospective Study of Divorce and Parent-Child Relationships," *Journal of Marriage and the Family* 58 (May 1996), pp. 356–357; Robert E. Emery and Michele Tuer, "Parenting and the Marital Relationship," in Tom Luster and Lynn Okagaki, eds., *Parenting. An Ecological Perspective* (Hillsdale, N.J.: Lawrence Erlbaum, 1993), p. 135.

17. Richard Weissbourd, "Divided Families, Whole Children," *American Prospect* (Summer 1994), p. 69.

18. E. Mavis Hetherington, "Coping with Family Transitions: Winners, Losers, and Survivors," in *Annual Progress in Child Psychiatry and Child Development* (New York: Brunner/Maze1, 1990), pp. 237–239.

19. Hetherington, "Coping with Family Transitions," p. 221.

20. Marilyn Coleman and Lawrence H. Ganong, "Family Reconfiguring Following Divorce," in Steve Duck and Julia T. Wood, eds., *Confronting Relationship Challenges,* vol. 5 (Thousand Oaks, Calif: Sage, 1995), pp. 81–85. See also: Acock and Demo, *Family Diversity and Well-Being,* p. 224; Paul R. Amato, Laura Spencer Loomis, and Alan Booth, "Parental Divorce, Marital Conflict, and Offspring Well-being During Early Adulthood," *Social Forces* 73, no. 3 (March 1995), p. 895; Nan Marie Astone and Sara S. McLanahan, "Family Structure, Parental Practice and High School Completion," *American Sociological Review* 56 (June 1991), p. 318; Forehand et al., "Interparental Conflict and Parental Divorce," p. 392.

21. Furstenberg and Cherlin, *Divided Families,* p. 71. Ronald L. Simons and Associates, *Understanding Differences Between Divorced and Intact Families: Stress, Interaction, and Child Outcome* (Thousand Oaks, Calif: Sage, 1996), pp. 208, 210, 222. For an argument that it is almost entirely family processes rather than divorce per se that cause poor outcomes, see Teresa M. Cooney and Jane Kurz, "Mental Health Outcomes Following Recent Parental Divorce: The Case of Young Adult Offspring," *Journal of Family Issues: The Changing Circumstances of Children's Lives* 17, no. 4 (July 1996), p. 510.

22. Furstenberg and Cherlin, *Divided Families,* p. 21.

23. Janet Johnston, "Family Transitions and Children's Functioning," in Philip Cowan et al., eds., *Family, Self, and Society: Toward a New Agenda for Family Research* (Hillsdale, N.J.: Lawrence Erlbaum, 1993); Amato, "Life-Span Adjustment of Children to Their Parents' Divorce," p. 175; James Bray and Sandra Berger, "Noncustodial Father and Paternal Grandparent Relationships in Stepfamilies," *Family Relations* 39 (1990), p. 419.

24. Weissbourd, "Divided Families, Whole Children," p. 68.

25. Philip A. Cowan, Carolyn Pape Cowan, and Patricia Kerig, "Mothers, Fathers, Sons, and Daughters: Gender Differences in Family Formation and Parenting Style," in Cowan et al., eds., *Family, Self, and Society,* p.186; Sharon Wilsnack, Albert Klasson, and Brett Schurr, "Predicting Onset and Pernicity of Women's Problem Drinking: A Five-Year Longitudinal Analysis," *American Journal of Public Health* 81 (1991), pp. 305–318.

26. Jennifer Clark and Bonnie Barber, "Adolescents in Postdivorce and Always-Married Families: Self-Esteem and Perceptions of Fathers' Interest," *Journal of Marriage and the Family* 56 (1994), p. 609.

27. Susan Gano-Phillips and Frank D. Fincham, "Family Conflict, Divorce, and Children's Adjustment," in Mary Anne Fitzpatrick and Anita L. Vangelisti, eds., *Explaining Family Interactions* (Thousand Oaks, Calif: Sage, 1995), p. 207.

28. Emery and Tuer, "Parenting and the Marital Relationship," pp. 138–139.

29. Constance Ahrons, *The Good Divorce: Keeping Your Family Together When Your Marriage Comes Apart* (New York: Harper Perennial, 1994), p. 6; Amato, "Life Span Adjustment of Children to Their Parents' Divorce," p. 167.

30. Joyce A. Arditti and Michaelena Kelly, "Fathers' Perspectives of Their Co-Parental Relationships Postdivorce: Implications for Family Practice and Legal Reform," *Family Relations* 43 (January 1994), p. 65; Furstenberg and Cherlin, *Divided Families,* pp. 26–27; Kevin P. Kurkowski, Donald A. Gordon, and Jack Arbuthnot, "Children Caught in the Middle: A Brief Educational Intervention for Divorced Parents," *Journal of Divorce and Remarriage* 20, no. 3/4 (1993), p.149; Constance Ahrons and R. B. Miller, "The Effect of Postdivorce Relationship on Paternal Involvement: A Longitudinal Analysis," *American Journal of Orthopsychiatry* 63 (1993).

31. Ahrons, *The Good Divorce,* p. 82; Emery and Tuer, "Parenting and the Marital Relationship," p. 145. See also Melinda Blau, *Families Apart: Ten Keys to Successful Co-parenting* (New York: G. P. Putnam's Sons, 1993).

32. James H. Bray and Charlene E. Depner, "Perspectives on Nonresidential Parenting," in Charles E. Depner and James H. Bray, eds., *Nonresidential Parenting: New Vistas in Family Living* (Newbury Park, Calif: Sage, 1993), pp. 6–7.

33. Paul R. Amato, "Father-Child Relations, Mother-Child Relations, and Offspring Psychological Well-Being in Early Adulthood," *Journal of Marriage and the Family* 56 (November 1994), p. 1039; Susan Chollar, "Happy Families: Who Says They All Have to Be Alike?" *American Health* (July/August 1993); Simons and Associates, *Understanding Differences Between Divorced and Intact Families,* p. 224; Bonnie L. Barber, "Support and Advice from Married and Divorced Fathers: Linkages and Adolescent Adjustment," *Family Relations* 43 (1994), p. 433.

34. William Goode, *World Changes in Divorce Patterns* (New Haven, Conn.: Yale University Press, 1993), pp. 330, 345; Robert Emery, "Divorce Mediation: Negotiating Agreements and Renegotiating Relationships," *Family Relations* 44 (1995); Cheryl Buehler and Jean Gerard, "Divorce Law in the United States: A Focus on Child Custody," *Family Relations* 44 (1995).

35. "Letters to the Editor," *New York Times,* December 31, 1995.

36. Andrew Cherlin, "Remarriage as an Incomplete Institution," *American Journal of Sociology* 84 (1978); Mark A. Fine, "A Social Science Perspective on Stepfamily Law: Suggestions for Legal Reform," *Family Relations* 38 (1989); Andrew Schwebel, Mark Fine, and Maureena Renner, "A Study of Perceptions of the Stepparent Role," *Journal of Family Issues* 12 (1991); Mark A. Fine and David R. Fine, "Recent Changes in Laws Affecting Stepfamilies: Suggestions for Legal Reform," *Family Relations* 41 (1992); Andrew Cherlin and Frank Furstenberg, "Stepfamilies in the United States: A Reconsideration," *American Review of Sociology* 20 (1994), p. 378.

37. Virginia Rutter, "Lessons from Stepfamilies," *Psychology Today* (May/June 1994), pp. 66–67; Lynn White, "Growing Up with Single Parents and Stepparents: Long-Term Effects on Family Solidarity," *Journal of Marriage and the Family* 56 (1994), p. 946.

RESPONSE QUESTIONS

1. What assumptions does Coontz seem to make about "traditional" families and modern family life at the beginning of her essay? Explain why you agree or disagree with these assumptions. To what extent are your first impressions altered or confirmed by reading the complete essay?

2. Coontz quotes a spokesperson for the Institute for American Values who speaks of a "post-marriage society." What is meant by this term? What are your views on the role of marriage in society?

3. In paragraph 7, Coontz quotes Barbara Whitehead just as Whitehead quotes Coontz in the previous essay. Why do these two writers refer to one another? After reading both essays, explain whether you believe they have represented each other fairly.

4. The writer gives much attention to the consequences of divorce. On the whole, do you think she overstates or minimizes the risks?

GUIDELINES FOR ANALYSIS

1. A great variety of primary and secondary sources are cited in the text. Which of these sources do you consider most authoritative and reliable? Why do you trust these sources more than the others?

2. In paragraph 8, Coontz stresses "*not* that children in divorced families have more problems but that *more* children of divorced parents have problems." What conclusions does she draw from this distinction? What are its implications for single-parent families?

3. In addition to what Coontz reveals about her subject, this essay can be studied for her investigative methods. On what grounds does Coontz question the research on divorce? What alternative explanations of the research does she offer?

4. Notice how the author uses transitions to link the sections of her essay. Find examples where she makes particularly smooth connections.

5. Compare Coontz's writing style to Goleman's, Sullivan's, or Hite's. How would you characterize her methods of research and reporting?

QUESTIONS OF CULTURE

1. Coontz makes an effort to represents different perspectives. What points of view are represented? How balanced is her representation? How does her use of terms like "divorce culture," "family value crusaders," and "pop psychologists" affect the balance?

2. The research cited in this essay does not distinguish between ethnic or racial groups. Do you think it is a good idea to treat Americans as a single culture when studying patterns of divorce? Explain your thoughts.

1. List what most people consider to be the consequences of divorce. Which of these supposed effects appear to be best supported by research?

2. What do your personal observations tell you about the issues raised in Coontz's essay? What research could you do to test the validity of these observations?

PREVIEW

Alice Walker is one of the leading figures in contemporary American literature and a strong voice among African American women. Born in 1944, the youngest of eight children in a poor southern family, she grew up with a deep appreciation for her cultural heritage of storytelling and personal relationships. A childhood accident at the age of eight left her blind and disfigured in one eye. Although this condition was partly corrected years later, she found herself isolated from the course of everyday life, a position that enabled her to become a keen, compassionate observer. An outstanding student, she attended Spelman College in Atlanta and Sarah Lawrence in New York, where she became active in the civil rights movement. She also began to write poetry, fiction, and nonfiction. Her works include *In Love and Trouble* (short stories, 1973), *In Search of Our Mothers' Gardens* (prose, 1983), *The Color Purple* (a novel, 1983), *A Poem Traveled Down My Arm* (poetry, 2003), and *Now Is the Time to Open Your Heart: A Novel* (2003). "Everyday Use" was originally published in *In Love and Trouble*.

Everyday Use
By Alice Walker

I will wait for her in the yard that Maggie and I made so clean and wavy yesterday afternoon. A yard like this is more comfortable than most people know. It is not just a yard. It is like an extended living room. When the hard clay is swept clean as a floor and the fine sand around the edges lined with tiny, irregular grooves, anyone can come and sit and look up into the elm tree and wait for the breezes that never come inside the house.

Maggie will be nervous until after her sister goes: she will stand hopelessly in corners, homely and ashamed of the burn scars down her arms and legs, eying her sister with a mixture of envy and awe. She thinks her sister has held life always in the palm of one hand, that "no" is a word the world never learned to say to her.

You've no doubt seen those TV shows where the child who has "made it" is confronted, as a surprise, by her own mother and father, tottering in weakly from backstage. (A pleasant surprise, of course: What would they do if parent and child came on the show only to curse out and insult each other?) On TV mother and child embrace and smile into each other's faces. Sometimes the mother and father weep, the child wraps them in her arms and leans across the table to tell how she would not have made it without their help. I have seen these programs.

Sometimes I dream a dream in which Dee and I are suddenly brought together on a TV program of this sort. Out of a dark and soft-seated limousine I am ushered into a bright room filled with many people. There I meet a smiling, gray, sporty man like Johnny Carson who shakes my hand and tells me what a fine girl I have. Then we are on the stage and Dee is embracing me with tears in her eyes. She pins on my dress a large orchid, even though she has told me once that she thinks orchids are tacky flowers.

In real life I am a large, big-boned woman with rough, man-working hands. In the winter I wear flannel nightgowns to bed and overalls during the day. I can kill and clean a hog as mercilessly as a man. My fat keeps me hot in zero weather. I can work outside all day, breaking ice to get water for washing; I can eat pork liver cooked over the open fire minutes after it comes steaming from the hog. One winter I knocked a bull calf straight in the brain between the eyes with a sledge hammer and had the meat hung up to chill before nightfall. But of course all this does not show on television. I am the way my daughter would want me to be: a hundred pounds lighter, my skin like an uncooked barley pancake. My hair glistens in the hot bright lights. Johnny Carson has much to do to keep up with my quick and witty tongue.

But that is a mistake. I know even before I wake up. Who ever knew a Johnson with a quick tongue? Who can even imagine me looking a strange white man in the eye? It seems to me I have talked to them always with one foot raised in flight, with my head turned in whichever way is farthest from them. Dee, though. She would always look anyone in the eye. Hesitation was no part of her nature.

"How do I look, Mama?" Maggie says, showing just enough of her thin body enveloped in pink skirt and red blouse for me to know she's there, almost hidden by the door.

"Come out into the yard," I say.

Have you ever seen a lame animal, perhaps a dog run over by some careless person rich enough to own a car, sidle up to someone who is ignorant enough to be kind to him? That is the way my Maggie walks. She has been like this, chin on chest, eyes on ground, feet in shuffle, ever since the fire that burned the other house to the ground.

Dee is lighter than Maggie, with nicer hair and a fuller figure. She's a woman now, though sometimes I forget. How long ago was it that the other house burned? Ten, twelve years? Sometimes I can still hear the flames and feel Maggie's arms sticking to me, her hair smoking and her dress falling off her in little black papery flakes. Her eyes seemed stretched open, blazed open by the flames reflected in them. And Dee. I see her standing off under the sweet gum tree she used to dig gum out of; a look of concentration on her face as she watched the last dingy gray board of the house fall in toward the red-hot brick chimney. Why don't you do a dance around the ashes? I'd wanted to ask her. She had hated the house that much.

I used to think she hated Maggie, too. But that was before we raised money, the church and me, to send her to Augusta to school. She used to read to us without pity; forcing words, lies, other folks' habits, whole lives upon us two, sitting trapped and ignorant underneath her voice. She washed us in a river of make-believe, burned us with a lot of knowledge we didn't necessarily need to know. Pressed us to her with the serious way she read, to shove us away at just the moment, like dimwits, we seemed about to understand.

Dee wanted nice things. A yellow organdy dress to wear to her graduation from high school; black pumps to match a green suit she'd made from an old suit somebody gave me. She was determined to stare down any disaster in her efforts. Her eyelids would not flicker for minutes at a time. Often I fought off the temptation to shake her. At sixteen she had a style of her own: and knew what style was.

I never had an education myself. After second grade the school was closed down. Don't ask my why: in 1927 colored asked fewer questions than they do now. Sometimes Maggie reads to me. She stumbles along good-naturedly but can't see well. She knows she is not bright. Like good looks and money, quickness passes her by. She will marry John Thomas (who has mossy teeth in an earnest face) and then I'll be free to sit here and I guess just sing church songs to myself. Although I never was a good singer. Never could carry a tune. I was always better at a man's job. I used to love to milk till I was hooked in the side in '49. Cows are soothing and slow and don't bother you, unless you try to milk them the wrong way.

I have deliberately turned my back on the house. It is three rooms, just like the one that burned, except the roof is tin; they don't make shingle roofs any more. There are no real windows, just some holes cut in the sides, like the portholes in a ship, but not round and not square, with rawhide holding the shutters up on the outside. This house is in a pasture, too, like the other one. No doubt when Dee sees it she will want to tear it down. She wrote me once that no matter where we "choose" to live, she will manage to come see us. But she will never bring her friends. Maggie and I thought about this and Maggie asked me, "Mama, when did Dee ever have any friends?"

15   She had a few. Furtive boys in pink shirts hanging about on washday after school. Nervous girls who never laughed. Impressed with her they worshiped the well-turned phrase, the cute shape, the scalding humor that erupted like bubbles in lye. She read to them.

When she was courting Jimmy T she didn't have much time to pay to us, but turned all her faultfinding power on him. He *flew* to marry a cheap city girl from a family of ignorant flashy people. She hardly had time to recompose herself.

When she comes I will meet—but there they are!

Maggie attempts to make a dash for the house, in her shuffling way, but I stay her with my hand. "Come back here," I say. And she stops and tries to dig a well in the sand with her toe.

It is hard to see them clearly through the strong sun. But even the first glimpse of leg out of the car tells me it is Dee. Her feet were always neat-looking, as if God himself had shaped them with a certain style. From the other side of the car comes a short, stocky man. Hair is all over his head a foot long and hanging from his chin like a kinky mule tail. I hear Maggie suck in her breath. "Uhnnnh," is what it sounds like. Like when you see the wriggling end of a snake just in front of your foot on the road. "Uhnnnh."

Dee next. A dress down to the ground, in this hot weather. A dress so loud it hurts my eyes. There are yellows and oranges enough to throw back the light of the sun. I feel my whole face warming from the heat waves it throws out. Earrings gold, too, and hanging down to her shoulders. Bracelets dangling and making noises when she moves her arm up to shake the folds of the dress out of her armpits. The dress is loose and flows, and as she walks closer, I like it. I hear Maggie go "Uhnnnh" again. It is her sister's hair. It stands straight up like the wool on a sheep. It is black as night and around the edges are two long pigtails that rope about like small lizards disappearing behind her ears.

20   "Wa-su-zo-Tean-o!" she says, coming on in that gliding way the dress makes her move. The short stocky fellow with the hair to his navel is all grinning and he follows up with "Asalamalakim, my mother and sister!" He moves to hug Maggie but she falls back, right up against the back of my chair. I feel her trembling there and when I look up I see the perspiration falling off her chin.

"Don't get up," says Dee. Since I am stout it takes something of a push. You can see me trying to move a second or two before I make it. She turns, showing white heels through her sandals, and goes back to the car. Out she peeks next with a Polaroid. She stoops down quickly and lines up picture after picture of me sitting there in front of the house with Maggie cowering behind me. She never takes a shot without making sure the house is included. When a cow comes nibbling around the edge of the yard she snaps it and me and Maggie and the house. Then she puts the Polaroid in the back seat of the car, and comes up and kisses me on the forehead.

Meanwhile Asalamalakim is going through motions with Maggie's hand. Maggie's hand is as limp as a fish, and probably as cold, despite the sweat, and she keeps trying to pull it back. It looks like Asalamalakim wants to shake hands but wants to do it fancy. Or maybe he don't know how people shake hands. Anyhow, he soon gives up on Maggie.

"Well," I say. "Dee."

"No, Mama," she says. "Not 'Dee,' Wangero Leewanika Kemanjo!"

"What happened to 'Dee'?" I wanted to know.

"She's dead," Wangero said. "I couldn't bear it any longer, being named after the people who oppress me."

"You know as well as me you was named after your aunt Dicie," I said. Dicie is my sister. She named Dee. We called her "Big Dee" after Dee was born.

"But who was she named after?" asked Wangero.

"I guess after Grandma Dee," I said.

"And who was she named after?" asked Wangero.

"Her mother," I said, and saw Wangero was getting tired. "That's about as far back as I can trace it," I said. Though, in fact, I probably could have carried it back beyond the Civil War through the branches.

"Well," said Asalamalakim, "there you are."

"Uhnnnh," I heard Maggie say.

"There I was not," I said, "before 'Dicie' cropped up in our family, so why should I try to trace it that far back?"

He just stood there grinning, looking down on me like somebody inspecting a Model A car. Every once in a while he and Wangero sent eye signals over my head.

"How do you pronounce this name?" I asked.

"You don't have to call me by it if you don't want to," said Wangero.

"Why shouldn't I?" I asked. "If that's what you want us to call you, we'll call you."

"I know it might sound awkward at first," said Wangero.

"I'll get used to it," I said. "Ream it out again."

Well, soon we got the name out of the way. Asalamalakim had a name twice as long and three times as hard. After I tripped over it two or three times he told me to just call him Hakim-a-barber. I wanted to ask him was he a barber, but I didn't really think he was, so I didn't ask.

"You must belong to those beef cattle peoples down the road," I said. They said "Asalamalakim" when they met you, too, but they didn't shake hands. Always too busy: feeding the cattle, fixing the fences, putting up salt lick shelters, throwing down hay. When the white folks poisoned some of the herd the men stayed up all night with rifles in their hands. I walked a mile and a half just to see the sight.

Hakim a barber said, "I accept some of their doctrines, but farming and raising cattle is not my style." (They didn't tell me, and I didn't ask, whether Wangero (Dee) had really gone and married him.)

We sat down to eat and right away he said he didn't eat collards and pork was unclean. Wangero, though, went on through the chitlins and corn bread, the greens and everything else. She talked a blue streak over the sweet potatoes. Everything delighted her. Even the fact that we still used the benches her daddy made for the table when we couldn't afford to buy chairs.

"Oh, Mama!" she cried. Then turned to Hakim-a-barber. "I never knew how lovely these benches are. You can feel the rump prints," she said, running her hands underneath her and along the bench. Then she gave a sigh and her hand closed over Grandma Dee's butter dish. "That's it!" she said. "I knew there was something I wanted to ask you if I could have." She jumped up from the table and went over in the corner where the churn stood, the milk in it clabber by now. She looked at the churn and looked at it.

"This churn top is what I need," she said. "Didn't Uncle Buddy whittle it out of a tree you all used to have?"

"Yes," I said.

"Un huh," she said happily. "And I want the dasher, too."

"Uncle Buddy whittle that, too?" asked the barber.

50   Dee (Wangero) looked up at me.

"Aunt Dee's first husband whittled the dash," said Maggie so low you almost couldn't hear her. "His name was Henry, but they called him Stash."

"Maggie's brain is like an elephant's," Wangero said, laughing. "I can use the chute top as a centerpiece for the alcove table," she said, sliding a plate over the chute, "and I'll think of something artistic to do with the dasher."

When she finished wrapping the dasher the handle stuck out. I took it for a moment in my hands. You didn't even have to look close to see where hands pushing the dasher up and down to make butter had left a kind of sink in the wood. In fact, there were a lot of small sinks; you could see where thumbs and fingers had sunk into the wood. It was beautiful light yellow wood, from a tree that grew in the yard where Big Dee and Stash had lived.

After dinner Dee (Wangero) went to the trunk at the foot of my bed and started rifling through it. Maggie hung back in the kitchen over the dishpan. Out came Wangero with two quilts. They had been pieced by Grandma Dee and then Big Dee and me had hung them on the quilt frames on the front porch and quilted them. One was in the Lone State pattern. The other was Walk Around the Mountain. In both of them were scraps of dresses Grandma Dee had worn fifty and more years ago. Bits and pieces of Grandpa Jattell's Paisley shirts. And one teeny faded blue piece, about the size of a penny matchbox, that was from Great Grandpa Ezra's uniform that he wore in the Civil War.

55   "Mama," Wangero said sweet as a bird. "Can I have these old quilts?"

I heard something fall in the kitchen, and a minute later the kitchen door slammed.

"Why don't you take one or two of the others?" I asked. "These old things was just done by me and Big Dee from some tops your grandma pieced before she died."

"No," said Wangero. "I don't want those. They are stitched around the borders by machine."

"That'll make them last better," I said.

60   "That's not the point," said Wangero. "These are all pieces of dresses Grandma used to wear. She did all this stitching by hand. Imagine!" She held the quilts securely in her arms, stroking them.

"Some of the pieces, like those lavender ones, come from old clothes her mother handed down to her," I said, moving up to touch the quilts. Dee (Wangero) moved back just enough so that I couldn't reach the quilts. They already belonged to her.

"Imagine!" she breathed again, clutching them closely to her bosom.

"The truth is," I said, "I promised to give them quilts to Maggie, for when she marries John Thomas."

She gasped like a bee had stung her.

65   "Maggie can't appreciate these quilts!" she said. "She'd probably be backward enough to put them to everyday use."

"I reckon she would," I said. "God knows I been saving 'em for long enough with nobody using 'em. I hope she will!" I didn't want to bring up how I had offered Dee (Wangero) a quilt when she went away to college. Then she had told me they were old-fashioned, out of style.

"But they're *priceless!*" she was saying now, furiously; for she has a temper. "Maggie would put them on the bed and in five years they'd be in rags. Less than that!"

"She can always make some more," I said. "Maggie knows how to quilt."

Dee (Wangero) looked at me with hatred. "You just will not understand. The point is these quilts, these quilts!"

70 "Well," I said, stumped. "What would you do with them?"

"Hang them," she said. As if that was the only thing you could do with quilts.

Maggie by now was standing in the door. I could almost hear the sound her feet made as they scraped over each other.

"She can have them, Mama," she said, like somebody used to never winning anything, or having anything reserved for her. "I can 'member Grandma Dee without the quilts."

I looked at her hard. She had filled her bottom lip with checkerberry snuff and gave her face a kind of dopey, hangdog look. It was Grandma Dee and Big Dee who taught her how to quilt herself. She stood there with her scarred hands hidden in the folds of her skirt. She looked at her sister with something like fear but she wasn't mad at her. This was Maggie's portion. This was the way she knew God to work.

75 When I looked at her like that something hit me in the top of my head and ran down to the soles of my feet. Just like when I'm in church and the spirit of God touches me and I get happy and shout. I did some thing I never done before: hugged Maggie to me, then dragged her on into the room, snatched the quilts out of Miss Wangero's hands and dumped them into Maggie's lap. Maggie just sat there on my bed with her mouth open.

"Take one or two of the others," I said to Dee.

But she turned without a word and went out to Hakim-a-barber.

"You just don't understand," she said, as Maggie and I came out to the car.

"What don't I understand?" I wanted to know.

80 "Your heritage," she said. And then she turned to Maggie, kissed her, and said, "You ought to try to make something of yourself, too, Maggie. It's really a new day for us. But from the way you and Mama still live you'd never know it."

She put on some sunglasses that hid everything above the tip of her nose and chin.

Maggie smiled; maybe at the sunglasses. But a real smile, not scared. After we watched the car dust settle I asked Maggie to bring me a dip of snuff. And then the two of us sat there just enjoying, until it was time to go in the house and go to bed.

RESPONSE QUESTIONS

1. Describe the narrator. What do you find most significant about her age, physical condition, background, and personality?

2. Compare the two sisters physically and intellectually. How much of their divergent personalities can be attributed to these qualities or to other factors?

3. When their former house burned down, Dee and Maggie behaved in different ways. How does the mother characterize their responses to the fire and the house? What do these differences reveal about the three women as a family?

4. "Everyday Use" can be read as a story about family values. What values do you think are affirmed or questioned?

5. Explain the meaning of the story's title. Why do you think it is dedicated "to your grandmamma?"

GUIDELINES FOR ANALYSIS

1. How objectively does the mother tell her story? What judgments does she make about her children? What are her judgments based on?

2. The mother has a habit of comparing Maggie and Dee to different animals. What do these comparisons suggest about her attitudes toward each of her children?

3. The mother's narration occasionally changes tense forms, shifting back and forth among past, present, and future. It also shifts from the first person ("I"), to the second person ("you") and third person ("she," "they"). What makes these shifts appropriate in a short story like "Everyday Use" while they might be considered unacceptable in an essay?

4. Trace the central conflict in the story from its first appearance to its crisis, or high point. What opposing forces are at work? Explain why you think the conflict is finally resolved, reversed, or left unsettled.

QUESTIONS OF CULTURE

1. Compare the outlook of young African Americans in 1927, when "colored asked fewer questions," and 1973, when the story was first published. What changes are reflected in Dee's new name and her interest in artifacts like churn tops and quilts?

2. Reread the description of the quilt. Explain why it might be considered a "cultural artifact." What does such a quilt tell us about the culture that produced it?

3. Imagine a family debate about the meaning of heritage. What sides would the mother, Maggie, Dee, and Hakim be likely to take in the debate?

IDEAS FOR YOUR JOURNAL

1. Rewrite a portion of the story from Dee's or Maggie's point of view. Try to capture the new narrator's speech patterns as well as her particular attitudes and observations.

2. Apply what you have learned about families from any of the research essays in this chapter to "Everyday Use." What observations can you make about emotional intelligence, the role of birth order, or new family forms?

A STUDENT WRITER IN ACTION

Preview

Mutsumi Oishi was born in Tokyo, Japan. After completing a two-year degree at a Japanese junior college as an English major, she worked for two years to save enough funds to live and study abroad. She came to New York at twenty-two and continued studying English at CUNY/ Hunter College for a year. "However," she writes, "I soon had to find a job to support myself. Since then, I have been very lucky landing various good jobs and meeting supportive friends, including my husband in New York."

When Mutsumi decided to return to school for a degree in business and accounting, she enrolled at Westchester Community College. With a full-time job and family responsibilities, she took evening, weekend, or online classes each semester. The following essay, in which she investigates the pros and cons of raising children in two languages, follows the format of an I-Search Paper. She begins the essay by clarifying the topic and her personal connections to it, then describes her search for answers to her topic questions. Her first draft focuses on primary sources: interviews with parents and site visits to schools. In her final draft, she integrates what she learned from articles, books, and other secondary sources. The questionnaire that she prepared for the interviews appears in the appendix of her final essay. Her sources are listed on the Works Cited page, which follows the guidelines of the Modern Language Association. This process involved many successive drafts and a lot of time, but Mutsumi found it all worthwhile: "I love learning new things and I plan to continue my education throughout my life," she says.

DISCOVERING

Q: How did you come up with the idea for your essay?

A: As I watched my daughter's daily struggle learning Japanese, I always wanted to know how others handle raising their own children as bilingual or multilingual. When the assignment was posted, I tried to find a theme that I was interested in on a daily basis. I immediately thought that this was a great opportunity to interview others and research on the issue.

PLANNING

Q: Say a little about how you prepare yourself to write, where you do your writing, and how you get yourself into the right frame of mind.

A: I did brainstorming mostly while I was commuting. I also used the 30 to 45 minutes wait time during my daughter's after-school activities for listing questions for interviews, finding the right persons to interview, or freewriting. I keep my notebook everywhere I go so that I can write ideas or a few sentences before I forget them. Many bits of ideas or phrases on the notes later helped in constructing my essay.

I did most of my writing at very early mornings while my family was still at sleep. I think that four o'clock in the morning is the perfect time to organize my thoughts, write, or study. I used my notes from previous days to refresh my thoughts for various writing assignments. Of course, I was not always in the mood to write an essay, but I had to force myself to write something within the hours that I can use for my writing. It certainly was challenging.

DEVELOPING

Q: Once you settled on the main subject, how did you go about organizing your ideas and developing your first draft?

A: Writing a first paragraph is always the hardest thing for me. It took a while to complete the thesis statement for this essay, as well. Once the first paragraph was somewhat done, I moved on to the rest of the essay at a faster pace. I created an outline in the beginning, and it definitely helped to organize my thoughts. Completing the essay was a slow and complex process because each step of planning, interviewing, organizing, drafting, and revising took a long time.

Because I needed to use primary sources for my first draft, I spent lots of time preparing questionnaires. After the actual interviews were completed, I also needed to spend a great amount of time reviewing their answers. I carefully chose which interviews to focus on and which ones to use as supporting my thesis.

I do not have any particular methods for building paragraphs; however, I try to make transitions between paragraphs as smooth as possible. I often make several versions of my draft by switching the order of paragraphs to see which version will flow more naturally or logically. Computer technology and a program such as *Word* really help to do this process easily.

REVISING

Q: How much revising did you do?

A: I do many revisions on my writing, in general. I often leave my writing out for a day or two, and then come back to review with fresh eyes, if the time allows.

I did much revising on this particular essay by myself and with others' help. I visited the writing center at the campus as often as I could, and I received advice and suggestions from different tutors. Having different tutors to go over the first stage of drafts really helped me to organize my thought and focus what I should write.

PROOFREADING AND ADVICE

Q: Do you give any special attention to completeness, unity, structures, continuity, or style? How do you proofread your work for errors?

A: I tried to make my thesis as clear as possible by including information I gathered through my primary and secondary sources. Although the essay was not a long one, I wanted it to be complete. I also paid special attention to continuity, because I often found my paragraphs hopping from one topic to another without smooth transitions.

I do not have any technique for proofreading; therefore, I just read many times looking for errors. I also made many visits to the writing center to have different tutors for proofreading. I hate admitting it, but I do make errors, especially on articles, prepositions, and word order, maybe because English is not my native language.

Q: Looking back, what would you say was your most important goal in writing the essay? What were your biggest obstacles, and how did you tackle them? How do you feel now about the results?

A: I do not have much opportunity to write essays. The memos and letters I write on a daily basis are all somewhat short. Therefore, writing this essay using primary and secondary sources was a challenging assignment. Once I choose my thesis, I actually enjoyed preparing questionnaires and conducting interviews. I just wanted to write a good completed essay.

My biggest obstacle was how to select a handful of data from the mountains of information I collected. All the information and interviews from different resources were interesting and important. However, not all could fit into my essay. The process of selecting information was time consuming and difficult. I learned a lot by going over the information one by one.

Q: Finally, did you learn anything about yourself while writing the essay? What advice would you give to other student writers?

I am probably a slow writer. I like writing, but the writing process takes up so much time. I do not mind writing about something that I am interested in. I just have to spend more time and plan ahead making sure I can finish assignments before due dates. When I complete a paragraph or essay, I can get great satisfaction.

I believe that finding something that you are truly interested in is a key for writing. I would suggest relating an assigned topic to anything that you really like or dislike, and then you should be able to find something to write about.

1. Native speakers of English use "for" or "of" instead of "on" in this expression.
2. This is an example of an "inverted pyramid" paragraph. You begin with a broad generalization and gradually narrow the idea to your specific topic sentence. It is a useful strategy, although it can sometimes slow down the momentum if you take too long to get to the main idea.
3. Can you relate this statement more clearly to the previous sentence?
4. Wrong verb form. Either delete the -ing ending, or delete the word "to."
5. This is where the essay really gets interesting for me, when something important and personal is at stake.

BENEFITS OF RAISING MULTILINGUAL CHILDREN

By Mutsumi Oishi

First Draft (with Instructor's Comments)

In this global society, we often hold high expectations on[1] children with multilingual and multicultural backgrounds as future international leaders in every field. We experience rapid technological improvements on a daily basis, and easy communication with people from around the world seems to make our world appear smaller and smaller. English has become the universal language over the last few decades. However, understanding native language is still a key to understanding its cultural background from the particular country or area of the world. We can understand culture, history, race, religion, heritage and behavior of people through learning their language. When children explore more than one cultural background at an early age, I believe they tend to accept more aspects of the differences. Therefore, I support the idea of raising children to speak more than one language, as it can be extremely beneficial to their lives.[2]

Although children are believed to have a tendency toward learning languages quicker and easier than adults, learning two or more languages and understanding multiple cultures, at the same time, are very challenging tasks. Through my experience of raising my daughter as bilingual in English and Japanese, I have experienced my own struggle and frustration over this challenge. I, also, learned English as my second language after I established my primary language, Japanese.[3] Therefore, I will focus specifically the two languages of English and Japanese, at this time.

My daughter and I have a battle to finishing[4] homework every Friday night for the weekend Japanese school, which she attends on Saturdays. My husband and I decided to enroll our daughter in the weekend Japanese school five and a half years ago, so that she could learn and experience its language and culture. The decision seemed perfect. We thought that as long as she attended the school, she would master the language with no difficulties. However, we were proven wrong.[5] Learning two different languages at the same time is more than tough or difficult; it is almost impossible unless both the parents and the child totally commit to learning and mastering the language. We are still learning and struggling to balance our expectations.

I have known many families in a similar situation, through the school and community, trying to offer both the languages and the cultures of English and Japanese, here in Westchester County, New York. I met Takako Sato, as my daughter's abacus teacher six years ago. Abacus is a traditional Japanese instrument for performing calculations by sliding counters along bamboo rods. Her abacus lesson also offers mental calculations by imaging an abacus on the right hand side of brain. Takako has been teaching abacus to children over 30 years in New York, married a Japanese electrician and has four sons from age 14 to 33. She expressed that although she and her husband try to offer the same to all four sons, each son has learned Japanese in a different way and the fluency level varies, as well. Her oldest son now works very closely with Japanese clients; therefore, his conversation in Japanese has improved, finally, to the business level. Takako claims that all four sons' primary language is English because she and her husband always wanted them to achieve academic success, just as one of the students in the local school. While they sent all four sons to the weekend Japanese school, they didn't force their sons to master both languages to the same level. The parents' intention was just to teach basic Japanese language and culture while they were young, and then they could study further if they wanted later on. Their simple approach worked for the two older sons, and as a result, they both took advanced level Japanese language courses at Columbia University.

As a part of introducing Japanese culture, Takako has taught abacus to all four sons. Her sons made many Japanese friends and have experienced cultural events throughout the school curriculums and other related activities. Takako believes that all those experiences enriched her sons' lives and gave broad views of society, in general. At the end of interview,[6] I felt good about raising bilingual children.

My neighbor introduced Mr. & Mrs. Terada to me a few years ago at her dinner party. Annie Terada, the third generation of Japanese-Americans, speaks fluent English with no accent. Soon after the dinner, I found out that they brought up their daughter with a single language, English. I remember that I was curious to know more about their decision choosing English over Japanese; however, I didn't feel comfortable enough asking personal questions at that time. My neighbor later mentioned to me that their daughter graduated from Harvard University with a music degree,[7] and she now plays a violin professionally in Los[8] Angeles philharmonic orchestra.

Since all my other primary resources support the idea of raising bilingual children, I felt that it is[9] necessary to interview Annie's point of view. Over the phone, Annie explained to me that she and her husband's decision. They felt that the difference of two languages, English and Japanese, is so great that it would be unbearable for them to teach and for their daughter to learn. Annie, a professor, teaches Japanese language courses at an American college, and had a concrete opinion about teaching two extremely different languages. She knew that the family would stay in the United States; therefore she wanted her daughter to excel academically in English. She also knew that in some cases, a bilingual child more often develops his language skills at a much slower pace than a single language child. A reason for the delay of learning process is believed to be caused by learning two different languages simultaneously.

6. Missing article

7. This information certainly underscores the case for learning one language at a time. Good example.

8. Missing article

9. Use the past tense of this verb to be consistent with the verb "felt."

10. It is better to use the definite article "the" here, since you are speaking about two specific languages. The indefinite article ("a") is used for general instances.

11. Use the -ing form of this verb here.

12. Comma splice error. Use a semicolon to join two independent clauses.

13. Missing article

14. Missing article

15. Missing article

16. After all you have written, I'm surprised that you conclude with this belief. Do you have stronger, more specific reasons for multilingual education than general idea of being "beneficial"?

Annie also states that a[10] logic pattern of two languages is far distant from one other. She then, gave me an interesting example of sentence structure in two languages. "I am not going out because it's raining outside," must be translated in Japanese as, "Rain is falling, and therefore I am not going out." Annie supports to teach[11] a child a single language, in order for him to have critical thinking skills while he is young. Nevertheless, she agrees that being bilingual or bicultural certainly can be beneficial later on. Annie had her education through colleges in the United States, and then she obtained a master degree in Japanese language from a university in Japan. She hated to attend the weekend Japanese school,[12] however, she admits that she still remembers a few things, "The things you learned at an early age won't be erased, and they stick to your head."

One of definitions[13] of "bilingual" from Merriam-Webster[14] Dictionary is, "using or able to use two languages especially with equal fluency." Four out of five interviewees I communicated support the idea of raising children to speak more than one language at home. However, all four admit that the two languages their children use are not equally taught and learned. The children's primary language is English and they work hard and struggle learning their second language, Japanese. Three interviewees, with their children aged from 4 to 13, answered my question of daily usage on two languages as 90% English vs. 10% Japanese or 80% English vs. 20% Japanese. Although parents are not nearly satisfied with the current result of children's progress on learning two languages, they believe in a long term benefit rather than an immediate result.

One interviewee stressed one of benefits of being bilingual[15] person: "Understanding parents' native language is crucial path to know parents' cultural backgrounds. Unless you learn the language, it's hard to understand culture, history, and tradition." I learned both the hardship and advantage of mastering two languages from the interviews. They all have different problems and struggles on a daily basis. However, I realize that they are all seeking a long term benefit for their children. I still believe in the idea of raising children[16] to speak more than one language, which can be beneficial to their lives.

Final Draft

In this global society, we often have high expectations for children with multilingual and multicultural backgrounds as future international leaders in every field. We experience rapid technological improvements on a daily basis, and easy communication with people from around the world seems to make our world appear smaller and smaller. English has become the universal language over the last few decades. However, understanding a native language is still a key to understanding the cultural background from a particular country or area of the world. We can understand culture, history, race, religion, heritage, and behavior of people through learning their language. When children explore more than one cultural background at an early age, I believe they tend to accept more aspects of the differences. Therefore, I support the idea of raising children to speak more than one language, as it can be extremely beneficial to their lives.

Although children are believed to have a tendency toward learning languages more quickly and easily than adults, learning two or more languages and understanding multiple cultures at the same time are very challenging tasks. Through the experience of raising my daughter as bilingual in English and Japanese, I have experienced my own struggle and frustration over this challenge. I learned English as my second language only after I established my primary language of Japanese. Therefore, I was interested to know whether it is better to learn two languages at the same time or one after the other.

My daughter and I have a battle finishing homework every Friday night for the weekend Japanese school, which she attends on Saturdays. My husband and I decided to enroll our daughter in the weekend Japanese school five and a half years ago, so that she could learn and experience its language and culture. The decision seemed perfect. We thought that as long as she attended the school, she would master the language with no difficulties. However, we were proven wrong. Learning two different languages at the same time is more than difficult; it is almost impossible unless both the parents and the child totally commit to learning and mastering the language. We are still learning and struggling to balance our expectations.

I have known many families in similar situations through the school and community. They struggle with trying to offer both the languages and the cultures of English and Japanese here in Westchester County, New York. I met Takako Sato, my daughter's abacus teacher, six years ago. Abacus is a traditional Japanese instrument for performing calculations by sliding counters along bamboo rods. Her abacus lesson also offers mental calculations by imaging an abacus on the right side of brain. Takako has been teaching abacus to children for over thirty years in New York, is married a Japanese electrician, and has four sons from ages fourteen to thirty-three. She said that although she and her husband tried to offer the same to all four sons, each son has learned Japanese in a different way, and the fluency level varies, as well. Her oldest son now works very closely with Japanese clients; therefore, his conversation in Japanese has improved to the business level. Takako claims that all four sons' primary language is English because she and her husband always wanted them to achieve academic success, as students in the local school. While they sent all four sons to the weekend Japanese school, they didn't force them to master both languages at the same level. The parents' intention was to teach basic Japanese language and culture while they were young so that later on they could study further if they wanted to. Their simple approach worked for the two older sons, and as a result, they both took advanced-level Japanese language courses at universities.

As a part of introducing Japanese culture, Takako has taught abacus to their four sons. They made many Japanese friends and participated in cultural events throughout the school, in addition to other related activities. Takako believes that all those experiences enriched her sons' lives and gave broad views of society, in general. After the one-and-a-half-hour interview, I felt somewhat relieved by her relaxed attitude toward raising her sons in the bilingual environment. In addition, I was convinced that I made the right decision teaching the two languages because all her sons turned out to be well-rounded persons.

My research confirmed many positive correlations between learning a language and living within its cultural environment. A Japanese biweekly news publication, *U.S. Front Line,* had a special feature on "Thinking about languages for your children—Monolingual, Bilingual, or Multilingual." It listed ten key factors to help children learn the two languages, and one of the main factors is to place the children in an environment directly reflecting its culture. It concluded that using games, songs, or plays, and having friends in the same environment certainly helps young children to learn the languages in a very effective way. It also urged parents to be tolerant of mistakes that children make through the learning process (Suyama 15). After all, no one learns a language within a short period of time. It takes years to teach and learn a language.

My neighbor introduced Mr. and Mrs. Terada to me a few years ago at a dinner party. Annie Terada, a third-generation Japanese American, speaks fluent English with no accent. Soon after the dinner, I discovered that they brought up their daughter with a single language: English. I remember that I was curious to know more about their decision choosing English over Japanese; however, I didn't feel comfortable asking personal questions at that time. My neighbor later mentioned to me that her daughter graduated from Harvard University with a degree in English Literature, and she now plays the violin professionally in the Los Angeles Philharmonic.

Since all my other primary resources support the idea of raising bilingual children, I felt that it was necessary to interview Annie about her point of view. Over the phone, Annie explained her position. She and her husband felt that the differences between the two languages, English and Japanese, are so great that it would not be a wise idea for them to teach and for their daughter to learn Japanese. Annie, an instructor, teaches Japanese-language courses at colleges and had a concrete opinion about teaching two extremely different languages. She knew that the family would stay in the United States; therefore, she wanted Annie to excel academically in English. She also knew that in some cases, a bilingual child more often develops his language skills at a much slower pace than a single-language child. One reason for the delay in the learning process is believed to be the confusion of learning two different languages simultaneously.

Annie also stated that the logic patterns of the two languages are distant from one other. She then gave me an interesting example of sentence structure in two languages. "I am not going out because it's raining outside" must be translated in Japanese as "Rain is falling, and therefore I am not going out." Annie supports teaching a child a single language in order for him to establish critical thinking skills while he is young.

The example Annie mentioned disturbed me; however, I had to admit that she was right. English is a direct language. When someone asks you an opinion, you need to indicate your point in the beginning of the reply, so that he understands where you are heading. You can add details later on as the conversation moves on. Nancy Sakamoto, an English teacher in Japan, points this out: "The Japanese way is to approach the central point gradually, by beginning at a distant point, and then filling in the picture by adding details. [. . .] After the whole picture has been filled in, the central point is finally reached" (Sakamoto 75). Afterward, Annie's decision to educate her daughter only in English seemed a rational explanation.

Nevertheless, Annie agrees that being bilingual or bicultural certainly can be beneficial later on. She had her education through colleges in the United States, and then she obtained a master's degree in Japanese language from a university in Japan. She was forced to attend the weekend Japanese school for a short period of time while she was seven or eight years old and absolutely hated it; however, she admits that she still remembers a few things: "The things you learned at an early age won't be erased, and they stick to your head."

One of the definitions of "bilingual" from the Merriam-Webster Dictionary is "using or able to use two languages especially with equal fluency." Four out of the five people I communicated with supported the idea of raising children to speak more than one language at home. However, all four acknowledged that the two languages their children use are not equally taught and learned. The children's primary language is English, and they work hard and struggle with learning their second language, Japanese. Three people, with children ranging from four to thirteen in age, answered my questions about their daily usage of the two languages. The ratio of English to Japanese spoken in their homes ranges from 9:1 to 8:1. Although these parents are not nearly satisfied with the current result of their children's progress learning two languages, they believe in a long-term benefit rather than an immediate result.

Daniel Chapman and my husband, Etsuji, have been practicing and teaching Kendo, the Japanese martial art of fencing with bamboo swords, to adults and children for over a decade in Westchester County. Dan first learned about Kendo while he was teaching English in Osaka, Japan, and continued to learn this extremely traditional and disciplined sport. He met his wife, Hitomi in Japan, and they have two daughters, thirteen and ten years old. They have been living in Westchester County for the last ten years. At home, Dan speaks in English and Hitomi speaks in Japanese. Their daughters use two languages simultaneously communicating with their parents. The girls seem to be confident and well balanced in dealing with two languages and cultures. I often find their names listed as winners of Japanese composition contests in the newsletter issued by the Japanese weekend school. I asked Hitomi if there are any secrets of success in educating two daughters in the bilingual environment. She replied to me, "I really can't pinpoint it because each child learns languages differently."

Hitomi Chapman is always very involved with her daughters' education in Japanese; however, I had no idea that she had actually obtained a master's degree in psycholinguistics. She explained to me that although she acquired her knowledge of psycholinguistics, she uses a rather simple and straightforward approach in teaching Japanese to her two daughters. She has read books in Japanese every single day to her daughters, ever since they were born. She chooses books to read very carefully from different fields and interests. One thing I found particularly interesting was that neither Hitomi nor Dan used any baby talk. They always speak with their daughters the same way they speak with other adults: at normal speed. According to Hitomi, the period of time a child uses simple language is very short; therefore, she and her husband skipped that period in Japanese and English altogether. The parents tried to keep the initial learning process as simple as possible and introduced two languages in a natural way. They truly understand the challenge and hardship of learning the two languages, as both Hitomi and Dan mastered English and Japanese respectively after their primary languages were already established. Hitomi stressed one of the benefits of learning the two languages: "Understanding parents' native language is a crucial path to know parents' cultural backgrounds. Unless you learn the language, it's hard to understand culture, history, and tradition."

I learned both the hardships and advantages of mastering two languages from these interviews and research. The people I interviewed all have different problems and struggles on a daily basis. However, I realize that they are seeking long-term benefits for their children. None of them cited an economic benefit or a practical benefit as a primary goal for teaching the two languages. Rather, they stressed the importance of learning a different point of view for daily living. I feel that the introduction of two different languages and cultures is only a beginning to learning about various cultures and people around the world. Consequently, I believe in the idea of raising children to speak more than one language, which can be beneficial to their development as well-rounded individuals and successful members of society.

Works Cited

Boschen, Chika. "Re: Bilingual Education." E-mail to the author. 5 Nov. 2003

Chapman, Hitomi. Telephone interview. 5 Nov. 2003

Mellor, Haruko. "Re: Bilingual Education." E-mail to the author. 6 Nov. 2003

Sakamoto, Nancy, and Reiko Naotsuka. *Polite Fictions: Why Japanese and Americans Seem Rude to Each Other.* Tokyo: Kinseido, 1982.

Sato, Takako. Personal interview. 3 Nov. 2003.

Suyama, Mikiko. "Thinking about Languages for Your Children." *U.S. Front Line* 5 Oct. 2003: 9+.

Terada, Annie. Telephone interview. 5 Nov. 2003.

Appendix: Interview Questions

Interviewee's information

Name _____ Age _____

Occupation _____

Place of Birth _____

Nationality _____

Your languages (Indicate bilingual or primary and secondary if applicable)

_____

Spouse of interviewee's information

Name _____ Age _____

Occupation _____

Place of Birth _____

Nationality _____

Your languages (Indicate bilingual or primary and secondary if applicable)

_____

Children of interviewee's information

Age _____   Gender   M   or   F

Place of Birth _____

Grade/Graduated:

_____

Age _____   Gender   M   or   F

Place of Birth _____

Grade/Graduated:

_____

1. Do (Did) you raise your children as bilingual?

Yes => Indicate two languages:

_____ and _____

Do you think that your children use two languages on a daily basis in the ratio of

50/50 (50% _____ 50% _____)

60/40 (60% _____ 40% _____)

70/30 (70% _____ 30% _____)

80/20 (80% _____ 20% _____)

90/10 (90% _____ 10% _____)

No => What language did you choose to raise your children? _____

What language did you decide not to teach your children? _____

Please list the reasons for your choice.

_____

_____

2. Who made the decision on educating your children as bilingual or non-bilingual?

☐ Yourself   ☐ Your spouse   ☐ Both of you

3. Who is (was) leading the education of your children as bilingual?

☐ Yourself   ☐ Your spouse   ☐ Both of you

4. Why did you choose to raise your children as bilingual?

To share two different languages, cultures, and heritages from parents?

To teach two languages as a skill for your children?

To provide more opportunities and possibilities for your children's future?

To have your children be prepared for a global environment?

Others => please give detailed reasons

5. What are the benefits of being a bilingual person?

Cultural Enrichments

Tradition/Heritage

Practical

Economic

Global/International

Others

Can you please explain how your children learn two languages?

7. Do (Did) they also have any trouble learning two languages?

If so, please provide a few examples of troubles and difficult situations.

8. What are your children's attitudes toward learning two languages?

9. Have your children ever resented learning two languages? If so, please explain.

10. Do (Did) you have any trouble teaching two languages at the same time?

If so, please provide a few examples of troubles and difficult situations.

11. What are (were) your expectations of your children's language skills? (fluency, etc.)

12. Do you think that your children have succeeded in mastering two languages, as per your expectations?

☐ Yes => Please provide a few examples of key factors for the success.

☐ No => Please try to explain your reasons. Were your expectations too high?

13. Do you recommend raising a child as a bilingual individual when he/she has the opportunity?

☐ Yes => Please support your recommendation.

☐ No => Please support your opinion.

14. Other comments

Thank you for your time.

CONSIDERATIONS FOR YOUR OWN WRITING

1. What did you learn about bilingual education from this student essay? After reading it, what more would you like to know?

2. Where in the essay were you most engaged? How did the writer try to keep your attention? Given your own experience (or inexperience) with bilingual education, what connections did you make to the topic while reading the essay?

3. When describing her composing process, Mutsumi stresses her efforts to make smooth transitions and write "a complete essay." What evidence can you find that she succeeded? What else could she have done to achieve continuity and completeness?

4. Mustumi begins her essay with a general paragraph on the importance of bilingual education, then moves to a more specific statement of her topic on learning English and Japanese simultaneously. What is gained by including the first paragraph? What might have been gained if she had started the essay with her second paragraph?

5. The writer decided to follow the format of an I-Search essay, describing her personal investigation of the topic step by step. A more traditional research paper would have been more objective, leaving out the subjective "I" and organizing information more logically than chronologically. What are the advantages and disadvantages of these two formats?

6. Notice how the writer combines primary and secondary sources. How much does she tell you about the people she interviewed? What does she learn from each of them? What kinds of information does she get from printed sources?

7. Look through the questionnaire in the Appendix. What kinds of questions did Mutsumi prepare for her interviews ahead of time? Which questions seem most useful in her final draft?

8. Mutsumi uses several different media for her research, including a book, a journal, the computer, the telephone, and face-to-face communication. What other media might she have used? Which medium seems most useful in her research?

9. Notice how the writer follows the MLA guidelines. Does her text include parenthetical citations for both primary and secondary sources? What information for these sources is included on the Works Cited page?

Evaluation Checklist

Use the following checklist to evaluate your investigative essay.

Topic. Is the topic clear? Does the essay offer a particular thesis, slant, or interesting perspective on the topic? Is the topic too broad or narrow to be covered in an essay of this length?

Content. What kind of information does the essay offer to answer the central topic question? Is the information from reliable sources? Have you made good use of primary and secondary sources? Are the results from interviews or surveys integrated smoothly into the essay? Is there a balance of information to support each section of the essay? Have you used too many or too few sources?

Audience. Have you assumed too little or too much knowledge on the part of your reader? Are specialized terms defined? Have you addressed common perceptions about the topic? Is the essay written in language that the reader can readily understand?

Structure. Is there a clear beginning, middle, and end? Does your opening offer an engaging introduction to the topic? Does the conclusion tie together the threads of the investigation in a memorable way? Are the parts of the essay sensibly arranged? An outline of the essay's organization may help to see this organization more clearly. It may also help to highlight transitions. Are smooth connections made from one part to the next?

Style. Are your language and tone appropriate for an essay of this kind? Do you guide your reader through an informed investigation of your topic as opposed to dominating the material or being overwhelmed by it?

Format. Have you followed the format of an I-Search Paper or a traditional academic research paper? What does the final essay look like? Does it have a proper heading, title, and Works Cited page? Are all sources properly documented, including those that are summarized and paraphrased as well as quoted? Are sources identified with tag lines and parenthetical citations? Are quotation marks used for short, direct quotes but omitted from long, indented quotations?

Research on the Web

The Internet is full of helpful Web sites on conducting research. Teachers, consultants, and professional writers offer the benefit of their experience free of charge. Here are a few links to get you started.

A Student's Guide to Research with the WWW
http://www.slu.edu/departments/english/research/
This tutorial guide was created for first-year composition students at St. Louis University. It offers abundant help with finding, navigating, and evaluating Web sources.

Style Sheets for Citing Internet Sources
http://www.lib.berkeley.edu/TeachingLib/Guides/Internet/Style.html
The University of California at Berkeley shows how to document sources using MLA, APA, Chicago, and other academic formats.

Library Research Skills
http://www.umuc.edu/library/tutor/intro.html
This site from the University of Maryland features a tutorial on more traditional library research—finding books, articles, and reference works—as well as research on the Web.

Seven Steps of the Research Process
http://www.library.cornell.edu/okuref/research/skill1.htm
Cornell University Library outlines a simple, effective strategy for preparing a research paper step by step.

Avoiding Plagiarism
http://owl.english.purdue.edu/handouts/research/r_plagiar.html
Purdue's Online Writing Lab (OWL) makes some clear distinctions to help students avoid the pitfalls of plagiarism.

Investigative Reporters and Editors
http://www.reporter.org/
Catch a glimpse of what professional investigative reporters do by logging on to this organization's Web site.

Harvard Family Research Project
http://www.gse.harvard.edu/~hfrp/
Find out how a major university approaches research on child development, family functioning, and communities.

Taking Stock

- Compare your approach to research before and after reading this chapter. What have you learned about organizing an investigation, finding good sources, and documenting your findings in a well-focused report?

- Retrace the steps you took while completing the assignment for this chapter. What were the biggest challenges? What tools and strategies helped the most? What new methods are you likely to use in future research?

- Review the readings and screenings that you analyzed. What do you consider to be the most interesting and important information that you learned about the changing family? What would you like to know more about?

- What evidence of research have you begun to notice in the media messages around you, including television, movies, magazines, newspapers, and the Internet? What standards have you formed for evaluating the quality of such research?

- Where in your life—at home, in school, in your communities, at work—can you foresee needs and opportunities for further documented investigations?

CHAPTER 7

Reaction Shots: Evaluating Our Consuming Choices

America has been called a consumer culture. We are constantly bombarded by messages encouraging us to consume. Eat this food, take these pills, get that CD, buy that car. Economists study our patterns of consumption. Sociologists note how much of our social interaction revolves around consumer choices, and psychologists affirm the truism that we are what we consume. But do we know why we choose some products and not others? Even if we have good reasons for our choices, are they really what motivate us when we order that super-size cheeseburger or gravitate toward the SUV in the auto dealer's showroom?

Of course, many of our daily judgments are not about purchases or products. We are continually sizing up people, criticizing places, and evaluating events. Often we are asked to explain our assessments—in writing and through other media. In this chapter, you'll be exploring why you make the judgments that you make. You'll become more aware of your evaluation process so you can avoid mindless choices and make powerful, informed decisions. You'll also learn ways to support your judgments with evaluative criteria, appropriate evidence, and robust reasoning—methods that will make these judgments sounder in themselves and more persuasive to others.

Making judgments is not something that we deliberately learn. It's automatic behavior. We walk through our lives saying "yes . . . no . . . no . . . maybe . . . definitely not" to nearly everyone and everything we meet. The assessments never stop. Most of the time, we don't think about the reasons for our judgments. We go on dispensing them as mindlessly as vending machines: nice car, weird haircut, great song, miserable day.

Even if someone asks us why we liked the movie or don't care for that new kid on the block, our reasons are not always within easy reach. Sometimes we have to dig deep to unearth the thinking behind our first impressions. Sometimes the reasons we come up with seem more like rationales—reasonable explanations manufactured to justify our first impressions—than the authentic chain of events that actually led to our reaction. Often enough, our reasons don't seem to matter. The world is full of people looking for the bottom line. Will we buy it? Does the movie rate a thumb up or a thumb down? Are we voting for or against?

Yet when our judgments continue unexamined, we fail to see the flaws or limitations in our thinking. There is a moment in the movie *Primary Colors* that illustrates how people make decisions by reflex rather than by reflection. A campaign worker has been unsuccessful handing out free leaflets to voters on the street. He follows pedestrians doggedly, but nobody wants to take what he is offering. Then he makes up a sign: "Take One, Get One Free!" In no time, the leaflets are all gone. What the pedestrians have responded to is the form, not the content of the sign. The words sound like a bargain, although a more thoughtful reading would reveal the fracture in their logic.

Making automatic, unexamined judgments can have more serious consequences. Harvard psychologist Ellen Langer gives numerous examples in her book on *Mindfulness*. She describes a boy who jumped into an empty pool, an airplane that crashed after its crew unthinkingly checked the anti-ice controls on their take-off roster, and her own grandmother, who died of a brain tumor after being incorrectly diagnosed with Alzheimer's disease—all victims of what Dr. Langer calls *premature cognitive commitments:* actions that follow routine expectations without time for evaluating them. While these cases are extreme, Langer points out that ordinary mindlessness can have a cumulative damaging effect on everyday life. When we make judgments based on a confining mind-set rather than on facts, we superimpose our biases on the world, we force people into molds, and we forfeit our own freedom. We deny to others and to ourselves the futures that are hidden from view by our past. Awareness is the key to mindfulness. We can't take charge of something if we're not aware of it. By revealing the mechanism that runs our responses, critical awareness gives us access to the controls.

SCENARIOS FROM LIFE

Consider how the following occasions call for mindful judgments.

- After only one week of classes, a student in your general psych class asks you out. The student seems to be just your type, so you agree. Within days you're congratulating yourself on your good luck. But after a few dates, your dream starts to look like a nightmare. You begin to notice unappealing habits and personal traits that you missed before. You wonder how your first impressions could have been so wrong.

- A new art show opens on campus, and your art instructor assigns you to review it. How will you assess the works of art on exhibit? How will you apply what you have learned about art to the new show? What format will you follow for your review?

- You've been promoted to a supervisory position at your new job. Among your new responsibilities is the task of evaluating employees. What criteria will you use to make your judgments? What standards should be met? How will you organize your evaluative report?

- Where would you like to live right after college graduation? Would kind of residence and neighborhood would you prefer? Compare your current standards and ideals to those you are likely to have when you hold a full-time job. How might they change if you get married and have children? How would you specify what you are looking for to a real estate agent at each stage of your life?

WHY WRITE TO EVALUATE?

Evaluative writing is a way of making judgments mindful. When you write an evaluation of something for somebody, you do more than give it a simple thumbs up or down. You clarify the thinking that led to your assessment. You might examine your assumptions and preconceptions. You might describe the categories or criteria by which you judged your subject and show how the subject measures up to your standards for each criterion. You might explain why you chose these categories and standards. You might offer evidence to support your choices. In other words, the process of showing someone else in writing how you arrived at your assessment makes you more conscious of your own values and evaluative thinking. You become aware of alternatives, and this awareness can liberate you from the unconscious drives that run your daily life.

Written evaluations take many forms. At work, you may be asked to evaluate a new plan or another employee. At school, you may have a chance to evaluate your courses and instructors. If you are in the market for a new computer or a car, you will probably be interested in consumer reports that evaluate those products. If you are interested in movies, books, or music, you check out the reviews. Each of these forms of evaluation requires more than a simple yes or no judgment.

True, your final purpose in reading a review is to decide whether or not to buy the CD or see the movie, but you also want the reviewer's reasons. You want to know what the movie is like, whether it offers action or romance, whether the actors give a good performance, and so on. You want to know whether the reviewer values what you look for in a film and whether this film has those qualities. For an employee evaluation, where the stakes are higher, your requirements are likely to be more precise. The criteria for judgment may be explicitly spelled out: professional qualifications, personal qualities, interaction with others, productivity. Within each criterion, a rating scale may be specified. For example, professional qualifications may be measured in years of experience and educational degrees. Productivity may be assessed in terms of publications (for a professor), units sold (for a salesperson), or annual profit (for an investor). The evaluation may include common standards to ensure that judgments are applied evenly from employee to employee, especially when the judgments have important consequences. The salesperson gets a bonus when she sells X units; the lawyer becomes a partner after Y years of producing Z-dollar profits. Consequential decisions call for responsible judgments that can be supported and explained.

The readings, videos, and writing options for this unit are intended to help you understand the nature of evaluation. As you observe how judgments are made and justified in the media, as you watch yourself forming judgments in your daily life, pay close attention to the roles played by misconceptions, questionable logic, unsupported claims, and irrelevant evidence. Notice when the judges simply make assertions and when they support their claims with evidence and reasoning. Notice when they clarify their values explicitly and when the beliefs that underlie their reasoning are hidden or implied. Ask yourself whom you believe. What makes them credible? How do they establish their authority?

Critical thinking is a state of mind. More accurately, it is a state of mindfulness, the mind watching itself. It takes a lot of conscious effort to to do this, but the result is that you go through life awake, without missing things big or small. (By the way, if you noticed the double *to*'s in the last sentence, you are already more mindful than most readers.)

WRITING OPTIONS

Option 1: The Critical Review

A critical review evaluates something in terms that can be recognized as objective. That is, it reviews the merits and shortcomings of its subject by offering evidence and reasons beyond your automatic, personal reaction. Your goal is to clarify the thoughts behind your judgments so that readers will understand how you arrived at your final evaluation—and perhaps even agree with you.

For your topic, you might choose an intangible subject—like a new movie, rock concert, or restaurant—or a consumer product, like the latest model of a sports car. Use the critical tools of analysis, comparison, and definition. Identify your evaluative criteria—the traits you look for when you judge restaurants or cars—and decide how well your subject measures up to those criteria. Compare your subject to others of its kind: to other romantic comedies, similar restaurants, or competing brands. Define any terms that readers might be familiar with.

When you write your review, keep in mind your purpose and your audience. What do your readers already know about such things? What will help them to understand how you arrived at your conclusions? How will you establish your credibility? What style is likely to keep them engaged while allowing you to speak in a comfortable voice?

Option 2: Snap Judgments

Can you remember a time when you misjudged a person, product, or idea? Your first impressions may have seemed factual and definitive, but later on you realized that your judgment was premature. As time went on, you learned more, saw things from a new perspective, or changed your standards. Maybe you were able to correct the damage. Maybe it was too late. This option will give you a chance to reflect on a personal example of snap judgments and to acknowledge what you learned from the experience.

This writing option is a lot like "Writing to Remember" in Chapter 3, but your focus here will be on uncovering the chronology of mindfulness. Pay close attention to the roles played by evidence, justification, rationales, and reasoning. Notice how you were misled or entrapped by circumstances, unquestioned assumptions, rigid categories, unexamined standards, and the momentum of routine. Notice what freed you. Notice what was gained and what was lost.

MEDIA OPTION: REVIEWER'S WEB SITE

The Internet is full of judgments and evaluations. Professionals and amateurs use it every day to post their opinions on every conceivable subject. It's a particularly good place to find reviews of movies, music, books, and thousands of consumer products. This option is an opportunity to put your own reviews on the Web. By designing a Reviewer's Web site, you can make your evaluative writing available to thousands, even millions of potential readers.

For your topic, choose an area in which you have a special interest. Maybe your Web site will specialize in reviews about hip-hop or cult movies or campus cultural events. You get to write the reviews and present them to an audience of Internet users who share your interest. Your project may continue well after your composition course is over.

Since creating a Web site requires special equipment and technical knowledge, this option is intended for students who already have experience with Web design. If you have that experience, you know how important it is to follow the principles of good composition described in Chapter 2. You need to think about your topic, audience, and purpose. You also need to think in terms of clarity, unity, completeness, continuity, structure, and style, although some of these principles are handled somewhat differently on the Web. Clarity is often a matter of careful page layout and succinct text. Unity often means following consistent conventions of placement, font selection, color, links, and graphics. The structure of a Web site is the arrangement of its component Web pages. Continuity is achieved through an orderly system of links, allowing readers to navigate smoothly from page to page. For more on reading and writing Web sites, see Chapter 1 and Chapter 2.

ACCESS. In addition to Internet access, you'll need space for your Web site on the World Wide Web. You'll need permission to upload your files to a server, a computer that is always running on the Web, which may be provided by your school or a commercial Internet Provider like AOL.

SOFTWARE. All Web pages use the HTML (Hypertext Markup Language) protocol, which provides consistency among users and enables them to jump from page to page by means of hypertext links. An easy way to create an HTML file is to write a document using Microsoft Word and save it as a Web page. More sophisticated pages and entire Web sites can be created with authoring tools like FrontPage and Dreamweaver.

STYLE. Writing for the Web is different from writing for print. Since users scan pages quickly, you should express your ideas simply and concisely. Web writers typically use short sentences and bullets or numbered lists. They highlight key terms and concepts, limiting one idea to a single screen. Your content pages—the actual reviews—are likely to be longer, but most readers will expect a clear statement of your main points before they have to scroll for more. Don't overload the screen with lots of multimedia gimmicks: dazzling images, animation, and sound effects that seem nifty to you but may overwhelm most users.

LAYOUT. Think in terms of screens. Place important information at the top. Use color and graphics consistently and sparingly (some users may be color-blind or visually impaired). Web designers provide headings and subheadings as guides. They often divide the screen into separate frames, with navigation aids (links) arranged under the heading or along the side and site information at the bottom. The content area is the largest frame and usually includes a scroll bar. It's often wise to sketch out each page before creating it on the computer.

WEB SITE STRUCTURE. Plan the relationship of your pages with a site map. Web designers often use a hierarchical organization; pages with more general information are arranged above pages with specific information. Transitions between pages are provided in the form of hyperlinks.

CREATE AN ALPHA VERSION. Most authoring systems allow you to test your Web site before launching it on the Web. This in-house version is called the *alpha phase,* the equivalent

of a rough draft. Save each Web page as a separate HTML file. Follow your structural plan to link the pages on your site.

REVISE. Let your friends perform a trial run of your Web site. Watch what they do as they navigate through your Web pages, and let them tell you what they're thinking as they read. You'll learn a lot about effective Web design and clear communication by observing how different users interact with your Web site.

www.mhhe.com/costanzo

Visit the Web site for a tutorial on designing a Web page.

STUDY MODELS. Check out some of the more popular review Web sites like rottentomatoes.com (for film reviews), music-critic.com, or cnet.com (for technology products). This is a good way to pick up tips about Web design while reading about your favorite topics.

TIPS ON EVALUATIVE WRITING

DISCOVERING

If you're writing a critical review, your topic might be a work of art, like a movie or a photograph. It might be a product, like the latest fashion in jeans or some new electronic device. It might be a performance, like a concert or a sports event. Choose something in which you are genuinely interested and that you feel reasonably qualified to judge.

If you decide to write about a snap judgment, search your memory for moments when you acted mindlessly. When did you jump to conclusions that you later regretted? When did you accept an idea before considering it carefully—with unexpected consequences? Reading Ellen Langer's essay, "When the Light's On and Nobody's Home," may help to prime your memory.

PLANNING

For Option 1, make arrangements to spend time with your topic. Much of your success as a reviewer will depend on careful observation and analysis. If you choose a movie, you should probably see it more than once. If you choose a product, you may want to test it under varying conditions.

It's often a good idea to take notes on your experience. Some of these notes will be subjective, detailing what the experience is like for you. But you may also consider other points of view. Later on, your notes will help to give your readers a full account of the work, product, or event that you're reviewing. The notes will also furnish you with specific evidence for supporting your judgments.

For Option 2, your notes will be based on memory rather than direct observation. Record not only what happened but also why it happened. If your subject is an idea, like an earlier belief that you could never learn to swim, that cigarettes are cool, or that you were unlovable, consider what people or events contributed to that belief. What evidence did you have to support those early impressions? What changed? What enabled you to see things differently? Trace the path of incidents and consciousness that led you to discard the old idea for a new one.

DRAFTING

For the review, analyzing your topic into parts may help to establish your criteria for evaluating it. People in the market for computers look for speed, capacity, reliability, special features, and product support. What do moviegoers, sports fans, or music lovers look for? You may also want to include background information or comparisons. What do you know about history or the people involved that might cast light on your topic? What similar products, works, or events might help to place your topic in perspective?

For Option 2, you might begin by reconstructing the scene of the crime. Where were you in your life when you first encountered the victim of your misconceptions? Describe the circumstances so that your readers understand your state of mind at the time. If your subject is a person, what did he or she look like to you? Details about clothing, mannerisms, speech, and setting can help to make the moment come alive. Be sure to explain why as well as how your judgment changed. Were you confronted by new evidence to contradict your earlier impressions? Did something happen to change your point of view? Were you aware of some change in your thinking?

REVISING

When you revise your review, use the yardsticks of your purpose and your audience to measure what you've written. What do your readers already know about such things? What will help them to understand how you arrived at your conclusions? How will you establish your credibility? What style is likely to keep them engaged while allowing you to speak in a comfortable voice?

The same is true for Option 2. Reread your draft from the readers' point of view. Will they be able to follow your chronology from start to finish? Have you avoided confusing shifts in time and tense? Have you provided enough background information for them to appreciate what happened? Have you provided clear transitions between the parts that narrate your experience and the parts that explain its significance?

Judging and Evaluating across the Media

PRINT

Consumer Reports
Car & Driver
Music reviews
Sports columns
Course evaluations
U.S. News Ultimate College Guide
Zagat Survey

TELEVISION

Ebert and Roeper
Antiques Roadshow
Judge Judy

RADIO

All Songs Considered
Jim Cramer's Real Money
Movie Talk
A Fistful of Soundtracks

INTERNET

CNet
cnet.com
Metacritic
Metacritic.com

Readings and Screenings: Consuming Choices

Spend a few minutes at the magazine rack in your local library or bookstore, and you'll see how much print is devoted to the task of judging and evaluating. Many monthly publications feature columns that review special topics of interest, from art exhibits and sports events to the newest fashions and the latest music CDs. Quite a few books, like *Zagatsurvey* and *Leonard Maltin's Movie & Video Guide,* compile hundreds of restaurant or movie reviews year after year. On the Internet, a Web site like metacritic.com will regularly update reviews of movies, DVDs, music, books, and games. In fact, all forms of media offer their own evaluative instruments, and they often evaluate each other.

No doubt you have your own favorite sources of reviews to help you make decisions. Some, like the *New York Times,* may rely on professional critics; some, like *Zagat,* depend on amateur reviews and public opinion surveys. Others, like metacritic.com, combine professional and nonprofessional assessments. Perhaps you have contributed to this steady stream of judgments. Or maybe you ignore all the reviews and make up your own mind independently.

The readings and screenings in this chapter share a common purpose, to make us more conscious of the choices that we make. All too often, explains Ellen Langer, our judgments are automatic reactions rather than reasoned evaluations. Langer, a research psychologist, illustrates the consequences of mindless choices with both serious and comic instances from daily life. In *The Persuaders,* an eye-opening PBS documentary on the marketing industry, Douglas Rushkoff interviews a wealthy market researcher who has learned to exploit gaps between the stated motives of consumers and their unconscious drives. Clotaire Rapaille has created a lucrative career by selling corporations the hidden "codes" to consumer choices. In "Danish," science writer David Bodanis demonstrates how mindless we can be about our eating habits. His humorous, eye-opening look at the ingredients in one of America's favorite breakfast foods will make some readers reevaluate their daily diet. Wendell Berry, a prolific poet and novelist, invites us to open our eyes even wider before we eat. If we knew where our food comes from, he advises, we might enjoy it more. Mary Kuntz explores how young activists are fighting back, undermining million-dollar advertising campaigns with parody ads for Dispepsi and Joe Chemo. In a pointed work of fiction, Toni Cade Bambara tells the story of a Harlem teacher whose students learn a tough lesson about consumer culture and economic class. The readings conclude with three reviews of *The Matrix,* revealing how different critics saw the film when it first appeared on the nation's screens.

PREVIEW

Have you ever found yourself driving on an unfamiliar road wondering how you got there, or have you ever purchased something without knowing why? Driving on autopilot and making automatic judgments are forms of what Ellen Langer calls "mindlessness." A professor of psychology at Harvard University, Dr. Langer has been studying this phenomenon for many years. Her popular book, entitled *Mindfulness,* is the product of more than fifty experiments and much research into the nature of unconscious decision making. In it she explores the roots of mindless behavior, showing how it affects our work and personal relationships. She also explains how to counteract the dangers of stereotyping, the banality of uncreative thinking, and the tedium of aging. The following selection is taken from Chapter 2 of *Mindfulness* (New York: Addison-Wesley, 1989).

When the Light's on and Nobody's Home
By Ellen Langer

Out of time we cut "days" and "nights," "summers" and "winters." We say *what* each part of the sensible continuum is, and all these abstract *whats* are concepts.
The intellectual life of man consists almost wholly in his substitution of a conceptual order for the perceptual order in which his experience originally comes.
William James, "The World We Live In"

Imagine that it's two o'clock in the morning. Your doorbell rings; you get up, startled, and make your way downstairs. You open the door and see a man standing before you. He wears two diamond rings and a fur coat, and there's a Rolls Royce behind him. He's sorry to wake you at this ridiculous hour, he tells you, but he's in the middle of a scavenger hunt. His ex-wife is in the same contest, which makes it very important to him that he win. He needs a piece of wood about three feet by seven feet. Can you help him? In order to make it worthwhile he'll give you $10,000. You believe him. He's obviously rich. And so you say to yourself, how in the world can I get this piece of wood for him? You think of the lumber yard; you don't know who owns the lumber yard; in fact you're not even sure where the lumber yard is. It would be closed at two o'clock in the morning anyway. You struggle but you can't come up with anything. Reluctantly, you tell him, "Gee, I'm sorry."

The next day, when passing a construction site near a friend's house, you see a piece of wood that's just about the right size, three feet by seven feet—a door. You could have just taken a door off its hinges and given it to him, for $10,000.

Why on earth, you say to yourself, didn't it occur to you to do that? It didn't occur to you because yesterday your door was not a piece of wood. The seven-by-three foot piece of wood was hidden from you, stuck in the category called "door."

This kind of mindlessness, which usually takes more humdrum forms—"Why didn't I think of Susan? She can unclog sinks"—could be called "entrapment by category." It is one of three definitions that can help us understand the nature of mindlessness. The other two, which we will also explain, are automatic behavior and acting from a single perspective.

Trapped by Categories

5 We experience the world by creating categories and making distinctions among them. "This is a Chinese, not a Japanese, vase." "No, he's only a freshman." "The white orchids are endangered." "She's his boss now."

In this way, we make a picture of the world, and of ourselves. Without categories the world might seem to escape us. Tibetan Buddhists call this habit of mind "The Lord of Speech":

> We adopt sets of categories which serve as ways of managing phenomena. The most fully developed products of this tendency are ideologies, the systems of ideas that rationalize, justify and sanctify our lives. Nationalism, communism, existentialism, Christianity, Buddhism—all provide us with identities, rules of action, and interpretations of how and why things happen as they do.[1]

The creation of new categories, as we will see throughout this book, is a mindful activity. Mindlessness sets in when we rely too rigidly on categories and distinctions created in the past (masculine/feminine, old/young, success/failure). Once distinctions are created, they take on a life of their own. Consider: (1) First there was earth. (2) Then there was land, sea, and sky. (3) Then there were countries. (4) Then there was Germany. (5) Now there is East Germany versus West Germany. The categories we make gather momentum and are very hard to overthrow. We build our own and our shared realities and then we become victims of them—blind to the fact that they are constructs, ideas.

If we look back at the categories of an earlier age, once firmly established, it is easier to see why new ones might become necessary. The Argentinean writer Jorge Luis Borges quotes from an ancient Chinese encyclopedia in which the animals are classified as "(a) belonging to the Emperor, (b) embalmed, (c) tame, (d) suckling pigs, (e) sirens, (f) stray dogs, (g) included in the present classification, (h) frenzied, (i) innumerable, (j) drawn with a very fine camel brush, (k) et cetera, (l) having just broken the water pitcher, (m) that from a long way off look like flies."[2] To be mindless is to be trapped in a rigid world in which certain creatures always belong to the Emperor, Christianity is always good, certain people are forever untouchable, and doors are only doors.

Automatic Behavior

Have you ever said "excuse me" to a store mannequin or written a check in January with the previous year's date? When in this mode, we take in and use limited signals from the world around us (the female form, the familiar face of the check) without letting other signals (the motionless pose, a calendar) penetrate as well.

Once, in a small department store, I gave a cashier a new credit card. Noticing that I hadn't signed it, she handed it back to me to sign. Then she took my card, passed it through her machine, handed me the resulting form, and asked me to sign it. I did as I was told. The cashier then held the form next to the newly signed card to see if the signatures matched.

10 Modern psychology has not paid much attention to how much complicated action may be performed automatically, yet as early as 1896 Leon Solomons and Gertrude Stein looked into this question. (This was the Gertrude Stein who, from 1893 to 1898, was a graduate student in experimental psychology at Harvard University, working under William James [and who later wrote poetry and prose as a member of an American expatriate group in Paris].) They studied what was then called "double personalities" and which later came to be known as "split personalities," and proposed that the mindless performance of the second personality was essentially similar to that of ordinary people. Ordinary people also engage in a great deal of complex behavior without consciously paying attention to it. Solomons and Stein conducted several experiments in which they were their own subjects, demonstrating that both writing and reading could be done automatically. They succeeded in writing English words while they were otherwise caught up in reading an absorbing story. With much practice, they were even able to take dictation automatically while reading. Afterward, they were completely unable to recall the words they had written but were

nevertheless quite certain they had written something. To show that reading could take place automatically, the subject read aloud from a book while a captivating story was read to him or her. Again they found that, after a lot of practice, they could read aloud unhampered while giving full attention to the story being read to them.

Solomons and Stein concluded that a vast number of actions that we think of as intelligent, such as reading and writing, can be done quite automatically: "We have shown a general tendency on the part of normal people, to act, without any express desire or conscious volition, in a manner in general accord with the *previous habits* of the person."[3]

An experiment I conducted in 1978 with fellow psychologists Benzion Chanowitz and Arthur Blank explored this kind of mindlessness.[4] Our setting was the Graduate Center at the City University of New York. We approached people using a copying machine and asked whether they would let us copy something then and there. We gave reasons that were either sound or senseless. An identical response to both sound and senseless requests would show that our subjects were not thinking about what was being said. We made one of three requests: "Excuse me, may I use the Xerox machine?"; "Excuse me, may I use the Xerox machine because I want to make copies?"; "Excuse me, may I use the Xerox machine because I'm in a rush?"

The first and second requests are the same in content—What else would one do with a copying machine except make copies? Therefore if people were considering what was actually being said, the first two requests should be equally effective. Structurally, however, they are different. The redundant request ("Excuse me, may I use the Xerox machine because I want to make copies?") is more similar to the last one ("Excuse me, may I use the Xerox machine because I'm in a rush?") in that both state the request and give a reason. If people comply with the last two requests in equal numbers, this implies attention to structure rather than conscious attention to content. That, in fact, was just what we found. There was more compliance when a reason was given—whether the reason sounded legitimate or silly. People responded mindlessly to the familiar framework rather than mindlessly attending to the content.

Of course, there are limits to this. If someone asked for a very large favor or if the excuse were unusually absurd ("because an elephant is after me"), the individual would be likely to think about what was said. It is not that people don't hear the request the rest of the time; they simply don't think about it actively.

In a similar experiment, we sent an interdepartmental memo around some university offices. The message either requested or demanded the return of the memo to a designated room—and that was all it said.[5] ("Please return this immediately to Room 247," or "The memo is to be returned to Room 247.") Anyone who read such a memo mindfully would ask, "If whoever sent the memo wanted it, why did he or she send it?" and therefore would not return the memo. Half of the memos were designed to look exactly like those usually sent between departments. The other half were made to look in some way different. When the memo looked like those they were used to, 90 percent of the recipients actually returned it. When the memo looked different, 60 percent returned it.

When I was discussing these studies at a university colloquium, a member of the audience told me about a little con game that operated along the same lines. Someone placed an ad in a Los Angeles newspaper that read, "It's not too late to send $1 to ———," and gave the person's own name and address. The reader was promised nothing in return. Many people replied, enclosing a dollar. The person who wrote the ad apparently earned a good sum.

The automatic behavior in evidence in these examples has much in common with habit.[6] Habit, or the tendency to keep on with behavior that has been repeated over time, naturally implies mindlessness.

However, as we will see in the following chapter, mindless behavior can arise without a long history of repetition, almost instantaneously, in fact.

Acting from a Single Perspective

So often in our lives, we act as though there were only one set of rules. For instance, in cooking we tend to follow recipes with dutiful precision. We add ingredients as though by official decree. If the recipe calls for a pinch of salt and four pinches fall in, panic strikes, as though the bowl might now explode. Thinking of a recipe only as a rule, we often do not consider how people's tastes vary, or what fun it might be to make up a new dish.

The first experiment I conducted in graduate school explored this problem of the single perspective. It was a pilot study to examine the effectiveness of different requests for help. A fellow investigator stood on a busy sidewalk and told people passing by that she had sprained her knee and needed help. If someone stopped she asked him or her to get an Ace bandage from the nearby drugstore. I stood inside the store and listened while the helpful person gave the request to the pharmacist, who had agreed earlier to say that he was out of Ace bandages. After being told this, not one subject, out of the twenty-five we studied, thought to ask if the pharmacist could recommend something else. People left the drugstore and returned empty-handed to the "victim" and told her the news. We speculated that had she asked for less specific help, she might have received it. But, acting on the single thought that a sprained knee needs an Ace bandage, no one tried to find other kinds of help.

As a little test of how a narrow perspective can dominate our thinking, read the following sentence:

Final folios seem to result from years of dutiful study of texts along with years of scientific experience.

Now count how many F's there are, reading only once more through the sentence.

If you find fewer than there actually are (the answer is given in the notes),[7] your counting was probably influenced by the fact that the first two words in the sentence begin with F. In counting, your mind would tend to cling to this clue, or single perspective, and miss some of the F's hidden within and at the end of words. Highly specific instructions such as these or the request for an Ace bandage encourage mindlessness. Once we let them in, our minds snap shut like a clam on ice and do not let in new signals.

Notes

1. C. Trungpa, *Cutting Through Spiritual Materialism* (Boulder and London: Shambhala, 1973).

2. T'ai P'ing, *Kuang Chi* [Extensive Records Made in the Period of Peace and Prosperity] (978 A.D.), as cited in Jorge Luis Borges, *Libro de Los Seres Imaginarios* (Buenos Aires: Editorial Kiersa S.A., Fauna China, 1967), p. 88. "Commitment," *Journal of Personality and Social Psychology* 41 (1981): 1051–1063.

3. L. Solomons and G. Stein, "Normal Motor Automation," *Psychological Review* 36 (1896): 492–572.

4. E. Langer, A. Blank, and B. Chanowitz, "The Mindlessness of Ostensibly Thoughtful Action: The Role of Placebic Information in Interpersonal Interaction, *Journal of Personality and Social Psychology* 36 (1978): 635–642.

5. Ibid.

6. To understand the more complex relationship between automatic information processing and mindlessness, compare E. Langer, "Minding Matters," in L. Berkowitz, ed., *Advances in Experimental Social Psychology* (New York: Academic Press, in press) and W. Schneider and R. M. Schiffrin, "Controlled and Automatic Human Information Processing: 1. Detection, Search, and Attention," *Psychological Review* 84 (1977): 1–66.

7. The correct answer is 8. A similar quiz was printed on the business card of the Copy Service of Miami, Inc.

RESPONSE QUESTIONS

1. Based on the title of this selection, what did you expect it to be about? At what point in your reading was Langer's purpose clear?

2. Where in your life have you found yourself acting "mindlessly"? How common is this kind of behavior?

3. What are the three forms of mindlessness described by Langer? Define each form, and give examples from your personal observation.

4. Try duplicating the Solomon and Stein experiment in automatic behavior by reading and writing simultaneously. Report back on the results.

5. Many of the psychology experiments described in the essay involve unsuspecting people. How ethical are such experiments? What guidelines do you think experimenters should follow when working with the public?

GUIDELINES FOR ANALYSIS

1. Why does Langer begin the essay with the story of a treasure hunt? How effective is this introduction?

2. Which of Langer's examples were most helpful in clarifying her ideas? What makes these examples particularly helpful?

3. Langer cites historical experiments, literature, and her own personal experience to develop her ideas about mindlessness. How convincing are these sources? If you find any of them questionable, explain why.

QUESTIONS OF CULTURE

1. Langer emphasizes the downside of mindlessness, how it can cause problems or mislead us in our daily lives. What are the benefits of such thinking? In what circumstances or cultures might it be useful to think automatically, in terms of categories, or from a single perspective?

2. Do you think the kinds of behavior described here are universal, or are they more apt to apply to certain societies? For example, are we more distracted by multimedia messages today than our ancestors were? Are hunters who depend for their survival on a single-minded pursuit of game more mindful than those who have modern multitasking jobs?

IDEAS FOR YOUR JOURNAL

1. Design your own experiment to test mindless behavior and report on your findings.

2. Keep a log of your mindless activity. How many instances can you count in a single week?

PREVIEW

How mindful are Americans when they go shopping? Do they really know the reasons for their consumer choices? According to Clotaire Rapaille, a French psychologist and marketing consultant, most people have no clue to their own motives. Dr. Rapaille believes that consumers are driven by concealed desires, which explain why some drivers in Manhattan own Hummers and

Americans refrigerate their cheese. In the following selection from PBS's *Frontline,* Dr. Rapaille and other researchers explain how advertisers tap into the unconscious brain for hidden codes that will help to sell their products.

www.mhhe.com/costanzo

Visit the Web site to see the video excerpt.

Since 1983, PBS's *Frontline* has gained national recognition and respect for its investigative reports on public affairs, giving television journalists the opportunity to explore complex, controversial issues in depth. "The Persuaders," a ninety-minute documentary on current marketing and advertising practices, was originally broadcast on *Frontline* on November 9, 2003. The transcript and video excerpt (available on *The Writer's Eye* companion Web site) are from Segment Four of the documentary, titled "The Science of Selling."

PARTIAL TRANSCRIPT FOR VIDEO DOCUMENTARY, "THE PERSUADERS"

DOUGLAS RUSHKOFF: Far away from the boardrooms of the entertainment industry, in places like this nondescript office park outside Boston, the nitty-gritty work of selling starts with a simple questionnaire about bread.

INTERVIEWER: And now what do you see as the disadvantages to eating grain-based foods?

DOUGLAS RUSHKOFF: Today, faced with a nation hooked on low-carb diets, the baked goods industry needs to find out just how Americans feel about their products.

INTERVIEWER: I'm going to read you some different emotions. I've got a whole list of them here. For each one of them, I just want you to tell me yes or no as to whether you think you feel that emotion when you're eating white bread, OK? The first one is accepting. Do you feel accepting when you're eating white bread?

5   INTERVIEWEE: Yeah, I would say yes.

INTERVIEWER: Affectionate?

INTERVIEWEE: No.

INTERVIEWER: Lonely?

INTERVIEWEE: No.

10   INTERVIEWER: Disappointed?

INTERVIEWEE: No.

INTERVIEWER: Afraid?

INTERVIEWEE: No.

INTERVIEWER: Trusting?

15 INTERVIEWEE: No, I don't think that would be an issue.

INTERVIEWER: Would you feel uncertain?

INTERVIEWEE: Yeah, a little uncertain. I've got one question. Can I ask a question? The question was, "When you eat bread, do you feel lonely?" Have you found people that say, yes, they feel lonely when they're eating bread?

INTERVIEWER: Not a lot on this one.

DOUGLAS RUSHKOFF: Welcome to the strange world of market research—

20 CLOTAIRE RAPAILLE, Market Research Guru: Now, we have to be careful because that's not politically correct to say women—

DOUGLAS RUSHKOFF: —where those who claim to have figured out the hidden desires of consumers are treated as gurus.

CLOTAIRE RAPAILLE: We all come from a woman. We all spend nine months inside of a woman, so women are expert in the inside. Translation: When a woman buys a car, the first thing she is looking at is, do they have cupholders?

DOUGLAS RUSHKOFF: Dr. Clotaire Rapaille lives in a baronial mansion in upstate New York. *Fortune 500* companies and their advertising agencies flock there to drink French champagne, admire Rapaille's many cars and listen with rapt attention to his insights on the irrational mind of the American shopper.

CLOTAIRE RAPAILLE: And we have to understand for each product what the dynamic is behind that. What is it that people are really buying there? We still have people that buy things they don't really need. Sometimes a product is not expensive enough.

25 DOUGLAS RUSHKOFF: What sets Rapaille apart from many other market researchers is his belief that consumers are driven by unconscious needs and impulses.

CLOTAIRE RAPAILLE: My experience is that most of the time, people have no idea why they're doing what they're doing. They have no idea. So they're going to try to make up something that makes sense. Why do you need a Hummer to go shopping? "Well, you know, in case I need to go off road." Well, you live in Manhattan. Why do you need a four-wheel drive in Manhattan? "Well, you know, sometime I go out and I go in"—I mean, this is—you don't need to be a rocket scientist to understand that this is disconnected. This has nothing to do with what the real reason is for people to do what they do.

DOUGLAS RUSHKOFF: Rapaille began his career as a psychiatrist in Europe studying autism.

CLOTAIRE RAPAILLE: My training with autistic children is that I had to understand what these kids were trying to tell me with no words, because they don't speak. Wow! So then, that's part of my training. How can I decode this kind of behavior which is not a word?

DOUGLAS RUSHKOFF: Rapaille claims that there are unconscious associations for nearly every product we buy buried deep in our brains.

30 CLOTAIRE RAPAILLE: One of my discoveries was that when you learn a word—whatever it is, coffee, love, mother—the first time you understand, you imprint the meaning of this word, you create a mental connection. And so actually, every word has a mental highway. I call that a code, an unconscious code in the brain.

DOUGLAS RUSHKOFF: Corporations love the idea of buying a single key to the psyches of vast numbers of consumers, a simple "code" that lies behind millions of individual decisions. Rapaille gave up psychiatry and says he has never looked back.

CLOTAIRE RAPAILLE: I have 50 of the *Fortune 100* companies as clients.

MAN: I saw that. That's very impressive.

DOUGLAS RUSHKOFF: Tonight Rapaille has been invited to speak to the Luxury Marketing Council of America.

35 GREGORY FURMAN, Chairman, Luxury Marketing Council: The premise of the council has been to bring the smartest minds in marketing together and help us all figure out ways to get money from the customers with the most money.

DOUGLAS RUSHKOFF: Rapaille has been commissioned by a handful of big companies like Boeing and Acura to "break the code on luxury."

GREGORY FURMAN: We're just delighted to have you with us.

CLOTAIRE RAPAILLE: Thank you. Thank you. *[applause]* I don't believe what people say. So some people listen to what they say and they say, "Well, do you want to buy that? Do you want to do this?" I don't believe what people say. I want to understand why they do what they do.

I found this word, and with that I want to understand you guys. And this is the word. I hope I didn't make a mistake. The right spelling?

40 DOUGLAS RUSHKOFF: To crack the code on luxury, Rapaille conducts a series of focus groups.

CLOTAIRE RAPAILLE: I'm serious. That's what I want to understand, how you feel about it. And anything for me is interesting.

WOMAN: Money?

CLOTAIRE RAPAILLE: Money!

DOUGLAS RUSHKOFF: He takes his subjects on what he hopes will be a three-stage psychic journey, past reason, through emotion to the primal core, where Rapaille insists all purchasing decisions really lie.

45 CLOTAIRE RAPAILLE: We start with the cortex because people want to show how intelligent they are. So give them a chance. We don't care what they say,

When people try to sell you luxury things, what kind of word do they use?

MAN: Well made.

CLOTAIRE RAPAILLE: Well made.

Nothing new there. And then we have a break. They're usually very happy with themselves. "Oh, we did a good job," and so on. When they come back, now we're going to the emotions. And I tell them, "You're going to tell me a little story, like if I was a 5-year-old from another planet."

50 INTERVIEWEES: Once upon a time— *[laughter]*

CLOTAIRE RAPAILLE: So suddenly, they are into a mindset that is completely different. They don't try to be logical or intelligent, they just try to please the 5-year-old from another planet.

MAN: I will send you and your entire family to Maui.

CLOTAIRE RAPAILLE: They don't understand what they're doing anymore. Good! That's what I want. At the end of the second hour, when we go to the break, they say, "This guy is crazy. What is he doing? I thought I understood what we were doing. Now I don't understand anything. I mean, I get paid to do that?" This is excellent. This is what I want.

MAN: We're going to be chosen for a new reality show.

55 WOMAN: That's what it is, a reality show! Wait, there's 19 of us?

MAN: They're going to give you a million dollars, and they want to see how you spend it!

CLOTAIRE RAPAILLE: Then when they come back for the third hour, then there is no more chairs. "Uh-huh! What is going on here? How come no chairs?" And I explain to them that I would like them to try to go back to the very first time that they experienced what we're trying to understand.

DOUGLAS RUSHKOFF: Rapaille is hunting for our primal urges. He's after what he calls the "reptilian hot buttons" that compel us to action.

CLOTAIRE RAPAILLE: It's absolutely crucial to understand what I call "the reptilian hot button." My theory is very simple. The reptilian always win. I don't care what you're going to tell me intellectually, give me the reptilian.

60   RAPAILLE EMPLOYEE: So I'm going to turn off the lights now, and we're going to all relax together.

CLOTAIRE RAPAILLE: I want you to be in a mindset a little bit like the one you had when you wake up in the morning. You'll be surprised to see that things come back to your mind that you forgot sometime for 20, 30 years. It's amazing.

DOUGLAS RUSHKOFF: The scribbles of consumers in the semi-darkness, half-remembered words and pictures associated with "luxury," somehow become Rapaille's keys to unlocking the luxury code.

CLOTAIRE RAPAILLE: Once you get the code, suddenly, everything start making sense. I understand why this car sells, this car doesn't sell. You know, I understand why—why a small $29,000 Cadillac cannot sell. You know, I understand why. Because it's off code. Oh!

DOUGLAS RUSHKOFF: Over the years, Rapaille has told car makers to beef up the size of their SUVs and tint the windows because the code for SUVs is domination. He told a French company trying to sell cheese to Americans that they were off-code.

CLOTAIRE RAPAILLE: In France, the cheese is alive. You never put the cheese in the refrigerator because you don't put your cat in the refrigerator. It's the same. It's alive. If I know that in America the cheese is dead—and I have been studying cheese in almost 50 states in America I can tell you, the cheese is dead everywhere—then I have to put that up front. I have to say, "This cheese is safe, is pasteurized, is wrapped up in plastic." I know the plastic is a body bag. "You can put it in the fridge." I know the fridge is the morgue. That's where you put the dead bodies, eh? And so once you know that, this is the way you market cheese in America.

RESPONSE QUESTIONS

1. After showing us a consumer being interviewed about bread, commentator Douglas Rushkoff welcomes us to "the strange world of market research." What makes the interview seem strange? Why do you think Rushkoff begins the segment at this point? How does the rest of the segment explain the interviewer's questions?

2. How did Dr. Rapaille's early psychiatric training with autistic children prepare him for a career in marketing research? What did he learn about wordless behavior?

3. Dr. Rapaille believes that consumers are motivated by unconscious needs and impulses, what he calls "reptilian hot buttons." Considering the advertisements that you know, how accurate does this insight seem to you?

4. What was your immediate assessment of Dr. Rapaille as you watched the video or read the transcript? On what details (his appearance, voice, surroundings? his title? what he said?) did you base this first impression? Would you have had the same response if you had read or watched the segment in a different order? What tentative conclusions can you draw about your interaction with printed texts and moving images? Can your conclusions be related to Rapaille's point about logic and emotion?

GUIDELINES FOR ANALYSIS

1. Contrast the "nondescript office park" where consumers are interviewed with the baronial mansion where Rapaille entertains his clients. What does the décor of these two locations suggest about the roles of buyers and marketers in our economy?

2. Notice how the documentary moves back and forth between Rushkoff and Rapaille. What does each contribute to your understanding of the segment's main ideas?

3. Follow the "three-stage psychic journey" through which Rapaille leads his focus groups. Why does he seek to disarm their rational faculties?

4. Compare "The Persuaders" to one of the printed essays in this chapter. How is each text organized? What do they say about mindless choices, consumers' relationship to food, or the advertising industry?

QUESTIONS OF CULTURE

1. Rapaille explains that cheese is alive in France but dead in the United States. How does he arrive at this conclusion, and what does it imply about French and American attitudes toward food? What other differences can you think of in the consumer habits of diverse cultures?

2. Advertisers claim that they need bold new strategies because American consumers have become cynical and impervious to ads. How far should marketers and advertisers be allowed to pursue their strategies? To what ethical principles should they be held accountable?

IDEAS FOR YOUR JOURNAL

1. Make a list of items you have purchased recently, and give the reasons for your choices. Then try to apply the principle of unconscious motives to your list. If Rapaille were hired to explain your choices, what emotional needs, buried desires, or influential images might he identify?

2. Elsewhere in "The Persuaders," Rushkoff observes: "We Americans value our freedom of choice—choice in the marketplace of goods, and choice in what has become a marketplace of ideas. When the same persuasion industry is engaged to influence these very different kinds of decision-making, it's easy for our roles as consumers and our roles as citizens to get blurred." Where have you seen this blurring of roles? What dangers do you see when candidates hire marketers to run their political campaigns? Do some freewriting on this topic to explore what citizens might do in the face of this worrisome trend.

PREVIEW

Among our everyday consuming choices are the decisions that we make about food. How much attention do we give to what we put into our bodies? Investigating a common breakfast item like a Danish pastry can turn up some surprises, as David Bodanis demonstrates.

Born in Chicago, Bodanis studied mathematics, physics, and economics at the University of Chicago before moving to Europe, where he began his career as a journalist. His first book, *The Secret House* (1987), offered a scientific look at everyday experience, revealing the extraordinary things we take for granted in an ordinary day. His next book, *The Secret Family* (1997), became the basis of an award-winning documentary about the astonishing world inside an ordinary human being. While he continues to pay attention to the details of our daily lives, Bodanis also serves as an international consultant, advocating a sustainable, environmentally sound economy. "Danish" is excerpted from *The Secret Family: Twenty-Four Hours Inside the Mysterious World of Our Minds and Bodies* (New York: Simon & Schuster, 1997).

Danish
By David Bodanis

The microwave buzzes, and the Danish—having, with a typical 2.45 MHz motor, been pummeled precisely 147 billion times in its one minute inside—is ready.

It looks delicious, icing glazed and caramelized, steaming with butter-rich vapors. Some people would deduce from this, that it's made of things like fresh icing and flour and butter. But that's no more likely than the family's fresh orange juice being made with fresh oranges. What we call Danish pastries—the Danes call them Viennese bread—couldn't be produced in mass quantities without some substitutions along the way.

The first thing to work on is that icing. It's hard to keep icing sugar enticingly white so the bakery company will just slap some white paint on. That's why dollops of titanium dioxide—the same chemical in the buckets of leftover white latex paint in the garage—form a good part of that gloopily delicious white substance on top. Where some brown, caramel-suggestive swirls are needed, brown waxes, including the indelible rosin used on violin bows, are often used.

Most of the rest of what's inside is pretty well known: flour, sugar, nuts, and oils. An ordinary bakery pecan roll can easily contain more fat than you'd get from a plate of eggs, bacon, and pancakes doused in margarine. But Danish pastry also needs to have what food psychologists (these are not researchers who interview foods—such people exist, but are generally only seen during visiting hours—but rather ones who ask others how they feel about foods) call "enhanced mouth-feel."

5   The simplest additive here, used in the most inexpensive Danish pastries, is made with dried extract of red algae, bleached so that no red color shows. It's cheap enough, just go to the right beach and there it is, and it does add a little of the desired stickiness. But this algae's quality isn't very high, and can also produce what's politely called "abdominal distention" if eaten in too great a quantity. Processed chicken feathers or the scraped belly stubble from scalded pig carcasses are often added to these lowest-price pastries, as their extracted proteins help in softening the flour that's used.

If you can afford a slightly better grade of Danish pastry there's likely to be a superior algal seaweed inside: the *chondrus* species. It's so much better and so useful for adding smoothness, that some is often used in cosmetics, which is something to think about when chewing a Danish while trying to put on mascara. But it's still nothing compared to the third and highest grade of mouth-feel enhancer. This is the high molecular weight polysaccharide called galactomannan. (Do not read any further if you like expensive Danish pastries.) Galactomannan is produced by processing the pods of a tree which originally grew in the Mediterranean region. It is an immensely sticky substance, ideal for mouth-feel needs. The tree, however, was also cultivated thousands of years ago. And who would have needed something so sticky in those years before it was included in Danish pastries?

When the Pharaohs of ancient Egypt died and had their brains pulled out through their noses and were embalmed, it was important that they be securely wrapped for their voyage into the land of death. This meant thick burial shrouds. What held those burial shrouds together, surviving so well, with stickiness so undiminished by the centuries that you can still pull out the active molecules from just above the mummified bodies in museums today? It was galactomannan.

Most of the family can't taste any of these extras, and they eat contentedly: nostril skins twisting wide and rib cages convulsively expanding—our heart rate almost always briefly speeds up when we sniff food—to help whirl the spurts of air needed for proper appreciation of these delicious vapors. About 20 percent of the population, however, are termed super tasters. Super tasters have more taste buds than other adults—about 9,000 is the average adult figure—and they even have more taste buds than the elevated numbers children have. Very occasionally a man possesses this anomalous inheritance, but more often the sole super taster in a family is going to be the wife. (No one knows why women are better tasters. One idea is that it could be a way of detecting very low-level bacterial infections in food which wouldn't matter normally, but could be important during pregnancies.)

It's a lonely life. You end up spending certain mealtimes asking your husband, in whispers so as not to upset the children, if he's sure, really sure, he hasn't detected that smell you're sure is there. You will smell milk going sour a day or so before anyone else, and notice when someone left onions on the bread board a week ago. No one, ever, will believe you. This sensitivity is even stronger near a woman's monthly period, for the nose's inner lining thins slightly then, and incoming vapors are more acutely detected.

10   If the parents are distressed at their kids' eagerness in gorging on the Danish, they can take heart from an Ohio study done on children in the hospital. When the children were given their choice of any food to eat, they began as you'd expect, loading up on chocolate cake and other sweets for the first few days. But within a week—so long as there were no reprimands from the nurses—almost all of the children ended up willfully gobbling plain bread and fruit and—even the boys did this!—lots of chewy vegetables.

RESPONSE QUESTIONS

1. What did you find most surprising, interesting, or troubling in this selection? How would you summarize what you learned from your reading?

2. What other foods might be candidates for this kind of evaluative analysis? How much do you already know about the process of producing them?

3. Has your taste for Danish pastry or other processed foods changed as a result of reading "Danish"? Trace your responses to the essay from beginning to end. Do you find yourself agreeing or resisting the author's intentions?

4. Compare "Danish" to the essays by Ellen Langer and Wendell Berry in this chapter. What connections can you make to the concepts of mindlessness and responsible eating?

GUIDELINES FOR ANALYSIS

1. Who are the intended readers of this essay? How can you tell? How does Bodanis try to make his topic interesting? In addition to making an informative assessment of Danish pastry, what other purposes does the writer seem to have in mind?

2. Pay attention to the writer's organizing strategy. Notice where he begins, how he ends, and how he links each section of the essay. What logic can you find behind the structure of his essay? Given the writer's purposes, how effective is this arrangement?

3. Bodanis uses terms like "enhanced mouth-feel" and "food psychologists." Where do these terms come from, and what do they mean? What do they imply about the food industry?

4. Judge the judge. Is this essay evenhanded in its treatment of the topic? How dangerous are the ingredients that Bodanis identifies? Are their amounts significant? Is it reasonable to draw comparisons between two products just because they contain the same additives? What conclusions do you draw about the writer's approach?

QUESTIONS OF CULTURE

1. "Danish" can be read as an indictment of mass consumption culture. Why do you think Danish pastries and other fast foods are so popular today? Who consumes these foods and who produces them? Speculate about the benefits and risks in terms of health and the economy.

2. Why are such foods allowed by the government? What role do you think the government should play?

3. Near the end of this selection, Bodanis speaks of "supertasters," noting that more women than men belong to this group. What broad distinctions does he make between men and women? Explain why you agree or disagree.

1. Think of another common food item—such as Jell-O, chewing gum, hot dogs, or fruit juice—and do your own research. Investigate the ingredients on the label, check the Internet watch groups, and scan the consumer magazines for inside information.

2. Create a personal food profile. List the things you look for in foods. What are your criteria for choosing what you eat, and what standards do you try to uphold? Then list your favorite foods. How well does your food philosophy dictate your actual food choice?

PREVIEW

Wendell Berry offers a broad look at the choices we make as consumers. As a native of Kentucky and a farmer, Berry developed an intimate knowledge of how things grow and a deep appreciation for where food comes from. A poet, novelist, and essayist as well as a farmer, he has taught English at New York University and the University of Kentucky and has written more than thirty books. The following essay is from *What Are People For?* (North Point, 1990).

The Pleasures of Eating

By Wendell Berry

Many times, after I have finished a lecture on the decline of American farming and rural life, someone in the audience has asked, "What can city people do?"

"Eat responsibly," I have usually answered. Of course, I have tried to explain what I meant by that, but afterwards I have invariably felt that there was more to be said than I had been able to say. Now I would like to attempt a better explanation.

I begin with the proposition that eating is an agricultural act. Eating ends the annual drama of the food economy that begins with planting and birth. Most eaters, however, are no longer aware that this is true. They think of food as an agricultural product, perhaps, but they do not think of themselves as participants in agriculture. They think of themselves as "consumers." If they think beyond that, they recognize that they are passive consumers. They buy what they want—or what they have been persuaded to want—within the limits of what they can get. They pay, mostly without protest, what they are charged. And they mostly ignore certain critical questions about the quality and the cost of what they are sold: How fresh is it? How pure or clean is it, how free of dangerous chemicals? How far was it transported, and what did transportation add to the cost? How much did manufacturing or packaging or advertising add to the cost? When the food product has been manufactured or "processed" or "precooked," how has that affected its quality or price or nutritional value?

Most urban shoppers would tell you that food is produced on farms. But most of them do not know what farms, or what kinds of farms, or where the farms are, or what knowledge of skills are involved in farming. They apparently have little doubt that farms will continue to produce, but they do not know how or over what obstacles. For them, then, food is pretty much an abstract idea—something they do not know or imagine—until it appears on the grocery shelf or on the table.

5 The specialization of production induces specialization of consumption. Patrons of the entertainment industry, for example, entertain themselves less and less and have become more and more passively dependent

on commercial suppliers. This is certainly true also of patrons of the food industry, who have tended more and more to be mere consumers—passive, uncritical, and dependent. Indeed, this sort of consumption may be said to be one of the chief goals of industrial production. The food industrialists have by now persuaded millions of consumers to prefer food that is already prepared. They will grow, deliver, and cook your food for you and (just like your mother) beg you to eat it. That they do not yet offer to insert it, prechewed, into our mouth is only because they have found no profitable way to do so. We may rest assured that they would be glad to find such a way. The ideal industrial food consumer would be strapped to a table with a tube running from the food factory directly into his or her stomach.

Perhaps I exaggerate, but not by much. The industrial eater is, in fact, one who does not know that eating is an agricultural act, who no longer knows or imagines the connections between eating and the land, and who is therefore necessarily passive and uncritical—in short, a victim. When food, in the minds of eaters, is no longer associated with farming and with the land, then the eaters are suffering a kind of cultural amnesia that is misleading and dangerous. The current version of the "dream home" of the future involves "effortless" shopping from a list of available goods on a television monitor and heating precooked food by remote control. Of course, this implies and depends on, a perfect ignorance of the history of the food that is consumed. It requires that the citizenry should give up their hereditary and sensible aversion to buying a pig in a poke. It wishes to make the selling of pigs in pokes an honorable and glamorous activity. The dreams in this dream home will perforce know nothing about the kind or quality of this food, or where it came from, or how it was produced and prepared, or what ingredients, additives, and residues it contains—unless, that is, the dreamer undertakes a close and constant study of the food industry, in which case he or she might as well wake up and play an active and responsible part in the economy of food.

There is, then, a politics of food that, like any politics, involves our freedom. We still (sometimes) remember that we cannot be free if our minds and voices are controlled by someone else. But we have neglected to understand that we cannot be free if our food and its sources are controlled by someone else. The condition of the passive consumer of food is not a democratic condition. One reason to eat responsibly is to live free.

But if there is a food politics, there are also a food esthetics and a food ethics, neither of which is dissociated from politics. Like industrial sex, industrial eating has become a degraded, poor, and paltry thing. Our kitchens and other eating places more and more resemble filling stations, as our homes more and more resemble motels. "Life is not very interesting," we seem to have decided. "Let its satisfactions be minimal, perfunctory, and fast." We hurry through our meals to go to work and hurry through our work in order to "recreate" ourselves in the evenings and on weekends and vacations. And then we hurry, with the greatest possible speed and noise and violence, through our recreation—for what? To eat the billionth hamburger at some fast-food joint hellbent on increasing the "quality" of our life? And all this is carried out in a remarkable obliviousness to the causes and effects, the possibilities and the purposes, of the life of the body in this world.

One will find this obliviousness represented in virgin purity in the advertisements of the food industry, in which food wears as much makeup as the actors. If one gained one's whole knowledge of food from these advertisements (as some presumably do), one would not know that the various edibles were ever living creatures, or that they all come from the soil, or that they were produced by work. The passive American consumer, sitting down to a meal of pre-prepared or fast food, confronts a platter covered with inert, anonymous substances that have been processed, dyed, breaded, sauced, gravied, ground, pulped, strained, blended, prettified, and sanitized beyond resemblance to any part of any creature that ever lived. The products of nature and agriculture have been made, to all appearances, the products of industry. Both eater and eaten are thus in exile from biological reality. And the result is a kind of solitude, unprecedented in human experience, in which the eater may think of eating as, first, a purely commercial transaction between him and a supplier and then as a purely appetitive transaction between him and his food.

10   And this peculiar specialization of the act of eating is, again, of obvious benefit to the food industry, which has good reasons to obscure the connection between food and farming. It would not do for the consumer to know that the hamburger she is eating came from a steer who spent much of his life standing deep in his own excrement in a feedlot, helping to pollute the local streams, or that the calf that yielded the veal cutlet on her plate spent its life in a box in which it did not have room to turn around. And, though her sympathy for the slaw might be less tender, she should not be encouraged to meditate on the hygienic and biological implications of mile-square fields of cabbage, for vegetables grown in huge monocultures are dependent on toxic chemicals—just as animals in close confinements are dependent on antibiotics and other drugs.

The consumer, that is to say, must be kept from discovering that, in the food industry—as in any other industry—the overriding concerns are not quality and health, but volume and price. For decades now the entire industrial food economy, from the large farms and feedlots to the chains of supermarkets and fast-food restaurants, has been obsessed with volume. It has relentlessly increased scale in order to increase volume in order (probably) to reduce costs. But as scale increases, diversity declines; as diversity declines, so does health; as health declines, the dependence on drugs and chemicals necessarily increases. As capital replaces labor, it does so by substituting machines, drugs, and chemicals for human workers and for the natural health and fertility of the soil. The food is produced by any means or any shortcuts that will increase profits. And the business of the cosmeticians of advertising is to persuade the consumer that food so produced is good, tasty, healthful, and a guarantee of marital fidelity and long life.

It is possible, then, to be liberated from the husbandry and wifery of the old household food economy. But one can be thus liberated only by entering a trap (unless one sees ignorance and helplessness as the signs of privilege, as many people apparently do). The trap is the ideal of industrialism: a walled city surrounded by valves that let merchandise in but no consciousness out. How does one escape this trap? Only voluntarily, the same way that one went in: by restoring one's consciousness of what is involved in eating; by reclaiming responsibility for one's own part in the food economy. One might begin with the illuminating principle of Sir Albert Howard's *The Soil and Health,* that we should understand "the whole problem of health in soil, plant, animal, and man as one great subject." Eaters, that is, must understand that eating takes place inescapably in the world, that it is inescapably an agricultural act, and that how we eat determines, to a considerable extent, how the world is used. This is a simple way of describing a relationship that is inexpressibly complex. To eat responsibly is to understand and enact, so far as one can, this complex relationship.

What can one do? Here is a list, probably not definitive:

1. Participate in food production to the extent that you can. If you have a yard or even just a porch box or a pot in a sunny window, grow something to eat in it. Make a little compost of your kitchen scraps and use it for fertilizer. Only by growing some food for yourself can you become acquainted with the beautiful energy cycle that revolves from soil to seed to flower to fruit to food to offal to decay, and around again. You will be fully responsible for any food that you grow for yourself, and you will know all about it. You will appreciate it fully, having known it all its life.

2. Prepare your own food. This means reviving in your own mind and life the arts of kitchen and household. This should enable you to eat more cheaply, and it will give you a measure of "quality control": you will have some reliable knowledge of what has been added to the food you eat.

3. Learn the origins of the food you buy, and buy the food that is produced closest to your home. The idea that every locality should be, as much as possible, the source of its own food makes several kinds of sense. The locally produced food supply is the most secure, the freshest, and the easiest for local consumers to know about and to influence.

4. Whenever possible, deal directly with a local farmer, gardener, or orchardist. All the reasons listed for the previous suggestion apply here. In addition, by such dealing you eliminate the whole pack of merchants, transporters, processors, packagers. and advertisers who thrive at the expense of both producers and consumers.

5. Learn, in self-defense, as much as you can of the economy and technology of industrial food production. What is added to food that is not food, and what do you pay for these additions?

6. Learn what is involved in the best farming and gardening.

7. Learn as much as you can, by direct observation and experience if possible, of the life histories of the food species.

The last suggestion seems particularly important to me. Many people are now as much estranged from the lives of domestic plants and animals (except for flowers and dogs and cats) as they are from the lives of the wild ones. This is regrettable, for these domestic creatures are in diverse ways attractive; there is much pleasure in knowing them. And farming, animal husbandry, horticulture, and gardening, at their best, are complex and comely arts; there is much pleasure in knowing them, too.

15   It follows that there is great displeasure in knowing about a food economy that degrades and abuses those arts and those plants and animals and the soil from which they come. For anyone who does know something of the modern history of food, eating away from home can be a chore. My own inclination is to eat sea-

food instead of red meat or poultry when I am traveling. Though I am by no means a vegetarian, I dislike the thought that some animal has been made miserable in order to feed me. If I am going to eat meat, I want it to be from an animal that has lived a pleasant, uncrowned life outdoors, on bountiful pasture, with good water nearby and trees for shade. And I am getting almost as fussy about food plants. I like to eat vegetables and fruits that I know have lived happily and healthily in good soil. not the products of the huge, bechemicaled factory-fields that I have seen, for example, in the Central Valley of California. The industrial farm is said to have been patterned on the factory production line. In practice, it looks more like a concentration camp.

The pleasure of eating should be an extensive pleasure, not that of the mere gourmet. People who know the garden in which their vegetables have grown and know that the garden is healthy will remember the beauty of the growing plants, perhaps in the dewy first light of morning when gardens are at their best. Such a memory involves itself with the food and is one of the pleasures of eating. The knowledge of the good health of the garden relieves and frees and comforts the eater. The same goes for eating meat. The thought of the good pasture and of the calf contentedly grazing flavors the steak. Some, I know, will think it bloodthirsty or worse to eat a fellow creature you have known all its life. On the contrary, I think it means that you eat with understanding and with gratitude. A significant part of the pleasure of eating is in one's accurate consciousness of the lives and the world from which food comes. The pleasure of eating, then, may be the best available standard of our health. And this pleasure, I think, is pretty fully available to the urban consumer who will make the necessary effort.

I mentioned earlier the politics, esthetics, and ethics of food. But to speak of the pleasure of eating is to go beyond those categories. Eating with the fullest pleasure—pleasure, that is, that does not depend on ignorance—is perhaps the profoundest enactment of our connection with the world. In this pleasure we experience and celebrate our dependence and our gratitude, for we are living from mystery, from creatures we did not make and powers we cannot comprehend. When I think of the meaning of food, I always remember these lines by the poet William Carlos Williams, which seem to me merely honest:

> There is nothing to eat,
>   seek it where you will,
>   but the body of the Lord.
> The blessed plants
>   and the sea, yield it
>   to the imagination
> intact.

RESPONSE QUESTIONS

1. What does Berry mean when he says, "Eating is an agricultural act"? How does he believe people can transform themselves from passive consumers to responsible eaters?

2. In paragraph 9, Berry describes advertisements in which "the food wears as much makeup as the actors." What ads or commercials come to mind? What purposes are served by advertising that disguises the real nature of food?

3. Berry wants to make us more mindful about eating. How is his purpose similar to Ellen Langer's in "When the Light's on and Nobody's Home"?

4. In what sense can it be good "to eat a fellow creature you have known all its life"? Do you agree with Berry's view in the next to final paragraph?

5. In addition to crying for awareness, the essay calls for action. Which of the proposed actions are you prepared to take toward restoring the pleasures of eating?

GUIDELINES FOR ANALYSIS

1. Berry's main idea can be summed up in two words: "eat responsibly." How does he expand this concept in the structure of his essay? What subtopics help to develop his idea of responsible eating?

2. In paragraph 4, Berry says that for most shoppers "food is pretty much an abstract idea." How does he make food more concrete? What illustrations and examples help the most?

3. Throughout his essay, Berry makes analogies. He compares industrial food to industrial sex and eating places to filling stations. He speaks of food aesthetics, food ethics, and the politics of food. What is the point of these analogies?

4. Compare this selection to Bodanis's essay, "Danish." In what sense do they share a common purpose? How do they differ in focus and style? What makes each essay effective in evaluating consumer products?

QUESTIONS OF CULTURE

1. Berry describes a consumer culture in which the food industry deliberately keeps people ignorant of the foods they eat. Who benefits from such a culture? Who loses out, and what do they lose?

2. In economic terms, Berry points out that volume and price replace quality and health as capital replaces labor. Explore the ideological implications of the view expressed in paragraph 11.

3. Many of Berry's suggestions have been adopted by the "slow food movement," which proposes to replace fast food with deliberate, pleasurable dining experiences. What other movements are aligned with his agenda?

IDEAS FOR YOUR JOURNAL

1. Record your eating habits. How often do you eat fast foods at home or away? When do you grow or prepare your own food? How well do you know the origins of what you eat?

2. Keep a log of the food advertisements and commercials you encounter in a day. How much of what Berry says about the food industry can you find in these ads?

PREVIEW

Our consumer culture can become so voracious that it sometimes seems to consume itself. In the following essay, Mary Kuntz assesses some recent trends in advertising. Anti-advertising activists have launched campaigns on several fronts to counteract the flood of ads that saturates our media-heavy culture. Meanwhile, advertisers have learned to respond in kind, creating their own parody ads to poke fun at each other and co-opt the culture jam. Kuntz's essay first appeared in the Marketing section of *Business Week* in 1998. Mary Kuntz is now a senior editor at *Business Week*.

Is Nothing Sacred in the Ad Game?

By Mary Kuntz

In Northern California, a band recently released *Dispepsi,* a CD pieced together from bits of music, ads, and interviews to create a scathing (and entertaining) commentary on the nation's second-largest soft-drink company. In New Jersey, a coalition of artists alters billboards in minority neighborhoods, adding touches such as a banner on a Newport cigarette ad that reads "Healthy profits don't always require living customers." And *Adbusters,* a nine-year-old Canadian quarterly devoted to the art of the "culture jam"—as such rearranged anti-advertising ads are called— reaches 30,000 subscribers, mostly in the U.S.

With sales messages assaulting us in every possible venue, it's no wonder that there's a growing cadre of activists who simply loathe ads and the industry that perpetrates them. What is more surprising is the growing sophistication of the backlash. Thanks to the advent of desktop publishing and the Internet, these grassroots critics are increasingly fighting Madison Avenue with the industry's own techniques. Just look at the fake ad on the back cover of *Stay Free!,* a tiny New York-based 'zine that critiques consumer culture. The typeface and photography look like the familiar Dewars campaign featuring attractive, sophisticated young imbibers, but the tagline reads: "Remember how liquor used to make you vomit?"

Corporate America's reaction to these lampoons is muted. "No comment," says Jan Sharkansky, a spokesperson for Calvin Klein Cosmetics Co., when asked about an *Adbusters* "ad" that shows a muscle-bound young man peering intently down his fashionable underwear under the headline "Obsession." Others in the ad community say they're barely aware of culture jammers and that, in any case, there's no advantage to trying to stop such small fry.

But while advertisers may be oblivious to the politics and polemics behind culture jam-

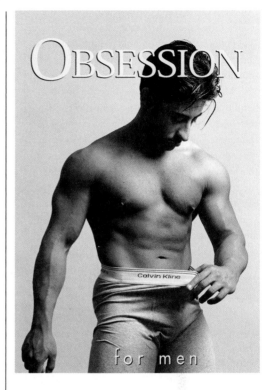

ming, they have been quick to intuit the value of a clever parody. Copping the same hip, ironic attitudes and playing to the same consumer cynicism, big-time marketers have begun to lampoon one another. "It punctures the pomposity because you're telling people something real," says David Suissa, chairman and executive creative director for Suissa Miller Advertising Inc., which produced a series of parody ads for Boston Chicken Inc. last year mocking Calvin Klein's anorexic models.

"Killing the Planet"

Adland's embrace of parody has blunted one of the culture jammers' favorite weapons, but not their ardor. Take 29-year-old Carrie Mclaren.

A record promoter by day, she publishes *Stay Free!*—with such articles as "Singled Out: An alarmist look at ultra-targeted marketing"—largely at her own expense. Why? "It's not just advertising, it's the overall commercialization of the planet," she says. Others cite ecological concerns. "We believe that our corporate culture is unsustainable," says Kalle Lasn, *Adbusters'* editor and founder. "Economic progress is killing the planet."

Mark Hosler of Negativland, the Bay Area band that released *Dispepsi,* also believes that the sheer volume of advertising is degrading to the mental and physical environment. "It isn't that advertising per se is evil, it's the amount of it that's going on," says Hosler, whose band coined the term "culture jamming." He argues that the wealth and might of giant marketers makes it difficult for opposing viewpoints to be heard. The aim of culture jamming: to break through that clutter by playing off the powerful messages and icons already out there.

There's also a political strand. Cicada Corps of Artists, the New Jersey group, alters tobacco and liquor billboards in minority neighborhoods, which they say receive a disproportionate share of such advertising. Defacing billboards is illegal, but group member Pedro Carvajal believes their activities are justified: "Alternatives have been taken away because they [advertisers] have all the money. We had to go underground."

Advertisers say the backlash from fringe groups is simply too puny to register on their radar screens. Maybe, but some parody protest ads have begun showing up in more traditional media. During a labor dispute with a Miller Brewing Co. distributor in St. Louis three years ago, the Teamsters put up a billboard mocking a Miller ad. Instead of two bottles of beer in a snowbank with the tagline "Two Cold," the ad showed two frozen workers in a snowbank labeled "Too Cold: Miller canned 88 St. Louis workers." Ron Carver, coordinator of strategic campaigns for the Teamsters, says the union has since used similar parodies in

disputes to great effect. "When you're doing this, you're threatening multimillion-dollar ad campaigns," he says.

Tobacco lampoons have also moved into the mainstream. Scott Plous, a psychology professor at Wesleyan University, is incensed at what he sees as the blatant appeal to kids by Big Tobacco. So a few years ago, he countered with his own cartoon character, Joe Chemo, who bears more than a passing resemblance to a certain familiar dromedary. With the help of various antismoking groups, Joe Chemo has moved from the pages of *Adbusters* to billboards in downtown Seattle, posters in public schools, and T-shirts given away to kids.

Lawsuits

Many big brands aren't as willing to shrug off the spoofs when they're done nationally by a fellow marketer. Digital Equipment Corp.'s discomfort with rival Hewlett-Packard Co.'s parody was understandable. Running just once in a few national publications, the ad replaced the "Digital" in the company's trademark red blocks with the word "worried?" in the same typeface. Appealing to customers left anxious by DEC's recent merger with Compaq Computer Corp., the ad brought in millions of dollars of business, says Nick Earle, marketing manager for HP's Enterprise Systems Group. Digital's response: a letter to HP alleging trademark infringement and demanding a halt to the ads.

Even mainstream ad parodies that aren't launched by rivals often seem to result in allegations and lawsuits. Mattel's sensitivity on the subject of Barbie is legendary. The company moved quickly to quash a recent Nissan ad that featured Barbie-and-Ken-like dolls. And Nike Inc., whose attitude-filled commercials have made it a favorite parody target, found nothing humorous about a recent campaign by Candie's Inc. for colorful new sneakers featuring actress Jenny McCarthy. The tagline: "Just Screw it." Nike fired off a cease-and-desist letter.

Heineken USA Inc. avoided litigation by taking parody a step further. A campaign for its Amstel brand involved billboards and TV spots denouncing it as an evil import from "free-thinking" Amsterdam. The campaign, supposedly by the fictitious Americans for Disciplined Behavior, won publicity when the prank was uncovered.

As the loop closes, it's getting harder to tell those who parody from those who are parodied, partly because it is virtually impossible to shame Madison Avenue. Two years ago, Negativland's Hosler got a call from hip Portland-based ad agency Wieden & Kennedy Inc. raving about the band's work and asking if it would like to make a spot for Miller. "I think they were sort of mystified about why we turned them down," he says. And that may be the ultimate irony. Advertisers crave a hip, cutting-edge attitude—even if it comes from their most ardent detractors.

RESPONSE QUESTIONS

1. Mary Kuntz refers to a number of people who dislike advertising and fear the cumulative effect of ads on the media environment. Do you share their views and concerns? Explain your opinion of the advertising industry today.

2. How does the author define *culture jam?* What examples does she give? Give your own examples of culture jamming based on your experience with media.

3. Identify an ad that you believe deserves to be jammed. What makes the ad a prime target?

4. Kuntz concludes, "it's getting harder to tell those who parody from those who are parodied." Do you agree? What examples can you offer to support your observation?

GUIDELINES FOR ANALYSIS

1. Kuntz begins by identifying groups in three different geographical areas that actively oppose ads. Where in her essay does she return to these three groups? How does she use these examples to develop her thesis about culture jamming?

2. The author describes both anti-advertising activists and big-time marketers. What trends does she see between these two groups? How does she relate these trends in the organization of her essay? What other groups does she include?

3. The essay originally appeared in *Business Week*. What steps has the author taken to appeal to readers of this magazine?

4. Kuntz makes regular use of topic sentences, transitions, and quotations. Which paragraphs begin with topic sentences to introduce subtopics? Which paragraphs begin with transitional sentences to bridge the gap between subtopics? Which paragraphs end with a quotation that summarizes a key idea?

QUESTIONS OF CULTURE

1. What does the term *culture jamming* imply about our culture? Identify the cultural beliefs that modern advertising practices promote. What values are being threatened?

2. Kuntz describes a group in New Jersey that illegally alters billboards in minority neighborhoods. What political motives can you see in this action? Do you think that such underground activities are justified when the activists have fewer resources than their opponents? Explain.

1. There is an Adbusters parody on page 42 of the Introduction. Visit Adbusters' Web site at www.adbusters.org for more examples. Find one or two parodies that you like, and explain why you think each parody works.

2. Create your own ad spoof, or plan an anti-ad campaign. Describe how you would proceed to publicize the spoof or launch the campaign.

3. Imagine you are working for an advertising agency. How might you respond to culture jamming of the products that you represent?

PREVIEW

Toni Cade Bambara was born in 1939 in New York City and raised in the poor neighborhoods of Harlem, Bedford-Stuyvesant, and Jersey City, New Jersey. An enthusiastic and able student, she majored in English at Queens College and studied theatre in Italy. Early in her career she worked for the New York State Department of Social Welfare, but later turned to writing and teaching. In the 1960s, Bambara was active in the civil rights movement, becoming a strong advocate for racial equality and social justice. Her short stories, novels, and anthologies often center on African American women whose experiences move them to new levels of social consciousness. These works include *Gorilla, My Love* (1972), *The Salt Eaters* (1980), *If Blessing Comes* (1987), and *Deep Sightings and Rescue Missions: Fiction, Essays, and Conversations* (1996). She died of cancer in 1995. "The Lesson" originally appeared in *Gorilla, My Love*.

The Lesson
By Toni Cade Bambara

Back in the days when everyone was old and stupid or young and foolish and me and Sugar were the only ones just right, this lady moved on our block with nappy hair and proper speech and no makeup. And quite naturally we laughed at her, laughed the way we did at the junk man who went about his business like he was some big-time president and his sorry-ass horse his secretary. And we kinda hated her too, hated the way we did the winos who cluttered up our parks and pissed on our handball walls and stank up our hallways and stairs so you couldn't halfway play hide-and-seek without a goddamn gas mask. Miss Moore was her name. The only woman on the block with no first name. And she was black as hell, cept for her feet, which were fish-white and spooky. And she was always planning these boring-ass things for us to do, us being my cousin, mostly, who lived on the block cause we all moved North the same time and to the same apartment then spread out gradual to breathe. And our parents would yank our heads into some kinda shape and crisp up our clothes so we'd be presentable for travel with Miss Moore, who always looked like she was going to church though she never did. Which is just one of the things the grownups talked about when they talked behind her back like a dog. But when she came calling with some sachet she'd sewed up or some gingerbread she'd made or some book, why then they'd all be too embarrassed to turn her down and we'd get handed over all spruced up. She'd been to college and said it was only right that she should take responsibility for the young ones' education, and she not even related by marriage or blood. So they'd go for it. Specially Aunt Gretchen. She was the main gofer in the family. You got some ole dumb shit foolishness you want somebody to go for, you send for Aunt Gretchen. She been screwed into the go-along for so long, it's a blood-deep natural thing with her. Which is how she got saddled with me and Sugar and Junior in the first place while our mothers were in a la-de-da apartment up the block having a good ole time.

So this one day Miss Moore rounds us all up at the mailbox and it's puredee hot and she's knockin herself out about arithmetic. And school suppose to let up in summer I heard, but she don't never let up. And the starch in my pinafore scratching the shit outta me and I'm really hating this nappy-head bitch and her goddamn college degree. I'd much rather go to the pool or to the show where it's cool. So me and Sugar leaning on the mailbox being surly, which is a Miss Moore word. And Flyboy checking out what everybody brought for lunch. And Fat Butt already wasting his peanut-butter-and-jelly sandwich like the pig he is. And Junebug punchin on Q.T.'s arm for potato chips. And Rosie Giraffe shifting from one hip to the other waiting for somebody to step on her foot or ask her if she from Georgia so she can kick ass, preferably Mercedes'. And Miss Moore asking us do we know what money is like we a bunch of retards. I mean real money, she say, like it's only poker chips or monopoly papers we lay on the grocer. So right away I'm tired of this and say so. And would much rather snatch Sugar and go to the Sunset and terrorize the West Indian kids and take their hair ribbons and their money too. And Miss Moore files that remark away for next week's lesson on brotherhood, I can tell. And finally I say we oughta get to the subway cause it's cooler an' besides we might meet some cute boys. Sugar done swiped her mama's lipstick, so we ready.

So we heading down the street and she's boring us silly about what things cost and what our parents make and how much goes for rent and how money ain't divided up right in this country. And then she gets to the part about we all poor and live in the slums which I don't feature. And I'm ready to speak on that, but she steps out in the street and hails two cabs just like that. Then she hustles half the crew in with her and hands me a five-dollar bill and tells me to calculate 10 percent tip for the driver. And we're off. Me and Sugar and Junebug and Flyboy hangin out the window and hollering to everybody, putting lipstick on each other cause Flyboy a faggot anyway, and making farts with our sweaty armpits. But I'm mostly trying to figure how to spend this money. But they are fascinated with the meter ticking and Junebug starts laying bets as to how much it'll read when Flyboy can't hold his breath no more. Then Sugar lays bets as to how much it'll be when we get there. So I'm stuck. Don't nobody want to go for my plan, which is to jump out at the next light and run off to the first bar-b-que we can find. Then the driver tells us to get the hell out cause we there already. And the meter reads eighty-five cents. And I'm stalling to figure out the tip and Sugar say give him a dime. And I decide he don't need it bad as I do, so later for him. But then he tries to take off with Junebug foot still in the door so we talk about his mama something ferocious. Then we check out that we on Fifth Avenue and everybody dressed up in stockings. One lady in a fur coat, hot as it is. White folks crazy.

"This is the place, " Miss Moore say, presenting it to us in the voice she uses at the museum. "Let's look in the windows before we go in."

5   "Can we steal?" Sugar asks very serious like she's getting the ground rules squared away before she plays. "I beg your pardon," say Miss Moore, and we fall out. So she leads us around the windows of the toy store and me and Sugar screamin, "This is mine, that's mine, I gotta have that, that was made for me, I was born for that," till Big Butt drowns us out.

"Hey, I'm goin to buy that there."

"That there? You don't even know what it is, stupid."

"I do so," he say punchin on Rosie Giraffe. "It's a microscope."

"Whatcha gonna do with a microscope, fool?"

10   "Look at things."

"Like what, Ronald?" ask Miss Moore. And Big Butt ain't got the first notion. So here go Miss Moore gabbing about the thousands of bacteria in a drop of water and the somethinorother in a speck of blood and the million and one living things in the air around us is invisible to the naked eye. And what she say that for? Junebug go to town on that "naked" and we rolling. Then Miss Moore ask what it cost. So we all jam into the window smudgin it up and the price tag say $300. So then she ask how long'd take for Big Butt and Junebug to save up their allowances. "Too long," I say. "Yeh," adds Sugar, "outgrown it by that time." And Miss Moore say no, you never outgrow learning instruments. "Why, even medical students and interns and," blah, blah, blah. And we ready to choke Big Butt for bringing it up in the first damn place.

"This here costs four hundred eighty dollars," say Rosie Giraffe. So we pile up all over her to see what she pointin out. My eyes tell me it's a chunk of glass cracked with something heavy, and different-color inks dripped into the splits, then the whole thing put into a oven or something. But for $480 it don't make sense.

"That's a paperweight made of semi-precious stones fused together under tremendous pressure," she explains slowly, with her hands doing the mining and all the factory work.

"So what's a paperweight?" asks Rosie Giraffe.

15   "To weigh paper with, dumbbell," say Flyboy, the wise man from the East.

"Not exactly," say Miss Moore, which is what she say when you warm or way off too. "It's to weigh paper down so it won't scatter and make your desk untidy." So right away me and Sugar curtsy to each other and then to Mercedes who is more the tidy type.

"We don't keep paper on top of the desk in my class," say Junebug, figuring Miss Moore crazy or lyin one.

"At home, then," she say. "Don't you have a calendar and a pencil case and a blotter and a letter-opener on your desk at home where you do your homework?" And she know damn well what our homes look like cause she nosys around in them every chance she gets.

"I don't even have a desk," say Junebug. "Do we?"

20   "No. And I don't get no homework neither," says Big Butt.

"And I don't even have a home," say Flyboy like he do at school to keep the white folks off his back and sorry for him. Send this poor kid to camp posters, is his specialty.

"I do," says Mercedes. "I have a box of stationery on my desk and a picture of my cat. My godmother bought the stationery and the desk. There's a big rose on each sheet and the envelopes smell like roses."

"Who wants to know about your smelly-ass stationery," say Rosie Giraffe fore I can get my two cents in.

"It's important to have a work area all your own so that . . ."

25   "Will you look at this sailboat, please," say Flyboy, cuttin her off and pointin to the thing like it was his. So once again we tumble all over each other to gaze at this magnificent thing in the toy store which is just big enough to maybe sail two kittens across the pond if you strap them to the posts tight. We all start reciting the price tag like we in assembly. "Hand-crafted sailboat of fiberglass at one thousand one hundred ninety-five dollars."

"Unbelievable," I hear myself say and am really stunned. I read it again for myself just in case the group recitation put me in a trance. Same thing. For some reason this pisses me off. We look at Miss Moore and she lookin at us, waiting for I dunno what.

"Who'd pay all that when you can buy a sailboat set for a quarter at Pop's, a tube of glue for a dime, and a ball of string for eight cents? It must have a motor and a whole lot else besides," I say. "My sailboat cost me about fifty cents."

"But will it take water?" say Mercedes with her smart ass.

"Took mine to Alley Pond Park once," say Flyboy. "String broke. Lost it. Pity."

30 "Sailed mine in Central Park and it keeled over and sank. Had to ask my father for another dollar."

"And you got the strap," laugh Big Butt. "The jerk didn't even have a string on it. My old man wailed on his behind."

Little Q.T. was staring hard at the sailboat and you could see he wanted it bad. But he too little and somebody'd just take it from him. So what the hell. "This boat for kids, Miss Moore?"

"Parents silly to buy something like that just to get all broke up," say Rosie Giraffe.

"That much money it should last forever," I figure.

35 "My father'd buy it for me if I wanted it."

"Your father, my ass," say Rosie Giraffe getting a chance to finally push Mercedes.

"Must be rich people shop here," say Q.T.

"You are a very bright boy," say Flyboy. "What was your first clue?" And he rap him on the head with the back of his knuckles, since Q.T. the only one he could get away with. Though Q.T. liable to come up behind you years later and get his licks in when you half expect it.

"What I want to know is," I says to Miss Moore though I never talk to her, I wouldn't give the bitch that satisfaction, "is how much a real boat costs? I figure a thousand'd get you a yacht any day."

40 "Why don't you check that out," she says, "and report back to the group?" Which really pains my ass. If you gonna mess up a perfectly good swim day least you could do is have some answers. "Let's go in," she say like she got something up her sleeve. Only she don't lead the way. So me and Sugar turn the corner to where the entrance is, but when we get there I kinda hang back. Not that I'm scared, what's there to be afraid of, just a toy store. But I feel funny, shame. But what I got to be shamed about? Got as much right to go in as anybody. But somehow I can't seem to get hold of the door, so I step away from Sugar to lead. But she hangs back too. And I look at her and she looks at me and this is ridiculous. I mean, damn, I have never ever been shy about doing nothing or going nowhere. But then Mercedes steps up and then Rosie Giraffe and Big Butt crowd in behind and shove, and next thing we all stuffed into the doorway with only Mercedes squeezing past us, smoothing out her jumper and walking right down the aisle. Then the rest of us tumble in like a glued-together jigsaw done all wrong. And people lookin at us. And it's like the time me and Sugar crashed into the Catholic church on a dare. But once we got in there and everything so hushed and holy and the candles and the bowin and the handkerchiefs on all the drooping heads, I just couldn't go through with the plan. Which was for me to run up to the altar and do a tap dance while Sugar played the nose flute and messed around in the holy water. And Sugar kept givin me the elbow. Then later teased me so bad I tied her up in the shower and turned it on and locked her in. And she'd be there till this day if Aunt Gretchen hadn't finally figured I was lyin about the boarder takin a shower.

Same thing in the store. We all walkin on tiptoe and hardly touchin the games and puzzles and things. And I watched Miss Moore who is steady watchin us like she waitin for a sign. Like Mama Drewery watches the sky and sniffs the air and takes note of just how much slant is in the bird formation. Then me and Sugar bump smack into each other, so busy gazing at the toys, 'specially the sailboat. But we don't laugh and go into our fat-lady bump-stomach routine. We just stare at that price tag. Then Sugar run a finger over the whole boat. And I'm jealous and want to hit her. Maybe not her, but I sure want to punch somebody in the mouth.

"Watcha bring us here for, Miss Moore?"

"You sound angry, Sylvia. Are you mad about something?" Givin me one of them grins like she tellin a grown-up joke that never turns out to be funny. And she's lookin very closely at me like maybe she plannin to do my portrait from memory. I'm mad, but I won't give her that satisfaction. So I slouch around the store bein very bored and say, "Let's go."

Me and Sugar at the back of the train watchin the tracks whizzin by large then small then gettin gobbled up in the dark. I'm thinkin about this tricky toy I saw in the store. A clown that somersaults on a bar then does chin-ups just cause you yank lightly at his leg. Cost $35. I could see me askin my mother for a $35 birthday clown. "You wanna who that costs what?" she'd say, cocking her head to the side to get a better view of the hole in my head. Thirty-five dollars could buy new bunk beds for Junior and Gretchen's boy. Thirty-five dollars and the whole household could go visit Grand-daddy Nelson in the country. Thirty-five dollars would pay for the rent and the piano bill too. Who are these people that spend that much for performing clowns and $1000 for toy sailboats? What kinda work they do and how they live and how come we ain't in on it? Where we are is who we are, Miss Moore always pointin out. But it don't necessarily have to be that way, she always adds then waits for somebody to say that poor people have to wake up and demand their share of the pie and don't none of us know what kind of pie she talking about in the first damn place. But she ain't so smart cause I still got her four dollars from the taxi and she sure ain't gettin it. Messin up my day with this shit. Sugar nudges me in my pocket and winks.

45   Miss Moore lines us up in front of the mailbox where we started from, seem like years ago, and I got a headache for thinkin so hard. And we lean all over each other so we can hold up under the draggy ass lecture she always finishes us off with at the end before we thank her for borin us to tears. But she just looks at us like she readin tea leaves. Finally she say, "Well, what did you think of F. A. O. Schwartz?"

Rosie Giraffe mumbles, "White folks crazy."

"I'd like to go there again when I get my birthday money," says Mercedes, and we shove her out the pack so she has to lean on the mailbox by herself.

"I'd like a shower. Tiring day," say Flyboy.

Then Sugar surprises me by sayin, "You know, Miss Moore, I don't think all of us here put together eat in a year what that sailboat costs." And Miss Moore lights up like somebody goosed her. "And?" she say, urging Sugar on. Only I'm standin on her foot so she don't continue.

50   "Imagine for a minute what kind of society it is in which some people can spend on a toy what it would cost to feed a family of six or seven. What do you think?"

"I think," say Sugar pushing me off her feet like she never done before cause I whip her ass in a minute, "that this is not much of a democracy if you ask me. Equal chance to pursue happiness means an equal crack at the dough, don't it?" Miss Moore is besides herself and I am disgusted with Sugar's treachery. So I stand on her foot one more time to see if she'll shove me. She shuts up, and Miss Moore looks at me, sorrowfully I'm thinkin. And somethin weird is goin on, I can feel it in my chest. "Anybody else learn anything today?" lookin dead at me. I walk away and Sugar has to run to catch up and don't even seem to notice when I shrug her arm off my shoulder.

"Well, we got four dollars anyway," she says. "Uh hun."

"We could go to Hascombs and get half a chocolate layer and then go to the Sunset and still have plenty money for potato chips and ice cream sodas."

"Uh hun."

55   "Race you to Hascombs," she say.

We start down the block and she gets ahead which is O.K. by me cause I'm going to the West End and then over to the Drive to think this day through. She can run if she want to and even run faster. But ain't nobody gonna beat me at nuthin.

RESPONSE QUESTIONS

1. How old do you think the narrator is? Recall your own outlook on school at that age. To what extent can you identify with the narrator?

2. Most of the narrator's friends and relatives have nicknames. What kind of relationships do these nicknames suggest? How attentive is the narrator to these relationships?

3. When Miss Moore asks her class if they know what money is, the narrator responds sarcastically. What is the point of Miss Moore's question? How does it prepare the narrator (and readers) for the lesson that follows?

4. Why does the narrator feel shame on entering F. A. O. Schwartz? How do the other children respond at first to the expensive toys? Why does the narrator want to punch somebody after watching Sugar touch the toy boat?

5. Although "The Lesson" is a work of fiction, it points to certain truths about consumer culture in America. How might Wendell Berry, Mary Kuntz, or one of the other essayists in this chapter respond to the story's theme or themes?

GUIDELINES FOR ANALYSIS

1. How does the narrator characterize her teacher? What sets Miss Moore apart from others in her community? Why does the narrator say she hates Miss Moore?

2. Describe the story's setting. Where and when does it take place? What is the narrator's attitude toward her environment at the beginning of the story? Do you see any changes in this attitude?

3. The narrator often speaks in the third person of "we" and "us." Who is she referring to? To what degree is the narrator identified with a group? To what extent does she appear to be an individual?

4. The conflict in the story can be said to start even before Miss Moore announces the class trip. What forces are in conflict? Where do they come to a climax? Is there a recognition scene, where the narrator understands the true nature of her condition? If so, what lesson does she understand?

QUESTIONS OF CULTURE

1. When the class arrives at Fifth Avenue, Sugar asks, "Can we steal?" How serious do you think she is? What attitude about private property is implied by her question?

2. Sociologists sometimes speak of the "culture of poverty." What values, practices, and beliefs do you associate with such a culture?

3. A rich person can feel poor, and a poor person can feel rich. Explain why you agree or disagree with this statement, and apply your answer to the story.

4. Rosie says, "White folks crazy." Sugar says, "This is not much of a democracy if you ask me." Why do you think the children make these statements? What judgments about race and politics can you find in the story?

1. Recall a time when you wanted something beyond your means. What did you want, and how did it feel that you could not afford it? What lessons have you learned about money, wants, and values since then?

2. Read one or two reviews of a product you consider to be excessively expensive. Then write a critique, not of the product but of the system that produced it.

PREVIEW: THREE FILM REVIEWS: *THE MATRIX*

Here are three reviews of *The Matrix* from the date of its original release in 1999. Since then, the movie has been seen by millions of people around the world, discussed and watched over and over again on video and DVD. *The Matrix* has generated two feature-length sequels, a popular

video game, animation shorts, and many imitations. How accurately did the early reviewers predict this phenomenon? As you compare these three reviews, consider their intended audiences as well as their distinctive purposes and styles. Notice what conceptions about movies and writing they have in common as well as how they differ. Which of the reviews do you consider best in terms of your criteria for a good movie review?

Dennis Lim reviews films for the *Village Voice,* a newsweekly based in New York City that has advocated "free-form, high-spirited and passionate journalism" since 1955. Roger Ebert, film critic for the *Chicago Sun-Times* since 1967 and co-host of a popular television show, is the only motion picture critic to have won the Pulitzer Prize for distinguished criticism (in 1975). Janet

Maslin, a film critic for the *New York Times* for many years, has recently turned to writing book reviews. Her own books include *Portraits of Love: Great Romances of the 20th Century* (2002).

Grand Allusions

by Dennis Lim

Working off the transcendently paranoid, made-for-movies premise that reality might be the grandest illusion of all, *The Matrix* comes on like an all-or-nothing mindfuck, hot-wired into the intense existential panic that courses through millennial anxiety attacks like *The Truman Show* and dystopian sci-fi trips from Philip K. Dick to last year's inventively convoluted *Dark City.* But the second film by Andy and Larry Wachowski (the brothers' follow-up to *Bound,* their obnoxious lesbian-chic-for-straight-guys neo-noir) turns out to be a tunnel-visioned crowd pleaser, and the spook factor that initially juices the movie evaporates in the interests of quick-fix set pieces. With big guns. And kick boxing.

There's plenty of plot to spill, so in the broadest possible terms: the world is in deep shit, but oh look, a Savior is on hand. *The Matrix* wears this biblical allusion like a bumper sticker, with a dopey, self-congratulatory smirk. The metaphor gets even more insane when you consider that The One (as he's repeatedly referred to) is, um, Keanu Reeves. In yet another blankly effortful performance, Reeves plays a computer nerd nicknamed Neo, who's led to his dubious destiny by a couple of enigmatic, leather-clad figures: the vixenish Trinity (Carrie-Anne Moss, underacting an underwritten role) and the stoic Morpheus (a no-bullshit Laurence Fishburne). They toy with Keanu's pretty little head for a while, but when the revelations arrive, they're suitably momentous, so I won't give

them away—suffice to say, it's not really 1999 after all.

The Matrix has all the makings of a cult—for starters, there's the too-much-information syndrome that fanboys revel in. Their central idea is vivid and enormously suggestive, but the Wachowskis' screenplay is composed mostly of mile-a-minute gobbledygook and mystic hogwash, and while the natural temptation is to deconstruct the mess, I suspect the film won't get any more coherent on subsequent viewings (finally, a movie tailor-made for Keanu's perpetual look of befuddlement). Virtual reality is relatively fresh and obviously fertile terrain for movies (it's the theme of David Cronenberg's upcoming *eXistenZ,* which is both more playful and more ingenious), and here, you wish it was more than simply a neat way of introducing really cool effects.

Ultimately, *The Matrix* settles for technically dazzling

comic-book shtick. Some might count this as a good thing, but I'm not a fan of the Wachowskis' more-is-more aesthetic, which they unleashed in the inappropriately florid *Bound,* and which has since turned even more grotesque. The visual effects (especially a shooting technique called "bullet-time photography" that applies animation tricks to live action) are impressive, but the movie's overall style is wearing. The camera (or computer program, as the case may be) calls attention to itself more than to what's within the frame, all swooping overheads and nutty angles. The John Woo on-speed shoot-outs and martial-arts tomfoolery, though tongue-in-cheek, are similarly histrionic (even if the virtual-reality context provides some sort of explanation for the gravity-defying acrobatics). The cumulative effect is perversely deflationary: long before it's over, the film has flushed the paranoia from its system.

The Matrix
by Roger Ebert

"The Matrix" is a visually dazzling cyberadventure, full of kinetic excitement, but it retreats to formula just when it's getting interesting. It's kind of a letdown when a movie begins by redefining the nature of reality, and ends with a

shoot-out. We want a leap of the imagination, not one of those obligatory climaxes with automatic weapons fire.

I've seen dozens if not hundreds of these exercises in violence, which recycle the same tired ideas: Bad guys fire thousands of rounds, but are unable to hit the good guy. Then it's down to the final showdown between good and evil—a mar-

tial arts battle in which the good guy gets pounded until he's almost dead, before he finds the inner will to fight back. Been there, seen that (although rarely done this well).

Too bad, because the set-up is intriguing. "The Matrix" recycles the premises of "Dark City" and "Strange Days," turns up the heat and the volume, and borrows the gravity-defying choreography of Hong Kong action movies. It's fun, but it could have been more. The directors are Larry and Andy Wachowski, who know how to make movies (their first film, "Bound," made my 10 best list in 1996). Here, with a big budget and veteran action producer Joel Silver, they've played it safer; there's nothing wrong with going for the Friday night action market, but you can aim higher and still do business.

Warning; spoilers ahead. The plot involves Neo (Keanu Reeves), a mild-mannered software author by day, a feared hacker by night. He's recruited by a cell of cyber-rebels, led by the profound Morpheus (Laurence Fishburne) and the leather-clad warrior Trinity (Carrie-Anne Moss). They've made a fundamental discovery about the world: It doesn't exist. It's actually a form of Virtual Reality, designed to lull us into lives of blind obedience to the "system." We obediently go to our crummy jobs every day, little realizing, as Morpheus tells Neo, that "Matrix is the wool that has been pulled over your eyes—that you are a slave."

5 The rebels want to crack the framework that holds the Matrix in place, and free mankind. Morpheus believes Neo is the Messianic "One" who can lead this rebellion, which requires mind power as much as physical strength. Arrayed against them are the Agents, who look like Blues Brothers. The movie's battles take place in Virtual Reality; the heroes' minds are plugged into the combat. (You can still get killed, though: "The body cannot live without the mind"). "Jacking in" like this was a concept in "Strange Days" and has also been suggested in novels by William Gibson ("Idoru") and others. The notion that the world is an artificial construction, designed by outsiders to deceive and use humans, is straight out of "Dark City." Both of those movies, however, explored their implications as the best science fiction often does. "Dark City" was fascinated by the Strangers who had a poignant dilemma: They were dying aliens who hoped to learn from human methods of adaptation and survival.

In "Matrix," on the other hand, there aren't flesh-and-blood creatures behind the illusion—only a computer program that can think, and learn. The Agents function primarily as opponents in a high-stakes computer game. The movie offers no clear explanation of why the Matrix-making program went to all that trouble. Of course, for a program, running is its own reward—but an intelligent program might bring terrifying logic to its decisions.

Both "Dark City" and "Strange Days" offered intriguing motivations for villainy. "Matrix" is more like a superhero comic book in which the fate of the world comes down to a titanic fist-fight between the designated representatives of good and evil. It's cruel, really, to put tantalizing ideas on the table and then ask the audience to be satisfied with a shoot-out and a martial arts duel. Let's assume Neo wins. What happens then to the billions who have just been "unplugged" from the Matrix? Do they still have jobs? Homes? Identities? All we get is an enigmatic voice-over exhortation at the movie's end. The paradox is that the Matrix world apparently resembles in every respect the pre-Matrix world. (I am reminded of the animated kid's film "Doug's 1st Movie," which has a VR experience in which everything is exactly like in real life, except more expensive.)

Still, I must not ignore the movie's virtues. It's great-looking, both in its design and in the kinetic energy that powers it. It uses flawlessly integrated special effects and animation to visualize regions of cyberspace. It creates fearsome creatures, including mechanical octopi. It morphs bodies with the abandon of "Terminator II." It uses f/x to allow Neo and Trinity to run horizontally on walls, and hang in the air long enough to deliver karate kicks. It has leaps through space, thrilling sequences involving fights on rooftops, helicopter rescues and battles over mind control.

And it has performances that find the right notes. Keanu Reeves goes for the impassive Harrison Ford approach, "acting" as little as possible. I suppose that's the right idea. Laurence Fishburne finds a balance between action hero and Zen master. Carrie-Anne Moss, as Trinity, has a sensational title sequence, before the movie recalls that she's a woman and shuttles her into support mode. Hugo Weaving, as the chief Agent, uses a flat, menacing tone that reminded me of Tommy Lee Jones in passive-aggressive overdrive. There's a well-acted scene involving Gloria Foster as the Oracle, who like all Oracles is maddeningly enigmatic.

"The Matrix" did not bore me. It interested me so much, indeed, that I wanted to be challenged even more. I wanted it to follow its material to audacious conclusions, to arrive not simply at victory, but at revelation. I wanted an ending that was transformational, like "Dark City's," and not one that simply throws us a sensational action sequence. I wanted, in short, a Third Act.

The Reality Is All Virtual, and Densely Complicated

by Janet Maslin

Action heroes speak volumes about the couch-potato audiences that they thrill. So it's understandable that "The Matrix," a furious special-effects tornado directed by the imaginative brothers Andy and Larry Wachowski ("Bound"), couldn't care less about the spies, cowboys and Rambos of times gone by. Aiming their film squarely at a generation bred on comics and computers, the Wachowskis stylishly envision the ultimate in cyberescapism, creating a movie that captures the duality of life a la laptop. Though the wildest exploits befall this film's sleek hero, most of its reality is so virtual that characters spend long spells of time lying stock still with their eyes closed.

In a film that's as likely to transfix fans of computer gamesmanship as to baffle anyone with quaintly humanistic notions of life on earth, the Wachowskis have synthesized a savvy visual vocabulary (thanks especially to Bill Pope's inspired techno-cinematography), a wild hodgepodge of classical references (from the biblical to Lewis Carroll) and a situation that calls for a lot of explaining.

The most salient things any prospective viewer need know is that Keanu Reeves makes a strikingly chic Prada model of an action hero, that the martial arts dynamics are phenomenal (thanks to Peter Pan–type wires for flying and inventive slow-motion tricks), and that anyone bored with the notably pretentious plotting can keep busy toting up this film's debts to other futuristic science fiction. Neat tricks here echo "Terminator" and "Alien" films, "The X-Files," "Men in Black" and "Strange Days," with a strong whiff of "2001: A Space Odyssey" in the battle royale being waged between man and computer. Nonetheless whatever recycling the brothers do here is canny enough to give "The Matrix" a strong identity of its own.

Mr. Reeves plays a late-20th-century computer hacker whose terminal begins telling him one fateful day that he may have some sort of messianic function in deciding the fate of the world. And what that function may be is so complicated that it takes the film the better part of an hour to explain. Dubbed Neo (in a film whose similarly portentous character names include Morpheus and

Trinity, with a time-traveling vehicle called Nebuchadnezzar), the hacker is gradually made to understand that everything he imagines to be real is actually the handiwork of 21st-century computers. These computers have subverted human beings into batterylike energy sources confined to pods, and they can be stopped only by a savior modestly known as the One.

We know even before Neo does that his role in saving the human race will be a biggie. (But on the evidence of Mr. Reeves's beautiful, equally androgynous co-star, Carrie-Anne Moss in Helmut Newton cat-woman mode, propagating in the future looks to be all business.) The film happily leads him through varying states of awareness, much of it explained by Laurence Fishburne in the film's philosophical-mentor role. Mr. Fishburne's Morpheus does what he can to explain how the villain of a film can be "a neural interactive simulation" and that the Matrix is everywhere, enforced by sinister morphing figures in suits and sunglasses. "The Matrix" is the kind of film in which sunglasses are an integral part of sleekly staged fight scenes.

With enough visual bravado to sustain a steady element of surprise (even when the film's most important Oracle turns out to be a grandmotherly type who bakes cookies and has magnets on her refrigerator), "The Matrix" makes particular virtues out of eerily inhuman lighting effects, lightning-fast virtual scene changes (as when Neo wishes for guns and thousands of them suddenly appear) and the martial arts stunts that are its single strongest selling point. As supervised by Yuen Wo Ping, these airborne sequences bring Hong Kong action style home to audiences in a mainstream American adventure with big prospects as a cult classic and with the future very much in mind.

RESPONSE QUESTIONS

1. If you've already seen *The Matrix,* jot down your general impressions. What do you remember most about the film? What positive and negative elements can you point to?

2. What should be included in a good movie review? How much of the plot should it give away? How subjective should the writing be? What should it tell you about the movie's acting, locations, and other cinematic qualities?

GUIDELINES FOR ANALYSIS

1. How well do the three reviews meet your standards of a good film review? What criteria does each reviewer seem to emphasize? What does each reviewer appreciate most and dislike most about the film?

2. What evidence from the film does each reviewer give to support the evaluation? Notice how much attention each gives to the film's plot, acting, special effects, and other cinematic elements.

3. Compare the writing styles of these reviewers. What do these styles assume about the readers of the *Village Voice,* the *Chicago Sun-Times,* and the *New York Times?*

QUESTIONS OF CULTURE

1. *The Matrix* grossed more than $171 million in the United States alone during its first year and over half a billion dollars worldwide. How do you explain discrepancy between these

essentially negative reviews and the box office sales? How can you account for the film's popularity abroad?

2. What makes a cult classic? Describe the subcultures for which *The Matrix* might have a special appeal. What would they find of value in the film?

IDEAS FOR YOUR JOURNAL

1. Write your own review of *The Matrix* or one of its two sequels, *The Matrix Reloaded* and *The Matrix Revolutions*.

2. Consult Karen Haber's anthology of essays, *Exploring the Matrix* (St. Martin's Press, 2003), or *"The Matrix" and Philosophy* (Open Court, 2002), edited by William Irwin. Why do you think the writers in these books take the film so seriously? Do you agree with their assessments?

A STUDENT WRITER IN ACTION

Preview

James Gerace is an enthusiastic hockey fan. Born and raised in New Rochelle, New York, he began watching the game at age nine and has played since he was eleven. When he graduates from college with a major in sports management, he would like to enter the field as a professional manager.

What follows is a brief account of James's writing process followed by his first and final draft. His first draft includes the instructor's comments so you can trace the changes that he made.

DISCOVERING

Q: How did you come up with the idea for your essay?

A: When I read up on the assignment for that week, I sought the advice of my girlfriend. She is one of the best writers I know, and I usually go to her for help when I am stumped for an idea. It didn't take her any time at all to suggest writing a season review of the Rangers since she knows how much I follow them and enjoy analyzing hockey in general. Once I had the idea it pretty much all came together.

PLANNING

Q: Say a little about how you prepare yourself to write and how you organize your thoughts.

A: To be honest, I don't exactly go by the book with my preparation for writing. I am usually stuck working most of the week and especially this past semester, I had to do a good amount of my draft writing while working. However, once it becomes time to write a final draft, I like to just go to my room and sit in bed with my laptop. Sometimes I will light a couple candles or put on some music to keep myself from becoming tense.

I used a little brainstorming to come up with the order in which I wanted to present my review but once I did that I basically wrote freely for about an hour and that was it. I basically just began writing about the team and players and then vented my feelings as a fan. Once I did that my paper sort of formed by itself.

DEVELOPING

Q: How did you develop your first draft?

A: My rough draft was basically about my feelings for the team and their coaches and managers plus information and knowledge of the players and team stats over the last several years. Once I had all those ideas on paper, I organized them step by step and turned it into a final paper that I really thought I did a good job with once I proofread it.

REVISING

Q: Tell me about your process of revising.

A: I did not do too much revising with this particular paper. I knew exactly what I wanted to say and how I wanted to say it, so I didn't feel that I should hold back. When it comes to the topic of hockey, and especially the team I wrote about, I become very opinionated and have a good amount to say. While I wrote I had to remind myself that I needed to stay neutral and not really reveal myself as a fan or overstate my opinion. This is one of those topics I could probably just write forever about since it's one of my biggest interests.

Q: What did you learn about yourself while writing this essay? What advice would you give to other student writers?

A: Completeness is something I worried about while writing this. I usually have a great deal to say about hockey, and while I am putting my thoughts on paper I worry that I am leaving something out. Other than that, I try my best to spell-check and reread my work when I am done with any paper. Structure is one of those things that I spend time trying to perfect too. I tried to make this paper flow from one topic to the next as best I could.

CONCLUSIONS AND ADVICE

Q: Looking back, what would you say was your most important goal in writing the essay? What were your biggest obstacles, and how did you tackle them? How do you feel now about the results?

A: My most important goal was to provide the reader with enough information to understand the agenda at hand for the team. I tried to write it so that even if a person with very little hockey knowledge read it, they would basically get the main ideas that this team underachieved, has talent, and needs to do a few certain things in order to succeed. As I said, I tried not to show favoritism. I also didn't want to say anything negative without facts to prove my points. I was very satisfied with the end results.

Q: Finally, did you learn anything about yourself while writing the essay? What advice would you give to other student writers?

A: This paper opened my eyes to the idea of sports writing a little bit more. It really restored my confidence in writing. As for advice to other students, I can only say to write about things that you truly enjoy when given the opportunity. When you are writing, it is ok to just write freely and really get as many of your ideas and thoughts as possible onto the page or screen. The paper I wrote is proof that sometimes a legitimate love for something can translate into a good paper.

RANGER HOCKEY REVIEW

By James Gerace

First Draft (with Instructor's Comments)

As the 2003-2004 NHL season approaches,[1] many fans in the tri-state area are getting mentally prepared for another season of New York Ranger hockey. This season marks the ten year[2] anniversary of the rangers taking the league by storm and overcoming every thing in their path to become Stanley Cup champions. However, that sweet memory has been soured for most fans after a six[3] consecutive year without a playoff berth. With a seemingly dominant team on paper, and a league leading eighty million dollar payroll,[4] it is a surprising situation in the eyes of fans and analysts.

Behind a veteran head coach and with a new sense of defensive responsibility, the rangers are getting set for the regular season. Thus far, when most of the starting line up has played, the team has been exceptional[5] going 2-0 with ten goals for and three against. Still, the team has[6] a whole can be summed up in a word;[7] uncertainty.

Despite the two wins;[8] the rangers have also suffered three awful losses during their preseason, while giving up a mind boggling sixteen goals in the three games and also showing signs early on that they have not repair[9] the many broken tools of last season.

Last season turned out to be both disappointing for fans and quite embarrassing for the team as a season highlighted by injury and underachievement from veteran star players came to an end just last April. At times they installed a false sense of hope into the minds of fans, with winning streaks and some consistent play every now and again. However, just as the previous five years had gone, last year closed up[10] with the rangers watching the playoffs on TV.

Some of the biggest problems for this team needing to be addressed in the off season included discipline, defensive responsibility, and special teams play.[11] As if this were not enough, they also received little help offensively from some of their highest paid forwards who were brought in to score goals and lead the team as an offensive threat.

Discipline was probably one of the most significant problems. The Rangers ranked in the top five for teams with the most penalties last year and it cost them. They had the 29th ranked penalty killing out of a thirty team league. Meanwhile, the Columbus Blue Jackets, a team that is on its third year of existence and was ranked third for most penalties, had the seventh ranked penalty kill in the league. In short, if you are going to take the penalties then kill them off, if you cannot, it is time for a more disciplined game plan.

Next on the list of things to address was most likely their weak and unstable defense. While teams like the New Jersey Devils executed a defensive mastery of their opponents night in and night out, the team on the other side of the river was out of position on a

Instructor's Comments

1. I like the way your first sentence orients the reader in relation to your topic.

2. Use a hyphen to connect two words when they work together to modify a noun.

3. Do you mean "sixth"?

4. Use hyphens to connect the words that work together as adjectives to describe "payroll."

5. Would a comma help your readers here?

6. typo?

7. Use a semicolon to join two sentences into one. Here you need a colon or a comma.

8. incorrect use of semicolon

9. wrong verb tense

10. Is this word necessary?

11. This is a good topic sentence. It helps to organize your essay by identifying three clear criteria of judgment, which I as a reader expect to learn about in the following paragraphs.

nightly basis, Most of the time opposing teams hardly had to break a sweat to move into the Rangers' zone or to get in front of the net. This led to the "blue shirts" having the highest goals against average in the league for the third time in seven years.

If the help of new assistant coach Tom Renney does not go unused, then the new season will bring forth a team that concentrates on defense as a five man unit and knows where their[12] team mates are on the ice at all times.

While defense and discipline are the foundation of any successful team[13] in the present day of hockey, the Rangers have other issues to sort out as well.

Their top scoring lines, which now consist of former all stars Eric Lindros, Martin Ruchinsky, Alex Kovalev and Anson Carter, among the top six, have failed to be consistent enough to get carry the team to the playoffs for the first time since 1997. With goal scoring doubts and career worst stats last year, some of these players, namely Lindros, will be looking for a chance to prove that they are still among the elite in the world. Lindros specially will be looking forward to erasing last year's poor performance in addition to the choice words fans and critics had for him last year in regards to his talent and capability. In order to succeed at the job in hand, Lindros and the others will have to keep their cool, and not try to change their style of play every night as they did last year.

And as is the case with this team and all time, just when you think it can not be any worse, there is always something else. Their interim head coach from last year, president and general manager Glenn Sather, has decided to retain the position and will be behind the bench for a full season. While Sather is indeed the man who led the Oilers to their dynasty and four Stanley Cups in the mid- eighties, Sather is now in his sixties and has not had the pressure of a full season as head coach since the early nineties. Although he feels that his record speaks for itself, his three years in New York as GM of the team has put him on top of the NY fans' hit list and there is no doubt in anyone's mind that an unsuccessful year as head coach will have people calling for Sather's dismissal once and for all.

All in all,[14] this is undoubtedly a potential season for disaster[15] for the New York Rangers. It is a season that will be filled with questions and uncertainties for the first half of the year until their position among other teams is clear. With all the tools necessary for success and with all the bad luck and injuries that has plagued them for almost a decade, this year will certainly have fans gearing up for yet another season without a post season appearance. Whether it happens or not,[16] rests solely on their efforts this season

Final Draft

As the 2003–2004 NHL season approaches, many fans in the tri-state area are getting mentally prepared for another season of New York Ranger hockey. This season marks the ten-year anniversary of the Rangers taking the league by storm and overcoming every-

12. Use a singular pronoun to agree with the antecedent noun (a team).

13. This is a good bridge sentence to link the previous paragraph to the one that follows.

14. You sum up the main points nicely in this concluding paragraph.

15. Should these words be rearranged?

16. There is no need for a comma between the verb and its subject.

thing in their path to become Stanley Cup champions. However, that sweet memory has been soured for most fans after a sixth consecutive year without a playoff berth. With a seemingly dominant team on paper, and a league-leading eighty million dollar payroll, it is a surprising situation in the eyes of fans and analysts.

Behind a veteran head coach and with a new sense of defensive responsibility, the Rangers are getting set for the regular season. Thus far, when most of the starting line-up has played, the team has been exceptional, going 2–0 with ten goals for and three against. Still, the team as a whole can be summed up in a word: uncertainty.

Despite their two wins, the Rangers have also suffered three awful losses during their preseason, while giving up a mind-boggling sixteen goals in the three games. They also showed signs early on that they have not repaired the broken tools of last year.

Last season turned out to be both disappointing for fans and quite embarrassing for the team. A season highlighted by injury and underachievement from veteran star players came to a close without much fight. At times they instilled a false sense of hope into the minds of fans, with winning streaks and some consistent play every now and again. However, just as the previous five years had gone, last year came to a close with the Rangers watching the playoffs on television.

Some of the biggest problems for this team needing to be addressed in the off-season included discipline, defensive responsibility, and special-team play. As if this were not enough, they also received little help offensively from some of their highest-paid forwards. They were brought in to score goals and lead the team as an offensive threat.

Discipline was probably one of the most significant problems. The Rangers ranked in the top five for teams with the most penalties last year, and it cost them. They had the twenty-ninth-ranked penalty killing out of a thirty-team league. Meanwhile, the Columbus Blue Jackets, a team that is in its third year of existence and was ranked third for most penalties, had the seventh-ranked penalty kill in the league. In short, if you are going to take the penalties, then kill them off; if you cannot, it is time for a more disciplined game plan.

Next on the list of things to address was most likely their weak and unstable defense. While teams like the New Jersey Devils executed a defensive mastery of their opponents night in and night out, the team on the other side of the river was out of position on a nightly basis. Most of the time, opposing teams hardly had to break a sweat to move into the Rangers' zone or to get in front of the net. This led to the "blue shirts" having the highest goals-against average in the league for the third time in seven years. So what will it take for this team to work to the best of its potential?

If the help of new assistant coach Tom Renney does not go unused, then the new season will bring forth a team that concentrates on defense as a five-man unit and where everyone knows where his teammates are on the ice at all times.

While defense and discipline are the foundation of any successful team in the present day of hockey, the Rangers have other issues to sort out as well. Their top-scoring lines now consist of former All Stars Eric Lindros, Martin Ruchinsky, Alex Kovalev, and Anson Carter, among the top six. However, last season they failed to be consistent enough to carry the team to the playoffs for the first time since 1997.

With goal-scoring doubts and career-worst stats last year, some of these players will be looking for a chance to prove that they are still among the elite in the world. Lindros especially will be looking forward to erasing last year's poor performance. In addition, he will try to make the fans and critics eat the choice words they had for him last year in regards to his talent and capability. In order to succeed at the job in hand, Lindros and the others will have to keep their cool and not try to change their style of play every night as they did last year.

As is the case with this team at all times, just when you think it cannot be any worse, there is always something else. Their interim head coach from last year, president and general manager Glenn Sather, has decided to retain the position and will be behind the bench for a full season. While Sather is indeed the man who led the Oilers to their dynasty and four Stanley Cups in the mid-eighties, Sather is now in his sixties and has not had the pressure of a full season as head coach since the early nineties. Although he feels that his record speaks for itself, his three years in New York as GM of the team has put him on top of the New York fans' hit list, and there is no doubt in anyone's mind that an unsuccessful year as head coach will have people calling for Sather's dismissal once and for all.

All in all, this is undoubtedly a potential season for disaster for the New York Rangers. It is a season that will be filled with questions and uncertainties for the first half of the year until their position among other teams is clear. With all the tools necessary for success, fans can only hope this is the breakthrough year for the New York Rangers. However, with all the inconsistencies, bad luck, and injuries that have plagued them for almost a decade, this year will certainly have fans gearing up for yet another season without a post-season appearance. Whether it happens or not rests solely on their efforts come the first game of the 2003–2004 season on October tenth.

CONSIDERATIONS FOR YOUR OWN WRITING

1. How well has James Gerace mastered the form and language of a sports review? What do you expect this genre of writing to include? What kinds of words and sentences do sports writers generally prefer?

2. What criteria does the writer use for evaluating the team's performance? By what standards does he judge the players, the managers, and their season? How clear are these criteria and standards? How dependable do they seem to you?

3. Whether or not you are a hockey fan, notice how the writer tries to keep up your interest in the topic. How does James seek to maintain a lively flow of words? Where is his writing most or least engaging? Describe the essay's overall tone.

4. Pay attention to the kinds of errors that appear in James's first draft. What patterns do you see? How has he repaired these errors in his final draft?

Evaluation Checklist

1. What helped you to understand the writer's point of view? Where were you most or least engaged?

2. Does the essay leave out anything you need to know? What would make the essay more complete?

3. What came across as the essay's main idea, its central focus? If the essay is a review, how clear is the writer's assessment of the topic? If the essay is about a snap judgment, how clear is the difference between the writer's first and final judgments? Where is the main idea most clearly presented?

4. List any problems you had following the text from start to finish. Does the writer give clear reasons for his or her judgments? How valid do the writer's criteria and standards seem to you, and how well are they applied to the topic at hand?

5. What do you remember most after reading the draft?

Reviews on the Web

The Internet is a great source of reviews, past and current. Here are a few of the many Web sites that evaluate movies, music, art, and books.

Movie Reviews
http://www.rottentomatoes.com/
http://movies.nytimes.com/pages/movies/index.html

Music Reviews
http://www.music-critic.com/
http://www.rollingstone.com/

Art Reviews
http://www.haberarts.com/myintro.htm
http://www.villagevoice.com/art/

Book Reviews
http://www.nytimes.com/pages/books/
http://www.nybooks.com/

Helpful Web site on Creating Web sites:
http://www.jessett.com

Blogs
http://www.blogger.com

Taking Stock

Take a moment to review what you have learned about judging and evaluating from this chapter.

1. Where in your future work, personal life, and community activities will you need to evaluate someone or something and clarify your assessment to someone else?

2. How has this chapter helped to prepare you for these needs? How have you sharpened your powers of judgment? What new tools have you acquired?

3. How many of the following words have you added to your critical vocabulary: *assessment, assumption, assortment, criteria (criterion), standards, preconceptions, reasoning, rationale, evidence, fact, opinion, stereotype, rating scale, logic, inductive reasoning, deductive reasoning, objective, subjective?* You should be able to define them and put them to good use.

4. Based on the feedback from your instructor, classmates, and peer reader, what methods and techniques seem to work best for you?

5. What did you learn about evaluative writing from the readings? Consider the way these readings define a topic, establish criteria for judging the topic, and apply prescribed standards. In your judgment, which of the readings did the best job of evaluating something or someone? How did you arrive at this assessment?

6. What did you learn about the topic that you wrote about or reviewed in your Web site? What would you still like to learn about this topic?

7. Think about the various topics presented in the readings and screenings. What is the most important thing you learned from them about the way Americans make choices in our consumer culture?

CHAPTER 8

Split Screen: Resolving the Gender Wars

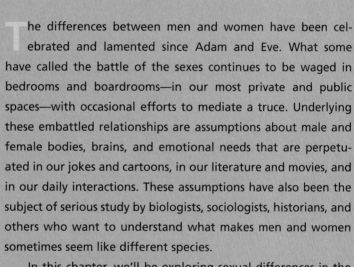

The differences between men and women have been celebrated and lamented since Adam and Eve. What some have called the battle of the sexes continues to be waged in bedrooms and boardrooms—in our most private and public spaces—with occasional efforts to mediate a truce. Underlying these embattled relationships are assumptions about male and female bodies, brains, and emotional needs that are perpetuated in our jokes and cartoons, in our literature and movies, and in our daily interactions. These assumptions have also been the subject of serious study by biologists, sociologists, historians, and others who want to understand what makes men and women sometimes seem like different species.

In this chapter, we'll be exploring sexual differences in the context of debate. Why are men and women so often at odds with each other? What makes those sparks fly across the gender divide? Are the differences, real or imagined, reconcilable? How can we understand all points of view and the reasoning behind them? Before turning to such questions, before examining specific arguments, let's consider the nature of argument itself. How are some people able to win others over to their point of view? What enables them to resolve disputes? How do they achieve the power to persuade?

The art of persuasion weaves many threads through the fabric of everyday life. Commercials persuade us to buy products, family and friends persuade us to modify behavior, written editorials and articles persuade us that one idea has more merit than another. Often we are the ones who do the persuading. We convince our boss that we deserve a raise. We propose solutions to community problems. We seek to influence a stranger to see things from our point of view. Learning how to make persuasive arguments and how to analyze the arguments of others is part of the art of living.

All arguments are not alike. On the street or in the workplace, some arguments sound less like persuasion than coercion, efforts to dominate the opposition through manipulation and force. On radio and TV, some programs posing as debates turn out to be shouting matches; in the end, they tell us more about the speakers than about the issues. Nor is it always easy to distinguish one kind of argument from another. Shows that look like documentaries may turn out to be "infomercials," lengthy advertisements for a product endlessly endorsed by attractive actors. Even in print, writers often blend news and personal opinion, blurring the boundaries between reporting and editorializing. This is not to say that contemporary forms of persuasion cannot be entertaining, informative, or even enlightening. It does suggest, however, that we need to understand the form and purpose of an argument if we are not to be confused or taken in.

The main purpose of this chapter is to give you guided practice analyzing and constructing persuasive arguments. You will be encouraged to examine arguments in a variety of media, from poster ads to commercials, from radio talk shows like *Talk of the Nation* and *Counterspin* to television news shows where opposing sides face off in showdown segments, from magazine articles to the op-ed page of your daily newspaper. Most of the readings and screenings in this chapter focus on the gender wars, efforts to sharpen or resolve conflicts between men and women in society. Meanwhile, you will be preparing a written essay or an oral presentation in which you take a stand on a controversial issue or seek to resolve a dilemma.

SCENARIOS FROM LIFE

- Your best friends are getting married. You know they love each other, but they keep getting caught up in a conflict. Whenever she speaks to him about her problems, he immediately offers a solution. He means to be helpful, but she just wants him to listen. Meanwhile, your male friend is resistant to any suggestions about changing his appearance, speech, or habits. He interprets her efforts to nurture his growth as accusations of incompetence. What can you do to resolve this conflict and maybe save the marriage?

- Your history grade will be based on a group project. The other students in your group want to do an oral report that you consider boring. You have a better idea, a multimedia presentation that will combine period photographs, documentary film, archival texts, and computer graphics. How can you persuade the others that your idea is in their best interests as well as yours?

- There is a plan to build a group home for delinquent adolescents in your neighborhood. The Department of Social Welfare is putting its weight behind the plan. Many of the residents oppose it vigorously. To head off a nasty confrontation, you decide to write a letter to the local newspaper.

- There is a new opening at work, and you believe that you're the right person for the job. The C.E.O. has asked for a written description of your qualifications. What can you write that will persuade her to promote you to the new post?

WHY WRITE TO PERSUADE?

Have you ever been part of a discussion that began as an inquiry and ended as an inquisition? You may have entered with an open mind, expecting to exchange ideas, perhaps to resolve some major issues, but at a certain point you realized that everyone was not speaking or listening in the same way. You realized that the conversation had become a form of confrontation and that the goal was not to share but to win. When this happened, you may have felt angry, invalidated, betrayed. It may be that someone in the conversation had shifted gears, propelling you unwillingly into combat. It is also possible, however, that your conversation partner held a different notion of what arguments should be. He or she assumed from the beginning that the purpose of talking was not to weigh the merits of your views but to prove you wrong. In that case, you were playing by different rules.

When people enter arguments with different expectations, when they mistake one form of disagreement for another, the results can range from stalemate to disaster. That is one reason why professionals in the field of conflict resolution seek to establish formal guidelines for disputes, settling them through methods like negotiation, adjudication, arbitration, and mediation. Each method of resolving conflicts follows predictable procedures. In **negotiation,** the disputants bargain with each other voluntarily toward a middle ground. In **mediation,** a third party helps them reach a mutually satisfying agreement. In **arbitration,** they present their cases to a third party whom they have chosen to decide on the issue. In **adjudication,** an appointed judge listens to both sides and provides the final word. There is a big difference between mediation, which focuses on common interests, and adjudication, which emphasizes adversarial roles, but in each case the opponents are likely to reach a resolution because they have agreed from the beginning to abide by the same rules.

In less formal settings, like the playground or the dining room, the patterns of argument are rarely spelled out so precisely, but they may be clear to those who know how to read the clues. When Uncle Frank chews on his cigar, you know his mind is set to win or lose. When your friends use words like "so what you're saying is" and "got it," you recognize that they are more interested in clarifying each other's positions than in scoring points. By being attentive to such hints of visual and verbal language, you become a better reader of the scripts that underlie all arguments. And you form a better map of the ground on which to build your own arguments.

As you move through the stages of your composing process, keep in mind what you have learned about persuasion in the media and elsewhere in your life. Persuasive writing, particularly essay writing, has much in common with other forms of argument, but it also differs in important ways. Do you watch television or listen to the radio with the same critical attention that you give to written texts? Do you accept, even seek the same level of emotional heat from your TV set as you do from articles on controversial issues? Do you apply the same standards of judgment to street corner debates and to written arguments? Such questions should help you to decide when your writing ought to be in sync with nonprint forms of persuasion and when it shouldn't be.

This chapter builds directly on concepts in Chapter 7. For that assignment, you wrote about a snap judgment or you reviewed a product, a performance, or a work of art. You examined your judgments and refashioned them into a clear, organized evaluation of your topic. In this chapter, your topic will be an issue, some moral or political controversy that has not yet been resolved. You will be examining the issue, taking a stand, and writing a persuasive essay to present your position in a favorable light. Or you will be looking at the issue from outside, proposing a solution that all sides might agree to. This means that you will need to consider other points of view as well as your own. The case you build—and your ability to convince your readers—will rest largely on a thoughtful appraisal of conflicting arguments. And it will draw on the persuasive power of your writing voice.

In other words, the key to powerful persuasion is attentive listening. If you want people to come over to your viewpoint, it helps to understand where they are coming from. People want their needs and concerns to be heard. By appealing to their interests, you are more likely to get their attention and influence their beliefs. You may never finally "resolve" the issue that you chose to write about. Few issues are resolvable in absolute terms. But you may resolve some of the underlying anxieties for your readers. Or you may reframe the issue in such a way that your readers understand and appreciate your position or solution. They might even come to see that, while they view things from different vantage points, their feet rest on a common ground.

WRITING OPTIONS

One reason for disagreement is that people enter arguments with different sets of rules. They don't even know that they are playing incompatible games in the same arena. One side might be thinking of the exchange as a contest, where the final goal is to win. Another side might be thinking of the exchange as a discussion in which the goal is a friendly compromise. Yet another side might be engaged in an inquiry with the goal of mutual understanding or a collaborative discovery of truths. So it is a good idea to identify the nature of the game before stepping onto the field. This way, you agree on the kind of disagreement you are having.

In this book, we have been using the term *format* to refer to the games that people play through various texts. When the purpose is persuasion, a television text may adopt the format of a commercial, a public service announcement, a talk show, or a news program highlighting opposing sides. Even these broad formats have distinctive variations. Some commercials use a "hard sell"; others sell by offering information or entertainment. Jim Lehrer presents controversies in a very different format from that used by Morley Safer or Jerry Springer. The same is true of written texts. You probably know newspaper columns that thrive on ridiculing, or "dissing," the opposition. You also have come across columns that regularly seek genuine solutions to world or local problems. Whether you are reading a text or writing one, you should be clear about the expectations built into its format.

Remember, too, that persuasive writing is rarely separate from other kinds of writing. In the course of developing an argument to support your claim, you may find yourself recalling past events (Chapter 3), describing current conditions (Chapter 4), analyzing those conditions (Chapter 5), reporting facts and ideas gleaned from outside sources (Chapter 6), evaluating the validity of information and opposing views (Chapter 7), and even imagining the future (Chapter 9). Look at these writing options as opportunities to draw creatively on what you have already learned in order to advance your thoughts and communicate them persuasively.

Option 1: Taking a Position

For this assignment, you will take a stand on a controversial issue and write an essay arguing the merits of your position. The main purpose of a position paper is to present a strong case for your view, supporting it with evidence and logical reasoning. Usually, a convincing position paper takes into account opposing points of view, demonstrating why those viewpoints seem less valid than your own. When you arrive at your conclusion, your readers should arrive with you.

Before writing your first draft, you will want to inform yourself about the issue. Talk to people, do some exploratory reading, notice how the topic is treated in the electronic media. Consider all sides of the issue carefully. Even if you disagree with some viewpoints, your position will be stronger if you consider opposing arguments. It will also help if you gather supporting material: the statistics, theories, examples, and other evidence with which to build your case. Formal research may not be required, but a persuasive essay tends to be more convincing when it includes documented information. Refer to the companion Web site for details on citing sources.

www.mhhe.com/costanzo

Research and citation guidelines are provided on the Web site.

When you draft your essay, be sure to define the controversy clearly. What is the main problem as you see it? What claims do the opposing sides make? What solution or solutions do you propose? Why do you believe that your proposal makes good sense? A common pattern for effective written arguments states a precise position, or thesis, compares it to competing claims, and supports it with convincing evidence. Such an argument uses logic to appeal to a reasonable audience. It distinguishes between facts, which can be verified, and inferences, which are matters of speculation or opinion. The section Tips on Writing Persuasively offers more ideas on planning, drafting, and revising your paper.

While you are writing, keep your purpose and your audience firmly in mind. A position paper is not a form of warfare or demolition. Although you may find yourself drawing on information and techniques from nonprint settings, remember that written arguments have their own expectations and conventions. Since an essay is always accessible to critical rereadings, unlike a conversation or a radio debate, it requires more attention to language, thought, and organization. Your credibility as a writer depends partly on your tone or "voice." If you write in a reasonable tone that is respectful of your reader, and if you establish your authority with clear thinking and accurate information, you are more likely to achieve your purpose. At best, you will persuade readers to accept your point of view; at least, you will help them understand how you arrived at your position.

Option 2: Resolving a Conflict

When two sides find it difficult to agree in an ongoing dispute, they sometimes seek the assistance of a mediator, a third party who is not involved in the dispute. The mediator's role is to help both sides reach a resolution. This may be some middle ground satisfactory to everyone or an entirely new solution that the disputing sides could not envision on their own. Because the mediator is not attached to any particular position and because the mediator's goal is a fair, mutually acceptable resolution, this approach often produces positive results.

Roger Fisher and William Ury give a good example in their best seller, *Getting to Yes:*

Consider the story of two men quarreling in a library. One wants the window open and the other wants it closed. They bicker back and forth about how much to leave it open: a crack, halfway, three-quarters of the way. No solution satisfies them both.

Enter the librarian. She asks one why he wants the window open: "To get some fresh air." She asks the other why he wants it closed: "To avoid the draft." After thinking a minute, she opens wide a window in the next room, bringing in fresh air without a draft. (40)

For this paper, you act as the mediator between opposing sides of a debate. You seek to understand the positions of both sides, to clarify their underlying interests, and to appreciate their immediate and long-range concerns. At the same time, you invent new options that might resolve the disagreement and consider them in the light of objective standards. In this way, you get to practice principles and skills of conflict resolution that will serve you well in nearly every arena of your daily life.

Your topic may be a personal disagreement (like a dispute over a salary, a possession, or a grade) or a global conflict (between hostile nations, competing ideologies, or groups with different goals, like ecologists and land developers). Choose a topic in which you have a genuine interest but about which you can be reasonably objective. Your purpose is not to take sides; it is to reconcile the opposing sides.

The essay should include a clear description of the conflict and present each side's point of view. You might begin with a brief history of the dispute to show what led to the problem. Since there are at least two sides to every argument, you should summarize the main positions of each side. Find out what the people involved really think by investigating their beliefs through reading, live interviews, broadcasts, or the Internet. Try to present each position as accurately and strongly as if it were your own. Show that you understand not only what the conflicting sides believe and why they believe it but also how they feel.

The theory of "principled negotiation" outlined in *Getting to Yes* offers a useful format for this essay. Although Fisher and Ury stress the importance of understanding the emotions involved in any problem, they caution mediators to separate the problem from the people. They also advise mediators to separate positions from their underlying motives. That is what the librarian does when she discovers that one reader wants fresh air while the other wants to avoid a draft. By identifying the original interests that led to their opposing positions, she is able to find a solution invisible to both. Fisher and Ury describe two more steps that are useful in any conflict resolution: brainstorming a number of options and judging them by objective standards. The options should serve the mutual interests of both parties. The standards for selecting the most promising option should be fair and objective. These concepts of principled negotiation are described further in a special section on page 379, Resolving Conflicts.

MEDIA OPTIONS

The media options for this chapter take the form of oral presentations, a traditional medium for developing arguments and settling disputes.

Option 1: The Debating Game

Stage a debate on a controversial topic between two groups. One side argues in favor of a particular position while the other side argues against it. Before the debate, each group tries to furnish its spokesperson with as many facts and ideas as it can to support its position. Let a third group judge the winning side, explaining the reasons for its judgment. A variation is to let the two competing groups exchange positions and begin again, this time arguing for the other side.

Option 2: The Mediation Game

Take a controversial issue (maybe the same issue you chose for debate) and set up a procedure for resolving it. Instead of a judge, select a mediator (or team of mediators) whose job is to reconcile opposing sides. The mediator might begin by interviewing the parties in conflict, listening to their complaints, clarifying their positions, and searching for the underlying interests. Once all parties are heard, the mediator might lead all parties to brainstorm possible alterna-

tives, focusing on the problem not the people, and work out some objective measures to weigh the best alternatives. In this game, there is no total loser; everybody wins something.

TIPS ON WRITING PERSUASIVELY

Writing a persuasive essay is much like writing any other essay. In a sense, each of your earlier essays has sought to persuade your readers of something: the power of a reconstructed memory, the accuracy of a description, the cogency of an analysis, or the thoroughness of your research. So the writing options in this chapter are not entirely new. What makes them persuasive essays is the degree to which you concentrate on developing a convincing argument. This means paying particular attention to positions (assertions, claims, opinions) and support (factual evidence, testimony, reasoning). It means listening to and accounting for objections, motives, and underlying needs. And it means developing confidence in your own authority as you learn more about a topic, gain a deeper understanding of the people involved, and practice the art of appealing to the best interests of your audience.

DISCOVERING

FIND A TOPIC Look for your topic in the world around you, or let a topic find you. Notice what you feel strongly about, what angers or inspires you. What do you find yourself arguing about lately? What are the big issues in your community, on talk shows, or in the news? What are the leading controversies in politics, business, religion, education, entertainment, or sports? Which of these controversies do you really care about?

Here are some categories that might spark a response:

- Gender (sexual harassment, gays in the military, same-sex marriage)
- Race and ethnicity (affirmative action, immigration policy)
- Social issues (gun control, prison reform, capital punishment, teen pregnancy)
- Ethical and moral issues (euthanasia, abortion, animals in research)
- Freedom of expression (media and violence, pornography, homeland security)
- The environment (global warming, genetically modified foods, endangered species)

NARROW AND REFINE YOUR TOPIC Once you have identified a broad category of interest, focus on a particular position (Writing Option 1) or problem (Writing Option 2). A **position statement** usually takes the form of a declarative sentence, an assertion that can be debated. It might be an assertion of fact ("Sport Utility Vehicles are Dangerous."), of values ("Doctor-Assisted Suicide Is Immoral."), or policy ("Resolved: Capital Punishment Should Be Abolished."). In this case, your task is to support the assertion as persuasively as you can. A **problem statement** usually takes the form of a question. It poses some dilemma as a problem to be solved. This might be a negotiable dispute (a request for a raise), a difference to be settled (a disagreement over property), or a conflict to be resolved (the family curfew). Here your task is to present all sides accurately and to propose an arrangement acceptable to each side. Your essay should persuade the concerned parties that your proposal is fair, feasible, and in everyone's best interest.

DO YOUR HOMEWORK This is an interactive assignment. Get out in the field and find out what others have to say about your topic. Interview some of the people involved. Read what they write and listen to their views on the electronic media. Separate the facts from the opinions, the evidence from the conclusions. Probe beyond surface statements to underlying assumptions and beliefs. Listing and clustering can help you at this stage. You might list pros and cons in separate columns. You might classify opinions into different groups. This gives you an organized awareness of the competing perspectives to take into account.

PLANNING

BUILD YOUR CASE If you are writing a position paper, look over the facts and reasons that might support your assertion. Pick the strongest points and gather evidence for each point. Can you think of examples that your reader will appreciate? Are these examples relevant, accurate, and sufficiently detailed? Can you cite statistics, facts, and outside authorities to reinforce each point? As you construct your case point by point, consider possible counterpoints. What might the opposition say to dispute your claims? How solid are your facts? How tight is your reasoning? Have you anticipated their objections well enough to convince an outside party that your position is stronger?

If you propose to settle a dispute, be sure you have a clear picture of the problem and a firm understanding of each side. Use questions to guide your interviews or secondary research. What is the nature of the conflict? When and how did it arise? Who is involved? What positions do they take and what explanations do they give? What needs and feelings are at work? Look beyond the entrenched positions for underlying interests. What led each party to decide on its position? Are their basic interests (as opposed to their positions) compatible with the opposing party's interests? Generate a list of possible options. Consider which options are most likely to work. Propose to judge these options by some objective standards. Are they practical? Are they fair to each side? Select the most promising option as your proposal and decide how you will sell it to the disputing groups. What would it take to gain their acceptance? What special needs and desires can you appeal to? What words and ideas are most likely to move them? What trigger terms should you avoid?

DRAFTING

A persuasive argument can take many shapes depending on your topic, audience, and style. Here are two examples of how you might organize your essay.

Position Paper

>Introduction (Describe the issue, assert your position, establish your authority, appeal to the reader.)
>
>Reason 1 with evidence
>
>Possible objections and your refutation
>
>Reason 2 with evidence
>
>Possible objections and your refutation
>
>Reason 3 with evidence
>
>Objections and refutation
>
>Conclusion: summarize your key points

Proposal Paper

>Introduction (Identify the problem and your relationship to it.)
>
>Describe competing positions
>
>Explain reasons for competing claims
>
>Consider options
>
>Recommend a solution
>
>Spell out strengths of proposed solution
>
>Explain what each side stands to gain
>
>Conclusion: forecast the future

When drafting your essay, pay close attention to your tone. Your readers are most likely to be persuaded if you project a reasonable, understanding, authoritative voice that appeals directly to their deeply felt needs. This voice, together with your use of logical transitions, will connect the parts of your essay into a unified whole.

REVISING

Let your paper stand a while before rereading it with a fresh eye. Read it several times, each time from the perspective of a different stakeholder. Or show it to readers who represent different sides of the dispute.

Comb through your language for metaphors and clichés that might conflict with your main message. If you want to reconcile opposing sides, avoid terms that sound provocative and combative. Stay away from "trash talk." It is also a good idea to weed out unnecessary terms like "frankly," "naturally," and "of course," which may insult your readers.

Check your final draft against the list of errors that you tend to make. If you document sources, be sure to consult the MLA, APA, or Chicago guidelines for proper format.

SPECIAL SECTION: RESOLVING CONFLICTS

In her book, *The Argument Culture,* Deborah Tannen voices her concern about the many oppositional forms of persuasion that dominate communication today. In the press, on television, in government, in schools, and elsewhere in American life, she finds an overwhelming tendency to polarize differences by framing them as debates, contests, "showdowns," "battles," and other forms of confrontation. The cumulative effect, she says, is that differences are magnified rather than resolved. "Our spirits are corroded by living in an atmosphere of unrelenting contention—an argument culture" (3).

While Tannen acknowledges the entertainment value of controversy and the truth value of constructive criticism, she questions "the *automatic* use of adversarial forms—the assumption that it's always best to address problems and issues by fighting over them" (26). She points out that a win-or-lose mentality can trample important truths in the hot pursuit of victory or a desperate evasion of defeat. When we do battle "for the sake of argument," the real issues become casualties of war. Even when we hold that "there are two sides to every argument," we limit our options, obscuring the complexities of an issue and screening possible solutions that may lie along another path. Tannnen's essay, "For Argument's Sake," appears on page 383.

Deborah Tannen is not the first to question the value of hostile argument. In *The Art of Negotiating,* an early classic in the field, Gerald Nierenberg shows that negotiation is most successful when it is a "cooperative enterprise" from which all parties emerge with some needs satisfied (39, 46). Nierenberg proposes a "Need Theory of Negotiation," one that recognizes the basic human needs motivating all bargaining positions, including physiological needs (like hunger and fatigue), safety and security, love and belonging, esteem, self-actualization (the need to be all one can be), curiosity (the need to know and understand), and beauty. Nierenberg describes persuasive techniques that address one group's needs in order to fulfill another group's needs. He stresses the importance of understanding what the situation looks like from other points of view, adding that "Listening is as much a persuasive technique as speaking" (132).

Roger Fisher and William Ury reaffirm the value of persuasive listening in *Getting to Yes,* which is based on a system of "principled negotiation" developed at the Harvard Negotiation Project. Fisher and Ury offer a four-point approach to negotiating differences that can also serve as a convenient outline for writing a persuasive essay. Their approach is particularly well suited for an essay that seeks to resolve a conflict (Writing Option 2) rather than to take a position in opposition to another side (Writing Option 1). Briefly stated, their approach focuses on four elements of negotiation:

> People: Separate the people from the problem
>
> Interests: Focus on interests, not positions.
>
> Options: Generate a variety of possibilities before deciding what to do.
>
> Criteria: Insist that the result be based on some objective standard. (10–11)

Understanding people is a key to principled negotiation. What the opposing sides think and how they feel are not just part of the problem; according to Fisher and Ury, they are the problem. So the first step in resolving differences is to appreciate the emotions and beliefs involved. Learn how each side perceives the issues and acknowledge their perceptions. Interview some of the interested parties, read what they have written, and listen to their filmed or televised accounts. Try to paraphrase what you hear in your own words while preserving the original facts and spirit. The goal here is to represent both sides as they see themselves. Acknowledgment is not the same as agreement. By making the underlying feelings and assumptions explicit and showing that you really understand them, you are not necessarily legitimizing them, but you are affirming people's rights to their points of view. In a tense confrontation, this can relieve much of the urgency to be heard and understood, and it diffuses the need for face-saving and self-defense. This allows you to concentrate on the issues themselves. As Fisher and Ury put it, acknowledgment lets you refocus the attack on the problem, not the people.

Often a problem exists because people have dug into incompatible positions. Like the two library patrons who fought over the window, they fail to see beyond their positions to the motives that led to those positions. If they considered why they chose their positions in the first place, they might discover mutual interests. And since any interest can be satisfied by more than one position, they might find new options that could please all sides. To uncover underlying interests, Fisher and Ury recommend the simple strategy of asking why. Why did each side decide on its position? What chain of events and reasoning led to their demands? What results did each side imagine if its demands were or were not met? Notice that the word "why" points in two directions: backward toward the past and forward toward the future. So look for both causes and consequences. Like Nierenberg, Fisher and Ury point out that all people are motivated by basic needs, including security, economic well-being, a sense of belonging, recognition, and control over their own lives. Try to identify the most important interests of both sides. Does the athlete want a higher salary because he wants to bolster his prestige or because he fears that his career might suddenly end if he were injured or suffered a losing streak? Does the team owner really need to keep down operating costs or does she fear that she will look weak if she "caves in"? There are many possible reasons (needs) for every position, but each need may be satisfied by more than one position. Having established the basic needs, a creative mediator is free to invent a set of new solutions.

The next step, then, is to devise new options for mutual gain. The athlete and owner might agree to a contract that ties salary to ticket sales, a way of sharing risk and profits. Or the owner might approve of a salary increase over several years. Or the contract might include a bonus for every game in which the athlete scores so many points. Fisher and Ury suggest generating as many options as possible. Brainstorming is a good technique for this stage. By postponing judgment or decision making, you free your imagination and keep an open mind. Try imagining what different kinds of people might suggest: a lawyer, a police officer, a child, a feminist, a romantic, a Jerry Seinfeld, or an Oprah Winfrey. Try changing the scope of the proposed agreement. Can it be broken down into smaller parts? What if a great deal more were at stake? Try expanding the pie before dividing it. Or try dividing the pie according to taste. One party might like the filling; another might prefer the crust.

Once you have listed a number of possible options, consider them in the light of objective standards. That is, measure them against broad principles that are reasonable and fair. If you are mediating between the owner of a totaled car and an insurance company, you might turn to several criteria, including the car's replacement cost, its book value, and its original cost minus depreciation. Each of these criteria has been used regularly to establish the fair value of a used car. If you are negotiating about a grade, what standards of assessment might be applied? A good question to ask here is "What is your theory?" How did each side arrive at its position? What principles did each side apply? Are those principles impartial and appropriate? If you are mediating an actual dispute instead of simply writing about one, Fisher and Ury suggest that you involve all sides in the search for objective standards well before you try to settle on an option. That way the standards become genuine tools of assessment rather than conveniences to justify a predetermined position. When you do write about a proposed resolution of a conflict, be sure to clarify your standards. Explain the criteria that make your proposed solution a matter of principle and not sheer will.

The ability to resolve differences without alienating or damaging the opposing sides is an important part of what Michael Goleman calls emotional literacy, and it can be learned as a positive alternative to aggression or passivity (*Emotional Intelligence* 264–68, 276–79). Cultivating the skills of conflict management may prove to be a welcome antidote to the culture of argument that dominates the current scene.

PRINT

Magazine ads

Billboards

Op-ed pages, editorials, and editorial cartoons

Newsweek's "My Turn" and op-ed pages of the *New York Times*

Position papers

Legal briefs

TELEVISION

Commercials

Infomercials

Jerry Springer

RADIO

Talk of the Nation

The Rush Limbaugh Show

The Randi Rhodes Show

The Sean Hannity Show

The Majority Report

INTERNET

The National Review Online
http://www.nationalreview.com

DailyKos
http://www.dailykos.com

The Huffington Post
http://www.huffingtonpost.com

Michelle Malkin
http://www.michellemalkin.com

Instapundit.com
http://www.instapundit.com

Readings and Screenings: Engendering Conflicts and Solutions

In recent years, the Internet has become one of the most active—and interactive—arenas for debating issues and resolving conflicts. Among the most popular sites are National Review Online and Daily Kos. NRO is a Web version of the popular conservative magazine founded in 1955 by William Buckley. Daily Kos, founded by Markos Moulitsas Zuniga (its name derives from the second syllable in his name), appeals to liberals and progressives. In addition to articles, both sites feature political blogs (short for Web logs): electronic journals where people post their personal commentaries day by day. Fueled by an abundant supply of contributors and readers (NRO attracts about a million visitors a day, Daily Kos nearly half as many), these blogs are rich sources of persuasive writing, good places to study the art of stating a position and developing an argument.

You'll find more traditional efforts to persuade you in the op-ed pages of your newspaper, in television commercials and magazine ads, in radio talk shows and political cartoons. Take stock of your own experience with persuasive media. Where do you usually turn to find support for your opinions? Where do you encounter texts that challenge your views? Where do the media vie for your attention and try to sell you something? Where do the media seek to solve or add to the conflicts in your life?

One site of persistent conflict in modern life is the arena of gender relations. Journalists routinely talk about the battle of the sexes. Self-help books speak of men and women as if they came from different planets. Most of the readings and screenings in this chapter focus on the differences between males and females. We begin with an essay by Deborah Tannen, well known for her research on gender differences. Her essay is followed by a selection by John Gray, the author of *Men Are from Mars, Women Are from Venus,* and an essay by Natalie Angier, who argues that Gray's popular teachings are simplistic and dangerously misleading. Canada's popular radio program, *Quirks & Quarks,* probes more deeply by asking scientists whether male and female brains are really different. The next pair of readings takes up the issue in a lighter vein. In "I Want a Wife," Judy Brady questions patriarchal expectations of women in a provocative reversal. Dave Barry's "Guys vs. Men" playfully proposes a category that is neither man nor woman. The differences between men and women are explored further in a video segment from *ABC News Nightline,* which discusses the role of women in combat. The section concludes with a classic short story by Ernest Hemingway, "Hills Like White Elephants," in which unspoken conflicts percolate through the dialogue of a young couple with a problem that is never named.

PREVIEW

In our newspapers, on television, in the workplace and our homes as well as in our courts and classrooms, our language reflects "an adversarial frame of mind [which] rests on an assumption that opposition is the best way to get things done." This observation on American public discourse by Deborah Tannen, a prominent linguist, led to her 1999 book *The Argument Culture: Stopping America's War of Words*. A summary of Tannen's views on the culture of argument introduces the readings in this chapter on persuasion, conflict resolution, and the battle of the sexes.

Deborah Tannen is best known for her studies of how men and women communicate. Her best-selling book, *You Just Don't Understand* (1990), helped to raise public awareness of gender differences in conversational styles. Tannen's subsequent books have focused on gender relations in the workplace (*Talking from 9 to 5*, 2001) and the role of language in families (*I Only Say This Because I Love You*, 2002).

Dr. Tannen teaches in the Linguistics Department at Georgetown University, where she holds the rank of University Professor. She lectures widely and has appeared on television shows like *The NewsHour with Jim Lehrer, 20/20, 48 Hours, CBS News, ABC World News Tonight, Oprah, Good Morning America, CNN, Larry King,* and *Hardball*. Her articles also appear regularly in the press, including the *New York Times, Newsweek, Time, USA Today,* and *People*. The following article appeared in the *Washington Post* on March 15, 1998.

For Argument's Sake

By Deborah Tannen

I was waiting to go on a television talk show a few years ago for a discussion about how men and women communicate, when a man walked in wearing a shirt and tie and a floor-length skirt, the top of which was brushed by his waist-length red hair. He politely introduced himself and told me that he'd read and liked my book *You Just Don't Understand,* which had just been published. Then he added, "When I get out there, I'm going to attack you. But don't take it personally. That's why they invite me on, so that's what I'm going to do."

We went on the set and the show began. I had hardly managed to finish a sentence or two before the man threw his arms out in gestures of anger, and began shrieking—briefly hurling accusations at me, and then railing at length against women. The strangest thing about his hysterical outburst was how the studio audience reacted: They turned vicious—not attacking me (I hadn't said anything substantive yet) or him (who wants to tangle with someone who screams at you?) but the other guests: women who had come to talk about problems they had communicating with their spouses.

My antagonist was nothing more than a dependable provocateur, brought on to ensure a lively show. The incident has stayed with me not because it was typical of the talk shows I have appeared on—it wasn't, I'm happy to say—but because it exemplifies the ritual nature of much of the opposition that pervades our public dialogue.

Everywhere we turn, there is evidence that, in public discourse, we prize contentiousness and aggression more than cooperation and conciliation. Headlines blare about the Starr Wars, the Mommy Wars, the Baby Wars, the Mammography Wars; everything is posed in terms of battles and duels, winners and losers, conflicts and disputes. Biographies have metamorphosed into demonographies whose authors don't just portray their subjects warts and all, but set out to dig up as much dirt as possible, as if the story of a person's life is contained in the warts, only the warts, and nothing but the warts.

It's all part of what I call the argument culture, which rests on the assumption that opposition is the best way to get anything done: The best way to discuss an idea is to set up a debate. The best way to cover news is to find people who express the most extreme views and present them as "both sides." The best way to begin an essay is to attack someone. The best way to show you're really thoughtful is to criticize. The best way to settle disputes is to litigate them.

It is the automatic nature of this response that I am calling into question. This is not to say that passionate opposition and strong verbal attacks are never appropriate. In the words of the Yugoslavian-born poet Charles Simic, "There are moments in life when true invective is called for, when it becomes an absolute necessity, out of a deep sense of justice, to denounce, mock, vituperate, lash out, in the strongest possible language." What I'm questioning is the ubiquity, the knee-jerk nature of approaching almost any issue, problem or public person in an adversarial way.

Smashing heads does not open minds. In this as in so many things, results are also causes, looping back and entrapping us. The pervasiveness of warlike formats and language grows out of, but

also gives rise to, an ethic of aggression: We come to value aggressive tactics for their own sake—for the sake of argument. Compromise becomes a dirty word, and we often feel guilty if we are conciliatory rather than confrontational—even if we achieve the result we're seeking.

Here's one example. A woman called another talk show on which I was a guest. She told the following story: "I was in a place where a man was smoking, and there was a no-smoking sign. Instead of saying 'You aren't allowed to smoke in here. Put that out!' I said, 'I'm awfully sorry, but I have asthma, so your smoking makes it hard for me to breathe. Would you mind terribly not smoking?' When I said this, the man was extremely polite and solicitous, and he put his cigarette out, and I said, 'Oh, thank you, thank you!' as if he'd done a wonderful thing for me. Why did I do that?"

I think this woman expected me—the communications expert—to say she needs assertiveness training to confront smokers in a more aggressive manner. Instead, I told her that her approach was just fine. If she had tried to alter his behavior by reminding him of the rules, he might well have rebelled: "Who made you the enforcer? Mind your own business!" She had given the smoker a face-saving way of doing what she wanted, one that allowed

him to feel chivalrous rather than chastised. This was kinder to him, but it was also kinder to herself, since it was more likely to lead to the result she desired.

Another caller disagreed with me, saying the first caller's style was "self-abasing." I persisted: There was nothing necessarily destructive about the way the woman handled the smoker. The mistake the second caller was making—a mistake many of us make—was to confuse ritual self-effacement with the literal kind. All human relations require us to find ways to get what we want from others without seeming to dominate them.

The opinions expressed by the two callers encapsulate the ethic of aggression that has us by our throats, particularly in public arenas such as politics and law. Issues are routinely approached by having two sides stake out opposing positions and do battle. This sometimes drives people to take positions that are more adversarial than they feel—and can get in the way of reaching a possible resolution. I have experienced this firsthand.

For my book about the workplace, "Talking from 9 to 5," I spent time in companies, shadowing people, interviewing them and having individuals tape conversations when I wasn't there. Most companies were happy to proceed on a verbal agreement setting forth certain ground rules: Individuals would control the taping, identifying names would be changed, I would show them what I wrote about their company and change or delete anything they did not approve. I also signed confidentiality agreements promising not to reveal anything I learned about the company's business.

Some companies, however, referred the matter to their attorneys so a contract could be written. In no case where attorneys became involved—mine as well as theirs—could we reach an agreement on working together.

Negotiations with one company stand out. Having agreed on the procedures and safeguards, we expected to have a contract signed in a matter of weeks. But six months later, after thousands of dollars in legal fees and untold hours of everyone's time, the negotiations reached a dead end. The company's lawyer was demanding veto power over my entire book; it meant the company could (if it chose) prevent me from publishing the book even if I used no more than a handful of examples from this one company. I could not agree to that. Meanwhile, my lawyer was demanding for me rights to use the videotapes of conversations any way I wanted. The company could not agree to that; it

meant I could (if I chose) put videotapes of their company on national television, make them look bad, reveal company secrets and open them up to being sued by their own employees.

The people I was working with at the company had no desire to pass judgment on any part of my book that did not involve them, and I had no intention of using the videotapes except for analysis. These extreme demands could have been easily dismissed by the principals—except they had come after months of wrangling with the language of drafts passed back and forth. Everybody's patience and good will had worn out. The adversarial nature of the legal process had polarized us beyond repair.

Requiring people to behave like enemies can stir up mutual enmity that remains long after a case has been settled or tried, and the lawyers have moved on. Because our legal system

is based on the model of ritual battle, the object—like the object of all fights—is to win, and that can interfere with the goal of resolving disputes.

The same spirit drives the public discourse of politics and the press, which are increasingly being given over to ritual attacks. On Jan. 18, 1994, retired admiral Bobby Ray Inman withdrew as nominee for secretary of defense after several news stories raised questions about his business dealings and his finances. Inman, who had held high public office in both Democratic and Republican administrations, explained that he did not wish to serve again because of changes in the political climate—changes that resulted in public figures being subjected to relentless attack. Inman said he was told by one editor, "Bobby, you've just got to get thicker skin. We have to write a bad story about you every day. That's our job."

SENATE DEBATE IN NEW JERSEY: WAR OF WORDS
IN A BATTLE OVER A RACETRACK, UNEXPECTED ALLIANCES

Slap for Kim faces U.N. stall
Brit big rips U.S. on Gitmo

BUSH RIPS DEMS AS 'PART OF CUT & RUN'

Capo: Gotti Sr. ignited a war

Fox News Chief Says Clinton Comments Assault Journalists

$9M SLAP AT YONKERS YUCKWAY

Woodward vs. Rumsfeld: The Bushies' Civil War

CAPTAIN 5-F-R-5 AS YANKS RIP TIGERS

They're back on the Attack
(Electronica pioneers return to U.S. after eight-year absence)

Bird Bashers
(Carlos has enjoyed success vs. Cards)

B.C. HOSTS VA. TECH IN KEY ACC BATTLE

Faso fires away / Slams Eliot over Hevesi in debate

Everyone seemed to agree that Inman would have been confirmed. The news accounts about his withdrawal used words such as "bizarre," "mystified" and "extraordinary." A *New York Times* editorial reflected the news media's befuddlement: "In fact, with the exception of a few columns, . . . a few editorials and one or two news stories, the selection of Mr. Inman had been unusually well received in Washington." This evaluation dramatizes just how run-of-the-mill systematic attacks have become. With a wave of a subordinate clause ("a few editorials . . ."), attacking someone personally and (from his point of view) distorting his record are dismissed as so insignificant as to be unworthy of notice.

The idea that all public figures should expect to be criticized ruthlessly testifies to the ritualized nature of such attack: It is not sparked by specific wrongdoing but is triggered automatically.

I once asked a reporter about the common journalistic practice of challenging interviewees by repeating criticism to them. She told me it was the hardest part of her job. "It makes me uncomfortable," she said. "I tell myself I'm someone else and force myself to do it." But, she said she had no trouble being combative if she felt someone was guilty of behavior she considered wrong. And that

is the crucial difference between ritual fighting and literal fighting: opposition of the heart.

It is easy to find examples throughout history of journalistic attacks that make today's rhetoric seem tame. But in the past, such vituperation was motivated by true political passion, in contrast with today's automatic, ritualized attacks—which seem to grow out of a belief that conflict is high-minded and good, a required and superior form of discourse.

The roots of our love for ritualized opposition lie in the educational system that we all pass through. Here's a typical scene: The teacher sits at the head of the classroom, pleased with herself and her class. The students are engaged in a heated debate. The very noise level reassures the teacher that the students are participating. Learning is going on. The class is a success.

But look again, cautions Patricia Rosof, a high school history teacher who admits to having experienced just such a wave of satisfaction. On closer inspection, you notice that only a few students are participating in the debate; the majority of the class is sitting silently. And the students who are arguing are not addressing subtleties, nuances or complexities of the points they are making or disputing. They don't have that luxury because they want to win

the argument—so they must go for the most dramatic statements they can muster. They will not concede an opponent's point—even if they see its validity—because that would weaken their position.

This aggressive intellectual style is cultivated and rewarded in our colleges and universities. The standard way to write an academic paper is to position your work in opposition to someone else's. This creates a need to prove others wrong, which is quite different from reading something with an open mind and discovering that you disagree with it. Graduate students learn that they must disprove others' arguments in order to be original, make a contribution and demonstrate intellectual ability. The temptation is great to oversimplify at best, and at worst to distort or even misrepresent other positions, the better to refute them.

I caught a glimpse of this when I put the question to someone who I felt had misrepresented my own work: "Why do you need to make others wrong for you to be right?" Her response: "It's an argument!" Aha, I thought, that explains it. If you're having an argument, you use every tactic you can think of—including distorting what your opponent just said—in order to win.

Staging everything in terms of polarized opposition limits

the information we get rather than broadening it. For one thing, when a certain kind of interaction is the norm, those who feel comfortable with that type of interaction are drawn to participate, and those who do not feel comfortable with it recoil and go elsewhere. If public discourse included a broad range of types, we would be making room for individuals with different temperaments.

But when opposition and fights overwhelmingly predominate, only those who enjoy verbal sparring are likely to take part. Those who cannot comfortably take part in oppositional discourse—or choose not to—are likely to opt out.

But perhaps the most dangerous harvest of the ethic of aggression and ritual fighting is—as with the audience response to the screaming man on the television talk show—an atmosphere of animosity that spreads like a fever. In extreme forms, it rears its head in road rage and workplace shooting sprees. In more common forms, it leads to what is being decried everywhere as a lack of civility. It erodes our sense of human connection to those in public life—and to the strangers who cross our paths and people our private lives.

RESPONSE QUESTIONS

1. Deborah Tannen says that "in public discourse, we prize contentiousness and aggression more than cooperation and conciliation." What examples does she offer to support this thesis?

2. Do you agree or disagree that we live in "an argument culture"? On what evidence do you base your view?

3. Explain what Tannen means by "ritual fighting." How does she trace this aggressive style to our educational system? Where in your own schooling have you been rewarded for intellectual aggression or for cooperative thinking?

4. Reread the section where Tannen describes the woman who addressed a smoker near a no-smoking sign. Do you think the woman's response to the smoker was emotionally intelligent or "self-debasing?" How would you have handled the situation?

5. Where, in your opinion, is it best to stand up and fight for a position, and where is it best to resolve differences through more cooperative means?

GUIDELINES FOR ANALYSIS

1. Tannen begins by describing something that happened on a television talk show. How does she use this incident to introduce her topic and herself? What does the incident illustrate about the argument culture?

2. Tannen finds oppositional behavior particularly strong in politics, law, and the workplace. How much space does she devote to these and other arenas of modern life? Given her purpose and audience, would more examples have been helpful?

3. Tannen quotes Charles Simic to point out that sometimes adversarial language is necessary. Where else does she qualify her thesis? Do such qualifications dilute or strengthen her case?

4. Would it be accurate to say that Tannen presents an "argument" against the argument culture? What are the features of a written argument? How closely does she follow the

conventional formats of aggressive rhetoric or develop alternative methods for resolving differences through writing?

QUESTIONS OF CULTURE

1. Is the "ethic of aggression" equally strong in all countries? Where in the world are societies based more on cooperation and conciliation? How do you rate the United States as a promoter of oppositional or cooperative thinking both at home and abroad?

2. Although Tannen does not focus on gender differences in this essay, she has spent most of her career studying the differences between men and women. To what extent do you believe that arguing and other forms of opposition are features of male behavior? Give evidence to support your view.

IDEAS FOR YOUR JOURNAL

1. Write a letter to the author responding to the essay. Explain why you agree or disagree with her ideas. If you disagree, try two forms of writing: one from a tough adversarial position, the other seeking to persuade her to your point of view by non-aggressive means.

2. Check out the language in several newspapers, magazines, television shows, or video games. How many references to conflict, opposition, and aggression can you find? How often are disagreements staged in oppositional formats (as debates, shouting matches, or contests)? When are differences expressed in combative terms (like "the battle of the sexes" or "a verbal duel")?

PREVIEW

John Gray's book about male-female relationships, *Men Are from Mars, Women Are from Venus,* became a national best seller when it appeared in 1992. Since then, Mars and Venus have become household terms in the ongoing battle of the sexes. Gray plays with the idea that men and women are from different planets, but he offers serious advice for overcoming misunderstandings and resolving disputes. The following selection, taken from the second chapter of his book, may be read as a study in conflict resolution. Gray begins by defining the problem, stating the positions of both parties, and suggesting solutions that might be acceptable to each party. Notice how he tries to understand the perspectives and feelings of both men and women without invalidating either group. Notice, too, how he gives background information that might help to explain one group's point of view to the other. Not everyone agrees with Gray's explanations or advice, but watch how he tries to persuade you to follow a certain course of thinking.

Gray's education has been nontraditional. He lived as a monk for nine years, receiving a B.A. and M.A. in Creative Intelligence from Maharishi European Research University. His doctorate in psychology and human sexuality is from Columbia Pacific University (a non-accredited private correspondence school). Many of his observations about couples come from the therapy sessions and seminars he has conducted for some twenty-five years. Dr. Gray lives with his wife and three daughters in Mill Valley, California. His other books include *Mars and Venus in the Bedroom* (1997), *Mars and Venus in the Workplace* (2002), and *Mars and Venus in Love* (2002).

Mr. Fix-It and the Home-Improvement Committee
By John Gray

The most frequently expressed complaint women have about men is that men don't listen. Either a man completely ignores her when she speaks to him, or he listens for a few beats, assesses what is bothering her, and then proudly puts on his Mr. Fix-It cap and offers her a solution to make her feel better. He is confused when she doesn't appreciate this gesture of love. No matter how many times she tells him that he's not listening, he doesn't get it and keeps doing the same thing. She wants empathy, but he thinks she wants solutions.

The most frequently expressed complaint men have about women is that women are always trying to change them. When a woman loves a man she feels responsible to assist him in growing and tries to help him improve the way he does things. She forms a home-improvement committee, and he becomes her primary focus. No matter how much he resists her help, she persists—waiting for any opportunity to help him or tell him what to do. She thinks she's nurturing him, while he feels he's being controlled. Instead, he wants her acceptance.

These two problems can finally be solved by first understanding why men offer solutions and why women seek to improve. Let's pretend to go back in time, where by observing life on Mars and Venus—before the planets discovered one another or came to Earth—we can gain some insights into men and women.

Life on Mars

Martians value power, competency, efficiency, and achievement They are always doing things to prove themselves and develop their power and skills. Their sense of self is defined through their ability to achieve results. They experience fulfillment primarily through success and accomplishment.

5   Everything on Mars is a reflection of these values. Even their dress is designed to reflect their skills and competence. Police officers, soldiers, businessmen, scientists, cab drivers, technicians, and chefs all wear uniforms or at least hats to reflect their competence and power.

They don't read magazines like *Psychology Today, Self,* or *People.* They are more concerned with outdoor activities, like hunting, fishing, and racing cars. They are interested in the news, weather, and sports and couldn't care less about romance novels and self-help books. They are more interested in "objects" and "things" rather than people and feelings. Even today on Earth, while women fantasize about romance, men fantasize about powerful cars, faster computers, gadgets, gizmos, and new more powerful technology. Men are preoccupied with the "things" that can help them express power by creating results and achieving their goals.

Achieving goals is very important to a Martian because it is a way for him to prove his competence and thus feel good about himself. And for him to feel good about himself he must achieve these goals by himself. Someone else can't achieve them for him. Martians pride themselves in doing things all by themselves. Autonomy is a symbol of efficiency, power, and competence.

Understanding this Martian characteristic can help women understand why men resist so much being corrected or being told what to do. To offer a man unsolicited advice is to presume that he doesn't know what to do or that he can't do it on his own. Men are very touchy about this, because the issue of competence is so very important to them.

Because he is handling his problems on his own, a Martian rarely talks about his problems unless be needs expert advice. He reasons: "Why involve someone else when I can do it by myself?" He keeps his problems to himself unless he requires help from another to find a solution. Asking for help when you can do it yourself is perceived as a sign of weakness.

10 However, if he truly does need help, then it is a sign of wisdom to get it. In this case, he will find someone he respects and then talk about his problem. Talking about a problem on Mars is an invitation for advice. Another Martian feels honored by the opportunity. Automatically he puts on his Mr. Fix-It hat, listens for a while, and then offers some jewels of advice.

This Martian custom is one of the reasons men instinctively offer solutions when women talk about problems. When a woman innocently shares upset feelings or explores out loud the problems of her day, a man mistakenly assumes she is looking for some expert advice. He puts on his Mr. Fix-It hat and begins giving advice; this is his way of showing love and of trying to help.

He wants to help her feel better by solving her problems. He wants to be useful to her. He feels he can be valued and thus worthy of her love when his abilities are used to solve her problems.

Once he has offered a solution, however, and she continues to be upset it becomes increasingly difficult for him to listen because his solution is being rejected and he feels increasingly useless.

He has no idea that by just listening with empathy and interest he can be supportive. He does not know that on Venus talking about problems is not an invitation to offer a solution.

Life on Venus

15 Venusians have different values. They value love, communication, beauty, and relationships. They spend a lot of time supporting, helping, and nurturing one another. Their sense of self is defined through their feelings and the quality of their relationships. They experience fulfillment through sharing and relating.

Everything on Venus reflects these values. Rather than building highways and tall buildings, the Venusians are more concerned with living together in harmony, community, and loving cooperation. Relationships are more important than work and technology. In most ways their world is the opposite of Mars.

They do not wear uniforms like the Martians (to reveal their competence). On the contrary, they enjoy wearing a different outfit every day, according to how they are feeling. Personal expression, especially of their feelings, is very important. They may even change outfits several times a day as their mood changes.

Communication is of primary importance. To share their personal feelings is much more important than achieving goals and success. Talking and relating to one another is a source of tremendous fulfillment.

This is hard for a man to comprehend. He can come close to understanding a woman's experience of sharing and relating by comparing it to the satisfaction he feels when he wins a race, achieves a goal, or solves a problem.

20 Instead of being goal oriented, women are relationship oriented; they are more concerned with expressing their goodness, love, and caring. Two Martians go to lunch to discuss a project or business goal; they have a problem to solve. In addition, Martians view going to a restaurant as an efficient way to approach food: no shopping, no cooking, and no washing dishes. For Venusians, going to lunch is an opportunity to nurture a relationship, for both giving support to and receiving support from a friend. Women's restaurant talk can be very open and intimate, almost like the dialogue that occurs between therapist and patient.

On Venus, everyone studies psychology and has at least a master's degree in counseling. They are very involved in personal growth, spirituality, and everything that can nurture life, healing, and growth. Venus is covered with parks, organic gardens, shopping centers, and restaurants.

Venusians are very intuitive. They have developed this ability through centuries of anticipating the needs of others. They pride themselves in being considerate of the needs and feelings of others. A sign of great love is to offer help and assistance to another Venusian without being asked.

Because proving one's competence is not as important to a Venusian, offering help is not offensive, and needing help is not a sign of weakness. A man, however, may feel offended because when a woman offers advice he doesn't feel she trusts his ability to do it himself.

A woman has no conception of this male sensitivity because for her it is another feather *in* her hat if someone offers to help her. It makes her feel loved and cherished. But offering help to a man can make him feel incompetent, weak, and even unloved.

On Venus it is a sign of caring to give advice and suggestions. Venusians firmly believe that when something is working it can always work better. Their nature is to want to improve things. When they care about someone, they freely point out what can be improved and suggest how to do it. Offering advice and constructive criticism is an act of love.

Mars is very different. Martians are more solution oriented. If something is working, their motto is don't change it. Their instinct is to leave it alone if it is working. "Don't fix it unless it is broken" is common expression.

When a woman tries to improve a man, he feels she is trying fix him. He receives the message that he is broken. She doesn't realize her caring attempts to help him may humiliate him. She mistakenly thinks she is just helping him to grow.

Give Up Giving Advice

Without this insight into the nature of men, it's very easy for a woman unknowingly and unintentionally to hurt and offend the man she loves most.

For example, Tom and Mary were going to a party. Tom was driving. After about twenty minutes and going around the block a few times, it was clear to Mary that Tom was lost. She finally suggested that he call for help. Tom became very silent. They eventually arrived at the party, but the tension from that moment persisted the whole evening. Mary had no idea of why he was so upset.

From her side she was saying, "I love and care about you, so I am offering you this help."

From his side, he was offended. What he heard was "I don't trust you to get us there. You are incompetent!"

Without knowing about life on Mars, Mary could not appreciate how important it was for Tom to accomplish his goal without help. Offering advice was the ultimate insult. As we have explored, Martians never offer advice unless asked. A way of honoring another Martian is *always* to assume he can solve his problem unless he is asking for help.

Mary had no idea that when Tom became lost and started circling the same block, it was a very special opportunity to love and support him. At that time he was particularly vulnerable and needed some extra love. To honor him by not offering advice would have been a gift equivalent to his buying her a beautiful bouquet of flowers or writing her a love note.

After learning about Martians and Venusians, Mary learned how to support Tom at such difficult times. The next time he was lost, instead of offering "help" she restrained herself from offering any advice, took a deep relaxing breath, and appreciated in her heart what Tom was trying to do for her. Tom greatly appreciated her warm acceptance and trust.

Generally speaking, when a woman offers unsolicited advice or tries to "help" a man, she has no idea of how critical and unloving she may sound to him. Even though her intent is loving, her suggestions do offend and hurt. His reaction may be strong, especially if he felt criticized as a child or he experienced his father being criticized by his mother.

For many men, it is very important to prove that they can get to their goal, even if it is a small thing like driving to a restaurant or party. Ironically he may be more sensitive about the little things than the big. His feelings are like this: "If I can't be trusted to do a small thing like get us to a party, how can she trust me to do the bigger things?" Like their Martian ancestors, men pride themselves on being experts, especially when it comes to fixing mechanical things, getting places, or solving problems. These are the times when he needs her loving acceptance the most and not her advice or criticism.

Learning to Listen

Likewise, if a man does not understand how a woman is different, he can make things worse when he is trying to help. Men need to remember that women talk about problems to get close and not necessarily to get solutions.

So many times a woman just wants to share her feelings about her day, and her husband, thinking he is helping, interrupts her by offering a steady flow of solutions to her problems. He has no idea why she isn't pleased.

For example, Mary comes home from an exhausting *day*. She wants and needs to share her feelings about the day.

40   She says, "There is so much to do; I don't have any time to myself."
Tom says, "You should quit that job. You don't have to work so hard. Find something you like to do."
Mary says, "But I like *my* job. They just expect me to change everything at a moment's notice."
Tom says, "Don't listen to them. Just do what you can do."
Mary says, "I *am!* I can't believe I completely forgot to call my aunt today."
45   Tom says, "Don't worry about it, she'll understand."
Mary says, "Do you know what she is going through? She needs me."
Tom says, "You worry too much, that's why you're so unhappy."
Mary angrily says, "I am not always unhappy. Can't you just listen to me?"
Tom says, "I *am* listening."
50   Mary says, "Why do I even bother?"

After this conversation, Mary was more frustrated than when she arrived home seeking intimacy and companionship. Tom was also frustrated and had no idea what went wrong. He wanted to help, but his problem-solving tactics didn't work.

Without knowing about life on Venus, Tom didn't understand how important it was just to listen without offering solutions. His solutions only made things worse. You see, Venusians never offer solutions when someone is talking. A way of honoring another Venusian is to listen patiently with empathy, seeking truly to understand the other's feelings.

Tom had no idea that just listening with empathy to Mary express her feelings would bring her tremendous relief and fulfillment. When Tom heard about the Venusians and how much they needed to talk, he gradually learned how to listen.

When Mary now comes home tired and exhausted their conversations are quite different. They sound like this:

55   Mary says, "There is so much to do. I have no time for me."
Tom takes a deep breath, relaxes on the exhale, and says, "Humph, sounds like you had a hard day."
Mary says, "They expect me to change everything at a moment's notice. I don't know what to do."
Tom pauses and then says, "Hmmm."
Mary says, "I even forgot to call my aunt."
60   Tom says with a slightly wrinkled brow, "Oh, no."
Mary says, "She needs me so much right now. I feel so bad."

Tom says, "You are such a loving person. Come here, let me give you a hug."

Tom gives Mary a hug and she relaxes in his arms with a big sigh of relief. She then says, "I love talking with you. You make me really happy. Thanks for listening. I feel much better."

Not only Mary but also Tom felt better. He was amazed at how much happier his wife was when he finally learned to listen. With this new awareness of their differences, Tom learned the wisdom of listening without offering solutions while Mary learned the wisdom of letting go and accepting without offering unsolicited advice or criticism.

65 To summarize the two most common mistakes we make in relationships: (1) A man tries to change a woman's feelings when she is upset by becoming Mr. Fix-It and offering solutions to her problems that invalidate her feelings. (2) A woman tries to change a man's behavior when he makes mistakes by becoming the home-improvement committee and offering unsolicited advice or criticism.

In Defense of Mr. Fix-It and the Home-Improvement Committee

In pointing out these two major mistakes I do not mean that everything is wrong with Mr. Fix-It or the home-improvement committee. These are very positive Martian and Venusian attributes. The mistakes are only in timing and approach.

A woman greatly appreciates Mt Fix-It, as long as he doesn't come out when she is upset. Men need to remember that when women seem upset and talk about problems is not the time to offer solutions; instead she needs to be heard, and gradually she will feel better on her own. She does not need to be fixed.

A man greatly appreciates the home-improvement committee as long as it is requested. Women need to remember that unsolicited advice or criticism—especially if he has made a mistake—make him feel unloved and controlled. He needs her acceptance more than her advice, in order to learn from his mistakes. When a man feels that a woman is not trying to improve him, he is much more likely to ask for her feedback and advice.

Understanding these differences makes it easier to respect our partner's sensitivities and be more supportive. In addition we recognize that when our partner resists us it is probably because we made a mistake in our timing or approach. Let's explore this in greater detail.

When a Woman Resists a Man's Solutions

70 When a woman resists a man's solutions he feels his competence is being questioned. As a result he feels mistrusted, unappreciated, and stops caring. His willingness to listen understandably lessens.

By remembering that women are from Venus, a man at such times can instead understand why she is resisting him. He can reflect and discover how he was probably offering solutions at a time when she was needing empathy and nurturing.

Here are some brief examples of ways a man might mistakenly invalidate feelings and perceptions or offer unwanted solutions. See if you can recognize why she would resist:

1. "You shouldn't worry so much."
2. "But that is not what I said."
3. "It's not such a big deal."
4. "OK, I'm sorry. Now can we just forget it."
5. "Why don't you just do it?"
6. "But we do talk."
7. "You shouldn't feel hurt, that's not what I meant."

8. "So what are you trying to say?"
9. "But you shouldn't feel that way."
10. "How can you say that? Last week I spent the whole day with you. We had a great time."
11. "OK, then just forget it."
12. "All right, I'll clean up the backyard. Does that make you happy?"
13. "I got it. This is what you should do."
14. "Look, there's nothing we can do about it."
15. "If you are going to complain about doing it, then don't do it."
16. "Why do you let people treat you that way? Forget them."
17. "If you're not happy then we should just get a divorce."
18. "All right, then you can do it from now on."
19. "From now on, I will handle it."
20. "Of course I care about you. That's ridiculous."
21. "Would you get to the point?"
22. "All we have to do is . . ."
23. "That's not at all what happened."

Each of these statements either invalidates or attempts to explain upset feelings or offers a solution designed suddenly to change her negative feelings to positive feelings. The first step a man can take to change this pattern is simply to stop making the above comments. To practice listening without offering any invalidating comments or solutions is, however, a big step.

By clearly understanding that his timing and delivery are being rejected and not his solutions, a man can handle a woman's resistance much better. He doesn't take it so personally. By learning to listen, gradually he will experience that she will appreciate him more even when at first she is upset with him.

When a Man Resists the Home-Improvement Committee

75

When a man resists a woman's suggestions she feels as though he doesn't care; she feels her needs are not being respected. As a result, she understandably feels unsupported and stops trusting him.

At such times, by remembering that men are from Mars, she can instead correctly understand why he is resisting her. She can reflect and discover how she was probably giving him unsolicited advice or criticism rather than simply sharing her needs, providing information, or making a request.

Here are some brief examples of ways a woman might unknowingly annoy a man by offering advice or seemingly harmless criticism. As you explore this list, remember that these little things can add up to create big walls of resistance and resentment. In some of the statements the advice or criticism is hidden. See if you can recognize why he might feel controlled.

1. "How can you think of buying that? You already have one."
2. "Those dishes are still wet. They'll dry with spots."
3. "Your hair is getting kind of long, isn't it?"
4. "There's a parking spot over there, turn [the car] around."
5. "You want to spend time with your friends, what about me?"
6. "You shouldn't work so hard. Take a day off."
7. "Don't put that there. It will get lost."
8. "You should call a plumber. He'll know what to do."

9. "Why are we waiting for a table? Didn't you make reservations?"
10. "You should spend more time with the kids. They miss you."
11. "Your office is still a mess. How can you think in here? When are you going to clean it up?"
12. "You forgot to bring it home again. Maybe you could put it in a special place where you can remember it."
13. "You're driving too fast. Slow down or you'll get a ticket."
14. "Next time we should read the movie reviews."
15. "I didn't know where you were." (You should have called.)
16. "Somebody drank from the juice bottle."
17. "Don't eat with your fingers. You're setting a bad example."
18. "Those potato chips are too greasy. They're not good for your heart."
19. "You are not leaving yourself enough time."
20. "You should give me more [advance] notice. I can't just drop everything and go to lunch with you."
21. "Your shirt doesn't match your pants."
22. "Bill called for the third time. When are you going to call him back?"
23. "Your toolbox is such a mess. I can't find anything. You should organize it."

When a woman does not know how to directly ask a man for support or constructively share a difference of opinion, she may feel powerless to get what she needs without giving unsolicited advice or criticism. . . . To practice giving acceptance and not giving advice and criticism is, however, a big step.

By clearly understanding he is rejecting not her needs but the way she is approaching him, she can take his rejection less personally and explore more supportive ways of communicating her needs. Gradually she will realize that a man wants to make improvement when he feels he is being approached as the solution to a problem rather than as the problem itself.

80 If you are a woman, I suggest that for the next week [you] practice restraining from giving *any* unsolicited advice or criticism. The men in your life not only will appreciate it but also will be more attentive and responsive to you.

If you are a man, I suggest that for the next week you practice listening *whenever* a woman speaks, with the sole intention of respectfully understanding what she is going through. Practice biting your tongue whenever you get the urge to offer a solution or change how she is feeling. You will be surprised when you experience how much she appreciates you.

RESPONSE QUESTIONS

1. Do you believe there are essential differences between men and women in relationships? If so, what are they? Give an example from your own experience (or a film, story, or historical event) that illustrates how men and women interpret the same experiences differently—or similarly.

2. According to Gray, men and women resist each other's efforts to improve them or to solve their problems. Why do men resist "improvement"? Why do women resist "solutions"?

3. Where in the essay does the author distinguish between what women and men are most interested in? Judging from your own experience, how accurate are these distinctions?

4. Read through the two lists of quotes. Check the ones that sound most familiar, and explore the hidden advice or criticism.

5. How useful do you find Gray's suggestions for solving conflicts? Which of his explanations would be most helpful to men? To women? Please explain your choices.

GUIDELINES FOR ANALYSIS

1. Why does the author say that men and women come from different planets? What purpose does this exaggeration serve?

Visual Prompt

2. Trace the essay's methods of resolving conflicts. Where does Gray state the problem and define his terms? Where does he give examples? What explanations does he offer for the positions taken by men and women? Where does he qualify or summarize his observations? What solutions does he offer?

3. In the long run, how balanced is Gray's presentation? Does he take sides, or does he acknowledge all points of view objectively and equally before offering advice?

4. *Men Are from Mars and Women Are from Venus* has sold over eight million copies in the United States and many more abroad. How do you account for the popularity of this book?

5. Consider the history of the Mars and Venus myth. See, for example, paintings of Mars and Venus, like Veronese's *Mars and Venus United by Love* pictured here. How does the myth fit Gray's essay? Is there anything that doesn't fit or that seems out of place?

QUESTIONS OF CULTURE

1. Some readers find Gray's characterizations to be stereotypical, even sexist. Explain why you agree or disagree.

2. Gray does not distinguish between different ages, nationalities, or ethnic groups. Do you think he should? How well would his observations apply to Swedish couples, for example, or Koreans, or gay and lesbian relationships?

3. Gray's writing belongs to a genre known as self-help books. What features do such books have in common? Who produces them, who reads them, and who gains what from whom?

IDEAS FOR YOUR JOURNAL

1. Make your own list of familiar statements men and women make to each other. Translate what is really being said (or heard) between the lines.

2. Try following Gray's advice, and report on the results.

PREVIEW

Natalie Angier, a Pulitzer Prize–winning journalist, was the mother of a young girl when John Gray's book came out. Born in 1958, she studied English, physics, and astronomy at the University of Michigan and Barnard College before going to work for various science magazines and joining the *New York Times* in 1990. Her provocative books on science and contemporary issues include *Natural Obsessions* (1988), *The Beauty of the Beastly* (1995), and *Woman: An Intimate Geography* (2000).

The following article appeared in the *New York Times*. Although Angier does not refer specifically to *Men Are from Mars, Women Are from Venus,* she does take issue with the idea that men and women are from different planets. Watch how she builds an argument, basing her position on personal experience, observation about our culture, and some research.

Condemning Our Kids to Life on Mars or Venus

By Natalie Angier

As a mother of a 2-year-old child, I am rather too intimately acquainted with a large, purple TV dinosaur named Barney. I know the lyrics to a number of the show's exhortatory songs (my personal favorite: "It's time to CLEAN UP! CLEANUP! 'Cause we want to do our share!"), and I've attended to the carefully selected multisociocultural cast. The rotating group of children has included whites, blacks, Chinese, Koreans, Hispanics, Arabs, kids in wheelchairs, a blind girl, a boy with a hearing aid, chubby kids, identical twin kids.

But if there is one thing I have never seen amid the peppy junior rainbow coalition it is a child whose sex is at all ambiguous, who is not, in other words, clearly and unmistakably either a girl or a boy. Virtually all the girls have long, luxurious hair, the boys short. And though the girls do wear pants, they as often wear dresses, accoutred with nifty striped knee socks or prim white anklets.

Such stylistic options are obviously not open to the Barney boys, who are close to horror-struck when they pay an imaginary visit to Scotland and meet a male bagpipe player wearing a kilt. "Don't worry," the man assures them. "This is just for special occasions; normally I dress just like you."

In recent months, it has become almost fashionable to toss around terms like "transgender" and "meta-sexual." A fall issue of the liberal digest, *Utne Reader,* is emblazoned with a picture of a man with breasts and a woman without. "It's 2 A.M.," a cover headline says. "Do you know what sex you are? Does anybody?"

The media has given wide play to the cause of intersexuals, or hermaphrodites, who reject the notion of the binary sex code and all surgical attempts to enforce it. Glam rock and its androgynous spoofery is back, sort of. We love gender-benders, crossdressers, and gay men and lesbians when they're well-behaved. They're so interesting and cute, and they remind us of how complex and interdigitating the concepts of maleness and femaleness can be. How far we've progressed; how nuanced is our thinking!

Except, that is, when it comes to our children. For our children, the categorical distinctions we make between male and female remain inviolate, more so, in a sense, than ever before. After a brief period in the 1970's and early 1980's of questioning infant apartheid by pink and blue, the world has "rediscovered" just how different boys and girls really are. And if you're a parent, you can't get away from the drumbeat of La Difference. On commercial television, the advertisements for boys' toys roar, "Smash 'em, hate 'em, annihilate 'em!" while the jingles for girls' toys are so taffy-sweet you'll go running for the dental floss.

It's not just the crass media. Everybody reinforces the old truisms. I go to a party of standard, middle-class Nature Conservancy donor-card types, and an older boy takes away my daughter's cup of milk. I jokingly warn my daughter, "You've got to watch out for those older kids." No, the boy's mother says. It's because he's a boy. A moment later, an older girl grabs away my daughter's cup of milk, but, um, that does not count.

I take my daughter shopping at the local food co-op and wend my way through aisles of bulk organic kasha and woven hemp shopping bags, and still the store clerks must comment on how "good" and "nice" little girls are. "If my son were here," one said, "he'd be pulling everything off the shelves!" Later, when I get home and my daughter sends an avalanche of books crashing to the floor and clobbers the cat with a wooden block, I consider calling the clerk and offering a child swap, but, hey, my daughter's longish hair is awfully pretty.

Behind the mounting insistence that boys will be boys and girls will behave, by birth and by genotype, is, I believe, the rising popularity of fields like behavioral genetics and evolutionary psychology, which habitually reach sweeping conclusions about deep human nature on the basis of the scantiest of data. Geneticists find behavioral differences between two sets of girls with a chromosomal condition called Turner's syndrome, and the next thing you know they're speculating grandly about a gene for

social graciousness, which girls have but boys don't.

Evolutionary psychologists distribute questionnaires to college students about what qualities they find attractive in the opposite sex, and the male students say they like kind, funny, intelligent, considerate, attractive women; and the female students say they like kind, funny, intelligent, considerate, industrious men; and evolutionary psychologists conclude, "Ah ha! Men and women really are different after all—men want comely mates, women want ambitious mates, and it has been thus since that mystical, all-powerful Stone Age."

So if women aim to please, and men aim to get ahead, we may see such behaviors as the fruits of sexual selection, the need for each sex to respond to the desires of the other. Which, when scaled down to suit our presexual children, works out roughly as: boys are naturally aggressive; girls are naturally solicitous.

On average, of course, scientists are always careful to speak of averages rather than absolutes. But still, there you are, and there's my girl, deemed "nice" by nature, and there's the boy gestating in the belly of a friend of mine, who will, a mother of sons assures my friend, "be a radical change" from the daughter my friend already had. Barbara Mackoff, a psychologist in Seattle and the

author of *Growing a Girl: Seven Strategies following a Strong, Spirited Daughter,* points out that we are now using our children to fight the old battle of the sexes. "The new question is, Who has it worse, boys or girls?" she said. "Who is more shortchanged by society?"

On the one hand, girls are said to suffer a crushing loss of self-cofidence at puberty, and thus to be at a disadvantage relative to boys. On the other hand, a new line of argument says that boys are worse off, for they suffer from comparatively high rates of conduct disorder, are more likely to be put on medications like Ritalin, and have a higher risk of being truants and high school dropouts.

"It's a new war, but the weapons we're using are the same ones we've always used in the battle of the sexes, and it always comes down to nature versus nurture," Dr. Mackoff said. "Those who argue that boys are shortchanged by this culture insist that boys will be boys by nature." As an example, she cites another recent book, *The Wonder of Boys,* in which the author, Michael Gurian, insists that boys are rambunctious and high-spirited not because they watch too many crush 'em, mush 'em TV commercials or any other such "politically correct" reason, but because, yes, testosterone makes them do it.

Well, some similar psycho-irritant—estrogen? choler? Saturn in retrograde?—makes me resent the persistent emphasis on sexual dialectics, particularly when it is writ small and applied to my daughter and her peers. Are there "innate" sex differences? Possibly, on average, with a staggering amount of overlap. Ho hum!

"There are so many conflicting theories about sex differences that may never be resolved," Dr. Mackoff said. "But we don't have to deny that sex differences may exist, or tackle that problem to the ground, to recognize that the biggest difference between girls and boys is in how we treat them. There is where our effort and focus should be. As long as we dwell obsessively on sex differences, we're going to put limits on our kids and shortchange every one of them."

Let me tell you a few things about my girl. She loves to play with toy animals and insects and already can name as many species as the average zoology student. She loves books about practically anything. She's fascinated by mechanical vehicles: cars, trucks, planes, vans, ditch-diggers, cherry pickers. She likes dressing up in her mother's shoes and wearing her mother's lipstick. She can throw a ball beautifully but is not much of a climber. She can draw a perfect circle. She keeps asking when we're going to take her to the dentist.

From birth, she has struck me and my husband as being straight down the middle, neither girlish nor boyish by any standard template. Of course, she is only an N of one, as scientists say, an anecdote, and not proof of anything. Eventually, the science of human nature and of sex differences may get so sophisticated that it actually has something useful to tell her about herself.

And maybe someday Barney will come to work in a skirt.

RESPONSE QUESTIONS

1. Angier says that boys and girls are clearly differentiated in all the children's TV shows that she has seen. Why does she see this as a problem?

2. Angier's title is an allusion to John Gray's book, *Men Are from Mars, Women Are from Venus.* Compare her views on the differences between men and women to the views expressed in Gray's essay on page 389. Why does she believe that we are "condemning our kids to life on Mars and Venus"?

3. In the middle of her essay, Angier summarizes the research of evolutionary psychologists. What does she think of their work? What reasons does she give for her point of view?

4. Trace your ongoing conversation with the author while reading this essay. Where do you find yourself resisting or agreeing with her argument?

5. Reread the author's description of her child. Does she sound like the little girls you know?

GUIDELINES FOR ANALYSIS

1. In paragraph 5, the author writes, "We love gender-benders, crossdressers, and gay men and lesbians when they're well-behaved. They're so interesting and cute, and they remind us how complex and interdigitating the concepts of maleness and femaleness can be." How would you describe the tone of her writing here? Where else do you find this tone in her writing?

2. The author begins and ends with a reference to Barney. Why do you think she frames her essay in this way?

3. Angier makes observations based on commercial television, a party, and a local food co-op. What points are illustrated by these examples? What other examples does she offer?

4. How would you rate this essay on its use of persuasive strategies? Consider the author's examples, her reasoning, the authorities to whom she refers, and her use of her own child as anecdotal evidence. Where is the essay most or least effective as an argument?

QUESTIONS OF CULTURE

1. Angier describes the characters on a certain television children's show as "a carefully selected multisociocultural cast." How true is this of children's programs today? Compare the ethnic and social diversity of these programs with their predecessors.

2. Use Angier's description of her little girl as the starting point for making two lists: traits that you associate with girls and traits that you associate with boys. Where do these associations come from? How widely are they shared?

IDEAS FOR YOUR JOURNAL

1. Imagine a conversation between John Gray and Natalie Angier. What would they say to each other about gender differences? What positions would they be likely to take, and how might they argue or attempt to resolve their differences?

2. What if children's programming began to reflect the sexual ambiguity that Angier finds in the modern adult world? What might the consequences be for children, their families, and society at large?

PREVIEW

On January 14, 2005, Harvard's President Lawrence Summers made public remarks about mental ability and gender that sent shock waves through academia and eventually led to his resignation. Speaking at a conference on diversity, Dr. Summers suggested that intrinsic differences in aptitude for science and engineering might explain the scarcity of women in these fields more than socialization. In the controversy that followed his speech, men and women from diverse fields and institutions joined in a national debate, raising pointed questions about inequities in testing and careers. What do scientists say about this issue? Does research really support Dr. Summers's statement? Are there significant differences between male and female brains?

Bob McDonald, host of Canada's popular radio program *Quirks and Quarks,* posed these and other questions to prominent professors of psychology. The following transcript is from a radio documentary broadcast on April 20, 2005, by CBC radio, a commercial-free, publicly owned corporation that also airs its programs on the Internet. As you read this excerpt from the transcript or listen to the entire broadcast (available on the companion Web site), notice the voices of persuasion and reconciliation at work.

www.mhhe.com/costanzo

To listen to the audio for this program, visit the book's Web site.

TRANSCRIPT OF CBC'S *QUIRKS AND QUARKS:* "MALE AND FEMALE BRAINS"

BOB MCDONALD (HOST OF CBC RADIO'S QUIRKS AND QUARKS): Hello, I'm Bob McDonald. Welcome to Quirks and Quarks on CBC Radio One. Leading today's program, Venus versus Mars. Are male and female brains really different? Also on the program, attack of the sea hare. When a spray is more than a perfume. Plus, ant attack with a torture rack, and some islet insight into treating diabetes. All this and more today, on Quirks and Quarks.

(MUSIC)

BOB MCDONALD: Many a comedian has made a handsome living poking fun at the differences between men and women. How is it, men ask, that women can talk on the phone for hours on end with a girlfriend they just saw for lunch? And why is it women wonder that men just can't seem to grasp the concept that an empty toilet paper roll needs replacing with a full one?

MCDONALD: But there were no jokes to be heard earlier this year when the President of Harvard University, Larry Summers, suggested that perhaps men and women not only have different character traits, but have different intellectual abilities as well. While trying to explain why there are so few women in faculties like mathematics, physics, chemistry and engineering, Dr. Summers said that there were, what he called, issues of intrinsic aptitude. He seemed to imply that women, by nature, are not as good at those disciplines as men. The response to Dr. Summers' comments was fast and furious. Critics demanded that Summers step down, and he was forced to issue a public apology. Harvard is one the most prestigious universities in the world, and having its president suggest that women can't do math was just too much for many people.

MCDONALD: But others thought this could be the beginning of a debate that needed to be heard. After all, of the 32 offers of tenure made by Harvard's Faculty of Arts and Sciences last year, only four went to women. Why is that? In a society that's characterized by the closing of gender gaps, perhaps it's not unreasonable to ask why a few of them so stubbornly persist. It's likely that there are still some lingering biases and barriers against women, but what about biology? Men and women evolve to fulfill very different roles, after all. We know there are plenty of physiological differences between the sexes. So is it really so far-fetched to suggest that there could also be differences between what a male brain can do and what a female brain can do?

5 MCDONALD: Two different scientific camps have emerged on this issue. One side argues that even if there are indeed neurological differences between men and women, they're outweighed by social pressures. It's discrimination and stereotyping, they'd say, that are keeping women away from these remaining academic heights.

MCDONALD: The other camp would argue that biological differences cannot be discounted, producing if not innate differences in ability, then at least innate differences in interests, which could affect career choices. But to try to answer any of these questions, it seems we should start by taking a look at the very organ at the centre of the debate, the brain itself.

MCDONALD: Dr. Richard Haier is a professor of psychology at the University of California Irvine, and he's in the business of studying sex differences in the brain, because he thinks that if we know what the differences are, then we can develop better treatment for diseases of the brain. But his findings might also be relevant to the discussion of cognitive ability. Traditionally, scientists believe that intelligence resided in the so-called grey matter of the brain, and that men had more of this brain tissue. But according to Dr. Haier, grey matter is not the only game in town.

DR. RICHARD HAIER (PROFESSOR OF PSYCHOLOGY AT THE UNIVERSITY OF CALIFORNIA IRVINE): We used magnetic resonance imaging, MRI, to make structural images of the brains of about 53 normal volunteers. We then used the MRI images to determine the amount of grey matter and white matter throughout the brain. The brain has two kinds of tissue. The grey matter is where the processing is done, where the brain work is done. The white matter is like the wiring that connects different parts of the brain to each other. And we can use MRIs to determine the amount of grey matter and white matter tissue in every spot in the brain. These spots are called voxels. And we can then correlate the amount of grey or white matter in each voxel to IQ. And when we did this, we found a number of areas where brain tissue was correlated to intelligence. In men, most of those areas were in the grey matter. In women, most of those areas were in the white matter.

MCDONALD: The curious part of Dr. Haier's research is that even though the brain architecture differed between the sexes, it wasn't related to any difference in intelligence. So men and women might have different brain anatomy, but their capacity for cognitive processing is the same. But Dr. Haier still doesn't quite know how it is that two different brain architectures can produce the exact same results.

10 HAIER: It may be that if you have more wiring, this could be like having a higher speed cable connection for your computer when you access the inter-

net, that you might be processing information faster along the wiring, and therefore you need less processing power . . . that the speed makes up for having less processing power. We don't really know how this works. It might be that women have more efficient brains when it comes to processing information, because they seem to need less brain matter to obtain equal levels of . . . cognitive processing.

MCDONALD: These findings do not surprise Dr. Simon Baron-Cohen. He's a professor of psychology and psychiatry at Cambridge University. Based on psychological and behavioral tests, he's developed a theory suggesting that there are two very distinct brain types, a male and a female, and that men and women are biologically predisposed to be good at different things.

DR. SIMON BARON-COHEN (PROFESSOR OF PSYCHOLOGY AND PSYCHIATRY AT CAMBRIDGE UNIVERSITY): Essentially I've been studying the idea that in women and girls there is a greater drive to empathize, and in boys and men there's a greater drive to systemize. And we know what empathy's all about, being able to tune into other people's feelings, imagine their thoughts and to respond appropriately. But systemizing is a relatively new idea, and it's all about having a fascination with how systems work, whether we're talking about machines or mathematics.

MCDONALD: Dr. Baron-Cohen has found that men are usually better at visual spatial tasks. For example, 3-D computer games or reading maps. Women, on the other hand, are often better at the tasks that are not about objects, but about people, such as identifying the emotional state of a person based on the expression in their eyes. But, not always Dr. Baron-Cohen cautions. Men can have a more female brain, and women can have a more male brain. A more female brain doesn't make you any less of a man, of course, but, he says, the makeup of your brain does, in part, determine what you're good at, and therefore, which areas of work you're likely to gravitate towards, or how good you are at math. More importantly, he says, these differences are not just a result of the input we get from our environment as we grow up. They're present at birth, which indicates that they're at least partly biological.

BARON-COHEN: We've done one study which looked at newborn babies on the first day of life, looking at boys and girls to see whether they have a preference for looking at social objects like people's faces or mechanical objects like a mechanical mobile suspended above the crib. And we find these sex differences are present even at birth. Boys preferring to look at the mechanical object, and girls preferring to look at the face.

15 MCDONALD: But others question both the findings and the implications of Dr. Baron-Cohen's work. One of them is Dr. Elizabeth Spelke, a psychology professor at Harvard University. She does not subscribe to the idea that male and female brains are innately different in any significant way. And she questions the methods used in his tests. In any event, in her own work she's produced opposite results from Dr. Baron-Cohen's. She's found no indication of different interests in infant boys and girls.

DR. ELIZABETH SPELKE (PROFESSOR OF PSYCHOLOGY AT HARVARD UNIVERSITY): We do studies in a number of domains. One that I've looked at for about 30 years concerns infants' understanding of objects and their mechanical properties. Infancy is this fascinating period where we put together our basic intuitive understandings of how the mechanical world behaves, how objects behave when they hit each other, how they move, what kinds of forces change their motions, and so forth. In all of these cases we see infants developing knowledge at an exciting rate. They start out, already at birth, able to perceive objects, to represent objects when they're hidden, and they've already quickly come to learn about their properties. We see boys and girls understanding the same things, learning the same things, paying attention to objects with the same intensity throughout this period of development.

MCDONALD: There's a large body of widely quoted research that suggests that boys and girls perform differently on academic tests depending on the subject. We've probably all heard it paraphrased at some point that girls are doing better than boys in arts, and that boys are doing better than girls in math. But Dr. Spelke says the methods used to assess these performances often contain inherent biases that will affect the results. Biases, she says, are often so deeply engrained in our culture and in ourselves, that we don't even know they're there. But they still affect how we perceive things, including how we perceive ourselves. She quotes a study of Asian schoolgirls to illustrate her point.

SPELKE: This was a study in which girls who were Asian were given a timed math test. And shortly before they were given the test they were asked a set of questions. And they were run in two different conditions. In one condition, the questions focused on their Asian identity, when did your family emigrate from Asia, come to the United States, and so forth. For the other group, the questions focused on their feminine identity. And then everyone was given the test. The reason they set up those two sets of questions is that in this group the stereotype is that Asians are good at math and that girls are bad at math. And they found that these Asian girls performed better on this math test when they . . . their questions had led them to think of themselves as Asian, [than] when their questions led them to think of themselves as female.

MCDONALD: The foundation for biases like these is often laid by the parents in a child's early years. Often through such innocent activities as play. But play is an important part of cognitive development in children. So the kind of play, or the toys kids play with, can actually influence their brain development. Since parents almost automatically and unconsciously provide gender-specific toys to their children, this could easily explain why boys prefer to play with trucks, and girls prefer to play with dolls. Those are the toys they've been encouraged to play with after all. But perhaps that's not the whole story. Dr. Gerianne Alexander is a Canadian scientist who's now an assistant professor of psychology at Texas A&M University. She thinks about sex differences along the same lines as Dr. Baron-Cohen. So in an experiment with vervet monkeys she tested the idea that toy preferences might have a biological component to them as well.

20 DR. GERIANNE ALEXANDER (ASSISTANT PROFESSOR OF PSYCHOLOGY AT TEXAS A&M UNIVERSITY): We presented toys that we knew were differentially preferred by boys and girls one at a time to the animal groups, and we videotaped them, and we later coded interactions or contact with these different toys. And our analysis showed that the male animals spent more time, relative to the female animals, with toys that are typically preferred by boys. And the female vervet spent more time with toys that are typically preferred by girls, compared to their male counterparts. So the data were consistent with what we see in children. But of course in these animals we know that they're not socialized to show these preferences, and really probably have no idea that they were interacting with, say a truck, because presumably they wouldn't know what a truck was. And so this is sort of compelling evidence, I think, consistent with the idea that there are these biological influences on children's toy preferences.

MCDONALD: In other words, the male monkeys preferred playing with trucks, and the female monkeys liked playing with dolls. And they clearly weren't influenced by their parents. So what might explain this innate difference in preference? Well, for one thing, we know there are environmental factors that can influence our biology, such as our hormone balance. According to Dr. Baron-Cohen, animal studies have shown that higher levels of the male hormone testosterone at the fetal stage can shape brain development and influence differences between the sexes. So he looked at human babies to see if the same was true for them.

BARON-COHEN: What we find is if you follow up those babies after they're born, those babies who had a higher level of fetal testosterone make less eye contact when they're toddlers and are slower to develop language when you measure that at two years old. So these are striking differences related to hormones, and they also relate to being male and female. Obviously males produce a lot more testosterone than females. And we find differences in eye contact and language development, with girls developing faster than boys on both of those measures.

MCDONALD: So, if hormones at least influence the difference between male and female brains, then perhaps the biological explanation for toy preferences is to be found in the hormonal balance as well. Dr. Alexander says that for both humans and many animal species, there's evidence to suggest that male hormone levels at the prenatal stage affect preferences for certain play styles after birth.

ALEXANDER: If you look at boys or males of a lot of different species, they rough and tumble more than females. And that rough and tumble, that prefer- ence for that active play, is influenced by these higher levels of androgens during prenatal life. So one idea is that maybe these toys allow themselves or permit higher levels of these active play styles that are preferred by boys. So that would be one idea.

25 ALEXANDER: The other possibility is related to what toys may contribute to the development of cognitive abilities. And people have suggested that toys preferred by boys afford opportunities for exploring object motion and con- struction. So a ball moves, a truck moves. And that these experiences with movement or with manipulating shapes might be attractive to males, more attractive to males than say to females. And then interacting with these toys then allows boys to develop spatial abilities.

MCDONALD: The point here is that if boys have more experience with motion and mechanics at a young age, they're more likely to gravitate towards those fields, such as engineering or math that require those abilities. But does that entirely explain the lack of women at the top of the academic ladder in certain fields of science? Probably not. Although men have slightly bigger brains, a discovery that, for a long time, kept the misconception alive that men are smarter than women, today scientists know that men and women are of equal intelligence, general intelligence that is. However, Larry Summers, the Harvard president, was wondering specifically about the ability to do mathematical reasoning at the very high levels required to become a profes- sor of physics or engineering, for instance. And here there do seem to be more males at the very top of the scale. This has been a subject of an ongoing study that started over four decades ago at Johns Hopkins University. It's known as The Study of Mathematically Precocious Youth, and it follows a population of gifted children from childhood into adult life. The goal is to identify the key factors that lead to academic achievement. Dr. Haier was involved with the study as a young graduate student, and says the results are so far intriguing, especially when they revisited some of those children 20 years later. The men and women report equal levels of job satisfaction, but different career choices.

HAIER: Interestingly a disproportionate number of the women went into fields like law and medicine. So more of the mathematically precocious boys, 20 years later, are working as math professors or . . . engineers, and more of the women are working as doctors and lawyers. The women in the mathematical precocious study were doing the math at this very high end just as well as the boys, and it goes back to the point . . . the erroneous stereotype that women can't do this. Woman can do it, there just aren't as many. And among the women who can do math at the high end, 20 years later when you ask them why they do law or medicine instead of engineering, they report things like, well, I like people more than things, and I don't like engineering. It's not that they can't do it, they just don't like it.

MCDONALD: So, it appears that all through elementary school, high school and college, girls are able to do math just as well as boys. But at some point during the course of their education, as their male peers go on to do graduate work in physics or math, even the most mathematically gifted women often choose to apply their abilities elsewhere. But why? Dr. Spelke thinks the answer is pretty simple.

SPELKE: If you had looked at what was happening when I was a student 30 years ago, many, many fewer women were going into biology and medicine. I think one of the differences there is there's been a social change in our perception of what is appropriate for a person of one or the other gender to do. And we see that reflected in people's expressed interests. So I'm not sure what would happen to our interests if it suddenly became widely considered to be ok for a woman to be a computer scientist, or a physicist. But I think looking at changes that have occurred in the past suggest that those interests might be very valuable.

30 MCDONALD: So, that leaves us with two camps who are still in wide disagreement. Dr. Spelke would say that any biological differences between the sexes are outweighed by social pressures and cultural influences. On the other

hand, people like Dr. Baron-Cohen and Dr. Alexander, are ready to attribute a lot more of the psychological differences between men and women to our biology. At the very least, Dr. Alexander says, we shouldn't be afraid of the idea that men and women are different. No one is saying one is better than the other, or smarter than the other. It could just be, as Dr. Haier suggested, that men and women simply have different brain architectures doing the same job. But Dr. Baron-Cohen stresses that we're not all biology. It's not just a choice of nature or nurture. Most scientists today agree it's a combination of the two. So even if you were born with a predisposition to play with either trucks or dolls, no one's saying those interests can't be influenced by parents or culture. After all, rumors are that even Einstein liked to play with dolls when he was young.

(MUSIC) . . .

RESPONSE QUESTIONS

1. Before you read the transcript or listen to the audio, take stock of your own views about intelligence. What do you already know or believe about the nature of male and female brains? Where do your knowledge and beliefs come from? Notice how the radio documentary affirms or challenges your preconceptions. What new information or ideas have you learned from "Male and Female Brains"? What else do you still want to know, and where would you go to find it?

2. What positions do the four psychologists take? What makes them authorities? What evidence and reasons do they offer in support of their positions? Their studies range from brain anatomy and hormone levels to infant behavior and experiments with monkeys. Whom do you find most convincing, and why?

3. Do any voices seem missing from the conversation? Is there anyone else you would have chosen for the interviews, and what would they have contributed?

GUIDELINES FOR ANALYSIS

1. The lead-in mentions Mars, Venus, and gender jokes and then moves from a light tone to more serious issues raised by Dr. Summers's talk. What other shifts in tone can you point to? On the whole, how would you describe this program's style? How does it compare to other talk shows that you know?

2. What role (or roles) does Bob McDonald assume? At what point in the program does he summarize (condense) or paraphrase (put into his own words) what experts say? When does he link their comments to the program's central topic? Where does he ask questions ("but what about biology?"), make inferences ("He seemed to imply"), or label people ("Critics demanded")? Is he generally neutral, or does he take sides?

3. A good radio documentary, like a well-written essay or documentary film, is carefully composed. Notice how the various pieces of this program were assembled after the interviews took place. What decisions were made about the show's beginning, middle, and ending? How else might the material have been selected and arranged?

QUESTIONS OF CULTURE

1. In *The Argument Culture* and "For Argument's Sake" (see pages 379 and 383), Deborah Tannen claims that the media contribute to a climate of aggression by using combative language and focusing on two opposing sides for every issue. To what degree does *Quirks and Quarks* resort to these antagonistic tactics or seek, instead, to give a balanced presentation of multiple viewpoints? What strategies of mediation or debate can you find in McDonald's commentary to support your analysis?

2. Dr. Elizabeth Spelke refers to a study of Asian schoolgirls in which the girls scored differently on math tests when focusing on their Asian identity than when focusing on their feminine identity. What point is she making about testing and cultural identity? How well does this point agree with your previous reading or personal experience?

IDEAS FOR YOUR JOURNAL

1. If you have access to children, observe their behavior along gender lines. What differences, if any, do you observe between the boys and the girls? What inferences (logical conclusions) can you draw from these observations? What experiments might test your conclusions more scientifically?

2. Check out CBC's Web page for this program (available at http://www.cbc/ca/quirks/archives/04-05/apr30.html), which offers links to Dr. Summers's speech and Web sites for the experts interviewed by Bob McDonald. Then create your own scenario for a radio documentary based on this material.

PREVIEW

Born in 1937 in San Francisco, Judy Brady attended the University of Iowa and received a B.F.A. in painting. Since then, as a freelance writer, Judy Brady has written essays on topics such as union organizing, abortion, and the role of women in society. Her most popular essay is "I Want a Wife," which originally appeared in *Ms.* magazine in 1971. Here she takes on the topic of gender roles and stereotypes with a distinctive sense of humor.

I Want a Wife

By Judy Brady

I belong to that classification of people known as wives. I am A Wife. And, not altogether incidentally, I am a mother.

Not too long ago a male friend of mine appeared on the scene fresh from a recent divorce. He had one child, who is, of course, with his ex-wife. He is obviously looking for another wife. As I thought about him while I was ironing one evening, it suddenly occurred to me that I, too, would like to have a wife. Why do I want a wife?

I would like to go back to school so that I can become economically independent, support myself, and, if need be, support those dependent upon me. I want a wife who will work and send me to school. And while I am going to school I want a wife to take care of my children. I want a wife to keep track of the children's doctor and dentist appointments. And to keep track of mine, too. I want a wife to make sure my children eat properly and are kept clean. I want a wife who will wash the children's clothes and keep them mended. I want a wife who is a good nurturant attendant to my children, who arranges for their schooling, makes sure that they have an adequate social life with their peers, takes them to the park, the zoo, etc. I want a wife who takes care of the children when they are sick, a wife who arranges to be around when the children need special care, because, of course, I cannot miss classes at school. My wife must arrange to lose time at work, and not lose the job. It may mean a small cut in my wife's income from time to time, but I guess I can tolerate that. Needless to say, my wife will arrange and pay for the care of the children while my wife is working.

I want a wife who will take care of my physical needs. I want a wife who will keep my house clean. A wife who will pick up after me. I want a wife who will keep my clothes clean, ironed, mended, replaced when need be, and who will see to it that my personal things are kept in their proper place so that I can find what I need the minute I need it. I want a wife who cooks the meals, a wife who is a good cook. I want a wife who will plan the meals, do the necessary grocery shopping, prepare the meals, serve them pleasantly, and then do the cleaning up while I do my studying. I want a wife who will care for me when I am sick and sympathize with my pain

and loss of time from school. I want a wife to go along when our family takes a vacation so that someone can continue to care for me and my children when I need a rest and change of scene.

I want a wife who will not bother me with rambling complaints about a wife's duties. But I want a wife who will listen to me when I feel the need to explain a rather difficult point I have come across in my course of studies. And I want a wife who will type my papers for me when I have written them.

I want a wife who will take care of the details of my social life. When my wife and I are invited out by my friends, I want a wife who will take care of the babysitting arrangements. When I meet people at school that I like and want to entertain, I want a wife who will have the house clean, will prepare a special meal, serve it to me and my friends, and not interrupt when I talk about the things that interest me and my friends. I want a wife who will have arranged that the children are fed and ready for bed before my guests arrive so that the children do not bother us. I want a wife who takes care of the needs of my guests so that they feel comfortable, who makes sure that they have an ashtray, that they are passed the hors d'oeuvres, that they are offered a second helping of the food, that their wine glasses are replenished when necessary, that their coffee is served to them as they like it. And I want a wife who knows that sometimes I need a night out by myself.

I want a wife who is sensitive to my sexual needs, a wife who makes love passionately and eagerly when I feel like it, a wife who makes sure that I am satisfied. And, of course, I want a wife who will not demand sexual attention when I am not in the mood for it. I want a wife who assumes the complete responsibility for birth control, because I do not want more children. I want a wife who will remain sexually faithful to me so that I do not have to clutter up my intellectual life with jealousies. And I want a wife who understands that my sexual needs may entail more than strict adherence to monogamy. I must, after all, be able to relate to people as fully as possible.

If, by chance, I find another person more suitable as a wife than the wife I already have, I want the liberty to replace my present wife with another one. Naturally I will expect a fresh, new life; my wife will take the children and be solely responsible for them so that I am left free.

When I am through with school and have a job, I want my wife to quit working and remain at home so that my wife can more fully and completely take care of a wife's duties.

My God, who *wouldn't* want a wife?

RESPONSE QUESTIONS

1. What assumptions about wives are embedded in Brady's essay? Give job titles to the various tasks that such wives perform. How would these jobs be classified in today's society?

2. The author begins many of her sentences with "I want" and "I need." What is the effect of this repetition on your reading? What distinctions can you make between selfish desires and legitimate needs after reading the essay?

3. Brady identifies herself as a wife and mother. How are these roles linked? To what extent does she imply that a husband is a kind of child?

4. How fair is Brady's characterization of husbands and wives? What has she exaggerated or omitted? If she is not seeking a balanced presentation, what is her purpose?

GUIDELINES FOR ANALYSIS

1. The announced occasion for Brady's essay is a visit by a divorced man. How does this help to frame what follows? What difference does it make that her thoughts come to her while ironing?

2. Note how Brady organizes her essay. What is the order of development? How else might the essay have been structured?

3. Describe Brady's writing style. What makes it different from the other essays in this chapter? How much more or less persuasive would Brady be if she presented a more straightforward argument or a list of complaints? What are the advantages and disadvantages of developing a position as Brady does or trying to resolve a conflict as John Gray does in "Mr. Fix-It"?

4. "I Want a Wife" was originally published in *Ms.* magazine in 1971. What were the prevailing attitudes about women's roles among readers at that time? Do the traditional roles described in the essay still hold true today? Should they? Support your view with reasons.

QUESTIONS OF CULTURE

1. Brady begins by classifying herself. Where do the categories come from? Who is responsible for creating and sustaining this system of classification?

2. How are a wife's roles defined in the Bible, Koran, Torah, or other religious texts with which you are familiar? Compare these definitions with Brady's.

3. Consider how an anthropologist might approach Brady's description of family roles. What connections might be made to societies of hunter-gatherers or other cultures?

IDEAS FOR YOUR JOURNAL

1. Write "I Want a Husband," reversing the perspective of Brady's essay.

2. Imagine a man performing the wifely duties described in "I Want a Wife." What scenes would be included in your Mr. Mom scenario?

PREVIEW

Dave Barry is best known as a humorist. His columns in the *Miami Herald* and his lighthearted books have delighted many readers with their playful, self-mocking wit. Barry was born in Armonk, New York, in 1947. After graduating from Haverford College with a major in English, he worked for a local newspaper, tried teaching writing to businesspersons for a while, then joined the staff of the *Miami Herald*, where he has been since 1983. He received the Pulitzer Prize for Commentary in 1988 and has written a number of popular books, including a novel, *Big Trouble* (1999). The following selection is taken from the introduction to *Dave Barry's Complete Guide to Guys: A Fairly Short Book* (1996).

Guys vs. Men

By Dave Barry

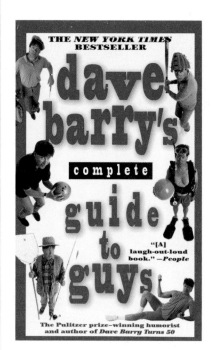

THE *NEW YORK TIMES*
BESTSELLER

dave barry's

complete

guide to guys

"[A] laugh-out-loud book." —*People*

The Pulitzer prize–winning humorist and author of *Dave Barry Turns 50*

This is a book about guys. It's *not* a book about men. There are already way too many books about men, and most of them are *way* too serious.

Men itself is a serious word, not to mention *manhood* and *manly.* Such words make being male sound like a very important activity, as opposed to what it primarily consists of, namely, possessing a set of minor and frequently unreliable organs.

But men tend to attach great significance to Manhood. This results in certain characteristically masculine, by which I mean stupid, behavioral patterns that can produce unfortunate results such as violent crime, war, spitting, and ice hockey. These things have given males a bad name.[1] And the "Men's Movement," which is supposed to bring out the more positive aspects of Manliness, seems to be densely populated with loons and goobers.

So I'm saying that there's another way to look at males: not as aggressive macho dominators; not as sensitive, liberated, hugging drummers; but as guys.

And what, exactly, do I mean by "guys"? I don't know. I haven't thought that much about it. One of the major characteristics of guyhood is that we guys don't spend a lot of time

5

pondering our deep innermost feelings. There is a serious question in my mind about whether guys actually *have* deep innermost feelings, unless you count, for example, loyalty to the Detroit Tigers, or fear of bridal showers.

But although I can't define exactly what it means to be a guy, I can describe certain guy characteristics, such as:

Guys Like Neat Stuff

By "neat," I mean "mechanical and unnecessarily complex." I'll give you an example. Right now I'm typing these words on an *extremely* powerful computer. It's the latest in a line of maybe ten computers I've owned, each one more powerful than the last. My computer is chock full of RAM and ROM and bytes and megahertzes and various other items that enable a computer to kick data-processing butt. It is probably capable of supervising the entire U.S. air-defense apparatus while simultaneously processing the tax return of every resident of Ohio. I use it mainly to write a newspaper column. This is an activity wherein I sit and stare at the screen for maybe ten minutes, then, using only my forefingers, slowly type something like:

Henry Kissinger looks like a big wart.

I stare at this for another ten minutes, have an inspiration, then amplify the original thought as follows:
Henry Kissinger looks like a big fat wart.

Then I stare at that for another ten minutes, pondering whether I should try to work in the concept of "hairy."

This is absurdly simple work for my computer. It sits there, humming impatiently, bored to death, passing the time between keystrokes via brain-teaser activities such as developing a Unified Field Theory of the universe and translating the complete works of Shakespeare into rap.[2]

In other words, this computer is absurdly overqualified to work for me, and yet soon, I guarantee, I will buy an *even more powerful* one. I won't be able to stop myself. I'm a guy.

Probably the ultimate example of the fundamental guy drive to have neat stuff is the Space Shuttle. Granted, the guys in charge of this program *claim* it has a Higher Scientific Purpose, namely to see how humans function in space. But of course we have known for years how humans function in space: They float around and say things like: "Looks real good, Houston!"

No, the real reason for the existence of the Space Shuttle is that it is one humongous and spectacularly gizmo-intensive item of hardware. Guys can tinker with it practically forever, and occasionally even get it to work, and use it to place *other* complex mechanical items into orbit, where they almost immediately break, which provides a great excuse to send the Space Shuttle up *again*. It's Guy Heaven.

Other results of the guy need to have stuff are Star Wars, the recreational boating industry, monorails, nuclear weapons, and wristwatches that indicate the phase of the moon. I am not saying that women haven't been involved in the development or use of this stuff. I'm saying that, without guys, this stuff probably would not exist; just as, without women, virtually every piece of furniture in the world would still be in its original position. Guys do not have a basic need to rearrange furniture. Whereas a woman who could cheerfully use the same computer for fifty-three years will rearrange her furniture on almost a weekly basis, sometimes in the dead of night. She'll be sound asleep in bed, and suddenly, at 2 A.M., she'll be awakened by the urgent thought: *The blue-green sofa needs to go perpendicular to the wall instead of parallel, and it needs to go there RIGHT NOW.* So she'll get up and move it, which of course necessitates moving other furniture, and soon she has rearranged her entire living room, shifting great big heavy pieces that ordinarily would require several burly men to lift, because there are few forces in Nature more powerful than a woman who needs to rearrange furniture. Every so often a guy will wake up to discover that, because of his wife's overnight efforts, he now lives in an entirely different house.

(I realize that I'm making gender-based generalizations here, but my feeling is that if God did not want us to make gender-based generalizations, She would not have given us genders.)

Guys Like a Really Pointless Challenge

Not long ago I was sitting in my office at the *Miami Herald*'s Sunday magazine, *Tropic,* reading my fan mail,[3] when I heard several of my guy coworkers in the hallway talking about how fast they could run the forty-yard dash. These are guys in their thirties and forties who work in journalism, where the most demanding physical requirement is the ability to digest vending-machine food. In other words, these guys have absolutely no need to run the forty-yard dash.

But one of them, Mike Wilson, was writing a story about a star high-school football player who could run it in 4.38 seconds. Now if Mike had written a story about, say, a star high-school poet, none of my guy coworkers would have suddenly decided to find out how well they could write sonnets. But when Mike turned in his story, they became *deeply* concerned about how fast they could run the forty-yard dash. They were so concerned that the magazine editor, Tom Shroder, decided that they should get a stopwatch and go out to a nearby park and find out. Which they did, a bunch of guys taking off their shoes and running around barefoot in a public park on company time.

This is what I heard them talking about, out in the hall. I heard Tom, who was thirty-eight years old, saying that his time in the forty had been 5.75 seconds. And I thought to myself. This is ridiculous. These are middle-aged guys, supposedly adults, and they're out there *bragging* about their performance in this stupid juvenile footrace. Finally I couldn't stand it anymore. "Hey!" I shouted. "I could beat 5.75 seconds."

20

So we went out to the park and measured off forty yards, and the guys told me that I had three chances to make my best time. On the first try my time was 5.78 seconds, just three-hundredths of a second slower than Tom's, even though, at forty-five, I was seven years older than he. So I just *knew* I'd beat him on the second attempt if I ran really, really hard, which I did for a solid ten yards, at which point my left hamstring muscle, which had not yet shifted into Spring Mode from Mail-Reading Mode, went, and I quote, "pop."

I had to be helped off the field. I was in considerable pain, and I was obviously not going to be able to walk right for weeks. The other guys were very sympathetic especially Tom, who took the time to call me at home where I was sitting with an ice pack on my leg and twenty-three Advil in my bloodstream, so he could express his concern.

"Just remember," he said, "you *didn't beat my time."* There are countless other examples of guys rising to meet pointless challenges. Virtually all sports fall into this category, as well as a large part of U.S. foreign policy. ("I'll bet you can't capture Manuel Noriega!" "Oh *YEAH??*")

Guys Do Not Have a Rigid and Well-Defined Moral Code

This is not the same as saying that guys are bad. Guys *are* capable of doing bad things, but this generally happens when they try to be Men and start becoming manly and aggressive and stupid. When they're being just plain guys, they aren't so much actively evil as they are *lost.* Because guys have never really grasped the Basic Human Moral Code, which I believe was invented by women millions of years ago when all the guys were out engaging in some other activity, such as seeing who could burp the loudest. When they came back, there were certain rules that they were expected to follow unless they wanted to get into Big Trouble, and they have been trying to follow these rules ever since, with extremely irregular results. Because guys have never *internalized* these rules. Guys are similar to my small auxiliary backup dog, Zippy, a guy dog[4] who has been told numerous times that he is *not* supposed to (1) get into the kitchen garbage or (2) poop on the floor. He knows that these are the rules, but he has never really understood why, and sometimes he gets to thinking: Sure, I am *ordinarily* not supposed to get into the garbage, but obviously this rule is not meant to apply when there are certain extenuating[5] circumstances, such as (1) somebody just threw away some perfectly good seven-week-old Kung Pao Chicken, and (2) I am home alone.

And so when the humans come home, the kitchen floor has been transformed into GarbageFest USA, and Zippy, who usually comes rushing up, is off in a corner disguised in a wig and sunglasses, hoping to get into the Federal Bad Dog Relocation Program before the humans discover the scene of the crime.

25 When I yell at him, he frequently becomes so upset that he poops on the floor.

Morally, most guys are just like Zippy, only taller and usually less hairy. Guys are aware of the rules of moral behavior, but they have trouble keeping these rules in the forefronts of their minds at certain times, especially the present. This is especially true in the area of faithfulness to one's mate. I realize, of course, that there are countless examples of guys being faithful to their mates until they die, usually as a result of being eaten by their mates immediately following copulation. Guys outside of the spider community, however, do not have a terrific record of faithfulness.

I'm not saying guys are scum. I'm saying that many guys who consider themselves to be committed to their marriages will stray if they are confronted with overwhelming temptation, defined as "virtually any temptation."

Okay, so maybe I *am* saying guys are scum. But they're not *mean-spirited* scum. And few of them—even when they are out of town on business trips, far from their wives, and have a clear-cut opportunity—will poop on the floor.

Guys Are Not Great at Communicating Their Intimate Feelings, Assuming They Have Any

This is an aspect of guyhood that is very frustrating to women. A guy will be reading the newspaper, and the phone will ring; he'll answer it, listen for ten minutes, hang up, and resume reading. Finally his wife will say: "Who was that?"

30 And he'll say: "Phil Wonkerman's mom."
(Phil is an old friend they haven't heard from in seventeen years.)
And the wife will say, "Well?"
And the guy will say, "Well what?"
And the wife will say, "What did she *say?*"

35 And the guy will say, "She said Phil is fine," making it clear by his tone of voice that, although he does not wish to be rude, he is trying to read the newspaper, and he happens to be right in the middle of an important panel of "Calvin and Hobbes."

But the wife, ignoring this, will say, "That's all she said?"

And she will not let up. She will continue to ask district-attorney-style questions, forcing the guy to recount the conversation until she's satisfied that she has the entire story, which is that Phil just got out of prison after serving a sentence for a murder he committed when he became a drug addict because of the guilt he felt when his wife died in a freak submarine accident while Phil was having an affair with a nun, but now he's all straightened out and has a good job as a trapeze artist and is almost through with the surgical part of his sex change and recently became happily engaged to marry a prominent member of the Grateful Dead, so in other words he is fine, which is *exactly* what the guy told her in the first place, but is that enough? No. She wants to hear *every single detail.*

Or let's say two couples get together after a long separation. The two women will have a conversation, lasting several days, during which they discuss virtually every significant event that has occurred in their lives and the lives of those they care about, sharing their innermost thoughts, analyzing and probing, inevitably coming to a deeper understanding of each other, and a strengthening of a cherished friendship. Whereas the guys will watch the play-offs.

This is not to say the guys won't share their feelings. Sometimes they'll get quite emotional.

40 "That's not a FOUL??" they'll say.

Or: "YOU'RE TELLING ME THAT'S NOT A FOUL???"

I have a good friend, Gene, and one time, when he was going through a major medical development in his life, we spent a weekend together. During this time Gene and I talked a lot and enjoyed each other's company immensely, but—this is true—the most intimate personal statement he made to me is that he has reached Level 24 of a video game called "Arkanoid." He had even seen the Evil Presence, although he refused to tell me what it looks like. We're very close, but there is a limit.

You may think that my friends and I are Neanderthals, and that a lot of guys are different. This is true. A lot of guys don't use words at all. They communicate entirely by nonverbal methods, such as sharing bait.

Are you starting to see what I mean by "guyness"? I'm basically talking about the part of the male psyche that is less serious and/or aggressive than the Manly Manhood part, but still essentially very male. My feeling is that the world would be a much better[6] place if more males would stop trying so hard to be Men and instead settle for being Guys. Think of the historical problems that could have been avoided if more males had been able to keep their genderhood in its proper perspective, both in themselves and in others. ("Hey, Adolf, just because you happen to possess a set of minor and frequently unreliable organs, that is no reason to invade Poland.") And think how much happier women would be if, instead of endlessly fretting about what the males in their lives are thinking, they could relax, secure in the knowledge that the correct answer is: very little.

45 Yes, what we need, on the part of both genders, is more understanding of guyness. And that is why I wrote this book. I intend to explore in detail every major facet of guyhood, including the historical facet, the sociological facet, the physiological facet, the psychosexual facet, and the facet of how come guys spit so much. Every statement of fact you will read in this book is either based on actual laboratory tests, or else I made it up. But you can trust me. I'm a guy.

EXAMPLE CHART	
Men	Guys
Vince Lombardi	Joe Namath
Oliver North	Gilligan
Hemingway	Gary Larson
Columbus	Whichever astronaut hit the first golf ball on the Moon
Superman	Bart Simpson
Doberman pinschers	Labrador retrievers
Abbott	Costello
Captain Ahab	Captain Kangaroo
Satan	Snidely Whiplash
The pope	Willard Scott
Germany	Italy
Geraldo	Katie Couric

STIMULUS-RESPONSE COMPARISON CHART: WOMEN VS. MEN VS. GUYS

Stimulus	Typical Woman Response	Typical Man Response	Typical Guy Response
An untamed river in the wilderness.	Contemplate its beauty.	Build a dam.	See who can pee the farthest off the dam.
A child who is sent home from school for being disruptive in class.	Talk to the child in an effort to determine the cause.	Threaten to send the child to a military academy.	Teach the child how to make armpit farts.
Human mortality	Religious faith	The pyramids	Bungee jumping

[1] Specifically, "asshole."

[2] To be or not? I got to know Might kill myself by the end of the show.

[3] Typical fan letter: "Who cuts your hair? Beavers?"

[4] I also have a female dog, Earnest, who never breaks the rules.

[5] I am taking some liberties here with Zippy's vocabulary. More likely, in his mind, he uses the term mitigating.

[6] As measured by total sales of this book.

RESPONSE QUESTIONS

1. Some readers find Barry's writing funny, offhandedly shrewd, even comforting; others find it silly or offensive. How do you respond to his writing style? Discuss the value—and risks—of using humor to persuade.

2. How much of yourself (or people you know) do you find in Barry's description of "guy-ness"? What serious issues and real insights about gender roles can you see behind the lightheartedness?

3. Barry counts on a familiar stereotype when he writes, "there are few forces in Nature more powerful than a woman who needs to rearrange furniture." How serious does he seem to be about making (and apologizing for) "gender-based generalizations"? Compare his distinctions between men and women to those made by John Gray, Natalie Angier, or other writers in this chapter.

4. Identify some of the other stereotypes in Barry's writing. What purposes do they serve?

5. In the final paragraph of his introduction, the author announces, "what we need, on the part of both genders, is more understanding of guyness." After reading to this point, explain whether you would want to read the rest of his book.

GUIDELINES FOR ANALYSIS

1. The author plays with distinctions between men and guys throughout his writing. What distinctions does he make? How does he try to clarify the differences?

2. Reread Barry's story about the forty-yard dash. Notice how he uses this extended anecdote to show how guys rise "to meet pointless challenges." What other examples might help to illustrate his point?

3. Occasionally, Barry captures situations in long sentences like this: "So I just *knew* I'd beat him on the second attempt if I ran really, really hard, which I did for a solid ten yards, at which point my left hamstring muscle, which had not yet shifted into Spring Mode from Mail-Reading Mode, went, and I quote, 'pop.'" How does the writer regard himself here? What makes the sentence funny? Find similar sentences in his writing.

4. Barry refers to Zippy, his "auxiliary backup dog," in order to explain the moral limitations of guys. How does the comparison between dogs and humans work? Do you find this analogy enlightening, insulting, reassuring, trivializing, or simply funny?

QUESTIONS OF CULTURE

1. Is there really a "culture of guyhood"? According to Barry, what practices and customs are valued in this culture? What beliefs about machines, competition, and feelings underlie these practices?

2. Compare the dialogue between Phil and his wife to the conversations between Martians and Venusians in John Gray's chapter from *Men Are from Mars, Women Are from Venus*. How accurately do these interactions reflect the way men and women you know really communicate?

IDEAS FOR YOUR JOURNAL

1. In his "Stimulus-Response Comparison Chart," Barry imagines how women, men, and guys might respond to a child being sent home from school for disruptive behavior. How would you use your mediation skills to resolve the issue between any two of these groups?

2. Add a stimulus or two to the chart. Identify a few situations, and imagine how women, men, and guys are likely to respond.

PREVIEW

Since 1980, *ABC News Nightline* has been bringing the day's controversial issues into America's homes. A typical program is divided into two segments. The first part presents a brief documentary report on the topic featuring an investigative reporter out in the field, talking with experts and gathering background information. The second part is similar to a debate. An anchor like Ted Koppel, speaking from the studio, addresses questions to two or three authorities by satellite and leads a kind of "conversation" to explore the topic.

www.mhhe.com/costanzo

View this video excerpt and others on the Web site.

The following discussion, hosted by Forrest Sawyer, was aired during the first Gulf war, when Congress was considering whether women should be allowed to participate in combat. Notice how Sawyer both encourages controversy and mediates conflicting points of view.

TRANSCRIPT OF TV NEWSMAGAZINE, *NIGHTLINE:* "WHAT ARE THE DIFFERENCES BETWEEN MEN AND WOMEN?"

SAWYER: Joining us now from our New York studio is retired Army Colonel David Hackworth, the highly decorated veteran who happened to write this week's cover story in *Newsweek* on women in combat; from our Washington studio, author and anthropologist Beryl Lieff Benderly, who says it is not a wise decision to allow women to fight; and from our affiliate WPRI in Providence, Rhode Island, Anne Fausto-Sterling, a biologist at Brown University who says that women do, indeed, have the stamina needed in combat.

Let us focus first, if I may, on the physical aspects of this question. Dr. Fausto-Sterling, do women have what's necessary to go into combat?

ANNE FAUSTO-STERLING, Brown University: I think it's important to realize that things like flying combat, flying airplanes are mostly technological. There isn't an issue of brute strength involved. And so much of our military activity is based on advanced technology and not brute strength that that's really a false issue.

SAWYER: Yeah, but what about when you get right down there in the trenches, I mean, would you draw a line anywhere at all or would you say hand-to-hand, toe-to-toe fighting is all right?

5 Dr. FAUSTO-STERLING: I think I would say that it depends on the individual, that there are a wide variety of abilities among men and among women, and that it's up to our military to train and screen individuals to see that they're capable of doing what would be expected of them.

SAWYER: Ms. Benderly, focusing simply on the physical questions, I think most people would probably say that men can lift and tote more, that they have more strength and can endure in that fashion more, but do women have what it takes to be in the trenches?

BERYL LIEFF BENDERLY, Author/Anthropologist: Well, I would agree with what Dr. Fausto-Sterling said. There's tremendous variation, and I don't know. I think it would depend on which women you were talking about. Not every man has what it takes, either.

SAWYER. All right. Colonel Hackworth, there you are. Some women could go into combat, just like some men can go into combat. Is that right?

Col. DAVID HACKWORTH, *Newsweek:* Well, I've interviewed 351 women for my piece over the last four weeks. I found some damned capable ones, Forrest, that I wouldn't want to arm-wrestle with, so there are some tough ones out there. It's a question of standards. Right now in the military there's dual standards, one standard for women, one standard for men. Uniformly, I found, among both women and men, they wanted one standard. They didn't want the deck stacked in favor of women.

10 SAWYER: Do you—you would agree that women should fly combat planes? Does that include flying jets where they can pull nine gravities?

Col. HACKWORTH: Well, I couldn't make that call, because I've never flown a jet. My daughter was in the Coast Guard in helicopters for four years. She's five-foot-one and did very well. A woman can do just about anything if she sets her mind to it, and look at our frontier women.

SAWYER: But I want you to be clear now. You were talking about trench fighting. I'm hearing you say, I think, that it's all right.

Col. HACKWORTH: Not on the ground. There are women that are capable. I have met quite a few in the past few weeks, during interviews, that could be very competent combat soldiers, but the interesting thing is, in my interviews, I ended up each one asking the women—and I went to the elite 18th Airborne Corps and spent a lot of time—does anybody want to be in direct combat? And I didn't get a volunteer, men or women.

SAWYER: Dr. Fausto-Sterling?

15 Dr. FAUSTO-STERLING: Yeah, I mean, I think that the important point is that it's not a question of what people are capable of. I mean, the question of whether or not women or men are going to fight in battle is a question that's essentially a political and moral question.

Ms. BENDERLY: Exactly. Exactly.

SAWYER: Well, I'm not sure that everybody's going to agree with you on that. I think there are an awful lot of officers of Colonel Hackworth's generation who will say, "No, it's not a political question. We aren't sure that there's a women who's going to be able to lift and tote a 200-pound dog soldier who's gotten into trouble back out of there." What do you think of that, Colonel Hackworth?

Col. HACKWORTH: Well, the bottom line is the attitude, and I found again and again with male soldiers that they had ingrained in them a respect for women and they couldn't stand seeing a woman blasted away, which I found interesting, because the one government where women were used as front-line combat soldiers, 1948, Israeli army, it failed because not that the women didn't fight properly, but the men couldn't handle seeing women blown apart. It just destroyed the cohesion of the unit, destroyed the spirit of the unit.

SAWYER: Ms. Benderly, something about the emotional interaction is the problem, he's saying.

20   Ms. BENDERLY: I would phrase it slightly differently. I think that it's not so much a question of whether women can fight, whether women are capable of fighting. I think it's a question of what kind of society we want to be. I think it's a question of social policy, of whether it's the best use of women and men to have women fighters. Personally, I think it isn't, because this discussion is very often phrased in terms of whether women are strong enough, strong as men, as if the real reason that men societies send young men into combat is that they're stronger. And I think that there's fair amount of anthropological study that indicates the real basic reason that societies send young men into combat isn't necessarily that they're stronger, but that they're expendable in a way that young women are not expendable.

SAWYER: All right. Let's hold it right there. We're going to come back in just a moment and talk about other aspects of this question, when we return.

(Screen graphic: Women in the Military: WWII, 2.2%; Korea, 1.3%; Vietnam, 1.1%; Gulf war, 11.2%)

SAWYER: Our topic is the differences between men and women and women in combat. And Ms. Benderly, help me understand something you just said. I think you said that the reason we send young men into combat and not women along with them is because they're expendable.

Ms. BENDERLY: That's exactly right.

SAWYER: I suspect they don't feel so expendable.

25   Ms. BENDERLY: No, but socially, in a sense, they are. Certainly they don't feel expendable, and certainly no human being is really, in a sense, morally expendable. But from the standpoint of society, think about what happened in World War I, between France and England, when they essentially hemorrhaged an entire generation of young men into the trenches and were ready to go again in 1939. Now, if they had hemorrhaged an entire generation of young women into the trenches, that would have been the end or very severe damage to the countries. The women are, in a sense—young women are, in a sense, the future of any society. This is why societies protect them.

SAWYER: Professor Fausto-Sterling, do you buy that argument? After all, it wouldn't be that many women who are in combat in the first place.

Dr. FAUSTO-STERLING: The argument makes me nervous, let me say, because again it reduces the issue to a fundamental question of the difference in reproductive systems, and I can—I mean, I can see the point that Ms. Benderly is making, but it—again, I think it has much more to do with a broader moral and political set of decisions, which do have to do with our assessment of what men are worth and what women are worth in our culture. But it has to do with our idea that we need—that we're supposed to protect women and somehow keep them safe. And that's an outmoded Victorian idea.

Ms. BENDERLY: Well, I don't mean to protect women in the sense that they are delicate, but protect the future society because it's simply a fact that women bear the next generation, and men don't. I'm not saying that individual women are weaker than others or require protection in the same sense.

SAWYER: But Ms. Benderly, you know, I think there are going to be a lot of women who will say, "Well, thank you very much, I appreciate that, but if I happen to be the one that wants to go into combat, I don't need you to protect me."

30   Ms. BENDERLY: Well, that's an argument—I have not really—thinking about this question, this is a very difficult question to answer with an either/or. What I think I'm trying to do is raise the point that this is more than just an issue of individual desires or individual abilities or even individual rights. It's really a question of policy for the society.

SAWYER: Colonel Hackworth, help me out here. When we're talking about women in the military and women in positions that we haven't traditionally thought of them as being in, are there some things—for instance, combat—are there some things which they can do better than men?

Col. HACKWORTH: Well, my experience is, I think women are a lot quicker than men, and they're certainly, in the military, a lot more educated. I think there's nothing that a woman couldn't do. Will Rogers once said that a woman could do anything a man can, including fighting a war. And I look back at my grandmother, who raised me, who was a frontier woman. She could just about do anything. If we want to change the whole mores of our society, we want to make our women like men, then let's go for it, and I can't, for the best of me, try to work out—having spent eight years on a battlefield—why a woman would want to do the worst damn thing a man is forced to do, and that is to be in combat. And I think another thing is the definition of combat, Forrest. To you it's not just a shell whistling over, a Scud smacking down next to you, it's getting belly-to-belly with an enemy, with a bayonet, with a club, with your hands, with a knife, and cutting his throat. And men have been doing that for 40 million years and it's going to take some education before women are able to do that little chore.

SAWYER: But your point is that education could take place if society wanted it to happen.

Col. HACKWORTH: If we want to change our whole society, it sure could.

35   Dr. FAUSTO-STERLING: I don't think—I mean, I think it's again wrong that men have been doing it for 40 million years, organized warfare.

Ms. BENDERLY: It's wrong that anyone's been doing it.

Dr. FAUSTO-STERLING: Yeah, I mean, it's—organized warfare is quite a recent activity.

Dr. BENDERLY: That's true.

Dr. FAUSTO-STERLING: And it's an activity we have control over. We cannot do it.

40   Ms. BENDERLY: This is true.

Dr. FAUSTO-STERLING: And that maybe is the more essential point.

Col. HACKWORTH: But what do you mean by recent? What do you mean by recent? Let's go from the biblical terms, from the time at Moses led Egypt—

Dr. BENDERLY: But that was only about 7,000 years ago. That's only 7,000 years ago.

Dr. FAUSTO-STERLING: Yeah.

45   Col. HACKWORTH: —I don't—yeah—well

SAWYER: Hold on just a second, let's just refocus this. I mean, the history of warfare is not really going to get us anywhere. I think, Professor Fausto-Sterling, what Colonel Hackworth is saying is that warfare has been around for a long time, and I think everybody would like to see it disappear, but those who go into the military recognize that they are signing on for the potential of war, and we saw that in the Persian Gulf. And the question is whether women who see combat as a potential way to move up the ladder and not going into combat as a way to hold them down the ladder, whether that should be permitted. Now, we've seen that Congress has said yes, in terms of flying, but what about the rest of it?

Dr. FAUSTO-STERLING: See, I don't think that women as a group who have made those choices that you suggest should be categorically denied what they might view as advancement potential. I mean, I think there may be a problem with them being in the military to begin with, or with anybody being in the military, but once there, as you said, decisions about what people can do should be based on their individual abilities and not on whether they belong to one sex or the other.

SAWYER: Ms. Benderly, I asked Colonel Hackworth just a moment ago if there's some things that women do better than men. Now, when we're looking at the mental array, when we're looking at those questions, do you see that women would approach problems, on average, in a different way, and therefore could do jobs better?

Ms. BENDERLY: I couldn't answer that question because I don't think there's such a thing as an average man or an average woman. I think it's entirely a matter of which woman you're talking about as compared to which man. One thing I did want to respond to that the colonel said, and also there's an implication in the film, as well, at the beginning of the show that warfare somehow arose out of male aggression, and I wanted to underscore the point that Dr. Fausto-Sterling was making, which is that war really grows out of state societies and political structures; it really has nothing to do with male aggression. It has to do with political organization.

50 SAWYER: Colonel Hackworth, let me leave you with the last word. We've got about 20, 25 seconds here. Do you anticipate, now that Congress has made this move in terms of women flying combat aircraft, that it will continue on into other avenues that we haven't seen before?

Col. HACKWORTH: No, I don't. I think what the bottom line is, that a presidential commission will come out of this. All of the studies from the Gulf, the lessons learned, will come out. The military's going through a great restructuring. I think after this restructuring, with the end of the cold war and the incredible cutback, we'll find out what the role is of the military for women.

SAWYER: All right, sir. All right. I thank you all three for a very good conversation.

Dr. FAUSTO-STERLING: You're very welcome.

Ms. BENDERLY: Thank you.

1. The announced topic of this program is women in the military. Forrest Sawyer poses the question, "Should women be allowed on the front lines?" How would you answer the question? What evidence and reasons can you offer to support your view?

2. Sawyer's guests include David Hackworth, a retired army colonel; Beryl Lieff Benderly, an author and anthropologist; and Dr. Anne Fausto-Sterling, a biologist at Brown University. What did you anticipate each guest would say about the topic? What were your expectations based on? How closely did their expressed professional, moral, and political views fit your preconceptions?

3. Early on, Dr. Fausto-Sterling calls the physical aspects of combat "a false issue." What does she mean? What do the other guests say about brute strength and the ability of women to handle the physical demands of military life?

4. Two of the guests are women, and one is a man. Does this affect the balance of views represented in the show? How closely are the women aligned? How do Col. Hackworth's references to his daughter, his pioneer grandmother, and the women he interviewed for his article in *Newsweek* affect his position as a male combatant? Does the anchor remain objective even though he is a man?

5. What do you consider to be the most persuasive arguments presented in the show?

GUIDELINES FOR ANALYSIS

1. Sawyer's role can be compared to that of the moderator of a public debate or the writer of a persuasive essay. He introduces the topic, frames the issues, and selects questions to be answered by the experts. He often repeats, summarizes, qualifies, and rephrases what the experts say. Sometimes he tries to channel what has been said in a new direction. Where does Sawyer fill his role most skillfully? Where should he have handled things differently?

2. What gives the three guests authority to speak on the topic? Who did you find most credible? What evidence or line of reasoning did you find most persuasive?

3. How organized is the discussion? Is there a logical progression in the flow of ideas, or do they evolve randomly? How much structure should there be in a program of this kind?

4. Describe the tone of *ABC News Nightline*. Compare it to other television shows that present different sides of controversial issues. Describe the audiences and intentions of these shows. To what extent are these programs informative, convincing, or entertaining?

5. Compare the transcript to the video. To what extent are you influenced by how the speakers look and sound on television? How do the graphics, backdrops, and other visual elements affect what is said? Do the speakers and arguments appear equally convincing on the page and on the screen?

QUESTIONS OF CULTURE

1. Explore the social, political, and economic issues raised by Benderly and Fausto-Sterling. How much merit do you see in the claims that men are socially expendable and that women

have a right to compete equally with men for military promotion. Does it matter whether individual variations outweigh gross differences in gender?

2. The *Nightline* program aired in July of 1991, during the first Gulf war when Congress voted to allow female pilots to fly combat missions. At the end of the show, Sawyer asked Col. Hackworth whether further legislation would "continue into other avenues that we haven't seen before." What changes in warfare and the American military have you seen since 1991? How would you answer Sawyer's question today?

3. What do the three guests say about the morality of combat? Do they agree that warfare is morally wrong? How relevant are the arguments that male aggression is a biological constant or that war is a political decision? What do you believe?

IDEAS FOR YOUR JOURNAL

1. Imagine you were producing a special edition of *Nightline* at your college. What controversial topic would you choose? Whom would you select for the anchor? Who would be the guests? What would you expect the dialogue to be like?

2. Write a response to Col. Hackworth, Ms. Benderly, or Dr. Fausto-Sterling explaining why you agree or disagree with his or her opinions. Use your response as the starting point for an essay on women in the military.

3. Examine the views of two guests who seem to disagree and write a letter trying to resolve their differences. Acknowledge the areas of disagreement, and identify any common ground you see. Appeal to their mutual concerns and commitments. Suggest how they might shift their individual positions to be consistent with a larger, common goal.

PREVIEW

Ernest Hemingway was born in Oak Park, Illinois, in 1899 and died in Idaho in 1961. His father was a doctor and his mother a musician who had given up her career to care for their six children. His early years were comfortably upper middle class, with a stable home and summers at the family cottage in Michigan. After high school, Hemingway worked as a reporter in Kansas City. At the age of nineteen, even before the United States entered World War I, he volunteered as an ambulance driver in Italy, where he was seriously wounded at the front. This did not prevent him from serving as a war correspondent during the Greco-Turkish War, the Spanish Civil War, and World War II. An enthusiastic sportsman and an aficionado of bullfighting, he was drawn repeatedly to situations that tested his courage as a man. From his experiences came the novels and stories that made him world famous, including *The Sun Also Rises* (1926), *A Farewell to Arms* (1929), *For Whom the Bell Tolls* (1940), and *The Old Man and the Sea* (1952). The following work of fiction is from his early collection of short stories, *Men without Women* (1927).

Hills Like White Elephants

By Ernest Hemingway

The hills across the valley of the Ebro were long and white. On this side there was no shade and no trees and the station was between two lines of rails in the sun. Close against the side of the station there was the warm shadow of the building and a curtain, made of strings of bamboo beads, hung across the open door into the bar, to keep out flies. The American and the girl with him sat at a table in the shade, outside the building. It was very hot and the express from Barcelona would come in forty minutes. It stopped at this junction for two minutes and went on to Madrid.

"What should we drink?" the girl asked. She had taken off her hat and put it on the table.

"It's pretty hot," the man said.

"Let's drink beer."

5   "Dos cervezas," the man said into the curtain.

"Big ones?" a woman asked from the doorway.

"Yes. Two big ones."

The woman brought two glasses of beer and two felt pads. She put the felt pads and the beer glasses on the table and looked at the man and the girl. The girl was looking off at the line of hills. They were white in the sun and the country was brown and dry.

"They look like white elephants," she said.

10   "I've never seen one," the man drank his beer.

"No, you wouldn't have."

"I might have," the man said. "Just because you say I wouldn't have doesn't prove anything."

The girl looked at the bead curtain. "They've painted something on it," she said. "What does it say?"

"Anis del Toro. It's a drink."

15   "Could we try it?"

The man called "Listen" through the curtain. The woman came out from the bar.

"Four reales."

"We want two Anis del Toro."

"With water?"

20   "Do you want it with water?"

"I don't know," the girl said. "Is it good with water?"

"It's all right."

"You want them with water?" asked the woman.

"Yes, with water."

25   "It tastes like licorice," the girl said and put the glass down.

"That's the way with everything."

"Yes," said the girl. "Everything tastes of licorice. Especially all the things you've waited so long for, like absinthe."

"Oh, cut it out."

"You started it," the girl said. "I was being amused. I was having a fine time."

30 "Well, let's try and have a fine time."

"All right. I was trying. I said the mountains looked like white elephants. Wasn't that bright?"

"That was bright."

"I wanted to try this new drink. That's all we do, isn't it—look at things and try new drinks?"

"I guess so."

35 The girl looked across at the hills.

"They're lovely hills," she said. "They don't really look like white elephants. I just meant the coloring of their skin through the trees."

"Should we have another drink?"

"All right."

The warm wind blew the bead curtain against the table.

40 "The beer's nice and cool," the man said.

"It's lovely," the girl said.

"It's really an awfully simple operation, Jig," the man said. "It's not really an operation at all."

The girl looked at the ground the table legs rested on.

"I know you wouldn't mind it, Jig. It's really not anything. It's just to let the air in."

45 The girl did not say anything.

"I'll go with you and I'll stay with you all the time. They just let the air in and then it's all perfectly natural."

"Then what will we do afterward?"

"We'll be fine afterward. Just like we were before."

"What makes you think so?"

50 "That's the only thing that bothers us. It's the only thing that's made us unhappy."

The girl looked at the bead curtain, put her hand out and took hold of two of the strings of beads.

"And you think then we'll be all right and be happy."

"I know we will. You don't have to be afraid. I've known lots of people that have done it."

"So have I," said the girl. "And afterward they were all so happy."

55 "Well," the man said, "if you don't want to you don't have to. I wouldn't have you do it if you didn't want to. But I know it's perfectly simple."

"And you really want to?"

"I think it's the best thing to do. But I don't want you to do it if you don't really want to."

"And if I do it you'll be happy and things will be like they were and you'll love me?"

"I love you now. You know I love you."

60 "I know. But if I do it, then it will be nice again if I say things are like white elephants, and you'll like it?"

"I'll love it. I love it now but I just can't think about it. You know how I get when I worry."

"If I do it you won't ever worry?"

"I won't worry about that because it's perfectly simple."

"Then I'll do it. Because I don't care about me."

65 "What do you mean?"

"I don't care about me."

"Well, I care about you."

"Oh, yes. But I don't care about me. And I'll do it and then everything will be fine."

"I don't want you to do it if you feel that way."

The girl stood up and walked to the end of the station. Across, on the other side, were fields of grain and trees along the banks of the Ebro. Far away, beyond the river, were mountains. The shadow of a cloud moved across the field of grain and she saw the river through the trees.

"And we could have all this," she said. "And we could have everything and every day we make it more impossible."

"What did you say?"

"I said we could have everything."

"We can have everything."

"No, we can't."

"We can have the whole world."

"No, we can't."

"We can go everywhere."

"No, we can't. It isn't ours any more."

"It's ours."

"No, it isn't. And once they take it away, you never get it back."

"But they haven't taken it away."

"We'll wait and see."

"Come on back in the shade," he said. "You mustn't feel that way."

"I don't feel any way," the girl said. "I just know things."

"I don't want you to do anything that you don't want to do—"

"Nor that isn't good for me," she said. "I know. Could we have another beer?"

"All right. But you've got to realize—"

"I realize," the girl said. "Can't we maybe stop talking?"

They sat down at the table and the girl looked across at the hills on the dry side of the valley and the man looked at her and at the table.

"You've got to realize," he said, "that I don't want you to do it if you don't want to. I'm perfectly willing to go through with it if it means anything to you."

"Doesn't it mean anything to you? We could get along."

"Of course it does. But I don't want anybody but you. I don't want any one else. And I know it's perfectly simple."

"Yes, you know it's perfectly simple."

"It's all right for you to say that, but I do know it."

"Would you do something for me now?"

"I'd do anything for you."

"Would you please please please please please please please stop talking?"

He did not say anything but looked at the bags against the wall of the station. There were labels on them from all the hotels where they had spent nights.

"But I don't want you to," he said, "I don't care anything about it."

"I'll scream," the girl said.

The woman came out through the curtains with two glasses of beer and put them down on the damp felt pads. "The train comes in five minutes," she said.

"What did she say?" asked the girl.

"That the train is coming in five minutes."

105　The girl smiled brightly at the woman, to thank her.

"I'd better take the bags over to the other side of the station," the man said. She smiled at him.

"All right. Then come back and we'll finish the beer."

He picked up the two heavy bags and carried them around the station to the other tracks. He looked up the tracks but could not see the train. Coming back, he walked through the barroom, where people waiting for the train were drinking. He drank an Anis at the bar and looked at the people. They were all waiting reasonably for the train. He went out through the bead curtain. She was sitting at the table and smiled at him.

"Do you feel better?" he asked.

110　"I feel fine," she said. "There's nothing wrong with me. I feel fine."

RESPONSE QUESTIONS

1. Describe the two main characters. How much information is given directly by the narrator? What can you tell about them from their conversation and behavior? What do you know of their past? Which character do you feel closest to, and why?

2. The main source of conflict is never named. What is the "awfully simple operation" referred to by the man? How do the two characters regard this operation?

3. Read a section of the dialogue aloud. How can you tell who is speaking at each point? What clues about tone does the writer provide? Explain any insights about the characters' personalities and attitudes that you get from your reading.

4. Consider what the other readings or screenings in this chapter say about the differences between men and women. Which essay do you find most helpful in explaining the dynamics between the man and the girl in this story? What do you find helpful?

5. Who do you think will win the conflict? What, if anything, is resolved at the end?

GUIDELINES FOR ANALYSIS

1. Hemingway used to say that good writing could be made even stronger by leaving things out. He compared such writing to an iceberg with only one-eighth visible above the surface. What does he leave out in this story?

2. The second sentence sets up an opposition between two sides of the river. What other oppositions do you find in the story? Relate these contrasting elements to the story's central conflict.

3. Notice how often the characters look away. What do they look at, and where in their conversation do these looks occur? What meanings can you attribute to these glances?

4. Some readers see the white hills as symbols. Explain why you agree or disagree. What is the significance of a white elephant? What else in the story do you consider to be symbolic?

QUESTIONS OF CULTURE

1. In the 1920s, when this story was written, Americans were enjoying a period of great prosperity. Women finally acquired the right to vote. Prohibition made the consumption of

alcohol illegal. How do these and other facts you know about the 1920s help to illuminate the story?

2. Hemingway sets his story in Spain and occasionally uses Spanish words. How important is it to know the meaning of these words? What significance, if any, do you see in the Spanish setting?

IDEAS FOR YOUR JOURNAL

1. Imagine this story as a film. How would you cast the central characters? What would guide your choice of location and set design? What would the camera show? What clues does Hemingway provide to help the actors with their lines? What sound effects and music would you add?

2. As a good friend of the couple, you decide to write a letter to them in Spain. Using your best mediating skills, how would you try to resolve their conflict as impartially as possible?

A STUDENT WRITER IN ACTION

Preview

Originally from the North of England, Kathryn Diamond came to the United States with an au pair program, working in the household of an American family while she became acquainted with life on this side of the Atlantic. During her first year in upstate New York, she met Matt, the young man who would become her husband. When they married four years later, she moved permanently to the United States and began working toward a degree in early childhood education. An enthusiastic devotee of the arts, she dreams of introducing first-graders to great music, theatre, painting, movies, and books.

What follows is Kathryn's own account of her writing process followed by her first and final draft. Her first draft includes the instructor's comments and a working outline so you can trace the changes that she made.

DISCOVERING

Q: How did you come up with the idea for your essay?

A: The topic of the essay came from my professor. She gave us an article about genetic engineering that was strongly against GE and asked us to write a response to the article in the classical style of argument. The whole class did a week of independent research on the topic, then shared our findings and had class discussions about the pros and cons. Finally, we each took an individual stance on the issue of genetic engineering—for or against—and began to draft our arguments.

PLANNING

Q: Say a little about how you prepare yourself to write and how you organize your thoughts.

A: I do my writing either on my home computer or on a computer in the lab located in the college library. Either way, I prefer a quiet place. Occasionally I listen to music at home while writing, but more often than not I find it distracting. I write much better in the evening, as I think that knowing time is getting away from me helps to focus my concentration. A firm deadline is crucial. A "sometime in the next two weeks" deadline means I will leave it till the last minute, whereas a "Tuesday 13th or you drop a grade" deadline inspires me to knuckle down sooner.

Q: Once you settled on the main subject, how did you go about organizing your ideas?

A: Our professor taught us to start with an issue question and a clear claim or thesis. If you can't sum up in one sentence what your essay is about, then you don't know what your essay is about. It is important to have a claim because it will keep your focus narrow and on track as you write. It's too easy to get sidetracked onto interesting details that don't add anything to your argument.

I did extensive Internet research on the subject to find supporting evidence. I also interviewed my mother about the subject because she is a sheep/cow/pig farmer who uses organic feed for her animals. When I had decided on my supporting points, I went through my research and labeled them 1, 2 or 3; this showed me where I had enough information and where I was lacking.

Finally, I drafted an outline, which summarized the introduction (the issue question and my position), my supporting evidence, and competing claims (when you look at opposing points of view), which I then argued against in my counterclaim, and ended with a conclusion.

DEVELOPING

Q: How did you develop your first draft?

A: I use the outline as my template for the essay. I open it in Microsoft Word and write over and around it to keep me on track. I start with the supporting points, as I find introductions hard to write at first. I always cite my sources as I go. Even though it can break my train of thought I find it much easier to do this while I write than at the end. It also ensures that I won't forget or miss anything. At some point during or just after writing the support section, I get grounded in the subject well enough to write the introduction. I end with the conclusion and then start to proofread the essay.

As far as transitions go, I just try to keep the argument unified as a whole, while keeping my supportive points distinct from each other. I will use signal phrases like "First, let me explain . . . ," "Next, there is the problem of . . . ," and "Finally, some people . . ." to show where the points begin.

REVISING

Q: Tell me about your process of revising.

A: I did some revising as I was writing. I found that my final point could be merged successfully with the competing claim and final counterclaim to make it stronger. I also decided that my quotes and backing sources for my second point were not strong enough. I realized that I was quoting a student, not a university as I had originally thought. I did some additional research and found better evidence for my point in a government document.

My method of writing is like an organized "stream of consciousness" style, with quotes and sources used liberally to back up my points. This means that I have to be very thorough about proofreading, as I often have incomplete thoughts, fragmented sentences, and errors with tense.

In order to keep a fresh perspective, I like to go back to the essay a day or two later and reread it. While reading it, I try to pretend it is someone else's essay and that I don't know anything about the subject. In doing this I try to pick up some of those "incomplete thought" errors. Also, I will occasionally ask my husband to proofread the final draft—he usually catches a couple of things.

CONCLUSIONS AND ADVICE

Q: What did you learn about yourself while writing this essay? What advice would you give to other student writers?

A: I learned that I am able to dive into a subject that is completely new to me, research it, form my own opinion, and write cohesively about it; in short, I learned how to write a college paper.

The advice I would give to students is start the research and outline of your essay early. Documented essays always take longer to write than you think they will, so aim to finish it at least a week before deadline; this will also give you time to revise it if necessary. The Internet is a valuable research tool, but be careful about citing your sources. Print a copy of anything you use, make sure the entire URL prints out on the bottom of the page. PDF files won't print it at all, so make sure you write it down. Highlight any sections you reference or quote. This will all help you to accurately cite your sources.

Finally, find a subject or an element of an assigned subject that you are passionate about. The stronger you feel about a subject, the easier it is to write about it.

OUTLINE

Issue Question:

Are genetically modified foods safe enough for mainstream public consumption?

Position:

I agree with Turner that we need to know much more about the long-range effects of genetically modified foods.

Supporting Reasons:

The genetic modification/engineering of foods has been an insidious part of farming for many years without the awareness of the general public. ("Breeding-out" weaknesses and disease — does it do as much harm as it does good?)

No one really knows what the long-term effects of genetic engineering will be on the environment. (Genetic engineering is a "young" science.)

Governments are not doing enough research into the effects and dangers of genetic engineering, choosing instead to see a miracle cure for disease and starvation.

Supporting Evidence:

England's National Scrapie Plan

Genetically Modified Organisms (GMOs)

Hawaiian mongoose problem

Golden Rice

Roundup Ready Soya

Competing Claims:

Some say that genetic engineering is the answer to the starving millions in Africa.

Counterclaim:

There is still not enough known about these seeds, etc. They could disrupt the already delicate balance of nature in that region.

Conclusions:

The possibilities for the genetic engineering of foods are amazing and far-reaching; however, there is far too much that isn't yet known about their long-term effects on the environment. Governments and scientists need to do more research on, and less mainstreaming of, genetically engineered foods.

1. I like the way you introduce your topic with a clear, provocative question.

2. If you're following the MLA guidelines for citing sources in your text, you need only identify a source (by author or title) with enough information to find it on your Works Cited page, where full details are given.

3. This summary of Turner's argument is a good way to position your own thoughts on the topic.

4. You should give the cited page number in parentheses at the end of your summary or quote.

5. Can you sharpen this point? Why is one thing better than another?

PROGRESS OR POISON: DOES GENETIC ENGINEERING TAKE MORE THAN IT GIVES?

by Kathryn Diamond

First Draft (with Instructor's Comments)

Are genetically modified foods safe, or even necessary?[1] In the article entitled "Playing with Our Food" in Better Nutrition (June 2000),[2] health reporter Lisa Turner states,[3] ". . . the potential *dangers* to humans and the environment are substantial." Briefly, she argues that genetic engineering is a new and dangerous science, about which little is known. She claims that there are real safety concerns about many of the practices and results of this "weird science". She also emphasizes that the public has a right to know what is in their food, and what the potential risks are to their health. (***)[4]

I agree with Turner that we need to know much more about the long-term effects of genetically modified foods. In this day and age, any kind of science is automatically seen as progress, and progress in turn is automatically assumed to be a good thing. However, I strongly believe that although genetic engineering may be progress, it isn't necessarily a change for the better. Genetic engineering is an unstable modern version of ancient breeding techniques. It is dangerous and unpredictable, and simply does not achieve its desired and well vaunted results. Progress is one thing, but human interference in the natural order of things is quite another.[5]

First, let me point out that genetic engineering has been a part of farming for many years. When the subject of genetic engineering is broached, it immediately brings to mind images of test tubes and laboratories. The reality can be very different, much more insidious, and completely unknown to the public at large. Farmers have used breeding to improve upon the genetic make-up of their animals as far back as anthropologists can tell. To this day, the debate rages over the genetic connection between domesticated dogs and their wolf and coyote cousins. However, there are much more recent examples.

In England there is a government sponsored program called the National Scrapie Plan. According to CBS Technologies of Wales, "Scrapie is a fatal disease affecting sheep and goats. It causes neurological disorders within the brain and central nervous system." (1)[6] Scrapie has been an officially recognized disease for over 10 years, but little is known about what causes it. The best that scientists have been able to do as far as preventing it is to devise a test for the *susceptibility* of an animal to the disease. When an animal has been found to be susceptible to the disease, the farmer or breeder is required to destroy it. This may seem logical, but consider this carefully for a moment: the sheep may *possibly,* one day—or may not—contract the disease; therefore, they are destroying it *just in case*. If this logic were applied to humans, people at risk for Alzheimer's disease would not be allowed to procreate, and would be required to participate in assisted suicide.[7] How ludicrous!

I have spoken to an English farmer about this program. Hazel Thornton is a sheep farmer who is very proud of her award-winning flock. She understands the need for diligence where disease is concerned, particularly in the wake of problems with Foot & Mouth Disease in recent years. However, she has serious reservations about the long-term benefits that this kind of preventative program can offer:

> "[8]The problem is that when you breed-out disease, you can also lose some valuable traits along with the bad ones. A sheep that is diagnosed with Scrapie susceptibility can very well be your best specimen. It can be a real blow to the healthy blood-line of a flock to lose your prizewinning stud ram. Unfortunately, the government would rather look at the possible bad, than the actual good." (Thornton)[9]

Another problem with genetic engineering is that no-one really knows what the long-term effects will be on the environment. On its website, the activist group Greenpeace details its philosophy concerning genetic engineering and the environment, "Genetic engineering enables scientists to create plants, animals and micro-organisms by manipulating genes in a way that does not occur naturally. These genetically modified organisms (GMO) can spread through nature and interbreed with natural organisms, thereby contaminating non 'GE' environments and future generations in an unforeseeable and uncontrollable way. Their release is 'genetic pollution' and is a major threat because GMOs cannot be recalled once released into the environment."[10] ("Campaign Overview")

I think that Greenpeace makes a valid point.[11] Introducing any new species into an ecological system can have a catastrophic effect. Consider the classic example of the Indian Mongoose being introduced into Hawaii in 1883. The mongoose was originally introduced to the island in the hope of controlling the rat and snake populations. However, there were disastrous consequences for the indigenous wildlife. A report on 'Harmful Non-Indigenous Species in the United States', commissioned by U.S. Congress[12]

6. Cite the title or author as listed on your Works Cited page.

7. Your analogy to humans drives your point home here.

8. No quotation marks are needed when you use the indented format for long quotations.

9. This parenthetical citation is not necessary since you have clearly identified the speaker above.

10. Use indented format for this long quote

11. Good transition.

12. Add commas before and AFTER interrupters.

acknowledges that the mongoose, " . . . was supposed to control rats in sugar cane fields, but has come to prey on birds, including the Hawaiian goose . . . and at least seven other endangered species." (236–238)

There is just no way to know the long-term effects of introducing a new species of seed into an ecological system. Genetic engineering is a very young science, and much of it is still a mystery. The bottom line is: if you can't control a 16¥ mongoose, how can you control the spread of seeds? How can you prevent a new type of plant from destroying the habitat of the native ones? How do you know that your 'new and improved' corn won't create a new, deadly disease and wipe out local wildlife? Even Congress emphasizes,

> "Many harmful introductions probably would not have occurred had the damage they caused been anticipated in advance. But little advance evaluation of potential harmful effects was performed for many [Non-indigenous Species] intentionally released in the past. Even when advance evaluations have been performed, however, they often have done a poor job of anticipating effects. Scientists generally agree that predicting the role and effects of a species in a new environment is extremely difficult." (61)

So even our government agrees with me; that the introduction of a new species into an existing ecological system is unpredictable and can end in disaster. Why then, does the government insist on forging ahead with genetic engineering? The answer, of course, is money.

Governments around the world are talking a good talk about ending world hunger through the miracle of genetic engineering. The truth of the matter is that the only people benefiting from this miracle are the fat cat corporate executives,[13] who are only concerned with lining their pockets. Take 'golden rice' for example. This genetically modified rice was supposed to end hunger, while simultaneously preventing blindness in children because of its rich vitamin content. It seemed like the perfect solution, and was even endorsed by former President Bill Clinton,[14] "If we could get more of this golden rice . . . out to the developing world, it could save 40,000 lives a day, people that are malnourished and dying," The only problem is: golden rice simply doesn't work. According to Greenpeace, "Nutrition science, however, suggests that golden rice alone will not greatly diminish vitamin A deficiency and associated blindness. . . . People whose diets lack [fats and proteins] or who have intestinal diarrheal diseases—common in developing countries—cannot obtain vitamin A from golden rice." Even though it doesn't solve the problem of blindness, it should still solve the problem of hunger, except for one big problem: time.[15] Again, Greenpeace asserts, "According to its developers, 'Golden Rice' will not be available for local planting until 2005 at the earliest. Other scientists point out that proper research and testing would probably take much longer." ("Golden Rice" 1-2)

13. Where do you support this assertion about "fat cats"?

14. If you're quoting Clinton here, make that clear and identify your source.

15. Can you sharpen this transition?

The possibilities and potential for genetically engineered food are amazing and far-reaching, however, there is far too much that isn't yet known about their[16] long-term effects on the environment.[17] Governments and scientists need to do more research on, and less mainstreaming of, genetically engineered foods. The risks are too great, and the benefits are practically non-existent. Nature has not been improved upon, only tampered with; the delicate ecological balance of our world has not been respected, it has been threatened; and hunger has not been eradicated, only momentarily lessened. We cannot stand by and let science run roughshod over nature. Whenever mankind has pushed too far too fast, there have been serious consequences. This is a truth that has been respected and revered in both religion and politics throughout history. It is time to give nature the same kind of respect before it is too late.[18]

Works Cited[19]

"Campaign Overview—Genetic Engineering" Greenpeace. 15 Oct. 2004
    <http://www.greenpeace.org/international_en/campaigns/intro?campaign_id=3942>

"Golden Rice" Greenpeace. 15 Oct. 2004
    <http://weblog.greenpeace.org/ge/archives/Reality%20v%20Fiction.pdf>

"Scrapie: The Facts." CBS Technologies. 29 April, 2004, 17 Oct. 2001
    <http://www.cbstechnologies.co.uk/docs/pdf/Scrapie.pdf>

Thornton, Hazel. Personal interview. 10 Oct. 2004.

U.S. Congress, Office of Technology Assessment, *Harmful Non-Indigenous Species in the United States, OTA-F-565* (Washington, DC: U.S. Government Printing Office, Sept. 1993)

Final Draft

Are genetically modified foods safe, or even necessary? In an article entitled "Playing with Our Food," health reporter Lisa Turner states, ". . . the potential *dangers* to humans and the environment are substantial." Briefly, she argues that genetic engineering is a new and dangerous science, about which little is known. She claims that there are real safety concerns about many of the practices and results of this "weird science." She also emphasizes that the public has a right to know what is in their food, and what the potential risks are to their health (24–26).

I agree with Turner that we need to know much more about the long-term effects of genetically modified foods. In this day and age, any kind of science is automatically seen as progress, and progress in turn is automatically assumed to be a good thing. However, I strongly believe that although genetic engineering may be progress, it isn't necessarily a change for the better. Genetic engineering is an unstable modern version of ancient breeding techniques. Furthermore, it is dangerously unpredictable and could have lasting repercussions in nature. Finally, genetic engineering simply does not achieve its desired and well-vaunted result of ending world hunger. Progress is one thing, but human interference in the

16. Agreement problem ("food" is singular)
17. Can you say this more directly?
18. Consider rewriting this section to reflect your particular focus on safety and the public good. Remember your opening question.
19. These are good sources, but where is Turner's article?

natural order of things is quite another. The interference of scientists in the matter of food and crop production is an unnecessary evil that the world would be better off without.

First, let me point out that genetic engineering has been a part of farming for many years. When the subject of genetic engineering is broached, it immediately brings to mind images of test tubes and laboratories. The reality can be very different, much more insidious, and completely unknown to the public at large. Farmers have used breeding to improve upon the genetic makeup of their animals as far back as anthropologists can tell. To this day, the debate rages over the genetic connection between domesticated dogs and their wolf and coyote cousins. However, there are much more recent examples.

In England there is a government-sponsored program called the National Scrapie Plan. According to CBS Technologies of Wales, "Scrapie is a fatal disease affecting sheep and goats. It causes neurological disorders within the brain and central nervous system" ("Scrapie" 1). Scrapie has been an officially recognized disease for over ten years, but little is known about what causes it. The best prevention scientists have been able to devise is a test for the *susceptibility* of an animal to the disease. When an animal has been found to be susceptible to the disease, the farmer or breeder is required to destroy it. This may seem logical, but consider this carefully for a moment: the sheep may *possibly,* one day—or may not—contract the disease; therefore, they are destroying it *just in case.* If this logic were applied to humans, people at risk for Alzheimer's disease would not be allowed to procreate and would be required to participate in assisted suicide. How ludicrous!

I have spoken to an English farmer about this program. Hazel Thornton is a sheep farmer who is very proud of her award-winning flock. She understands the need for diligence where disease is concerned, particularly in the wake of problems with foot-and-mouth disease in recent years. However, she has serious reservations about the long-term benefits that this kind of preventative program can offer:

> The problem is that when you breed-out disease, you can also lose some valuable traits along with the bad ones. A sheep that is diagnosed with Scrapie susceptibility can very well be your best specimen. It can be a real blow to the healthy bloodline of a flock to lose your prizewinning stud ram. Unfortunately, the government would rather look at the possible bad, than the actual good. (Thornton)

Another problem with genetic engineering is that no one really knows what the long-term effects will be on the environment. On its Web site, the activist group Greenpeace details its philosophy concerning genetic engineering and the environment:

> Genetic engineering enables scientists to create plants, animals and micro-organisms by manipulating genes in a way that does not occur naturally. These genetically modified organisms (GMO) can spread through nature and interbreed with natural organisms, there-

by contaminating non-"GE" environments and future generations in an unforeseeable and uncontrollable way. Their release is "genetic pollution" and is a major threat because GMOs cannot be recalled once released into the environment. ("Campaign Overview")

I think that Greenpeace makes a valid point. Introducing any new species into an ecological system can have a catastrophic effect. Consider the classic example of the Indian mongoose being introduced into Hawaii in 1883. The mongoose was originally introduced to the island in the hope of controlling the rat and snake populations. However, there were disastrous consequences for the indigenous wildlife. A report on "Harmful Non-Indigenous Species in the United States," commissioned by the U.S. Congress, acknowledges that the mongoose ". . . was supposed to control rats in sugar cane fields, but has come to prey on birds, including the Hawaiian goose . . . and at least seven other endangered species" (236–38).

What is true of animals is also true of plants. If you can't control a sixteen-inch mongoose, how can you control the spread of seeds? How can you prevent a new type of plant from destroying the habitat of the native ones? How do you know that your "new and improved" corn won't create a new, deadly disease and wipe out local wildlife? Even Congress emphasizes,

> Many harmful introductions probably would not have occurred had the damage they caused been anticipated in advance. But little advance evaluation of potential harmful effects was performed for many [non-indigenous species] intentionally released in the past. Even when advance evaluations have been performed, however, they often have done a poor job of anticipating effects. Scientists generally agree that predicting the role and effects of a species in a new environment is extremely difficult. (61)

So even our government agrees with me; the introduction of a new species into an existing ecological system is unpredictable and can end in disaster. Why then, does the government insist on forging ahead with genetic engineering? The answer, of course, is money.

Governments around the world talk a good talk about ending world hunger through the miracle of genetic engineering. However, the truth of the matter is that the only people benefiting from this miracle are the fat cat corporate executives, who are only concerned with lining their pockets. Take "golden rice" for example. This genetically modified rice was supposed to end hunger, while simultaneously preventing blindness in children because of its rich vitamin content. It seemed like the perfect solution and was even endorsed by former president Bill Clinton, who promised "If we could get more of this golden rice . . . out to the developing world, it could save 40,000 lives a day, people that are malnourished and dying" (qtd. in "Golden Rice" 1). The problem is: golden rice simply doesn't work.

According to Greenpeace, "Nutrition science . . . suggests that golden rice alone will not greatly diminish vitamin A deficiency and associated blindness. . . . People whose diets lack [fats and proteins] or who have intestinal diarrheal diseases—common in developing countries—cannot obtain vitamin A from golden rice." Not only does this new rice fail to prevent blindness, it also falls far short of ending world hunger. Again, Greenpeace asserts, "According to its developers, 'Golden Rice' will not be available for local planting until 2005 at the earliest. Other scientists point out that proper research and testing would probably take much longer" ("Golden Rice" 1).

Meanwhile, executives from Zeneca, the company which hopes to produce the rice, are using scare tactics to garner support. This is clearly shown when Dr. Adrian Dubock, one such executive, talks about his product: "The levels of pro-vitamin A that the inventors . . . have achieved, are sufficient to provide the minimum level of pro-vitamin A to prevent the development of irreversible blindness affecting 500,000 children annually. . . . One month delay = 50,000 blind children [a] month" ("Golden Rice" 1–2).

Comments like this only serve one purpose: that is to scare the general public so that they will not object or ask too many awkward questions when the government passes out lucrative subsidies and tax breaks to companies like Zeneca. Trade laws and regimes are being manipulated in favor of big corporations and are trampling the local farmers' productivity. These problems are not just hurting the little guy, but entire countries are also being affected. Greenpeace claims, "Subsidized exports, artificially low prices and WTO legalized dumping by the rich companies characterize the current unfair model of agricultural trade faced by poor countries" ("Feeding the World").

These companies could argue that they are providing a way for Third World countries to escape from poverty and starvation. But who is really reaping the benefits?

Consider the case of Argentina, where they began planting genetically engineered Roundup Ready (RR) soya in 1996. Although the quantity of their crops has doubled, the number of starving people in the country has also experienced a sharp increase. This is mainly due to the locally produced crops, which fed farmers and the surrounding villagers, being replaced by the RR soya. The soya is then exported instead of being used to feed hungry people at home.

It is the same old story: the rich get richer, and the poor get poorer. Does it have to be this way?

The possibilities and potential for genetically engineered food are amazing and far-reaching, but far too little is known about their long-term effects on the environment. Governments and scientists need to do more research on, and less mainstreaming of, genetically engineered foods. The risks are too great, and the benefits are, at present, practically nonexistent. Nature has not been improved upon, only tampered with; the delicate ecological balance of our world has not been respected, it has been threatened; and hunger has not been eradicated, only momentarily lessened. We cannot stand by and let science run roughshod over nature. Whenever humankind has pushed too far too fast, there have been serious consequences. This is a truth that has been respected and revered in both religion and politics throughout history. It is time to give nature the same kind of respect before it is too late.

Works Cited

"Campaign Overview—Genetic Engineering" *Greenpeace*. 15 Oct. 2004
<http://www.greenpeace.org/international_en/campaigns/intro?campaign_id=3942>.

Ezcurra, Emiliano. "Record Harvest, Record Hunger." Greenpeace. June 2002. 15 Oct. 2004
<http://www.greenpeace.org/international_en/multimedia/download/1/11328/0/recordharvest.pdf>.

"Feeding the World—Facts versus Fiction" *Greenpeace*. 15 Oct. 2004
<http://www.greenpeace.org/international_en/campaigns/intro?campaign_id=3994&print=1>.

"Golden Rice" *Greenpeace*. 15 Oct. 2004
<http://weblog.greenpeace.org/ge/archives/Reality%20v%20Fiction.pdf>.

"Scrapie: The Facts." *CBS Technologies*. 29 April, 2004, 17 Oct. 2004
<http://www.cbstechnologies.co.uk/docs/pdf/Scrapie.pdf>.

Thornton, Hazel. Personal interview. 10 Oct. 2004.

Turner, Lisa. "Playing with Our Food: Genetic Engineering and Irradiation." *Better Nutrition* June 2000. Rpt. in *Writing Arguments*. Ed. John D. Ramage, John C. Bean, and June Johnson. New York: Pearson Education, 2004.

U.S. Congress, Office of Technology Assessment, *Harmful Non-Indigenous Species in the United States, OTA-F-565* (Washington, DC: U.S. Government Printing Office, Sept. 1993).

CONSIDERATIONS FOR YOUR OWN WRITING

1. What did you already know about genetic engineering before reading Kathryn's essay? Did her writing change your view in any way? Please explain.

2. What are the main points to support her argument? Which of these supportive points do you find most persuasive? What might make her argument even more convincing?

3. Find the section of the essay where the writer presents an opposing view and counters it. How effective is this part of her argument?

4. Compare Kathryn's composing process to your own. Do you have similar habits for preparing yourself to write or for planning, drafting, and revising your work? How has her description helped you to clarify, confirm, or change your own approach to writing persuasive essays?

5. Kathryn follows a traditional pattern for writing a persuasive essay, or argument. What does this pattern include? How does her use of an outline help her to plan, research, and draft the essay?

6. Kathryn explains that documented essays often require more time and attention than essays without outside sources. What tips does she offer for doing the necessary research and citation? What are her strategies for managing time?

Evaluation Checklist

Use this checklist to help you—or another student—evaluate your persuasive essay.

- If the essay is about conflict resolution, it should clarify the central problem, present each side of the conflict, explain the concerns of each party, and propose reasonable options that might help to solve the problem. How accurately, fairly, and completely have you done these things?

- If the essay is a position paper, it should identify a controversial issue and present a strong case for one point of view, supporting this view with convincing evidence and reasoning. How well does your writing accomplish these goals?

- Given your readers' views on the topic, have you taken into account their best interests and beliefs? Will they need more background information, examples, or explanations to follow your line of reasoning?

- What makes this paper persuasive? What might make it even more persuasive?

- How would you describe the essay's tone? Is the writing voice engaging? Is it appropriate to your topic and point of view?

Taking Stock

Take a moment to review what you have learned from this chapter.

1. Where in your future work, personal life, and community activities might you be called on to resolve a dispute or clarify a position in writing or in speech?

2. In what ways do you now feel better equipped for these occasions? How have you sharpened your powers of mediation and persuasion?

3. Try to define these terms: mediation, negotiation, objective, subjective, assertion, assumption, verifiable facts, opinions, evidence, refutation, interests, position, resolution.

4. Think about the various perspectives on genre represented in this chapter. What did you learn about the differences between men and women? Have any of your views changed as a result of what you read, viewed, wrote, or discussed in class?

5. Consider the process you went through for the writing assignment or oral presentation. What steps will you probably take again in future writing? What will you do differently?

The Web of Persuasion

The following Web sites are among the many online resources that focus on the arts of persuasion and conflict resolution.

Persuasive and Logical Writing
http://www.uvsc.edu/owl/handouts.html
Utah Valley State College list tips for writing persuasively, from choosing a topic to using sources.

Propaganda Techniques
http://library.thinkquest.org/C0111500/proptech.htm
ThinkQuest's online library describes traditional tools of persuasion, such as bandwagon, glittering generalities, and name calling.

Speech Gems
http://www.speechgems.com/persuaders.html#Examples
A company specializing in communications tools offers explanations and examples of persuasive techniques for public speaking.

Media Literacy Clearinghouse
http://www.frankwbaker.com
Designed chiefly for educators, Frank Baker's Web site keeps expanding with links to good sites about analyzing different media.

OJPCR
http://www.trinstitute.org/ojpcr/
The *Online Journal of Peace and Conflict Resolution* publishes full-text articles about peaceful efforts to resolve disputes throughout the world.

Mediate.com
http://www.mediate.com/index.cfm
This Web site features articles by professional mediators on a variety of conflict areas. It is also a marketplace for mediators.

Conflict in Cyberspace
http://www.rider.edu/~suler/psycyber/conflict.html
A psychotherapist offers advice on resolving conflict online.

CHAPTER 9

Fast-Forward: Predicting and Proposing Future Worlds

"Prediction is very hard, especially when it's about the future."—Yogi Berra

In these fast-changing times, it isn't easy to foresee what lies ahead without a crystal ball, but the outlook can be made clearer with some careful planning. That's why farsighted city planners create detailed blueprints for projects like Fresh Kills Parkland. In spring 2006, New York City unveiled an ambitious proposal to convert the huge Fresh Kills Landfill on Staten Island into a public space for recreation, sports, and art. The site will be three times the size of Manhattan's Central Park, a "living landscape" comprising wetlands, waterways, dry lowlands, and maritime forests. Such ambitious plans call for meticulous preparation. The landfills must be sealed and made safe for public use. The long-term impact on the environment must be studied. Someone must design an infrastructure of roads and drainage systems. Adequate funding must be in place. The master plan must be flexible enough to accommodate changes over the next thirty years. You can trace the evolution of the Fresh Kills project by visiting the New York City Department of City Planning Web site at http://www.nyc.gov/html/dcp/html/fkl/fkl2c.shtml.

In the earlier chapters of this book, most of what you have been writing, reading, and viewing has focused on past or current events. You have been reconstructing memories. You have been describing, analyzing, and evaluating things around you. You have been investigating contemporary issues and considering solutions to problems that already exist. In this chapter you'll be turning to the future, looking forward to the options that lie ahead of you and the people in your life. You'll be using writing as an instrument for *speculation* (literally for observing the landscape from the high ground of a watchtower) to get a clearer view of the paths that might be taken in the coming months and years.

We'll begin with some questions. Where in your life are you expected to make predictions? What kinds of familiar texts (books, magazines, movies, computer programs, television and radio shows) offer visions of the future? What tools do you already have to help you speculate about coming events? Where, for example, do your images of the future come from? What are your methods for making the important decisions in your life? The goal of this chapter is to sharpen your speculative abilities so that you can have clearer images of the possibilities and make more empowering choices.

To predict (from Latin, *praedicare*) means to say (*dicare*) what will happen before (*prae*) it does. You make a prediction every time you guess out loud where a certain road will lead or what will happen if you insert tab A into slot B. You make predictions when you conjecture what will be on Friday's test or when you look up at the morning sky and speculate about the evening's weather.

Whether we are aware of it or not, a prediction usually is based on some kind of theory, the ideas that we hold to and the process of reasoning that we follow. Although we may not be in the habit of examining our theories, it is often a good thing to know what they are, especially when the stakes are high. If we are going to invest our life's savings in the stock market or our life's happiness in a personal relationship, it is worth paying attention to the assumptions behind our decisions. If we intend to act on our predictions, it is often also worth creating a proposal. To propose (from the Latin word, *proponere,* to set forth) means to lay out as a plan. A good proposal offers a realistic, systematic course of action to achieve a desired goal. Proposals give us blueprints for building solid futures out of possibilities.

SCENARIOS FROM LIFE

- In Thursday's chemistry lab, you will be conducting a new experiment. The instructor has asked you to formulate a hypothesis predicting the results. You are expected to describe in writing what will happen when you follow the procedures and explain the theory that accounts for the anticipated outcomes.

- An empty lot in your neighborhood is filling up with trash. It has become an eyesore and may present a serious health hazard. You decide to write an editorial offering several ideas for what can be done for the benefit of the community.

- Where would you like to be ten years from now? What are your dreams, and how will you achieve them? The time has come to set down these thoughts—in a letter to the person you want to marry, who is attending another school.

- The construction company you work for is competing for a major city project. Your job is to write the project proposal. Your proposal must communicate the architect's inspiring vision, but it must also be realistic and show how your company plans to complete the work effectively, within the budget, and on time.

WHY WRITE TO PREDICT AND PROPOSE?

Ever since the invention of writing, people have explored and announced their predictions through the written word. We find them in almanacs, horoscopes, and regular features of magazines, like *Newsweek*'s "Periscope" or *Wired*'s "Found: Objects from the Future." We find them in works of science fiction, like Orwell's *1984* and Ursula LeGuin's "The Left Hand of Darkness," or in works of prophecy like Nostradamus's *Centuries* (first printed in 1555), Alvin Toffler's *Future Shock,* and John Naisbitt's *Megatrends.* With each new medium of communication, the speculative voice has taken on new forms. Think of television programs like *Twice in a Lifetime* or movies like *The Matrix.* The tide of speculative texts swells at predictable times, like the start of a new year or the beginning of a new millennium, but its persistence at all times and in all media demonstrates a basic human need.

Of course, not all predictions or proposals are equally convincing, nor are they meant to be. We will be paying close attention in this chapter to what makes some predictions more persuasive and robust than others. You will have a chance to take stock of your own forecasting tools and to add the tools that others use to your personal repertoire. Some of these tools are tried and true techniques of the trade, like charts, graphs, and maps. Some, like Tarot cards and crystal balls, are of more questionable validity. But your most powerful instrument, one that you already own, is your imagination. Remember that imagination takes many forms. It can be gradual and deliberate, like working out a theory axiom by axiom or word by word. Much science and philosophy is conducted in this way. It can also be quick and instinctive. You don't need lengthy reasoning when you see bricks begin to fall from a dilapidated bridge in a high wind. It can even take the form of music or a dance, the body's rhythms leading the mind to speculative breakthroughs.

The quotation by Yogi Berra that begins this chapter may seem to be absurdly simple. After all, what else could prediction be about if not the future? What else could make predicting so difficult but the fact that the future is still unknown? Yet Berra's pronouncements have a way of revealing ironic truths that lie beneath the obvious. If we probe a little more deeply into the source of our predictions, if we ask where our speculations come from, we might find that our images of the future come largely from the past. Seen in this way, what makes prediction so hard is not the unknown but the images of life that we know all too well, much like a jar of flies that keep flying round in circles long after the lid has been removed. We are caught up in patterns of thinking that have become so routine, bound to feelings so deeply invested in earlier experiences that truly fresh futures are unimaginable. A good way to free your imagination—one that you will have a chance to practice in this chapter—is to liberate your thinking from routine habits of mind.

WRITING OPTIONS

Option 1: What If?

What if the *Titanic* had missed that iceberg? What if the Civil War had ended in two separate countries instead of in preserving the United States? Or what would your personal life be like if it had taken a different twist at some crucial turning point in your past? It is natural to speculate about what might have been. Doing so gives us a chance to undo our past mistakes in our imagination or to trace the course of unlived possibilities.

Lots of movies imagine alternative pasts. Martin Scorsese's *The Last Temptation of Christ* (1988) pictures what might have happened if Christ had chosen not to die on the cross. Frank

Capra's *It's a Wonderful Life* (1946) includes a scene in which the hero has a vision of his town as it might have been if he had never been born. Robert Zemeckis's *Back to the Future* movies (1985–1990) are all about returning to the past to change the future. Some television shows have offered regular speculations of this kind. The Discovery Channel's *What If?* combined documentary film with fiction to imagine history that never had a chance to happen, such as what might have occurred if Martin Luther King had lived to become the first African American president. The ongoing plot of *Early Edition* centered on a man who gets his newspaper delivered one day early and uses it to change tomorrow's news.

For this writing option, you will do some imaginative time travel. Select a decisive moment in the past when events could have taken one of several forking paths. Then imagine a scenario that tells what might have been. Your moment might be a familiar point in history or it might be a moment in your personal life, but it should be a major turning point, a bend in the road with major consequences. Try to show as well as tell how events would unfold from that point on. Picture the world as it would look: how people might act, what a camera might see, the places and things that might figure as important. Be specific. Give close-ups as well as long shots. Your scenario should be realistic. That is, use what you know about people, history, geography, and cultural habits to construct a likely story, one that readers will not find impossible to believe. Like good science fiction, your historical fiction can be based on sound reasoning and credible details and still allow you to exercise your imagination.

Option 2: Envisioning a Future

We all face big decisions in our lives. Some are as predictable as choosing a college, a marriage partner, a place to live, a change in career. Other choices arise unexpectedly, as startling as the deer that leaps into the road ahead. For this writing option, you will imagine a future that lies on the other side of a decision in your life. You will select some choice that you must face within the next six months and imagine the consequences of choosing a particular path.

This assignment will be most valuable if the decision is genuinely important to you. You may be struggling with a personal relationship that requires a decisive action. You may be wondering how your life will change if you move. You may be considering a new job or a major purchase. The process of writing can help you clarify the options available to you. It can help you visualize more precisely a possibility that until now has been just a vague impression. It may also help you work through some of the feelings that arise in the face of significant change.

Your essay might take the form of a scenario. That is, you might describe the sequence of events that are likely to follow your decision. Or your essay might take the form of a proposal, focusing on the way your decision will be carried out. Whatever form it takes, give attention to the context of your decision. What background information do readers need to know about you and your circumstances to appreciate what this decision means to you? What emotions does it bring up for you? Give attention also to the realistic outcomes of your decision. What is likely to change? What might remain the same? What will life be like for you and others once the proposed changes go into effect?

MEDIA OPTION: COMPOSING LYRICS

As an alternative to writing an essay about the future, try casting your vision in the form of lyrics for a song. Composing lyrics is a little like writing poetry. The words carry a certain melody, flow with a tempo, evoke images, convey a mood. The language of lyrics is often less concentrated than the language of poetry, less intense, so that it doesn't compete with the music that carries much of the song's meaning and emotion.

Some lyricists write the words before the music. Others hear the music first and may try to match words to the tune while humming it or playing it in their head. The music may not be a matter of specific notes and chords. It may be more of a tempo and a mood: a melancholy ballad, a staccato rap, or a sensual tango. Are you writing a song that drifts lazily along, lashes out in anger, or pulsates with energy? Let the emotional cadence suggest the words.

Some people like to keep a lyrics notebook. They jot down ideas as they occur and let them incubate. Ideas might come at any time, or they might be coaxed by flipping through the pages of a book at random, scanning pictures in a magazine, or handling items in a drawer. Usually, a strong concept, a striking image, or a haunting feeling will stay with you. When that happens, listen to what it says. Let it lead you where it wants to go. Your job is to keep it alive and on course.

One songwriter begins with the title. He listens to conversations or snatches of dialogue from the radio, and a phrase will catch his attention. It will resonate with something inside him, and the rest is a matter of discovering what the title is about. What's the story in "Tequila Sunrise" or the message in "A Bottle of Red"?

A good lyricist is attuned to the weight of words, their cadence, and their color. Listen to the word "twenty" when you say it. Which of the two syllables do you stress? It would be unnatural to emphasize the second syllable, so you'd place the word where it fits the rhythm of your line. Meter is the rhythm of a line of verse. If you want a metrical pattern in your lyrics, pay attention to the alternating stresses of your syllables. Some lyricists like to use rhyme, but many songs are fine without them. Often a few internal rhymes, as opposed to a regular rhyme scheme, are enough to give the words a sense of unity. No rhyme at all is probably better than the forced clichés of love and dove or June and moon.

Songwriters are also attentive to alliteration and assonance. Alliteration is the repetition of initial consonant sounds, like the **h** in "**h**ip-**h**op" or the **s** in "I **s**at upon the **s**etting **s**un." Assonance is the repetition of internal vowel sounds, like the long **a** sounds in "You c**a**me and you g**a**ve without t**a**king" or "L**a**tely he's t**a**ken to p**a**inting the castle walls brown." If not overdone, these sound effects can make a line more melodic and more memorable.

Use words that paint pictures in the mind. If you're describing a future, set the scene. Listeners usually relate more strongly to a few specific images than to abstractions. This does not mean that it is always better to be direct. Sometimes ambiguity can be inviting, allowing room for the audience to participate in the making of the song's meaning, and leaving listeners with a provocative, perhaps troubling question instead of a pat answer.

As with any kind of writing, composing lyrics takes practice. It also helps to listen to other people's lyrics with a writer's ear. Give yourself the time to write and the permission to fail.

TIPS ON WRITING PREDICTIONS AND PROPOSALS

Predicting and proposing call for both imagination and reasoning, talents that you have been developing as you've read and worked through previous chapters. For the writing options in this chapter, you will be drawing on visual powers that you exercised when you reconstructed a memory (Chapter 3) or described something after close observation (Chapter 4). This time, what you visualize will be an imagined future rather than an actual occurrence. You will also be using the abilities to analyze, investigate, and evaluate that you practiced in Chapters 5, 6, and 7 to the extent that your vision of the future is coherent, informed, and realistic. Furthermore, you may continue to build on your skills of resolving and persuading (Chapter 7). Writing to predict, like writing to persuade, requires you to establish credibility. Writing to propose, like writing to resolve an issue or a problem, requires that you work out a feasible plan. So much of what you have already learned will be helpful to you here.

DISCOVERING

LISTING. Try making lists of possible subject areas and topics.

For Option 1 ("What If?"), list subject areas that interest you, like history, biology, technology, or politics. Under each subject area, begin listing turning points: important events that might have produced different outcomes if things had turned out differently. For example:

BIOLOGY

What if humans had no thumbs?

What if ants were more intelligent than humans?

What if cats could fly?

What if dinosaurs never died off?

What if people had eyes in the back of their heads?

HISTORY

What if Hitler had won the war?

What if Spain, and not England, had settled the Atlantic colonies?

What if the Turks had conquered Europe in the Middle Ages?

What if the planned attacks of September 11 had been discovered in time?

For Option 2 ("Envisioning a Future"), make a list of tough decisions that lie ahead for you. Here are some decisions that other students have faced:

Should I move to Florida?

What if I dropped out of school?

Should I quit my job?

Should I get married now or wait until after graduation?

What major should I choose?

MODEL TEXTS Read through some articles or books that make predictions. Or watch a movie like *Run, Lola,*

Run or *Sliding Doors,* which offer alternative story lines. The essays and video selections for this chapter may also give you some ideas for your own topic.

FREEWRITING Write for twenty minutes without stopping on any of the following topics to prime the pump of your imagination. If you feel resistance at any point, ask yourself, "Why am I resisting this?" and write whatever comes to mind.

Imagine a world without _____ (computers, sports, language, racism). Fill in the blank.

Your friend commits the crime of _____ and seeks your help. What is your response?

Where would you like to be in twenty years?

If I could redesign the human body, what would I change?

What if you really got what you've been asking for from _____ (your boyfriend, your boss, your parents)?

If you had a magic undo button, what would you undo in your life? How would life be different?

VISUALIZATION Try this twenty-minute exercise in imagination. Sit comfortably with your eyes closed and let your mind float free. First, focus on your breathing. Breathe deeply to exhale the day's preoccupations and inhale fresh images. Imagine you are rising, buoyed up above the landscape, over the horizon, to a promising new place. Let yourself see this place in rich detail. Notice what things look like here. If there are any people, what they are doing? If this place has a building, where is the entrance? What do you see, hear, smell, or feel when you enter? How are the rooms furnished? How are they lit? Move through your imaginary set, providing props and costumes as you go. Does anything or anyone seem missing? Let your mind complete as much of the picture as possible. When the exercise is over, jot down any particulars that might give you a head start on the assignment.

CLEARING THE STAGE Sometimes we get so caught up in the emotional brambles of the past that we make little headway toward the future. Ironically, the best way to move forward at such times can be to move backward to that point where we got stuck and unhitch ourselves. The process is a bit like traveling back to the future in your mind's own movie so that you can change part of the script that prevents you from making progress. By facing and mentally "undoing" a key moment in your past or in history, you liberate fresh possibilities for your future. The undoing can occur when you imagine an alternative path or a different way of viewing events, like reinterpreting a bad grade as a sign that you were poorly prepared instead of hopelessly stupid. Or it can occur when you keep reviewing what happened until it loses its power, like repeatedly hitting the replay button on a videotape that shows you missing an easy shot at a goal. Once you really acknowledge your bad luck (or bad timing), you are ready to get back on the field and kick the ball instead of yourself.

STRUCTURE Consider possible ways to organize your draft.

Move from the past to the future.

Explore the consequences of two (or more) alternative futures. (For example, what would happen if you quit your job and what would happen if you stayed?)

Weigh the pluses and minuses of what you propose. (What would you gain if you quit the job and what would you lose?)

Imagine your goal already achieved (the prediction); then fill in the steps to get you there (the proposal). These steps might include specific actions to take and measures of your progress.

FORMAT You may want to follow the style and structure of a familiar type of writing, like a fable, a project proposal, a film scenario, science fiction, a Choose-Your-Own-Adventure, or *The Farmer's Almanac.*

DEVELOPMENT Describe your vision of the future in concrete visual terms. Be specific about locations, personalities, and actions. Use analogies, metaphors, and examples to develop your ideas. It may be important to describe the emotional consequences of your decision and to explore its implications for other people.

REVISING

ESTABLISH CREDIBILITY Reread your essay from the perspective of a skeptic, someone who doubts what you predict. How can you establish your authority? What could you add (or delete) to make your speculation more convincing?

BE CLEAR AND COMPLETE Would a reader who knows little of your subject be able to understand what you envision? What background information would help? What examples or explanations would make your essay easier to follow?

USE GOOD REASONING Check the steps in your thinking. Does one idea flow logically from another? Is there a theory behind your vision? Are your assumptions and conclusions consistent with the theory?

Readings and Screenings: Fast-Forward to the Future

Steven Spielberg's *Minority Report* (2002) envisions a future world in which genetically altered police officers have the ability to arrest killers before they commit crimes. It's a fast-paced world where buildings reach vertiginous heights amid a maze of superhighways and the law gets entangled in technology. Can someone be tried for murder if the would-be murderer is caught before the crime takes place? In Spielberg's *Artificial Intelligence: AI* (2001), global warming has drowned the coastal cities of the world. Retreating into the American heartland, scientists have created a child robot with such real feelings that a grieving mother adopts him as her own—until her true son returns. Science fiction films like these offer images of cities and societies as utopias or dystopias, gleamingly perfect or hopelessly flawed.

Where else do we get our visions of the future? Imaginative fiction is a staple of literature, comic books, and television shows as well as films. But our media also give us more down-to-earth views in the form of popular science magazines, environmental impact studies, demographic projections, economic forecasts, and speculative essays.

Two of the readings in this chapter are grouped with videos. Robert Frost's familiar poem, "The Road Not Taken," raises questions about alternative pathways in our personal lives. "Dan Brooks," a commercial for Seiko, uses a similar idea to make a point about the importance of timing. The utopian lyrics of John Lennon's "Imagine" are paired with a Pepsi commercial that plays with the distinctly nonlyrical imagination of a teenage boy. The longer readings present four/five very different visions of the future. Martin Luther King's celebrated speech, "I Have a Dream," offers his impassioned plea for equality and social justice. Rachel Carson's "Fable for Tomorrow" pictures a world devastated by ecological disaster. Cyberculture guru Kevin Kelly foresees the creation of a dynamic "universal library" on the Internet in "Scan This Book?" And Marvin Minsky's article, "Will Robots Inherit the Earth?" answers his question with a cheerful "yes." Finally, Kurt Vonnegut's futuristic story, "Harrison Bergeron," takes the idea of equality to ironic extremes. Whether skeptical or optimistic, all of these works use the tools of speculation and imagination to envision future worlds.

PRINT

Books:
The Farmer's Almanac
Future Shock
Megatrends
What If: Eminent Historians Imagine What Might Have Been

Science Fiction:
1984
Brave New World
Fahrenheit 451

Magazines:
Popular Science
Wired

TELEVISION

Weather Channel

Science Fiction programs:
Battlestar Galactica
Stargate SG-1
Twice in a Lifetime

MOVIES

It's a Wonderful Life
Back to the Future
Run, Lola, Run
Sliding Doors
Science fiction films

INTERNET

World Future Society
http://www.wfs.org/
Mapping Your Future
www.mapping-your-future.org/

"The Road Not Taken" (1915), by one of America's foremost poets, has become one of the best known "What If" scenarios. Although often taken as a simple statement of regret for life's unchosen path, the poem is less straightforward and merits a closer reading.

Robert Frost was born in San Francisco in 1874. At the age of eleven, he moved to New England and became interested in poetry in high school. Although he attended Dartmouth College, and later Harvard, he never earned a formal degree. Instead, he wandered from job to job, working as a teacher, cobbler, dairy farmer, reporter, and editor. Meanwhile, he was writing the poems that would make him world famous. In 1895, Frost married Elinor Miriam White, and the couple settled in New Hampshire. In 1912, he took his family to England, where he widened his circle of reading and literary acquaintances before returning to the United States three years later. During his lifetime, he was awarded the Pulitzer Prize four times and was named poet laureate from 1958 to 1959. He died in 1963.

The Road Not Taken,
by Robert Frost

Two roads diverged in a yellow wood,
And sorry I could not travel both
And be one traveler, long I stood
And looked down one as far as I could
5   To where it bent in the undergrowth;
Then took the other, as just as fair,
And having perhaps the better claim,
Because it was grassy and wanted wear;
Though as for that the passing there
10   Had worn them really about the same,
And both that morning equally lay
In leaves no step had trodden black.
Oh, I kept the first for another day!
Yet knowing how way leads on to way,
15   I doubted if I should ever come back.
I shall be telling this with a sigh
Somewhere ages and ages hence:
Two roads diverged in a wood, and I—
I took the one less traveled by,
20   And that has made all the difference.

RESPONSE QUESTIONS

1. Describe the speaker of the poem. What can you tell about the speaker's age, gender, and personality?

2. How are the two roads contrasted? In what way are they "about the same"? What reasons does the speaker give for taking "the one less traveled by"?

3. Why does the speaker say, "I shall be telling this with a sigh"? Why has the speaker's decision "made all the difference"?

4. Some readers regard the poem as an assertion of individualism. Some read it as a drama about indecision and the irreversibility of choice. What evidence can you find for each of these interpretations? What other readings can you offer?

GUIDELINES FOR ANALYSIS

1. Examine the particulars of the poem: the yellow wood, the undergrowth, the grass, or "the leaves no step had trodden black." What special meanings do you find in these details?

2. What do you notice about Frost's use of words that makes this poem so memorable? Identify the rhyme scheme by marking each new end rhyme with a different letter. Identify the metrical pattern by marking alternating stressed and unstressed syllables. Identify any unusual choices in vocabulary or sentence structure.

3. How would you describe the poem's tone? What makes it sound sad, regretful, defiant, or ironic?

QUESTIONS OF CULTURE

1. Did you picture the speaker as a man or a woman? Would it make a difference if you thought the poem were written by Emily Dickinson or Maya Angelou? Why or why not?

2. Frost's poetry is usually connected with New England. What lifestyle do you associate with that part of the United States? To what extent do you consider Frost's work regional or universal?

IDEAS FOR YOUR JOURNAL

Write about a personal decision that you have made or must make in the future. What were (or are) the alternatives? Imagine each choice as a different road, and describe the road in physical terms. Would it be lined with trees, filled with potholes, paved with silver? What differences can you foresee as a consequence of your decision?

PREVIEW

If you were hired to make a commercial for a company that sold expensive wristwatches, what features might you advertise? How might you emphasize those features in your ad? When DDB Needham Worldwide won the account for Seiko watches, the New York advertising agency came up with a 60-second story about a man named Dan Brooks. Watch the commercial and compare it to Frost's poem, "The Road Not Taken."

www.mhhe.com/costanzo

View this commercial on the Web site.

COMMERCIAL: DAN BROOKS

Voice-over narration: "One day Dan Brooks was walking down the street minding his own business when he was about to walk into a beautiful woman: The woman who would have his three children. The woman who would graduate law school and go on to become a successful politician. The woman who would go on to change his life forever . . . but rather than insisting on a Seiko, Dan settled for an ordinary watch, and unfortunately, Dan was running one second late."

RESPONSE QUESTIONS

1. Did the ending of this ad surprise you? Where did you think it was going? What guided your expectations?

2. Recall a time when you missed an opportunity because you were too early or too late. What might have been different if your timing were more fortunate?

GUIDELINES FOR ANALYSIS

1. Notice how the story is told in words and moving images. How important is the voice-over narration to our understanding of the images we see and their significance?

2. What visual decisions (about casting, clothing, location, camera angle, framing, the length of each shot) contribute to the story? How do these decisions help to shape our response?

3. What do you think was the aim of this commercial? Do you think it achieved this purpose? Why or why not?

QUESTIONS OF CULTURE

1. How important is it to know the time of day? When do you need to consult a clock or a watch? Could you get along without one?

2. Consider how different cultures place different values on timeliness. How would this ad appeal to people in South America, Africa, Europe, or Asia? How might the script be rewritten for those markets?

"Dan Brooks" is a story of "what might have been." Imagine an alternate scenario. If Dan could go back in time, what do you think he would change and how might his future be different?

John Winston Lennon was born in Liverpool, England, in 1940. Although raised largely by his strict and dutiful Aunt Julia, he spent much time with his free-spirited mother, who taught him how to play the banjo and enjoyed his playful companionship until her death in 1958. In school, John was an indifferent student, more interested in art and music than in academic life. In 1957, he joined a group of musicians who would become the Beatles. Their first album appeared in 1962, and two years later they were guests on *The Ed Sullivan Show.* Soon the world knew about Beatlemania. The Beatles played together until 1970, evolving through a progression of musical styles from buoyant rock and roll to transcendental meditation, defining their generation and shaping popular music for decades to come. Lennon died in 1980, shot on a New York City street by a deranged fan. One of his most enduring songs is "Imagine." Released in 1971, nine years before his violent death, it envisions a utopian future of community and peace.

Imagine,
by John Lennon

Imagine there's no heaven
It's easy if you try
No hell below us
Above us only sky
5   Imagine all the people
Living for today . . .
Imagine there's no countries
It isn't hard to do
Nothing to kill or die for
10 And no religion too
Imagine all the people
Living life in peace . . .
You may say I'm a dreamer
But I'm not the only one
15 I hope someday you'll join us
And the world will be as one
Imagine no possessions
I wonder if you can
No need for greed or hunger
20 A brotherhood of man
Imagine all the people
Sharing all the world . . .
You may say I'm a dreamer
But I'm not the only one
25 I hope someday you'll join us
And the world will live as one.

RESPONSE QUESTIONS

1. How appealing do you find the message about unity, equality, and peace in Lennon's refrain?
2. What view of religion is implied in the song? How might the belief in an afterlife affect "living for today"?
3. Why might Lennon believe that there would be "nothing to kill and die for" without countries? What view of politics, governments, and nationalities lies behind such a belief?
4. The fourth stanza hints at economic issues around possessions, possessiveness, and poverty. What are they?
5. What if Lennon's dream were to come true? What would such a world look like in realistic terms?

GUIDELINES FOR ANALYSIS

1. "Imagine" was written to be heard, not read. Listen to the original recording if you can. How do the lyrics match the music? What's missing from the words on the page?
2. Compare the language of Lennon's lyrics to Frost's poem and Martin Luther King's speech. What features do they have in common? How do they differ? Consider techniques and qualities like repetition, rhythm, ambiguity, irony, precision, and specific details.

QUESTIONS OF CULTURE

1. Who has the most to gain from Lennon's utopia? Who has the most to lose?
2. Imagine the people you know or have read about who might actually work for or against such a world. What role do their age, gender, occupation, race, religion, or nationality play in your thinking?

IDEAS FOR YOUR JOURNAL

Compose your own lyrics. Describe a dream that you have had, or imagine a future world that you would like to see. In your choice of words and tempo, try to capture the spirit of your vision.

PREVIEW

Pepsi commercials usually radiate messages of youth, vitality, and pleasure. Think of all the "Joy of Pepsi" ads with Britney Spears or the more recent, hip "Pepsi: It's the Cola" campaign. The commercial featured here was meant to appeal to young teenagers who are often asked the annoying adult question, "What do you want to do when you grow up?" The ad shows a high school student imagining his future until his companion brings him back to the moment. It was created by Joseph Pytka Productions, of Venice, California, a long-time agency for Pepsi.

COMMERCIAL: BE YOUNG, HAVE FUN

(SFX: CARS PASSING BY) BOY #1:
Hey, man. What do 'ya wanna do?
BOY #2: I don't know.

I'm thinking maybe finish high
school..and college. (BKGD MUSIC:
FAST-PACED) Wife. House.

Kids. (SFX: BABY YELPS) Station
wagon. (SFX: LAWNMOWER) Riding
mower!

Having in-laws over for a
barbecue. (SFX: SMOKE)

I guess I'll give up Pepsi and
start drinking prune juice. (SFX:
ELECTRICAL WIRE SHORT IN ATTIC) Or
rewire the attic. (SFX: SCREAM
FROM BEING ELECTROCUTED) Join the

lodge. Bowl on Wednesdays. (SFX:
BOWLING BALL PINS KNOCKED DOWN)
Work off the 'ol gut. Kiss a
little butt at the office. (TO
EXECUTIVE) Sir uh, nice tie.

Make middle management. (SFX: HE
WADES IN WATER) Or hang it up, and
head on down to Miami. (SFX: ROAR
OF CAR) Buy some white shoes and

pants that come up to my chest and
complain about the government
full-time. (MUSIC STOPS) BOY #1:
No, man.

I mean, what do you want to do
this afternoon? BOY #1 (THINKS):
Oh. The beach! (MUSIC RESUMES AS
ROCK 'N ROLL) Eh man, before your
future

gets here, you know what you gotta
do.

(SFX: MALE VO LAUGHS) BOY #2: I
love it!!!!

(MUSIC ENDS) (SFX: KISSING EFFECT)

RESPONSE QUESTIONS

1. Did you find this commercial amusing or annoying, or did you have some other response? What specifically made you feel this way?

2. Notice which of life's moments (marriage, riding a mower, flattering the boss) were chosen for the sequence of growing up. Which of these scenes did you like most? Why?

3. What other scenes would you include if you were in charge of the creative team that made this ad?

GUIDELINES FOR ANALYSIS

1. At what point did you get the advertisement's central message? Would this have been a better ad if it were shorter or longer? Why?

2. For what age group do you think the Pepsi ad was created? What decisions about casting, language, editing, and music might appeal to this group?

3. The imaginary chronology of life (from marriage to retirement) is framed by shots of two teenagers sitting on a curb. What does this structure emphasize about the future and the present? How does this structure relate to the printed words near the end of the ad ("Be young. Have fun. Drink Pepsi.")?

QUESTIONS OF CULTURE

1. Where do children get their images of adulthood? How important do those images turn out to be?

2. How much of the future imagined by these kids involves consumer goods? Compare their vision to John Lennon's song, "Imagine." What differences do you see between a materially oriented culture and a society based on intangible values?

FOR YOUR JOURNAL

Think of some expectations you had about growing older that turned out to be wrong. What was wrong with them?

PREVIEW

A hundred years after Lincoln freed the slaves, Martin Luther King, Jr., delivered one of the most important speeches in modern times. On the steps of the Lincoln Memorial on August 28, 1963, he addressed a vast assembly of Americans marching for civil rights, recalling the promise of their heritage and calling on them to take steps to fulfill that promise. His dream of universal freedom and equality inspired millions and served as a guiding vision for political activism.

I Have a Dream,
by Martin Luther King, Jr.

Five score years ago, a great American, in whose symbolic shadow we stand signed the Emancipation Proclamation. This momentous decree came as a great beacon light of hope to millions of Negro slaves who had been seared in the flames of withering injustice. It came as a joyous daybreak to end the long night of captivity. But one hundred years later, we must face the tragic fact that the Negro is still not free.

One hundred years later, the life of the Negro is still sadly crippled by the manacles of segregation and the chains of discrimination. One hundred years later, the Negro lives on a lonely island of poverty in the midst of a vast ocean of material prosperity. One hundred years later, the Negro is still languishing in the corners of American society and finds himself an exile in his own land.

So we have come here today to dramatize an appalling condition. In a sense we have come to our nation's capital to cash a check. When the architects of our republic wrote the magnificent words of the Constitution and the Declaration of Independence, they were signing a promissory note to which every American was to fall heir.

This note was a promise that all men would be guaranteed the inalienable rights of life, liberty, and the pursuit of happiness. It is obvious today that America has defaulted on this promissory note insofar as her citizens of color are concerned. Instead of honoring this sacred obligation, America has given the Negro people a bad check which has come back marked "insufficient funds." But we refuse to believe that the bank of justice is bankrupt. We refuse to believe that there are insufficient funds in the great vaults of opportunity of this nation.

5   So we have come to cash this check—a check that will give us upon demand the riches of freedom and the security of justice. We have also come to this hallowed spot to remind America of the fierce urgency of now. This is no time to engage in the luxury of cooling off or to take the tranquilizing drug of gradualism. Now is the time to rise from the dark and desolate valley of segregation to the sunlit path of racial justice. Now is the time to open the doors of opportunity to all of God's children. Now is the time to lift our nation from the quicksands of racial injustice to the solid rock of brotherhood.

It would be fatal for the nation to overlook the urgency of the moment and to underestimate the determination of the Negro. This sweltering summer of the Negro's legitimate discontent will not pass until there is an invigorating autumn of freedom and equality. Nineteen sixty-three is not an end, but a beginning. Those who hope that the Negro needed to blow off steam and will now be content will have a rude awakening if the nation returns to business as usual. There will be neither rest nor tranquility in America until the Negro is granted his citizenship rights.

The whirlwinds of revolt will continue to shake the foundations of our nation until the bright day of justice emerges. But there is something that I must say to my people who stand on the warm threshold which leads into the palace of justice. In the process of gaining our rightful place we must not be guilty of wrongful deeds. Let us not seek to satisfy our thirst for freedom by drinking from the cup of bitterness and hatred.

We must forever conduct our struggle on the high plane of dignity and discipline. We must not allow our creative protest to degenerate into physical violence. Again and again we must rise to the majestic heights of meeting physical force with soul force.

The marvelous new militancy which has engulfed the Negro community must not lead us to distrust of all white people, for many of our white brothers, as evidenced by their presence here today, have come to realize that their destiny is tied up with our destiny and their freedom is inextricably bound to our freedom.

10   We cannot walk alone. And as we walk, we must make the pledge that we shall march ahead. We cannot turn back. There are those who are asking the devotees of civil rights, "When will you be satisfied?" We can never be satisfied as long as our bodies, heavy with the fatigue of travel, cannot gain lodging in the motels of the highways and the hotels of the cities. We cannot be satisfied as long as the Negro's basic mobility is from a smaller ghetto to a larger one. We can never be satisfied as long as a Negro in Mississippi cannot vote and a Negro in New York believes he has nothing for which to vote. No, no, we are not satisfied, and we will not be satisfied until justice rolls down like waters and righteousness like a mighty stream.

I am not unmindful that some of you have come here out of great trials and tribulations. Some of you have come fresh from narrow cells. Some of you have come from areas where your quest for freedom left you battered by the storms of persecution and staggered by the winds of police brutality. You have been the veterans of creative suffering. Continue to work with the faith that unearned suffering is redemptive.

Go back to Mississippi, go back to Alabama, go back to Georgia, go back to Louisiana, go back to the slums and ghettos of our northern cities, knowing that somehow this situation can and will be changed. Let us not wallow in the valley of despair. I say to you today, my friends, that in spite of the difficulties and frustrations of the moment, I still have a dream. It is a dream deeply rooted in the American dream.

I have a dream that one day this nation will rise up and live out the true meaning of its creed: "We hold these truths to be self-evident: that all men are created equal." I have a dream that one day on the red hills of Georgia the sons of former slaves and the sons of former slaveowners will be able to sit down together at a table of brotherhood. I have a dream that one day even the state of Mississippi, a desert state, sweltering with the heat of injustice and oppression, will be transformed into an oasis of freedom and justice. I have a dream that my four children will one day live in a nation where they will not be judged by the color of their skin but by the content of their character. I have a dream today.

I have a dream that one day the state of Alabama, whose governor's lips are presently dripping with the words of interposition and nullification, will be transformed into a situation where little black boys and black girls will be able to join hands with little white boys and white girls and walk together as sisters and brothers. I have a dream today. I have a dream that one day every valley shall be exalted, every hill and mountain shall be made low, the rough places will be made plain, and the crooked places will be made straight, and the glory of the Lord shall be revealed, and all flesh shall see it together. This is our hope. This is the faith with which I return to the South. With this faith we will be able to hew out of the mountain of despair a stone of hope. With this faith we will be able to transform the jangling discords of our nation into a beautiful symphony of brotherhood. With this faith we will be able to work together, to pray together, to struggle together, to go to jail together, to stand up for freedom together, knowing that we will be free one day.

15   This will be the day when all of God's children will be able to sing with a new meaning, "My country, 'tis of thee, sweet land of liberty, of thee I sing. Land where my fathers died, land of the pilgrim's pride, from every mountainside, let freedom ring." And if America is to be a great nation, this must become true. So let freedom ring from the prodigious hilltops of New Hampshire. Let freedom ring from the mighty mountains of New York. Let freedom ring from the heightening Alleghenies of Pennsylvania! Let freedom ring from the snowcapped Rockies of Colorado! Let freedom ring from the curvaceous peaks of California! But not only that; let freedom ring from Stone Mountain of Georgia! Let freedom ring from Lookout Mountain of Tennessee! Let freedom ring from every hill and every molehill of Mississippi. From every mountainside, let freedom ring.

When we let freedom ring, when we let it ring from every village and every hamlet, from every state and every city, we will be able to speed up that day when all of God's children, black men and white men, Jews and Gentiles, Protestants and Catholics, will be able to join hands and sing in the words of the old Negro spiritual, "Free at last! Free at last! Thank God Almighty, we are free at last!"

RESPONSE QUESTIONS

1. When was the last time you read or heard Martin Luther King's speech? What do you remember most about it? After rereading the text, identify those passages that strike you most strongly today. How do you explain the effect on you?
2. The speech includes King's vision of the future. Where is this vision described?
3. What other famous speeches have you read or listened to? Based on your experience, what do you expect from a good speech? Read King's words both silently and aloud. Do you think it is more effective as a written text or as a speech?

GUIDELINES FOR ANALYSIS

1. What was King's guiding purpose in making this speech? What do you think he wanted to accomplish? Where does this purpose become clearest to you?
2. Who is King addressing? At what points does he refer to specific groups of listeners? Do you think these specific references limit the audience to which his message might appeal?
3. At one point, King compares the promise of freedom to a bad check. Where does he use analogies? What purposes do they serve?
4. Find examples of repetition and parallelism (sentences that begin the same way) in the speech. What is the effect of these techniques? Is this repetition more effective when read silently or aloud?
5. Notice which parts of the speech refer to the past, which to the future, and which to the present. How are past, future, and present related in the speech? What principles of organization guide the progression of his speech?

QUESTIONS OF CULTURE

1. King concludes with the words of a Negro spiritual. What other features of his speech do you associate with African-American traditions?

2. How close are we to realizing King's vision today, more than forty years after the speech was made? What progress has been made by African-Americans? How much freedom, justice, and equality is enjoyed by other groups?

FOR YOUR JOURNAL

1. When was the last time you heard a public speech performed? What was the occasion and what was your response?

2. If you were selected to give the commencement speech at your graduation, what would you say to your fellow graduates? What kind of future do you envision for them? What advice would you give them about following their dreams?

PREVIEW

A fable is a short, fictitious story made to teach a moral lesson. It is usually written in simple language and often features animals, gods, or inanimate objects as characters. "Fable for Tomorrow" is a warning, an ominous prediction of what might happen if we ignore the silent danger signs that threaten our environment.

Marine biologist, nature writer, and ecologist, Rachel Carson (1907–64) grew up in the rural river town of Springdale, Pennsylvania, where she learned to love the natural beauty that surrounded her. After graduating from the Pennsylvania College for Women (now Chatham College) in 1929, she studied at the Woods Hole Marine Biological Laboratory and received a master's degree in zoology from Johns Hopkins University in 1932. During the Depression, she worked for the U.S. Bureau of Fisheries and supplemented her income writing articles on natural history for the *Baltimore Sun*. She developed a unique style that combined poetic expression with scientific exactitude, gradually rising to become editor-in-chief of publications for the U.S. Fish and Wildlife Service. Her fascination with the ocean and profound respect for all forms of aquatic life inform three of her most famous books, *Under the Sea Wind* (1941), *The Sea Around Us* (1951, a national best seller), and *The Edge of the Sea* (1955). "Fable for Tomorrow" is her introduction to *The Silent Spring*, written in 1962.

Fable for Tomorrow
By Rachel Carson

There was once a town in the heart of America where all life seemed to live in harmony with its surroundings. The town lay in the midst of a checkerboard of prosperous farms, with fields of grain and hillsides of orchards where, in spring, white clouds of bloom drifted above the green fields. In autumn, oak and maple and birch set up a blaze of color that flamed and flickered across a backdrop of pines. Then foxes barked in the hills and deer silently crossed the fields, half hidden in the midst of the fall mornings.

Along the roads, laurel, viburnum and alder, great ferns and wildflowers delighted the traveler's eye through much of the year. Even in winter the roadsides were places of beauty where countless birds came to feed on the berries and on the seed heads of the dried weeds rising above the snow. The countryside was, in fact, famous for the abundance and variety of its bird life, and when the flood of migrants was pouring through in spring and fall people traveled from great distances to observe them. Others came to fish the streams, which flowed clear and cold out of the hills and contained shady pools where trout lay. So it had been from the days many years ago when the first settlers raised their houses, sank their wells, and built their barns.

Then a strange blight crept over the area and everything began to change. Some evil spell had settled on the community: mysterious maladies swept the flocks of chickens; the cattle and sheep sickened and died. Everywhere was a shadow of death. The farmers spoke of much illness among their families. In the town the doctors had become more and more puzzled by new kinds of sickness appearing among their patients. There had been several sudden and unexplained deaths, not only among adults but even among children, who would be stricken suddenly while at play and die within a few hours.

There was a strange stillness. The birds, for example—where had they gone? Many people spoke of them, puzzled and disturbed. The feeding stations in the backyards were deserted. The few birds seen anywhere were moribund; they trembled violently and could not fly. It was a spring without voices. On the mornings that had once throbbed with the dawn chorus of robins, catbirds, doves, jays, wrens, and scores of other bird voices there was now no sound; only silence lay over the fields and woods and marsh.

5   On the farms the hens brooded, but no chicks hatched. The farmers complained that they were unable to raise any pigs—the litters were small and the young survived only a few days. The apple trees were coming into bloom but no bees droned among the blossoms, so there was no pollination and there would be no fruit.

The roadsides, once so attractive, were now lined with browned and withered vegetation as though swept by fire. These, too, were silent, deserted by all living things. Even the streams were now lifeless. Anglers no longer visited them, for all the fish had died.

In the gutters under the eaves and between the shingles of the roofs, a white granular powder still showed a few patches; some weeks before it had fallen like snow upon the roofs and the lawns, the fields and streams.

No witchcraft, no enemy action had silenced the rebirth of new life in this stricken world. The people had done it themselves.

This town does not actually exist, but it might easily have been a thousand counterparts in America or elsewhere in the world. I know of no community that had experienced all the misfortunes I described. Yet every one of these disasters has actually happened somewhere, and many real communities have already suffered a substantial number of them. A grim specter has crept upon us almost unnoticed, and this imagined tragedy may easily become a stark reality we all shall know.

RESPONSE QUESTIONS

1. What is the "evil spell" mentioned in the third paragraph? Why doesn't the author give it a specific name?

2. What explanation can you give for the white powder described near the end of the essay?

3. Carson ends by saying that "every one of these disasters has actually happened somewhere." Do you know of any places where such things have occurred or are still happening?

GUIDELINES FOR ANALYSIS

1. Why does Carson call this a fable? What words or techniques make it sound like other fables that you know?

2. The author describes "a spring without voices." What examples does she give to illustrate this silence?

3. Where in the essay does Carson create a picture? Which descriptions are most powerful? What gives them their power?

4. What is the effect of the author stepping into the story in the final paragraph? What would the story lose without her presence?

QUESTIONS OF CULTURE

1. After *The Silent Spring* was published, Carson was attacked by the chemical industry, which had high stakes in DDT and the other pesticides whose ill effects she was exposing to the public. Among other things, they published a parody of her book that pictured a future overrun by insects, famines, and disease because chemical controls had been banned. Where do you see this debate between environmentalists and industry today? What arguments can you make for both sides?

2. Although legislation has limited some of the more hazardous practices in countries like the United States, many developing nations do not have regulations on their heavy industry. Where in the world is the environment most in danger? Present reasons why poorer countries should or should not be expected to follow the same expensive measures as richer countries to protect their natural resources.

IDEAS FOR YOUR JOURNAL

Revise Rachel Carson's fable for our own times. What "grim specters" threaten the natural harmony of our tomorrow? What will our children's world look and sound like if our generation fails to heed the warning signs?

PREVIEW

In 2005, Google began scanning thousands of books and making them available online. The significance of this project caught the attention of cyberculture guru Kevin Kelly, who speculated that much more was at stake than access to digital texts. For Kelly, Google's initiative signaled the revival of an ancient dream, a universal library, but with a modern twist. In "Scan This Book?" he explores the global implications of what could be one of the most ambitious undertakings of our time.

Kevin Kelly has made a career of envisioning futures and living into them. Born in 1952, his early interests in writing, photography, and conservation led him to publish the popular *Whole Earth Catalog* in the 1980s, an unorthodox compendium of articles reviewing hardware, power tools, books, and software that promote self-education. In 1993, he helped to launch *Wired* magazine and served as executive editor until 1999. A keen observer of digital culture, Kelly has gained a worldwide reputation for spotting technological trends and contributing to their momentum. In his influential book *Out of Control* (Addison-Wesley, 1994), he explores how machines, the economy, and other human inventions are becoming biological. In *New Rules for the New Economy* (Penguin, 1998), he offers a provocative forecast for the wired global marketplace. Kelly's writing has appeared in publications such as the *New York Times,* the *Economist, Time, Science,* and *Esquire;* his photographs have appeared in *Life* and other American national magazines. The following excerpt appeared in the *New York Times Magazine* on May 14, 2006.

Scan This Book?

Kevin Kelly

In several dozen nondescript office buildings around the world, thousands of hourly workers bend over table-top scanners and haul dusty books into high-tech scanning booths. They are assembling the universal library page by page.

The dream is an old one: to have in one place all knowledge, past and present. All books, all documents, all conceptual works, in all languages. It is a familiar hope, in part because long ago we briefly built such a library. The great library at Alexandria, constructed around 300 B.C., was designed to hold all the scrolls circulating in the known world. At one time or another, the library held about half a million scrolls, estimated to have been between 30 and 70 percent of all books in existence then. But even before this great library was lost, the moment when all knowledge could be housed in a single building had passed. Since then, the constant expansion of information has overwhelmed our capacity to contain it. For 2,000 years, the universal library, together with other perennial longings like invisibility cloaks, antigravity shoes and paperless offices, has been a mythical dream that kept receding further into the infinite future.

Until now. When Google announced in December 2004 that it would digitally scan the books of five major research libraries to make their contents searchable, the promise of a universal library was resurrected. Indeed, the explosive rise of the Web, going from nothing to everything in one decade, has encouraged us to believe in the impossible again. Might the long-heralded great library of all knowledge really be within our grasp?

Brewster Kahle, an archivist overseeing another scanning project, says that the universal library is now within reach. "This is our chance to one-up the Greeks!" he shouts. "It is really possible with the technology of today, not tomorrow. We can provide all the works of humankind to all

the people of the world. It will be an achievement remembered for all time, like putting a man on the moon." And unlike the libraries of old, which were restricted to the elite, this library would be truly democratic, offering every book to every person.

But the technology that will bring us a planetary source of all written material will also, in the same gesture, transform the nature of what we now call the book and the libraries that hold them. The universal library and its "books" will be unlike any library or books we have known. Pushing us rapidly toward that Eden of everything, and away from the paradigm of the physical paper tome, is the hot technology of the search engine.

1. Scanning the Library of Libraries

Scanning technology has been around for decades, but digitized books didn't make much sense until recently, when search engines like Google, Yahoo!, Ask and MSN came along. When millions of books have been scanned and their texts are made available in a single database, search technology will enable us to grab and read any book ever written. Ideally, in such a complete library we should also be able to read any article ever written in any newspaper, magazine or journal. And why stop there? The universal library should include a copy of every painting, photograph, film and piece of music produced by all artists, present and past. Still more, it should include all radio and television broadcasts. Commercials too. And how can we forget the Web? The grand library naturally needs a copy of the billions of dead Web pages no longer online and the tens of millions of blog posts now gone— the ephemeral literature of our time. In short, the entire works of humankind, from the beginning of recorded history, in all languages, available to all people, all the time.

This is a very big library. But because of digital technology, you'll be able to reach inside it from almost any device that sports a screen.

From the days of Sumerian clay tablets till now, humans have "published" at least 32 million books, 750 million articles and essays, 25 million songs, 500 million images, 500,000 movies, 3 million videos, TV shows and short films and 100 billion public Web pages. All this material is currently contained in all the libraries and archives of the world. When fully digitized, the whole lot could be compressed (at current technological rates) onto 50 petabyte hard disks. Today you need a building about the size of a small-town library to house 50 petabytes. With tomorrow's technology, it will all fit onto your iPod. When that happens, the library of all libraries will ride in your purse or wallet—if it doesn't plug directly into your brain with thin white cords. Some people alive today are surely hoping that they die before such things happen, and others, mostly the young, want to know what's taking so long. (Could we get it up and running by next week? They have a history project due.) Technology accelerates the migration of all we know into the universal form of digital bits. Nikon will soon quit making film cameras for consumers, and Minolta already has: better think digital photos from now on. Nearly 100 percent of all contemporary recorded music has already been digitized, much of it by fans. About one-tenth of the 500,000 or so movies listed on the Internet Movie Database are now digitized on DVD. But because of copyright issues and the physical fact of the need to turn pages, the digitization of books has proceeded at a relative crawl. At most, one book in 20 has moved from analog to digital. So far, the universal library is a library without many books.

But that is changing very fast. Corporations and libraries around the world are now scanning about a million books per year. Amazon has digitized several hundred thousand contemporary books. In the heart of Silicon Valley, Stanford University (one of the five libraries collaborating with Google) is scanning its eight-million-book collection using a state-of-the art robot from the Swiss company 4DigitalBooks. This machine,

the size of a small S.U.V., automatically turns the pages of each book as it scans it, at the rate of 1,000 pages per hour. A human operator places a book in a flat carriage, and then pneumatic robot fingers flip the pages—delicately enough to handle rare volumes—under the scanning eyes of digital cameras.

Like many other functions in our global economy, however, the real work has been happening far away, while we sleep. We are outsourcing the scanning of the universal library. Superstar, an entrepreneurial company based in Beijing, has scanned every book from [200] libraries in China. It has already digitized 1.3 million unique titles in Chinese, which it estimates is about half of all the books published in the Chinese language since 1949. It costs $30 to scan a book at Stanford but only $10 in China.

Raj Reddy, a professor at Carnegie Mellon University, decided to move a fair-size English-language library to where the cheap subsidized scanners were. In 2004, he borrowed 30,000 volumes from the storage rooms of the Carnegie Mellon library and the Carnegie Library and packed them off to China in a single shipping container to be scanned by an assembly line of workers paid by the Chinese. His project, which he calls the Million Book Project, is churning out 100,000 pages per day at 20 scanning stations in India and China. Reddy hopes to reach a million digitized books in two years.

The idea is to seed the bookless developing world with easily available texts. Superstar sells copies of books it scans back to the same university libraries it scans from. A university can expand a typical 60,000-volume library into a 1.3 million-volume one overnight. At about 50 cents per digital book acquired, it's a cheap way for a library to increase its collection. Bill McCoy, the general manager of Adobe's e-publishing business, says: "Some of us have thousands of books at home, can walk to wonderful big-box bookstores and well-stocked libraries and can get Amazon.com to deliver next day. The most dramatic effect of digital libraries will be not on us, the well-booked, but on the billions of people worldwide who are underserved by ordinary paper books." It is these underbooked—students in Mali, scientists in Kazakhstan, elderly people in Peru—whose lives will be transformed when even the simplest unadorned version of the universal library is placed in their hands.

2. What Happens When Books Connect

The least important, but most discussed, aspects of digital reading have been these contentious questions: Will we give up the highly evolved technology of ink on paper and instead read on cumbersome machines? Or will we keep reading our paperbacks on the beach? For now, the answer is yes to both. Yes, publishers have lost millions of dollars on the long-prophesied e-book revolution that never occurred, while the number of physical books sold in the world each year continues to grow. At the same time, there are already more than a half a billion PDF documents on the Web that people happily read on computers without printing them out, and still more people now spend hours watching movies on microscopic cellphone screens. The arsenal of our current display technology—from handheld gizmos to large flat screens—is already good enough to move books to their next stage of evolution: a full digital scan.

Yet the common vision of the library's future (even the e-book future) assumes that books will remain isolated items, independent from one another, just as they are on shelves in your public library. There, each book is pretty much unaware of the ones next to it. When an author completes a work, it is fixed and finished. Its only movement comes when a reader picks it up to animate it with his or her imagination. In this vision, the main advantage of the coming digital library is portability—the nifty translation of a book's full

text into bits, which permits it to be read on a screen anywhere. But this vision misses the chief revolution birthed by scanning books: in the universal library, no book will be an island.

Turning inked letters into electronic dots that can be read on a screen is simply the first essential step in creating this new library. The real magic will come in the second act, as each word in each book is cross-linked, clustered, cited, extracted, indexed, analyzed, annotated, remixed, reassembled and woven deeper into the culture than ever before. In the new world of books, every bit informs another; every page reads all the other pages.

In recent years, hundreds of thousands of enthusiastic amateurs have written and cross-referenced an entire online encyclopedia called Wikipedia. Buoyed by this success, many nerds believe that a billion readers can reliably weave together the pages of old books, one hyperlink at a time. Those with a passion for a special subject, obscure author or favorite book will, over time, link up its important parts. Multiply that simple generous act by millions of readers, and the universal library can be integrated in full, by fans for fans.

In addition to a link, which explicitly connects one word or sentence or book to another, readers will also be able to add tags, a recent innovation on the Web but already a popular one. A tag is a public annotation, like a keyword or category name, that is hung on a file, page, picture or song, enabling anyone to search for that file. For instance, on the photo-sharing site Flickr, hundreds of viewers will "tag" a photo submitted by another user with their own simple classifications of what they think the picture is about: "goat," "Paris," "goofy," "beach party." Because tags are user-generated, when they move to the realm of books, they will be assigned faster, range wider and serve better than out-of-date schemes like the Dewey Decimal System, particularly in frontier or fringe areas like nanotechnology or body modification.

The link and the tag may be two of the most important inventions of the last 50 years. They get their initial wave of power when we first code them into bits of text, but their real transformative energies fire up as ordinary users click on them in the course of everyday Web surfing, unaware that each humdrum click "votes" on a link, elevating its rank of relevance. You may think you are just browsing, casually inspecting this paragraph or that page, but in fact you are anonymously marking up the Web with bread crumbs of attention. These bits of interest are gathered and analyzed by search engines in order to strengthen the relationship between the end points of every link and the connections suggested by each tag. This is a type of intelligence common on the Web, but previously foreign to the world of books.

Once a book has been integrated into the new expanded library by means of this linking, its text will no longer be separate from the text in other books. For instance, today a serious nonfiction book will usually have a bibliography and some kind of footnotes. When books are deeply linked, you'll be able to click on the title in any bibliography or any footnote and find the actual book referred to in the footnote. The books referenced in that book's bibliography will themselves be available, and so you can hop through the library in the same way we hop through Web links, traveling from footnote to footnote to footnote until you reach the bottom of things

Next come the words. Just as a Web article on, say, aquariums, can have some of its words linked to definitions of fish terms, any and all words in a digitized book can be hyperlinked to other parts of other books. Books, including fiction, will become a web of names and a community of ideas.

Search engines are transforming our culture because they harness the power of relationships, which is all links really are. There are about 100 billion Web pages, and each page holds, on average, 10 links. That's a trillion electrified connections coursing through the Web. This tangle of relationships is precisely what gives the Web its immense force. The static world of book knowledge is about to be transformed by the same elevation of relationships, as each page in a book discovers other pages and other books. Once text is digital, books seep out of their bindings and weave themselves together. The collective intelligence of a library allows us to see things we can't see in a single, isolated book.

When books are digitized, reading becomes a community activity. Bookmarks can be shared with fellow readers. Marginalia can be broadcast. Bibliographies swapped. You might get an alert that your friend Carl has annotated a favorite book of yours. A moment later, his links are yours. In a curious way, the universal library becomes one very, very, very large single text: the world's only book.

RESPONSE QUESTIONS

1. What does Kelly mean by a "universal library"? If the Egyptians fell short of building one 2,300 years ago, when there were far fewer texts, why does he believe that we can achieve this goal today?

2. In paragraph 4, Kelly quotes an archivist who compares the scanning project to putting a man on the moon. Why does he think a universal library is so important? Explain why you do or don't agree.

3. According to the author, not only will digital technology make more books accessible, but it also will "transform the nature of what we now call the book" (paragraph 5). In what ways does he believe electronic texts differ from printed texts?

4. In addition to changes in the nature of books, Kelly says that the authorship and readership of electronic texts involve radical changes as well. How do features like links and tags alter the way books can be authored and read?

5. Kelly emphasizes the positive possibilities of scanned books. What negative consequences can you predict? On the whole, does the idea of a universal digital library seem more beneficial or detrimental to you?

GUIDELINES FOR ANALYSIS

1. Kelly's essay begins with a close up of technologists at work, then pulls back for a wider view of the dream they are working toward. Watch how he keeps zooming back and forth between specific details and big ideas throughout his writing. Does he offer a balanced presentation of facts and generalities? How important is it to do so in an essay of this kind?

2. Notice the first sentence of each paragraph. Some sentences run on for half a paragraph; others are only two words long. Some are topic sentences; introducing the main idea, while others serve as transitions, linking one paragraph to the next. Highlight these sentences so you can identify their separate functions, and tell what sentence strategies you might use in your own writing.

3. Kelly has a knack for provocative, memorable statements, such as "all libraries will ride in your purse" (paragraph 7), "no book will be an island" (paragraph 13), and "[digital] books seep out of their bindings and weave themselves together" (paragraph 20). What does he mean by such statements? Which of his predictions do you find realistic or far-fetched?

QUESTIONS OF CULTURE

1. Kelly mentions that much scanning is outsourced to countries like India and China. He also notes that a universal library can bring special benefits to the developing world. Do you imagine that digital technologies will help to close the gap between poor and wealthy nations or widen it?

2. In what sense can print-based literacy and digital literacy be said to belong to different cultures? Consider the kinds of thinking and communicating associated with traditional books and electronic texts. What is being lost or gained in the shift from one culture to another?

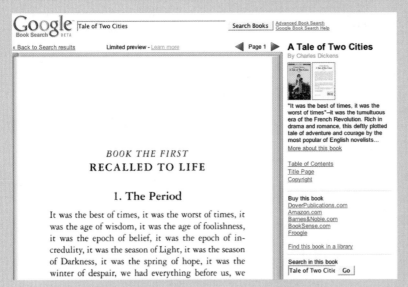

IDEAS FOR YOUR JOURNAL

1. Go online to Google Book Search (http://www.google.com/books), and browse through the collection or look up a few key terms. Jot down your personal impressions. How does this experience compare to the act of browsing in a traditional library or searching through the contents and indexes of conventional books?

2. If you could insert links (to other parts of the same

text or other texts) and tags (public annotations in the form of comments, pictures, or songs) into Kelly's essay, what would you add? How would this change the essay for other readers?

3. The selection excerpted here is from a longer article. "Scan This Book?" goes on to consider other trends and issues, including copyright, piracy, and plagiarism. Read the complete article if you can and discuss some of the ethical problems posed by widespread scanning.

PREVIEW

Marvin Minsky (born in 1927), a professor at the Massachusetts Institute of Technology, is best known for his ingenious speculations about humans and machines. A pioneer in the field of artificial intelligence, he has made important technical contributions to the development of cognitive theory, neural networks, robotics, and related areas. What makes his work distinctive is the way he draws on contributions from a variety of divergent fields and shares his ideas beyond the province of specialists. In *The Society of Mind* (1985), Minsky proposed that intelligence is not the product of a single mechanism but the intricate interaction of many diverse agents. The following article appeared in *Scientific American* in 1994.

Will Robots Inherit the Earth?

By Marvin Minsky

> Early to bed and early to rise,
> Makes a man healthy and wealthy and
> wise.
> —Ben Franklin

Everyone wants wisdom and wealth. Nevertheless, our health often gives out before we achieve them. To lengthen our lives, and improve our minds, in the future we will need to change our bodies and brains. To that end, we first must consider how normal Darwinian evolution brought us to where we are. Then we must imagine ways in which future replacements for worn body parts might solve most problems of failing health. We must then invent strategies to augment our brains and gain greater wisdom. Eventually we will entirely replace our brains—using nanotechnology. Once delivered from the limitations of biology, we will be able to decide the length of our lives—with the option of immortality—and choose among other, unimagined capabilities as well.

In such a future, attaining wealth will not be a problem; the trouble will be in controlling it. Obviously, such changes are difficult to envision, and many thinkers still argue that these advances are impossible—particularly in the domain of artificial intelligence. But the sciences needed to enact this transition are already in the making, and it is time to consider what this new world will be like.

Health and Longevity

Such a future cannot be realized through biology. In recent times we've learned a lot about health and how to maintain it. We have devised thousands of specific treatments for particular diseases and disabilities. However, we do not seem to have increased the maximum length of our life span. Franklin lived for 84 years and, except in popular legends and myths, no one has ever lived twice that long. According to the estimates of Roy Walford, professor of pathology at UCLA

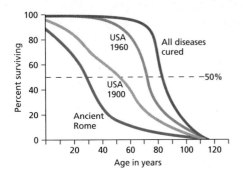

Medical School, the average human life span was about 22 years in ancient Rome; about 50 in the developed countries in 1900, and today stands at about 75. Still, each of those curves seems to terminate sharply near 115 years. Centuries of improvements in health care have had no effect on that maximum.

Why are our life spans so limited? The answer is simple: Natural selection favors the genes of those with the most descendants. Those numbers tend to grow exponentially with the number of generations—and so this favors the genes of those who reproduce at earlier ages. Evolution does not usually favor genes that lengthen lives beyond that amount adults need to care for their young. Indeed, it may even favor offspring who do not have to compete with living parents. Such competition could promote the accumulation of genes that cause death.

For example, after spawning, the Mediterranean octopus (*O. Hummelincki*) promptly stops eating and starves to death. If we remove a certain gland though, the octopus continues to eat, and lives twice as long. Many other animals are programmed to die soon after they cease reproducing. Exceptions to this include those long-lived animals, like ourselves and the elephants, whose progeny learn so much from the social transmission of accumulated knowledge.

We humans appear to be the longest-lived warm-blooded animals. What selective pressure might have led to our present longevity, which is almost twice that of our other primate relatives? This is related to wisdom! Among all mammals, our infants are the most poorly equipped to survive by themselves. Perhaps we needed not only parents, but grandparents too, to care for us and to pass on precious survival tips.

Even with such advice, there are many causes of mortality to which we might succumb. Some deaths result from infections. Our immune systems have evolved versatile ways to deal with most such diseases. Unhappily though, those very same immune systems often injure us by treating various parts of ourselves as though they, too, were infectious invaders. This blindness leads to diseases such as diabetes, multiple sclerosis, rheumatoid arthritis, and many others.

We are also subject to injuries that our bodies cannot repair. Namely, accidents, dietary imbalances, chemical poisons, heat, radiation, and sundry other influences can deform or chemically alter the molecules inside our cells so that they are unable to function. Some of these errors get corrected by replacing defective molecules. However, when the replacement rate is too slow, errors accumulate. For example, when the proteins of the eyes' lenses lose their elasticity, we lose our ability to focus and need bifocal spectacles—one of Franklin's inventions.

The major causes of death result from the effects of inherited genes. These genes include those that seem to be largely responsible for heart disease and cancer, the two largest causes of mortality, as well as countless other disorders such as cystic fibrosis and sickle cell anemia. New technologies should be able to prevent some of these disorders by finding ways to replace those genes.

Perhaps worst of all, we suffer from defects inherent in how our genetic system works. The relationship between genes and cells is exceedingly indirect; there are no blueprints or maps to guide our genes as they build or rebuild the body. As we learn more about our genes, we will hopefully be able to correct, or at least postpone many conditions that still plague our later years.

Most likely, eventual senescence is inevitable in all biological organisms. To be sure, certain species (including some varieties of fish, tortoises, and lobsters) do not appear to show any systematic increase of mortality rate with age. These animals seem to die mainly from external causes, such as predators or a lack of food. Still, we have no records of animals that have lived for as long as 200 years—although this does not prove that none exist. Walford and many others believe that a carefully designed diet, one seriously restricted in calories, can significantly increase a human's life span—but cannot prevent our ultimate death.

Biological Wearing-Out

As we learn more about our genes, we will hopefully be able to correct, or at least postpone many conditions that still plague our later years. However, even if we found cures for each specific disease, we would still have to deal with the general problem of "wearing out." The normal function of every cell involves thousands of chemical processes, each of which sometimes makes random mistakes. Our bodies use many kinds of correction techniques, each triggered by a specific type of mistake. However, those random errors happen in so many different ways that no low-level scheme can correct them all.

The problem is that our genetic systems were not designed for very long-term maintainance. The relationship between genes and cells is exceedingly indirect; there are no blueprints or maps to guide our genes as they build or rebuild the body. To repair defects on larger scales, a body would need some sort of catalogue that specified which types of cells should be located where. In computer programs it is easy to install such redundancy. Many computers maintain unused copies of their most critical "system" programs, and routinely check their integrity. However, no animals have evolved like schemes, presumably because such algorithms cannot develop through natural selection. The trouble is that error correction then would stop mutation—which would ultimately slow the rate of evolution of an animal's descendants so much that they would be unable to adapt to changes in their environments.

Could we live for several centuries simply by changing some number of genes? After all, we now differ from our evolutionary relatives, the gorillas and chimpanzees, by only a few thousand genes—and yet we live almost twice as long. If we assume that only a small fraction of those new genes caused that increase in life span, then perhaps no more than a hundred or so of those genes were involved. Still, even if this turned out to be true, it would not guarantee that we could gain another century by changing another hundred genes. We might need to change only a few of them—or we might have to change a good many more.

Making new genes and installing them is slowly becoming feasible. But we are already exploiting another approach to combat biological wear and tear: replacing each organ that threatens to fail with a biological or artificial substitute. Some replacements are already routine. Others are on the horizon. Hearts are merely clever pumps. Muscles and bones are motors and beams. Digestive systems are chemical reactors. Eventually, we will solve the problems associated with transplanting or replacing all of these parts.

When we consider replacing a brain though, a transplant will not work. You cannot simply exchange your brain for another and remain the same person. You would lose the knowledge and the processes that constitute your identity. Nevertheless, we might be able to replace certain worn out parts of brains by transplanting tissue-cultured fetal cells. This procedure would not restore lost knowledge—but that might not matter as much as it seems. We probably store each fragment of knowledge in several different places, in different forms. New parts of the brain could be retrained and reintegrated with the rest—and some of that might even happen spontaneously.

Limitations of Human Wisdom

Even before our bodies wear out, I suspect that we run into limitations of our brains. As a species we seem to have reached a plateau in our intellectual development. There's no sign that we're getting smarter. Was Albert Einstein a better scientist than Newton or Archimedes? Has any playwright in recent years topped Shakespeare or Euripides? We have learned a lot in two thousand years, yet much ancient wisdom still seems sound—which makes me suspect that we haven't been making much progress. We still don't know how to deal with conflicts between individual goals and global interests. We are so bad at making important decisions that, whenever we can, we leave to chance what we are unsure about.

Why is our wisdom so limited? Is it because we do not have the time to learn very much, or that we lack enough capacity? Is it because, as in popular legend, we use only a fraction of our brains?

Could better education help? Of course, but only to a point. Even our best prodigies learn no more than twice as quickly as the rest. Everything takes us too long to learn because our brains are so terribly slow. It would certainly help to have more time, but longevity is not enough. The brain, like other finite things, must reach some limits to what it can learn. We don't know what those limits are; perhaps our brains could keep learning for several more centuries. Ultimately, though, we will need to increase their capacity.

The more we learn about our brains, the more ways we will find to improve them. Each brain has hundreds of specialized regions. We know only a little about what each one does—but as soon as we find out how any one part works, researchers will try to devise ways to extend that organ's capacity. They will also conceive of entirely new abilities that biology has never provided. As these inventions accumulate, we'll try to connect them to our brains—perhaps through millions of microscopic electrodes inserted into the great nerve-bundle called the *corpus callo-*

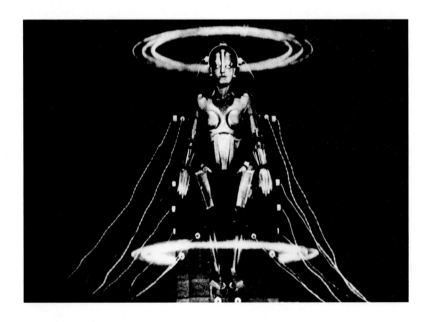

sum, the largest data-bus in the brain. With further advances, no part of the brain will be out of bounds for attaching new accessories. In the end, we will find ways to replace every part of the body and brain—and thus repair all the defects and flaws that make our lives so brief.

Needless to say, in doing so, we'll be making ourselves into machines.

Does this mean that machines will replace us? I don't feel that it makes much sense to think in terms of "us" and "them." I much prefer the attitude of Hans Moravec of Carnegie Mellon University, who suggests that we think of those future intelligent machines as our own "mind-children."

In the past, we have tended to see ourselves as a final product of evolution—but our evolution has not ceased. Indeed, we are now evolving more rapidly—although not in the familiar, slow Darwinian way. It is time that we started to think about our new emerging identities. We now can design systems based on new kinds of "unnatural selection" that can exploit explicit plans and goals, and can also exploit the inheritance of acquired characteristics. It took a century for evolutionists to train themselves to avoid such ideas—biologists call them "teleological" and "Lamarckian"—but now we may have to change those rules!

Replacing the Brain

Almost all the knowledge that we learn is embodied in various networks inside our brains. These networks consist of huge numbers of tiny nerve cells, and even larger numbers of smaller structures called synapses, which control how signals jump from one nerve cell to another. To make a replacement of your brain, we would need to know something about how each of your synapses relates to the two cells it bridges. We would also have to know how each of those structures responds to the various electric fields, hormones, neurotransmitters, nutrients and other chemicals that are active in its neighborhood. Your brain contains trillions of synapses, so this is no small requirement.

Fortunately, we would not need to know every minute detail. If that were so, our brains wouldn't work in the first place. In biological organisms, generally each system has evolved to be insensitive to most details of what goes on in the smaller subsystems on which it depends. Therefore, to copy a functional brain, it should suffice to replicate just enough of the function of each part to produce its important effects on other parts.

Suppose that we wanted to copy a machine, such as a brain, that contained a trillion components. Today we could not do such a thing (even were we equipped with the necessary knowledge) if we had to build each component separately. However, if we had a million construction machines that could each build a thousand parts per second, our task would take only minutes. In the decades to come, new fabrication machines will make this possible. Most present-day manufacturing is based on shaping bulk materials. In contrast, the field called "nanotechnology" aims to build materials and machinery by placing each atom and molecule precisely where we want it.

By such methods, we could make truly identical parts—and thus escape from the randomness that hinders conventionally made machines. Today, for example, when we try to etch very small circuits, the sizes of the wires vary so much that we cannot predict their electrical properties. However, if we can locate each atom exactly, then those wires will be indistinguishable. This would lead to new kinds of materials that current techniques could never make; we could endow them with enormous strength, or novel quantum properties. These products in turn will lead to computers as small as synapses, having unparalleled speed and efficiency.

Once we can use these techniques to construct a general-purpose assembly machine that operates on atomic scales, further progress should be swift. If it took one week for such a machine to make a copy of itself, then we could have a billion copies in less than a year.

These devices would transform our world. For example, we could program them to fabricate efficient solar energy collecting devices and apply these to nearby surfaces, so that they could power themselves. In this way, we could grow fields of micro-factories in much the same way that we now grow trees. In such a future, we will have little trouble attaining wealth, but rather in learning how to control it. In particular, we must always take care when dealing with things (such as ourselves) that might be able to reproduce themselves.

Limits of Human Memory

If we want to consider augmenting our brains, we might first ask how much a person knows today. Thomas K. Landauer of Bell Communications Research reviewed many experiments in which people were asked to read text, look at pictures, and listen to words, sentences, short passages of music, and nonsense syllables. They were later tested in various ways to see how much they remembered. In none of these situations were people able to learn, and later remember, more than about 2 bits per second, for any extended period. If you could maintain that rate for twelve hours every day for 100 years, the total would be about three billion bits—less than what we can store today on a regular 5-inch Compact Disk. In a decade or so, that amount should fit on a single computer chip.

Although these experiments do not much resemble what we do in real life, we do not have any hard evidence that people can learn more quickly. Despite those popular legends about people with "photographic memories," no one seems to have mastered, word for word, the contents of as few as one hundred books—or of a single major encyclopedia. The complete works of Shakespeare come to about 130 million bits. Landauer's limit implies that a person would need at least four years to memorize them. We have no well-founded estimates of how much information we require to perform skills such as painting or skiing, but I

don't see any reason why these activities shouldn't be similarly limited.

The brain is believed to contain the order of a hundred trillion synapses—which should leave plenty of room for those few billion bits of reproducible memories. Someday though it should be feasible to build that much storage space into a package as small as a pea, using nanotechnology.

The Future of Intelligence

Once we know what we need to do, our nano-technologies should enable us to construct replacement bodies and brains that won't be constrained to work at the crawling pace of "real time." The events in our computer chips already happen millions of times faster than those in brain cells. Hence, we could design our "mind-children" to think a million times faster than we do. To such a being, half a minute might seem as long as one of our years, and each hour as long as an entire human lifetime.

But could such beings really exist? Many thinkers firmly maintain that machines will never have thoughts like ours, because no matter how we build them, they'll always lack some vital ingredient. They call this essence by various names—like sentience, consciousness, spirit, or soul. Philosophers write entire books to prove that, because of this deficiency, machines can never feel or understand the sorts of things that people do. However, every proof in each of those books is flawed by assuming, in one way or another, the thing that it purports to prove—the existence of some magical spark that has no detectable properties.

I have no patience with such arguments. We should not be searching for any single missing part. Human thought has many ingredients, and every machine that we have ever built is missing dozens or hundreds of them! Compare what computers do today with what we call "thinking." Clearly, human thinking is far more flexible, resourceful, and adaptable. When anything goes even slightly wrong within a present-day computer program, the machine will either come to a halt or produce some wrong or worthless results. When a person thinks, things are constantly going wrong as well—yet this rarely thwarts us. Instead, we simply try something else. We look at our problem a different way, and switch to another strategy. The human mind works in diverse ways. What empowers us to do this?

On my desk lies a textbook about the brain. Its index has about 6,000 lines that refer to hundreds of specialized structures. If you happen to injure some of these, you could lose your ability to remember the names of animals. Another injury might leave you unable to make any long-range plans. Yet another kind of impairment could render you prone to suddenly utter dirty words, because of damage to the machinery that normally censors that sort of expression. We know from thousands of similar facts that the brain contains diverse machinery.

Thus, your knowledge is represented in various forms that are stored in different regions of the brain, to be used by different processes. What are those representations like? In the brain, we do not yet know. However, in the field of Artificial Intelligence, researchers have found several useful ways to represent knowledge, each better suited to some purposes than to others. The most popular ones use collections of "If-Then" rules. Other systems use structures called "frames"—which resemble forms that are filled out. Yet other programs use web-like networks, or schemes that resemble tree-like scripts. Some systems store knowledge in language-like sentences, or in expressions of mathematical logic. A programmer starts any new job by trying to decide which representation will best accomplish the task at hand. Typically then, a computer program uses only a single representation and if this should fail, the system breaks down. This shortcoming justifies the common complaint that computers don't really "understand" what they're doing.

But what does it mean to understand? Many philosophers have declared that understanding (or meaning, or consciousness) must be a basic, elemental ability that only a living mind can possess. To me, this claim appears to be a symptom of "physics envy"—that is, they are jealous of how well physical science has explained so much in terms of so few principles. Physicists have done very well by rejecting all explanations that seem too complicated, and searching, instead, for simple ones. However, this method does not work when we're dealing with the full complexity of the brain. Here is an abridgment of what I said about understanding in my book, *The Society of Mind:*

> If you understand something in only one way, then you don't really understand it at all. This is because, if something goes wrong, you get stuck with a thought that just sits in your mind with nowhere to go. The secret of what anything means to us depends on how we've connected it to all the other things we know. This is why, when somcone learns "by rote," we say that they don't really understand. However, if you have several different representations then, when one approach fails you can try another. Of course, making too many indiscriminate connections will turn a mind to mush. But well-connected representations let you turn ideas around in your mind, to envision things from many perspectives until you find one that works for you. And that's what we mean by thinking!

I think that this flexibility explains why thinking is easy for us and hard for computers, at the moment. In *The Society of Mind,* I suggest that the brain rarely uses only a single representation. Instead, it always runs several scenarios in parallel so that multiple viewpoints are always available. Furthermore, each system is supervised by other, higher-level ones that keep track of their performance, and reformulate problems when necessary.

Since each part and process in the brain may have deficiencies, we should expect to find other parts that try to detect and correct such bugs.

In order to think effectively, you need multiple processes to help you describe, predict, explain, abstract, and plan what your mind should do next. The reason we can think so well is not because we house mysterious spark-like talents and gifts, but because we employ societies of agencies that work in concert to keep us from getting stuck. When we discover how these societies work, we can put them inside computers too. Then if one procedure in a program gets stuck, another might suggest an alternative approach. If you saw a machine do things like that, you'd certainly think it was conscious.

The Failures of Ethics

This article bears on our rights to have children, to change our genes, and to die if we so wish. No popular ethical system yet, be it humanist or religion-based, has shown itself able to face the challenges that already confront us. How many people should occupy Earth? What sorts of people should they be? How should we share the available space? Clearly, we must change our ideas about making additional children. Individuals now are conceived by chance. Someday, though, they could be "composed" in accord with considered desires and designs. Furthermore, when we build new brains, these need not start out the way ours do, with so little knowledge about the world. What sorts of things should our mind-children know? How many of them should we produce—and who should decide their attributes?

Traditional systems of ethical thought are focused mainly on individuals, as though they were the only things of value. Obviously, we must also consider the rights and the roles of larger-scale beings—such as the super-persons we call cultures, and the great, growing systems called sciences, that help us to understand other things. How many such entities do we want? Which are the kinds that we most need? We ought to be wary

of ones that get locked into forms that resist all further growth. Some future options have never been seen: Imagine a scheme that could review both your and my mentalities, and then compile a new, merged mind based upon that shared experience.

Whatever the unknown future may bring, already we're changing the rules that made us. Although most of us will be fearful of change, others will surely want to escape from our present limitations. When I decided to write this article, I tried these ideas out on several groups and had them respond to informal polls. I was amazed to find that at least three quarters of the audience seemed to feel that our life spans were already too long. "Why would anyone want to live for five hundred years? Wouldn't it be boring? What if you outlived all your friends? What would you do with all that time?" they asked. It seemed as though they secretly feared that they did not deserve to live so long. I find it rather worrisome that so many people are resigned to die. Might not such people be dangerous, who feel that they do not have much to lose?

My scientist friends showed few such concerns. "There are countless things that I want to find out, and so many problems I want to solve, that I could use many centuries," they said. Certainly, immortality would seem unattractive if it meant endless infirmity, debility, and dependency upon others—but we're assuming a state of perfect health. Some people expressed a sounder concern—that the old ones must die because young ones are needed to weed out their worn-out ideas. However, if it's true, as I fear, that we are approaching our intellectual limits, then that response is not a good answer. We'd still be cut off from the larger ideas in those oceans of wisdom beyond our grasp.

Will robots inherit the earth? Yes, but they will be our children. We owe our minds to the deaths and lives of all the creatures that were ever engaged in the struggle called Evolution. Our job is to see that all this work shall not end up in meaningless waste.

RESPONSE QUESTIONS

1. Minsky maintains that Darwinian evolution accounts for our current life span, yet imposes limits on human longevity. Why does he believe that biology alone cannot lead to the kind of future he envisions?

2. This essay first appeared in 1994. What advances in genome studies, genetic engineering, computer science, and other fields over the last ten years have either confirmed or contradicted Minsky's claims and predictions?

3. What restrictions on human intellectual development does Minsky perceive? What options does he foresee to overcome these limitations?

4. According to Minsky, it will be easy to attain wealth in the future; the problem will be learning how to control it. What does he mean by this? What else will be a challenge to control?

5. Minsky's vision of a world inherited by robots is essentially optimistic. What makes him so hopeful? Explain why you share or do not share his optimism. What does he fail, perhaps, to take into account?

GUIDELINES FOR ANALYSIS

1. The author begins with a well-known saying by Ben Franklin. How does the quotation help to introduce the topic and set up the central thesis? Where else does Minsky refer to Franklin in the essay?

2. One of Minsky's organizing strategies is to pose a series of questions and to answer them. How relevant are his questions? How clear and convincing are his answers?

3. Trace the analogies between humans and computers that run through the essay. According to Minsky, how are humans and computers similar and how do they differ? What future does he imagine for combining minds and machines?

4. Why is Minsky impatient with those who argue that computers will never think? How does he define thinking? What does he believe to be the key to effective thinking?

5. Near the end of his essay, the author tells how he tested his ideas with different groups. What kinds of readers did he have in mind? Point to specific passages and composing strategies that show he tried to address the knowledge level, interests, and concerns of these readers.

QUESTIONS OF CULTURE

1. When describing a future generation of intelligent machines as "mind-children," Minsky asks, "Who should decide their attributes?" Consider the ethical implications of his vision. How do you think his question should be answered?

2. Minsky says that his scientist friends are more curious about the future than fearful of change. Do you agree with his distinction between scientists and nonscientists? To what degree might the "culture of science" encourage such differences in attitude?

3. If human bodies and brains are gradually replaced by nanotechnology, what will happen to the distinctions of gender, social class, and ethnicity? If they disappear, what divisions are likely to replace them?

1. Write a story in which Minsky's predictions are realized and robots inherit the earth. The narrator might be a human or a robot.

2. Argue against Minsky's claim that computers can really learn to think. What evidence can you offer to refute the idea of machine intelligence?

PREVIEW

Kurt Vonnegut, Jr., was born in Indianapolis in 1922 into a family of prominent freethinkers with strong beliefs in pacifism and civil responsibility. In 1943, his undergraduate studies at Cornell University were interrupted by the draft. Vonnegut entered military service and was captured by Germans forces during the Battle of the Bulge. Through a series of ironic circumstances that would inform much of his writing, he survived the Allied bombing of Dresden in 1945 while imprisoned in a slaughterhouse. This incident became the inspiration for *Slaughterhouse Five* (1969), a novel that mixes history with science fiction, fantasy, and wry observations on human fallibility. After the war, he pursued (unsuccessfully) a graduate degree in anthropology and worked for a while at General Electric, where the motto was "Progress Is Our Most Important Progress." Vonnegut did not share GE's optimistic vision of a future enhanced by technology. In his short stories, essays, and novels—including *Piano Player* (1952), *The Sirens of Titan* (1959), *Cat's Cradle* (1963), and *Breakfast of Champions* (1973)—he drew bleakly comic portraits of a world trapped in a relentless cycle of inhumanity. "Harrison Bergeron" was originally published in 1961.

Harrison Bergeron,
by Kurt Vonnegut

The year was 2081, and everybody was finally equal. They weren't only equal before God and the law. They were equal every which way. Nobody was smarter than anybody else. Nobody was better looking than anybody else. Nobody was stronger or quicker than anybody else. All this equality was due to the 211th, 212th, and 213th Amendments to the Constitution, and to the unceasing vigilance of agents of the United States Handicapper General.

Some things about living still weren't quite right, though. April for instance, still drove people crazy by not being springtime. And it was in that clammy month that the H-G men took George and Hazel Bergeron's fourteen-year-old son, Harrison, away.

It was tragic, all right, but George and Hazel couldn't think about it very hard. Hazel had a perfectly average intelligence, which meant she couldn't think about anything except in short bursts. And George, while his intelligence was way above normal, had a little mental handicap radio in his ear. He was required by law to wear it at all times. It was tuned to a government transmitter. Every twenty seconds or so, the transmitter would send out some sharp noise to keep people like George from taking unfair advantage of their brains.

George and Hazel were watching television. There were tears on Hazel's cheeks, but she'd forgotten for the moment what they were about.

5   On the television screen were ballerinas.

A buzzer sounded in George's head. His thoughts fled in panic, like bandits from a burglar alarm.

"That was a real pretty dance, that dance they just did," said Hazel.

"Huh," said George.

"That dance—it was nice," said Hazel.

10   "Yup," said George. He tried to think a little about the ballerinas. They weren't really very good—no better than anybody else would have been, anyway. They were burdened with sashweights and bags of birdshot, and their faces were masked, so that no one, seeing a free and graceful gesture or a pretty face, would feel like something the cat drug in. George was toying with the vague notion that maybe dancers shouldn't be handicapped. But he didn't get very far with it before another noise in his ear radio scattered his thoughts.

George winced. So did two out of the eight ballerinas.

Hazel saw him wince. Having no mental handicap herself, she had to ask George what the latest sound had been.

"Sounded like somebody hitting a milk bottle with a ball peen hammer," said George.

"I'd think it would be real interesting, hearing all the different sounds," said Hazel a little envious. "All the things they think up."

15   "Um," said George.

"Only, if I was Handicapper General, you know what I would do?" said Hazel. Hazel, as a matter of fact, bore a strong resemblance to the Handicapper General, a woman named Diana Moon Glampers. "If I was Diana Moon Glampers," said Hazel, "I'd have chimes on Sunday—just chimes. Kind of in honor of religion."

"I could think, if it was just chimes," said George.

"Well—maybe make 'em real loud," said Hazel. "I think I'd make a good Handicapper General."

"Good as anybody else," said George.

20   "Who knows better than I do what normal is?" said Hazel.

"Right," said George. He began to think glimmeringly about his abnormal son who was now in jail, about Harrison, but a twenty-one-gun salute in his head stopped that.

"Boy!" said Hazel, "that was a doozy, wasn't it?"

It was such a doozy that George was white and trembling, and tears stood on the rims of his red eyes. Two of the eight ballerinas had collapsed to the studio floor, were holding their temples.

"All of a sudden you look so tired," said Hazel. "Why don't you stretch out on the sofa, so's you can rest your handicap bag on the pillows, honeybunch." She was referring to the forty-seven pounds of birdshot in a canvas bag, which was padlocked around George's neck. "Go on and rest the bag for a little while," she said. "I don't care if you're not equal to me for a while."

25   George weighed the bag with his hands. "I don't mind it," he said. "I don't notice it any more. It's just a part of me."

"You been so tired lately—kind of wore out," said Hazel. "If there was just some way we could make a little hole in the bottom of the bag, and just take out a few of them lead balls. Just a few."

"Two years in prison and two thousand dollars fine for every ball I took out," said George. "I don't call that a bargain."

"If you could just take a few out when you came home from work," said Hazel. "I mean—you don't compete with anybody around here. You just set around."

"If I tried to get away with it," said George, "then other people'd get away with it—and pretty soon we'd be right back to the dark ages again, with everybody competing against everybody else. You wouldn't like that, would you?"

30   "I'd hate it," said Hazel.

"There you are," said George. "The minute people start cheating on laws, what do you think happens to society?"

If Hazel hadn't been able to come up with an answer to this question, George couldn't have supplied one. A siren was going off in his head.

"Reckon it'd fall all apart," said Hazel.

"What would?" said George blankly.

35   "Society," said Hazel uncertainly. "Wasn't that what you just said?"

"Who knows?" said George.

The television program was suddenly interrupted for a news bulletin. It wasn't clear at first as to what the bulletin was about, since the announcer, like all announcers, had a serious speech impediment. For about half a minute, and in a state of high excitement, the announcer tried to say, "Ladies and Gentlemen."

He finally gave up, handed the bulletin to a ballerina to read.

"That's all right—" Hazel said of the announcer, "he tried. That's the big thing. He tried to do the best he could with what God gave him. He should get a nice raise for trying so hard."

40   "Ladies and Gentlemen," said the ballerina, reading the bulletin. She must have been extraordinarily beautiful, because the mask she wore was hideous. And it was easy to see that she was the strongest and most graceful of all the dancers, for her handicap bags were as big as those worn by two-hundred-pound men.

And she had to apologize at once for her voice, which was a very unfair voice for a woman to use. Her voice was a warm, luminous, timeless melody. "Excuse me—" she said, and she began again, making her voice absolutely uncompetitive.

"Harrison Bergeron, age fourteen," she said in a grackle squawk, "has just escaped from jail, where he was held on suspicion of plotting to overthrow the government. He is a genius and an athlete, is under-handicapped, and should be regarded as extremely dangerous."

A police photograph of Harrison Bergeron was flashed on the screen—upside down, then sideways, upside down again, then right side up. The picture showed the full length of Harrison against a background calibrated in feet and inches. He was exactly seven feet tall.

The rest of Harrison's appearance was Halloween and hardware. Nobody had ever born heavier handicaps. He had outgrown hindrances faster than the H-G men could think them up. Instead of a little ear radio for a mental handicap, he wore a tremendous pair of earphones, and spectacles with thick wavy lenses. The spectacles were intended to make him not only half blind, but to give him whanging headaches besides.

45   Scrap metal was hung all over him. Ordinarily, there was a certain symmetry, a military neatness to the handicaps issued to strong people, but Harrison looked like a walking junkyard. In the race of life, Harrison carried three hundred pounds.

And to offset his good looks, the H-G men required that he wear at all times a red rubber ball for a nose, keep his eyebrows shaved off, and cover his even white teeth with black caps at snaggle-tooth random.

"If you see this boy," said the ballerina, "do not—I repeat, do not—try to reason with him."

There was the shriek of a door being torn from its hinges.

Screams and barking cries of consternation came from the television set. The photograph of Harrison Bergeron on the screen jumped again and again, as though dancing to the tune of an earthquake.

50   George Bergeron correctly identified the earthquake, and well he might have—for many was the time his own home had danced to the same crashing tune. "My God—" said George, "that must be Harrison!"

    The realization was blasted from his mind instantly by the sound of an automobile collision in his head.

    When George could open his eyes again, the photograph of Harrison was gone. A living, breathing Harrison filled the screen.

    Clanking, clownish, and huge, Harrison stood—in the center of the studio. The knob of the uprooted studio door was still in his hand. Ballerinas, technicians, musicians, and announcers cowered on their knees before him, expecting to die.

    "I am the Emperor!" cried Harrison. "Do you hear? I am the Emperor! Everybody must do what I say at once!" He stamped his foot and the studio shook.

55   "Even as I stand here" he bellowed, "crippled, hobbled, sickened—I am a greater ruler than any man who ever lived! Now watch me become what I can become!"

    Harrison tore the straps of his handicap harness like wet tissue paper, tore straps guaranteed to support five thousand pounds.

    Harrison's scrap-iron handicaps crashed to the floor.

    Harrison thrust his thumbs under the bar of the padlock that secured his head harness. The bar snapped like celery. Harrison smashed his headphones and spectacles against the wall.

    He flung away his rubber-ball nose, revealed a man that would have awed Thor, the god of thunder.

60   "I shall now select my Empress!" he said, looking down on the cowering people. "Let the first woman who dares rise to her feet claim her mate and her throne!"

    A moment passed, and then a ballerina arose, swaying like a willow.

    Harrison plucked the mental handicap from her ear, snapped off her physical handicaps with marvelous delicacy. Last of all he removed her mask.

    She was blindingly beautiful.

    "Now—" said Harrison, taking her hand, "shall we show the people the meaning of the word dance? Music!" he commanded.

65   The musicians scrambled back into their chairs, and Harrison stripped them of their handicaps, too. "Play your best," he told them, "and I'll make you barons and dukes and earls."

    The music began. It was normal at first—cheap, silly, false. But Harrison snatched two musicians from their chairs, waved them like batons as he sang the music as he wanted it played. He slammed them back into their chairs.

    The music began again and was much improved.

    Harrison and his Empress merely listened to the music for a while—listened gravely, as though synchronizing their heartbeats with it.

    They shifted their weights to their toes.

70   Harrison placed his big hands on the girl's tiny waist, letting her sense the weightlessness that would soon be hers.

    And then, in an explosion of joy and grace, into the air they sprang!

    Not only were the laws of the land abandoned, but the law of gravity and the laws of motion as well.

    They reeled, whirled, swiveled, flounced, capered, gamboled, and spun.

    They leaped like deer on the moon.

75   The studio ceiling was thirty feet high, but each leap brought the dancers nearer to it.

    It became their obvious intention to kiss the ceiling. They kissed it.

And then, neutraling gravity with love and pure will, they remained suspended in air inches below the ceiling, and they kissed each other for a long, long time.

It was then that Diana Moon Glampers, the Handicapper General, came into the studio with a double-barreled ten-gauge shotgun. She fired twice, and the Emperor and the Empress were dead before they hit the floor.

Diana Moon Glampers loaded the gun again. She aimed it at the musicians and told them they had ten seconds to get their handicaps back on.

80   It was then that the Bergerons' television tube burned out.

Hazel turned to comment about the blackout to George. But George had gone out into the kitchen for a can of beer.

George came back in with the beer, paused while a handicap signal shook him up. And then he sat down again. "You been crying," he said to Hazel.

"Yup," she said.

"What about?" he said.

85   "I forget," she said. "Something real sad on television."

"What was it?" he said.

"It's all kind of mixed up in my mind," said Hazel.

"Forget sad things," said George.

"I always do," said Hazel.

90   "That's my girl," said George. He winced. There was the sound of a rivetting gun in his head.

"Gee—I could tell that one was a doozy," said Hazel.

"You can say that again," said George.

"Gee—" said Hazel, "I could tell that one was a doozy."

RESPONSE QUESTIONS

1. Vonnegut describes a world in which "everyone was finally equal." What is wrong with this picture of the future?

2. Describe the Bergerons. What kind of life do they lead? Argue the case that they are contented with their life or that they are really unhappy. What makes their son Harrison so different?

3. Identify the kinds of handicaps that people have in the year 2081. What purposes do these handicaps serve? Does the Handicapper General have a handicap? Why or why not?

4. Compare Vonnegut's vision of the future to Marvin Minsky's in "Will Robots Inherit the Earth?" What makes one writer pessimistic and the other optimistic?

GUIDELINES FOR ANALYSIS

1. A satire ridicules human vices, follies, abuses, or stupidities. Is this a satire on the idea of equality, on people like the Bergerons, or on other targets? How can you tell?

2. Although, like "Fable for Tomorrow," this story depicts a world gone wrong, Vonnegut's writing is very different from Rachel Carson's. What makes his writing style different? How would you characterize his sense of humor, his use of dialogue, and his narrative voice?

3. "Harrison Bergeron" has many of the elements that we expect in a work of fiction. It contains some exposition (background information we need to understand what happens), a

central conflict (struggle between opposing forces), a complication (the point where this conflict begins), a crisis (highpoint in the action), and a resolution (when the conflict ends). Identify these elements in the story. Compare the author's treatment of these elements to other stories you have read.

QUESTIONS OF CULTURE

1. George and Hazel are shown in front of the television set. Make a case for seeing their interaction as a spoof on modern television culture.

2. When Hazel asks George to remove part of his handicap, he warns that this would lead "to the dark ages again." Explain his line of reasoning. Does he have a point? What other proposals have been made in the past to solve the problem of "people competing against everybody else"?

IDEAS FOR YOUR JOURNAL

1. Imagine a scenario that might lead up to the future described in this story. What historical events would probably have to take place before there could be a United States Handicapper General? What other changes to the Constitution might be made before Amendment 211?

2. Write a story set in 2081 when one of the world's problems has been solved with devastating results. Imagine a future in which the wrong things have been done for the right reasons.

A STUDENT WRITER IN ACTION

Preview

"What if I were born male instead of female?" An assignment in English 101 prompted Monique Bonfiglio to think about the life she might have led if her sex chromosome were XY instead of XX. Although she treats gender differences with a light touch, she is not unmindful of the serious issues involved.

Monique was born in Yonkers, New York, and currently resides in Rockland County, thirty minutes north of New York City. Monique is a communications major at Westchester Community College who enjoys reading and writing. After graduation from WCC, she plans to transfer to a four-year college, perhaps in New York City. "I aspire to have a career doing what I love, and that is to write," she says. "Expressing myself in creative form provides me with enjoyment and peace of mind."

DISCOVERING

Q: How did you arrive at the idea for your essay?

A: Last semester I took a class called the psychology of human sexuality, which has given me incredible insight into societal gender issues. Since then, I have found myself constantly exploring and questioning gender roles that have been assigned to males and females. After brainstorming, I came up with various ideas regarding male and female qualities. I asked myself this question, "If I was born a male, would my life be easier or more difficult"? I decided to play with the idea and it turned into an essay.

PLANNING

Q: Say a little about how you prepare yourself to write and how you organize your thoughts.

A: I carry a small tape recorder around with me wherever I go because ideas come to me at the strangest moments. I'll be driving or in a crowded room and all of a sudden my mind wanders and I come up with the most creative ideas. If I do not immediately capture them, the ideas are lost. I do not exactly prepare myself to write; the ideas prepare me. I write everywhere: at home on my computer, at work or on the subway in my note pad. Even on vacation I bring writing tools with me. When I feel my creative juices flowing I'll stop what I'm doing and write. If I sit myself down and say, "Okay, it is time to write," nothing good comes out of it.

DEVELOPING

Q: How did you develop your first draft? Do you have any methods for building paragraphs? How did you arrive at your beginning and ending?

A: I am a firm believer in the effectiveness of freewriting in inspiring creative ideas. My essay started out as an exercise in freewriting. I came up with the idea—what if I was born male instead of female?—and I just wrote until the ideas were flowing consistently. Amazingly it all came together; one thought lead to another and another until I had enough material to organize an essay.

By looking over some freewriting pieces I devised a first draft that was worlds away from what the piece is now. In my first draft I explored three different "what if" scenarios about a paragraph or two each in length. My paragraphs start with a single idea and are finished when that idea is fully expressed. Usually the last sentence in my paragraph is a transition to the next or an indication that the thought has been completely expressed. In my opinion, trying too hard to structure paragraphs a certain way subtracts from the substance of a piece of writing. I feel the task of evaluating paragraph structure should take place during revision.

REVISING

Q: Tell me about your process of revising. What did you delete, add, move around, or otherwise change? And what were you thinking when you made the changes?

A: Revising is as much a part of writing as the creative process itself. My introduction was omitted, as was the other two "what if" scenarios I had explored. I decided to focus purely on the male female situation after some constructive criticism offered by a professor. The only way to know what readers think of your writing is to ask them. I try to have my pieces critiqued by as many people as possible from different age groups and social classes. I ask that my peers, teachers, co-workers, and family read my creations and offer not only criticism but advice as well. I like to know what kind of thoughts and emotions are inspired in other people through my writing. I often ask, "What was your favorite part?" When I made the changes to my piece I considered them positive revisions that would make my point more clear.

Q: Do you give any special attention to completeness, unity, structure, continuity, or style? How do you proofread your work for errors?

A: I always take completeness, unity, structure, continuity, and style into consideration when writing. Depending on the subject I am writing about, some of these factors become more significant. For example, if I were writing about death, I would want to focus more on unity, making sure that the mood was consistent throughout the piece. If I were writing a piece for submission to a magazine, I would probably focus more on the style of my writing.

I find proofreading to be challenging and prefer to have my work proofread by someone other than myself. I am the worst possible speller and tend to get lost in substance rather than noticing grammatical errors. When I do proofread my work, I read it over and over again until it seems flawless.

ADVICE

Q: Looking back, what would you say was your most important goal in writing the essay? What were your biggest obstacles, and how did you tackle them? How do you feel now about the results?

A: My most important goal was to demonstrate my skills as a writer. I would say that my biggest obstacle was getting it from the first draft to what it is today. I did this by reading the piece repeatedly and asking myself how it could be clearer and more to the point. I made efforts not to stray from the main idea and tried not to lose sight of my purpose. I am satisfied with the end result. The piece addresses some serious issues while remaining playful and entertaining.

Q: Finally, did you learn anything about yourself while writing the essay? What advice would you give to other student writers?

A: While writing this essay, I learned that I am still perplexed by societal gender issues and that it is quite difficult to clearly express some of the ideas I explored in my piece.

As an aspiring writer I would have to say the most important advice I can give student writers is to engage in freewriting activities. By doing this you can explore the deep caverns of your mind, finding useful ideas that you can offer to the world. The more you write, the easier it becomes to express your ideas clearly.

BOYS DON'T CRY,

by Monique Bonfiglio

Monique's First Draft (with Instructor's Comments)

"What if" . . . such a simple combination of words but when attached to certain scenarios, what profound thought and speculation is[1] inspired. Wondering what ifs can cause the brain to go off on a tangent beckoning for the deepest contents of the mind to come forth and penetrate reality. When we consider the "what it" of life, we are invoking the evolution of imagination[2] and asking to be taken to a place other than here, a time other than now. Wondering "what if" can certainly drive a person crazy

1. Be sure the verb agrees with its subject, which is plural here

2. Are we invoking imagination or its evolution?

3. Instead of telling us what you will attempt to do, why don't you just do it?

4. I like the way you make the hypothetical idea of gender change personal and specific. I can visualize the differences as you describe them.

5. Here (and throughout your essay) you often switch to "was" instead of using "were." I suggest that you use "were" more consistently whenever you are speculating about what might have been.

6. Your method of combining funny and serious examples is very engaging.

7. Comma splice

8. Is this the word you want? Does it strike the right tone here?

9. spelling

because unanswered questions are a burden to the mind and choices confirmed wrong disturb the spirit. On the other hand, exploring the "what ifs" reminds us of the infinite possibilities and that actions, intentional or not, have consequences. This is real; I will attempt to participate in this thought process with every intention of distorting reality while crediting fate.[3]

What if I were born male rather than female? I would answer to another name and my grace and beauty would have been substituted with strength and masculinity. These chandelier earrings[4] would certainly not dangle appropriately from my attentive ears; my ears would not even be attentive if I were a man. Maybe my skin would not be so soft, and tendrils of hair would definitely not reach the middle of my back whose deep curve would be absent if I were not a woman. If I was[5] born a man, I would be exempt from the duties of motherhood; this would certainly subtract from who I am. If I was not female it is possible that I would place more worth on power and possession than on peace, praise, and appreciation. My fascination in couture and cosmetics may have been omitted from my genes if I were born a male rather than a female. The word JUICY would not be scrolled across the back of these pants[6] that snugly squeeze my buttock, which would not jiggle as it does if I were a man. Maybe, if I was a boy, I would be closer to my brother and he and I would share clothes as my sister and I do. Perhaps if I were a man, I would have been denied access to my sensitive side, afraid to let the world see me cry; maybe I would make women cry.

I am not a man though,[7] I am a woman. I cherish my femininity and consider my girly[8] qualities to be nothing but assets that compliment[9] who I am inside and out. Considering what if I was born a man rather than a woman has allowed me to explore an alternative to my existence although I merely scratched the surface of how my fate would be altered if I were born a man. This scenario leaves many questions unanswered and demands future attention which will be allocated when appropriate (maybe when I am bored).

What if yesterday, while driving home from school, I slammed my car into that red pickup truck in front of me? If I impacted it with enough force, certainly those ladders, made of steel, resting insecurely and unfastened in the trucks bed, would crash abruptly through my windshield. Before I could think or even understand what has happened, the ladders would probably pierce my skull. Most likely I would encounter a fourth of a second of intense, invading pain before exhaling it out of my body through my last breath. The driver of the tuck may blame himself for not securing the ladders; he was probably only traveling a short distance. The scene would have impressed upon his mind, robbing his sanity; he would be unable to forget the sight of me, blood gushing, and steel rods protruding from my distorted face. Maybe he would lie or make excuses or accusations that I was on a cell phone and that he had not stopped short in front of me.

My family would miss me and maybe some would feel guilty for not telling me they love me in a while. My casket would definitely be closed at the funeral where so many have gathered to mourn my tragic untimely[10] death. Perhaps, as time passes, my existence would be pushed further and further from everyday life that what I looked like, how I smelled, and my embrace Could only be remembered when the utmost effort was exerted in doing so. Maybe my poetry, songs, and artwork would be worth something to the world if I was taken off the face of the Earth.

I was behind it, but I did not hit that red pickup truck yesterday; I did not die. Considering what if I had has made me appreciate being alive right now. I have been reminded of how delicate human life is and how unpredictable fate can be. While I was behind the truck I actually imagined the ladders crashing through my windshield, killing me. What haunting thoughts those were running through my head; it made me pay closer attention while driving.

What if drugs were legal? Would more people use them or less? Certainly drugs would be safer because their production and distribution could be monitored and regulated by some organization, probably the Federal Government.[11] Perhaps some drugs like Marijuana, steroids, and cocaine would be legal and others such as heroin, LSD, and crack would not be, or maybe they will all be legitimate, placed in some read the label and use at your own risk category with prescription drugs and cigarettes. Certainly, doctors would go back to prescribing cocaine as a form of numbing medicine as they had prior to the illegalization[12] of the drug. It would still be used in cough medicine and Coca Cola as it has in the past. Maybe people would be more laid back, happier, more content, or would we be a nation of incompetent addicts who's[13] most productive and prosperous industry was drugs? If drugs were legal maybe we would produce them here rather than having them transported from South America as they are; the economy would improve and there would be less of a reliance on foreign product. Other drug producing nations would suffer upon the loss of their largest customer, America. Would law enforcement officials, athletes, and politicians admit using drugs if they were legal? Fewer children would turn to drugs in subconscious acts of rebellion for, if drugs were allowed, there would be nothing rebellious about using them.

Drugs are not legal though and I doubt they will ever be entirely. This does not mean people do not use them. Drugs are as much a part of American society as sitcoms and soap operas. Each generation has experienced the effects of drug use whether it be first hand or as spectators. In America, there is a supposed "war on drugs", we are losing[14] because no matter how much of the budget is allocated towards combating drug use, trafficking, and distribution, it will prevail.[15]

10. Separate Items in a series with a comma.

11. No uppercase is needed here unless this is a proper name. The same is true of marijuana

12. Do you mean "prohibition"?

13. spelling

14. spelling
15. This phrasing sounds awkward. Can you say it another way?

16. This is cute, but I think you may have lost the focus and momentum of your essay here. Try another ending.

What if this torturous toothache was not a reality and I was not on prescribed Vicodin;[16] would I still be contemplating these ridiculous possibilities? Probably not.

Monique's Final Draft

What if I were born male rather than female? I would answer to another name and my grace and beauty would have been substituted with strength and masculinity. These chandelier earrings would certainly not dangle appropriately from my attentive ears; my ears would not even be attentive if I were a man. My long, delicate, fingernails certainly would not glow passion pink if they grew from the rough hands of a man. Maybe my skin would not be so soft and tendrils of hair would definitely not reach the middle of my back, whose deep curve would be absent if I were not a woman.

Leg and armpit shaving would not even cross my mind if I were a man. I doubt I would spend eight dollars a week on eyebrow waxing. If I were born a man instead of a woman, oral contraceptives would not be of my immediate concern. Instead, I would simply keep a condom or two in my wallet, for sexually transmitted disease and AIDS would still be my concern if I were of the opposite sex. In my masculinity, I would be exempt from the duties of motherhood; this would certainly subtract from who I am. If I were a man, subconsciously I would be relieved and comforted by the idea that I was not a member of the sex who has been burdened with the duty of giving birth.

If I were not female it is possible that I would place more worth on power and possession than on peace, praise, and appreciation. My fascination with couture and cosmetics might have been omitted from my genes. I would seek answers and advice from the pages of *Playboy* and *GQ* rather than *Glamour* and *Vogue* magazines, probably paying more attention to the pictures and advertisements than to the substance of the articles.

The word JUICY would not be scrolled across the back of these pants that snugly squeeze my buttocks, which would not jiggle if I were a man. If I were not female, I would place less importance on my walk-in closet, organized so precisely with a spot for every shoe, belt, and accessory; a man's wardrobe could not possibly occupy half of it. If I were a man I would not need this blowdryer nor would these hot rollers be necessary. I could even do without this eyelash curler.

Maybe, if I were a boy, I would be closer to my brother and he and I would share clothes as my sister and I do. If I *were* a boy, and *did* share clothes with my brother, the exchange would be quite different, lacking the elaborate emotions and accessories of sisterhood. There would have been no Barbie, no Easy Bake Oven, but I still would have grown up on the Smurfs and *Sesame Street*. Most likely, if I were a man, I would fear intimacy and commitment rather than strive for it as most women do. Perhaps if I were a man, I would have been denied access to my sensitive side, afraid to let the world see me cry; maybe I would make women cry.

How would body image affect me if I were a man? I would not have to worry that my breasts were imperfect, my hips were too large, or that my feet were not pretty, but maybe I *would* slave at Ballys to have bulging biceps, triceps, and calves. Perhaps if I were male I could take pride in a beer belly as a symbol of masculinity, for most men assume the bigger the better. Maybe not, for some men take creotine in pursuit of a solid body and dread the possibility of inheriting an abdominal middle-age spread. If I were a man I would definitely fear the departure of my hair, or maybe it would not bother me because concern about appearance is a feminine trait.

As society evolves and gender identity moves forth into the public spotlight as a subject of speculation, it is only right to question what is male and what is female. It is unfair to say men do not cry, but at the same time that is what we are taught. Men should be strong and fearless as women are considered meek and gentle, so where do sensitive men and powerful women come in? I am a woman but that does not prevent the surge of testosterone in my body that inspires strength, anger, and excitement.

Occasionally I raise my voice, take on leadership roles, and even get dirty; does this make me manly or less feminine? I think not. If I were born male rather than female, maybe I would be the same person with different accessories.

CONSIDERATIONS FOR YOUR OWN WRITING

1. Monique's first draft began as an exercise in freewriting. What topics emerged from the flow of ideas? What parts of the draft do you find most engaging? What makes them interesting to you?

2. Monique decided to focus on one of several possible topics for her final essay. Do you think she made a good choice? How has she developed this topic? What has she added, moved, or removed?

3. Describe the essay's tone. How seriously does the writer treat the topic of sexual difference? Would this be a better essay if the topic were explored in greater depth?

4. Monique followed a suggestion to start the essay without an introductory paragraph on "what if" scenarios. What difference does this make to you as a reader? Which opening paragraph do you prefer?

5. How do you interpret the final sentence? Is this a good way to conclude the essay? Explain why or why not.

6. Has Monique given a fair account of the differences between men and women? Where do you agree or disagree most? What would you change if you were writing on this topic?

Evaluation Checklist

Test your essay with a reader by asking the following questions.

1. What did you like most about the writer's use of imagination?

2. What was hard to follow or accept?

3. Where would visual description, factual information, or other details help you to envision the future in this essay?

4. How has the writer arranged things? Would another arrangement be more effective?

5. Identify any words or phrases that got in the way.

6. Circle any spelling, punctuation, or grammar errors.

7. What else needs more attention?

8. What is the most important point that you are left with?

Taking Stock

Step back and review what you have learned about imagining the future from this chapter.

1. Where in your study, work, personal life, and community activities will you need to make predictions and offer proposals? How will you be called on to communicate your vision in writing and other media?

2. How has this chapter helped to prepare you for these needs? How have you sharpened your ability to speculate, forecast, estimate, form hypotheses, and write proposals? Which of these skills would you still like to improve?

3. What did you learn from the readings and screenings about poetry, lyrics, speculative essays, film scenarios, and commercials? Identify one or two strategies that you would like to try out.

4. Consider the topic of your essay or song. What do you understand about this topic now? What would you still like to learn about it? What have you learned about your own imagination?

5. Think about the various topics presented in the readings and screenings. What is the most important thing you learned about the future?

Futures on the Web

The Internet, sometimes called the gateway to the future, has lots to say about the world we are becoming. Follow its forking paths to help you predict and propose creative possibilities.

Map Your Future
http://www.mapping-your-future.org/
Sponsored by a group of guaranty agencies affiliated with the Federal Family Education Loan Program (FFELP), this site offers advice for selecting a school, paying for it, and pursuing a career.

World Future Society
http://www.wfs.org/
This nonprofit educational organization publishes an online magazine about the social and technological developments shaping the future.

Future of Music Coalition
http://www.futureofmusic.org/
This collaborative effort by groups in several fields monitors trends and issues in the music world.

Wired
http://www.wired.com/
This popular e-zine and magazine often prints articles about the future of technology.

Peace and Future Research
http://www.transnational.org/
This is a think tank dedicated to conflict mitigation and world peace.

Media Lab
http://www.media.mit.edu/
A leader in shaping the future of media technology, MIT's Media Lab highlights projects by students and faculty of the Massachusetts Institute of Technology. Marvin Minsky is a member of the faculty.

Rand
http://www.rand.org/scitech/stpi/ourfuture/
A report on our environmental future from the RAND corporation, a nonprofit think tank.

CREDITS

TEXT CREDITS

Diane Ackerman. "How to Watch the Sky" from *A Natural History of the Senses* by Diane Ackerman. Copyright © 1990 by Diane Ackerman. Used by permission of Random House, Inc.

Maya Angelou. From *I Know Why the Caged Bird Sings* by Maya Angelou. Copyright © 1969 and renewed 1997 by Maya Angelou. Used by permission of Random House, Inc.

Natalie Angier. "Condemning Our Kids to Life on Mars and Venus," *New York Times,* November 24, 1998. © 1998 by The New York Times Co. Reprinted with permission.

"Anthropology" definition from *Webster's New World College Dictionary*, 4/e. Reprinted with permission of John Wiley & Sons, Inc.

Apple Computer commercial text: © Apple Computer, Inc. Used with permission. All rights reserved. Apple® and the Apple logo are registered trademarks of Apple Computer, Inc.

Toni Cade Bambara. "The Lesson" from *Gorilla, My Love* by Toni Cade Bambara. Copyright © 1972 by Toni Cade Bambara. Used by permission of Random House, Inc.

Dave Barry. From *Dave Barry's Complete Guide to Guys* by Dave Barry. Copyright © 1995 by Dave Barry. Used by permission of Random House, Inc.

Before the First Word excerpt used by permission of Designs for Learning, Inc.

Wendell Berry. "The Pleasures of Eating" from *What Are People For?* by Wendell Berry. Copyright © 1990 by Wendell Berry. Reprinted by permission of North Point Press, a division of Farrar, Straus and Giroux, LLC.

Deborah Blum. From "What Is the Difference Between Boys and Girls?" from *Life* July 1999. Copyright 1999 Life Inc. Reprinted with permission. All rights reserved.

David Bodanis. "Danish" by David Bodanis. Reprinted with the permission of Simon & Schuster Adult Publishing Group, from *The Secret Family: Twenty-Four Hours Inside the Mysterious World of Our Minds and Bodies* by David Bodanis. Copyright © 1997 by David Bodanis. All rights reserved.

Kathryn Bold. "The Old Man and the Flea" by Kathryn Bold. Reprinted from *Hemispheres* magazine. Used with permission by the author.

Judy Brady. "I Want a Wife" from *Ms.* 1:1, December 31, 1971. Copyright © 1970 by Judy Brady. Reprinted by permission of Judy Brady.

Rachel Carson. "A Fable for Tomorrow," from *Silent Spring* by Rachel Carson. Copyright © 1962 by Rachel L. Carson, renewed 1990 by Roger Christie. Reprinted by permission of Houghton Mifflin Company. All rights reserved.

Sandra Cisneros. "Eleven" from *Woman Hollering Creek*. Copyright © 1991 by Susan Cisneros. Published by Vintage Books, a division of Random House, Inc., and originally in hardcover by Random House, Inc.

Reprinted by permission of Susan Bergholz Literary Services, New York. All rights reserved.

Continental Insurance Company. Text from Continental Insurance commercial. Reproduced by permission of CAN.

Stephanie Coontz. "Putting Divorce in Perspective" from *The Way We Really Are* by Stephanie Coontz. Copyright © 1992 by Basic Books, a Division of HarperCollins Publishers, Inc. Reprinted by permission of Basic Books, a member of Perseus Books, LLC.

Daily Kos Logo: www.dailykos.com. Used with permission.

John Davidson. From "Menace to Society" by John Davidson from *Rolling Stone* February 22, 1996. © Rolling Stone LLC 1996. All Rights Reserved. Reprinted by permission.

Annie Dillard. "Seeing," Chapter 2 from *Pilgrim at Tinker Creek* by Annie Dillard, pp. 14–34. Copyright © 1974 by Annie Dillard. Reprinted by permission of HarperCollins Publishers.

William J. Doherty. "Rituals of Passage: Weddings" from *Intentional Family* by William Doherty. Copyright © 1997 by Addison-Wesley Publishing Company. Reprinted by permission of Da Capo Press, a member of Perseus Books, LLC.

Roger Ebert, "The Matrix," from the Roger Ebert column by Roger Ebert. Copyright © 2003 The Ebert Company. Reprinted with permission of Universal Press Syndicate. All rights reserved.

First Person Plural excerpt provided courtesy of P.O.V. / American Documentary, Inc.

N. Scott Momaday. "The Way to Rainy Mountain" from *The Way to Rainy Mountain,* 1969. University of New Mexico Press. Used with permission.

NRO Logo: Reprinted with permission of National Review, Inc.

Susan Orlean. "The American Man at Age Ten" from *Esquire,* December 1992. Used with permission by Susan Orlean.

Anna M. Quindlen. "On a SoHo Street, a Feast for Body and Soul." *New York Times,* June 5, 1982. © 1982 by The New York Times Co. Reprinted by permission.

Nancy Sakamoto. From *Polite Fictions: Why Japanese and Americans Seem Rude to Each Other* by Nancy Sakamoto. Copyright © 1982 by Nancy Sakamoto. Reprinted with the permission of Kenseido Publishing Company, Ltd.

Esmeralda Santiago. From *When I Was Puerto Rican* by Esmeralda Santiago. Copyright © 1993 by Esmeralda Santiago. Reprinted by permission of Da Capo Press, a member of Perseus Books, LLC.

William Stafford. "Ask Me" © 1977, 1998 by the Estate of William Stafford. Reprinted from *The Way It Is: New & Selected Poems* with the permission of Graywolf Press, Saint Paul, Minnesota.

Frank J. Sulloway. "Birth Order and Personality" from *Born to Rebel* by Frank J. Sulloway. Copyright © 1996 by Frank J. Sulloway. Used by permission of Pantheon Books, a division of Random House, Inc.

Deborah Tannen. From *The Argument Culture* by Deborah Tannen. Copyright © 1997 by Deborah Tannen. Used by permission of Random House, Inc.

Kurt Vonnegut, Jr. "Harrison Bergeron" by Kurt Vonnegut, from *Welcome to The Monkey House* by Kurt Vonnegut, Jr. Copyright © 1961 by Kurt Vonnegut, Jr. Used by permission of Dell Publishing, a division of Random House, Inc.

Alice Walker. "Everyday Use" from *In Love & Trouble: Stories of Black Women.* Copyright © 1973 by Alice Walker. Reprinted by permission of Harcourt, Inc.

Barbara Dafoe Whitehead. "From Death to Divorce" by Barbara Dafoe Whitehead. This essay is a selection from "Dan Quayle is Right" (© 1993 by Barbara Dafoe Whitehead c/o Writers Representatives LLC, New York, NY, all rights reserved), an essay that was first published in *The Atlantic Monthly,* April 1993, beginning page 47 and ending page 60. It has been retitled "From Death to Divorce" for this volume. Reprinted by permission of Writers Representatives LLC.

PHOTO CREDITS

INDEX